HIDDEN DISGRACE

HIDDEN DISGRACE

*Revealing the Distress Signals
Covered by North American Indian Myths*

David J. Fierst

About the Cover

An upside-down national ensign, or flag, is known internationally to seamen as a distress signal. There have been from time to time upside-down flags placed on flagpoles at various places on the Pine Ridge Indian Reservation in South Dakota and at other sites of protest.

The feathery object depicted as draped in front of the flag is known as a dream catcher. Various Indian nations have their own variations of the purpose behind dream catchers, but in some instances, it is believed they protect children from bad dreams. Since the bulk of the Indian persons described in this book are Lakota, it is useful to remember the dream catcher idea did not originate with that nation. The idea for the artistic rendering originated with Bethany L. Fierst.

Copyright © 2020 by David J. Fierst
LCCN: 2020901042

All rights reserved. This book, or parts thereof,
may not be reproduced in any form without permission.

Paperback ISBN 978-1-63337-374-7
E-book ISBN 978-1-63337-375-4

Printed in the United States of America
1 3 5 7 9 10 8 6 4 2

Grateful acknowledgment is made for permission to reprint material from the following:

Indians in Unexpected Places by Philip J. Deloria, published by the University Press of Kansas copyright ©2004. www.Kansaspress.ku.edu. Used by permission of the publisher.

From *LIONS OF THE WEST* by Robert Morgan copyright © 2011 by Robert Morgan. Reprinted by permission of Algonquin Books of Chapel Hill. All rights reserved.

Not for Sale by Kevin Hancock copyright © 2015. Seventh Power Press. Reprinted by permission of the author.

Black Elk's Religion by Clyde Holler copyright ©1995. Reprinted by permission of Syracuse University Press.

Lakota Portraits: Lives of the Legendary Plains People by Joseph Agonito copyright © 2011. Reprinted by permission of the publisher.

Excerpts from *Great Plains* by Ian Frazier. Copyright ©1989 by Ian Frazier. Reprinted by permission of Farrar, Straus & Giroux.

Original Instructions Edited by Melissa K. Nelson, published by Inner Traditions International and Bear & Co., copyright © 2008. All rights reserved. http://www.Innertraditions.com. Reprinted with permission of publisher.

TABLE OF CONTENTS

Author's Note	IX
Preface • SuAnne Big Crow — The "Shooting Star" of Pine Ridge: Part I	XV
Introduction	1
Ch. 1 • Anna Mae Pictou-Aquash — The "Lost Bird" of Wounded Knee: Part I	33
Ch. 2 • Columbus — We Hardly Knew Thee	47
Ch. 3 • John O'Sullivan — In the Eye of the Storm of Manifest Destiny	61
Ch. 4 • Ward Churchill — Who Are Indians and What Are They Up to Anyway?	73
Ch. 5 • William Henry Harrison — Tippecanoe, Tyler, Jefferson, and the Rest, Too	91
Ch. 6 • Colonel John Chivington — "Buffalo Bill" Cody: Part I	97
Ch. 7 • Helen Hunt Jackson — With Friends Like This…	109
Ch. 8 • S. C. Gwynne and Terry Mort — The Savage Indians Got What They Deserved	131
Ch. 9 • From Crazy Horse to the Crazy Horse Monument — Who's Kidding Whom?	151
Ch. 10 • Searching for Spiritual Meaning in the Land of John Dunbar — Crazy Horse Redux	159
Ch. 11 • A Short Essay on the Many Faces of Sitting Bull	175
Ch. 12 • "Libbie" Custer and "Buffalo Bill" Cody: Part II	183
Ch. 13 • Will the Real George A. Custer Please Stand Up?	191
Ch. 14 • The "Lost Bird" of Wounded Knee: Part II	205
Ch. 15 • Henry B. Whipple — "The Do Gooders Do Us More Harm"	213
Ch. 16 • The Mysterious Mormons	221
Ch. 17 • Raymond Yellow Thunder	225
Ch. 18 • Russell Means and His Strange Journey to the Heart of the American Dream	237
Ch. 19 • J. Edgar Hoover — The Guardian of "Freedom" and his Federal Bureau of Imperialism: Part I	255
Ch. 20 • Joseph Trimbach and the Federal Bureau of Imperialism: Part II	259
Ch. 21 • Joseph Trimbach and the Federal Bureau of Imperialism: Part III	273
Ch. 22 • Black Elk — An Unrecognized Symbol of Cultural Survival	291
Epilogue • SuAnne Big Crow — The "Shooting Star" of Pine Ridge: Part II	297
Afterword	317
Bibliography	325
Index	343
About the Author	361

Author's Note

The failure to contextualize honestly the facts of history, then, must be identified as one of the main kinds of Anti-Indianisms in literary expression.
Elizabeth Cook-Lynn, *Anti-Indianism in Modern America*[1]

In this book I have used the term Indian or American Indian to describe many of the people and the descendants of those people living in the Western Hemisphere at the time of Columbus' arrival in 1492. (Although the subtitle of this book refers to myths about North America, aspects of the history of indigenous people in South America are included as well.) This is true throughout unless the term "Native American" or other term appears in a direct quotation. There are many reasons I have made this choice of terminology, but one of the best is found in a quote from the book *Where White Men Fear to Tread*, co-written by late Indian activist Russell Means. He quoted a speaker at a conference: "We were enslaved as 'Indians,' we'll gain our freedom as Indians, and then we can call ourselves any damn thing we please!"[2]

Likewise, a large portion of this book contains descriptions of events involving a group of people commonly referred to as "Sioux" Indians. There are various explanations for the origin of this term, but some sources believe it is derived from the French word Nadouessioux, or "little snake." Means also quoted Ben Black Elk, the son of the famous Nicholas Black Elk, who provided another explanation: "It's time for us to quit being *Sioux*, a word that comes from another Indian nation and means 'cutthroat' [emphasis in original]."[3] Thus, while the word "Sioux" appears on many signs on the Pine Ridge Reservation, where I have visited many times, as a matter of personal preference I have done my best to avoid using this term, which I consider slightly awkward. When I asked a Pine Ridge resident why there was not more outcry against this word, she wisely replied that sometimes you must "pick your battles," or words to that effect. Nevertheless, I have chosen to avoid using "Sioux" unless it appears in a direct quotation or derivation of one.

The proper name for the people commonly referred to as the Sioux is Oceti Sakowin, which means Seven Council Fires. The Seven Council Fires are sometimes organized into three groups: Dakota, Nakota, and Lakota, each containing groupings of fires. The Dakota includes the four Council Fires Mdewakanton (Dwellers by the Sacred Lake), Wahpekute (Shooters Among the Leaves), Sisitonwan/Sisseton (People of the Marsh), and Wahpetonwan (Dwellers Among the Leaves). The Nakota includes the two Council Fires Ihanktown/Lower Yanktonai (People of the End) and Ihanktowana/Upper Yanktoni (People of the Little End). The Council Fire Tetonwan, also known as the Lakota, is subdivided into seven bands: Hunkpapa (Camps at the Horn), Sicangu/Brulé (Burnt Thigh), Itazipo/Sans Arc (Without Bows), Sihasapa (Blackfeet), Oglala (Scatters His Own), Oohenumpa (Two Kettles), and Minneconjou (Planters by the River). While this structure is relatively complex, the focus of the discussion in this book about Plains Indians centers primarily on the Oglala Lakota.[4]

Also, in terms of structure, this book is not a history book in the strictest sense of the term. It uses the stories of individuals, both Indian and white, as launching pads for broader discussions. Since obviously there was interaction between some of the characters in this study, there is some overlap between chapters. Likewise, since it is not a typical give-the-dates type history book, brief descriptions of three significant events are in order, since they are not necessarily presented in chronological sequence in the chapters of this book.

The first, to be discussed in some detail in the chapter on author Helen Hunt Jackson, is what is commonly referred to as the "Trail of Tears." This tragic event involved the forced relocation of Cherokee, Creek, Choctaw, Seminole, and Chickasaw Indian Nations from the Southeast United States to present-day Oklahoma. The movement started for the Choctaws in 1831 and ended with the movement of the Chickasaws in approximately 1847. Estimates of Cherokee deaths alone during this forced march range from 4,000 to 8,000.[5]

The second event, the Wounded Knee Massacre, occurred on the Pine Ridge Indian Reservation on December 29, 1890. On that day, approximately 300 Minneconjou Lakota along with their leader, Spotted Elk, known as "Big Foot," were killed by members of the United States 7th Cavalry and other United States units. Some historians refer to this event as Wounded Knee I. Likewise, in terms of chronology, the "Lost Bird" referred to in the first chapter on Anna Mae Aquash and referenced in other chapters was a baby found at the Wounded Knee Massacre site approximately four days after the slaughter. She was obtained from the Lakota, who initially cared for her right after she was found, by the deception of military officer Brigadier General Leonard Colby and raised primarily by his wife Clara.

The third event of significance occurred on February 27, 1973, when members of the American Indian Movement (AIM), other Indians, and their allies "occupied" the village of Wounded Knee, the location of the Massacre of December 29, 1890. The "occupation" involved these men and women being surrounded by heavily armed federal forces for days and held the attention of the entire world. Historians have sometimes referred to this event as Wounded Knee II. Throughout this book, the term "occupation" or any derivative thereof appears in quotes unless it is contained in a larger direct quotation, to highlight the issue of whether Indians can logically be described as "occupying" territory designated as their lands by treaty. Anna Mae Aquash participated in Wounded Knee II as one of the "occupiers" and was murdered sometime in late 1975 or early 1976 on the Pine Ridge Indian Reservation. Discussions regarding the reason for her death and the handling of its investigation remain emotionally charged to this day.

In terms of the theme of this book, as hopefully readers will understand, it is not intended to constitute an analysis of general race issues nor an analysis of issues facing contemporary women in the United States outside those facing Indian women. Rather, it is simply an attempt to generate discussion as to whether events in Indian history and, more importantly, Indians themselves, have been fairly depicted.

Likewise, while non-Indians have been critical of the American Indian Movement (AIM), in my opinion, the criticism is inappropriate when it extends beyond proven facts and involves editorializing. If Indian people have criticisms of AIM, that is another matter. From a personal standpoint, I would never have learned about the Wounded Knee Massacre or any events related to it had it not been for the AIM-led "occupation" of Wounded Knee in 1973 and the attendant publicity. As Mary Brave Bird, also known as Mary Crow Dog, said: "Some people loved AIM, some hated it, but nobody ignored it."[6] Once, while describing a talk by AIM stalwart Russell Means, the late, brilliant Lakota author Vine Deloria, Jr. said: "'As I was listening to Russell Means I continually looked around the room to see the faces of the people as he spoke. Almost every face shone with a new pride.'"[7]

Ultimately, my fervent hope is that this book will be considered among those paying Indians "…the uncommon tribute of taking their culture(s) seriously."[8] Or, as Vine Deloria, Jr. once advised: "We need the public at large to drop the myths in which it has clothed us for so long. We need fewer and fewer 'experts' on Indians. What we need is a cultural leave-us-alone agreement in spirit and in fact."[9] Another helpful viewpoint was expressed by Carolyn Niethammer in her fascinating biography of stalwart Navajo leader Annie Dodge Wauneka entitled *I'll Go and Do More*. Niethammer explained: "During those weeks on the reservation when I was not working, and my eyes needed a rest, I drove around the reservation as Annie had loved to do, and tried to look at it through her eyes."[10] While the main title of this book, *Hidden Disgrace*, suggests the facts of Indian history are somehow concealed, in reality, the facts are often generally known, but need to be placed in their proper "context." This process of placing events in "context" can be described to a large extent as eliminating "erasure," which historian Tricia Logan described as:

> an elegant method of revising history. Erasure, omission, or willful blindness pervasively and sometimes insidiously overlooks portions of a historical narrative in favor of a dominant narrative. Often hidden in plain sight, the missing voices of a historical narrative can reveal as much as what is visible.[11]

The main title of this book, as noted, is *Hidden Disgrace,* and was chosen some time ago. Likewise, while this book contains some discussion of the topic of genocide, it is not as extensive as many others on that specific subject. Nevertheless, the following quote, found toward the end of the research phase for this writing, is an apt description of the thought process applicable to this project:

> Exploring 'hidden genocides', or cases that have been pushed to the background or out of sight, provides one example of a critical genocide studies approach. The chapters in this book make the case over and over again that genocides in Indigenous North America have been hidden in precisely this way, a masking that is linked to the ways histories have been written.[12]

Fortuitously, in addition to Cook-Lynn's demand that we "contextualize" Indian history, she had words of encouragement: "Being critical of a colonial past does not suggest that all is wrong in the United States."[13]

ENDNOTES

1. Elizabeth Cook-Lynn, *Anti-Indianism in Modern America: A Voice from Tayekaya's Earth* (Chicago: University of Illinois Press, 2001), p. 8.
2. Russell Means and Marvin Wolf, *Where White Men Fear to Tread* (New York: St. Martin's Griffin, 1995), p. 370.
3. Ibid., p. 209.
4. "Oceti Sakowin/Seven Council Fires" Akta Lakota Museum and Cultural Center (www.aktalakota.org). The website uses the spelling "Mniconjou" for the Planters by the River band. However, for the sake of uniformity, the spelling Minneconjou is used to be in conformity with its usage in the rest of the book. Will Peters, an Oglala Lakota immersed in his traditional culture and used as a reference source, currently refers to the Itazipo band as Itazipcola (No bows).
5. Vicki Rozema, *Voices from the Trail of Tears* (Winston-Salem, North Carolina: John F. Blair Publishing, 2003), p. 40.
6. Joy Harjo, Gloria Bird, Eds., Mary Brave Bird, "Mary Brave Bird" *Reinventing the Enemy's Language: Contemporary Native Women's Writings of North America* (New York: W.W. Norton & Co., 1977), p. 338.
7. Paul Chaat Smith and Robert Allen Warrior, *Like a Hurricane: The Indian Movement from Alcatraz to Wounded Knee* (New York: The New Press, 1996), p. 273.
8. Richard Drinnon, *Facing West: The Metaphysics of Indian-Hating and Empire Building* (Norman, Oklahoma: University of Oklahoma Press, 1997), p. 17.
9. Vine Deloria, Jr., *Custer Died for Your Sins: An Indian Manifesto* (New York: Avon Books, 1969), p. 34.
10. Carolyn Niethammer, *I'll Go and Do More: Annie Dodge Wauneka* (Lincoln, Nebraska, University of Nebraska Press, 2001), p. xvi. Interestingly enough, Niethammer observed that Annie and Esther Burnett Home: "…were both working mothers in an era when that was unusual anywhere in the United States." p. xxv.
11. Andrew Woolford, Jeff Benvenuto, Alexander Laban Hinton, Eds., Tricia E. Logan "Memory, Erasure, and National Myth" *Colonial Genocide in Indigenous North America* (Durham, North Carolina: Duke University Press, 2014), p. 149.
12. Woolford, Benvenuto, and Hinton, Eds., Alexander Laban Hinton, "Afterword - Colonial Genocide in Indigenous North America," *Colonial Genocide in Indigenous North America*, p. 327. Nevertheless, any discussions as to whether Indians in North America were victims of genocide often seem inevitably to morph into the argument the Jewish Holocaust was a unique event. There is no intention in this writing to address that issue, and any suggestion of an invitation to that debate is unintentional. Those interested in a robust discussion of the issue are urged to read volumes such as Ward Churchill's *A Little Matter of Genocide: Holocaust and Denial in the Americas 1492 to the Present* (San Francisco, California: City Lights Books, 1997) passem. A discussion of the controversies surrounding Ward Churchill himself appear in a later chapter.
13. Elizabeth Cook-Lynn, *A Separate Country: Postcoloniality and American Indian Nations* (Lubbock, Texas: Texas Tech University Press, 2012), p. 154.

Preface

SuAnne Big Crow
The "Shooting Star" of Pine Ridge: Part One

People think I teach these Ways because I want to go back to the days of chasing buffalo and living in Tipis, but I'm just talking about living in balance in two worlds.

Will Peters, Oglala Lakota[1]

Lakota Indian SuAnne Big Crow, who spent her short, eventful life on the Pine Ridge Indian Reservation in South Dakota, was a "shooting star" in two senses of the term. Her brief life of just under eighteen years was not only a symbolic "shooting star" that burned brightly and ended all too suddenly, but she was literally a "shooting star"—an All-American basketball player for the Pine Ridge High School Lady Thorpes. Her innocence and optimism often stood out in stark contrast to the despair and poverty that consistently stifle hope in this almost forgotten area of the remote state of South Dakota. During her sophomore season in high school, she averaged over 30 points a game, once scored a record-setting 67 points in a single game, and also set a state record for scoring for a single season—761.[2] To top it all off, at the end of that season she scored the winning basket in the South Dakota girls' basketball tournament championship game in Sioux City, South Dakota.[3]

Between her sophomore and junior years in high school, SuAnne went to Europe on an Indian Girls Basketball All Star Team. In a scenario that must seem all too eerily reminiscent to Indian people, on that trip SuAnne contracted a mysterious stomach illness. As if to set a precedent, during a Buffalo Bill's Wild West tour through Spain in the late 1880s, at least four of the Indians traveling with the troupe, which included many Lakota, died of a mysterious illness or illnesses. In the case of SuAnne, many who knew her believe she never was really 100 percent again after the trip and a sort of "darkness" entered her life. Nevertheless, her enthusiastic approach to living demonstrated that beauty, tragedy and chaos are intertwined in the lives of those who live together in this isolated area far from the mainstream of contemporary American life. SuAnne's life and the lives of other Pine Ridge residents are colorfully detailed in Ian Frazier's poignant book *On the Rez*.

SuAnne's hometown (considered a village) of Pine Ridge is part of the Pine Ridge Indian Reservation which contains several other small towns and villages including the village of Wounded Knee, the site of the infamous 1890 massacre. The reservation is 3,469 square miles in size, equivalent to the entire state of Connecticut. Pine Ridge Village is also the birthplace of the superb athlete Billy Mills who won a gold medal in the 10,000-meter race at the 1964 Tokyo Olympics.[4] The Pine Ridge Indian Reservation is more like a poverty-stricken developing country than anywhere else in the United States with the exception of other Indian reservations. Some Pine Ridge residents to this day at times fly U.S. flags upside down in what are known internationally as distress signals.

Yet, SuAnne's life seemed to be a beacon of hope for so many who lived and still live in this hardscrabble area. She possessed an enormous appetite for life and for food—it was said she could eat four Big Macs and four large fries in one sitting. She was also very outspoken against using alcohol and drugs and was elected homecoming queen during her senior year of high school. SuAnne's personality was larger than life: she was known to have a great sense of humor and loved to see how far she could go with pranks. One of SuAnne's teachers, Warfield Moose, said: "'She showed us a way to live on the earth.'"[5]

Sadly, however, as if to symbolize Black Elk's cry, as stated by John Neihardt in *Black Elk Speaks*, that: "…with running tears I must say now that the tree has never bloomed,"[6] SuAnne's earthly journey came to an end on February 9, 1992. On that day, she fell asleep while driving with her mother and crashed the car. In remembrance of her life, a recreation center on the eastern edge of the village of Pine Ridge is named the SuAnne Big Crow Center in her honor.[7] The marker above SuAnne's grave depicts a cheerful young woman; her final resting place is located just outside the eastern edge of the Re-Member facilities. Re-Member is a relief organization that facilitates humanitarian projects on the Pine Ridge Reservation such as building wheelchair ramps, skirting for trailers, and outhouses. Conditions are so harsh in some areas of Pine Ridge, Re-Member's provision of outhouses is one of the organization's most desired services.

The graveyard where SuAnne's remains lie is also a stark reminder of the harshness of life on the Pine Ridge Reservation. Near SuAnne's marker are the graves of one young man who didn't make it to his 24th birthday and another who didn't make it to his 22nd. The specific stories of the young men buried there are not known, and their identities remain anonymous to outsiders. However, for Indian youths on Pine Ridge in general, there is a palpable feeling of the presence of a: "…reckless fury that ends the lives of so many young Indians in car wrecks, in fights with knives or baseball bats, passed out in ditches alongside country roads on sub-zero nights."[8] Accidents and homicides are not the only hazards faced by Indian youths. In February 2015, Pine Ridge President John Yellow Bird Steele declared a state of emergency due to the number of teen suicides occurring there.[9]

Thus, perhaps the most remarkable aspect of SuAnne's life was that it was that of a typical teenager, albeit an extraordinarily successful one in a place that is anything but typical for many in the United States. The family and friends who survived SuAnne faced and continue to face enormous challenges just to survive. For example, one major problem in Pine Ridge is diabetes. Sadly, this threat to the longevity of the lives of South Dakota's Indian population has been known to the United States government for nearly a century. In 1928, the federal government issued the Meriam Report, which noted the diets of most Indians, including those on Pine Ridge, were notably lacking in fresh fruits, vegetables, and milk.[10] Thus, to cut through the layers of distortion foisted on the masses by historians and adequately explain the events and circumstances resulting in the poverty and chaos on Pine Ridge and other reservations is a challenging task, maybe even an impossible one. Yet, considering the myth of Indian savagery, and those other corresponding myths of Indian history, perhaps what is even more difficult for outsiders to comprehend is the success of people like SuAnne and the recent emerging sense of Indian pride. For the benefit of those like SuAnne, who is at rest and no longer struggles, and others who still struggle against massive odds, it is crucial to at least try set the record as straight as possible, not only to help heal the scars of Indian people, but for the benefit of whites and others as well.

There are so many idioms, phrases, and symbols in the language and culture of the United States arising from the bloated "Frontier Myth"—which sets the table for Indian history—it is commendable historians such as Richard Slotkin have lately striven to accurately report many aspects of that convoluted collection of tales.[11] As another example, historian Richard Drinnon explained during the Vietnam War, areas where the Viet Cong lurked were labeled "Indian Country."[12] To some extent even during the recent wars in Iraq and Afghanistan areas not controlled by United States forces were labeled "Indian Country" as well. Slotkin, quoting Martin Green, noted that myths are often transmitted in: "'coded message[s] from the culture as a whole to its individual members.'" Continuing Drinnon's line of thinking of using the "Indian Country" framework, during the Vietnam War, before missions, combat leaders urged their men to be prepared to play "'Cowboys and Indians.'"[13] On the other extreme from this depiction of Indians as, for example, "Stone Age Pagans on horseback,"[14] was the counter-cultural image of Indians as "Noble Savages."[15] Neither of these extreme depictions of Indians provides a satisfactory view, or even a useful starting point, for framing a realistic view of Indians and describing their cultures in any meaningful sense.

For example, the late Lakota Indian Vine Deloria, Jr., a brilliant writer, lawyer, and seminary graduate, outlined an aspect of the mythic view of what he called the "plight" of Indians. He humorously stated: "I once did a projection backward and discovered that evidently most tribes were entirely female for the first three hundred years of white occupation. No one, it seemed, wanted to claim a male Indian as a forbear." Deloria, Jr. reasoned: "A male ancestor has too much of the aura of the savage warrior, the unknown primitive, the instinctive animal, to make him a respectable member of the family tree."[16]

SuAnne's human, albeit bittersweet, story can serve as one gateway for examining these myths and unasked questions of Indian history as a whole. For example, when comparing the justification of westward expansion in the United States with the tenets of Darwin's evolutionary theory, it would be useful to question why the subtitle to his 1859 book, *On the Origin of Species by Means of Natural Selection or the Preservation of Favoured Races in the Struggle for Life*, is rarely stated. In that regard, historian James Wilson advised: "It is, perhaps, not surprising that Anglo-American commentators…should have seized on Darwin to explain the genocide of native Californians as an inevitable, biological process in which the morals and intentions of individual settlers were largely irrelevant."[17] If this hints at shining too critical a light on conventional accounts of Indian history, it is perhaps because the opinions of Indians themselves are rarely sought. Consider the eloquent and stark assessment of history and current affairs offered by M. Annette Jaimes, a Juaneno/Yaqui author:

> For the great mass of non-Indian Americans, those who wish not to be Nazis or the heirs to Nazism, and whose collective conscience might bestir itself to compel some positive alteration in the colonial relationship were the facts known to them, our present realities largely remain as far from sight and mind as the history upon which they are predicated. Only in bringing about a fundamental change in their [lack of] consciousness concerning the American Indian experience can we hope to gain the allies necessary to affect the genuine decolonization of Native North America. Only in attaining such understanding can they, in turn, be afforded the ability and opportunity to take the positions and undertake the activities of allies, distanced through their thinking and their deeds from the status quo.[18]

Some might recoil at Jaimes' references to Nazism as unduly strident and/or harsh. Others may argue the already existing pleas for de-mythologizing or de-savaging Indians have made any further excursions into this realm unnecessary. Nonetheless, at least in terms of various books reviewed in this book, there are still those who insist on viewing Indians such as Sitting Bull or Crazy Horse as either savages or as spectral creatures who may or may not have taken human form. Although no comprehensive inventory of writing about the spirituality of Indian leaders appears to exist, there is certainly significant evidence on the other end of the spectrum of the tendency to view Indians past and present as uncomprehending children or even "Stone Age Pagans." Thus, even though Indian people like SuAnne and a multitude of others have shown their capacity for successfully employing the skills considered valuable in Western society, in the words of history professor Patricia Nelson Limerick, the message of the full humanity of these resilient people has "not gotten through."[19]

ENDNOTES

1. Quote from Will Peters, Oglala Lakota. Will has used this saying frequently, so a specific date is not indicated.
2. Ian Frazier, *On the Rez* (New York: Picador, 2000), p. 225.
3. Ibid., p. 232.
4. Ibid., p. 194.
5. Ibid., p. 199.
6. John Neihardt, *Black Elk Speaks* (Lincoln, Nebraska: University of Nebraska Press, 1961), p. 279. Some question whether Black Elk actually stated this and believe it was an artistic invention of Neihardt. Nevertheless, the words convey a sense of sadness fitting for some situations on Pine Ridge.
7. Frazier, *On the Rez,* p. 197.
8. Thomas Powers, *The Killing of Crazy Horse* (New York: Vintage Books/A Division of Random House, 2010), p. xix.
9. Rebecca Klein "Native American School Mourning 4 Student Suicides Get Emergency Federal Aid" *HuffPost,* June 19, 2015.
10. Lewis Meriam, *The Meriam Report: The Problem of Indian Administration* (Brookings Institution, 1928), *passim*.
11. Richard Slotkin, *Fatal Environment: The Myth of the Frontier in the Age of Industrialization 1800-1890* (New York: Atheneum Publishers, 1985), *passim*.
12. Drinnon, *Facing West,* pp. 368, 451.
13. Slotkin, *Fatal Environment*, p. 16.
14. S. C. Gwynne, *Empire of the Summer Moon: Quanah Parker and the Rise and Fall of the Comanches, the Most Powerful Tribe in American History* (New York: Scribner, 2010), p. 319.
15. James Wilson, *The Earth Shall Weep: A History of Native America* (New York: Picador, 1998), p. 38.
16. Deloria, Jr. *Custer Died for Your Sins*, p. 11.
17. Wilson, *The Earth Shall Weep*, p. 235.
18. M. Annette Jaimes, Ed. "Introduction: Sand Creek: The Morning After *State of Native America: Genocide, Colonization, and Resistance* (Boston: South End Press, 1992), pp. 8-9.
19. Patricia Limerick, *The Legacy of Conquest: The Unbroken Past of the American West*, (New York: W.W. Norton & Co., 1987), p. 31.

Introduction

The stories of the Ghost Dance ceremonial, as the frenzied acts of a crazed Indian population that preceded the Wounded Knee Massacre *has* [sic] *been concocted by apologist historians as the rationale for the mass killing. This conspiracy theory is perpetuated even by present day historians* [emphasis in original].

Elizabeth Cook-Lynn, Anti-Indianism in Modern America[1]

On December 28, 1890, a group of approximately 300 beleaguered, bedraggled, and beaten Minneconjou Lakota Indians led by Spotted Elk, otherwise known as "Big Foot," neared the village of Pine Ridge in southwest South Dakota in hopes of finding food, shelter, and solace during one of the state's bitter winters. Before arriving at Pine Ridge, they were intercepted by soldiers of the 7th Cavalry and other federal units who were sent to quell the so-called "Ghost Dance" uprising. There were: "…weary-eyed mothers, gaunt and sad warriors, half famished children, hollowed eyed aged Indians with bowed heads and subdued expressions following the white captors to camp."[2] The next day, December 29, 1890, those 7th U.S. Cavalry troops, some of whom were once led by George A. Custer, and other United States troops, slaughtered these Minneconjou Lakota Indians with high-velocity rifles and Hotchkiss revolving cannons, which produced massive death, as the name would suggest.

Historian Jerome Greene described the madness: "When the soldiers brought a Hotchkiss gun forward to fire directly at these people, it became, in the words of Iron Hail [ironically], '…a storm of thunder and hail.'" Iron Hail also lamented: "'There went up from these dying people a medley of death songs that would make the hardest heart weep.'"[3] As the rounds showered onto the helpless, starving Lakota perishing in the agonizing cold that tragic day: "Abdomens and skulls were exploded like so many watermelons. The bullets severed limbs like leaves from trees."[4] Louise Weasel Bear sadly explained: "'We tried to run, but they shot us like we were a buffalo. I know there are some good white people, but the soldiers must be mean to shoot children and women, Indian soldiers would not do that to white children.'"[5] This disgraceful event and dark stain on the United States flag was initially called a "battle" but eventually became known as the Wounded Knee Massacre. As stated in the Author's Note, Wounded Knee is located on the Pine Ridge Indian Reservation and is about fifteen or so miles from the village of Pine Ridge.

At the time of this sad incident, L. Frank Baum, who later penned *The Wonderful Wizard of Oz*, served as the editor of the Aberdeen South Dakota *Saturday Pioneer*. He wrote these harsh words in the aftermath of this tragedy, published January 3, 1891:

> The *Pioneer* has before declared [after Sitting Bull's murder] that our only safety depends on the total extirmination [sic] of the Indians. Having wronged them for centuries, we had better, in order to protect our civilization, follow it up by one more wrong and wipe these untamed and untamable creatures from the face of the earth. In this lies (the) future safety of our settlers.[6]

Just two weeks prior to making this blood-curdling pronouncement, after the great Hunkpapa Lakota Sitting Bull's slaying on December 15, 1890, Baum had this to say in the *Saturday Pioneer*:

> The nobility of the Redskin is extinguished, and what few are left are a pack of whining curs who lick the hand that smites them. The Whites, by law of conquest, by justice of civilization, are masters of the American continent, and the best safety of the frontier settlers will be secured by the total annihilation of the few remaining Indians.[7]

Although a topic not often discussed in polite company, the justification of the slaughter of Indians as being beneficial for the safety of white settlers was not a thought first uttered by Baum. Eminent historian Richard Drinnon noted chronicler Philip Vincent in 1638 was assuring the New England colonists after the Pequot War: "'…of their peace, by killing the barbarians, better than our English Virginians were being killed by them. For having once terrified them, by severe execution of just revenge, they shall never hear of more harm from them…'" After pointing out extermination was not the only remedy for the "Indian problem," Vincent argued the Indians could also be enslaved. Drinnon explained that while Vincent may have outwardly addressed the question as to whether the Pequots were men or not in the affirmative, in reality: "…the loud and clear answer of the war was that Indians were truly animals that could be killed or enslaved at will."[8]

Of course, rationalizing the brutality unleashed upon the people Columbus and other explorers initially encountered in the Western Hemisphere was not solely the domain of journalists and other scribes. Baum's comments are remarkably like then-General George Washington's instructions to Major-General John Sullivan regarding taking peremptory action against the Haudenosee Indians in the mid-1770s:

> [you are] to lay waste all the settlements around…that the country may not be merely *overrun* but *destroyed* [emphasis in source]… You will not by any means listen to any overture of peace before the total ruin of their settlements is affected… *Our future security will be in their inability to injure us*…and in the terror with which the severity of the chastisement they receive will inspire them. Sullivan replied: the Indians shall see that there is malice enough in our hearts to destroy everything that contributes to their support [emphasis added].[9]

Some have suggested that in the writing of *The Wonderful Wizard of Oz*, Baum intentionally described an imaginary Kansas where no Indians existed.[10] Regardless, the troopers of the 7th Cavalry were part of a live flesh-and-blood organization who many believe exacted revenge for what happened at the Little Big Horn 14 years earlier, where Custer and over 265 of his men and Indian Scouts perished at the hands of Lakota and Cheyenne warriors.

Of course, Baum's article containing the harsh comments describing what was needed to complete the destruction of Indian resistance after December 29, 1890, was not the first emotionally charged account of a deadly conflict between the 7th Cavalry and Indians. The difference was earlier accounts, such as those written in the aftermath of what became known as "Custer's Last Stand" in 1876, described a scenario where the 7th Cavalry was the defeated foe, not the victors, over those Indians who were commonly referred to as the "Sioux" in many publications. In its July 6th edition, typical of most far-Western papers, the *Bismarck Tribune* printed an article which contained such descriptions of scenes after the battle as: "The squaws seem to have passed over the field and crushed the skulls of the wounded and dying with stones and clubs…the privates of some were cut off, while others bore traces of torture."[11] That the Indians involved in the battle believed they were defending their families and homeland was apparently beside the point. In announcing Custer's defeat in 1876, many other newspapers such as *The Denver Daily News* cried out for vengeance for Custer. Buffalo Bill's Wild West, ostensibly a show developed for entertainment purposes for the masses, further fueled the idea in American culture of avenging Custer by enacting the Little Big Horn battle as one of its climactic scenes and was "…met with near sacred veneration.[12]

Thus, Baum wasn't the only scribe worshiping at the altar of promoting the unleashing of unrestrained violence upon Indian people who had absolutely no ability to inflict any significant harm on settlers or other whites, perhaps just the most well-known. Others built on Baum's call for slaughter and basked in the reflected glow of the 7th Cavalry's acclaimed valor at Wounded Knee Creek. As evidence, a ceremony attended by more than 10,000 people was conducted at Ft. Riley, Kansas, on July 24, 1893, to dedicate a monument in honor of the troopers killed on December 29, 1890. It was proclaimed by a local bard that these men and their surviving comrades exhibited heroism by taking a stand against a "vast Indian conspiracy that had sworn death to all." The poet heightened the patriotic tone of the occasion by his following words:

> And now the Seventh with grateful sense
> Of highest service paid
> Erects her lofty monument
> Where martyred sons are laid.[13]

Kansas state legislator J.R. Burton, in his dedication oration, pointed out that "real Americans" understood the importance of Manifest Destiny and honored rather than reviled the 7th Cavalry for their conduct on December 29, 1890. Thus, the merciless slaughter of defenseless Indians, mostly old men, women, and children, was cheerily justified by the virtually religious doctrine of Manifest Destiny. The unfounded belief there was a "conspiracy" by "Ghost Dancing" leaders of a new religion to start a war against the

United States and settlers in the South Dakota region further justified the killing. Certainly, no one present wanted to advise the misty-eyed mourners that a good percentage of the "martyred sons" were killed, as noted, by what is now referred to as "friendly fire"—rounds fired by members of their own units. Perhaps the maudlin sentiments surrounding the loss of men on December 29, 1890, in Custer's beloved 7th were a continuation of the romanticized view of his defeat at the hands of Indian warriors (some argue by his own hand) 14 years earlier.

One young girl wrote in a letter to the *New York Herald* after Custer's death:

> My heart was filled with pity when I read the other night for mother the account in your paper of the awful slaughter done by the Indians on General Custer & his army... I would have given the world to have had one look at the fearless General Custer; and then he was so young and, as the papers say, so handsome. I could cry tears over his sad fate.[14]

Curiously, one publication produced for the fiftieth anniversary commemoration of Custer's 7th Cavalry's participation in the Battle of the Little Big Horn makes no mention of the Wounded Knee Massacre.[15] While only speculation, part of the lack of enthusiasm for linking the Little Big Horn Battle and identifying the motives for the slaughter at Wounded Knee could have been to diminish publicity for the shameful event by not connecting it to Custer. There also could have been the realization that Custer was not as popular with his men as he was with the general public, whose sentiments were reflected in the letter from the little girl.

The somber lines about the mighty deeds of the 7th Cavalry were not the first time a zesty little ditty was used to exaggerate military exploits during what were called the "Indian Wars" of the mid-19th century. The awkwardly labelled "Grattan Massacre" in what is now present-day Goshen County, Wyoming, occurred when Lieutenant John L. Grattan was killed along with 29 of his men after demanding the surrender of a Brulé Lakota man named High Foretop for the minor "crime" of killing and eating a sickly cow of a Mormon emigrant that had wandered into the Lakota village. Even though the Lakota offered as many as five horses in compensation for the cow, Grattan's impetuous nature led to the demise of his men and himself. After the battle, General Harney arrived on the scene to demand the surrender of the group of Indians who fought the first group of soldiers demanding the surrender of High Foretop.

Instead of a surrender, a confrontation erupted that resulted in Harney's men killing 86 Brulé, about half that number being women and children. In the aftermath of this carnage, which became known as the Battle of Ash Hollow, or Blue Water Creek, one wag wrote:

> We did not make a blunder,
> We rubbed out Little Thunder
> And we sent him to the other side of Jordan.[16]

Adding to the incongruousness of the lines was the fact that Little Thunder was not killed in the battle but taken prisoner. In the larger picture, in what became a pattern, since the Indians came out on the losing side of the conflict, the combat which gave rise to the writing of this creepy poem was labeled a battle, even considering the high level of Indian civilian casualties. And, as was the case in the murder of Raymond Yellow Thunder many years later, alcohol played a role, perhaps even a significant one, in creating chaos. Specifically, in the case of the "Grattan Massacre" a drunken interpreter exacerbated the tensions resulting in the fight over the sickly cow.[17]

The "vast Indian conspiracy" that was supposedly thwarted by the troops surrounding the Indians at Wounded Knee in December 1890 was claimed to be energized by those leading the "Ghost Dancers." Many, many historians regurgitate the fable that Indians on Pine Ridge were enthralled by the idea of the "Ghost Dance" and the corresponding belief that "ghost shirts" would make the wearers bulletproof. Not surprisingly, contemporary Indian leaders such as the late Russell Means scoffed at the notion, even claimed by Dee Brown, that the "Ghost Dance" precipitated the mass killings at Wounded Knee. Means argued the Wovoka "…taught his people to think and act like Indians." Means further asserted this was translated to become the theme of AIM: "Remain true to who you are, and you will find peace of mind."[18] Larry McMurtry, who won a Pulitzer Prize for his novel *Lonesome Dove,* in his eccentric book *Crazy Horse* scoffed at the notion the "Ghost Dance" was the precipitating cause of the Wounded Knee Massacre during the bitter cold winter in December 1890. He noted: "It is hard now to understand, except as paranoia, the overreaction to the Ghost Dance, or other, earlier expressions of Indian messianic or millennial religion." He added: "What they [proponents of the Ghost Dance] preached…was not so very different from what low-Protestant, millennial, evangelical, Holy Roller charismatics preach now to dirt-poor congregations throughout rural America."[19]

Lest non-Indians write off Means' comment as that of a "radical" or McMurtry's as far-fetched, consider that even after the shooting stopped in the aftermath of the Wounded Knee Massacre one writer explained: "How many guns the Indians had, the colonel [Forsyth, Commander of the Federal forces at Wounded Knee] did not know; *in fact no one has ever known."* Nevertheless, to assure the reader the killing of Big Foot and his followers was justified, Forsyth: "…could assume that well over half of the men had them." That it would have been a simple matter to stack and count the weapons of the slaughtered Indians seems an elusive thought to many. Perhaps it was an intentional oversight.[20]

Likewise, by placing the events leading up to that tragedy in "context" as demanded by Lakota writer and scholar Elizabeth Cook-Lynn, it eventually becomes evident the "Ghost Dance" can scarcely be considered a cause of the massacre at all. Inexperienced and greedy Indian agents, ambitious military officers, and perhaps the most overlooked of all as a cause, lying newspaper reporters, played significant roles in the buildup to the events of leading to the deaths of those at least 300 mostly unarmed Indians on December 29, 1890. Additionally, it has been claimed that federal troops imbibed from a: "…small keg of whiskey to toast the capture of Big Foot…[but]…According to all reports, the celebration was neither lengthy nor particularly boisterous."[21] However, there is a growing belief that alcohol consumed by federal forces played more of a factor in creating the resulting bloodbath on the morning of December 29, 1890, than previously admitted. It was noted by author Renée Sansom Flood that the keg of whiskey was 10 gallons in capacity and was taken to the soldiers surrounding the Indians at Wounded Knee the night of December 28.[22] To assist in placing the specific events surrounding the Wounded Knee Massacre in context, it is also useful to consider there is little in the recorded history of Lakota warfare with whites to suggest they habitually sought out face-to-face combat with an equal number of federal troops, much less when surrounded by vastly superior numbers. Likewise, Lakota warriors were not known to embrace the idea of conducting winter campaigns, perhaps one of the few exceptions being the Fetterman Fight in December 1866.

Thus, the desire to present an "accurate" picture of history, particularly Indian history, is often hampered by layers of distortion which block a clear understanding of the "context" of events. First and foremost, to borrow a phrase from Virginia Woolf's *The Elizabethan Lumber Room*, Indian historians often appear hampered by the disease of "sublime complacency"[23] when seeking the "truth." Fortunately, in addition to Indians with strong intellects such as the late Vine Deloria, Jr., and Elizabeth Cook-Lynn, exceptions on the white side of the equation such as Richard Drinnon, Bernard Bailyn, Patricia Limerick, and Richard Slotkin push for balanced views of events involving Indians. Nevertheless, "sublime complacency" can be so debilitating it thwarts even the thought of asking Indians for their side of the story of various events. As Ian Frazier, an excellent writer on Indian matters, once inexplicably stated: "'Well, I know that Indian writers have said critical things but I just have never thought about it.'"[24] This malady is more likely than not an outgrowth of the desire to avoid facing harsh truths about the treatment of the group of human beings who occupied North (and South) America at the time of Columbus' arrival in 1492. As Patricia Limerick cautioned: "Indian history is so complex, and involves such a proliferation of points of view, that an open mind is essential…historians have to be adept at putting together diverse versions of the same events."[25] Another label for discussions seemingly frozen in time might be the colorful phrase "discourse inertia."[26]

In the example of the Wounded Knee Massacre, why admit the 300-plus followers of Spotted Elk were slaughtered in a drunken orgy of violence? It better serves the attempt to quell the pangs of conscience to promote the absurd tale the killing was due to the desire to suppress the "outbreak" to be led by the "Ghost Dancers." Apparently, for many historians, explaining how the "Ghost Dancers" differed in their beliefs from some charismatic Christians as McMurtry noted is hardly worth the effort, even if the differences were indeed negligible. The idea that the Lakota in southwest South Dakota had anywhere to go after an "outbreak" would be laughable but for the horrible consequences these humans endured, and their descendants continue to collectively suffer.

One example of "sublime complacency" in early settler/Indian interactions can be understood by applying simple logic to the story of the Jamestown colony and its survival due to Indian agriculture. The extent of this Indian agriculture should be obvious; the first English colonies were only able to survive because the local Indians supplied them with maize and other products of the soil out of the surplus created by the Indians' agricultural acumen. Thus, it would seem an obvious conclusion that Indian agriculture at the time of the first contact with settlers was developed to the point it could create consistent surpluses. Yet, despite this evidence, 18th century international law theorists such as Emerich Vattel promoted the myth Europeans were justified in seizing vast tracts of land from Indians since: "…the earth must be cultivated because it belongs to the human race in general for its subsistence."[27] That there is strong evidence Indians developed substantial agricultural production in North America prior to the arrival of Europeans seemed beside the point to Vattel and those who endorse his precepts.

Another example of "sublime complacency" is found in the writing of Kass Fleisher, in her book *The Bear River Massacre and the Making of History*. Fleisher squandered an opportunity to explore whatever evidence she could discover to facilitate an examination of whether a mass rape of Indian women occurred after the slaughter at Bear River, Idaho, in January 1863. Undoubtedly, she should be applauded for her efforts in presenting a picture of the events which occurred on that cold winter day. Although there is no doubt of the killings, according to Fleisher herself the evidence of mass rape is less certain. Nonetheless, Fleisher, obviously a bright and well-educated individual, should question whether she got lost in attempting to recount events by forcing them to be viewed through what could be labeled a contemporary white "feminist" paradigm. For example, for almost all events in Indian history, the first question to be asked would seem to be whether there was an attempt to justify whatever action was taken by the whites through the quasi-religious doctrine of Manifest Destiny or some other rationalization. Unfortunately, Fleisher neglected this inquiry.[28]

However, it is difficult to find fault with Fleisher for casting blame for the atrocity at Bear River on the attitudes of the relentlessly aggressive white Euro-Americans involved. Nevertheless, she did not consider the possibility other non-male groups of that era had similar attitudes toward Indians. Renée Sansom Flood described preeminent feminist icon Susan B. Anthony in at least one instance as being less than charitable in her attitude toward an Indian female infant found on the killing fields of Wounded Knee in 1890, called "Lost Bird," in the aftermath of the slaughter. Fleisher explains Anthony did not believe "…all means of oppression must be fought together" as apparently her counterpart Elizabeth Cady Stanton did. Anthony believed if all the obstacles for equality were attacked at once, "…none would be truly conquered."[29] During the time period of the "Minnesota Uprising" of 1862, the editor of the *St. Cloud Democrat*, Jane Grey Swisshelm, held the view the Dakota Indians were: "…devils in human form who existed beyond the horizon of help or mercy."[30]

Further, Fleisher took umbrage with a comment of Indian activist Lakota Mary Crow Dog, who stated: "'…women's lib was a white, upper-middle class affair of little use to a reservation Indian woman. With all their good intentions some had patronized me, even used me as an exotic conversation piece at their fancy parties.'"[31] When reflecting on Mary Crow Dog's lack of enthusiasm for abortion and her "urge to procreate," Fleisher stated cynically: "When I read this [comment], all I am able to hear is the process of yet another uterus being co-opted for purposes of the state." What exactly this means is not altogether clear. Fleisher added: "I try to see this question from Crow Dog's perspective. I squint my eyes real hard, but I just can't do it,"[32] as if her specific understanding was the crucial element in Mary Crow Dog's well-being. Nevertheless, Lorelei Means explained this attitude as she saw it:

> White women…virtually demand that we give up our own traditions in favor of what they imagine their own to be… What we need to be is *more*, not less Indian. But every time we try to explain this to our 'white sisters,' we either get told we're missing the point—we're just dumb

Indians after all—or we're accused of self-hatred as women... maybe all this feminism business is just another extension of the same old racist, colonialist mentality [emphasis in original].

Janet McCloud further explained: "'Many Anglo women try, I expect in all sincerity, to tell us that our most pressing problem is male supremacy. To this, I have to say, with all due respect, *bullshit* [emphasis in original]."[33] As insightful historian David Stannard noted: "...common sense [in terms of Fleisher recognizing her circumstances differed vastly from Mary Crow Dog's] rarely succeeds in combating cultural conceit."[34] Further, as history professor Peter Stearns cogently explained: "Knowledge of cultural constructions of femininity and masculinity—including the diversity among different groups and societies and major changes in standards over time—is vital to understanding how people and societies function."[35]

In that regard, what Fleisher may not have understood, from the perspective of Indian women, they often believe they: "...have formed the very core of indigenous resistance to genocide and colonization since the first moment of conflict between Indians and invaders."[36]

Specifically, in the case of Mary Crow Dog, after her sister delivered a baby at the Rosebud tribal hospital, she was sterilized without her consent (the Rosebud Reservation is about 90 minutes from the Pine Ridge Reservation). Two hours later the baby died. Mary also relayed the story of her sister-in-law Delphine who was: "...a good woman who had lived a hard life, (and) was found dead in the snow, the tears frozen on her face. A drunken man had beaten her, breaking one of her arms and legs, leaving her helpless in a blizzard to die."[37] It seems obvious then, in the harsh reality of life on Indian reservations, what rights Indian women consider important diverge significantly from those of Fleisher, an English professor at Illinois State University (at the time of this writing). In essence, when Fleisher claimed she had "...identified myself as being 'feminist' in outlook,"[38] that obviously means something entirely different for many Indian women whose babies experience a higher degree of infant mortality than in other parts of the United States. Professor Fleisher exhibits that curious "open-mindedness" that always seems to exist in academic circles and ultimately manifests in people being viewed as right if their views don't differ with the intelligentsia.

Yet, Fleisher's discussion of racial prejudice in the United States, as well as in Naomi Shaefer Riley's book *The New Trail of Tears*,[39] serves an unintended purpose. Under the rubric of "sublime complacency," Fleisher's book on the Bear River Massacre contained a discussion of circumstances involving racism against black people (as well as Riley's to be discussed in the Epilogue). Fleisher specifically addressed the depiction of mistreatment blacks and women in Rosewood, Florida, in a film titled, aptly enough, *Rosewood*. In her one-size-fits-all view of minorities in the United States, she expended considerable ink discussing those events in 1923 as depicted in this film, but made mention of the theft of land occupied by Seminole Indians as the only connection at all to Indian people of any type and only then as an afterthought.[40] Discrimination against blacks in Florida is connected to events in Idaho 60 years earlier, but it is not clear exactly how.

It's as if in his 1985 book, *Fatal Environment*, Richard Slotkin anticipated this limited thinking when he stated: "...the ideology of Indian policy also reflects the values and presuppositions we tend to bring to the general problem of unassimilated racial and ethnic minorities." Fleisher assumed determining whether mass rapes of Indian women occurred in 1863 and understanding the exploitation of black people in Florida required the same analysis. Slotkin concluded his exploration of this paradigm with the explanation there was a distinction between the situation of blacks and that of Indians. He noted that due to Indians being considered part of political autonomous entities: "…it was deemed logical to categorize all crimes committed by Indians as social acts, that is, as acts of war. It was from this logic that the exterminationist case took off and compelled the Friends [of Indians] to deny the reality of white-Indian violence in the West."[41] While it would be illuminating for readers to read the rest of Slotkin's writing on this specific topic for themselves, it is reasonable to suggest he is saying that if Indians could be categorized as a group committing hostile acts, then declaring "war" on them was an easy step and could be done without having to make the effort to identify specific crimes with specific individuals. Federal Bureau of Investigation (FBI) agent Joseph Trimbach provided a contemporary example of this thinking when he flippantly announced the FBI was in a "war" with "militant Native Americans" during the 1973 "occupation" of Wounded Knee.[42]

Another observation regarding Fleisher and her foray into writing Indian history is that her effort exemplified the lack of zeal many exhibit when writing about the subject. She claimed that she: "…attempted to apply for a summer travel grant from the National Endowment for the Humanities…but I could not find three academic historians willing to write a letter in support of this work." Nonetheless, apparently, she received funding from what she called a "…white-chick community supported interdisciplinary research grant."[43] Based on her own comment, the book was primarily a "'tertiary' work," which she explained meant she got the: "…information from other people [mostly white men] who have studied primary works."[44] How her apparent disdain of Mary Crow Dog differed significantly from what she considered the skewed outlook displayed by "mostly white men" is one of many attitudes left unexplained. Fleisher's mistake, much like Hancock's (to be discussed later), was to interject too much of herself into the story of the Bear River Massacre. She asserted: "I have the right to tell the story of the Bear River Massacre and Rape." This is true. She continued, "It's my story too."[45] This is a trendy claim which at best merely obfuscates the understanding of the circumstances surrounding those events in Idaho on January 29, 1863. Hopefully, it is not a demonstration of how narcissism smothers rational discussions of events that did not involve the re-tellers of these events.

Fleisher, possessing a Ph.D. in English, also made a curious misstatement about the writing of the eccentric Ward Churchill. She claimed that Churchill was: "apparently unaware of the Bear River Massacre or he would have pointed out that Sand Creek [Colorado] happened because Bear River itself was immediately forgotten."[46] Putting aside the odd requirement of many to filter basic facts of history through Churchill's intellect (which admittedly occurs in this volume to some extent), and the need to embrace Churchill's work with caution, her statement about his not knowing about the Bear River Massacre is simply wrong. On pages 30 and 175 of *Since Predator Came*, published in 1995, nine years before Fleisher's book was published in 2004, Churchill referred to the Bear River Massacre.[47] Since Fleisher seemed to place significant faith in Churchill's writing, it is not an easily understandable mistake.

Fleisher is far from being the only author or historian whose writing suffers from an overreliance on what could best be classified as clichés. Helen Hunt Jackson, S. C. Gwynne, Joseph Trimbach and other writers whose works are critiqued in this essay seem satisfied with cardboard cutouts as representation of real Indians rather than developing even minimally sophisticated structures for viewing the lives of real people. Slotkin again provided a solid foundation for analysis of this type of exposition, this time in *Gunfighter Nation*. In that work he explained that for such authors (although he does not specifically mention those like Fleisher and Trimbach whose books were written after his book quoted here):

> the central symbols of the myth/ideological system are not representations of real-world values and conflicts but literary properties whose meaning is established by well understood conventions. And since he has no stake, either personal or ideological, in the outcome of the struggles he [or she] depicts [Fleisher's claims that the Bear River Massacre story was "my story too" notwithstanding]—Indians vs Whites, rustlers vs. cattlemen, Mormons vs. Gentiles—he is able to play freely with some of the basic myth/ideological conventions, including politically loaded categories like race and sex.[48]

In essence, and fortunately for future generations interested enough to explore Indian history, Slotkin, Drinnon, Bernard Bailyn, Patricia Limerick, and especially Vine Deloria, Jr., and his son Philip were not satisfied with superficial examinations of what happened when reviewing the events leading up to the conquest of the land that became the United States, North America, and South America by the Europeans and their descendants.

Adding to the layers of distortion of Indian history are seemingly well-intentioned labels and descriptions of events. The hanging of 38 Dakota Indians in Mankato, Minnesota, in 1862 after the uprising there is labeled the largest mass execution in United States history.[49] However, the unflinching use of this term deflects analysis of what a "mass execution" consists. Any expansive view of the term would suggest that in reality, the Wounded Knee Massacre was also a "mass execution" in that at least 300 virtually defenseless Indian men, women, and children were slaughtered at that time. Nevertheless, determining which massacre, i.e., "mass execution" is the worst is one positive step in the direction of reorganizing accounts of history and preparing to face the grim facts of what actually happened to indigenous people in the Western Hemisphere. In that regard, with this present attempt at the re-working of the paradigm of what in fact constitutes an accurate portrayal of Indian history in mind, Michael Bradley's "Author's Forewarning" to his intriguing book *The Columbus Conspiracy* is instructive. He explained his book: "…is not primarily based upon new research and new facts. It is based on a re-examination and re-interpretation of many facts long known to the specialists in the study of history and navigation."[50]

While Bradley's book might be dismissed as just the ramblings of another "conspiracy theorist," his urging of readers and historians to reexamine known information is valuable. Likewise, while this present book does contain some degree of original source material, the main thrust of the writing is to urge reexamination of events. Perhaps even as importantly, hopefully it will encourage evaluating the use of terms such as "massacre" and the much overused and ill-understood word "hostile" to describe primarily non-reservation Indians. Interestingly enough, Bradley's suggestion Columbus was a pirate is not as far-fetched as it might appear at first blush.[51] In his venerated volume *The Life and Voyages of Christopher Columbus,* Washington Irving described a scene which occurred within 24 hours of the arrival of Columbus and his men in the "New World." Irving wrote regarding Columbus and his men encountering some of the natives: "The avarice [greed] of the discoverers was quickly excited by the sight of small ornaments of gold, worn by some of the natives in their noses."[52] This indeed sounds like the thought processes of pirates, not the description of men who had more noble motives in mind.

Regarding Bradley's comment about "new research" etc., it is often argued the math and science skills of high school students in the United States have and continue to decline compared to the rest of the world. Likewise, can it be credibly argued the knowledge of United States history of these students or of the population in general is any more robust? While Bradley argued his views of Columbus are a "… re-examination and re-interpretation of many facts known to specialists" etc., he does not describe the broader picture of the general public being blissfully ignorant of many instances of the brutal treatment of large numbers of Indians, much less of individuals. As Fleisher, her biases notwithstanding, stated: "… history tells us as much or more about the teller, the cultural context of that teller's biases, and the telling itself—than it tells us about What Happened [which she unequivocally proves with her book]."[53] In this volume, there are plenty of questions about that phenomenon. Yet, how do you examine the biases of historians *who tell us nothing at all* about noteworthy occurrences? It is illogical to label the first, or near first, disclosure of events as revisionist history if the story has hardly or even never been told before at all.

Researching the issue of whether aspects of Indian history have been either deliberately or inadvertently hidden (which ultimately changes nothing about the underlying facts) leads to an unsettling conclusion. When considering who the "our" is in Baum's statement quoted at the beginning of this Introduction, it is clear he did not intend to include darker-skinned people in the concern over "our only safety." Some have questioned whether the Kansas of Baum's imagination included any Indians at all. In that vein, it is incontrovertible that for an entire century after the end of WWI in 1918, virtually all armed conflicts the United States have involved non-European, dark-skinned foes. While obviously the Second World War with Germany involved a European foe, the United States was simultaneously fighting the Japanese. If the Wounded Knee "occupation" of 1973 and surrounding events are classified as a "war," as claimed by former FBI Agent Joseph Trimbach, at that juncture the United States was fighting *two* darker-skinned "enemies" simultaneously—American Indians and the Viet Cong/North Vietnamese—at that time. While the "Cold War" arrayed the United States and some allies against the Soviet Union, arguably the closest the two nations came to direct confrontation was in Afghanistan in the early 1980s, the Cuban Missile Crisis of 1962, or during the Berlin Blockade of 1948-1949.

The understanding of how many indigenous people were present at the time Columbus "discovered" America, and why there are so few now, is a critical issue to be addressed shortly. However, there is also the issue of determining what the Indian people were really like at that time, which can be overlooked when considering the numbers matter. Importantly, new research has resulted in an increasing number of historians, researchers, etc. disputing that what the Europeans "discovered" was a desolate, sparsely land populated with a few "savages." For example, Charles Mann wrote the original inhabitants of North America: "…were not nomadic but built up and lived in some of the world's biggest and most opulent cities. Far from being dependent on big-game hunting, most Indians lived on farms. Others subsisted on fish and shellfish. As for the horses, they were from Europe."[54]

In that regard, Mann called into question the whole notion of European cultural and even military superiority. He noted that during the timeframe between the sixteenth and eighteenth centuries, contrary to the: "…master narrative… Europeans routinely lost [wars with indigenous groups] when they could not take advantage of disease and political fragmentation."[55] Mann also asked the obvious question: "If Christian civilization was so wonderful, why were its inhabitants all trying to settle somewhere else?"[56] University of California professor Dr. Andrea Smith provided an answer: "At the time of Columbus' exploits, European society was a dysfunctional system, racked by mass poverty, disease, religious oppression, war, and institutionalized violence."[57]

Fortunately, in her book on the Bear River Massacre, Fleisher, in commenting on how the general public learns history, asked the most critical question of all, "How are the stories being told?" She noted that most people don't have the opportunity to review original source documents such as letters and journals produced at or near the time of events. As such, she suggested we are heavily reliant (perhaps too heavily reliant?) on secondary sources such as books, and even "tertiary" level documents such as "…the blockbuster history genre Stephen Ambrose has popularized."[58] Another question arising from the unavailability of most people to view original source documents is this—what is being left out of books and who decides what is being left out? Peter Stearns commented in that regard: "…history does not rely on memorization, but rather involves the ability to select information from the available evidence, organize it, and draw meaningful conclusions from it."[59]

Yet, it is vital when considering the value of original source documents related to Indian history to question whether they are being used in their proper context. What the proper context is, is often the source of debate, but it at least as a minimum must be identified. In *Touched by Fire*, one of the seemingly endless number of the biographies of George A. Custer, Louise Barnett criticized the conclusion of historian Richard Slotkin about an episode in Custer's life. In *Fatal Environment*, Slotkin stated Custer was: "angling to acquire…an Indian agency and to purchase…a post tradership." Barrett explained in her view, Slotkin imagined the description of nefarious intent in a letter one Rufus Ingalls wrote to Custer where he stated, among other things: "We want to do a big thing in [sic] Black Hills…" Barnett indicated Slotkin misidentified the author of the letter as being Abraham Buford as opposed to Ingalls. Barnett also claimed the mistake was compounded by James Welch repeating it in *Killing Custer: The Battle of the Little Big Horn and the Fate of the Plains Indians*.[60]

Yet the real error, or at least overstatement, in the context of Indian history appears to have been committed by Barnett herself. While noting Slotkin's ultimately insignificant error, she does not expend any energy dissecting the impact of these trading posts on, to borrow from Welch, "…*the Fate of Plains Indians*." Custer's motives in desiring to get involved in Indian trading posts are ultimately similar to Columbus'—they are largely irrelevant in that whatever these motives consisted of, noble or not, indigenous culture was affected (or in Custer's case would have been affected by him). Nevertheless, Indians usually came out on the short end when trading with whites was involved. Even General William T. Sherman, hardly considered sympathetic to the plight of Indians, recognized the problem of Indians restricted to reservations, which he called: "…parcel[s] of land inhabited by Indians and surrounded by thieves."[61] Barnett's concerns about Custer's dealings are commendable, but the context of the events requires examining the larger question, for example, of how Indians were affected, or perhaps infected by disease, after contacts with whites.

Sometimes, if people are provided as close to as possible accurate and verifiable facts even without an explanation of the context, they can draw their own conclusions. For example, an individual named Scott Burgwin executed a statement that he was arrested by the FBI and other law enforcement types in Bend, Oregon, as his group was travelling from Eugene, Oregon in April 1973. His "crime" was that he was caught with a truckload of food and clothing he planned to transport to the Wounded Knee "occupiers" some 1,200 miles away.[62] In an another instance, original source documents claim that after her body was discovered in an exceptionally remote part of the Pine Ridge Reservation, not only were Anna Mae Aquash's hands cut off and shipped to Washington, D.C., to enable the FBI to identify her through fingerprints, but at some point her *fingers were cut off of her hands*.[63] In any event, facts such as the circumstances of Burgwin's arrest, and the dismemberment of Anna Mae, do not seem to find their way into the history books. To a large extent, the significance of those reported facts can be determined by conscientious readers if they are ever made aware of them.

Also, one of the critical tools needed for credibly contemplating white-Indian history is to examine what might be labeled the "blind spots" of failing to take Indian views into account—at all. It is a theme which will be repeated throughout this book. Certainly, there is no problem in having this book subjected to that same scrutiny. In any event, due to constant repetition of erroneous conclusions, and their apathetic acceptance by historians, these "blind spots" are often difficult to identify. For example, in the Introduction to the book written by Libbie Custer, the wife and then widow of General George A. Custer of the "Last Stand" fame, *Boots and Saddles,* Jane Stewart chided Ms. Custer for her: "…general tendency…to ignore completely or gloss over anything critical pertaining to her husband's life." Yet, just a few sentences previously Stewart participated in the same glossing-over in describing events on the Great Plains in 1876. She claimed the Indians there "disregarded" the "order" for all those in Sioux and Cheyenne country to come into the agencies, as reservations were sometimes called, before January 31, 1876, or be "classified as hostiles."[64] Putting aside the discussion of the mind-numbingly specious term "hostile" for a moment, the Indians saw the "order" entirely differently. William B. Matson reported in *Crazy Horse, The Lakota Warrior's Life and Legacy,* to the beleaguered Lakota, the "order" was: "…merely their acknowledgement that a big fight was coming, and their way to make it seem like we started it."[65]

The important task of humanizing Indians and deconstructing myths about them contains an additional challenge—to begin to address the question raised by Richard Drinnon. He asked about whites who now occupy the United States: "How have we become alienated from ourselves and from the land?"⁶⁶ This question coincides with the emergence of what some argue is the practice of acting as a "plastic medicine man"—someone intent on appropriating Indian spiritual practices—sometimes for profit. Lakota Scholar Vine Deloria, Jr., observed: "'White people in this country are so alienated from their own lives and so hungry for some sort of real life that they'll grasp at any straw to save themselves.'"⁶⁷

This phenomenon perhaps reached its zenith as the hippie era was finally dying out in the mid-seventies. Gary Snyder, a white poet, won a Pulitzer Prize for his 1975 book *Turtle Island*. Snyder more or less claimed he was an Indian Shaman, which drew scorn from Indians who argued he was ripping off Indian culture, among other things. As Buffy Sainte-Marie (a Cree and Canadian folk singer) once said of "hippie" types: "'They'll never be Indians. The white people never seem to realize they cannot suck the soul out of a race. The ones with the sweetest intentions are the worst soul suckers. [They need to be] the best white people they can be.'"⁶⁸

In humanizing Indians there is also the need to address the distorted perspective of whites who argue Manifest Destiny and/or Westward Expansion was inevitable or the product of forces outside the control of human agencies. A superlative and unique viewpoint for analyzing this dilemma is again found in Richard Slotkin's *Gunfighter Nation*, where he described the challenges facing what was called the National Commission on the Causes and Prevention of Violence which memorialized its conclusions in 1968:

> The Report [of the Commission] had the paradoxical tasks of criticizing those aspects of American life and history that have produced such frightening levels of social violence while defending American society from its demonization by leftist and European critics. It had to awaken Americans to a realization of what was wrong in their history and culture without intensifying their mood of angry despair—a mood that would make constructive reform impossible.⁶⁹

The Commission also performed its most important function when it: "…specifically criticized the exceptionalist myths by which Americans had rationalized their social violence."⁷⁰

When considering to decide if it is easy to cast too harsh a light on past events and attitudes, it is integral to remember Jefferson claimed—and his claim has been repeated countless times—not that the United States was a city on the side of the hill on the upward trend to a state of bliss, but that it *was* the "City on the Hill." There is no ambiguity in this proclamation, and it is a symbol of the belief in the truth of American Exceptionalism. People who repeated this and continue to repeat this phrase have no doubt the United States is the most upright, moral, democratic, and closest to heaven as an earthly place can ever get. Unfortunately, John F. MacArthur in *The Vanishing Conscience* asked the real question of Indian history, or more precisely, viewing the current state of Indian affairs:

> Is society becoming [or remaining] incapable of even thinking in terms of good and evil? Has the relativism of a humanistic culture rendered modern society wholly amoral?⁷¹

Until recently, the poultice of myths has been the remedy for the pangs of petrified consciences of whites ever-present but rarely acknowledged. Richard Slotkin advised: "…it is the function of myth to provide a formula for credence and faith, not an apparatus for critical analysis."[72] Fortunately, Robert F. Berkhofer, a former University of Michigan history professor, wrote one of the best books on Indian history—*The White Man's Indian*—to shine a light on the path through the fog of these myths. In his laser-like, focused analysis of Indian history, Berkhofer noted another historian engaged in: "…following the suggestion of D.H. Lawrence that Americans had always tried to exorcise the Indian demon in their midst only to fall prey to the demon of the continent." Even more critical to understanding Indian history, Berkhofer explained:

> In the course of surveying the voluminous secondary literature from several disciplines that I considered relevant to the topic, I was constantly struck by how often scholars seemed oblivious of research germane to their topics in other disciplines or how frequently they presented conclusions and themes about a historic period without being aware of similar patterns holding for another era.[73]

However, as will hopefully be made clear through the liberal use of the writing of those such as Slotkin and Limerick, the experiences of various ethnic groups are not necessarily interchangeable.

In regard to the preceding comments by Berkhofer, one simple fact rarely if ever rises to prominence in discussions about Indian history but puts just about every other aspect of the topic in perspective—by the time of former President John Quincy Adams' death in 1848: "The Mexican War had been won and the expansion to the West was complete… Now there was nowhere farther to expand."[74] This fact will be particularly relevant in the discussion of the Wounded Knee Massacre of 1890 and the alleged violent "breakout" planned by the Lakota. Thoughtful writers like Stew Magnuson have argued: "The thought of attacking anybody never crossed their [the Lakota's] minds. Most of the Pine Ridge Agency Population didn't believe in the Ghost Dance religion… They couldn't have broken out and attacked anyone had they wanted to."[75] After considering the reality of conquest by the whites and the precariousness of their situation, the question about the Lakota then correctly turns into: breakout to where?

Indeed, when examining the Wounded Knee Massacre and the events surrounding it, which is essentially one of the central topics of this book, careful readers realize the conventional explanations are *reductio ad absurdum*—i.e., as the term suggests, ultimately absurd. More details will be added in later chapters, but the summary of the explanation is that Spotted Elk—also known as "Big Foot"—while leading his people to Pine Ridge to seek provisions and shelter during a bitterly cold South Dakota winter, chose to march his people directly to where heavily armed soldiers were located instead of bypassing them to avoid a confrontation. Then, Big Foot's Minneconjou allowed themselves to be herded into a valley where they were completely surrounded by this heavily armed force outnumbering them by an estimated almost five-to-one ratio.[76] Subsequently, the Indian warriors used a shot arguably accidentally fired by a deaf man named Black Coyote, while wrestling with at least two soldiers, as a signal to attack with rifles hidden under blankets. Not a shred of evidence indicated any prior planning of this attack, but somehow this random rifle shot was determined to be the signal for the "ambush." Additionally, historians rarely highlight at the time the Minneconjou sprang this confrontation with the itchy trigger-fingered federal troops, "Big Foot" was completely incapacitated with pneumonia, and was determined to avoid trouble and stated so more than once. Further, as conventional accounts rarely highlight, the Minneconjou chose to conduct their uprising two weeks *after* the assassination of one of the most revered Indian leaders of all time, Sitting Bull, who was then no longer available to assist in leading any "outbreak."

Rex Alan Smith, in *Moon of Popping Trees,* which contained a typical account of the Wounded Knee Massacre, and from which quotes in previous paragraphs were taken, advised: "…in no other area of American history is true accuracy harder to achieve, nor has more inaccurate nonsense been written than in that pertaining to American Indians."[77] Nevertheless, Smith's claim: "…the army did not have the *slightest* intention of getting into a fight with the Indians that day at Wounded Knee [emphasis added],"[78] simply does not ring true. Likewise, barely three pages before granting absolution to the United States government for the dark stain on its flag, Smith quoted an order from the commanding general of the South Dakota region, General Nelson "Bearcoat" Miles, which instructed: "Disarm the Indians. Take every precaution to prevent their escape. If they choose to fight, destroy them."[79] Smith's claim the Wounded Knee Massacre was: "…*mostly a battle, partly a massacre, and entirely a tragic blunder* [emphasis in original]"[80] wilts under serious scrutiny.

Cries for revenge for Indians killing whites, even in mutual combat such as the Battle of Little Big Horn, fits that notion of needing to be aware of "similar patterns holding for another era" described by Berkhofer. A cry for bloody vengeance arose as a result of a series of attacks and counterattacks between the Indians and the newly arrived Europeans in New Amsterdam in 1640. The Raritan Indians attacked the settlement on Staten Island after the settlers apparently stole some beaver skins from an Indian who had too much to drink. During the Indians' emotionally charged attack, four settlers were killed, and their houses were set on fire. Willem Kieft, the singularly rigid and arrogant governor of New Amsterdam, viewed this as an opportunity to respond to the Indians' attack and as a rationalization for mass slaughter.

"[C]onfident that he had a justification for liquidating at least some of the most troublesome tribes," Kieft sent a combined force of 80 soldiers and sailors on the offensive against the Indians with the idea of imposing retribution. Kieft also, in a pattern to be replicated throughout the coming decades and centuries, engaged the services of the colony's Indian allies in his fight against the Raritans. Kieft not only encouraged them to "'cut off'" any Raritans but upped the ante for their participation by offering ten fathoms of wampum for each Raritan head delivered to Kieft's fort. If a Raritan head was presented which was proven to be directly linked to the killing of settlers on Staten Island, twice the reward was paid.

Kieft's forces themselves invaded the Raritans' village on Staten Island and killed several of them. To make certain the Raritans understood the superior morality of European culture, Kieft's men seized the brother of the Raritan leader and tortured him "'in his private parts with a piece of split wood.'" Kieft's forces also burned some villages and drove off livestock. To round out the festivities, an Indian ally arrived and: "'in great triumph, [brought] a dead hand hanging on a stick'" claimed to formerly be attached to the killer of some Dutch on Staten Island. Bernard Bailyn added: "Kieft's bloody zeal was appeased, but only for the moment."

The next year, 1641, a young warrior, committed to avenging the murder of an uncle, killed an old wheelwright living in north Manhattan, afterwards decapitating him and ransacking his house. Kieft demanded the perpetrator be produced for trial, but the local chief refused in view of the number of his tribesmen that had been slain by the colonists. Kieft subsequently campaigned for the authority "'to attack the Indians as enemies.'" In another phrase reminiscent of Baum's quote at the beginning of the Introduction, Kieft postulated: "'…the barbarous murder must be avenged for the sake and security of our lives and cattle.'" In one incident at Pevonia on the Jersey side of the Hudson River, Dutch soldiers massacred 80 Indians. In a scenario duplicated by Colonel John Chivington slightly over 220 years later, it was claimed by Cornelis Melyn (although argued by some to be an exaggeration):

> Infants were torn from their mother's breasts, and hacked to pieces in the presence of the parents, and pieces thrown into the fire and in the water, and other sucklings, being bound to small boards, were cut, stuck, and pierced, and miserably massacred to move a heart of stone. Some were thrown into the river, and when the fathers and mothers endeavored to save them, the soldiers would not let them come on land but made both parents and children drown.

It was later claimed the mother-in-law of the notorious secretary to Kieft, Cornelis van Tienhoven: "'amused herself in kicking about the heads of the dead men which had been brought in as bloody trophies of that midnight slaughter.'" A later raid in Westchester County by Dutch and English troops was led by Captain John Underhill, who had been previously involved with the slaughter of Pequots. He positioned his troops to surround a village of wigwams and proceeded to killed 180 of its inhabitants as they tried to escape. Others, estimated to be as many as 700, who remained in the village, were burned alive. One witness to the affair made the odd observation: "'What was most wonderful [was that] among this vast collection of men, women and children not one was heard to cry or to scream.'"[81]

John Demos, in his book on colonists captured by Indians and others, *Unredeemed Captive*, cautioned when reviewing events: "Historians must try to peel back its surface and touch the more complicated reality behind."[82] The instruction applies to other events and broader aspects of history as well. Even though Rex Alan Smith put much of the blame for the Wounded Knee Massacre on the Indians in his book *Moon of Popping Trees*, his comment regarding an incident involving a drunken interpreter: "…there are good reasons for believing the Indian version to be much closer to the truth"[83] is sound guidance when looking at any event or events in this broader panorama of Indian history. Even General "Bearcoat" Miles seemingly regretted the Wounded Knee Massacre and castigated those whom he held responsible for the slaughter, which belies the many claims the events of December 29, 1890, involved mutual combat. Nevertheless, the distortion in reporting events surrounding the Wounded Knee Massacre continues in recent writing. In his 2010 book, *Empire of the Summer Moon*, which was primarily about the Comanches, author S. C. Gwynne inexplicably concluded, with little explanation, why he thought the "Ghost Dance" was about the "annihilation or disappearance of whites."[84] Gwynne did not, among other things, note that much of the hysteria surrounding the "Ghost Dance" was generated by irresponsible newspaper reporters looking to interest readers in their paid-by-the-column news stories.

The subject of Demos' book, a review of the so-called "captivity narratives," provides an excellent platform for placing Indian events and history in "context" and to some extent unraveling the myth of Indian savagery. Demos noted that of all of what were considered the bad aspects of Indian captivity, one of: "...the worst is that some captives will come to *prefer* Indian ways [emphasis is original]."[85] Additionally, as Kenneth C. Davis noted in *America's Hidden History*: "One scholarly estimate counted more than 1,640 New Englanders taken hostage by Indians between 1675 and 1763." Davis added, as suggested by Demos, that not all the captives made dramatic escapes and killed their captors as one Hannah Dustin did. Some rejected the Puritan lifestyle altogether. Davis cited one study by historian Carol Burkin and noted: "'...at least one-third of the women taken to New France chose to remain, and at least 40 percent converted to Catholicism and married French husbands.'"[86]

The conversions to Catholicism were undoubtedly fueled by the pressure applied by Jesuit priests. Nonetheless, although Burkin's study indicated the captives married French husbands, the fact remains that many of the captives held by Indians in New England chose to remain with them even when given the opportunity to return to the Puritan-run settlements. Dr. Smith claimed: "Between 1675 and 1763, almost 40 percent of women who were taken captive by native people in New England chose to remain with their captors."[87] The "captivity narratives" are one of many useful tools for peeling back the surface myths and looking at the "...complicated reality behind."

Nevertheless, why does it matter, particularly for whites and other non-Indians, what happened in the ever-distant past? Historian Jack Norton provided one answer. He noted that when Indians killed whites, there was almost always swift and terrible retribution. However, when whites killed Indians, as in the case of the mass killing of Wiyots in California in the mid-19th century, there was no accountability. He continued:

> The legacy to us is the belief that our actions have no consequences. But, in truth, all of us still suffer the consequences of what happened here. Indians have been wounded in their psyches, their economy, and physically. Other Americans have been cheated of the truth and therefore of a piece of their own identity.[88]

Alfed W. Crosby, Jr., the author of *The Columbian Exchange—Biological and Cultural Consequences of 1492*, reiterated, in the very first sentence of his preface, Cook-Lynn's point of the importance of establishing the proper framework for viewing events in Indian history, and stated: "Nothing can be understood apart from context, and man is no exception."[89] Crosby also admonished us to understand the descriptions of the "sensational accomplishments" of the conquistadors: "...are so hypnotically interesting that most of us never shake loose from their surface fascination to seek the real significance of the events they depict."[90]

Robert Morgan, author of *Lions of the West*, acknowledged the reality of Westward Expansion was: "...a narrative of ruthlessness and greed on a cataclysmic scale." Yet, it seems ingrained as the irresistible urge of historians to glamorize white brutality. In that regard, Morgan continued: "...we cannot deny the poetry of the westward vision."[91] Morgan, seemingly trying to absolve the United States government of its responsibility for its harsh treatment of Indians, used Tolstoy as his foil. Morgan noted the famous

Russian writer wrote in *War and Peace*: "'The force that decides the fate of peoples does not lie in military leaders, not even in armies and battles, but in something else.'"[92] It is a clever quote, but is it a proper tool to evaluate the actions of human beings? For example, while it might appear the building of railroads across the Great Plains in the mid-19th century was simply the work of private entities, their development received the wholehearted blessing of government officials, particularly General William T. Sherman. All involved in this enterprise were human, earthly entities. Yet, as will be discussed in this book's chapter on Manifest Destiny, the pseudo-scientific idea of "'survival of the fittest'" permeated almost all facets of economic growth in the United States, particularly in the last half of the 19th century. The corollary to Andrew Jackson's notion that government should not intervene on the side of the rich meant that government had no business intervening on behalf of the downtrodden. Of course, it is doubtful if the government, without an ulterior motive, ever meaningfully intervened on behalf of the downtrodden, particularly if they happened to be Indians.

When the question arises as to whether Indians were the victims of genocide, a common deflecting response is that there was no "official" policy of genocide. In a sense this thought process is the myth under which the other myths outlined in this book thrive. For example, there are actually still current writers such as S. C. Gwynne, Terry Mort, and Naomi Schaefer Riley who have no qualms about suggesting that if Indians were mistreated, they were savages and got what they deserved only in response to their aggression. For another example, in discussing the "ownership" of the Black Hills of South Dakota in *Killing the White Man's Indian,* Fergus Bordewich stated the Lakota acquired this territory: "Quite simply, by force of arms—by naked conquest. They entered and they pushed aside whoever was there."[93] In other words, since he believed the Lakota took the territory from other Indians, settlers had the right to take the land from the Lakota and the consequences to them be damned. Although the specific situation of the history of the Black Hills of Bordewich's musings will be addressed throughout various sections of this book, this same type of reasoning is often generally applied to situations involving other Indian nations throughout United States history.

Likewise, even for chronic problems such as the current poverty on Indian reservations, there is a belief the simple solution to all of the dysfunction is to provide Indians the: "…opportunity to live lives of freedom and dignity in the land we all share."[94] Yet even a staunch supporter of encouraging Indians to forget the past and look to the future such as Fergus Bordewich noted one of the factors inhibiting economic growth on Indian reservations is their remoteness.[95] Nevertheless, how the Indians are responsible for their "remoteness" or how this obstacle is to be overcome is not meaningfully analyzed by Bordewich or rarely anyone else.

Unfortunately for the defenders of the white conquest of the Western Hemisphere, the crucial issue that sets white actions apart from those of Indians is that there is scant, if any, evidence to suggest Indians ever used God, the Creator, or any type of theological pretense to attempt to justify annihilation of enemies. Of course, there are instances where Indian warriors prayed for bravery, etc. Nevertheless, compare that to the theme of Western expansion under the guise of "Manifest Destiny" which reveals the ugly truth that whites often justified brutality under the rubric that God wanted it to be so. It is a troubling rationalization.

Further, Bordewich's own words disclose the chasm between the aggressive behavior of whites as opposed to that of Indians. He stated the Lakota "...pushed aside whoever was there." When another tribe was described as "pushed aside" it implies, at least by Bordewich's own phraseology, they were at least left intact enough as a unit to relocate. There is little comparison between warfare among Indian nations, to borrow the words of Theodore Roosevelt in describing the later 19th century Dawes Act allotment system, with the "'mighty pulverizing engine to break up tribal mass'"[96] used by whites to subjugate and imprison Indians in the ghastly reservation system. Something else that is usually overlooked in the rush to equate the dominance of the Lakota on the Plains with the dominance of Europeans over the entirety of North America is that the two main ingredients in the Lakota formula for dominance—horses and rifles—were introduced to them by Europeans.

Another element that is lacking in the comparison between white and Indian behavior is the recognition of the scale of the events. An event known as the "Trail of Tears" involved the forced relocation of an estimated 16,000 Indians from the Southeast United States to Oklahoma. There is little in the history of Indian-nation-to-Indian-nation interactions to compare the number of people involved in that immensely dark episode.

Sometimes, even in death, Indians could not escape the whites' continuing and ravenous appetite for more Indian land. In 1961, despite energetic opposition by Seneca leaders, the Kinzua Dam just north of the city of Pittsburgh was built, flooding much Seneca land, including Seneca leader Cornplanter's burial site. Where Cornplanter's and the remains of 3,000 other Senecas ended up is somewhat clouded in mystery, as the Army Corps of Engineers kept their plans about moving the remains a secret.[97] Of course, at times, without even the pretext of obtaining more land, the graves of Indians have simply been unapologetically ransacked to provide specimens for studies, exhibits for museums, and novelties for the entertainment of non-Indians.[98]

By the start of the 20th century, many Indians found themselves virtually imprisoned in a reservation system some believe was the model for Hitler's concentration camps, the evil device used to facilitate the extermination of Jews and other Hitler enemies in mid-20th century Europe.[99] Adding to the tragedy of Indian history, there have been countless stories and images presented about Indians over many years that are incomplete, inaccurate, and sometimes just false. And sometimes, enormously significant events in the lives of Indian nations are not mentioned at all. William Coleman, author of *Voices of Wounded Knee*, in the preface to that wonderful book, discussed the lack of teaching about the Wounded Knee Massacre. He stated: "I looked back to see my college days as a history major. I didn't remember any of my teachers mentioning the incident."[100]

Likewise, lesser-known incidents such as the incarceration of Indians at the Canton/Hiawatha Asylum for Insane Indians, the mass hanging of 38 Indians at Mankato, Minnesota, and others are barely whispered about at all. Yet, even the most diligent historians can miss even just mentioning key facts of well-known incidents. For example, is the fear of being labeled a "conspiracy theorist" too much to overcome to even mention claims of the possible Mormon role in the "Ghost Dance" craze? Likewise, is it too much to suggest the idea blaming the Wounded Knee Massacre on this so-called "Ghost Dance" craze, apparently involving an Indian prophet named Wovoka, as a mere pretext to slaughter more Indians and gain control over more of their lands? Who dares highlight the stories of drunkenness prior to the crazed actions of federal troops on the morning of December 29, 1890, in the remote Wounded Knee area of South Dakota?

Further, often where there are researched histories, there is a lack of "connecting the dots," or even pointing out the obvious. For example, Dillon Myer's name, unlike those of Crazy Horse, Sitting Bull, George Custer, and others, is not one normally associated with the vast and often relentlessly tragic history of the American Indian. Nonetheless, during World War II and for a period shortly thereafter, Myer was Director of the War Relocation Authority from 1942-1946. The War Relocation Authority was the organization responsible for overseeing the mass incarceration of Japanese Americans in the United States during that period. In May of 1950, he was appointed Bureau of Indian Affairs (BIA) Chief by President Harry Truman and served until the start of the Eisenhower Administration in 1953. Ironically, one of Myer's major programs was an attempt to end the Reservation System, commonly referred to as "termination."[101]

That is not to suggest Myer was a benevolent administrator with a heart filled with love toward Indians, since many, many Indians depended and still depend on government programs for survival. It is documented that his brittle nature extended to whites as well. In one episode during his tenure Myer forced the transfer of an Indian agent who had the temerity to merely suggest the BIA had failed to protect the water rights of the Pauite tribe of Utah. There was a tip-off during Myer's War Relocation Authority tenure that he was not going to be a big promoter of what we now loosely label "diversity." In that capacity, he required Japanese citizens considered "agitators" to be isolated from other detainees and be required to take loyalty oaths before being released from internment camps.[102] It would hardly seem surprising then to learn that Myer was a big proponent of assimilation—teaching Indians white culture—and the policy of "termination." The "termination" program was described by many as an effort to eradicate Indian cultures and sever ties between Indians and their tribal lands. For an Indian point of view, in his seminal book *Custer Died for Your Sins*, Vine Deloria, Jr., entitled a 22-page chapter "The Disastrous Policy of Termination" to highlight the importance of the assistance of the federal government for Indians.[103] One example of the harsh reality of the effects of termination involved the Menominee Indians of Wisconsin and their battle to keep a hospital open. This struggle for survival is described in detail in *Freedom with Reservation*, an intriguing book published in 1972.[104]

Yet, to arrive at a point where the story of events like the Wounded Knee Massacre and eventually 20th century Indian activism can be placed in anything resembling their proper contexts, it is useful to at least consider other myths of Indian history. Although the myths are not necessarily specifically articulated throughout this writing, hopefully the essence of the myths themselves are apparent. This was done intentionally so that a reader may, by analyzing the material presented, formulate other myths not even suggested. As such, this book is not a history book in the commonly thought of definition of the word, but it is historical; it might be considered a historiography. The book often uses the lives of individuals, both Indian and non-Indian, as entry points into the discussions of larger issues and myths. However, without question the stories of these individuals are worth telling for the sake of telling them alone without trying to establish larger points.

It may appear the myths are unrelated to one another. Yet the unifying theme of all of them is that their deconstruction is based at least partially on the idea that Indians have histories of their own apart from their roles as unwilling participants in the American/European conquest of North America. Even more important than that is to simply recognize Indians were and are human beings with joys, sorrows, and good and bad qualities just like the rest of humanity. In that regard as well, it is important to acknowledge there are indeed skilled Indian authors and thinkers—the late Vine Deloria, Jr., Joseph Marshall, and Elizabeth Cook-Lynn, to name a few—and they are used in this book as often as possible. Even the writing of controversial Ward Churchill, who some claim is not a "real" Indian, was a source of useful input for the discussion of Indian history.

Nonetheless, it is often the impulse of whites to want to, as historian George Kennan stated, appear "…more wise and noble than we really were…"[105] and that inhibits the influence of Indian writers and intellectuals. One author, Fergus Bordewich, dismissively noted that many Indian intellectuals have: "…a view of history [which] is unforgiving and rooted in a sense of permanent crisis."[106] This is the type of thinking that ends on the street to nowhere with road signs suggesting there was no genocide of Indians and no apology is ever necessary for what happened to Indians in the 500-plus years since Columbus made his first appearance in the Western Hemisphere. What is concerning is that Bordewich made his statement in 1996, not 1896. And while Churchill has been castigated for making some ill-conceived remarks about 9/11 and for possibly having no Indian "blood," he at least has been unrelenting in his raising the issue of genocide against Indians. Churchill's writing has value if for no other reason than to help keep this issue in the minds of American scholars, and more importantly, American citizens.

Indeed, Ward Churchill also provides a starting point for the discussion of who is and is not an Indian, which is not as easy a question to answer as it might seem. As to his analysis of Indian history, many readers with knowledge of contemporary Indian issues may recoil at the liberal use of quotes and analysis of events provided by Churchill as used in this book. He was heavily criticized for remarks made in an essay he wrote after 9/11 and was terminated from the University of Colorado, Boulder, more or less on charges of academic fraud (although some claim the firing was pretextual). Others have mocked his claims of being an "Indian." Yet, to dismiss his writing and comments about Indians being subjected to genocide and related matters eliminates a much-needed counterweight to the viewpoint of more "respectable" historians.

Consider the languid comment by Jerome A. Greene, a historian for the National Park Service, about the December 29, 1890, Wounded Knee Massacre in his book, *American Carnage*: "Although one might hesitate to use the word 'bloodlust' to explain what happened at Wounded Knee, the term is a clear reflection of how the events must have seemed to the Indians involved, particularly noncombatant women, children, and elderly men."[107] Greene does not explain why "one might hesitate." His tone more closely resembles that which would be found at tea-time by someone who found his tea not to his liking rather than one who is describing the unrestrained slaughter of unarmed, starving and freezing human beings, some of whom were chased down for miles before being shot.

Thus, to suppress the writings of Ward Churchill because of his less than well-received comments about 9/11 or for other reasons becomes the embodiment of the cliché "throwing out the baby with the bathwater." If Ward Churchill does not question the standard histories of Indian-white encounters, then who will? One of the distractions created by cries of "revisionist history" is that it diverts attention from analyzing whether certain events or series of events are accurately presented *at all*. Especially in the case of the notorious Wounded Knee Massacre, many alleged circumstances and theories surrounding causes never seem to see the light of day.

For example, wouldn't it be useful, as suggested above, for researchers and historians to review the letter buried in the microfilm of the National Archives containing the suspicions of an army major regarding Mormon involvement in stirring up trouble in 1890 among the Oglala Lakota and other bands?[108] Historian Robert Utley noted: "In the theology of the Church of Jesus Christ of Latter-Day Saints, Indians occupied a place of special significance, and Mormons took special interest in them." Utley also described the rumors regarding Wovoka's deception in creating ice in the Walker River in Nevada in the middle of the summer.[109] Yet, how many other rumors are addressed—*even to simply dismiss them as the musings of misguided conspiracy theorists?* Additionally, considering how far-fetched typical explanations for the Wounded Knee Massacre are, i.e., it was in a response to the "Ghost Dance," how far out can other explanations really be?

What is also seems lacking from much writing about the history of Indians, especially from the "Indians committed atrocities too" crowd, is the presentation of the sheer devastation unleashed upon vast segments of Indian population. For example, in the aftermath of King Philip's War, out of a Native population of approximately 20,000, at least 2,000 were killed in battle or died of their injuries, 3,000 died of sickness or starvation, 1,000 were shipped out of the country as slaves, and another 2,000 or so fled for any sanctuary other Indians could provide. The Native American population of southern New England sustained losses of between 60 to 80 percent.[110] Seemingly minor but ultimately consequential ethical questions are rarely examined as well. In one glaring example of duplicity, the Delawares in Pennsylvania signed a treaty with William Penn which contained a clause whereby the Propriety of Pennsylvania could have title to lands north of the Delaware River at Philadelphia: "'as far as a man can go in a day in a half.'" The Delawares had intended this to be as far as a man could go walking briskly for that long—most likely about 30 miles. However, in an interpretation that wouldn't even have occurred to Penn himself, the proprietors cleared a path northwest of the appropriate bend of the Delaware River. Then, a man was carefully selected for his endurance and athletic ability. On April 9, 1737, he commenced running as steadily and as fast as possible on this cleared pathway; by the end of the 36 hours he had covered 150 miles. The whites mockingly called the treaty from that point forward as the "'Walking Treaty.'"[111]

Interestingly, to review a phenomenon a little over a century later, one of the unexpectedly useful aspects of William Cody's traveling Buffalo Bill's Wild West was that it provided examples of how complicated the answer or answers to the seemingly simple question of who is an Indian could become. Although in the stage performance itself, cowboys played heroes and Indians played the villainous and antagonistic savages, behind the scenes the relationships were much more complex. First and foremost, at least some of the white cowboys had Indian families. William "Bronco Bill" Irving, a white cowboy, had a reputation as a top hand and superb horse rider in the Black Hills region. He also spoke fluent Lakota and was married to a Lakota woman named Ella Bissonett.[112] Curiously, the name Bissonette (with an "e") would figure prominently in events on the Pine Ridge Indian Reservation yet again another century later.[113]

Similarly, William "Billy" Bullock, who joined the Wild West in 1883, had a complex background even before then. His father, William G. Bullock, was a white merchant in Lakota country who married a Lakota woman. This marriage firmed up Bullock's political alliance with Red Cloud, who regarded him as a trusted ally and a go-between when Red Cloud negotiated with the United States government. Likewise, since 1877, Cody also relied heavily on John Y. Nelson, a white man who married into Red Cloud's family, to act as a go-between for Cody and his Indian entertainers. In the show itself, Nelson sometimes drove the Deadwood stage, which depicted a running battle between whites, Indians, and even Mexicans. Sometimes Nelson portrayed a hunter who returned to his family's cabin just in time to help stave off an attack by "savage" Indians. In any event, it was Nelson's real-life comfort in living in and between two cultures that made him so valuable to Cody.[114]

Yet, even those sympathetic to Indians such as Peter Nabokov can perhaps unknowingly support flimsy propositions such as, the Western Hemisphere was sparsely populated at the time of Columbus' arrival. In the very first section of *Native American Testimony*, Nabokov claimed that in 1492: "North America alone was home to an estimated two to ten million people."[115] Few seem to realize (or admit) the question of the indigenous population of North America or the Western Hemisphere at the time of Columbus' arrival is the question that sets the stage for discussing virtually all other myths or aspects of Indian history. The discussion is consistently thwarted for obvious reasons. If it could be credibly established there were, for the sake of discussion, 75 million indigenous people living in North America (or even the entire Western Hemisphere) at the end of the 15th century, then the question few want to address—what happened to all of them?—becomes the proverbial "elephant in the living room" during discussions about Indian history. In his fascinating book *1493*, Charles Mann argued without hesitation that when the Europeans arrived: "…the [western] hemisphere was full of Indians—tens of millions of them."[116] Likewise, the issue of how many indigenous people inhabited North and South America at the time of Columbus' "discovery" is more than a question to be debated in academic circles. It is a question of monumental significance that has been subject to highly political responses. If, as suggested by a growing number of researchers, the answer is a number much higher than the ten million at the high end of the range Nabokov suggested, it becomes difficult, maybe even impossible, to deny Indians in North and South America were victims of genocide.

Similarly, as in the case of the "Ghost Dance," there are many other instances where it is important to question the often illogical and even absurd conclusions presented to history students and the simply curious. For example, in *Killing the White Man's Indian*, a decidedly odd recalibration of the devastating impact of Westward Expansion on Indian nations, Bordewich claimed:

> Although many modern polemicists call upon Americans to regard the nation's treatment of the Indians as a pattern of deliberate 'genocide' the physical extermination of Native Americans was never an official policy of the United States government.[117]

Bordewich's argument is similar to what Tolstoy called "force that decides the fates of peoples" and that which Morgan claimed propelled Westward Expansion. This type of reasoning is what is referred to in law schools and elsewhere as "straw man" arguments. In essence, a "straw man" argument consists of developing a question regarding a nonexistent situation or problem, and then an answer to the nonexistent scenario is provided. Obviously, "straw man" arguments present no real answers to real questions. Of course, there is no evidence an "official policy" of genocide existed. From the simplest of misdemeanors to the most horrible of atrocities such as the "Final Solution" proposed for Jewish people and others in Europe, there is usually no specific written account of plans. Yet, by putting together a circumstantial case (and of course in the case of the Nazis, reviewing *Mein Kampf*), a coherent picture emerges. Bordewich's argument also obscured the reality that in cases such as not preventing gold miners from invading the Black Hills in the mid-1870s, the real crime for the government was *failing* to act.

Nevertheless, there is evidence of the mindset of at least one (then) soon-to-be-elected official as to his views on actively encouraging Westward Expansion. In a September 11, 1888, letter announcing his acceptance of the Republican nomination for President in the 1888 general election, Benjamin Harrison stated: "In the earlier years of our history public agencies to promote immigration were common. The pioneer wanted a neighbor with more friendly instincts than the Indian."[118] This is not the musing of someone who was going to fervently safeguard the rights of Indians.

Deloria, Jr., moreover, provided useful guidance as to how to reevaluate Indian history based on less well-known snippets such as those contained in Harrison's letter and records of other situations:

> Standard textbooks and histories concern themselves with the arrangement of historical artifacts—the dates, policies, movements, and institutions which mark the progress of the human transformation of the North American continent. Anthologies, for the most part, attempt to illustrate a general theme of the conflicting values that characterized the settlement of America. *The missing dimension in our knowledge is the informality of human experience, which colors all our decisions and plays an intimate and influential role in the historical experiences of our species* [emphasis added].[119]

As such, while Harrison's letter does not constitute an "official" policy of the United States, it leaves no doubt in a somewhat informal way as to what the soon-to-be president was thinking—the land should belong to the settlers.

In keeping with Deloria, Jr.'s suggestion to consider the "informality of human experience," the deconstruction of myths about Indian history is addressed in this book through the use of the stories of characters and even at times groups of characters involved in the process of Westward Expansion.

It includes some contemporary individuals as well. Agreeing with Deloria, Jr.'s premise, Albert K. Weinberg stated in the preface to *Manifest Destiny*: "… a study having to do with highly controversial issues of political history and morals demands treatment from an individual point of view."[120] The use of descriptions of the lives of more contemporary players like SuAnne also helps fulfill that purpose, although some readers might disagree with attributing certain information to certain individuals, or the order of presenting that information. And, while the history of Indians in the United States has been relentlessly tragic, it is hopeful the prayer attributed to Black Elk from *Black Elk Speaks* was not in vain:

> In sorrow I am sending a feeble voice, O Six Powers of the World. Hear me in my sorrow, for I may never call again. O make my people live![121]

ENDNOTES

1. Cook-Lynn, *Anti-Indianism in Modern America*, p. 191.
2. James McGregor, *The Wounded Knee Massacre from the Viewpoint of the Sioux* (Rapid City, South Dakota: Fenske Printing, 1940), p. 56.
3. Jerome Greene, *American Carnage: Wounded Knee, 1890* (Norman, Oklahoma: University of Oklahoma Press, 2014), p. 278. Curiously, Greene does not state the Indian man he stated was Iron Hail is better known as Dewey Beard. Powers, *The Killing of Crazy Horse*, p. xvi.
4. Steve Hendricks, *The Unquiet Grave: The FBI and the Struggle for the Soul of Indian Country* (New York: Thunder Mouth's Press, 2006), p. 60.
5. Dee Brown, *Bury My Heart at Wounded Knee: An Indian History of the American West* (New York: St. Martin's Press, 1970), p. 444.
6. Frazier, *On the Rez*, p. 281, n. 6.
7. David E. Stannard, *American Holocaust: The Conquest of the New World* (New York: Oxford University Press, 1992), p. 126.
8. Drinnon, *Facing West*, p. 50.
9. Roxanne Dunbar-Ortiz, *An Indigenous People's History of the United States* (Boston: Beacon Press, 2014), p. 77.
10. Mario Gonzalez and Elizabeth Cook-Lynn, *The Politics of Hallowed Ground: Wounded Knee and the Struggle for Indian Sovereignty* (Chicago: University of Illinois Press, 1999), p. 88.
11. James Welch (with Paul Stekler), *Killing Custer: The Battle of the Little Big Horn and the Fate of the Plains Indians* (New York: Penguin Books, 1994), pp. 191-192.
12. Louis K. Warren, *Buffalo Bill's America: William Cody and the Wild West Show* (New York: Vintage Books/A Division of Random House, 2005), p. 280.
13. David Grau, *Surviving Wounded Knee: The Lakotas and the Politics of Memory* (New York: Oxford University Press, 2016), p. 68.
14. Louise Barnett, *Touched by Fire: The Life, Death and Mythic Afterlife of George Armstrong Custer* (New York: Henry Holt & Co., 1996), p. 373.
15. Captain George J. McMurry, (Chaplain 7th Cavalry) "The Seventh Cavalry at the Fiftieth Anniversary of the Little Big Horn." Custer Collection Monroe, Michigan Public Library.
16. Rex Alan Smith, *Moon of Popping Trees: The Tragedy at Wounded Knee and the End of the Indian Wars.* (Lincoln, Nebraska: University of Nebraska Press, 1996), p. 31.
17. Ibid., pp. 19-22.
18. Means and Wolf, *Where White Men Fear to Tread*, p. 285.
19. Larry McMurtry, *Crazy Horse* (New York: Viking/Penguin Group, 1999), p. 123. Historian Stanley Vestal argued: "Of course the missionaries of long-established sects would not admit that the Ghost Dance was a Christian church [sic]. But their claim is absurd. For you cannot believe in the Second Coming of Christ unless you believe in the First. The Ghost Dance was entirely Christian—except

for the difference in rituals." Stanley Vestal *Sitting Bull: Champion of the Sioux* (Norman, Oklahoma: University of Oklahoma Press, 1932), p. 272.

20 Smith, *Moon of Popping Trees*, p. 181. In fact, Greene in *American Carnage* makes reference to an inventory of weapons taken at least as of the time the shooting started, p. 487 footnote 19.
21 Ibid., p. 179.
22 Renée Sansom Flood, *Lost Bird of Wounded Knee: Spirit of the Lakota* (New York: Scribner, 1995), p. 38. When Rex Alan Smith referenced a "small keg of whiskey" in his *Moon of Popping Trees* p. 179, he did not specify if he understood it to be a ten-gallon keg.
23 Virginia Woolf, "The Elizabethan Lumber Room" *The Common Reader*, 1925.
24 Cook-Lynn, *Anti-Indianism in Modern America*, p. 23.
25 Limerick, *The Legacy of Conquest*, p. 214.
26 D. Cober, "On Racist Discourse in S. C. Gwynne's Empire of the Summer Moon." *Ration of Common Humanity*. September 20, 2013.
27 Albert K. Weinberg, *Manifest Destiny: A Study of Nationalist Expansion in American History* (Chicago: Quadrangle Books, 1963), p. 97.
28 Kass Fleisher, *The Bear River Massacre and the Making of History* (Albany, New York: State University of New York Press, 2004), *passim*.
29 Ibid., p. 252.
30 Berg, *38 Nooses: Lincoln, Little Crow and the Beginning of the Frontier's End* (New York: Pantheon Books, 2012), p. 208.
31 Fleisher, *The Bear River Massacre*, p. 279.
32 Ibid., p. 287.
33 Jaimes, Ed., M. Annette Jaimes with Theresa Hailey "American Indian Women: At the Center of Indigenous Resistance in Contemporary North America." *The State of Native America*, p. 332.
34 Stannard, *American Holocaust*, p. 11.
35 Peter N. Stearns, *Meaning Over Memory: Recasting the Teaching of Culture and History* (Chapel Hill, North Carolina: University of North Carolina Press, 1993), p. 138.
36 Jaimes, Ed., M. Annette Jaimes with Theresa Hailey "American Indian Women: At the Center of Indigenous Resistance in Contemporary North America" *The State of Native North America*, p. 311.
37 Crow Dog, *Lakota Woman* (New York: Harper Collins, 1990), p. 4. Mary also referenced her mother being sterilized some years previous to this event at the Pine Ridge Hospital. pp. 8-9. Professor Andrea Smith cited a report that indicated: "Indian women on Pine Ridge in the Black Hills experience a miscarriage rate six times higher than the national average." *Conquest: Sexual Violence and American Indian Genocide* (Durham, North Carolina: 2005), pp. 66-67. (Citing Lakota Harden in her end notes), "Black Hills Paha Sapa Report," (Rapid City: South Dakota, 1980). This may provide some context for Mary Crow Dog's comments.
38 Fleisher, *The Bear River Massacre*, p. 285.

39 Naomi Schaefer Riley, *The New Trail of Tears: How Washington is Destroying American Indians* (New York: Encounter Books, 2016) *passim*.
40 Fleisher, *The Bear River Massacre*, p. 272-277.
41 Slotkin, *Fatal Environment*, p. 321.
42 Joseph Trimbach, *American Indian Mafia: An FBI Agent's True Story About Wounded Knee, Leonard Peltier, and the American Indian Movement (AIM)* (Parker, Colorado: Outskirts Press, 2009) p. 13.
43 Fleisher, *The Bear River Massacre*, pp. 304-305.
44 Ibid., p. 312.
45 Ibid., p. 305.
46 Ibid., p. 250.
47 Ward Churchill, *Since Predator Came: Notes from the Struggle for American Indian Liberation*, (Oakland, California: AK Press, 1995), pp. 30, 175.
48 Slotkin, *Gunfighter Nation*, p. 212.
49 Scott Berg, *38 Nooses: Lincoln, Little Crow and the Beginning of the Frontier's End* (New York: Pantheon Books, 2012), *passim*.
50 Michael Bradley, *The Columbus Conspiracy: An Investigation into the Secret History of Christopher Columbus* (Willowdale, Ontario, Canada: Hunslow Press, 1992), p. 5.
51 Ibid., p. 6.
52 Washington Irving, *The Life and Voyages of Christopher Columbus* (Hertfordshire, England: Wordsworth Editions Limited, 2008), p. 114.
53 Fleisher, *The Bear River Massacre*, p. xiii.
54 Charles C. Mann, *1491: New Revelations of the Americas Before Columbus* (New York: Vintage Books/A Division of Random House, 2005), p. 18. However, it is unlikely Mann meant to suggest *all* the indigenous inhabitants of North America at the time of Columbus' arrival were farmers.
55 Ibid., p. 104.
56 Ibid., p. 52.
57 Andrea Smith, *Conquest: Sexual Violence and American Indian Genocide* (Durham, North Carolina: Duke University Press, 2005), p. 17.
58 Fleisher, *The Bear River Massacre*, p. 124.
59 Stearns, *Meaning Over Memory*, p. 173.
60 Barnett, *Touched by Fire*, p. 268. The Slotkin quote is contained in endnote 54 for this page.
61 Hendricks, *Unquiet Grave*. p. 61.
62 Scott Burgwin, Affidavit dated March 31, 1973 (St. Paul, Minnesota: Minnesota Historical Society March 31, 1973).
63 Kenneth Tilsen, April 15, 1976 letter to FBI Director Clarence Kelly (St. Paul, Minnesota: Minnesota Historical Society April 15, 1976).
64 Elizabeth R. Custer, *Boots and Saddles: or Life in the Dakotas with General Custer* (Norman, Oklahoma: University of Oklahoma Press, 1961), p. xvii.

65 William Matson, *Crazy Horse: The Lakota Warrior's Life and Legacy* (Layton, Utah: Gibbs Smith, 2016), p. 90.
66 Drinnon, *Facing West*, p. xxix.
67 Ward Churchill, "Spiritual Hucksterism: The Rise of the Plastic Medicine Men," *Cultural Survival Quarterly Magazine*, June 2003.
68 Sherry Smith, *Hippies, Indians, and the Fight for Red Power* (New York: Oxford University Press, 2012), p. 81.
69 Slotkin, *Gunfighter Nation*, p. 555.
70 Ibid., p. 556.
71 John MacArthur, *The Vanishing Conscience: Drawing the Line in a No-Fault, Guilt Free World* (Dallas, Texas: Word Publishing, 1994), p. 57.
72 Richard Slotkin, *Regeneration through Violence: The Mythology of the American Frontier 1600-1860* (Norman, Oklahoma: University of Oklahoma Press, 1973), p. 13.
73 Robert Berkhofer, *The White Man's Indian: Images of the American Indian from Columbus to the Present* (New York: Vintage Books/A Division of Random House, 1979), p. xiv.
74 Robert Morgan, *Lions of the West: Heroes and Villains of the Westward Expansion* (Chapel Hill: Algonquin Books, 2011), p. 410.
75 Stew Magnuson, *The Death of Raymond Yellow Thunder and Other True Stories from the Nebraska-Pine Ridge Border Towns* (Lubbock, Texas: Texas Tech University Press, 2008), p. 120.
76 Grau, *Surviving Wounded Knee*, p. 62.
77 Smith, *Moon of Popping Trees*, p. vii.
78 Ibid., p. 182. Evidence this is an inaccurate conclusion is Thomas Powers' comment that as Spotted Elk's people were heading to Pine Ridge, the U.S. Cavalry was "…hot on their heels." This suggests the possibility the Minneconjou were driven toward Wounded Knee Creek to ensure they encountered the bulk of the U.S. forces. Powers, *The Killing of Crazy Horse*, p. xvi.
79 Ibid., p. 179.
80 Ibid., p. 1.
81 Bernard Bailyn, *The Barbarous Years: The Peopling of British North America: The Conflict of Civilizations* (New York: Alfred A. Knopf/A Division of Random House), pp. 219-221.
82 John Demos, *The Unredeemed Captive: A Family Story from Early America* (New York: Vintage Books/A Division of Random House, 1995), p. 122.
83 Smith, *Moon of Popping Trees*, p. 173.
84 S. C. Gwynne, *Empire of the Summer Moon*, pp. 299-300.
85 Demos, *The Unredeemed Captive*, p. 4.
86 Kenneth C. Davis, *America's Hidden History: Untold Tales of the Frist Pilgrims, Fighting Women, and Forgotten Founders Who Shaped a Nation*, (New York: First Smithsonian Books, Harper Collins Publishers, 2008), p. 52.
87 Smith, *Conquest*, p. 20.

88 Fergus Bordewich, *Killing the White Man's Indian: Reinventing Native Americans at the End of the Twentieth Century* (New York: Anchor Books/A Division of Random House, 1996), p. 54.
89 Alfred W. Crosby, *The Columbian Exchange: Biological and Cultural Consequences of 1492* (Greenwood, Connecticut: Greenwood Press, 1972), p. xiii.
90 Ibid., p. xiv.
91 Morgan, *Lions of the West*, p. xx.
92 Ibid., p. xxi. Similarly, Robert Remini, in his mostly apologetic book on President Andrew Jackson's Indian policy, argued Indian removal, or what became known as the "Trail of Tears," was "inevitable." Robert V. Remini, *Andrew Jackson and His Indian Wars* (New York: Penguin Putnam, Inc., 2001) p. 237.
93 Bordewich, *Killing the White Man's Indian*, p. 228.
94 Riley, *The New Trail of Tears*, p. xiii.
95 Bordewich, *Killing the White Man's Indian*, p. 340.
96 Charles Wilkinson, *Blood Struggle: The Rise of Modern Indian Nations* (New York: W.W. Norton & Co., 2005), p. 43.
97 Ibid., p. 116-117.
98 Vine Deloria, Jr. *God is Red: A Native View of Religion* (Golden, Colorado: Fulcrum Publishing, 1994), pp 13-18.
99 Neeta Lind, "Pine Ridge: American Prisoner of War Camp #334" *Daily Kos,* June 4, 2010. Hitler was also quoted as saying: "I don't see why a German who eats a piece of bread should torment himself with the idea that the soil which produced this bread has been won by the sword. When we eat wheat from Canada, we don't think about the despoiled Indians." Adolf Hitler, 2000, *Hitler's Table Talk, 1941-1944.* As quoted in Woolford, Benvenuto, Hinton, Eds. David B. MacDonald, "Genocide in the Indian Residential Schools." *Colonial Genocide in Indigenous North America*, p. 306.
100 William S.E. Coleman, *Voices of Wounded Knee* (Lincoln, Nebraska: Bison Books/University of Nebraska Press, 2000), p. x.
101 Richard Drinnon, *Keeper of Concentration Camps: Dillon S. Meyer and American Racism* (Berkeley, California: University of California Press, 1987), *passim*.
102 Ibid., pp. 78-80.
103 Deloria, Jr. *Custer Died for Your Sins*, pp. 60-82.
104 Deborah Shames, Ed., *Freedom with Reservation: The Menominee Struggle to Save Their Land and People* (Madison, Wisconsin: Impressions, Inc., 1972), *passim*.
105 Morgan, *Lions of the West*, p. xxiii.
106 Bordewich, *Killing the White Man's Indian*, p. 279.
107 Greene, *American Carnage*, p. 271.
108 E.R. Kellogg, "Commanding" October 27, 1890 letter, United States National Archives.
109 Robert M. Utley, *The Last Days of the Sioux Nation* (New Haven, Connecticut: Yale University Press, 1963), pp. 65-66.
110 Davis, *America's Hidden History*, p. 75.

111 Allan W. Eckert, *That Dark and Bloody River: Chronicles of the Ohio River Valley* (New York: Bantam Books, 1995), p. xxx.

112 Warren, *Buffalo Bill's America.* p. 403.

113 Means and Wolf, *Where White Men Fear to Tread,* pp. 252-253. Means described Gladys Bissonette as a prominent force at a meeting on February 27, 1973, in the decision to "occupy" Wounded Knee.

114 Warren, *Buffalo Bill's America*, p. 403.

115 Peter Nabokov, Ed., *Native American Testimony: A Chronicle of Indian-White Relations from Prophecy to Present* (New York, Penguin Books), 1978, p. 4.

116 Charles C. Mann, *1493: Uncovering the World Columbus Created* (New York: Vintage Books/A Division of Random House, 2011), p. 367.

117 Bordewich, *Killing the White Man's Indian*, p. 37.

118 Charles Hedges, Ed., *Speeches of Benjamin Harrison: Twenty Third President of the United States* (New York: United States Book Co., 1892), courtesy of the Indiana Historical Society.

119 Nabakov, *Native American Testimony*, p. xvii.

120 Weinberg, *Manifest Destiny*, p. vii.

121 Neihardt, *Black Elk Speaks*, p. 280. As will be discussed in a little more detail in the chapter on Black Elk, some researchers consider this prayer an invention of Neihardt, same as the quote attributed to Black Elk in the Preface.

CHAPTER 1

Anna Mae Pictou-Aquash
The "Lost Bird" of Wounded Knee: Part I

I know that I will be killed. They won't let an Indian like me live. The FBI has put a jacket on me. When I refused to cooperate with them, they spread the rumor that I was one of their informants…it doesn't matter if the FBI kills me or whether my life is snuffed out by one of our own people who believes the rumors the Feds have spread about me. It will always be the FBI who murders me.

Anna Mae Aquash
Dennis Banks and Richard Erdoes, *Ojibwa Warrior* [1]

It is said Lakota Elders believe the winds always howl when the body of a murder victim is disturbed. On the weekend of March 12, 1976, during the wake and funeral of Anna Mae Pictou-Aquash, a 30-year-old Micmac Indian, 30 mile-per-hour winds blasted across the section of the Pine Ridge Indian Reservation of South Dakota where this doleful memorial took place. The wind chilled the rickety Jumping Bull Hall containing the dejected mourners to such an extent they were forced to huddle around two stoves improvised from 50-gallon drums. Adding to the desperate atmosphere surrounding this grim event was the fact the mourners eventually moved to the Jumping Bull property itself, where eight months earlier one 18-year old Indian man, Joe Stuntz Killsright, and two FBI agents were killed during an intense shootout. The event also marked the second time the remains of Anna Mae were buried.[2] Certainly, the echoes of the story of "Lost Bird" can be heard in the telling of events of Anna Mae's life that was cut short all too suddenly.

In a sense Anna Mae's story, or at least the final chapter, didn't start with her journey toward Indian activism, but rather with the Indian Reorganization Act (IRA) of 1934. To a large extent the American Indian Movement's (AIM) story on Pine Ridge can be considered to have started there as well. AIM began in Minneapolis in 1968 to address police harassment of Indians there as well as to explore issues of sovereignty and culture. In essence, the IRA was an attempt to install Western-style governments on reservations to supplant the old chief system, or more accurately, a way of life based on listening to guidance provided by Elders. Many believe the "occupation" in 1973 had much of its genesis in the clash of these two very different methods of governing.

In considering accounts of the 1973 "occupation," it is useful not to gloss over the sketchy success of the IRA-created government on Pine Ridge at that time, if it was even a success at all. Currently, considering the intense problems still existing there, some would argue the situation has not improved much, if at all, since then. What is also important not to overlook is the prominence of Indian women in traditional tribal leadership and politics. Very early in 1973, Gladys Bissonnette, discussing then Tribal President Dick Wilson, said: "…past administrations…weren't quite as hard on us as this drunken fool we got now, who hasn't got the backbone to stand up and protect his Indians…" Grace Black Elk said: "'This Dick Wilson, he hates AIM people because they are doing what he should have been doing. So he's jealous of them, more jealous than anything else.'" Before anyone grasped the magnitude of the federal government's involvement in an Indian reservation in a remote region of South Dakota, Ellen Moves Camp queried: "'We all wonder why it is the government is backing him [Dick Wilson] up so much.'"[3]

In former FBI Agent Joseph Trimbach's book of FBI propaganda, *American Indian Mafia*, a sophomoric takeoff on the name American Indian Movement, the foreword by Richard Two Elk contained blame for AIM for virtually all the problems on the Pine Ridge Indian Reservation and argued: "These problems have only been compounded by the destructive legacy of [the] false heroes [of AIM]."[4] Trimbach began his introduction with what he considered a description of Anna Mae's last moments alive. Ever the jihadist against AIM, Trimbach concluded this section with: "Had she trusted the FBI they could have saved her. But when your friends become your enemies, it is hard to know whom to trust."[5] Then, in the opening chapter of his racist screed entitled "AIM is to Blame," Trimbach noted that even before closing arguments began in the 2004 trial of Arlo Looking Cloud, who was convicted of Anna Mae's murder, "…the unmistakable beacon of truth shown through the courtroom."[6] In Trimbach's estimation, Arlo's conviction and the subsequent third burial of Anna Mae in Nova Scotia closed the book on the story of Anna Mae Aquash.

Unfortunately for Trimbach, questions about Anna Mae's death, and her life, remain unanswered. Trimbach left out the description of many aspects of Anna Mae's story to cram it in to his preconceived and oversimplified narrative that the FBI was good, and AIM was bad. Anna Mae's story, like AIM's, and the story of Indian nations in general is far from simple. Even Trimbach's attempt to portray the early stages of Anna Mae's second reburial in Nova Scotia as the nostalgic reuniting of her with her two daughters and their father Jake Maloney appears to gloss over some of the difficulty involved in those circumstances. While there is no doubt the daughters, Deborah and Denise Maloney, grieved the loss of their mother, the family situation for Anna Mae was more complicated than Trimbach disclosed in his portrayal of a make-believe world inhabited by no real people. After Anna Mae's second daughter was born while she and Jake were living in Boston, Jake became involved romantically with a white woman. Anna Mae and Jake attempted to reconcile but eventually divorced. Although Anna Mae had legal custody, the girls moved in with their father and his new wife around 1973 after he remarried.[7] It is unclear how much contact the daughters had with Anna Mae from this point until Anna Mae's death at the end of 1975 or early 1976.

Surprisingly, considering how much venom Trimbach directed at AIM, he acknowledged the shaky legacy of the IRA on the Pine Ridge Reservation. He further acknowledged the IRA style of government rule was voted in there by a slim margin. He wryly noted: "…the process of electing Native leaders by majority rule was not well received by those who favored more traditional forms of tribal decision making." He even admitted that on some reservations, specifically noting Pine Ridge, that: "…tribal governments became havens for cronyism and misappropriation of funds."[8] Yet, rather than explore how to best resolve the conflict caused by Wilson's corruption as he seemingly recognized, he proceeded to support the Wilson regime against all opposition.

To provide some structure to analysis of these events, attorney Mario Gonzales and author Elizabeth Cook-Lynn noted: "The effort to obfuscate Indian history is a modern American compulsion, apparently, that cannot be resisted."[9] Another more direct way to state this is to say that ignoring the Indian point of view is simply a habit of whites. In *Wounded Knee 1973, A Personal Account*, Stanley Lyman, the former area director for the Pine Ridge Bureau of Indian Affairs (BIA), made many comments that if not completely indifferent to Indians, were actually hostile to them, and even simply bizarre. When Lyman was asked about the corruption of Dick Wilson, he argued it was "beside the issue"[10] although he never explained what the "issue" really was. Lyman stated to a *New York Times* reporter: "…the Indian system of selecting leadership did not provide leaders whom the government could deal with in a legal fashion, that is, with regards to agreements, treaties, and things of that kind."[11] Then, in a puzzling reversal in explaining the resistance of some Indians to certain federal legislation, Lyman stated: "…there has been a group left out; they have not been discriminated against in my opinion. This is the group that wants to go back to the old treaties. They do not recognize the Indian Reorganization Act or tribal government."[12]

It is certainly not something discussed by the United States government, but confirmation existed that the corruption, or at the very least, gross incompetence of Dick Wilson's tribal government was not "'beside the point.'" Ramon Roubideaux, a Lakota attorney who in 1952 was the first Indian licensed in the State of South Dakota to practice law, argued regarding the implementation of IRA-style governments on Indian reservations: "'…we have people with eighth grade educations running what are, in effect multi-million dollar corporations!" Giving some context to the motivations of the 1973 Wounded Knee "occupiers" Roubideaux continued: "Indians can do anything harmful to their own people and nothing happens… What we've done is let the worst thing that was created by the white man in the last one hundred years—tribal governments—have a power they simply do not deserve.'"[13]

Lyman's mocking comments about Indians wanting to go back to the times of treaties, viewed through the lens of morality, do not reveal a pleasant result. As MacArthur stated in *The Vanishing Conscience:* "Our society takes pleasure in its own wickedness. People are not ashamed of their sin; they boast about it."[14] Substitute treaty breaking for the word sin and you have a perfect paradigm to describe how breaking treaties was (and apparently still is) viewed. Is there any hint that Lyman, either personally or as a representative of the United States government, believed breaking the treaties he referred to in his sarcasm was cause for an apology, or even regret? As a reading of Trimbach's *American Indian Mafia* also reveals, he believed there is no reason for those who support the "American Way of Life" to feel shame over the treatment of Indians, much less there is an apology due.

Nevertheless, for a bright, ambitious young woman like Anna Mae, the energy she received from announcing her pride in her Indian heritage certainly directed her attention toward the conflict at Wounded Knee in 1973. After her divorce from Jake Maloney and entering a relationship with Nogeshik, Anna Mae became more aggressive in her efforts to become politically relevant in the growing Indian activist movement of the '60s and '70s. However, well before meeting Nogeshik, she seemed destined for achievement. In 1969, Anna Mae helped organize the Boston Indian Council, a program designed to assist Indians in overcoming alcoholism.[15] She made her first contact with AIM leader Russell Means at the *Mayflower II* demonstration in Boston Harbor in 1970. At this event, ostensibly organized to celebrate the 350th anniversary of the first Thanksgiving, Means, Dennis Banks and other AIM members occupied a replica of the original *Mayflower*.[16] After that, Anna Mae attended Wheelock College, a private institution in Boston, and ended up winning a scholarship to Brandeis University, although she did not attend the school.[17] She also taught children and performed social work in Roxbury, an African-American community in Boston.

Some believed Nogeshik fueled Anna Mae's Indian activism due to his flamboyant displays of Indian pride through his use of jewelry, clothing, and beadwork. In November 1972, Anna Mae participated in the Bureau of Indian Affairs Washington, D.C., headquarters occupation, the culmination of the Trail of Broken Treaties caravan.[18] When Anna Mae's mother first met Nogeshik, supposedly she exclaimed: "My God, Anna Mae! Where'd you get the last of the Mohicans?"[19] Shortly after this event she traveled with Nogeshik to Wounded Knee, South Dakota, to participate in a portion of the 71-day "occupation" of that historic site.

Anna Mae's journey to the "occupation" site included an eight-mile hike from a point where she and Nogeshik were dropped off by a van and included hiding from federal patrols during this trek. During the "occupation" itself, Anna Mae was recognized for her cool head and hard work. She participated in the nightly Indian patrols of the village and considered herself a female warrior. In April 1973 Anna Mae and Nogeshik were married in a traditional "Sioux" ceremony during the height of the "occupation."[20] Anna Mae's emergence as a female warrior and leader in AIM also increased her exposure to the FBI's aggressive tactics to disable AIM. Although the claims are vehemently denied by official FBI sources, AIM has been argued by many to have been a target, along with the Black Panthers, of the FBI's counterintelligence program—COINTELPRO. As suggested by the quote opening this chapter, one of the favorite tactics FBI critics claim was used against its enemies was "snitch jacketing." As also explained in the endnote for the quote heading this chapter, the idea of using a "snitch jacket" was to plant false information or documents on a loyal member of an organization with the purpose of making it seem as if the target was cooperating with the FBI.[21]

After the 1973 "occupation" ended, Anna Mae and Nogeshik returned to Boston where they tried to establish an AIM survival school. Since outside funding was unavailable for the project, Anna Mae moved to Ottawa, Canada, and became an authority on Indian culture.[22] One of the results of her efforts was the rediscovery of the traditional ribbon shirt. Anna Mae believed the idea of these garments began with the Micmacs, who developed them to brighten the drab clothing provided by missionaries. The shirts became so popular within AIM circles they were given away and it became impossible to maintain an inventory.[23] During this period, Anna Mae made several trips to the Russell Means/Dennis Banks trial in the United States District Court in Minnesota for charges made against them by the federal government for their roles in the 1973 "occupation." Much to the chagrin of Trimbach, after an almost eight-month trial, in July 1974, Federal District Judge Fred Nichols ultimately dismissed all the charges in the case.[24]

As far as the situation with Anna Mae, unravelling the story of the circumstances surrounding her death requires a state of mind that white historians usually seem unwilling to attempt—considering matters from an Indian point of view. In a rarely discussed aspect of Anna Mae's life, some Indians believed "Nawiziwin"—jealousy—surrounding her relationship with Dennis Banks—was a primary factor in creating the circumstances leading to Anna Mae's execution.[25] Undoubtedly, navigating the various claims and rumors surrounding Anna Mae's demise is a complicated and convoluted task. Rumors about the top leadership of AIM such as Means and Banks ordering her execution for being an informant have circulated for years, although no charges have ever been forthcoming. The conventional story about Anna Mae's murder was that she was taken against her will to Troy Lynn Yellow Wood's house in Denver. Subsequent to that, she was taken in a Ford Pinto to Pine Ridge and murdered.[26]

However, on top of everything else, the FBI fueled the paranoia on Pine Ridge by its unusual actions in investigating Anna Mae's death which also spawned numerous conspiracy theories since the first of two autopsies, conducted by W.O. Brown, was botched so badly. In a sworn affidavit (concerning this first autopsy), FBI Special Agent William Wood claimed:

> Due to the decomposition of the body, it was impossible to obtain fingerprints of the unidentified Indian female during the course of the autopsy, therefore, Doctor Brown severed the hands from the body and they were forwarded to the Latent Fingerprint Section of the Federal Bureau of Investigation Identification Division, Washington D.C., for purposes of identification. On March 2, 1976, I was advised by Nathan Merrick, Criminal Investigator, Bureau of Indian Affairs, Pine Ridge South Dakota, that the remains of the unidentified Indian female had been buried at Pine Ridge, South Dakota, prior to determination of the body's true identity.[27]

In this affidavit, Wood proposed his allegation Anna Mae was killed because AIM members believed she was an informant and also: "…requested that a court order be issued for the exhumation of Aquash's body for the purpose of obtaining complete x-rays of her remains, and further medical examination."[28] Regarding his request for a second examination of Anna Mae's body, his instincts proved correct. Anna Mae's second autopsy revealed a small-caliber bullet hole in the back of her skull, obviously in great contradiction to Dr. Woods' finding she died of "exposure." Steve Hendricks quipped: "Anna Mae had died of a different kind of exposure—as it turned out, exposure to a .32 caliber, copper-jacketed bullet."[29] Dr. Andrea Smith recounted a similar tale regarding the 2002 death of Ada Elaine Brown, the sister of Terri Brown, president of the Native Women's Association of Canada. Ada was found beaten to death and disfigured so badly her family didn't recognize her. After: "The autopsy report said the cause of death was a brain aneurysm..." Terri sarcastically quipped, "Yeah, because she was beaten to a pulp."[30]

As important as unraveling the tangled facts and circumstances involved in this sad tale is, it is critical not to lose sight of a large unanswered question: what was the FBI's purpose in being present in such numbers in this remote region of the United States in the first place? It may be difficult for non-Indians to grasp the mistrust Indians had for the federal government, and particularly the FBI, in the 1970s. The uninformed point of view of many white Americans robotically accepting the history of the conquest of Indian land in a positive light for the conquerors compounds the damage of what actually happened in Indian history. Although historian Hampton Sides' praise of *Empire of the Summer Moon* seems out of place,[31] he astutely noted in his foreword to Dee Brown's *Bury My Heart at Wounded Knee*, which presented the nasty underside of Indian history, that: "Few academics in the discipline of Western Americana warmed up to Brown's book... This middle-aged librarian, lacking the requisite Ph.D. in history, wasn't a member of their club."[32]

For whatever reason, the questioning about such circumstances as the presence of heavily armed FBI agents in large numbers on Pine Ridge in the 1970s has been lacking. Therefore, it becomes the realm of an individual such as a "radical" like Dennis Banks who described the situation on February 27, 1973, by noting: "Pine Ridge was swarming with FBI agents and U.S. marshals in blue jumpsuits. Already the first APCs—some carrying machine guns—were arriving to protect the government's darling [Dick Wilson] against big, bad AIM."[33] Likewise, despite all Ward Churchill's publicly acknowledged warts, he correctly pointed out that federal government interest in the Black Hills region and western South Dakota did not end with Custer's expedition and the subsequent flood of miners searching for gold in the 1870s. For example, in 1942, the northwestern one-eighth of Pine Ridge was impounded by the War Department to be used as an aerial gunnery range for WWII pilots. The land was never returned to the Lakota people; Churchill claimed the area contained a rich uranium deposit.[34]

Regarding the actual details of the last days of Anna Mae's life, many statements were made at the 2004 trial of Arlo Looking Cloud for her murder. According to this testimony, while Anna Mae was in Denver, a meeting was held at the home of Troy Lynn Yellow Wood to decide how to deal with Anna Mae as an accused informant. Robert Robideau was an avid follower of the Looking Cloud trial and was previously accused and ultimately acquitted of murdering the two FBI agents in 1975 on the Pine Ridge Reservation for which Leonard Peltier was ultimately convicted. Although Robideau himself was accused of being an informant, he stated John Trudell was the informant after Trudell testified at the Looking Cloud trial. In any event, Robideau reported that: "...Trudell testified that Looking Cloud confessed to him, in 1988, his role in Anna Mae's murder and also implicated John Graham as shooting Anna Mae in the head while she prayed."[35]

Perhaps for many reasons, few will be satisfied with the explanation for the killing of an intelligent, young, and beautiful Indian woman. Sadly, like Lost Bird before her, and SuAnne and Jancita Eagle Deer after her, regardless of the cause of her death, she also could be said to have been the object of the lament attributed to Black Elk that: "…with running tears I must say now that the tree has never bloomed."[36] Nevertheless, Anna Mae feared more earthly peril and noted not long before she was killed: "…if they take me back to South Dakota I'll be murdered."[37] As if to put an exclamation point on the gloomy tale of Anna Mae, as noted in the Introduction, in an April 15, 1976, letter to FBI Director Clarence Kelly, attorney Ken Tilsen questioned who ordered Anna Mae's hands removed from her body and noted the grisly, seemingly never reported detail, "…*all fingers had been severed from the hands* [emphasis added]."[38]

What has never been revealed before, at least in relation to Anna Mae's story, is that the FBI's ability to remotely identify homicide victims was developed long before her death. In the FBI's own centennial history appears the following account of the identification of Elizabeth Short, better known as the "Black Dahlia," whose murder occurred in 1947:

> The ensuing investigation was led by the L.A. Police Department. The FBI was asked to help *and it quickly identified the body—just 56 minutes in fact after getting blurred fingerprints via "Soundphoto"* [a primitive fax machine used by news services] *from Los Angeles* [emphasis added].[39]

It is difficult to believe in the almost 30 years from the time of Elizabeth Short's murder to Anna Mae's, the FBI's technical capabilities would not have improved and it would not have been able to identify Anna Mae remotely, despite Wood's claim "…it was impossible to obtain fingerprints."

As gloomily as the story of Anna Mae Aquash unfolded, it could be argued it was eclipsed in sordidness by that of Jancita Eagle Deer, which contained allegations of rape against a man who eventually became the governor of South Dakota, Bill Janklow. Many complain the allegations were never fully addressed; ultimately Jancita died under suspicious circumstances after being struck by a car. One version of the rape allegation was that on a Saturday night in January 1967 as a 15-year-old eighth grader, she was checked out of her dorm room at the BIA Boarding School in Mission, South Dakota, by then-Rosebud tribal attorney Bill Janklow. At that time, Janklow was assisting her in becoming the adopted daughter of John and Yvonne Arcoren and had also helped her become a student at the BIA Boarding School. Janklow was eventually elected South Dakota Attorney General in 1974 and governor in 1978. As governor, he served four terms of four years—from 1979 to 1987 and again from 1995 to 2003, making him the second longest serving governor in post-Constitution United States history. Paradoxically, given Janklow's continuous animosity toward the American Indian Movement, Janklow's father served as a prosecutor for the United States at the Nuremberg trials in Germany which were centered around the atrocities involving the Nazis and their treatment of Jews.

On that Saturday night in January 1967, Janklow brought Jancita to his home for a dinner with his family. At five minutes before eight, Janklow drove with Jancita the half mile downtown toward the dorm but arrived too early for the dance. According to Jancita's statement, Janklow then said: "'We might as well drive around until the dance starts,'" in response to which Jancita queried, "'Can I go to a movie?'" As the drive continued, Janklow then reportedly said, "'Wouldn't you rather drink with me?'" to which Jancita replied, "'I'd rather go to the dance.'" The account of the next events, which Janklow vehemently denied, involved Janklow driving Jancita a few miles west on U.S. Highway 18 and then turning the car north on a dirt road. After arriving at a secluded spot, Janklow stopped the car, pushed a lever which lowered the seat and next pushed Jancita down along with it as he continuously restrained her.[40] Janklow proceeded to unbutton Jancita's blouse as he proclaimed his love for her, all the while she was continuously hitting him. Janklow managed to pull Jancita's underwear off and then sexually assaulted her for approximately ten minutes. After the incident, an FBI investigation concluded: "'there is insufficient evidence to support the allegations of the victim, and said allegations are unfounded.'" The day after Jancita claimed she was raped, Jancita showed her dormitory matron, Catherine Bordeaux: "…a nickel-sized 'discoloration of the skin' on her upper left breast [and] a hickey on the right side of her neck." Jancita was not examined by a doctor regarding her allegations against Janklow until the following Monday morning, 36 hours after the alleged incident.[41]

In 1974, seven years after the alleged incident, AIM stalwart Dennis Banks filed a claim against Janklow in the Rosebud Tribal Court. Rosebud is an Indian Reservation about two hours east of Pine Ridge. Since tribal courts do not have jurisdiction over major crimes on reservations (see endnote 41), the allegation of rape was intertwined with other lesser charges and presented as a package of conduct unbecoming a member of the tribal bar. The other charges were drunken driving, disobeying police officers, perjury, and malpractice. As Banks' charges arose amid Janklow's contentious attorney general's race in South Dakota, it was revealed that as a juvenile, Janklow had a delinquency petition filed against him for an "assault" that involved several other juveniles victimizing a seventeen-year-old girl. At that time, Janklow was presented with the option of either entering jail or enlisting in military service. Janklow opted for entering the Marine Corps the day after being formally accused of the assault.[42]

The Rosebud Tribal disbarment proceedings, which Janklow did not attend, drew virtually no public attention. Nonetheless, one witness described an incident where Janklow was pulled over for erratic driving. Regarding the most serious rape charge of Jancita Eagle Deer, some type of medical records were produced that purportedly were consistent with her claim of sexual assault. At a press conference eight days prior to the election, Jancita was grilled by Janklow's attorney, Jeremiah Murphy. The following day, South Dakota newspapers ran stories claiming Janklow was being subjected to a smear campaign.[43] On April 4, 1975, Jancita was killed under suspicious circumstances—she was struck by a Pontiac GTO driven by a boy from a local prosperous white family from the town of Aurora—which never appeared to be thoroughly investigated.[44]

When revisiting the accounts of the lives and deaths of long-dead residents of southwest South Dakota, avoiding the temptation to become engulfed in paranoid thinking requires perpetual vigilance. Yet, top-flight investigative journalist Steve Hendricks, whose work has been liberally cited in this book, and who examined the role of the federal government in Anna Mae's murder and Jancita's likely homicide, explained: "…paranoia in Indian Country was not something the FBI cared to snuff."[45] Hendricks also observed the atmosphere in the region made it seem as if "Death clings to Wounded Knee."[46] It would not seem too much of an exaggeration to suggest that the women bystanders to the conflict there symbolically, if not literally, bore the brunt of the violence.

As in the situation of Anna Mae, the question which never gets answered satisfactorily is: what was Jancita's death really all about? And, as in the case of the proverbial bad penny, whenever there was turmoil within AIM and other quarters, the name of FBI informant Douglas Durham kept turning up. On the afternoon Jancita was killed, it was believed she was en route to Des Moines, Iowa, in a dark blue Chevy belonging to Durham's father. Many believed Durham used that car when he believed using his own car would be too conspicuous. Some also believed Durham, with whom Jancita apparently had a tempestuous relationship, pushed her out of the car, possibly while it was still moving. Disturbingly, another facet of the incident not investigated thoroughly (or much at all) was there were no skid marks from the car driven by the teenage boy prior to the point of impact. It is believed Jancita's body was thrown 150 feet; unsurprisingly, it is believed she was killed immediately upon impact with the car.[47]

The ignoble end to Janklow's political career lent credence to Jancita's claims and those of Janklow's other accusers. After his term as governor of South Dakota ended, Janklow was elected to the United States House of Representatives for a term which commenced January 3, 2003. On August 16, 2003, Janklow raced through a stop sign while driving near Trent, South Dakota, and struck a motorcycle driven by 55-year-old Randy Scott, killing him instantly. One accident reconstruction expert estimated Janklow's speed at the time of the collision as 70 miles per hour. On December 8, 2003, Janklow was convicted of second-degree manslaughter after a jury trial, even though most of the evidence of his prior speeding citations was excluded from the trial. He was sentenced to 100 days in jail out of a possible 3,650 and resigned his seat in Congress effective January 20, 2004. Janklow died of brain cancer on January 12, 2012. Hendricks noted in his precise and acerbic style: "For killing nobody, Sarah Bad Heart Bull, Dennis Banks, and Russell Means had been sentenced by South Dakota judges to multiples of Janklow's sentence."[48]

Other instances of the disparities in the administration of criminal justice mechanisms are found without a great deal of effort. Arthur Fleming, the head of the United States Commission on Civil Rights, wrote to the United States Justice Department inquiring about the lack of progress in investigating murders and other serious crimes on the Pine Ridge Reservation. Assistant U.S. Attorney Richard Thornburgh's July 12, 1976, letter in response contained this tepid claim:

> I would like to point out that with regard to crimes committed by an Indian against the person or property of another Indian, the FBI has responsibility to investigate the fourteen major felonies enumerated in Title 18 United States Code Section 1153. The FBI has neither the authority nor the resources to furnish day-to-day police protection on the various Indian reservations. This responsibility rests with the Bureau of Indian Affairs in the Department of Interior.[49]

In contrast, as Hendricks again sharply noted, as well as explained by FBI Agent Trimbach, within hours of the incident that resulted in the deaths of FBI Agents Coler and Williams in June 1975, Trimbach returned to Pine Ridge with a sniper team from Minneapolis. By the next day, he had assembled a force of camouflage-clad agents fully armed with automatic weapons such as M-16s and supported by armored personnel carriers, planes, and helicopters to confront the Indians at the Jumping Bull Ranch.

If there is anything of value at all to be gained from Anna Mae's sad tale, reflecting on her brief life raises questions regarding violence against Indian women as well as the roles of Indian women in contemporary Indian culture. Cook-Lynn believed: "Models of the relationship between feminism and violence described in the context of colonization and imperialism of the modern world are a study in complexity."[50] Although Anna Mae's violent death was the result of unique circumstances, Cook-Lynn also reported: "No discussion about women is complete without [addressing] the harrowing exposure to violence, which, they say, is rising on Indian reservations and has been for several decades, perhaps for all of the twentieth century." Cook-Lynn noted many causes are blamed for the chaos, including the Christian religion's prohibition against plural marriage, which she noted: "…was at the heart of the *tiospaye* system and, in spite of the criticism of it from such disciplines as religion and anthropology, may have been a buffer against violence in today's Indian societies."[51] In that regard, the inclination to blame the violence on the "…innate savagery of the Indian"[52] must be avoided in that violence against Indian women (by other Indians of the same nation) was not a pervasive issue until white society foisted the reservation system on Indians. Likewise, Dr. Smith argued that Indian boarding schools were the incubators of violence in Indian communities.[53]

Also, as suggested by Fleisher's previous comments, an equally complex issue is discerning the role of feminist thought in the lives of Indian women, a topic worthy of a great deal of study and thought. Cook-Lynn posited: "Most Native women are not feminists in that sense because they do not perceive tension between their own struggles and the community at large." Interestingly, Cook-Lynn, a supporter of the legacy of the American Indian Movement, stated: "…the male-dominated American Indian Movement of the mid-1960s did little to defend what may be called women's rights."[54] Nevertheless, as noted above and as discussed in the Introduction, Indian women have not necessarily been receptive to what has been labeled feminist theory. Women of All Red Nations (WARN) spokesperson Madonna Thunder Hawk saw "…feminist theory as a colonial assault on indigenous cultures."[55]

Endnotes

1. Dennis Banks and Richard Erdoes, *Ojibwa Warrior: Dennis Banks and the Rise of the American Indian Movement* (Norman, Oklahoma: University of Oklahoma Press, 2004), p. 353. The "jacket" Anna Mae was referring to is a shortened version of the term "snitch jacketing"—a practice of law-enforcement types like FBI agents convincing a targeted group like AIM that a person is an informant. The purpose is to sow paranoia and mistrust within the group whether the person is an informant or not. In the case of Anna Mae, the FBI detained her several times and then immediately released her on those occasions.
2. Joanna Brand, *The Life and Death of Anna Mae Aquash* (Toronto: James Lorimer & Co. Publishers, 1993), p. 141.
3. Peter Matthiessen, *In the Spirit of Crazy Horse: The Story of Leonard Peltier and the FBI's War on the American Indian Movement* (New York: Penguin Books, 1992), p. 62.
4. Trimbach, *American Indian Mafia*, p. viii.
5. Ibid., from the unnumbered Introduction page.
6. Ibid., p. 31.
7. Brand, *The Life and Death of Anna Mae Aquash*, p. 110.
8. Trimbach, *American Indian Mafia*, p. 53.
9. Gonzalez, Cook-Lynn, *The Politics of Hallowed Ground*, p. 204.
10. Stanley David Lyman, *Wounded Knee 1973: A Personal Account* (Lincoln, Nebraska: University of Nebraska Press, 1991), pp. 19-20.
11. Ibid., p. 151.
12. Ibid., pp. 152-153.
13. Bordewich, *Killing the White Man's Indian*, pp. 90-91.
14. John F. MacArthur, Jr., *The Vanishing Conscience*, p. 58.
15. Brand, *The Life and Death of Anna Mae Aquash*, p. 58
16. Ibid., p. 59.
17. Ibid., p. 60.
18. Ibid., p. 61.
19. Ibid., pp. 61-62.
20. Ibid., p. 63.
21. Ibid., p. 78.
22. Ibid., p. 111.
23. Ibid., pp. 113-114.
24. Hendricks, *The Unquiet Grave*, p. 140.
25. Ernestine Chasing Hawk, "Did Nawaziwin orchestrate the death of Anna Mae?" *Native Sun News*, March 30, 2016.
26. Trimbach, *American Indian Mafia*, pp. 23-24.
27. William B. Wood, FBI Agent, March 8, 1976 Affidavit describing events in the Anna Mae Homicide

Investigation, (St. Paul, Minnesota: Minnesota Historical Society, March 8, 1976). Hendricks noted that "Her decay was so severe that her fingerprints could not be taken at the hospital." *Unquiet Grave* p. 4.

28 Ibid.
29 Hendricks, *The Unquiet Grave*, p. 7.
30 Smith, *Conquest*, p. 31.
31 Gwynne, *Empire of the Summer Moon*, p. i.
32 Brown, *Bury My Heart at Wounded Knee*, p. xviii.
33 Banks and Erdoes, *Ojibwa Warrior*, p. 158.
34 Ward Churchill and Jim Vander Wall, *Agents of Repression: The FBI's Secret Wars Against the Black Panther Party and the American Indian Movement* (Boston, Massachusetts: South End Press, 1988), pp. 130-131.
35 Robert Robideau, "John Trudell, A Profile of Cowardice an FBI Informant Covers His Tracks in the Murder of Anna Mae Pictou Aquash," *Independent Media Center*, July 18, 2007.
36 Niehardt, *Black Elk Speaks*. p. 279.
37 Hendricks, *The Unquiet Grave*. p. 226.
38 Kenneth Tilsen, April 15, 1976 letter to FBI Director Clarence Kelly (St. Paul, Minnesota: Minnesota Historical Society April 15, 1976).
39 U.S. Federal Bureau of Investigation (2008), "The FBI: A Centennial History 1908-2008," p. 43.
40 Hendricks, *The Unquiet Grave*, pp. 147-148.
41 Ibid., pp. 149-150. The FBI has jurisdiction over cases involving most felonies committed by Indians against other Indians on Indian reservations pursuant to the Major Crimes of 1885. The original felony list included seven offenses: murder, manslaughter, rape, assault with intent to kill, arson, burglary, and larceny. The list of felonies has been expanded since the original law was passed. The impetus for creating this legislation was the United States Supreme Court overturning Crow Dog's murder conviction for lack of jurisdiction after he was found guilty of killing Spotted Tail on the Pine Ridge Indian Reservation. Wikipedia. See also the quote from Richard Thornburgh's July 12, 1976, letter to Arthur Fleming cited in part on page 41 referring to "fourteen major felonies." Obviously, since Janklow was not an Indian, the FBI considered it within their investigative jurisdiction to investigate Jancita's claims against Janklow.
42 Ibid., pp. 152-153.
43 Ibid., p. 155.
44 Ibid., pp. 194-195.
45 Ibid., p. 199.
46 Ibid., p. 335.
47 Ibid., p. 194.
48 Ibid., pp. 271-273 and pp. 283-288. Ironically, Janklow prosecuted Sarah Bad Heart Bull for her participation in the Custer Court House Riots for which she received a sentence of one to three years. p. 144. Although Means and Banks were also prosecuted for their participation in the riots, after their eight-month trial in federal court in Minneapolis for their Wounded Knee activities, this trial was almost anticlimactic.

49 Richard L. Thornburgh, July 12, 1976 letter to Arthur Fleming, Chairman of the United States Commission on Civil Rights, (St. Paul, Minnesota: Minnesota Historical Society July 12, 1976).
50 Cook-Lynn, *A Separate Country*, p. 98.
51 Ibid., p. 96.
52 Deloria, Jr. *Custer Died for Your Sins*. p. 102.
53 Smith, *Conquest*. p. 51. It does not appear the situation is going to resolve any time soon. On May 3, 2019, the Trump White House issued a proclamation, which stated in part: "…we draw attention to the horrible acts of violence committed against American Indian and Native Alaska people, particularly women and children." "White House issues proclamation for Missing and Murdered American Indian and Alaska Natives Awareness Day." Vincent Schilling, *Indian Country Today*, May 5, 2019. Recently the United States Senate passed a bill to assist in dealing with the epidemic of missing and murdered indigenous women. Trump is expected to sign the bill. Gilbert Cordova "Senate Bill Allocates Millions to Address Missing and Murdered Indigenous Women Epidemic" Channel 2, KTUU, Anchorage, Alaska, December 20, 2019.
54 Cook-Lynn, *A Separate Country*, p. 97.
55 Ibid., p. 98. Andrea Smith noted: "While the analysis and organizing of the environmental justice movement is exemplary, it often marginalizes women of color. That is, women of color are suffering from not only environmental racism but environmental sexism." Smith, *Conquest*, p. 69. She also noted at a talk she gave in Illinois on mining issues, she was asked: "'…don't you think the *real* reason Native peoples have environmental problems is because they're having too many children? [emphasis in original]'" *Ibid.*, p. 78.

CHAPTER 2

Columbus We Hardly Knew Thee

Having thus satisfied their consciences by offering the Native Americans a chance to convert to Christianity, the Spaniards then felt free to do whatever they wanted with the people they had just "discovered."

James Loewen, *Lies My Teacher Told Me*[1]

On October 12, 1991, Russell Means, other Indian individuals including members of the Colorado American Indian Movement, and Ward Churchill were arrested for blocking a Columbus Day Parade near the Colorado State Capitol building in Denver.[2] While in the second decade of the 21st century this may not seem particularly noteworthy, at that time it was a unique event for Denver. Never a hotbed of civil disobedience even during the tumultuous 1960s, the event was the most noteworthy spectacle involving Indians in the "Mile High" City since Indian-killing Colonel John Chivington and his men paraded through the Denver Opera House displaying the grisly trophies carved out of slaughtered Indians, possibly including up to 100 scalps taken after the killings at Sand Creek in 1864.[3]

The eventual all-misdemeanor charges of refusing to obey a lawful police order, obstructing a public thoroughfare, and disturbing the peace were ultimately related to the refusal of these individuals to obey police directives to remove themselves from blocking the parade. Those people arrested were supported by more than 300 additional protesters. At trial, in a significant upgrade from standard defenses for misdemeanors, a motion to dismiss with an extensive memorandum containing arguments the charges against those arrested were invalid based on various doctrines of international law, particularly the 1948 United Nations Convention on Punishment and Prevention of the Crime of Genocide, was filed. Also included in the memorandum was a discussion of the impact of Columbus' arrival in the "New World." Although the trial judge did not dismiss the charges based on this elaborate defense, the jury subsequently found the defendants not guilty at the conclusion of the trial on June 26, 1992. In post-verdict statements to the press, jurors stated they had been convinced by the defense it was the Columbus Day celebrants, and not the defendants, who were in the wrong.[4]

Ward Churchill, one of the defendants in the Columbus Day protest trial, noted that Columbus set sail for the "New World" "…fully expecting to encounter wealth belonging to others."[5] Yet, this observation in one form or another was not Churchill's alone, who many view as far too "extreme" or even dishonest to be taken seriously. Washington Irving, who penned a mostly flattering biography of Columbus, made a virtually identical observation. Irving noted the lust for gold and other riches, with the corresponding pain and madness associated with that state of mind, was present in Columbus and his crew practically from the first moments they arrived in the Western Hemisphere near the end of the 15th century. The lust for gold carried by the new arrivals was unleashed on the inhabitants of this newly "discovered" land to spread death and destruction, along with diseases like smallpox and cholera. Irving added that after Columbus returned to the Western Hemisphere the second time: "The white man had penetrated into the land. Avarice, and pride, and ambition, piercing care, and sordid labour [sic], and withering poverty, were soon to follow, and the indolent paradise of the Indian was about to disappear forever."[6]

One of the most intriguing aspects of Indian history is that agreement over events or circumstances of over 500 years ago remains elusive. Yet, there is now some consensus that at least during Columbus' lifetime, he was not always known by that name. He was purportedly known at some point during his life in Genoa, Italy, as Cristoforo Colombo. After he moved to Spain, he was referred to as Cristóbal Colón.[7] Yet, agreement regarding the issue of how many indigenous people resided in the Western Hemisphere at the time of Columbus' arrival remains unresolved, as does agreement over how they arrived in North America specifically in the first place. Vine Deloria, Jr., initially received significant criticism for his attack on the so-called Bering Strait theory, which posits Indians traveled over a land bridge from Asia to North America. Deloria, Jr., explained his skepticism: "'There's this perfect moment when the ice-free corridor magically appears just before the land bridge is covered by water. And the Paleo-Indians, who are doing fine in Siberia, suddenly decide to *sprint* over to Alaska.'" Deloria, Jr., further fleshed out opposition to the Bering Strait theory: "And then they *sprint* through the corridor, which just in time for them has been replenished with game. And they keep sprinting so fast that they overrun the hemisphere even faster than the Europeans did [emphasis in original].'" As if anticipating ridicule, Deloria, Jr., added: "And these are the same people who say traditional origin tales are improbable.'"[8]

Likewise, unraveling myths about Indian history requires viewing events from different angles. In that regard, recent authors such as Charles Mann, noted above, have called into question the whole notion of European cultural and even military superiority and has been receptive to Deloria, Jr.'s challenge to the Bering Strait theory. He stated that during the timeframe between the 16th and 18th centuries, contrary to the: "master narrative of post-contact history, Europeans routinely lost [wars with indigenous groups] when they could not take advantage of disease and political fragmentation" to incapacitate Indian groups.[9]

Nevertheless, accurately defining who Christopher Columbus really was remains elusive and it is hoped the depiction settles at the appropriate point between two wildly diverging descriptions. In the *Mysterious History of Columbus* John Noble Wilford explained:

Irving's *The Life and Voyages of Christopher Columbus*, published in 1829, was read avidly in the United States and contributed to the idealized image of the discoverer that dominated literature for more than a century and has not been entirely expunged. His soaring fancy produced a romance, more than a judicious biography.[10]

At the other end of the spectrum from Irving awaits Michael Bradley and his *Columbus Conspiracy*. Bradley suggested Columbus may have been a pirate with connections to the Knights Templar.[11] Obviously, this contradicted longstanding narratives of the events in Christopher Columbus' life; in reality, whatever story line is chosen does not alter the outcome of the conquest and colonization to which the original inhabitants of North and South America were continuously subjected after his arrival. Nonetheless, in some respects the outlines of Irving and Bradley overlap. Bradley provided some interesting, if speculative, explanations as to why Columbus was considered a "navigator of genius," to use a term repeated often by Irving. Bradley essentially argued Columbus knew he did not have the type of ships to make a journey all the way to China and intended to end up where he did all along. Not an easy sell.

Likewise, as suggested, agreement has yet to be reached as to the population density of the Western Hemisphere at the time of Columbus' arrival. Recently, as masterfully recounted in Charles Mann's *1491*, William Denevan, a geographer at the University of Wisconsin, and other researchers, have been arguing the Americas "discovered" by Christopher Columbus were more densely populated with indigenous people than previously believed; possibly "much more" densely populated.[12] The ramifications for those arguing for or against the conclusion that Indians in the Western Hemisphere were subjected to genocide are clear. If the Americas at the time of Columbus' arrival in the Western Hemisphere were highly populated with indigenous people, then the existence of a low population of Indians now means it becomes increasingly difficult to argue against them being subjected to genocide. For defenders of the intellectual and moral superiority of European culture, this position is, of course, untenable.

Mann also argued that Columbus didn't really "discover" anything at all and that what he stumbled upon was a highly developed system of agricultural production. Spanish invaders: "…were stunned to find warehouses overflowing with untouched cloth and supplies," and Mann explained the Incas had "managed to eradicate hunger." Mann concluded, quoting Peruvian novelist Mario Vargas Llosa, who was: "…no fan of the Inca,…[that] 'only a very small number of empires throughout the whole world have succeeded in achieving this feat.'"[13] Historian Alvin Josephy has been arguing a similar point for years and stated in *1492*: "History still teaches falsely that pre-Columbian America was a wilderness, a virgin land, virtually untenanted, unknown, and unused, waiting for the white explorers and pioneers, with their superior brains, brawn, and courage, to conquer and 'develop' it."[14] The concerning aspect of Josephy's world view is not that it is an exaggeration, or that it is "revisionist" history, but that he made it in 1991. In the 25-plus years since he penned those words, can it be argued his persuasive analysis has gained much traction? Josephy himself noted the reason for this when he stated, in relation to a description of the Carib Indians (who he believes were erroneously labeled cannibals) that Indian history has been a: "…misshapen collection of largely false, distorted, or half-true images that has passed for scholarship and has shaped the public's understanding of Indians and their universes."[15]

Further, the conventional belief about the conquest of North and South America to one degree or another involves the myth, or as the more scientifically inclined might say, paradigm, that in addition to being sparsely populated, those few Indians or natives present on those continents were nothing more than "savages" or pagans. But has the term ever really been fully defined or explored? Irving provided this description of Columbus' spirituality without considering those indigenous people he came in contact might have spiritual aspirations of their own. Irving stated that Columbus had:

> A deep religious sentiment mingled with his meditations…he looked upon himself as standing in the hand of Heaven, chosen from among men for the accomplishment of its high purpose; he read, as he supposed, his contemplated discovery foretold in Holy Writ, and shadowed forth darkly in the mystic revelations of the prophets. [He believed his role was] carrying the light of the true faith into benighted and pagan lands and gathering their countless nations under the holy dominion of the church.[16]

But what is to be understood regarding a "…deep religious sentiment…" that co-existed with the ability to inflict or at least endorse the infliction of intense suffering on other human beings? Hopefully, the answer to the question of what the only element is separating the Europeans from the native "savages" is not hypocrisy. Just taking one of the Ten Commandments—Thou shalt have no other gods before me—how does that square with virtually making a god out of gold, as some current historians have suggested the Europeans seemed to do?

In that regard, Charles Mann is among the new breed of historians not attempting to rationalize the cruelty employed by Europeans in their conquest of the Western Hemisphere. Interestingly, he put a twist on the notion that greed motivated the Europeans and suggested in *1491* at least the Spanish conquistadors were not "…so much gold crazy as status crazy." For example, Mann noted the explorer Francisco Pizarro was born into the lower echelons of Spanish nobility but hoped to gain titles and other rewards for his efforts in exploring the Western Hemisphere.[17] One way to accomplish this in that era was to bring something tangible back to Europe from expeditions. Gold and silver, being non-perishable, were eminently suitable for this purpose. Of course, considering the suffering unleashed in pursuit of these goods, it would certainly matter little to the conscripted native miners what motivation was involved in inflicting pain and harsh treatment on them.

Likewise, the belief Columbus' activities were ordained by God did not necessarily work to the advantage of the "non-Christian" natives. It has been claimed the Adelante of San Domingo, Columbus' brother Don Bartholomew, had a priest accompany him on his tours of the region. One of the primary functions of the priest was to administer confession so when rebellious individuals were arrested, they could be immediately hanged.[18] Irving, ever the fan, earlier in his book had argued that Don Bartholomew: "…though stern in his policy, was neither vindictive nor cruel in his nature."[19] As such, Irving suggested the summary execution story might have been an exaggeration; he most likely *just* threw the malcontents into dungeons awaiting trial.[20] As the saying goes, how troublesome a situation is depends on whose ox is being gored.

One of the great ironies of Columbus' story often overlooked is that Ferdinand and Isabella eventually reneged on their agreement to compensate him as generously as they originally intended. It could be argued they broke a "treaty"; after all, a treaty in its simplest form is simply an agreement. The initial plan for Columbus was that he was to be allowed to keep one tenth of whatever treasures—gold, silver, etc.—he "discovered" during his exploratory voyages. Whatever can be said about the spiritual nature of Christopher Columbus, it is undeniable that he struck a business deal with Spanish royalty. His desire to establish a monopoly on the riches he expected to find in the "New World" set in motion an exploitative attitude toward the Indian people he encountered there. Nevertheless, owing in part to Columbus' incompetence as a colonial administrator, and the desire of the royal couple to establish undisputed dominance in the lands newly explored at least by the Europeans, the King and Queen of Spain simply decided the original deal was too generous to honor. Much like the dispossession of American Indians of their land wreaked havoc on the psyches of their cultures, the breaking of this deal shattered Columbus' emotional stability.[21]

Considering that ultimately Indians were consistently labeled "savages," "wild," "hostile," etc., it is surprising to learn Columbus' initial descriptions of Indians to his royal sponsors, as understood by Peter Martyr, were enthusiastic and positive. He declared:

> 'It is certain' ...'that the land among these people is as common as the sun and water; and that 'mine and thine', the seeds of all mischief, have no place with them... They deal truly one with another, without laws, without books, and without judges. They take him for an evil and mischievous man who taketh pleasure in doing hurt to another.[22]

After wrecking his ship on the cacique of Guacanagari and encountering its residents, he stated in his journal: "'So loving, so tractable, so peaceable are these people that I swear to your majesties there is not in the world a better nation, nor a better land. They love their neighbors as themselves.'"[23] After Columbus' initial glowing descriptions of the Indians, he later attempted to justify his greed, brutality and enslavement of these unfortunate souls by claiming they were "'cruel,'" "'stupid,'" and: "'a people warlike and numerous, whose customs and religion are very different from ours.'"[24] Whether or not Columbus possessed the "deep religious sentiment" claimed by Irving, the penchant for Columbus and other Europeans was to justify every sort of cruelty in the name of God. With that type of rationalization in mind, Jake Page noted how eventually even the motivation provided by the "Christian message" changed over time. He noted as the "discoverers" of the "New World" steam-rolled through the Western Hemisphere: "After the ravages of European-borne diseases, the religion of the Europeans was the single most dangerous force the Indians across the entire hemisphere would ever face."[25]

Ironically, while history reveals whites and other Europeans would endure just about any pain or hardship to gather gold, silver, and other riches, Indians reserved their volunteering for intense suffering almost exclusively for spiritual pursuits such as the Sun Dance. Yet, in many cases Indians in what became North and South America sacrificed their very lives for the benefit of others pursuing riches. The lust for gold proved an ever-present reality for the Europeans and their descendants who subdued the Indians on both continents. For example, almost 400 years later in the Pacific Northwest in 1860, a gold strike occurred on Orofino Creek, a tributary of the Clearwater River north of Salmon River County in Idaho, considered at the time to be Nez Perce territory. Indian trader Elias dodged groups of Nez Perce long enough to lay claim to a gold strike and: "carried enough dust back to Walla Walla, Washington, to stimulate interest there." Historian Paula Marks added: "In a situation foreshadowing events in the Black Hills fifteen years later, the second group departing Walla Walla had to dodge not only Indians but United States troops sent to keep them off Indian property."[26]

What is seemingly less well known is the role the lust for gold played in the dark episode in United States history that eventually became known as the "Trail of Tears." In 1829, in one account, gold was discovered by an Indian youth living on Ward Creek (Georgia) who sold the pebble to a white trader who recognized the object as gold. As was typical, the news of the discovery of gold spread like wildfire and attracted a stampede of prospectors.[27] The greed of white men to take control of the gold fields was one more excuse for the Georgians to remind the federal government to take control of Cherokee lands.

Thus, perhaps no other issue differentiated the culture of Indians from white culture like that of gold; Indians thought gold made white people crazy. Prior to the start of the removal process of the Cherokees from Georgia, and after gold was discovered, there were some who believed: "Gold was as close to an earthly god as a man could find" and that "Gold makes its own laws." Part of the dilemma was that up until essentially the early 1800s, finding gold was one of the few ways wealth could be accumulated. During the period gold could be mined in Georgia, it even became a form of currency and miners often carried with them a pair of hand scales to facilitate that process. To the delight of bartenders and whiskey peddlers, it was well known at the time that three and one-half grains of gold was considered appropriate payment for a pint of whiskey.[28]

But, regardless of how Indians viewed the gold fever afflicting whites, by any objective standards, the lust and craziness over gold *was* virtually unlimited from the time of Columbus' arrival forward to the present day. In a camp in Montana in the late 1800s, one man searching for a lost pig was followed by a crowd of people convinced he was leading them to a gold strike. In another anecdote, after an old mountaineer buying supplies was heard saying: "'I have got about as good a thing as I want,'" an estimated 1,200 gold seekers followed him out of town in the snow and bitter cold. What these gold-crazed fools did not realize was that the grizzled old man was referring to his Blackfoot Indian wife, not a gold strike.[29]

As even a casual review of history discloses, gold was not the only substance which drove Europeans mad. Likewise, although the major focus of this book is North America, Indians in South America were also brutalized and exploited in the fanatical pursuit of mineral riches and subjected to the pain-inducing myth of European intellectual and cultural superiority. In April 1545, a man named Diego Gualpa, or Hualpa, was walking on a plateau in the Andes Mountains in South America, possibly looking for a lost llama. Apparently, as he stumbled on a high ridge and seized a shrub for balance, it came out of the shallow soil. Seeing the metallic sparkle where the shrub was pulled out led to the discovery of the largest silver strike in history—300 feet long, 13 feet wide, and 300 feet deep. Silver ore typically only contains a small percentage of pure silver, and this particular deposit was thought to have had as high as a 50 percent silver content. Yet the Spaniards who seized the opportunity to mine the silver initially had difficulty even developing a process to purify the silver without burning away much of the actual silver content. Eventually the Spaniards borrowed a process from the local indigenous people and learned how to process the silver ore at low temperatures with smelters fueled by dry grass and llama dung.

The town nearest the silver ore, Potosi, grew as populated as London or Amsterdam at that time and became the highest elevated, richest city in the world. Potosi became synonymous with excess with miners giving fortunes to beggars and spending enormous sums on swords, clothes, and obscenely lavish celebrations. In a bidding war over a single piece of fish being sold at a market, the two bidders eventually quit after the price reached 5,000 pesos, which was several years income for most Europeans at that time. In another bizarre episode reminiscent of Indian-abusing President Andrew Jackson's violent earlier life, a man showed up for a duel—except this man, certainly unlike Jackson—showed up in a mother-of-pearl-colored tunic decorated with diamonds, emeralds, and strands of pearls. At one Potosi celebration, a city street was literally lined with silver bars.[30]

Yet, as ostentatious as these displays of wealth became, they were exceeded in intensity by the inhumane and harsh treatment unleashed on native Indian miners. The cruelest suffering foisted on the natives began when the transplanted Europeans realized in the 1550s that mercury rather than heat could be used to purify silver ore. (It might be more accurate to state the process was rediscovered, since the Chinese had known about this technique for centuries.) The mercury ore was in Huancavelica, about 800 miles from Potosi. In an elaborate purification process that involved the use of saltwater, copper, heat, and mercury, the eventual result was pure silver. With the need for using Indians in the purification process of silver essentially eliminated, they could be treated exclusively as a source of labor for the hazardous task of mercury mining.

When retrieving the mercury, Indian miners entered the poorly ventilated mines with candles strapped to their foreheads. The hellish working environment was described as a place where: "Heat from the earth vaporized the mercury—a slow acting poison—so workers stumbled through the day in a lethal steam. Even in cooler parts of the mine they were hacking away at the ore with picks, creating a fog of mercury, sulfur, arsenic, and silica." It would not require a great deal of scientific research to convince reasonable people that even after one- or two-month stints in mercury mines—and workers often worked several—these workers suffered intensely from their exposure to mercury. One of the many side effects of mercury toxicity included intense shaking; unsurprisingly, even foremen and supervisors who did not spend as much time inside the mines as the workers were also casualties of mercury poisoning or toxicity.

Indian families became so desperate to avoid having family members work in the unforgiving death traps of the Huancavelica mercury mines that parents often maimed their children to make them unfit for the unrelenting demanding labor. Mercury poisoning or toxicity was so pervasive and frightful that when officials dug up the graves of miners in 1604, decomposed corpses left behind puddles of mercury. In addition to mercury poisoning or toxicity, miners succumbed to pneumonia, tuberculosis, silicosis (lesions in the lungs caused by the inhalation of silica dust), and asphyxiation caused by breathing carbon dioxide in badly ventilated tunnels.

Conditions in the Potosi silver mine weren't as immediately lethal as the Huancavelica mercury mines but were ultimately just as inhumane. In almost complete darkness, gangs of Indian miners carried up to 100-pound loads of ore up and down dangling rope and leather ladders. In the initial phases of the mining operation, the Indian slaves were given two weeks rest above ground for every week spent below the surface. Eventually the rest periods were eliminated by the Spaniards and when miners hit a patch of lower-quality ore, they were forced to work even harder to meet their silver quotas. Failure to meet the quotas brought forth punishment with whips, clubs, and stones. Anti-slavery activists of the day denounced the hellish pits of Potosi and one outraged priest wrote to the Spanish royal secretary: "If twenty healthy Indians enter on Monday, half come out on Saturday as cripples."[31]

In 1498, Columbus ventured to what he understood to be called Paria, a large peninsula in the northeast corner of present-day Venezuela. In what seemed a typical misunderstanding for Columbus, he believed this peninsula to be an island. Although it was usually gold which typically inflamed his lusting for riches, this time it was the sight of pearls wrapped around the arms of natives found on Paria which aroused Columbus and his crew to a near frenzy of greed. Columbus had read in Pliny (presumably the Elder, a Roman author, naturalist and natural philosopher born in 23 AD) that pearls were: "generated from drops of dew which fall into the mouths of oysters." So vivid were the images of riches to be gained from oysters found in Paria that Columbus gave the name Gulf of Pearls to one of its gulfs.[32]

One of the odd realizations about the history of indigenous people in the Western Hemisphere is there has been a growing amount of recognition regarding the cruelty inflicted on those souls who were steamrolled by western expansion in North America. However, there does not seem to be a corresponding awareness of the pain and suffering inflicted on Indians in South America as described above. A notable exception to the silence about injustices inflicted upon the indigenous people there, particularly the Spaniards, was by a Dominican priest, Bartoleme de las Casa, who wrote *A Brief Account of the Destruction of the Indies*. In addition to the horrors foisted upon Bolivian Indians forced to work in silver and mercury mines, in the 1880s, thousands of Brazilians were made slaves to those harvesting rubber in the form of latex from the species of trees known as Castilla elastic. Although the quality of the rubber collected from these trees, *caucho,* was of a lesser quality than other sources, it was at times possible to collect hundreds of pounds of latex from a single tree, thus compensating for the lower quality of rubber, or latex. However, the process of harvesting the rubber involved killing the trees. Thus, a premium was placed on being the first workers to enter a forested area, and the obvious goal of the overseers and owners of the operation became to harvest the most amount of rubber in the least amount of time. The health of the rubber workers was of no concern.

Since at least initially the arrival of the Europeans seemed to the indigenous peoples as the appearance of some kind of deities, the situation in South America was ripe for the exploitation of these overawed individuals. One of the primary abusers in the centuries after Columbus was Carlos Fitzcarrald, the son of an immigrant to Peru. In the late 1880s, Fitzcarrald began forcing thousands of Indians to harvest rubber from the caucho trees. At one point, after a Mashco Indian leader doubted the effectiveness of Fitzcarrald's pistol's bullets as opposed to arrows, Fitzcarrald and his men killed approximately 100 of these Mashco Indians. Additionally, Fitzcarrald gave no thought to the environmental impact of this rubber harvesting. Another brutal exploiter of South American Indians arrived on the rubber scene in the form of Julio Cesar Arana, the son of a Peruvian hat maker. In what was a typical scenario in South America, instead of paying high wages to lure workers from other regions, Arana simply enslaved local indigenous people to collect rubber for him. In addition, Arana had a gang of around 100 toughs from Barbados to do his bidding, particularly to control his slave force. However, at least partially due to the activities of some human rights activists from Britain, in what would seem a case of poetic justice, Arana's empire disintegrated, and he died penniless in 1952.[33]

Returning to events in North America, the tragic consequences of encouraging the concept of acquisitiveness spared no section of what eventually became the United States and reached the Great Plains, thousands of miles from where Columbus first landed. In the Dakota region in the early 1800s, particularly the area of the Teton tribes, white traders brought rifles, horses, steel knives and other goods to these Indians in exchange for buffalo robes, humps, and tongues. The rifles and horses enabled the Indian hunters to increase their ability to kill buffalo in great numbers over a wider range of territory, increasing pressure on the herds. The need for gunpowder, without which the guns were useless, further increased the Indians' dependence on trade. The greed of barterers in trading cheap-quality goods, bribing of government officials, availability of whiskey, and the ignoring of the concept of conservation fueled the prospect of conflict on the frontier between the two cultures.

Likewise, sometime after Columbus' arrival, Pueblo Elders had dire prophecies regarding the coming invasion of whites:

> Listen! Listen! The gray-eyed people are coming nearer and nearer. They are building an iron road. They are coming nearer every day. There will be a time when you will mix with these people. That is when the Grey Eyes are going to get you to drink black, hot water, which you will drink whenever you eat. Then your teeth will become soft. They will get you to smoke at a young age, so that your eyes will run tears on windy days, and your eyesight will be poor. Your joints will crack when you want to move slowly and softly. You will sleep on soft beds and not like to rise early.[34]

Yet, if the above warnings against materialism are considered a type of protest against Columbus, then Indian opposition to the virtual deification of Columbus began long before the protest in Denver in 1992. However, it was most likely the Indian activism of the 1960s and 1970s that crystallized and first drew attention to this viewpoint. After Lakota Indian Leonard Crow Dog was convicted and imprisoned for his participation in the Wounded Knee "occupation" of 1973, he was visited by the prison psychiatrist. When asked if he had any physical complaints, he said he had an irritation—the U.S. government was irritating him. Crow Dog then turned the tables on the examiner and queried: "Have you got a cure for breaking promises? Have you got a cure for lying?"[35] Crow Dog then responded to the question about what he thought about the then-upcoming bicentennial in 1976:

> Washington was a guy with short silk pants, a wig, and wooden teeth who kept slaves. Then Columbus. He thought he had landed in India—only ten thousand miles off course. Then Custer—without us you might have had him for president. You ought to be grateful. You people elected a Nixon, an Agnew. I'm humble. I'm satisfied with Sitting Bull and Crazy Horse.[36]

Of course, much like any other Indian who expressed dissatisfaction with the state of affairs pertaining to Indians, many have dismissed Leonard Crow Dog as nothing more than a fringe "militant" due to his involvement with the American Indian Movement. However, sober reflection reveals his points about Columbus and various founding father types are certainly worth considering. While Crow Dog's comments are the type often responded to with cries of "revisionist history," it is important to consider one logical point—there is no such thing. History is either accurate or it is not. Consider this quote from Irving's biography of Columbus:

> Without wishing to knock Columbus *off a pedestal which he richly deserves*, we may remind ourselves that a hero does not have to possess all the good qualities under the sun. A daring explorer and a *navigator of genius* may not be the perfect choice for the founder and governor of a new colony [emphasis added].[37]

The statement: "…[a] hero does not have to possess all the good qualities under the sun…" is another example of a "straw man" argument. Obviously, no human being possesses "…all the good qualities under the sun," but many have argued that Columbus may not have even been close. As is coming to light more and more, Columbus was cruel and greedy. It is fairly accurate to depict Columbus as a "daring explorer," but that label could easily be applied to other groups such as Vikings and pirates. These last two groups, like Columbus, ventured out in small (by today's standards) ships looking for loot, treasure, and perhaps notoriety.

As suggested by Leonard Crow Dog, to call Columbus a "navigator of genius" is at best an ambivalent proposition, perhaps difficult to embrace. The context of that statement would be easier to grasp had Irving described the efforts of other navigators and explorers of that era experiencing even less success in ending up where they intended. Even Irving agreed with the oddness of his own description when he noted the people of Columbus' day, including apparently Columbus himself, were: "…surprised at their own ignorance of the world around them."[38] Irving noted at one point while exploring the coast of Cuba, Columbus thought he was sailing along some point in Asia. In another instance, on August 19, 1498, Columbus arrived at: "…the island of Hispaniola…fifty leagues to the westward of the river Ozema, the place of his destination, and anchored on the following morning under the little island of Beata." Apparently, Columbus himself, caught up in his own beliefs regarding his superb navigational skills: "…was astonished to find himself so mistaken in his calculations."[39]

Recent writing has cast further doubt on Irving's assessment of Columbus as a "navigator of genius." In that regard, the methodical approach to sea exploration of the Vikings has been increasingly recognized in recent research. In *The Mysterious History of Columbus,* John Wilford cited Alfred Crosby's *Ecological Imperialism: The Biological Expansion of Europe, 900-1900*: "'Only a fool with a new theory would sail off into an ocean without a very specific idea of where he was going.'" In contrast, he explained, "'The Norse always had a specific idea'" of where they were headed.[40]

It becomes clear from a thorough reading of Irving's biography of Columbus that nothing in Irving's view would have knocked Columbus off the "pedestal which he so richly deserves." Columbus' second voyage to the "New World" involved a fleet of seventeen ships containing over 1,000 men. The activities involved with the exploration and inhabitation of various Caribbean islands during this period created such chaos and resentment that an insurrection arose among the natives of the islands Columbus was still convinced were the West Indies. Consequently, as noted by Granzotto, Columbus and his brother Bartholomew decided to lead a punitive expedition with the specific purpose of crushing the revolt, which evolved into a conflict lasting ten months. The war resulted in the capture of many natives—Five Hundred—who were doomed to become slaves, taken to Spain, and sold under horrible living conditions. They were displayed on the trading blocks in the nude and two hundred of them died in a very short time.[41]

In rationalizing Columbus taking 500 slaves back to Spain at the conclusion of this second trip, Irving proposed a form of what has become described in slang terms as the "Nuremberg Defense," i.e., 'I was just following orders." Irving argued that it was common at that time to make slaves out of "conquered" people, i.e.: "The customs of the times must be pleaded in his apology," particularly making those who were not Christians into vassals of the righteous. Irving continued: "…the practice had been sanctioned by the church itself,"[42] and that most learned theologians had pronounced all barbarous and infidel nations who shut their ears to the truths of Christianity fair objects of war and rapine, or captivity and eventual slavery. It would not be the last time brutalization of natives would be justified in the name of God. And, tellingly, in analyzing the Custer expedition into the Black Hills of South Dakota in 1874, it has come to light that the number of men and wagons used in that foray looking for gold and other minerals exceeded the number of men and wagons accompanying Custer on his way to what became known as the Battle of the Little Big Horn two years later. What is most valued is often discovered by observing what people do.

When taking a serious look at what Columbus brought to the "New World" it is often the foreshadowing of future events that is "discovered." Although Columbus was not directly involved in the incident in 1503, the pattern of future atrocities unleashed upon Indians in the Western Hemisphere was established, particularly in South Dakota not quite 400 years later. In that year of 1503, on the island of Xarangua: "Quarrels took place between the caciques [native leaders] and their oppressors" and: "…were immediately reported to the [local] governor as dangerous mutinies." Any resistance by the natives to the harsh, "capricious and extortionate exaction," was exaggerated and reported as "…a rebellious resistance to the authority of government." An "alarmist" or "mischief maker" persuaded Ovando, the territorial governor, that there existed a: "…*deep laid conspiracy among the Indians of this province to rise upon the Spaniards* [emphasis added]." Ovando set out for Xarangua along with 300 heavily armed foot soldiers and 70 horsemen to visit the cacique Anacaona under the pretext of friendship and of collecting the expected tribute. After receiving word of the impending visit, Anacaona gathered her subordinate caciques to ensure Ovando was received with "homage and distinction." Upon Ovando's arrival, Anacaona and her followers greeted Ovando with great flourish and fanfare. Irving described the scene as one where: "For several days the Spaniards were entertained with all the natural luxuries that the province afforded." Further: "National songs and dances and games were performed for their [the Spaniards] amusement, and there was every outward demonstration of the same hospitality, the same amity, that Anacaona had uniformly shown to white men."

Nonetheless, Ovando was persuaded by whisperers that Anacaona was secretly plotting a massacre of the Spaniards; historians are unable to provide an explanation for such a belief. Ovando was most likely influenced by the "unprincipled adventurers who infested the province." In a cautionary note worthy of repetition and requiring little modification for application throughout the centuries, Irving chided: "Ovando should have paused and reflected before he acted upon it. He should have considered the improbability of such an attempt by naked Indians against so large a force of steel-clad troops, armed with European weapons, and he should have reflected upon the general character and conduct of Anacaona."[43] Have historians of the Wounded Knee Massacre employed similar logic when examining the motives of Indians who participated in the "Ghost Dance?"

Ovando set up a jousting match for his soldiers on a Sunday afternoon in front of the house where he was staying. However, the cavalry and foot soldiers accompanying Ovando were given secret instructions to use real weapons instead of reeds or blunted tilting lances. It was also arranged to make it appear the foot soldiers were mere spectators, but they were actually instructed to attack the natives upon receipt of a prearranged signal. None of the native guests, including, of course, Anacaona and her beautiful daughter Higuena-mota, were armed. When Ovando saw that all the preparations for the ambush were completed, he gave the signal for the attack to begin. The caciques accompanying Anacaona were captured and tortured and the common people were massacred without regard to age or sex. Anacaona was carried off in chains to Santo Domingo. After a sham trial, she was unceremoniously hanged before a crowd of Spaniards.[44]

ENDNOTES

1. James W. Loewen, *Lies My Teacher Told Me: Everything Your American History Textbook Got Wrong* (New York: Touchstone Books/Simon and Schuster, 1995), p. 37.
2. Ward Churchill, *Indians Are Us: Culture and Genocide in Native North America* (Monroe, Maine: Common Courage Press, 1994), p. 11.
3. Welch (with Paul Stekler), *Killing Custer*, p. 144.
4. Churchill, *Indians Are Us*, p. 46 Editor's Note.
5. Ibid., p. 29.
6. Irving, *The Life and Voyages of Christopher Columbus*, p. 281.
7. Gianni Granzotto, *Christopher Columbus: The Dream and the Obsession* (Garden City, New York: Doubleday &Co., 1985), pp. 9-10.
8. Mann, *1491*. pp. 185-186.
9. Ibid., p. 104.
10. John Noble Wilford, *The Mysterious History of Columbus: An Exploration of the Man, the Myth, the Legacy* (New York: Knopf Doubleday Publishers, 1991) p. 39.
11. Bradley, *The Columbus Conspiracy*, p. 117.
12. Mann, *1491*, p. x.
13. Ibid., p. 84.
14. Alvin M. Josephy, Jr., "The Center of the Universe" in *America in 1492: The World of Indian Peoples Before the Arrival of Columbus*, Ed. Alvin M. Josephy (New York: Vintage Books/A Division of Random House, Inc. 1993), p. 6.
15. Ibid., pp. 4-5.
16. Irving, *The Life and Voyages of Christopher Columbus*, p. 31.
17. Mann, *1491*, p. 92 (footnote at bottom of the page).
18. Irving, *The Life and Voyages of Christopher Columbus*, p. 499. Irving's 692-page book does not have an index, but it appears the "Adelanto" described on this page is Don Bartholomew, Columbus' brother. Nevertheless, the obvious conclusion from the episode is the Spaniards' consistently justified cruel behavior because strict application of Catholic principles virtually required it.
19. Ibid., p. 461.
20. Ibid., p. 499. Irving did not specify the outcome of any trials.
21. Wilford, *The Mysterious History of Columbus*, p. 97.
22. Irving, *The Life and Voyages of Christopher Columbus*, p. 143.
23. *Ibid.*, p. 150.
24. Loewen, *Lies My Teacher Told Me*, p. 62.
25. Jake Page, *In the Hands of the Great Spirit: The 20,000-Year Old History of American Indians* (New York: Free Press/A Division of Simon and Schuster, 2003), p. 111.

26 Paula Mitchell Marks, *Precious Dust: The Saga of the Western Gold Rushes* (Lincoln, Nebraska: University of Nebraska Press, 1994), p. 38.
27 John Ehle, *Trail of Tears: The Rise and Fall of the Cherokee Nation* (New York: Anchor Books/A Division of Random House, 1988), p. 222. The other account of the discovery of gold was "a peculiar-looking stone" was found by a young black slave who showed it to his master, who then spread the news. Ibid., p. 222.
28 Ibid., pp. 222-223.
29 Marks, *Precious Dust*, p. 40.
30 Mann, *1493: Uncovering the World Columbus Created*, p. 179.
31 Ibid., p. 184.
32 Irving, *The Life and Voyages of Christopher Columbus*, pp. 410-413.
33 Mann, *1493: Uncovering the World the World Columbus Created*, pp. 328-329.
34 Peter Nabokov, Ed., *Native American Testimony*, p. 14.
35 Crow Dog, *Lakota Woman*, p. 230.
36 Ibid., p. 231.
37 Irving, *The Life and Voyages of Christopher Columbus*, p. xv.
38 Ibid., p. 9.
39 Ibid., p. 416.
40 Wilford, *The Mysterious History of Columbus*, p. 5.
41 Granzotto, *Christopher Columbus*, pp. 221-223.
42 Irving, *The Life and Voyages of Christopher Columbus*, p. 351.
43 Ibid., pp. 645-646.
44 Ibid., p. 648.

CHAPTER 3

John O'Sullivan
In the Eye of the Storm of Manifest Destiny

> The clashes and conflicts of Western history will always leave the serious individual emotionally and intellectually unsettled. In the nineteenth century West, speaking out for the human dignity of all parties to the conflicts took considerable nerve. It still does.
>
> Patricia Nelson Limerick, *The Legacy of Conquest*[1]

In a moment of exquisite callousness, in 1871 Interior Secretary Columbus Delano exhorted a group of Indians visiting Washington, D.C., to accept their fate by explaining the momentum of Westward Expansion by whites was unstoppable because, "'the Great Spirit has decreed it.'" Had the consequences of such attitudes, held by many, not been so tragic for Indians, the scene would have been comical. Although Delano was a proponent of Grant's "Peace Policy" regarding Indians, his sentiments did not differ from the military leaders of the day who essentially dominated the formulation of Indian "policy." Lieutenant-Colonel George Forsyth, a contemporary of the controversial George A. Custer, claimed: "'Barbarism must necessarily give way before advancing civilization.'" Another military man, echoing Tolstoy, claimed: "'…no human hand could stay the rolling tide of progress.'"[2] Custer himself described the Indians of that era in an essay at West Point as existing: "'…on the verge of extinction, standing on his last foothold, clutching his bloodstained rifle, resolved to die amidst the horrors of slaughter, and soon be talked of as a noble race who once existed but have now passed away.'"[3] It is no small irony Delano shares his first name with the man commonly identified as the person who "discovered" America.

It was said about Custer in 1984 that: "Even now, after a hundred years, his name alone will start an argument."[4] This comment about Custer points the way to an important question: why is the history of the role John O'Sullivan played in providing intellectual structure to Westward Expansion so obscure? While perhaps next to Columbus, Custer is the most famous (or infamous) character in the parade of history making up Westward Expansion, it is logical to assert that O'Sullivan was significantly more influential than Custer, at least intellectually. O'Sullivan's soon to be near-sacred mantra of Manifest Destiny appeared in the *United States Magazine and Democratic Review*, where he was editor, in its July-August 1845 edition in an article entitled "Annexation":

> Why, were other reasons wanting, in favor of now elevating this question of the reception of Texas into the Union, out of the lower region of our past party dissensions, up to its proper level of a high and broad nationality, it surely is to be found, found abundantly, in the manner in which other nations have taken to intrude themselves into it, between us and the proper parties to the case, in a spirit of hostile interference against us, for the avowed object of thwarting our policy and hampering our power, limiting our greatness and checking the fulfillment of our *manifest destiny to overspread the continent allotted by Providence for the free development of our yearly multiplied millions* [emphasis added].[5]

At the time O'Sullivan produced this essay, he was also editor of the *New York Morning News* and later became Minister to Portugal. He was lavishly praised by John St. Tammany as: "'...one of the ablest writers and most accomplished scholars and gentlemen of the times.'"[6]

The proposition that North and South America were sparsely populated at the time Columbus arrived in 1492 co-existed with the powerful social and political mantra of "Manifest Destiny." This slogan of invulnerability propelled the settlers, military, and railroad barons of that era to conduct a campaign of near annihilation of Indians and their culture. In his 1967 Pulitzer Prize-winning book *Exploration and Empire*, William Goetzman stated: "...the explorer was largely dedicated to lending a helping hand in the matter of Manifest Destiny."[7] Like so many other aspects of Euromerican thought regarding Indians, Goetzman's line suggested Manifest Destiny was an independent, almost live entity rather than a concept created by men. Likewise, is the concept of Manifest Destiny significantly different than the belief espoused by Columbus that he was ordained to "discover" a "New World"?

The repercussions of the belief in Manifest Destiny, aside from its impact on Indians, had some peculiar consequences on evaluating the roles of leaders throughout United States history. After General Winfield Scott led the extraordinarily successful military campaign resulting in the conquest of Mexico in 1847, Americans paid scant attention to Scott's accomplishments, giving little consideration to the possibility stated by one historian who believed he: "'may well have been the most capable soldier this country has ever produced.'" Americans more or less believed that Manifest Destiny was a living organism, a "...natural, inevitable process," and the actions of individuals necessarily mattered little.[8] That belief was pervasive throughout the 19th century (and beyond), and historians have often had little in terms of criticism of that mindset.

Thus, the belief that Manifest Destiny entitled Euromericans the unfettered right to dominate the Indian inhabitants of the Western Hemisphere virtually became a religion unto itself. As a case in point, George Ellis, a well-known 19th century cleric and author, used his position to put the seal of "God's" approval on crushing the spirit out of any Indians who had the audacity to survive the "Indian Wars" of the 1880s. He boldly claimed in much the same manner as L. Frank Baum:

> We [whites] have a full right, by our own best wisdom, and then even by compulsion, to dictate terms and conditions to them [the Indians]; to use constraint and force; to say what we intend to do, and what we must and shall do… This rightful power of ours will relieve us from conforming to any troublesome extent, the views and inclinations of the Indians whom we are to manage… [which are irrelevant and] …The Indian must be made to feel he is in the grasp of a superior.[9]

Author Armando Prats recalled a line written in his tenth-grade American history text which succinctly summarized this point in four words, "'The Indians hindered progress.'" He further explained when writing about movies depicting Indians and understanding the significance of this phrase: "There it is—stark, cruel, absolute in its Darwinian indifference. In the early days of my research into the Indian Western, three decades later, there was hardly an Indian to be seen that did more noble work than that of hindering progress." Prats bleakly concluded this maudlin description of Indians in United States society: "To be sure, he was ubiquitous, yet he was nearly invisible. He posed a formidable threat to the dreams of civilization, yet he was almost always faceless and voiceless."[10] Not to be outdone by any man of the era in terms of verbal harshness was Sarah Royce, author of *A Frontier Lady: Recollections of the Gold Rush and Early California.* She described an incident where her traveling party was stopped by Indians while traveling through Lakota Country. She cried: "'…[their] demands were unreasonable! The country we were traveling over belonged to the United States and…these red men had no right to stop us.'"[11]

There was, and continues to be, a seemingly endless supply of justifications for the refusal to acknowledge that Manifest Destiny was simply a rationalization to take Indian land. The comfort of the belief in Manifest Destiny assured white citizens they had the unequivocal right to the entire territory which eventually became the United States of America. In 1846, during the debate on annexing Oregon, one Representative McDowell asked: "What are the *natural limits* of the United States, where the impulse of *annexation* will cease of itself? Is not growth the normal state, also, of the Federal Union? [emphasis in original]." Of course, the claim that God's will required expansion of the boundaries of the United States hit a snag in the case of its claims regarding the Oregon Territory when the British wanted expansion too, just in the other direction. A British publicist claimed: "growth is now, and must for some time, continue to be the normal state of our existence in the East." The publicist also argued that growth should continue until Great Britain reached the "natural limits of the Empire."

There simply was no limit to the way Manifest Destiny fueled the competitive spirit lodged in the denizens of the United States, regardless if the fuel was labeled Manifest Destiny or not. One Representative Bedinger stated: "…in the growth cycle of states, America was in 'the vigor of youth' while Great Britain had 'passed her prime.'" One writer in the *Democratic Review* breathlessly exclaimed in verse:

> We cannot help the matter if we would
> The race must have expansion—we must grow
> Though every forward footstep be withstood
> And every inch of ground presents its foe…[12]

Even though the concept of Manifest Destiny may not have been specifically articulated by John O'Sullivan until 1845, it existed as part of an aggressive and growing young nation's consciousness well before that moment. In an 1838 essay in the *Democratic Review*, the same publication which published the essay coining the phrase Manifest Destiny, the following foreshadowing of the 1845 pronouncement was published:

> The far-reaching, the boundless future will be the era of American greatness. In its magnificent domain of space and time, the nation of many nations is *destined to manifest* to mankind the excellence of divine principles; to establish on earth the noblest temple ever dedicated to the worship of the Most High—the Sacred and the True. Its floor shall be a hemisphere—its roof the firmament of the star-studded heavens, and its congregation an [sic] Union of many Republics, comprising hundreds of happy millions, calling, owning no man master, but governed by God's natural and moral law of equality, the law of brotherhood—of 'peace and good will amongst men' [emphasis in original as inserted by Weinberg].[13]

Is it surprising, given the belief in God's sanction of Manifest Destiny, that during the various stages leading up to the "Trail of Tears," Andrew Jackson displayed uninhibited aggression in promoting his relocation policies? The leaders of the various Indian nations could be excused if they failed to see this travesty as the application of "God's natural and moral law of equality." Jackson's failure to acknowledge the Cherokees' role in defeating the Creek Indians in 1814, which prompted much bitterness on the part of the Cherokees, was anything but "moral." It was believed "…nothing appears to have stung the Cherokees more deeply" than the realization that their loyalty had been betrayed by Jackson.[14] The conquest of land occupied by Indians, i.e. "savages," as being justified by God's will was a belief held not only by national leaders, but by ordinary foot soldiers as well. Lieutenant James Calhoun, of Custer's 7th Cavalry, a prominent military unit in actions described throughout this book, once mused that after whites possessed the land:

> the hives of industry will take the place of dirty wigwams. Civilization will ere long reign supreme and throw heathen barbarianism into oblivion. Seminaries of learning will raise their proud cupolas far above the canopies of Indian lodges and Christian temples will elevate their lofty spires upward toward the azure sky while places of heathen mythology will sink to rise no more. This will be a period of true happiness.[15]

People who at times argued there was ample existing territory for the population of the United States had little credibility with those who believed in the inevitable expansion of the boundaries of the ever-growing United States of America. Additionally, what perhaps Indians who put the community foremost over the needs of the individual could never understand, was that on the frontier, democracy to whites meant there were no practical limits on those individuals who participated in greedy land grabs. Likewise, Richard Slotkin explained that the lines between those on the frontier who viewed Indians as simply "hinder[ing] progress" and ambitious businesspeople were blurred. He noted: "The virtues of the hunter/Indian fighter are primarily those of the entrepreneur, the man on the make. He is self-willed and self-motivated, and—if controlled at all—self-controlled." Slotkin also explained: "He is a man of exploit, not of patient labor."[16] And although James Donovan glossed over discussing the lack of rights afforded Indians after the "uprising" in Minnesota in 1862 in *A Terrible Glory*, he did astutely note: "In the post [Civil] War Gilded Age, money and its pursuit were all-important."[17]

The rightness of the belief in Manifest Destiny is inseparable from the pervasive myth that Europeans cleared out a wilderness and built cities from scratch. It is a corollary to the myth that Europeans "discovered" (mostly for our purposes) a North American continent uninhabited except for a small number of "savages." However, in reality, while Europeans often imposed new architectural styles and different ideas for urban planning in the "new" world, they frequently built their structures over existing Indian settlements rather than clearing out swaths of forest or wilderness. Additionally, nowhere does the myth of Europeans discovering a virgin wilderness awaiting the Europeans to fulfill their "Manifest Destiny" combust in historical reality as when examining indigenous peoples' use of fire to control the environment. As Shepard Krech III explained: "By the time Europeans arrived, North America was a manipulated continent. Indians had long since altered the landscape by burning or clearing woodland for farming and fuel." Krech concluded his analysis by arguing: "Despite European images of an untouched Eden, this nature was cultural not virgin, anthropogenic not primeval, and nowhere is this more evident than in the Indian uses of fire."[18]

While the term Manifest Destiny itself may not be much in vogue in academia these days, the concept still seemingly continues to infest to one degree or another virtually every non-Indian account of Indian history. Of course, even though the idea that whites were entitled by God to settle North (and South) America was used to dilute the descriptions of the most heinous and evil of acts, it is seemingly a rarely condemned feature of history. While individuals like Teddy Roosevelt have argued that practically any account of Indian history not involving Indians willingly accepting their total domination by white culture is "sentimental nonsense," it is the converse which is more likely to be true. It is "sentimental nonsense" and worse to gloss over claims of theft, torture, and murder as part of God's plan as ordained by Him through Manifest Destiny.

In recent history, warped echoes of the cries of Manifest Destiny can be found in an unexpected location: that of Indian gaming—in other words, casinos. As will also be discussed in a subsequent chapter, the issue of Indian gaming is intertwined with defining who is and is not an "Indian." In this regard, at times the belief that Indians should relinquish gambling profits from casinos has bordered on rabid. In a protest directed at proponents of Indian gaming, one thoughtless individual carried a sign stating: "We took your land—get over it." Arnold Schwarzenegger, during his first campaign for California governor in 2003, completely disregarded the nature of the relationships of tribes to the states. He aired campaign ads accusing Indians of failing to pay their "'fair share'" of casino profits to the state and vowed to pursue these funds once in office, and characterized the $130 million California tribes paid to the state at that time as part of a revenue-sharing agreement as paying "'virtually nothing to the state.'"[19] Perhaps this type of thinking is an outgrowth of the "reflexive" belief the system tilts in favor of Indians.[20]

Schwarzenegger's attitude about Indian gaming is like that of Grant and other government officials prior to the Black Hills Expedition of 1874—anything to alleviate a budget crisis was permissible. Just as California was experiencing a severe budget crisis in the early 2000s (which never seemed to end), the United States in the early 1870s was experiencing one of the worst financial periods in the history of the young nation. It was believed the discovery and eventual mining of gold could alleviate the effects of the crisis. Never mind the expedition led by Custer into the Black Hills was viewed by the Lakota as a blatant violation of the Ft. Laramie Treaty of 1868. Similarly, many states today now overlook any qualms about gambling, and in addition to supporting casinos, see Indian gaming profits as one more way to generate money for public purposes. Perhaps one major difference between the 1874 situation and the contemporary times lies in how Indian leaders view profits now. While Indian leaders saw little value in the gold from the Black Hills, they placed great value on the Black Hills as a sacred area. Conversely, many Indian leaders now see casino profits as a way to finance public health projects, water treatment facilities, etc. Unfortunately, in the case of the Black Hills, not only were the miners allowed to run wild looking for gold, but under the guise of Manifest Destiny the Black Hills were eventually taken as well.

Darwin's *Origin of Species*, which in one way or another at least helped justify the doctrine of "natural selection" and ultimately "survival of the fittest," was not published until 1859. However, ideas that the conquest of North America was inevitable were percolating years before that. They often appeared in the form of the belief that what eventually became the United States was a new Israel, and that when people were thinking of: "God's dispensations to America [they are] reminded of those to Israel." Jefferson stated in his inaugural address of 1805, "God led our forefathers, as Israel of old.'"[21]

One of the most chilling applications in the 19th and early 20th century of natural selection arose in what was loosely termed the "science" of eugenics. Eugenics was largely the concept driving the operation of the Canton/Hiawatha Asylum for Insane Indians in eastern South Dakota. In reality, there was nothing "natural" about the "selection" advocated by the disciples of eugenics, the "science" developed by Sir Francis Galton, a British biologist and Darwin's cousin.[22] Eugenics' proponents advocated that perhaps nature wasn't doing such a good job with evolution after all and it needed help to cull the "weak" or "undesirables" out of society to ensure more room for growth for the "strong." Even Darwin himself was not fond of the idea of eugenics and said, "'…leave things alone and all will come [out] right.'"[23] Nonetheless, the "science" of eugenics found a welcoming home in the hellish corridors of what came to be known as the Canton/Hiawatha Asylum for Insane Indians located in Canton, South Dakota. The Canton/Hiawatha Asylum was opened in 1901 with Oscar Gifford, former mayor of Canton and a South Dakota congressman, named its first superintendent. It mattered little to those making the appointment that Gifford had no medical background. The first employee "code" of over 40 rules indicated kicking, striking, shaking, or choking of patients were permissible methods of patient control.[24]

It takes little "imagination" (a term employed by writer Helen Hunt Jackson to be discussed shortly) to see eugenics as practiced at Canton/Hiawatha as a perfect tool for ensuring at least a small segment of Indians were engulfed in the tidal wave of Manifest Destiny. If traditional Indians resisted assimilation or becoming more of a part of "mainstream" United States society, all that was required for them to be committed to Canton/Hiawatha was to be labeled "feebleminded." If the Indians could be assimilated, then there would be little reminder of what was done to them in the name of "progress." Particularly in the case of Lakota Indians, shipping them across the state to Canton/Hiawatha and keeping them institutionalized in miserable conditions was one way of trying to erase from American consciousness that the Black Hills were once under the safekeeping of these proud people. There were so few procedural safeguards in place to ensure Indians were properly committed (if they ever were), and the sanitary and general living conditions were so deplorable, many found out at the Canton/Hiawatha Asylum the "…only sure way to leave was death."[25]

After the "insane" Indians arrived at Canton/Hiawatha, the "medical" practitioners there could go to work and ensure the Indians became model citizens to be returned to the reservations as examples of the benefits of embracing white culture. Indians who were torn away from their families and shipped there were not afforded anything remotely resembling due process at any point. The existence of the Canton/Hiawatha Asylum, that in reality was nothing more than a torture palace with no medical or therapeutic purpose, is still essentially an unknown dark episode in United States history. Even just one example of the treatment Indians received—forcing them to live in their own waste—should be enough to bring forth a feeling of shame in all but the most hard-hearted. However, unlike the writings of historians S. C. Gwynne and Helen Jackson, who actually suggested (as will be explained in later chapters) that Indian suffering was not worth describing, multiple examples of Indian mistreatment are provided to enhance understanding of the unrecognized abuses of the concept of Manifest Destiny in its more subtle forms.

For example, on November 8, 1917, Agnes Caldwell of the Kenosha Agency of Wisconsin was committed to the Canton/Hiawatha Asylum against her will with a diagnosis made by then-superintendent Dr. Hummer for "…being feebleminded with a distinct weakness for men…" Hummer believed she was a prime candidate for this commitment because this weakness for men: "…could result in the birth of numerous feebleminded or otherwise mentally deficient children." Caldwell wrote the Commissioner of the Indian Office in Washington, D.C., numerous times begging for her release, but, based on Hummer's "diagnosis," the commissioner denied her requests. Agnes gave birth to a baby girl at the Asylum who died of bronchial pneumonia in 1921, less than a year after she was born. This tragedy only compounded the mess created by Agnes' involuntary commitment. On top of everything else, Agnes' husband George tried to divorce her while she was at Canton/Hiawatha. After sixteen years of dehumanizing treatment, Agnes was released to try to pick up the pieces of what remained of her life.[26]

In another example of uninhibited cruelty, Edith Schroder, a Chippewa, was sent to Canton/Hiawatha by C.H. Gensler, Superintendent of the Lac du Flambeau agency in Wisconsin, who sought her admission and wanted her "diagnosed" as "feebleminded." "Evidence" of her "feeblemindedness," like the case of Agnes Caldwell, was her nearly annual giving birth to a child which Gensler believed made her a "'nuisance and menace to society.'" Hummer supported Gensler's belief that Schroder should be housed at Canton/Hiawatha because she was "diagnosed" as "feebleminded" and not insane. (The preference of the feebleminded diagnosis over that of insanity was not explained.) Schroder was committed at the Canton/Hiawatha Asylum until the 1930s when she was diagnosed as sane and recommended for immediate return to her reservation.[27] Fortunately, although too late to prevent the deaths of well over 100 patients, and the destruction of many more lives, the Canton/Hiawatha Asylum was closed in 1934.[28]

Thus, the connection between what came to be known as cultural genocide and the Canton/Hiawatha Asylum (or other similar institutions foisting assimilation on Indians such as boarding schools) is often overlooked, apparently since so many writers argue genocide means the complete annihilation of a group of people. In an unrelated matter, between 1907 and 1913, Kate Barnard, a commissioner of charities and corrections in Oklahoma, investigated and found, among other despicable acts, guardians of Indian children had committed normal Indian children to insane asylums while the guardians themselves collected royalties from oil land. In 1910 alone she intervened in nearly 200 cases where orphaned Indian children lost their land to unscrupulous land grabbers. After her discovery of the fraudulent commitment of children to the asylums, Barnard pushed a bill through the Oklahoma legislature making orphan Indian minors wards of the state. Powerful men in Oklahoma who liked the idea of getting rich from oil profits were not pleased with her efforts and drove her to a nervous collapse.[29]

What was starting to be lost for Indians at the Canton/Hiawatha Asylum and at the boarding schools was not only dignity and even life, but vast storehouses of knowledge through the loss of use of languages. As Elizabeth Woody noted in "By Our Hand, Through the Memory, the House Is More Than Form": "It may make some people uncomfortable to see how eradication of native languages through colonization has impacted massive stores of knowledge."[30] As hopefully will become apparent, without the resilience of some Indian nations, Manifest Destiny eventually almost turned the subjugation of Indian nations into complete actual and cultural genocide. Many argue it did.

President Teddy Roosevelt promoted the inherent rightness of Manifest Destiny long after the Plains and other Indians had been completely subjugated essentially using military force, destruction of buffalo herds, and the onslaught of settlers. During the Philippine Insurrection, fought from 1898 to 1902, United States forces killed a vast number of Filipinos, including elderly men, women, and children civilians. After the killing was concluded, one critic stated: "'They never rebel in Northern Luzon because there isn't anybody there to rebel.'"[31] During the 1904 Presidential election, the brutality and terror unleashed upon these islanders was not even remotely a liability during Roosevelt's reelection bid. In actuality, Roosevelt employed the notion of the "Frontier Myth"—that "real" Americans relished the idea of the conquest and subjugation of "inferior races"—to his advantage. Those who opposed aggressive imperialism, such as Roosevelt's opponent, William Jennings Bryan, were presented with: "…[the] more complex task of denying the validity of America's most potent national myth and then explaining why it had been wrong for our ancestors to dispossess the Indians." [32] He failed.

In the end, Manifest Destiny and its concomitant rationalization of the seizure of Indian lands or territory gained its momentum not as a result of supernatural forces. Rather, Manifest Destiny "succeeded" through the all-too-human actions and justifications of whites. One major belief system, to be analyzed in subsequent discussions in this book, contained the notion that Indians were simply incapable of governing themselves and converting them to Christianity and indoctrinating them in European culture was in their best interests. Another flimsy justification, which was amply demonstrated in the case of the Black Hills, was that Indians were not able to use land "productively" and could not tolerate others using it "productively" either. In the process of breaking up tribal holdings, the tribe was eliminated as the basic socio-economic group and replaced with—nothing. And no one seemed to consider: "Good intentions cannot make up for the resulting destruction of Indian families, Indian self-sufficient economies, Indian cultures, and Indian peoples themselves."[33]

ENDNOTES

1 Limerick, *The Legacy of Conquest*, p. 221.
2 Barnett, Louise, *Touched by Fire*, p. 115.
3 Evan Connell, *Son of the Morning Star* (New York: Harper & Row Publishers, 1984), p. 168 (also quoted in Barnett, *Touched by Fire*, p. 115).
4 Ibid., p. 106.
5 Weinberg, *Manifest Destiny*, p. 112.
6 Ibid., p. 111.
7 William H. Goetzmann, *Exploration and Empire: The Explorer and the Scientist in the Winning of the American West* (New York: The Norton Library/W.W. Norton & Co., 1966), p. xiii.
8 Morgan, *Lions of the West*, pp. 302-303.
9 Wilson, *The Earth Shall Weep*, p. 293.
10 Armando Prats, *Invisible Natives: Myth and Identity in the American Western* (Ithaca, New York: Cornell University Press, 2002), p. xiv.
11 Jeffrey Ostler, *The Lakota and the Black Hills: The Struggle for Sacred Ground* (New York: Penguin Books, 2010), p. 37.
12 Weinberg, *Manifest Destiny*, p. 194.
13 Ibid., p. 107. It is no small irony this comment foreshadowed the banner virtually mocking the dazed survivors of the Wounded Knee Massacre hanging in the Episcopal Mission on Pine Ridge: "PEACE ON EARTH GOOD WILL TO [sic] MEN." Brown, *Bury My Heart at Wounded Knee*, p. 445.
14 Ehle, *Trail of Tears*, p. 315.
15 Connell, *Son of the Morning Star*, p. 245.
16 Slotkin, *Fatal Environment*, p. 68.
17 James Donovan, *A Terrible Glory: Custer and the Little Big Horn: The Last Great Battle of the American West* (New York: Back Bay Books/Little Brown & Co., 2008), p. 102.
18 Shepard Krech, III, *The Ecological Indian-Myth and History* (New York: W.W. Norton & Co., 1999), p. 122.
19 Steven Andrew Light and Kathryn R.L. Rand, *Indian Gaming and Tribal Sovereignty: The Casino Compromise* (Lincoln, Nebraska: University of Kansas Press, 2005), pp. 124-125.
20 Wilkinson, *Blood Struggle*, p. 338.
21 Weinberg, *Manifest Destiny*, p. 40.
22 Todd Leahy, *They Called It Madness: The Canton Asylum for Insane Indians 1899-1934* (Baltimore: Publish America, 2009), p. 80.
23 Ibid., pp. 82-83.
24 Ibid., pp. 40-41.
25 Ibid., p. 99. Author Carla Joinson noted in the history of the institution nine patients were admitted pursuant to court order. Carla Joinson, *Vanished in Hiawatha, The Story of the Canton Asylum for Insane Indians* (Lincoln, Nebraska: University of Nebraska Press, 2016) p. 5.

26 Ibid., pp. 94-96. Caldwell also claimed Louis Hewling, a "former" staff member, was the father of a baby girl she conceived and delivered while at Canton/Hiawatha. There is some confusion about this account in that Hewling resigned a full year before the baby was born, and his continued access to Caldwell was not explained. Ibid., p. 95.
27 Ibid., pp. 87-88.
28 Ibid., pp. 167-168.
29 Flood, *Lost Bird of Wounded Knee*, p. 170.
30 Harjo, and Bird, Eds., Elizabeth Woody, "By Our Hand, Through the Memory, the House Is More Than Form." *Reinventing the Enemy's Language*, p. 514.
31 Slotkin, *Gunfighter Nation*, p. 119.
32 Ibid., p. 121.
33 George Tinker, *Missionary Conquest: The Gospel and Native American Cultural Genocide* (Minneapolis, Minnesota: Augsburg Fortress, 1993) p. 31.

CHAPTER 4

Ward Churchill
Who Are Indians and What Are They Up to Anyway?

By the time I was fourteen I understood the treatment of Indians was something people did not like to talk about plainly.

Thomas Powers, *The Killing of Crazy Horse*[1]

The "Indian" identity of "The Lost Bird of Wounded Knee" was never in doubt. The "Indian" identity of the controversial Ward Churchill, who has largely faded from sight due to various controversies, is often in doubt. For now, one aspect of "Lost Bird's" life, that of a Lakota Indian baby found in the aftermath of the slaughter at Wounded Knee on December 29, 1890, and raised by whites, provides a pathway to a subject glossed over even more often than the idea of Indian "savagery"—who is an Indian anyway? As such, a few comments from Renée Sansom Flood's riveting book *Lost Bird of Wounded Knee* provide guidance for the discussion.

In providing details of the circumstances of "Lost Bird's" life as an Indian child raised in white culture, Flood noted she "...had no model to look up to, no Indian face to look into except a wooden carving scowling in front of the cigar store."[2] As is commonly known, the typical name for some wooden carvings of Indians was and still is "cigar store Indian," a moniker with which she was insulted at times. She also became a symbol of how: "...colonizers attempted to defeat Indian people *and* to eradicate their identity and humanity. They attempted to transform Indian people into tobacco pouches, bridle reins or souvenirs—objects for the consumption of white people [emphasis in original]."[3] In "Lost Bird's" case, she was a living object of curiosity for whites to gawk at and of course ridicule as at various times in "Lost Bird's" life she was also called "'chinee,'" "'tar baby'," "'squaw,'" and "'nigger.'"[4]

While the expression "cigar store Indian" is hopefully regarded as offensive, caricatures of Indians abound in the current culture of the United States. Some slough off concerns about this type of labeling as "political correctness." However, Indians have concerns about labels such as these, as well as the use of Indian-looking mascots for sports teams. In the words of Glenn Morris, the head of Colorado AIM, this: "…is only the tip of a very huge problem of continuing racism against American Indians." Ward Churchill also found it difficult to view various members of the Kansas City Chiefs NFL football team at that time posing for a poster looking "'fierce'" and "'savage'" while wearing Indian regalia as participating in "'good clean fun.'"[5] Defining Indian identity is a dilemma that persisted long after the sad tale of "Lost Bird" came to its end. In the formative stages of the American Indian Movement its leadership decided to incorporate a spiritual component into the organization. With that goal in mind, the leadership also decided to visit then 25-year-old medicine man Leonard Crow Dog at the Rosebud Reservation in South Dakota. One of the first questions asked of Crow Dog was, "'What is an Indian?'"[6]

What is ultimately concerning about the demise of Ward Churchill's reputation is trying to find a replacement for him as a prominent purveyor of a "pro-Indian" perspective regarding current (and not so current events). Who, as the quote at the beginning of this chapter suggests, will ensure the writing of Indian history is subjected to rigorous analysis? The general public, with limited access (or conditioned to have limited interest) regarding news about events in remote South Dakota and other faraway locales, is reliant on those who filter reporting of events and news about Indians through whatever framework they choose to employ. Whether it is analyzing history, relatively current events, or Indian or Native American spirituality, writers, notably "non-Indian" ones, seem bent on avoiding logical conclusions as if they were the smallpox virus. One example of this phenomenon is found in Rolland Dewing's article "South Dakota Newspaper Coverage of the 1973 Occupation of Wounded Knee."[7]

Dewing is considered by many to be the apotheosis of Ward Churchill in terms of writing history about Indians. Among Dewing's credentials is a Ph.D. in history from Ball State University located in Muncie, Indiana. Yet, when reading Dewing's article, it is incumbent upon the reader to keep in mind Sir Arthur Conan Doyle's admonition, "There is nothing more deceptive than an obvious fact." One of the significant facts Dewing failed to highlight is that the entirety of the events described in his article, with the exceptions of the Custer Court House Riot story and the Wesley Bad Heart Bull incident, took place on the Pine Ridge Indian Reservation in South Dakota. This piece of information may not be as self-evident as it might appear. Dewing, an FBI agent named Joseph Trimbach, and others, in their hysteria to describe the desperate souls in the American Indian Movement at that time as virtually the biggest threat to democracy since the British sacked Washington, D.C., during the War of 1812, neglect to mention it in their writing. One of the few, and possibly the only, documents to highlight this particular aspect of South Dakota geography is *The Wounded Knee Massacre from Viewpoint of the Sioux*. As can be safely deduced from the book's title, the Wounded Knee Massacre took place in the same location as the "occupation," only 83 years earlier. As its author noted: "Why should these soldiers from the South interfere with their rights [of "Big Foot's band] to travel, in their own country. These poor bewildered people were *within the bounds of the Sioux Reservation*."[8]

Dewing never addressed the issue of the location of the "occupation" head on. Some "authors" such as Joseph Trimbach suggest circumspectly the massive force deployed against the Wounded Knee "occupiers" had something to do with the response to the trashing and looting of the Gildersleeve's Trading Post. Many sources claimed this enterprise was notorious for exploiting Indians; as confirmation of this claim it was noted during a Congressional hearing about his business practices that Clive Gildersleeve invoked his Fifth Amendment right not to testify 99 times.[9] Russell Means noted the store owners had no hesitation in displaying: "…[a] 19th century ledger of cattle receipts of Pine Ridge. 'The cavalry captain in charge had made up names for the Indians who received that beef': 'Shits in His Food,' 'She Comes Nine Times,' 'Fucks His Daughter,' and 'Maggot Dick,' to recall a few."[10] Aside from protecting the reputation of the junk-selling Gildersleeve's store, a coherent explanation for the exaggerated sense of emergency, the need to employ the most modern weaponry, and the deployment of the large number of FBI agents and U.S. Marshall's personnel on Pine Ridge, is lacking. Explanations generally involved the need to address the threat posed by AIM intending to start a large-scale revolt to a belief the "occupation" was the result of some type of Communist plot that needed to be thwarted.[11]

Dewing disagreed with the explanation of the circumstances surrounding the "occupation" provided by Robert Burnette and John Koster in their book, *The Road to Wounded Knee*. Dewing asserted: "…that the press did not dig actively for information to explain the real issues in the confrontation." Unfortunately, since he apparently disagreed with the synopsis provided by Burnette and Koster, Dewing did not make a summary of what he thought were the "real issues." However, Dewing noted Burnette and Koster believed press reports included: "…basic information concerning Wounded Knee and the American Indian Movement." Again, Dewing did not provide a synopsis of the other facts he believed were not presented in the court of public opinion.[12]

Nonetheless, Dewing managed to subtly editorialize his views by passing along without explanation other comments from various regional newspapers. He quoted the *Sioux Falls Argus Leader* as stating in its February 27, 1973, edition: "'The people who live on the Pine Ridge Reservation do not deserve being victims of the American Indian Movement's latest play for headlines based on the symbolism of names significant in Indian history. Neither do the people of South Dakota.'" Even the *Los Angeles Times* got into the act the following day by publishing an editorial cartoon which depicted Uncle Sam with an arrow shot through his knee. During the second week of March, 1973, the *Argus Leader* whined: "'…[the] saddest part of the whole sorry business is that the cause of good relations between Indians and white South Dakotans has been set back 30 years by what has happened at Wounded Knee.'"[13] Whether it is Dewing implying the members of AIM were criminals by calling the residents of Pine Ridge their "victims," or the more aggressive labeling of the AIM members as "militants," can it credibly be argued "militant" is anything other than a code name for "savage?"

Like many sources, the *Argus Leader* failed to describe what those "good relations" consisted of and how the intractable problems on the Pine Ridge Indian Reservation were the result of any actions of the American Indian Movement. Although it requires some searching, more AIM-friendly, if not ultimately more balanced, views of the reporting of Wounded Knee II can be unearthed. In a research paper entitled

Media Interpretations of Wounded Knee II: Narratives of Violence versus Sympathetic Coverage, Jana Cary-Alvarez undertook such an analysis. She noted, for example, the *Arizona Daily Star* published articles which: "…quoted parallels drawn by [Vernon] Bellecourt between the occupation of Wounded Knee and the American Revolution…" and: "…by allowing explanations of the Wounded Knee protest [such as Bellecourt's] into the account, the *Arizona Daily Star* challenged a conservative narrative of senseless violence."[14]

Likewise, what fantasy interpretation of history were the *Argus Leader* writers engaging in to claim AIM interfered with the "good relations" between the Indians living on Pine Ridge and the white citizens of South Dakota? *After* the Wounded Knee Massacre, a "Joint Resolution" signed by Governor Arthur C. Mellette on January 20, 1891, stated in part it was: "…the conviction of the legislature of the State of South Dakota that the immediate and complete suppression of armed hostilities against the Government is of vastly greater importance at the present moment than a theoretical solution of the various causes that may have led to the present critical situation."[15] There is a lot contained in that sentence, but nothing to suggest "good relations" with the Lakota was a priority or even a consideration of those South Dakota elected officials. Senator Tom Daschle's "efforts" in the 1990s in garnering an apology from the United States government for the Wounded Knee Massacre were a complete debacle. It was said at that time: "In addition to his opposition to an apology, he also remains adamantly opposed to the return of stolen lands in the Black Hills and has been unwilling to participate in any discussions concerning land reform."[16] In 2019, the Oglala Sioux Tribal Council passed a resolution banning South Dakota Governor Kristi Noem from the Pine Ridge Reservation. The ban, which legal experts contended was (and still is) enforceable, was in response to her support for legislation criminalizing aspects of Keystone XL pipeline protestors' behavior. Unsurprisingly, a major source of contention was Noem's failure to solicit the opinion regarding the matter.[17] These are not examples of good relations, but rather of the consistent inability of the representatives of the two cultures to communicate effectively.

Nonetheless, even after complaining how AIM created the multitude of problems on Pine Ridge and elsewhere, Dewing's readers were left to their own devices to understand how this occurred. Of course, the real reason there was no explanation how "AIM is to blame," to borrow FBI Agent Joseph Trimbach's juvenile rhyme, is because it is a monumentally difficult proposition to establish by any rational interpretation of historical events. The problems on Pine Ridge and other Indian reservations were (and are) longstanding, chronic problems as detailed in depth by the 1928 document entitled *The Meriam Report: The Problem of Indian Administration*, or simply the *Meriam Report*. The Institute for Government Research, better known as the Brookings Institution, possessing a stellar reputation for thoroughness and integrity, issued the *Meriam Report*, an 847-page analysis of problems in Indian communities, primarily reservations. Although in retrospect, the report appeared devoid of any doubts about the ability of white culture to cure the problems of Indians, it nevertheless was an attempt to thoroughly dissect the reasons for the difficult living conditions of indigenous people.

For example, on page 430, under the heading General Economic Conditions, were the following comments:

> Upon almost every reservation may be seen families living in poverty and yet possessed of potential resources, tribal, individual, or both, that if well utilized should yield a reasonable degree of comfort. One of the chief reasons for this state of affairs is that much of the Indian's property consists of land that is often arid, semi-arid, or mountainous, valuable chiefly for grazing, unsalable except in very large tracts, and often capable of little development for other agricultural purposes.[18]

The problems Indians suffered existed for decades, long before they were comprehensibly documented by the *Meriam Report*. In 1862, the Dakota Indians fought whites in Minnesota, which ultimately resulted in the hanging of 38 Indians after summary trials for their part, or at least what the military claimed was their part, in the conflict. As further retribution, the "Columns of Vengeance" of 1863-4 were intended to further punish Indians, many of whom had nothing to do with the 1862 fighting. At the conclusion of the campaign General Alfred Sully testified before Congress about the problems among Indian tribes including venereal disease, alcoholism, and smallpox, and other matters. He attributed those problems to the close contact these people had with whites from whom came "'…all the vices and few of the virtues.'" Astonishingly, even with the recognition of this circumstance, Sully was a zealous advocate of assimilation of Indians into white culture.[19]

Of course, heaping scorn and suspicion on AIM members has not been limited to individuals with obvious agendas of justifying their actions, such as Trimbach. FBI-friendly columnists Roland Evans and Robert Novak enjoyed taking shots at AIM, as demonstrated by this excerpt from an editorial:

> The tragedy is that the stupid and barbaric behavior of a few hundred militants who probably do not represent the aspirations and needs of the great mass of the Indians, could serve to obscure the real problems and legitimate hopes of their people.[20]

What "aspirations and needs" were not represented by AIM were not explained in this venom-filled tirade. It was not for nothing that Novak's nickname was "the Prince of Darkness." As would be expected, Vine Deloria, Jr., had a more positive view of the AIM-led event:

> Wounded Knee marked the first sustained modern protest by aboriginal peoples against the Western European interpretation of history, for the Oglala Sioux refused to accept the definitions which the American legal system had used to cover up the status of Indian tribes and make them appear to be merely a minor domestic problem of the United States.[21]

Following up that line of thinking, Deloria, Jr.'s son, Philip, noted for Indian undertakings in general: "Success is written off as an anomaly, a bizarre little episode that calls up a chuckle,"[22] a viewpoint that might explain the eventual indifference to the victory at the Wounded Knee "occupation" after the vast publicity generated by the event and some of the requests made by its leaders such as Means, Banks, and Bellecourt.

A news release from the Wounded Knee Legal Defense/Offense Committee provided a much more upbeat assessment of the "occupation" than that of Evans and Novak and warrants being quoted at length:

> The fact that the Wounded Knee confrontation was a clear-cut victory for the Indian people cannot be denied. The holding of a sizable portion of land by force against the military might of the U.S. Government was evidence of the determination and dedication of the people inside Wounded Knee. The U.S. Government was held off not only by the brilliant military defense of the area but also by the fact that the demands of the Indian people were widely supported by the people of the United States. For the first time in U.S. history a public opinion poll (the Harris Survey) showed that over 50% of the American people supported an armed uprising against the U.S. Government. The overwhelming support of the American people and Third World movements was probably the determining factor in preventing a second Massacre at Wounded Knee.

At the conclusion of the lengthy press release, another optimistic note was added:

> The occupation of Wounded Knee represented the beginning of a new era. The Oglala Sioux and their AIM supporters boldly thrust themselves into the consciousness of America and demanded the recognition of what was rightfully theirs—the United State's [sic] compliance with the terms of its treaties. The occupants of Wounded Knee resisted military pressure and starvation tactics for seventy-one days until the government agreed to review the obligations under the treaties and to re-evaluate the tribal government. The unity that prevailed at Wounded Knee was inspiring to Indian groups and Third World movements throughout the world. Indians everywhere demand control of their own reservations and lives; their voices have been ignored for too long. The resounding voices at Wounded Knee would not be muffled and have compelled us to recognize their demands. The echoes will reverberate throughout the entire Native American nation in the coming years.[23]

In large part due to the efforts of the FBI in tying up AIM members in court, the momentum from the "occupation" was soon dissipated. The press release quoted above is a reminder, along with the photographs and newsreels of that event, of the optimism generated by the efforts of AIM and its allies.

Further, what is the "tragedy" the writers Evans and Novak speak of regarding the issue of AIM's presence on Pine Ridge? It seems as if the "tragedy" was that somehow (apparently) the "takeover" or "occupation" of Wounded Knee by Russell Means and other Indian men and women prevented writers from all over the United States from writing on any aspect of current Indian affairs they chose prior to the "occupation." Like Trimbach's complaints about "…the false heroes of AIM…," Evans and Novak never explain how they were prevented from writing about Indian affairs because of the takeover. Did stray bullets from an FBI agent's rifle disable their typewriters? Were they taken hostage by AIM people, as Trimbach claims the Gildersleeves and others were? We are not so advised. Steve Hendricks provided a succinct and apt description of the situation after the "occupation" as he noted: "It is easy to forget in this chronicle of intrigue that the thousands of people who gave themselves to AIM did so for the noble goal of freeing a race from the grotesque miseries afflicting it." As a sad postscript he also noted: "Many of those miseries are with Indians still, almost as if AIM and its allied movements had never been."[24]

Nonetheless, a brief internet search does not disclose *any* books or extended series of articles by Evans and Novak over their lengthy Washington, D.C., careers about Indians living in the United States. Roland Evans was a writer in Washington, D.C., since 1945 and produced various opinion pieces in about four and a half decades there. Robert Novak's career started in D.C. in about 1957 and covered several decades as well. Although the Wounded Knee "occupation" lasted only 71 days, either of these giants of journalism had ample opportunity to write about the 500-year history of European-Indian interactions in the territory that became the United States. That mainstream writers and journalists have rarely, if ever, addressed the issue of Indian genocide in any form or other problems faced by Indians was and is problematic.

However, long after AIM ceased to function as a viable political force, chronic problems at Pine Ridge Reservation remain. For example, as reported in the February 9-10, 2019, *Wall Street Journal*, in an article entitled "Pedophile Doctor Left Trail of Suspicions—and Abuse," Stanley Patrick Weber practiced medicine on Pine Ridge for 21 years despite a virtual avalanche of sexual-assault allegations. Weber arrived in Pine Ridge in 1995 after suspicions of his pedophile activities arose at an Indian Health Service Hospital in Browning, Montana. Instead of being fired and/or referred for criminal charges, Weber was transferred to Pine Ridge. Interviews with former patients and court documents contained allegations that immediately upon his arrival at the reservation Weber: "…plied teen boys with money, alcohol and sometimes opioids, and coerced them into oral and anal sex with him in hospital exam rooms and at his government housing unit." Many of Weber's victims, some now well into adulthood and many with serious felony convictions, credibly claim his abuse ruined their lives.[25]

While Churchill has received much scorn from some corners for what many consider his pretending to be an Indian, the dividing line between who really is an Indian and who isn't is murkier than it appears upon closer examination. Robert Morgan noted in *Lions of the West*: "In manners, in clothes, in outlook, the mountain men [in the early 19th century] came to resemble the Indians as much as they did white men."[26] Adding to their acculturation to Indian lifestyles, these mountain men often also took Indian women for wives. Additionally, the question of who is and who isn't an Indian has ramifications well beyond considerations of historical context or what some might label over-sensitiveness or "political correctness." The question becomes more focused, as briefly discussed previously, when it comes to the question of money, as it does in any context, raised in recent times as to who is entitled to share in the profits from Indian gaming—i.e., casinos.

In California, with revenues from Indian gaming measured in billions of dollars, tribal membership continues to be a heated topic. For those not previously tribal members, they see the denial of their membership into the tribe the work of greedy present tribal members. Those present members see as questionable those recent applications for membership from descendants of those who abandoned the reservations during leaner times. After opening a casino in Southern California in 1995, the Pechanga Band of Luiseno Mission Indians witnessed a 2,000 percent increase in membership applications, prompting a temporary moratorium on new members by tribal leadership. Consequently, a group opposed to the moratorium protested its existence and filed suit in federal court seeking to stop the $10,000 per month payments to current Pechanga members. In 2004, as its annual casino profits approached $185 million, 130 members were dropped from tribal rolls, prompting another federal court challenge.[27]

Similarly, as the Pequot tribe in Connecticut experienced astounding success with their Foxwoods Resort casino, which opened in 1992, the legitimacy of the "Indianness" of the entire tribe came under scrutiny. Located just 110 miles from Boston and 130 miles from New York City, this casino at one time attracted over 40,000 visitors a day and garnered over $1 billion in annual revenues. In the early part of the 21st century, Foxwoods paid the state of Connecticut approximately $200 million under a revenue sharing agreement.[28] On that occasion attacks on the "Indianness" of the Pequots attracted much publicity. In *Without Reservation*, a law student named Jeff Benedict concluded current Pequot tribal members were not Pequots at all. Kim Eisler's book *Revenge of the Pequots* contained a theme of portraying Indians as unblushingly greedy as in Benedict's book. She additionally argued the Pequots were not Native American, but "Casino-American." At one point, Donald Trump said the Pequots: "'don't look like Indians to me and they don't look like Indians to Indians.'" In response to such comments, former tribal chair Richard "Skip" Hayward retorted that Benedict was "'a damn lunatic.'" Another tribal chair, Kenny Reels, said: "'We are tired of people trying to label us or paint what they want an Indian to look like.'"[29]

Some see casino-based economies as inconsistent with traditional "Indian" values and as evidence of the poisonous effects of contact with Europeans, beginning with Columbus and his single-minded pursuit of riches. Native journalist Tim Giago, a vocal critic of Indian gaming (and the American Indian Movement as well), argued that tribes involved with harvesting casino profits: "'…have turned into what they've deplored all their lives. They're bureaucracies and they're being run by attorneys and accountants—white attorneys and accountants.'" Authors Light and Rand claimed the Navajo nation has conspicuously chosen to avoid pursuing the development of Indian gaming. They have a story about Noqoilpi, or "'He who wins men,'" a gambler god who descended to the Pueblo people from the heavens. Noqoilpi's winnings eventually included the property and freedom of the Pueblos and eventually he enslaved them. Although a young Navajo eventually defeated Noqoilpi, presumably winning back freedom for his people, the story is considered a warning against gambling. Navajo healer Johnson Dennison commented:

> There are many Navajo mythologies about gambling and it's always been a part of Navajo culture, but it is associated with control and can make you go crazy… Gambling is not an honest way to make a living or to make money. It's a form of poverty.[30]

Interestingly enough, apparently some Navajo people overcame their revulsion to gambling, as a cursory internet search revealed the existence of multiple Navajo-controlled casinos as of October 2019.

Nevertheless, as important as determining who receives profits from Indian gaming is, its significance pales in comparison to the issue of blood quantum as the determining factor of "Indianness." The concept of "blood quantum" arose in conjunction with the United States government establishing a procedure for determining who received rations and other items. The general rule was that to be considered an Indian, the individual needed to have at least one fourth of "Indian blood." Particularly problematic, and unique to Indians, is the inability imposed by this process for Indian nations and tribes themselves to determine who is and is not a member. Some have suggested, quite convincingly, the use of the blood quantum mechanism is a deliberate attempt at genocide by literally defining Indians out of existence as intermarriage with whites and others continues throughout the decades and centuries.

A recent example of how convoluted the claim of Indian heritage can become involved Senator Elizabeth Warren of Massachusetts. As a result of a challenge to her claim of Indian heritage issued by President Donald Trump, Warren submitted to a DNA test. As a result of the DNA test which indicated she had an Indian ancestor six to ten generations ago, she argued that this result strongly suggested she had "Native American heritage." Cherokee Nation Secretary of State Chuck Hoskin, Jr., replied: "It makes a mockery out of DNA tests and its legitimate uses while also dishonoring legitimate tribal governments and their citizens, whose ancestors are well documented and whose heritage is proven."[31]

Ward Churchill is one of the few to raise the question of the effects of defining Indians by blood quantum and other matters of little notice in the "mainstream media" but of great importance to Indian culture. He is also often one of the lone voices of dissent to counter the purveyors of conventional Indian history and those who provided and continue to provide perfunctory approval to Indian policy in the United States. For example, Churchill aptly noted that Duane Schultz in *Month of the Freezing Moon: The Sand Creek Massacre of November 1864*, regurgitated the constant theme that "Indians committed atrocities too" spewed out by S. C. Gwynne, Terry Mort, Naomi Schaeffer Riley, and others. Churchill also noted that Schultz promoted the: "…standard of 'academic objectivity' which decreed that whenever one addresses the atrocities committed by the *status quo*, one is duty-bound to 'balance one's view' by depicting some negativity embodied in its victims [emphasis in original]."[32] As Allison Marie Goar emphasized in her master's thesis at Colorado State University in 2016, quoting from *Critical Race Theory: The Key Writings That Formed the Movement*, "Scholarship is inevitably political."[33]

Churchill sarcastically further argued that this requirement to "'balance one's view'" is "…an iron law of 'responsible scholarship.'" One example from Schultz's writing on Sand Creek Churchill cites in his book, quoting Duane Schultz, follows this pattern: "'[B]efore there were whites to rob and plunder and steal from, the [Indians] robbed and stole from each other. Before there were white men in the country to kill, they killed each other.'" Schultz was not finished: "'Before there were white women and children to scalp and mutilate and torture, the Indians scalped and mutilated and tortured the women and children of the enemies of their own race, (etc.).'" Churchill then explained as to the Sand Creek Massacre, in the view espoused by Schultz, the cause of the slaughter was the result of: "…the intrinsic bestiality of [the Cheyennes] [i.e.] the inherently horrible nature of the victims themselves."[34]

Richard Slotkin, perhaps a more "respected" historian than Churchill, reiterated his belief in the insistence of historians to erroneously perpetuate the victim-blaming process. In that regard, he harshly criticized one contributor to the "Violence" Commission report noted in the Introduction—Joe B. Frantz. Slotkin believed Frantz's argument that the Indian victims of frontier violence suffered their fates due to "inevitable conflicts" was both "tortuous and illogical." Slotkin was simply unrelenting in his criticism of Frantz's general view that while the "Indian Wars" were: "among the worst examples of frontier violence and [saw] them as the origins of present-day racial antipathies," and their tendency toward "cruelty and …'extermination,'" they were "'inescapable.'"[35] Richard Drinnon further argued: "How could a system of justice in the clearings be built upon a record of injustice in the wilderness? A society of Christian brotherhood erected upon its denial? Respect for law and order based on broken treaties, bribery and debauchery, and a thoroughgoing contempt for the natural right of natives?"[36]

One example of what Slotkin might have considered "victim blaming" can be found by comparing two accounts of the Wounded Knee Massacre. Philip Deloria, son of the noted Vine Deloria, Jr., took umbrage with the characterization of the Wounded Knee Massacre as an unfortunate occurrence. He argued: "…Wounded Knee was not simply an awful mistake, a miscalculation at a moment of extraordinary tension. The troops chased fleeing Lakotas for miles across the plains, hunting down and killing, not only men, but women and children, all of them already half-starved and exhausted."[37] Nevertheless, many authors are indeed ready to staunchly defend the notion the Wounded Knee Massacre was an "awful mistake."

For example, Robert Utley agreed with other writers that "Big Foot's" people wanted peace. Additionally, it bears repeating transcripts of witness statements recorded by Walter Camp indicate Big Foot stated: "'I have come to this reservation to avoid trouble and I will take the main road to the agency and join the peaceable people there.'"[38] Nevertheless Utley foisted blame on the victims of federal bullets by stating: "…[a] few unthinking young men, incited by a fanatical medicine man, lost control of themselves and created an incident." Utley added the obligatory slogan that: "Once fired upon, the soldiers fought back with a fury inspired by what they deemed Indian treachery. They did not deliberately kill women and children, although in a few instances more caution might have been exercised."[39]

A review of original source documents, however, throws considerable doubt upon Utley's claim that Indian women and children were not recklessly, and perhaps even intentionally, killed. A document authored by General Nelson Miles dated March 2, 1891, stated that regarding a Captain Godfrey: "…he did not think they [the soldiers] could see the Indians on account of the brush." The slightly awkward narrative continued:

> Persons who were on the ground and examined the brush declared that they were without leaves, and that persons could easily be identified in that locality at a distance of fifty yards. The weight of this excuse, however, is entirely destroyed by the fact that soldiers could see well enough to take deliberate and deadly aim and kill four persons with six shots, and so near were they as to burn the clothing and flesh of every victim, and one of their United States cartridge shells was found in the midst of the dead bodies.

Incredibly, but perhaps not surprisingly, Miles claimed: "In my opinion, however, Captain Godfrey was not responsible for this *crime*." Miles' justification for exonerating this Captain Godfrey of what he himself labeled a "crime" was that: "All the facts were not ascertained until the regiment was ordered out of this Division, and this incident was regarded in the same light as that of others which occurred in other parts of the field."[40]

It is unfortunate that Churchill's conflicts regarding plagiarism and other matters with the University of Colorado at Boulder's academic community did not raise a larger question: are historians (other than Churchill) *really* under an obligation to operate under a code of ethics—even an informal one? While academic institutions provide some oversight regarding the output of the professors in their employ, in this somewhat free society only the marketplace dictates the success or failure of independent authors. Even then, there is no assurance these scribes feel compelled to write the "truth" or even make their biases or sources of funding clear (although at times the biases become quite evident). For example, to his credit, Jerome Greene, the author of *American Carnage,* stated on his dust cover he was a retired Research Historian for the National Park Service.[41] Yet, even then, that disclosure may indicate to the reader that the writer is "objective" when that may or may not be the case. And, as James Loewen points out in *Lies My Teacher Told Me,* high school teachers in particular are at the mercy of publishing house conglomerates who are in no hurry to explore alternative explanations for events in history. As Loewen so pithily stated, quoting Michael Dorris: "…[when] learning about Native Americans, 'One does not start from point zero, but from minus ten.'"[42]

Churchill's role in interpreting United States history was to challenge those: "…[readers] in the twentieth century… [who associated] their glorious national history with a larger Western tradition… [which] pointed the way to democracy, individualism, rationality, and other virtues that would reach perfection across the Atlantic."[43] Palatable to the "status quo" or not, Churchill to a large extent had the skill to engage: "…many bright [readers], who tire of the propagandistic qualities of American history."[44] Likewise, while Churchill's obvious thorns of accusations of plagiarism and outright academic fraud have been exposed for all to examine in this age of instant news and internet information, his critics act as if: "…they themselves were free of political partisanship and were concerned only with defense of objective, civilized truth." In short: "…the unwillingness of many canonists [conventional historians] to recognize their own political agendas is troubling. It impedes sensible debate."[45]

Churchill's value as a contrarian becomes even more evident when reviewing accounts of recent historical events and encounters with the culture of Pine Ridge Indian Reservation in South Dakota. Bitter failure former FBI Agent Joseph Trimbach's amateurish *American Indian Mafia* portrayed the 1973 "occupation" with no more depth of analysis than a "cowboys and Indians" Saturday afternoon matinee. If this is considered an exaggeration, confirmation exists in Trimbach's evident pride in FBI Agent Robert Haefner: "…who kept his sense of humor during those trying times by drawing up a series of cowboy-and-Indian cartoons…"[46] and who described the FBI's deployment as: "…a semi-circle of vehicles as our perimeter defense just like in the old movies."[47] Philip Deloria noted the type of movies Haefner recreated in cartoon form: "…tended to fetishize the violent potential of the Indian, creating a particular array of racialized images and expectations against which members of an assumed audience might imagine themselves."[48] Jake Page asserted: "The fact that *most* American Indians by far were, at the time Columbus arrived, agricultural villagers who supplemented their crops with wild or semi-domesticated food never really sank in until recently [emphasis in original]."[49] Both Deloria and Page stated in sophisticated fashion the simple truth that myths die hard.

At the opposite end of the spectrum of describing Indians and Indian culture is well-meaning Kevin Hancock and his ill-considered claims of supernatural encounters, "in the land of Crazy Horse." In his book *Not for Sale*, Hancock viewed Indians as ethereal creatures with such a high degree of spirituality their feet barely touch the ground.[50] Unfortunately, it appeared in Hancock's worldview the primary purpose of Indians on Pine Ridge was to introduce whites to sacred Lakota traditions to enable these individuals to experience emotional and, of course, spiritual growth, with a minimum of study. That this exercise does little, if anything, to promote the well-being of Lakota people hardly seemed worth considering, although Hancock did make some superficial recommendations as to how to improve life on the Pine Ridge Reservation. A more complete analysis of both Trimbach's resentment-gorged tale of his view of Russell Means and his allies as brazen thieves, murderers, etc. Indians and Hancock's descriptions of his otherworldly encounters is found in later chapters.

Churchill's angry tirades against the domination of Indians by Western culture is a refreshing reminder that at the end of the day Indians are not savages nor spirit beings but human beings with both bad and good qualities, often embroiled in political battles for survival with whites. He consistently reminded his readers the crushing problems faced by Indians were often complex and for the most part the result of actions of greedy and dishonest whites. On a more specific and localized scale relative to Pine Ridge, Churchill publicized FBI counterintelligence program activities, given the obvious acronym COINTELPRO, directed against Indian "militants," that might have otherwise remained unknown. Churchill wrote about these matters in his book, co-authored with Jim Vander Wall, *Agents of Repression—The FBI's Secret Wars Against the Black Panther Party and the American Indian Movement*.[51] Likewise, in Seth Rosenfeld's well-written and well-researched *Subversives: The FBI's War on Student Radicals and Reagan's Rise to Power*, he provided tremendous detail regarding the FBI's efforts in spying on students at the University of California, Berkeley (Cal Berkeley) and to some extent Black Panthers in the 1960s. He also described Ronald Reagan's unsavory and cowardly efforts in informing on fellow actors while a member and the President of the Screen Actors' Guild.[52] Nevertheless, Rosenfeld did not discuss FBI efforts to infiltrate AIM using informants and other methods. Perhaps he believed the matter was beyond the scope of his book.

Churchill has had many detractors who accuse him of plagiarism and fraud. For example, in "Did the U.S. Army Distribute Smallpox Blankets to Indians? Fabrication and Falsification in Ward Churchill's Genocide Rhetoric," Thomas Brown shrieked: "Churchill has habitually committed multiple counts of research misconduct." Brown referred to the American Historical Association's Statements on Standards of Professional Conduct, which opens with the sentences: "*All* historians believe in honoring the integrity of the historical record. They do not fabricate evidence [emphasis added]."[53] Certainly it is no secret the beleaguered Churchill has created a myriad of problems for himself and received consistently harsh criticism for his ill-considered comments after 9/11 and his unnecessary claims of Indian heritage. Yet, if it is true, as George Orwell argued, "Omission is the most powerful form of lie," then Brown's article suggests a larger question—can historians get their "facts" straight, yet distort the context about what really happened? An analysis of S. C. Gwynne's *Empire of the Summer Moon* a few chapters hence as well as other writing described throughout this essay reveals this is not only possible but has happened and continues to occur with regularity.

Nevertheless, it is evident from the title of Brown's article alone that he has many negative comments to share with readers regarding Churchill. Considering the fallout Churchill experienced after he published his article "On the Justice of Roosting Chickens: Reflections on the Consequences of U.S. Imperial Arrogance and Criminality," Brown seems to have engaged in the all-American sport of kicking a man while he's down. Brown pulled no punches and summed up his views by claiming, "Every aspect of Churchill's tale is fabricated."[54] Yet, unintentionally or not, upon closer examination, the argument can be made the title suggests a story that is at a minimum incomplete. First of all, Brown's statements did not reflect the reality that whether or not white people *intentionally* transmitted the smallpox virus, after contact with Europeans, they suffered a devastating number of deaths after coming in contact with it. It is consistently argued Indians in North America: "…had almost no resistance to a whole range of diseases, from the common cold and measles to smallpox and bubonic plague, which had developed independently [from North America] in the Old World."[55]

Further, it is not clear whether Brown was suggesting whites prior to the formation of the country known as the United States never intentionally passed the smallpox virus to Indians, which many historians believe they did. It has been claimed that in 1763 one Captain Simeon Ecuyer, a British officer, facilitated at least one such episode. Ecuyer is believed to have caused the transmission of the smallpox virus to the Delaware Indians as he instructed his men to distribute two blankets and a handkerchief from the local smallpox hospital to these unsuspecting people. Unfortunately for the Delaware Indians, the trick worked, and their tribe was decimated by the attacks.[56] Brown also did not discuss other forms of what might be classified as chemical warfare, or just simply poisoning. For example, in the early 17th century, after the English concluded a treaty with rebellious Chiskiacks, they gave these unsuspecting Indians poison in honor of their "'eternal friendship'" and 200 Indians died as a result of this treachery.[57] During the "Columns of Vengeance" campaign conducted by federal troops in the aftermath of the Minnesota Uprising of 1862, soldiers left strychnine-laced beans for the Indians to discover in the remains of an encampment.[58]

Thus, the criticism of Churchill by Brown raises an even larger question: is any serious consideration simply given to the magnitude of the suffering and destruction experienced by Indians through disease, intentionally spread or not, or other forms of chemical/biological warfare? An analysis by James Wilson in his marvelous *The Earth Shall Weep* illustrates this point by noting that: "…[in] the First World War, for instance, which is often seen as the apotheosis of mass destruction, [there were] killed around 2 percent of the British population over a four-year period. Many Native American communities lost 75 percent or more of their members within just a few weeks," to which Wilson added "the kind of losses predicted for a nuclear holocaust."[59] This type of reasoning is indeed putting the events of Indian history into context, although it is difficult at times to find evidence of views of events separated from their political contexts. In the *Columbian Exchange*, Alfred Crosby quoted a 16th-century Dominican priest who virtually viewed smallpox as an implement of war and evidence of God's enmity toward Indians: "'When the Christians were exhausted from war, God saw fit to send the Indians smallpox, and there was a great pestilence in the city [Tlaxcala]…'"[60]

The Minnesota Uprising of 1862 itself serves as a portal into examining aspects of Indian history often overlooked. While hunger and deprivation were the primary reasons for the conflict, harsh attitudes of whites did nothing to dissipate the resentment of these beleaguered people. When the Indians complained of the lack of distribution of stored food, Indian Agent Andrew Myrick: "…responded as he often had to such sentiments: as far as he was concerned, the Indians could eat grass or their own shit."[61] Likewise, as disgraceful as it was to hang 38 Indians under those circumstances, or any circumstances, nothing about 19th century history suggests it was a particularly unique event. After a skirmish, General Phil Sheridan had nine Cascade Indians hanged for its "'salutary effect'" regardless of the circumstances of each case (or apparently questioning the legality of the action). Adding to the shamefulness of the already sordid affair, one of the men hanged had warned the whites of the upcoming battle.[62]

ENDNOTES

1. Thomas Powers, *The Killing of Crazy Horse*, p. xii.
2. Flood, *Lost Bird of Wounded Knee*, p. 160.
3. Smith, *Conquest*, pp. 116-117. Unfortunately, in the realm of establishing an Indian identity, like Ward Churchill, Dr. Smith created problems for her credibility by claims of Cherokee heritage which were vigorously challenged by Cherokee tribal representatives and others. Samantha Allen, "Tribes Blast 'Wannabe' Native American Professor." *The Daily Beast*, July 11, 2015. Churchill was specifically referred to in this article. See also David Shorter, "Four Words for Andrea Smith: 'I'm Not an Indian.'" *Indian Country Today*. July 1, 2015. Churchill is referred to in this article as well.
4. Flood, *Lost Bird of Wounded Knee*, p. 180.
5. Churchill, *Indians Are Us*, pp. 65-68.
6. Nabokov, Ed., Vernon Bellecourt "Birth of AIM," *Native American Testimony*, p. 376.
7. Rolland Dewing, "South Dakota Newspaper Coverage of the 1973 Occupation of Wounded Knee" (South Dakota Historical Society, Copyright, 1982). Article is undated.
8. McGregor, *The Wounded Knee Massacre from the Viewpoint of the Sioux*, p. 56.
9. Hendricks, *The Unquiet Grave*, p. 62.
10. Means and Wolf, *Where White Men Fear to Tread*, p. 263.
11. Lelo, *Newsletter* (warning against the perils of communism facing Pine Ridge) (St. Paul, Minnesota: Minnesota Historical Society March 26, 1973).
12. Dewing, "South Dakota Newspaper Coverage of the 1973 Occupation of Wounded Knee," pp. 49-50.
13. Ibid., p. 52.
14. Jana Cary-Alvarez, "Media Interpretations of Wounded Knee II: Narratives of Violence versus sympathetic coverage." *Sound Ideas* (Puget Sound, Washington: University of Puget Sound, 2013), p. 14.
15. Joint Resolution of the South Dakota Legislature Regarding Indian Outbreak, January 20, 1891. United States National Archives, Washington, D.C.
16. Mario Gonzales and Elizabeth Cook-Lynn, *The Politics of Hallowed Ground*, p. 52.
17. Jeremy Fugleberg, "Can Oglala Sioux Tribe ban Gov. Kristi Noem from reservation? Here's what the law says" *Sioux Falls Argus Leader* May 7, 2019. Fugleberg claimed the neglect on Noem's part was contrary to the "…tribe and state's history of valuable cooperation" but did not elaborate on the comment.
18. Meriam, *Meriam Report*. p. 430.
19. Paul N. Beck, *Columns of Vengeance: Soldiers, Sioux, and the Punitive Expeditions 1863-1864* (Norman, Oklahoma: University of Oklahoma Press, 2013), p. 248.
20. Ward and Vander Wall, *Agents of Repression*, p. 262.
21. Vine Deloria, Jr., *Behind the Trail of Broken Treaties: An Indian Declaration of Independence*. Austin, Texas, University of Texas Press, 2000, pp. 80-81.
22. Philip J. Deloria, *Indians in Unexpected Places* (Lawrence, Kansas: University Press of Kansas, 2004), p. 231.
23. Wounded Knee Legal Defense/Offense Committee and North American Media. Memorandum

describing the success of the Wounded Knee "occupation" (St. Paul, Minnesota: Minnesota Historical Society, undated).

24 Hendricks, *The Unquiet Grave*, p. 369.
25 Christopher Weaver, Dan Frosch, and Gabe Johnson, "Pedophile Doctor Left Trail of Suspicions—and Abuse" *Wall Street Journal,* February 9-10, 2019.
26 Morgan, *Lions of the West*, p. 312.
27 Light and Rand, *Indian Gaming and Tribal Sovereignty: The Casino Compromise*, p. 101.
28 Ibid., p. 108.
29 Ibid., pp. 109-110.
30 Ibid., p. 102.
31 David Choi and Ashley Collman, "'Inappropriate and Wrong': Cherokee Nation Official throws cold water on Elizabeth Warren's DNA test of Native American heritage." *Business Insider*, October 15, 2018.
32 Ward Churchill, Ed., M. Annette Jaimes, *Fantasies of the Master Race: Literature, Cinema, and the Colonization of American Indians* (Monroe, Maine: Common Courage Press, 1992), p. 116.
33 Crenshaw, Kimberle, eds. *Critical Race Theory: The Key Writings That Formed The Movement*. New York: New Press, 1995.
34 Churchill and Jaimes, *Fantasies of the Master Race*, pp. 116-117.
35 Slotkin, *Gunfighter Nation*, pp. 559-560.
36 Drinnon, *Facing West*, pp. 162-163.
37 Deloria, *Indians in Unexpected Places*, p. 24.
38 Walter Camp, "Interviews with Andrew Good Thunder, Little Hawk, No Flash, Louis Bordeaux," p. 524, Envelope 90. (Walter Camp Papers, Bloomington, Indiana, Lilly Library).
39 Utley, *The Last Days of the Sioux Nation*, p. 230.
40 General Nelson A. Miles, March 2, 1891, 2d Endorsement of correspondence regarding women and children killed at Wounded Knee Creek (Washington, D.C., United States National Archives). However, General Miles must not have been wholly satisfied with this conclusion. Nevertheless, he had previously designated a Court of Inquiry to investigate the conduct of commanding officer James Forsyth on the scene at Wounded Knee. The court exonerated Forsyth. He also authorized an inspector general investigation, but ultimately Forsyth was restored to command. Greene, *American Carnage,* pp. 319-323. Although I disagree with Greene's conclusion the massacre was not intentional, he provided a very thorough account of the Army investigations of the incident. As suggested by David Smits' research into "kill orders" noted in the chapter on S. C. Gwynne and Terry Mort, if there were in fact any orders of this type given, they would almost certainly be given orally. My conclusion the massacre was deliberate is based on the statements from current Pine Ridge residents, who in my opinion have nothing to gain by distorting the historical record.
41 Greene, *American Carnage* (inside dust cover in back). To his credit, however, Greene did provide significant facts surrounding the Wounded Knee Massacre, even though, as noted above, I disagree with his conclusion the slaughter was not intentional.

42   Loewen, *Lies My Teacher Told Me*, p. 93. It appears Dorris himself had his own complicated history. Elizabeth Cook-Lynn, in discussing the accusations of child abuse which were never fully investigated due to Dorris' suicide, stated: "In cases like these, it seems legitimate and necessary for critics and literary professionals to assess the influence of the personal life of a writer/scholar on his work, and to say what his professional contribution has been to literary studies in an era of unprecedented development of Native literatures." Cook-Lynn, *Anti-Indianism in Modern America*. p. 74. Cook-Lynn also had criticism of Churchill and stated: "Most Americans, even Churchill, see Indians as ghosts of the past, forever gone like wisps of the wind, or, if they must face the fact of their presence, as distorted images of themselves." Cook-Lynn, *A Separate Country*, p. 131.

43   Stearns, *Meaning Over Memory*, p. 76-77.

44   Ibid., p. 93.

45   Ibid., p. 61.

46   Trimbach, *American Indian Mafia*, p. 309.

47   Ibid., p. 310.

48   Deloria, *Indians in Unexpected Places*, p. 50.

49   Page, *In the Hands of the Great Spirit*, p. 109.

50   Kevin Hancock, *Not for Sale: Finding Center in the Land of Crazy Horse* (Casco, Maine: Seventh Power Press, 2015), *passim*.

51   Churchill and Vander Wall, *Agents of Repression, passim*.

52   Seth Rosenfeld, *Subversives: The FBI's War on Student Radicals, and Reagan's Rise to Power* (New York: Farrar, Strauss & Giroux, 2012), *passim*.

53   Thomas Brown, "Did the U.S. Army Distribute Smallpox Blankets to Indians? Fabrication and Falsification in Ward Churchill's Genocide Rhetoric." *Plagiary* (Ann Arbor, Michigan University Library).

54   Ibid.

55   Wilson, *The Earth Shall Weep*, p. 28.

56   Robert M. Utley and Wilcomb E. Washburn, *Indian Wars* (Boston: Houghton Mifflin Co., 1977), p. 98. In a fascinating essay regarding Indians in Canada, Kiera Ladner made this observation: "…it has been rumored by many that smallpox blankets made their way into the Hills, and many a person died from the diseases, poisons [strychnine], guns, and 'whiskey' that invaders [and possibly invading nations] brought into the Hills." Woolford, Benvenuto and Hinton, Eds., Kiera Ladner, "Political Genocide—Killing Nations through Legislation and Slow-Moving Poison," *Colonial Genocide in Indigenous North America*, p. 227. Ladner also suggested the use of placing smallpox germs in blankets was not an uncommon occurrence, although she does not specifically name the United States Army as the culprit. She also wrote: "…genocide in the Americas was not limited to physical acts of individualized destruction through instruments of death such as smallpox blankets," Ibid., p. 241. As it almost seems axiomatic Indians writers' perspectives were and are ignored, scant attention has been paid to the comment of Deloria, Jr.: "In the old days blankets infected with smallpox were given to the tribes to decimate them." Deloria, Jr., *Custer Died for Your Sins*, p. 60.

57 Wilson, *The Earth Shall Weep*, p. 71.
58 Beck, *Columns of Vengeance*, p. 127.
59 Wilson, *The Earth Shall Weep*, p. 75.
60 Crosby, *The Columbian Exchange*, p. 48.
61 Berg, *38 Nooses*, p. 29. It was claimed after he was killed and his body was discovered, his mouth was stuffed with grass. Ibid., p. 33.
62 Powers, *The Killing of Crazy Horse*, p. 110.

CHAPTER 5

William Henry Harrison
Tippecanoe, Tyler, Jefferson and the Rest Too

> He has excited domestic insurrections amongst us, and has endeavored to bring on the inhabitants of our frontiers, the *merciless Indian Savages,* whose known rule of warfare, is an undistinguished destruction of all ages, sexes, and conditions [emphasis added].
> Thomas Jefferson, Declaration of Independence,
> referring to the British King George inciting Indian tribes to attack colonial settlements[1]

On April 23, 1793, Ranger leader Captain Sam Brady challenged Major-General "Mad Anthony" Wayne to a shooting competition between Brady's men and Anthony's men. At that time, future President William Henry Harrison served as Anthony's aide-de-camp. Brady claimed any two of his Rangers could outshoot any 100 men of Anthony's choosing out of his army of 2,500. While drinking large quantities of alcohol during military service does not seem to be a fact often highlighted by historians, the wager between Brady and Anthony was a "…keg of good quality rum…" A mark was placed on a tree as a target about 80 yards from where the men stood.

As the contest unfolded with Anthony's men taking the first turn, about half of them were unable to even hit the tree; of the 50 shots that hit the tree, not one came within six inches of the black mark that made up the center of the target. When the Rangers took their turn, the first Ranger to shoot, Hezekiah Bukey, hit the outer edge of the center of the target. John Cuppy, up next, teased Bukey by snorting: "'How come you was so far away from the middle of that black mark, Ki? Reckon you're having a bad day.'" Cuppy proceeded to place a rifle ball about half an inch or so from dead center. Brady then turned to General Wayne and boasted: "'Well, General Wayne, what could you do if you had a hundred men such as these sharpshooters of mine?'" Naturally, due to Wayne's aggressive nature, he exulted: "'Captain Brady, I'll tell you this—I wish to God I had five hundred such men, who could put a bullet through an Indian's eye at that distance. Why, with such marksmen as that I could fight the very devil himself!'" Brady's men, of course, had won the coveted keg of rum.[2]

While much is made of the effects of alcohol on Indians, little mention is made of the effects on Indians as a result of whites, especially white soldiers, who consumed too much alcohol. While in *That Dark and Bloody River,* Allan Eckert did not expand on the theme of drinking in the frontier military, he did at least make the point that rum was the prize for the above described shooting contest. Nevertheless, he also noted in *Sorrow in Our Hearts: The Life of Tecumseh* British traders: "…treated the Indians abominably in many circumstances, flagrantly cheated them in their dealings and supplied them with far too much liquor which, in effect, gave them nothing of lasting value for their work."[3] It is increasingly believed excessive consumption of alcohol played a role, sometimes a significant one, in other white-Indian encounters. In the case of the beating death of Raymond Yellow Thunder in Gordon, Nebraska, in 1972, alcohol played a major role in fueling the nasty behavior of the white perpetrators. As will be noted in other portions of this book, at Wounded Knee, South Dakota, in December 1890, prominent sources are now noting the federal soldiers involved in that massacre were drinking "convivially" the night before and in the early morning hours of December 29, 1890, and may have simply been drunk at the time the shooting started.[4]

It has been noted that in the buildup to what eventually became known as the Grattan "Massacre" in 1854, the "'mixed blood'" interpreter Wyuse who was attached to Lieutenant Grattan's unit was believed to have had whiskey in his canteen instead of water and: "…was so drunk he had to be lifted onto his saddle." Perhaps due to the inexperience and impetuousness of 2nd Lieutenant J.L. Grattan, he and his men may have provoked a confrontation with the Lakota anyway. Nonetheless, Wyuse's drunkenness and resulting uninhibited hurling of insults at the already nervous Lakota did nothing to dissipate the hysteria surrounding the irrational anger of whites. The entire incident was an over-aggressive reaction of these whites seeking retribution from an Indian man named Straight Foretop who had killed a sickly cow owned by a Mormon man which had strayed into Straight Foretop's village.[5] In another incident on the Yankton Sioux Reservation, which some considered typical:

> General Sully came up [and] passed through the middle of our field, turned all his cattle and stock into our corn and destroyed the whole of it… The soldiers set fire to the prairie and burnt up four of our lodges and all there was in them …*the soldiers* [were] *very drunken* [sic] *and came to our place* [emphasis added].[6]

As to William Henry Harrison specifically, his name is not usually one that comes to mind when thinking about United States Presidents. Nevertheless, he serves as a stark reminder that *all* United States Presidents, prominent in history or not, had roles in developing or implementing some aspect of Indian policy. Harrison's aggressiveness, which was either learned or reinforced during his time with Wayne, to the detriment of Indians, combined with his belief: "…Indians [did not have] the capacity to live up to white standards." Like Andrew Jackson later: "…his only policy was to remove as many of them as possible." In 1809 he "negotiated" the treaty of Ft. Wayne which formalized the right of white possession of much of Indiana and Illinois for the purpose of white settlement. Echoing the rallying cry of Manifest

Destiny, Harrison proclaimed rhetorically: "'Is one of the fairest portions of the globe to remain...the haunt of a few wretched savages, when it seems destined by the Creator to support a large population and to be the seat of civilization?'" Two years later his forces crushed a large force of Shawnees led by Tenkswatawa at Tippecanoe Creek.[7] Harrison's successful 1840 presidential campaign used the slogan "Tippecanoe and Tyler Too," an obvious reference to his success at the 1811 battle.

While it would indeed be beneficial to develop a comprehensive list of the policies and actions of these men regarding Indians, a review of some of their actions can nevertheless be instructive. George Washington's activities and attitudes have been considered in modest detail in other sections of this book, therefore the starting point will be a brief description of the second President's, John Adams, apparent philosophy regarding Indians. To gain some understanding of Adams' attitude toward Indians, it is informative to revisit the writings of Thomas Morton, primarily through the contents of his unique book *New English Canaan*. Singularly perceptive, Morton noted the countryside in the eastern United States was beautiful like an English park due to the Indians' practice of burning off underbrush every spring and fall. Morton mistakenly accepted the view of William Alexander that the Indians had no religion and the plague of 1616-17 was an act of God clearing out natives to hasten English occupation of the region. Nevertheless, Morton, which made him unique for his times: "... in enthusiastic detail paid the Indians the uncommon tribute of taking their culture seriously."[8] Returning to Adams, although he displayed some curiosity about Morton's writing, he ultimately expressed a fairly conventional for that era view of individuals like Morton who he considered: "...defied well-ordered states [and who] put themselves outside civil society and [who] were the proper recipients of governmental wrath."

Adams also encapsulated in an accolade he bestowed on his family what could be a foreshadowing of what more formally became known as the concept or slogan of Manifest Destiny by exalting: "My family, I believe, have cut down more trees in America than any other name! What a family distinction!'"[9] Drinnon pointed to Hans Huth's argument in *Nature and the American* that the ax was the "'appropriate symbol of the early American attitude toward nature.'"[10] Drinnon further noted that Adams, along with his belief Morton had no real place in civilized society and his flashes of sympathy for actual Indians, had no qualms about the demise of Indians who he considered: "'...by disposition' cruel and bloody-minded...[and] no more fit for citizenship than black chattels [echoing the reasoning of *Dred Scott v. Sandford*]."[11]

In essence, despite his "whortleberries" of compassion for Indians which he displayed in his youth, and eulogizing in his anthem of Manifest Destiny how missionaries were involved in "'...dangerous and unwearied labors,'" he reverted to the typical mantra white society attempted to: "'...convert these poor, ignorant savages to Christianity...with...little success.'" Without noting any degree of irony in his musings, Adams declared: "'the Indians are as bigoted to their religion as the Mahometans are to their Koran, the Hindoos [sic] to their Shaster.'"[12] He concluded: "'...it is a principle of religion, at bottom, which inspires the Indians with such an invincible aversion both to civilization and Christianity. The same principle has excited their perpetual hostilities against the colonists and the independent Americans.'"

Drinnon explained: "In this remarkable paragraph Adams fused racism, nationalism, and Enlightenment bigotry into a whole that hardly commiserated with the Indians: If that was kindness, it was the kindness that kills."[13]

Thomas Jefferson, Adams' successor, whose visage adorns Mount Rushmore in the Black Hills of South Dakota, viewed himself as a protector of Indians.[14] However, as Drinnon pointed out: "The truth was that Jefferson had little understanding of Native American culture and less concern for its integrity."[15] Drinnon also noted that historian Heloise Abel claimed: "…the idea of removal originated with Jefferson…*after* the acquisition of Louisiana." Drinnon disagreed slightly in that he argued a February 27, 1803, letter to the aforementioned William Henry Harrison contained the comment: "Our settlements will gradually circumscribe and approach the Indians, and they will in time either incorporate with us as citizens of the United States, or *remove beyond the Mississippi*. The former is certainly termination [N.B!] of their history most happy for themselves.'" Likewise, Drinnon concluded: "His use of *termination* here directly anticipated the official policy of that name a century and a half later [emphasis in original]."[16]

Unfortunately, history has revealed Jefferson was as duplicitous as any President before or since when it came to matters involving Indians. Consider the words Jefferson directed to Handsome Lake, the great Seneca Prophet:

> You remind me, brother, of what I said to you when you visited me last winter, that the lands you then held would remain yours and shall never go from you but when you should be disposed to sell. This I now repeat and will ever abide by. We, indeed, are always ready to buy land; but we will never ask you but when you wish to sell… Go on then, brother, in the great reformation you have undertaken. Persuade our red brethren then to be sober, and to cultivate their lands; and their women to spin and weave for their families.

Nevertheless, less than two months after Jefferson's speech to Handsome Lake a memorandum entitled "Hints on the subject of Indian boundaries" began circulating. This little gem contained covert suggestions for extinguishing Indian title to land they refused to sell. Jefferson then sent a confidential message to Congress on: "…how to undermine Indian leaders who persisted 'obstinately in their dispositions.'" Drinnon also noted Jefferson secretly launched a systematic campaign of psychological warfare against the tribes.[17] While the foregoing is certainly not a comprehensive accounting of presidential actions detrimental to Indian interests, it contains some insight into the thought processes of these men, and subsequent chapters contain further elaboration on the actions of Presidents, particularly as to those of Andrew Jackson, U.S. Grant, and to some degree Harry Truman.

ENDNOTES

1 Declaration of Independence (U.S. 1776).
2 Eckert, *That Dark and Bloody River*, pp. 589-590.
3 Allan W. Eckert, *A Sorrow in Our Heart: The Life of Tecumseh* (New York: Bantam Books, 1992), p. 9.
4 Heather Cox Richardson, *Wounded Knee: Party Politics and the Road to an American Massacre* (New York: Basic Books/A Member of Perseus Books Group, 2010), p. 262.
5 Bob Drury and Tom Clavin, *The Heart of Everything That Is: The Untold Story of Red Cloud, An American Legend* (New York: Simon and Schuster, 2013), pp. 126-127.
6 Dunbar-Ortiz, *An Indigenous People's History of the United States*, p. 164.
7 Henry Warner Bowden, *American Indians and Christian Missions* (Chicago, Illinois: University of Chicago Press, 1981), p. 166.
8 Drinnon, *Facing West*, p. 17.
9 Ibid., p. 73.
10 Ibid., pp. 73-74.
11 Ibid., p. 75.
12 Ibid., p. 76.
13 Ibid., p. 77.
14 Ibid., p. 82.
15 Ibid., p. 92.
16 Ibid., p. 84, plus footnote.
17 Ibid., p. 86.

CHAPTER 6

Colonel John Chivington
"Buffalo Bill" Cody: Part I
and the Unending Myth of Indian Savagery

"EXTERMINATE THEM! EXTERMINATE THEM!"

Response to question asked at the Denver Opera House after Chivington's men paraded body parts of butchered Indians snatched from Sand Creek: "Would it be best…to try to 'civilize' Indians or simply exterminate them?"

David Stannard, *American Holocaust*[1]

In an orgy of violence and simultaneous exploding supernova of savage fury, on March 16, 1968, members of Company C, 1st Battalion, 20th Infantry Regiment, 11th Brigade of the 23rd (American) Infantry Division annihilated with rifle and machine gun fire between 347 and 504 unarmed civilians in two hamlets of Son My Village in the Quang Ngai Province of South Vietnam. The number of casualties proposed by U.S. Army investigators was 347, whereas the figure cited by local government officials was 504. According to some sources, before being killed, some of the women were gang-raped and after being killed, their bodies were mutilated. Twenty-six soldiers were charged with criminal offenses, but Platoon Leader William Calley was the only one convicted; he was found guilty of personally killing 22 villagers. Calley was originally sentenced to life in prison but only served three and one half years under house arrest. Many historians of that era believe the eventual disclosure of the incident increased the public's opposition to the Vietnam War, particularly after it was learned the United States Army attempted a cover-up. The slaughter became known as the My Lai Massacre.[2]

Halfway around the world slightly over 100 years earlier, at Sand Creek, Colorado, on November 29, 1864, between 130 and 200 Cheyenne and Arapaho Indians met similar fates at the hands of Colonel John

Chivington's Colorado Volunteers. Dee Brown, in *Bury My Heart at Wounded Knee*, claimed that after the shooting stopped: "105 Indian women and children and 28 men were dead."[3] Oddly, S. C. Gwynne, in his nasty polemic against 19th-century Comanches in Texas, *Empire of the Summer Moon*, argued Sand Creek was: "…the bloodiest, most treacherous, and least justified slaughter of Indians in American history. It would pass into legend and infamy under the name of the Sand Creek Massacre."[4] Gwynne also placed the casualty figure at 300, a much higher number than typically claimed.[5] Although academics have at times inexplicably recoiled at the comparison between the two events—My Lai and Sand Creek—due to the ferocity of the devastation bursting forth upon the unsuspecting villagers in both cases, comparisons were inevitable.

It is interesting Gwynne arrived at the number 300 in his estimate of casualties at Sand Creek, since the gruesome practice of "body counts" did not come into vogue until the Vietnam War (although those figures have been characterized as exaggerated). And the notoriety of the Sand Creek slaughter was eventually eclipsed by the horror at Wounded Knee in 1890. Yet, Sand Creek indeed contained the worst aspects of soldiering on the border between the whites on the already conquered frontier and the Indians on the verge of extinction—drunkenness, lack of training, and cowardice. Had Chivington's soldiers been properly trained and disciplined, even more Indians would likely have met their untimely deaths. As it happened, Dee Brown explained all-night whiskey drinking and poor marksmanship resulted in many Indians fleeing into the night unharmed and many soldiers being killed by other soldiers in what is now labeled "friendly fire."[6] The slaughter precipitated the end of peace talks with Indian leaders which began prior to the attacks, and Brown concluded: "In a few hours of madness at Sand Creek, Chivington and his soldiers destroyed the lives or the power of every Cheyenne or Arapaho chief who had held out for peace with the white man."[7]

To top it all off, John Chivington was a former Methodist minister turned apparent blood-lusting psychopath. He seemed to have more in common with Rasputin the Mad Monk of early 20th century fame than any conventional image of a man of the cloth. To the Indians: "…he appeared like a great bearded bull buffalo with a glint of furious madness in his eyes."[8] Chivington was infamous for advocating in a public speech in Denver prior to the massacre the killing and scalping of Indians including infants, stating, "'kill all—little and big—nits make lice.'"[9]

The uninhibited and unambiguous slaughter at Sand Creek was preceded by events and characters which provide a portal with which to view the complexity of life in and around the plains. In 1835, William Bent, a white trader, married Owl Woman, a beautiful woman from a prominent Cheyenne family headed by a Medicine Man named White Thunder. Such marriages were common in the early to mid-1800s between "Mountain Men" and these Indian women, with the Indians often viewing the arrangements as a doorway into financial improvement. A lieutenant from the United States Topographical Engineers was so struck by Owl Woman's beauty he asked her to pose for a watercolor portrait and described her as a "'remarkably handsome woman.'"[10]

William Bent was not just a run-of-the-mill "Mountain Man," but: "the master of the largest fur trading post on the southern plains." Although it was typical for these "Mountain Men" to abandon their

Indian wives upon returning to white society, William and Owl Woman remained together until her death in 1847. Although William took two of Owl Woman's sisters into their lodge, and one of them, Yellow Woman, bore a son named Charlie, he steadfastly loved Owl Woman. George Bent was born as the third child of William and Owl Woman on July 7, 1843.[11]

One of the significant events of George's life was his taking of a meeting with Chivington, along with his father William, some months prior to the Sand Creek Massacre. As is clear by the occurrence of the Sand Creek massacre itself, the meeting did not go well; one of Chivington's comments was, "I'm on the warpath." Chivington, who had no tolerance for intermarriages between whites and Indians, considered William Bent a "'squawman'" and, to add to the intimidating nature of the meeting, stood a foot taller than William. He was particularly repulsed by George, who he considered not only a half-breed, but a traitorous rebel since George fought for the South during the Civil War. Chivington was a singularly dangerous opponent for the Cheyennes and an especially dangerous hazard for the Bents. Not only did he command all the troops in the Colorado Military District, but he viewed "Killing Indians [as] God's work." His personal ambition to obtain the star of a brigadier general and possibly become a congressman further fueled his desire to spill the blood of those he considered God's enemies.[12]

The issue of joining Cheyenne warriors and fighting against whites was not such a simple one for George as fighting Indians was for Chivington. For one thing, George was half white. Although not necessarily related to the meeting with Chivington, the attacks in August 1864 by the combined Cheyenne Dog Soldier-Lakota alliance increased in their scope and intensity, signaling an escalation of tension in an already tense situation. After discussing various matters with Chivington, George was ready to fight—but more certain than ever he did not want to fight against the whites. George had lived amongst them, gone to school with them, and generally shared their lives back in Westport and St. Louis. He found it difficult to envision fighting against them and even more difficult to envision killing them. He was eager to fight as a Cheyenne warrior and share in the honors bestowed upon those who succeeded in combat, which to George meant fighting against Pawnees, Crow, and Utes.[13]

On the morning of the Colorado Volunteers' attack on the Indians at Sand Creek on November 29, 1864, Robert Bent, George's brother, was riding alongside Chivington. As they approached the Indian village, they saw an American flag waving and heard Black Kettle, the Indian leader, tell the people to stand near the flag. Sadly, unimaginable barbarity and brutality followed the first shots by the onrushing cavalry in spite of this signal of friendship. Indian women ran up to the stampeding soldiers with their breasts exposed to indicate they were not warriors but were all shot anyway as they begged for mercy. An Indian woman who was lying on the bank of a stream with a shattered leg caused by a bullet, raised her arm to fend off a soldier approaching with his saber drawn. The soldier struck her arm and broke it, and when she rolled over and raised her other arm, the soldier struck it with his saber and broke that one as well. The soldier departed and left the woman in her agonizingly painful condition.[14]

Some 30 or 40 women hiding in a depression sent out a little girl with a white flag toward the frenzied soldiers. The soldiers shot the little girl and proceeded to shoot the remaining women as well.

One pregnant Indian woman was ripped open and her unborn child was thrown like a rag doll beside her. Other women had their vaginas cut out; one soldier explained he was going to make a tobacco pouch out of the fruits of his barbaric behavior after he had cut off White Antelope's scrotum. Captain Silas S. Soule, one of the few officers to retain control of his men during the massacre, said of the horrors: "'You would think it impossible for white men to butcher and mutilate human beings as they did.'"[15]

Even S. C. Gwynne managed to note that subsequent to the Sand Creek Massacre, Chivington and his men displayed the bloody scalps and other body parts of the beleaguered Cheyennes and Arapaho slain to a standing room only crowd at the Denver Opera House. In attendance at the macabre celebration was Senator James Doolittle of Wisconsin, the Chairman of the Doolittle Committee investigating Indian-white affairs in the Western United States. As noted in the heading to this chapter, after the grisly parade concluded, there was a debate over whether to "civilize" Indians or simply exterminate them.[16] Sadly, Chivington's soldiers were certainly not the first to utilize parts of Indian bodies for utilitarian purposes. In the aftermath of the Andrew Jackson-led attack on Horseshoe Bend during the war against the Creeks in 1814, Jackson's men were seen: "…cutting long strips of skin from the bodies of the dead Indians to make bridle reins of them." To round out the carnage, it was noted Jackson's Indian scouts scalped the dead Creeks.[17]

To claim Chivington was only borrowing the practice of scalping from the Cheyennes or other Indians he encountered is to unthinkingly endorse the myth of Indian savagery in North America. In actuality, the account of scalping in Herodotus is believed to be the first ever recorded. Written in the 5th century B.C., in one passage containing a description of Parthians who removed the hair from fallen enemies to adorn their weapons and clothing, it was noted: "It is apparent that they use a sharp and very keen dagger by which they make a circle of flesh above the eye level…'" Two generations later Xenophon wrote after some of his men were killed on the way to the Mediterranean Sea that their hair was separated from their heads. Byzantine historian Precopius refers to a Count Belisarius being anxious about the behavior of certain of his auxiliary soldiers. These "wild" tribesmen tortured captives, removed the upper skin portion of the skull, treated it with oils, stuffed it with padding, and made it into a "'most grisly trophy."

Although Genghis Khan and his warriors in the 13th century were not believed to have engaged in the practice of scalping, they learned plaited human hair was less susceptible to rain and cold than rope or leather. Thus, human hair gathered from the skulls of the slain was used to operate catapults and siege engines. Spaniards arriving in the Western Hemisphere learned that Caribbean natives retrieved heads and hair from fallen foes. In that regard, one Captain Alvarado noticed the Guatemalans skinned the heads of captured conquistadors. Thus, although the practice of scalping is believed to have filtered up to North America as early as the 16th century, its timing and origins are unverified. It is not known with certainty whether the concept migrated up from Mexico, arose independently, or was brought to North America from elsewhere.[18] Nevertheless, to nonchalantly attribute the practice of scalping to Indians in North America without providing details or caveats is intellectually lazy.

What makes Gwynne's description (or lack thereof) of the Sand Creek Massacre and its aftermath so problematic, however, is that the perpetrators were whites. Apparently to him, Chivington and his soldiers were not "savages" or "Stone Age pagans" for their various acts of butchery, as he described the acts of Comanches. Instead, Gwynne awkwardly outlined the thinking of apparently many people of the day, who in his view considered killing Indians inconsequential:

> The army's distaste for Chivington had more to do with style and with the savagery of his raw recruits. He had, after all, attacked a village under truce. Otherwise, it was clear from the reaction on the raw frontier that it was long past time when it had become morally justifiable to kill Indian women and children.[19]

The question raised by the description of the Sand Creek Massacre becomes an obvious one—who were often the real "savages" on the borderlands between whites and Indians? In a statement to be fleshed out in a little more detail subsequently, in addition to his other unusual comments about the Sand Creek Massacre, Gwynne claimed: "There is little point in describing in detail what happened"[20] regarding the monstrous behavior of Chivington's soldiers. This, despite his earlier detailed descriptions of Comanche violence directed towards whites. Since the Sand Creek Massacre had nothing to do with the Comanches, why even discuss it at all if not to demonstrate whites were the real savages in many cases? Any honest reckoning discloses they were.

What Gwynne excluded by declining to "describe in detail what happened" was not only an account of the savage fury of the attack by Chivington's men, but the suffering of those who *survived*. George Bent stated after the attack at Sand Creek:

> That was the worst night I ever went through. There we were…without any shelter whatever and not a stick of wood to build a fire with. Most of us were wounded and half naked; even those who had had time to dress when the attack came, had lost their buffalo robes and blankets during the fight. The men and women who were not wounded worked all through the night, trying to keep the children and the wounded from freezing to death.[21]

And, as the attack at Sand Creek illustrated, in the chaotic world of Indian history, the American flag is an ever-present symbol, but a symbol of what, exactly? Civilization? Death? Colonization? In *An Indigenous Peoples' History of the United States*, Roxanne Dunbar-Ortiz recounted a story where she protested the use of a picture of a Navajo woman weaving a rug in the design of the "Stars and Stripes" as a cover photograph for a book entitled *Out of Many: A History of the American People*. Although the authors pointed out to her the picture was actually a real photograph, Dunbar-Ortiz persisted in her protest and the photograph was deleted from future editions. Apparently, Dunbar-Ortiz, without realizing how narrow this point of view is, believed the photograph too strongly reinforced what she called the "settler-colonialist" framework of U.S. history.[22] It is surprising that an author with the obvious sophistication of Dunbar-Ortiz would get caught up in promoting a one-dimensional portrayal of a nonexistent, monolithic Indian perspective on patriotism. Russell Means echoed Dunbar-Ortiz's sentiments and noted the international distress signal was the ship's national ensign flown upside-down and noted that AIM flew the U.S. flag upside-down.[23]

Nevertheless, is it possible for Indians that the United States flag simultaneously serves as both a symbol of oppression *and* hope?

Yet, despite her passion for promoting Indian well-being and recognitions of past atrocities and mistreatment of Indians, Dunbar-Ortiz is far too intelligent to be caught off guard, like: "…white radicals [who] were puzzled by the fervent patriotism of most Native communities, and their pride in military service."[24] As evidence, at the beginning of virtually every pow wow throughout the United States, the United States flag is prominently featured in the parade of veterans entering the arenas at these celebrations. Likewise, Clyde Holler noted Sun dances at the Rosebud Reservation in South Dakota in 1917 and 1918 were dedicated to World War I and a third in 1919 was dedicated to the Allied victory.[25] Undoubtedly, in contrast, in various locations on the Pine Ridge Reservation at times are flown upside-down United States flags. Clearly, an objective view of Indian history reveals the relationship between Indians and the United States government can be generally described at a minimum as complex.

Another anecdote from Thomas Mails' *Fools Crow* aptly demonstrated not only the patriotism of some Indians, but the richness and variety of Indian lives and careers in modern society. Mails recounted the story of Ed Magaw who flew for the United States Air Force (actually Army Air Corps) in World War II. Magaw came to Frank Fools Crow to ask for "medicine" to protect him during his missions; Mails stated Magaw conducted: "110 flying missions returning from all of them without a scratch." Mails concluded this episode by noting: "…[on Magaw's] last flight he saw a huge American flag wrapped around his airplane. He said the Yuwipi [spirit] people did that for him, to let him know he would return home unharmed."[26]

While it is commendable more "pro-Indian" or even simply "Indian" writers have stepped forward to proclaim their version of the truth, it is critical indeed to evaluate the context of the information. Unfortunately, if Dunbar-Ortiz's anger about the "settler-colonialist" system in place for Indians is justified, the picture protest does little to highlight the issue. Nevertheless, even if her anger over the use of the "Stars and Stripes" photograph is misplaced, she indirectly brings another point about Indian history to the surface.

The salient point about the United States flag is that it demonstrates what is irrefutably true about many aspects of white-Indian history—punching through the simple surface crust of appearances and myths usually reveals a more complex reality underneath. In addition to recognizing the uninhibited savagery of whites at various points during the 19th century, there is no better method for distancing people from the thinking that Indians are savages than to acknowledge the complexity of Indian societies. Those voices recognizing this reality have existed for quite some time, but they are usually drowned out by those who prefer the simplicity of the "noble savages" or just savage designation. Around 1819, Henry M. Brackenridge took a cruise on the Missouri River and noted how: "'…mistaken are those who look for primitive innocence in what they call the state of nature.'" Brackenridge added:

> They have amongst them their poor, their envious, their slanderers, their mean and crouching, their haughty and overbearing, their unfeeling and cruel, their weak and vulgar, their dissipated and wicked; and they have also, their brave and wise, their generous and magnanimous, their

rich and hospitable, their pious and virtuous, their frank, kind and affectionate, and in fact, all the diversity of characters that exists among the most refined people.[27.]

This volume may not have answers on how to encourage Western thinkers to place Indian history in its proper context, but it can serve as a point of reference for asking questions. Specifically, it can function as a platform to highlight an important question: why is it so difficult to view Indians simply as human beings and not as either "noble savages" or as savage savages? The writer Mark Twain provided an example of this phenomenon. As Slotkin explained when Twain reflected on his early life in *Roughing It,* he expected: "…to meet noble savages and behold [an] Edenic landscape, to befriend hunters of the Leatherstocking kind." As Twain's romantic vision is thwarted, he described his impressions of the fictitious "Goshoot" tribe (most likely a takeoff on the name of the Goshute tribe of Utah) as people who were "…treacherous, filthy, and repulsive…" and that: "They deserve pity, poor creatures; and they can have mine—at this distance."[28]

Of course, there is indeed the ever-present simple truth that whites took Indian land by stealth, subterfuge, and force. It is difficult to avoid this conclusion. Yet even in that process there were instances of Indians fighting Indians such as the Crow against the Lakota. Certainly, that in no way justifies the brutality inflicted by whites on Indians in the past (if in reality it has ever stopped). Yet, as forcefully pointed out by Winona LaDuke in *The Militarization of Indian Country,* a book cited by Dunbar-Ortiz herself, since the early 1900s, despite the harsh treatment inflicted on them, Indians served and continue to serve with distinction in the United States military. And those Indians typically served in numbers proportionally higher than any other segment of the United States population[29] and are particularly likely to serve in combat and other units assigned to hazardous duty.[30]

Whether or not military service is seen simply as means to temporarily escape the poverty on reservations is largely irrelevant regarding respect many Indians display toward the United States flag. As noted, it is no secret the honoring of military veterans is a featured aspect of all the thousands of all pow wows conducted across the United States every year, with the United States flag prominently displayed. As another demonstration of patriotism, during WWI, Plains Indians bought war bonds in large quantities. What is striking about this circumstance is that these people fished money out of perpetually empty pockets to promote democracy for the rest of the world while it barely existed for them. Some of the Lakota men who fought in the trenches of France during WWI came back to their reservations to find their allotments of land provided by the Dawes Act of 1887 sold out from under them for non-payment of taxes which accrued while they were off risking their lives.[31]

The more immediate problem for Indians living on reservations and elsewhere is how to deal with those suffering the negative after-effects of surviving combat, such as in Iraq, Afghanistan, and Vietnam. The results gained by exploiting the courage of these men and women comes with a high price tag. One raw fact of this honorable service in those highly stressful military occupational specialties is the pervasive existence of conditions such as Post Traumatic Stress Disorder (PTSD). Studies of Indian

Vietnam veterans in southwestern Indian nations has shown PTSD rates as high as 45 percent, while the rate for that condition reaches as high as 57 percent for Northern Plains Indians.[32]

Perhaps Dunbar-Ortiz's decidedly visceral reaction to the "Stars and Stripes" weaving Navajo woman's picture was due in part to the incredibly simplistic portrayal of white-Indian interactions in the story lines of movies in the late 1940s and early 1950s. While it is speculation, is it sensible to deny that those celluloid storybooks impacted the thinking of those in contemporary American culture? The formula in those films consisted of Indians who were either attacking or on the verge of attacking the virtuous white frontier agrarians who were only trying to establish farms and ranches for the betterment of all. Of course, just as it looked like the bloodthirsty Indians were about to get the best of those folks, the blue-clad U.S. Cavalry: "...atop their sweat-streaked but beautiful horses, stretched out flat, bugle blaring, guidon whipping straight behind them" had come: "...to rescue the poor beleaguered families, and in the process, give the savage miscreants the beatings of their lives."[33]

It was (and still is) difficult to determine when "entertainment" involving Indians stopped and the educational process began. Long before the celluloid cavalry began saving settlers from Indians on the war path, Buffalo Bill's Wild West was a component of what historian Eric Hobshawn labeled the "mass production of traditions." The producers of the show deliberately excluded the word "show" from the title of Buffalo Bill's Wild West to reinforce the concept the enterprise actually *was* the wild west (ironically, Louis Warren included "show" in the title of his book on Buffalo Bill). Buffalo Bill's Wild West's lasting legacy in Europe was its reinforcement of the images of Indians on the frontier as "noble savages" and perhaps just "savage savages..." Unfortunately, Buffalo Bill's Wild West was simply not designed to provide spectators an accurate understanding of Indian history, as it was an artful blend of fact and fiction. In addition, George Caitlin's Indian Gallery containing highly fictionalized encounters between whites and Indians was a popular attraction in Europe four decades before the arrival of Buffalo Bill's Wild West. Germans employed Indians for years as part of ethnological exhibits at zoos and by 1879, the Dresden Zoo contained a replica of an Indian village. American Indians also found steady employment in Germany through Buffalo Bill's Wild West circuses and sometimes sold crafts to make extra money.[34]

Even without deliberately claiming Indians are savages, currently there is no shortage of "scholarly" research by whites which either deliberately or inadvertently attempted to portray Indians as clueless savages, incapable of deciphering the complex and even not-so-complex interactions of white society. In *Blood Struggle*, Charles Wilkinson, referring to the analysis of an anthropologist named Kathleen Pickering, claimed that Indians who accumulated any type of material wealth would be accused by other Indians of "'starring around'" or "'going white.'" To further this hoary idea, Wilkinson cited Pickering to claim that to be a traditionalist, an Indian must more or less be: "...poor in money but rich in spirit and community support."[35] The disconnect between what experienced writers and researchers like Wilkinson and Pickering present as what might be considered "typical" Indian thinking and what Indians most likely think in modern times is baffling. It is simply not true Indians are incapable of succeeding in "modern" society. It is no wonder Vine Deloria, Jr., Means, and other Indians mocked anthropologists for decades.

Even a cursory review of Indian history discloses that the idea of "noble savages" who rejected all forms of financial success as claimed by Wilkinson is implausible. The implausibility is compounded by the apathy of historians who lumped all Indians living in the Western Hemisphere into one homogenous group rather than noting the individual characteristics of the various nations occupying the distinct regions on the two continents. For example, while Comanches and Kiowas attacked wagon trains traversing the Santa Fe Trail, Cheyennes and Arapaho often viewed the whites riding in their caravans as potential business partners. The whites traveling on this route were seeking furs and hides, while the Cheyennes and Arapaho were hoping for guns, powder, lead, cloth, and other goods brought by these newcomers.[36]

In recent descriptions of Indian nations possessing casinos, the pendulum has swung wildly in the opposite direction from the "noble savages" eschewing all forms of material gain. *National Review* editor Rich Lowry once argued:

> American Indians have always occupied an outsized place in our imagination, usually as a noble people at one with a pristine North American continent. It's time to upgrade the image. Forget buffalo, eagle feathers, and tribal dances. Think slots, Harrah's, and dirty politics.

The *Wall Street Journal* likewise childishly spouted: "'Bet by bet, the Indians are scalping customers for millions.'"[37]

Will Peters, an Oglala Lakota, as ardently devoted to the traditional Lakota teachings as possible, provided a more logical view of a modern-day Lakota man. He teaches school on the Pine Ridge Reservation and interacts with the mostly white volunteers who spend a week during the spring and summer months performing humanitarian tasks on the reservation for the Re-Member organization. As noted in the quote leading into the Preface, Will explained his view of traditional Indian values:

> People think I teach these Ways because I want to go back to the days of chasing buffalo and living in Tipis, but I'm just talking about walking in balance in two worlds.[38]

These are not the words of someone who is rejecting all forms of material gain for fear of being accused of "'starring around.'" However, it is also not the philosophy of someone rejecting all traditional Lakota values either.

Ironically, as discussed throughout this book, it often appeared that those on the frontier closest to Indians seemed to have the best grasp of the fact there were and are many different tribes and nations, as well as a variety of responses to white intrusion. For example, Kit Carson, who over his career as a scout and frontiersman engaged in ferocious combat and even perhaps indiscriminate killing of Indians, understood this concept well. However, in *Blood and Thunder*, Hampton Sides noted that from an early age Carson learned: "…there was no such thing as 'Indians', that tribes could be substantially and sometimes violently different from one another, and that each group must be dealt with separately, on its own terms."[39] Likewise, as is noted throughout this book, "Old Jules" Sandoz, a friend of the Lakota and an outcast from white society, and others rightfully scoffed at the paranoid notion that the Indians on Pine Ridge were somehow savages and wanted to fight the whites during the "Ghost Dance" period leading up to the Wounded Knee Massacre in December, 1890.[40]

It is still, as Gyasi Ross, noted Blackfeet author and attorney, pointed out, a common perception or belief that all Indians are the same. "Indian question? Ask the Indian guy!" Yet, the message that Indians are savages is always lurking. Ross noted there was always a curiosity about how he made it away from the rez. To him, this was:

> …interesting—I knew the people asking the questions had good intentions: they weren't asking in a malicious way. But there are two implicit messages in this question, and they are sneaky and ugly: 1) That the reservation is this place that needs to be escaped from, like a black hole, lest all hope and potential be sucked away. 2) That I was somehow different than the other people on the reservation because I was resourceful and smart enough to sneak away from the reservation's destructive power.[41]

Lumping all Indians together in one group serves another purpose—it makes it harder to pinpoint specific acts of brutality directed at a particular nation, for example, the Navajo. Nevertheless, in *Blood and Thunder*, Hampton Sides described in great detail Carson's 1864 campaign to force the Navajo in the Southwest to surrender and give up living their way of life and move to the Bosque Redondo in eastern New Mexico. The forced move to the Bosque Redondo was a similar concept to what became known as the "Trail of Tears," the movement of Indians in the Southeast United States to Oklahoma earlier in the 19th century. The Bosque Redondo movement was the brainchild of General James Henry Carleton who conceived of the idea after learning of the project to settle nearly 3,000 Emigdiano Indians to the Southern Joaquin valley along a river bottom near Ft. Tejon,[42] California. The Bosque Redondo, unsurprisingly, was a "massive failure"[43] and a disaster for the Navajo. There seem to be few, if any, exceptions to the damaging, heartbreaking situations created by whites who thought they knew how best Indians should live. The discussion in the next chapter on Helen Hunt Jackson brings into focus that myth.

ENDNOTES

1. Stannard, *American Holocaust*, p. 134. President Theodore Roosevelt said at a later time Sand Creek was: "'...as righteous and beneficial a deed as ever took place on the frontier.'" Ibid, p. 134.
2. "My Lai Massacre" Wikipedia. Many commentators have compared the My Lai Massacre to the Sand Creek Massacre. It has also been suggested the My Lai Massacre was similar to the "Trail of Tears." See Kenneth Stern, *Loud Hawk: The United States versus the American Indian Movement* (Norman, Oklahoma: University of Oklahoma Press, 2002), p. 42.
3. Brown, *Bury My Heart at Wounded Knee*, p. 91.
4. Gwynne, *Empire of the Summer Moon*, p. 220.
5. Ibid., p. 221.
6. Brown, *Bury My Heart at Wounded Knee*, p. 91.
7. Ibid., p. 92.
8. Ibid., p. 83.
9. David F. Halaas and Andrew E. Masich, *Halfbreed: The Remarkable True Story of George Bent: Caught Between the Worlds of the Indian and the White Man* (Cambridge, Massachusetts: Da Capo Press/A Member of the Perseus Books Group, 2004), p. 157.
10. Ibid., p. 24. Powers noted: "Living with both bands of Sioux was a large floating population of whites married to Indians. Officials spoke dismissively of them as 'squawmen.'" Powers, *The Killing of Crazy Horse*, p. 61.
11. Ibid., p. 39.
12. Ibid., pp. 121-122.
13. Ibid., p. 127.
14. Ibid., pp. 145-146.
15. Ibid., pp. 146-147.
16. Stannard, *American Holocaust*, p. 134.
17. Robert V. Remini, *Andrew Jackson and His Indian Wars* (New York: Penguin Putnam, Inc. 2001), p. 78.
18. Connell, *Son of the Morning Star*, pp. 162-163.
19. Gwynne, *Empire of the Summer Moon*, p. 221.
20. Ibid., p. 220.
21. Halaas and Masich, *Halfbreed*, p. 152.
22. Dunbar-Ortiz, *An Indigenous Peoples' History of the United States*, p. 6.
23. Means and Wolf, *Where White Men Fear to Tread*, p. 197.
24. Phillip Jenkins, *Dream Catchers: How Mainstream America Discovered Native Spirituality* (New York: Oxford University Press, 2004), p. 157.
25. Clyde Holler, *Black Elk's Religion: The Sun Dance and Lakota Catholicism* (Syracuse, New York: Syracuse University Press, 1995), p. 136.

26 Thomas E. Mails, *Fools Crow* (Lincoln, Nebraska: University of Nebraska Press, 1979), p. 52. One of the interesting aspects of this description is that Magaw saw "…a huge American flag wrapped around his airplane." Worthy of note is a Lakota Indian named Ed McGaa wrote a book wherein he described flying F-4 Phantom jets during the Vietnam War. Ed McGaa, *Spirituality for America: Earth Saving Wisdom from the Indigenous* (Hill City, South Dakota: Four Directions Publishing, 2013), *passim*.

27 Krech, *The Ecological Indian*, pp. 26-27. Curiously, a letter written by a Hugh Henry Brackenridge about an incident involving the capture of two men by Indians in 1782 contained the comment about Indians: "They have the shapes of men and may be of the human species, but certainly in their present state they approach nearer the character of Devils; take an Indian, is there any faith in him? Can you bind him by favor? Can you trust his word or confide in his promise?" Wilcomb E. Washburn, Ed., Hugh Henry Brackenridge, "The Animals, Vulgarly Called Indians," *The Indian and the White Man* (Garden City, New York: Anchor Books/Doubleday & Co., 1964), p. 116. As noted by Weinberg in *Manifest Destiny*, this Brackenridge had no qualms about advocating for the "extermination" of Indians. Weinberg, *Manifest Destiny*, p. 77.

28 Slotkin, *Fatal Environment*, p. 517.

29 Winona LaDuke, *The Militarization of Indian Country* (East Lansing, Michigan: Michigan State University Press, 2013), p. 9.

30 Ibid., p. 17.

31 Magnuson, *The Death of Raymond Yellow Thunder*, p. 173.

32 LaDuke, *The Militarization of Indian Country*, p. 17.

33 Welch (with Paul Stekler), *Killing Custer*, p. 98.

34 Warren, *Buffalo Bill's America*, pp. 353-354.

35 Wilkinson, *Blood Struggle*, p. 350.

36 Halaas and Masich, *Halfbreed*, p. 17. Interestingly, Gwynne does note: "…in addition to their prowess in war, the Comanches were great merchants and traders." *Empire of the Summer Moon*, p. 60.

37 Light and Rand, *Indian Gaming and Tribal Sovereignty The Casino Compromise*, p. 124.

38 Will Peters, Oglala Lakota.

39 Hampton Sides, *Blood and Thunder: The Epic Story of Kit Carson and the Conquest of the American West* (New York: Anchor Books/A Division of Random House, 2007), p. 12. Sides' choice of the word "violently" seems particularly odd in this context.

40 Magnuson, *The Death of Raymond Yellow Thunder*, p. 119.

41 Gyasi Ross, "Leaving the Reservation: Modern Day Assimilation," *Huffington Post*, updated May 19, 2014.

42 Sides, *Blood and Thunder*, p. 403. Sides also noted: "One more rationale, slightly hidden, propelled Carleton's enthusiasm for flushing the Navajos from their country. He smelled gold." Ibid., p. 408.

43 Ibid., p. 487.

CHAPTER 7

Helen Hunt Jackson
With Friends Like This...

> All I ask in this creation
> Is a pretty little wife and a big plantation
> Way up yonder in the Cherokee Nation
>   Popular early 19th century song
>   John Ehle *Trail of Tears*[1]

In her book ostensibly intended to shame white Americans about their treatment of Indians, *A Century of Dishonor*, Helen Hunt Jackson frequently made mystifying comments about those beleaguered people. Intentionally or not, she asserted the superiority of European culture over that of Indian culture by making statements such as, "Innate cruelty is not exclusively an Indian trait."[2] She further stated the positive point of the Ft. Laramie Treaty of 1868, flagrantly violated by the United States government almost as soon as it was signed, was: "The encouragement held forth in this treaty as one great motive in leading these people [who she described as the 'Sioux'] to break tribal influences, so deleterious to improvement, and adapt our democratic civilization."[3] This friend of the Indian noted without elaboration that people in the 1870s considered that General Custer was "murdered" at the Battle of the Little Big Horn.[4] In explaining why the "Sioux" were so willing to engage in "civilized labor," Jackson stated:

> That all this should be true of these wild, warlike Sioux, after so many years of hardships and forced wanderings and removals, is incontrovertible proof that there is in them a native strength of character, power of endurance, and indomitable courage, which will make of them ultimately a noble and superior race of people, if civilization will only give them time to become civilized, and Christians will leave them time and peace to learn Christianity.[5]

After all the laudatory claims of Jackson's book are reviewed, a reader is left wondering if those expending such praise have considered the plain meaning of the words she wrote such as those quoted above and to be quoted in the following pages. Jackson's essay is liberally adorned, without further explanation, with the word "hostile" to describe Indians in the 19th century not living on reservations. It can fairly be stated using the words of Indian scholar George Tinker that ultimately she, like missionaries, was: "…convinced of the superiority of [her] own culture, social structures, and technologies."[6] She also implied, to borrow again from George Tinker, she: "…did not see the conquest of the west as wrong or as an injustice to Indian people."[7] That appeared to be Jackson's view at least in the instances where Indians were afforded the opportunity to shed themselves of what she apparently considered pagan and superstitious beliefs and receive the endless blessings provided by conversion to Christianity. If there is any doubt Jackson firmly held to the belief in the superiority of her own culture, reading her own words should quickly dispel those doubts. She stated in the second page of the main text of her book: "Of the fairness of holding that ultimate sovereignty belonged to the civilized discoverer, as against the savage barbarian, there is no manner nor ground of doubt. To question this is feeble sentimentalism."[8]

Is it "revisionist history" to now question whether Jackson's views about the Indians in North America are, at a minimum, insensitive? Jackson, at least to contemporary readers, could seem unconcerned regarding how the indigenous people Columbus encountered upon his arrival in the Western Hemisphere were soon dispossessed of their lands as long as they were provided the opportunity to become "Christians." She essentially claimed the primary question to be considered when analyzing the eventual "honorableness of the United States dealing with the Indians" was: "What was the nature of the Indians' right to the country in which they were living when the continent of North America was discovered[?]" She did not specify what Indians she was referring to nor what country existed at that point in history. She suggested dismissing as "sentimentalists" those who argued the "Indians were the real owners of the soil." She also pronounced without equivocation regarding the right of ownership by either the Indians or the Europeans that: "The only authority on the point must be the view and usage as accepted by the great discovering Powers at the time of discovery, and afterwards in their disposition of the lands discovered." She explained that the Indians' "'right of occupancy'" was a: "right alienable in but two ways, either by purchase or conquest."[9] Defining the story of indigenous peoples only through the "fact" of their "discovery" by Europeans consigns them to be a "'people without history.'"

Likewise, Jackson's initial approach to describing how the Europeans acquired "title" to Indian land suggested a uniformity to this activity which did not exist. Even within the group of settlers from a single nation such as England, there was often disagreement. In discussing early Puritan settlements, two-time Pulitzer Prize-winning historian Bernard Bailyn explained:

> The first and most vital question the settlers faced was how the land—so vast, so apparently boundless, so providentially open for exploitation—would be possessed and used. They had lived in a realm where every acre was preciously possessed and where whole domains were preserved for landlords' recreation while tenants and subtenants cultivated plots whose yields were shared in rents. In the varieties of their regional origins they had had different

experiences in crop selections and land use. Now, in New England, cling as they might to the practices they had known, they had no choice but to reconsider the foundations of land distribution and exploitation.[10]

In his eloquent style, Bailyn added: "The differences [in process] mattered. In certain places distinctions created by English regional origins were easily reconciled and soon faded, but in others they persisted and led at times to difficult community relations and bitter controversies."[11] Likewise, one issue overlooked in the question of how the settlers acquired title to land and in all the hysteria concerning Puritans being turned into savages by heathen Indians, was poverty. In noting how Europeans depleted the resources on that continent from the 15th through the 17th centuries, in *Ecological Indian* Shepard Krech III noted: "poverty was as rife in the countryside as in expanding urban areas."[12] It appeared little changed as the Europeans arrived on the North American continent and foisted their culture upon Indians, resulting in chronic, decades-long poverty for the many of the conquered.

Yet, the notion that Europeans "discovered" America is an idea which refuses to go away. It is mystifying that more than 500 years after Columbus arrived in the Western Hemisphere and over 100 years after Jackson penned her treatise, writers cling to the notion that Columbus "discovered" America. It is as if letting go of that hoary premise would be like letting go of a safety rope and falling into an abyss. In 1985, Italian author Gianni Granzotto wrote regarding the pre-"discovery" Columbus: "Nothing even vaguely resembling America ever entered his mind. America was more than unforeseeable: it did not exist." Granzotto further mused: "Is this not perhaps how America came to be discovered, because no one, not even Columbus, knew it was there?"[13] No one? For Indians living in the Western Hemisphere at the time, learning Columbus rescued them from oblivion (if that even crossed anyone's mind) must have been equally as reassuring as learning Columbus shared with Queen Isabella: "…[a] desire for a new world, a vaster Christian universe."[14] In addition to the confusion many Europeans experienced concerning who owned land, in real life although Jackson was not particularly influential in the male-dominated Indian Rights Association (IRA), she was a supporter nonetheless. Like the group Jackson did belong to, the Women's National Indian Association (WNIA), the IRA fervently believed assimilation would benefit Indians. That assimilating Indians into Euro-American culture might result in extinguishing Indian culture seemed of little concern to Jackson or her contemporaries.

Adding to the mystical overtones of Granzotto's analysis is his recounting of the tale of the "unknown helmsman," the only survivor of a providential shipwreck who supposedly helped launch Columbus' career of "discovering" America. The essence of this mythic story involved a ship which was dismasted by an ocean storm and was randomly tossed about by the waves of the sea whereupon by chance the ship ran aground at Porto Santo, Spain, where Columbus was living. Columbus attempted to no avail to nurse the mysterious stranger back to health. As the man was breathing his last, he told Columbus: "…on the other side of the ocean there were other lands." Summoning his last bit of strength, the expiring man complied with Columbus' wish that he draw a map (what dying person doesn't draw maps?) of the yet to be fully "discovered" regions.[15] Columbus' biographer Ovieda stated in the first recorded account in 1535 of this undated event, "'in my opinion, none of this is true.'" Later versions of the story specifically identified the mysterious sailor as Alonso Sanchez, a native of Palos, most likely referring to a city in the Spanish province of Huelva.[16] Left unexplained by proponents of this legend is why, if Sanchez did indeed draw a map, he was not given more credit for guiding Columbus to the "discovery" of America.

The legend of the "unknown helmsman" parallels another mystical-sounding tale explaining Columbus' arrival in Portugal in 1476. The outline of the story, which author John Wilford claims is "probably true," began with Columbus shipping out with a fleet from Genoa bound for Lisbon and ultimately England. On August 13, 1476, the story went, the merchant fleet Columbus traveled in was attacked by French-Portuguese warships. The motive for the attack remains unclear in that Portugal and France were at peace with the city-state of Genoa at that time. Although three of the Genoese ships caught fire, sank, and many sailors drowned, Columbus latched on to an oar and managed to drag himself to shore. The people of Lagos fed, nursed, and sheltered Columbus and the other survivors.[17]

Intentionally or not, Columbus' tale of high adventure is reminiscent of the story of Apostle Paul surviving a shipwreck as recorded in Acts 27-28 of the New Testament. Particularly striking is the description of how Paul was treated after the ship ran ashore: "…the natives showed us unusual kindness for they kindled a fire and made us all welcome, because of the rain that was falling and because of the cold [NKJV]." Like Paul, many considered Columbus the chosen vessel (especially Columbus himself) to carry the message of Christ to new lands. Unfortunately for Columbus, it is difficult to ascribe his actions as successful insofar as advancing the gospel of Christ. No testimonials from Indians as to their gratitude for Columbus bringing the "good news" to North America have achieved prominence. The story of the "unknown helmsman" was not the last time belief in divine or mystical forces would shape perception of an event. In a series of violent encounters in 1636-1637 between settlers and Pequot Indians, English forces eventually surrounded the Indians hiding behind an earth and timber fort near Mystic, Connecticut. Captain John Mason, commander of the contingent surrounding the trapped Indians, believed it was God's judgment that: "'…in little more than one Hour's space was their impregnable Fort with themselves utterly Destroyed, to the number of six or seven hundred [capitalization as in original].'"[18]

Additionally, even years of additional scholarship and a Pulitzer Prize are no assurance that the notion Europeans "discovered" America and portions thereof is leaving American consciousness any time soon. In his 1967 Pulitzer Prize-winning book on history, *Exploration and Empire*, William Goetzman advised: "To speak of American 'discovery' of the Southwest [United States] is presumptuous." This would seem to be a breakthrough in terms of recognizing Europeans or Americans didn't "discover" America or at least the Southwest since there were already people living there. Unfortunately, after his promising comment, Goetzman continued by colorfully advising that the "American explorers" were: "…entering a region which for nearly three centuries had been the scene of spectacular and almost unbelievable feats of discovery by small parties of clanking Spanish knights and zealous, hard-bitten missionaries."[19]

Filtering the events of Indian history through the lens of believed European "discovery" of the "New World" or defining Indians almost exclusively through their contacts with whites did not begin with Helen Hunt Jackson and most certainly will not end there. Later, particularly when it came to analyzing the combat victories of Indian-led forces, notably those of Crazy Horse, inevitably they were ascribed to the moral failings of the whites or supernatural intervention of some sort as opposed to the superior fighting skill or strategy of Indian warriors. For example, Lakota author Joseph Marshall noted Indian warriors were taught at a young age to shoot as many as 20 arrows accurately in a minute. Yet, Marshall takes particular umbrage at the notion that Crazy Horse's life is defined as: "'[the] conqueror of Custer' version, the purveyor of violence ready to fight at the drop of a 'war' bonnet, his hate for white people dripping like venom." Marshall was explaining, of course, that in many accounts Crazy Horse had no identity except as an opponent of Custer: "Kill a famous white man and insure your place in history."[20]

Further, if exploration and discovery are considered synonyms, as they surely must be if common sense dictates, John Wilford's axiom, "…the corollary of exploration is imperialism," is an honest anvil to hammer on the views of "sympathetic" historians such as Jackson. Wilford added, and Columbus' actions verified the point: "Explorers have not been content to find; they must seize as well." Expanding on this point, in which he seemed to agree with Jackson, Wilford continued: "That which is discovered is there to be taken and used as the discoverer sees fit." And, as indigenous people most likely would certainly agree: "The prize becomes tarnished, and the discoverer with it." Wilford elaborated with an early example: "At La Isabela [an early city established by Columbus] the Spaniards turned on each other and the hapless Tianos. They expected harsh tribute from the Indians and, when the Indians began to die off from strife, exhaustion, and disease, they were replaced with slaves from Africa."[21]

Yet, an omission of a detailed description of the "Trail of Tears," as the removal of Cherokees and other Indians from the Southeast United States is often called—perhaps the most shameful of all the shameful episodes of Indian history—is the most bewildering aspect of Jackson's exposé. Describing this event, Jackson laconically stated: "To dwell on the picture of this removal is needless. The fact by itself is more eloquent than pages of detail and description could make it. No imagination so dull, no heart so hard as not to see and to feel, at the bare mention of such an emigration, what horrors and what anguish it must have involved." To put her view of how important Christian conversion was in the entire horror show, she explained, without a hint of irony: "Only a great magnanimity of nature, *strengthened by true Christian principle* could have prevented them from being changed into eighteen thousand bitter enemies [emphasis added]."[22] Christian principle indeed. Now, anyone criticizing Jackson's description, or more accurately lack of description, is likely either thought to lack an understanding of her era, or else is reprogrammed to stop entertaining thoughts of engaging in "revisionist history." Unsurprisingly, Jackson also did not comment on the Potawatomi "Trail of Death" in 1838, where 859 Potawatomi Indians were force-marched 660 miles from their homes in Plymouth, Indiana, to present-day Osawatomie, Kansas.[23]

Jackson apparently also did not consider it necessary "to dwell" on the circumstances of the Creek Indians after their war with the Andrew Jackson-led forces of the Tennessee Militia ended in 1814. This Creek War, which commenced in September 1813, ended six months later after Creek forces were annihilated at the Battle of Horseshoe Bend in March 1814. About 3,000 Creeks, estimated at about 15 percent of the Creek population, were killed over the course of the war. Nevertheless, Helen Jackson claimed the Creeks "suffered much less severely" than other Indians at the conclusion of the Revolutionary

War since they refused to side with the British.[24] It was only a matter of time for that circumstance to change. After the conclusion of the Horseshoe Bend Battle, the acts of mutilation of the dead Indians in 1814 were hardly different than the acts of Thomas West, known as Third Lord De La Warr, and his men in the early 17th century in Virginia. Bailyn noted that after West's men destroyed a Kecoughtan village, they: "cawsed the Indians heade to be Cutt of[f],' and then [West] was persuaded by his troops to allow them to kill the children, which they did by throwing them overboard and 'Shotingge owt their Braynes in the water' [spelling and capitalization as in source]."[25]

Unfortunately, no imagination, dull or not, is a substitute for an accurate reporting based on solid research of records of an event as significant as the "Trail of Tears." It is understandable that research into historical matters in Jackson's day was not what it is today (or at least should be). Considering the "Trail of Tears" is thought by some to be the cruelest of all the cruel episodes in Indian history, it was incumbent upon Jackson to describe the event in as much detail with the information she had available. Her claim that: "the fact by itself is more eloquent than pages of detail and description could make it" is at a minimum difficult to understand. Even Robert Remini stated: "…from start to finish the operation of the removal policy was a horror. Deliberate fraud, corruption, mismanagement, and theft marked almost every step in the process. The Indians were abused and mistreated."[26]

Even though Remini recognized the inherent cruelty surrounding the actions of those implementing the removal policy, he argued: "To his dying day on June 8, 1845, Andrew Jackson genuinely believed that what he accomplished [with the removal which was actually put into effect during Martin Van Buren's presidency] rescued these people from inevitable annihilation." Remini, realizing his statement could be considered far-fetched, and possibly ludicrous, added: "And although that statement sounds monstrous, and although *no one* in the modern world wishes to accept or believe it, that is exactly what he did. He saved the Five Civilized Nations from probable extinction."[27]

Apparently, even in some of the lofty realms of academia, where Professor Remini resided for most of his life, the desire to require words and phrases to have precise meanings has dissipated. Remini's statement that *no one* in the modern world "…wishes to accept or believe…" Jackson's removal-oriented actions saved the "…Five Civilized Nations from probable extinction…" is wrong on its face because *Remini himself accepted it*—obviously then, at least one person—Remini—believed it. Remini indeed elaborated on this point at length in volume three of his *Jackson and the Course of American Freedom*. The larger point, of course, is there is now no earthly means available to disprove Remini's argument that removal saved the Five Civilized Nations since nothing was ever seriously attempted. Remini acknowledged one of the courses of action available to Jackson to protect the integrity of the various Indian nations was to protect them in their eastern homelands. Yet, as noted, Remini claimed that Jackson: "…knew such a policy was doomed from the start and had fifteen years of personal experience to attest to its impossibility."[28] Unfortunately, history is devoid of any examples of Jackson's attempts to protect the integrity of native societies in the eastern United States.

Possibly the only way to extrapolate a different outcome than the one created by removal is to review the events near the conclusion of the "Creek War of 1836." In May 1836, a full-fledged war broke out in

Georgia between Creek warriors and the Georgia militia in the Chattahoochee Valley. As white squatters and speculators flooded Creek territory, frequently ejecting the natives from their homes before the besieged Indians had a chance to even pack their belongings, angry exchanges often resulted in shootings. Secretary of War Lewis Cass ordered General Thomas S. Jesup to assemble regulars and militia troops from Georgia and Alabama to subdue the Creeks and subsequently remove them. Remini noted: "It took close to ten thousand soldiers and several bloody engagements in July to stifle Creek armed resistance."[29] The question thus arises: what if a similar sized force was employed to deter white encroachment earlier in the process? The record is devoid of even an estimate of the size of the force needed to protect Indian communities and settlements. The record also indicated attempts to ward off encroachment, as seldom as they were, were weak at best.

Additionally, Remini's arguments that relocation was the only way to save the Indians in the Southeast United States is at best an oversimplification and at worst an outright falsehood. The Dawes Act of 1887 initially exempted the territory held by the same Five Civilized Nations which were relocated to Oklahoma. However, in 1898 Congress passed the Curtis Act which, similar to the Dawes Act, provided for the termination of Indian governments and the breaking up of their tribal holdings into allotments.[30] After all, in a vivid description of the Lakota, which could apply to the situation in Oklahoma as well, why should there be: "young Indians lying around in every attitude enjoying their freedom and the sunshine"[31] when there was money to be made for the whites?

The territory held by the Indians was originally about 19.5 million acres, about one-half of present Oklahoma. This area contained fertile farmland, abundant pine forests, functioning coal mines, and—perhaps ultimately most problematic for them—undeveloped oil reserves, which proved too much of a tempting target for stealing for whites to even try to resist. Thus, when the Curtis Act provided the opportunity to seize the wealth in this region, tens of thousands of non-Indians invaded Oklahoma to grab their share of the riches through means legal or otherwise. Corruption and theft were so rampant that individuals involved in defrauding Indians out of their property and mineral rights willingly accepted the titles of "grafters."[32]

Also obscured by the writing of Jackson, Remini, and others was the thinly veiled belief the problem for Indians was at the end of the day the simple fact of their very existence. Views that Indian wars or the "necessity" of Indian removal were caused almost exclusively as a result of settler encroachment or intrusion are seemingly buried in well-thought-out books such as Patricia Nelson Limerick's *The Legacy of Conquest*. For example, she outlined the views of General John Wool in the Pacific Northwest in 1857 who bluntly foisted the blame for Indian wars on settler intrusion. He extended this thought process even further by suggesting a moratorium on further white settlement in the Oregon interior. Limerick herself proposed a unique argument in analyzing the thought processes of whites in the mid19-th century after the Civil War by explaining: "…it was an easy transition of thought to move from the idea of humans held in an unjust and resented captivity to the idea of land and natural resources held in Indian captivity."[33]

Perhaps Jackson's unwillingness to provide "pages of detail and description" regarding the "Trail of Tears" reflected the attitude existing at that time to consider Indians not worth making much of a fuss about in written accounts (with numerous occurrences to follow throughout history). Another time silence was considered worth more than an actual description using words involved Comanche—the horse. Comanche, ridden by Captain Miles Keogh of the 7th Cavalry who died at the Battle of the Little Big Horn in 1876, was by legend the only "survivor" from the battle from the federal side. On April 10, 1878, Colonel Sturgis ordered "official status" for Comanche in an attempt to protect him from souvenir hunters, especially those who wanted snippets from his tail. In the dedication speech of the colonel for Comanche, he stated in part that Comanche's: "'…very silence speaks in terms more eloquent than words of the desperate struggle against overwhelming odds, of the hopeless conflict, and heroic manner in which all went down that day.'"[34]

Fortunately, in addition to Remini's summary, other writers do provide us "pages of details" about the "Trail of Tears." In *Voices from the Trail of Tears*, Vicki Rozema quoted from a June 18, 1838, letter written by a Colonel W. J. Worth who lamented a measles outbreak which precluded the use of buildings at Ft. Poinsett to house Indians under his charge. Rozema noted that: "Less than a month after the forced removal began, illness and death were attacking the camps and emigrant parties in epidemic proportions." Rozema also noted a steamboat collision where the *Monmouth* carrying 611 Creeks was cut in two by another steamboat which caused the drowning of over 300 of these men, women, and children. She likewise stated that General Winfield Scott ordered the forced emigrations to be suspended because of the heat and sickness arising during the summer season and because of the: "…complaints he was receiving from different quarters on how cruelly the emigration was being handled." Of course, what would Indian history be without the obligatory casting of blame for mistreatment on the Indians themselves? Rozema noted without explanation that the emigration was: "…severely handicapped by the weather and the obstinacy of the Cherokees."[35]

To further examine the horrors suffered by the Cherokees and the other Indians on the "Trail of Tears," and which Jackson declined to describe, it is important to reevaluate the commonly accepted figure of 4,000 deaths during this movement since it is now coming into question as being too low. Historian Russell Thornton studied mortality rates of the Cherokees during and immediately after the 1838 removal and calculated the number of deaths as being closer to 8,000.[36] Thornton arrived at this figure by not only including those who died on the march itself, but also who died shortly after arriving in the West. As historian John Ehle asserted, whether or not one accepts the government figures or believes the results of other calculations (such as those compiled by one Dr. Butler from Connecticut): "…deaths were numerous, suffering was intense and of equal importance the government of the Cherokees, once promising, was destroyed."[37] Why the destruction of a system of government was of "equal importance" to the deaths of human beings is left unaddressed (although it could be considered a form of genocide as suggested by the discussion at the end of the chapter).

Fortunately, Ehle's writing also promoted a story line regarding the "Trail of Tears" Jackson seemingly rejected, that Indians were not just props in the onward parade of people to be "Christianized," but human beings with stories of their own. After the mass movement to Oklahoma was complete, some of the Indians put in claims for monetary damages, but Ehle noted this attempt at reparations did not account for the personal losses such as:

> A favorite cow. A pet dog. The tree that had been a sapling when Mother married and now shaded the house and spring. The field Papa and my brothers cleared with fire and then beat the roasted roots with clubs and stone. The hearth, where the bread has been baked for many years.[38]

Although writing about a different situation, Scott Berg produced a description which could have been applicable to the "Trail of Tears" and many other miserable scenarios for Indians: "No aspect of the Indian Wars, however violent, was so painful to many Indians as [the] separation from culture, family, tribe, and lands."[39]

Unfortunately, Ehle's comments do not shed light upon Jackson's comment that: "...to dwell on the picture of this removal is needless." She also did not state "needless" for whom? Yet, Ehle himself fell into a strange intellectual quagmire by asserting the odd argument that removal: "...was less costly in human terms than an outright war, an alternative Indians would have found more understandable and which would have been consistent with their own history."[40] Ehle did not indicate which Indians would have thought war was more "understandable," or what a comment like this would mean to them.

Earlier in her book, prior to her non-description of the suffering experienced by Indian people on the "Trail of Tears," Jackson displayed a similar methodology. At that point, she described a treaty signed between the United States government and the Delaware Indians in 1778 at Ft. Pitt, Pennsylvania. She indicated by a footnote: "It is superfluous to say that these provisions were never carried out."[41] Why she just doesn't demonstrate with a few facts how the treaty was violated is not explained as well. Jackson expended more effort explaining the origin of the state of Delaware name as being a derivative of the name of the "...great English brave—Lord De la Ware."[42] Additionally, why Lord de Ware was considered "great" or how he became a "brave" was also left unexplained.

Yet, the greatest flaw in Jackson's logic is exhibited in her habitual implication and sometimes express statements of Indians living in a state of perpetual savagery prior to the arrival of Columbus. She argued: "There is no instance in all history of a race of people [the Cherokees] passing in so short a space of time from the barbarous stage to the agricultural and civilized."[43] Nevertheless, although First Nations scholars have addressed current scholarship in Indian matters, the comments could apply to Jackson's writing. Tirso Gonzales noted: "...the colonizer mentality, in one way or another, dwells in more than 90 percent of the human population on Earth..." and added: "First Nation scholars Marie Battiste and James Youngblood Henderson comment, in the following way, on Eurocentrism, 'It is the imaginative and institutional context that informs contemporary scholarship, opinion, and law. As a theory, it postulates the superiority of Europeans over non-Europeans.'"[44] It is a curious phenomenon indeed that although many praise Helen Hunt Jackson for highlighting cruel behaviors in many instances of the government dealing with Indians, none of them question her apparent assumption that European civilization was superior.

Other writers, perhaps unknowingly, fall into these odd explanations in describing the cruelty foisted on Indians. Roxanne Dunbar-Ortiz, in initially describing the practice of scalping by New England settlers, noted that "...scalp hunting became a lucrative commercial practice..." and: "Scalps and Indigenous children became a means of exchange, currency..." These comments about at least scalping suggest it was an open and obvious element of daily life in New England towns. Instead of leaving it at that, Dunbar-Ortiz then commented that was not the case in noting the practice of exchanging scalps and trading Indian children "…may have even created a black market."[45] Even with the uncertainty surrounding its history, it is instructive to note the practice of scalping had a long tradition in North America. During what was known as the "Mexican Period" of United States history, from 1835 to 1850, governors of some Mexican states developed a system of essentially paying cash bounties for scalps of virtually any dark-haired person.

Curiously, Bernard Bailyn, who as a Harvard history professor would not be considered a "radical," had no hesitation in fully outlining the brutality of settlers (and Indians) in New England in the 17th century. He described the situation as one where: "Sensibilities coarsened when brutality grew commonplace. The desecration of bodies, so much a part of the Indians' search for reciprocity in warfare and diplomacy, became for Europeans a search for domination."[46] Bailyn also noted regarding their relationship with Indians, Virginians: "'ransaked their Temples, Tooke down the Corpes of their deade kings from of[f] their Toombes,' engaged freely in scalping, and did not hesitate to decapitate their enemies in campaigns of terror [spelling as in source]." In sum, after noting other instances of brutality, such as a Captain Davis from Virginia who: "…stabbed an Indian 'queen' to death as a merciful alternative to burning her alive." Bailyn concluded: "Dismembered body parts—heads, hands, scalps, and torn off strips of skin—had become commonplace objects among such gentle people as the Pilgrims."[47]

At a minimum, for the sake of credibility and clarity, Dunbar-Ortiz should decide whether she believed the scalp hunting and trading of Indians as slaves was out in the open or somewhat hidden from view in a "black market." What is confusing is that, in Dunbar-Ortiz's account at least, there is no indication any authorities made any effort to put a stop to those barbaric practices. In fact, the bloody and mutilated corpses of the scalped Indians were referred to as "Redskins," suggesting few, if any, of the settlers recoiled in protest. As is well known, Redskins is the name of a National Football League team located in the capital of the United States. A headline from the *Canton Farm Leader* on January 23, 1934, announcing the closing of the Canton/Hiawatha Asylum for Insane Indians blared: "'no Redskins remain at what was once the only insane Indian institution in the world.'"[48]

Given how easily a "sympathetic" writer and advocate like Jackson labeled Indians resistant to white engulfment "hostiles," is it any wonder that the term Redskins was eventually considered an acceptable name for a nationally known team (even though it was the name of what remained of Indians who were stripped of their skin)? "Hostiles" can certainly be construed as the disrespectful label for Indians who were unwilling to wholly accept white domination/culture. In that regard, Armando Prats in *Invisible Natives,* quoting Robert Berkhofer's *White Man's Indian,* stated that there was a "'curious timelessness' that characterizes 'the white man's Indian,'" which perhaps unconsciously manifested itself in the use of these mascots. In essence, it is a way of claiming Indians desiring to retain meaningful aspects of their traditional culture are consigned to become relics of the past. It is logical to conclude from Prats' analysis a possible consequence of the use of these mascots is having Indians "conceived of as ahistorical and static."

Prats continued: "Not only does the Indian recede as white America carries out its foreordained advance, but he remains unchanging, 'iconic.' He is history's discard, an exile from the Western paradise."[49]

If there is any question that writers of Indian history have desensitized average people to the suffering of Indians, those who oppose removing Redskins as the team name for this NFL franchise usually do so on the basis the name is traditional. The question becomes: a tradition of what? A number of activities and language uses were traditional but have been discontinued due to their immoral and offensive natures. Slavery was a tradition for decades in the United States but was discontinued essentially at the conclusion of the Civil War.

One argument in favor of keeping the Indian-inspired mascots is that a poll taken by the *Washington Post* in early 2016 claimed 90 percent of Native Americans were not offended by the Redskins mascot. It was later determined only 44 percent of those surveyed by the *Post* belonged to tribes.[50] In response, *The Nation* disputed the poll and encapsulated its protest in an article entitled "On the Shameful and Skewed 'Redskins' Poll."[51] In another study conducted in 2016 by a professor from the University of Montana, it was demonstrated that Native American sports mascots often reinforced stereotypes in the minds of these *non*-Indian people. For example, residents of Cleveland, who had the Chief Wahoo as the symbol of their professional baseball team, were more likely to associate Native Americans with warlike traits than residents of other cities.[52] Fortunately, the Cleveland Indian organization decided to discontinue the use of this problematic symbol.[53]

As noted above, given that Jackson started her book with her endorsement of the concept that Columbus "discovered" the Western Hemisphere, it is hardly surprising her book does not now come across as particularly sympathetic to the plight of Indians. Nevertheless, the idea that Europeans "discovered" North and/or South America is so firmly embedded in history teachings about Indians, it is a source of confusion for many to "discover" that Indians such as the Lakota had a name for North America long before 1492—Turtle Island. It simply seems as if Jackson was virtually unrelenting and unapologetic in her unwillingness to even attempt to view events from the Indian perspective. Rather than write an understanding description of the desperation of the nearly starving Dakota Indians in Minnesota in 1862, she hinted they were simply hostile, uncomprehending savages:

> A sense of wrong in the past and distrust for the future was ever deepening in their minds, and preparing them to be suddenly thrown by any small provocation into an antagonism and hostility grossly disproportionate to the apparent cause.[54]

Yet, Jackson overlooked the situations where Indians disregarded the warnings made by Indian leaders who explained Indian nations who capitulated to whites without a fight were the first to be completely conquered.

Fortunately, recent analysis of history writing might suggest there is a trend toward redirecting the view endorsed by Helen Hunt Jackson that people around the world are important only to the extent they interacted with Westerners. In short, people and groups of people should be given a platform to tell their own stories, not just when they are "discovered." In *Meaning Over Memory*, Peter Stearns explained:

"The most important development of all, [in social history] however, has been an insistence that major areas of the world be viewed as historical actors in their own right and not simply as recipients of Western impulses and guidance." However, it will be left to others to bring attention to Indians as "actors in their own right" since he explained: "African history, to use the most notable example, did not begin with Western contact, and even in the age of active imperialism, Western contact did not define everything that was going on."[55]

In addition to her consistently Eurocentric perspective, Jackson also never seemed to question the inevitability of white conquest of North America. Describing an event on the Great Plains in 1857, she commented that: "The next year's records show the Government itself was aware that some measures must be taken to provide for the troublesome wild tribes of the prairie." This description is from Jackson's book purportedly sympathetic to the plight of Indians in the 19th century and not a propaganda piece promoting the virtues of Manifest Destiny. Jackson did not begin to hint the "wild" behavior might have something to do with the Indians' accurate belief the whites were there to dispossess them from the land used for hunting buffalo. She noted without irony: "The Indians themselves are deeply anxious and disturbed."[56]

Jackson's writing would be more logical if she had placed the adverb understandably before the phrase "deeply anxious and disturbed." Otherwise, it is made to appear the Indians got stirred up for no reason because that's just the way they were or that they reacted, as noted above, and as she stated in a later part of her book, with: "…an antagonism and hostility grossly disproportionate to the apparent cause."[57] In the paragraph following her "deeply anxious and disturbed" comment, in noting the Plains Indians were aware of tribes to the east ceding land, she argued: "…by an Indian's reasoning, in a few years these tribes will emigrate farther west, and, as a matter of necessity, occupy hunting grounds of the *wild* tribes [emphasis added]."[58] Although the pressure on the Plains Indians came more from whites seizing territory used for hunting and diminished buffalo herds rather than other Indians, the prediction precipitating the label "Indian's reasoning" proved accurate as to the loss of territory. Apparently, if a writer in the 19th century did not advocate the outright extermination of Indians, he or she was considered sympathetic to Indians, regardless of what was actually written.

It is often argued current readers do not understand the mores of 19th-century people and writers and are misunderstanding the circumstances of those times. For example, her constant choice of the word "wild" to describe Indian nations might be considered acceptable in her time. Unfortunately, to describe Indians as "wild" ignored the reality of the situation existing for Indians from the very early days of the formation of what eventually became the United States. One of the preeminent examples of what this means is found in examining the situation existing for the Shawnees and other Indian nations prior to the commencement of what is now known as the French and Indian War.

First and foremost, this circumstance demonstrated that at least the Shawnees were capable of making decisions and political calculations based on their analysis of the situation as opposed to sheer emotion or anger. In 1752, a French force led by Charles Michael de Langlade, a half-French, half-Ottawa Indian soldier, destroyed the village of Pickawillany, partially in retaliation for insults leveled against French envoys by Unemakemi, the Miami chief. During the attack, de Langlade personally assaulted Unemakemi, cutting out his heart while he was still alive and eating some of it.[59] Many other Indians were killed or captured and later executed. Despite this ferocious attack by the French on their allies, the Shawnees still considered the British the bigger threat to their maintaining control of their territory. While ultimately the Indians' choice to support the French during this conflict was a miscalculation, it was a calculated choice nonetheless.[60]

Examples like those of de Langlade notwithstanding, there is an unmistakable theme running through Jackson's writing of her belief that the ultimate good to be achieved for Indians was to become just like white people. According to Jackson's biographer, Valerie Sheer Mathis, the only legitimate debate for the future of Indians was whether it was better for them to become Catholic or Protestant. In describing the operation of the Women's National Indian Association (WNIA), she noted without hesitation that one goal of the WNIA was to "Christianize the American Indians, including those of California."[61] Of course, once again, Indians were not consulted about these spiritual issues. Nevertheless, Joseph Marshall told a story of why an old Indian man did not want to give up his round Tipi. The man explained in that dwelling: "…the white man's devil couldn't catch him in a corner." The ever-astute Marshall shrewdly noted: "[it] was not the white man's devil he was afraid of, however; he was afraid of the white man himself."[62]

Less well-known authors perpetuated the theme Indians were/are savages by constantly referring to well-planned Indian attacks and ambushes against armed soldiers as "massacres." In *Saga of Chief Joseph*, Helen Howard, for reasons she did not reveal, described the combat deaths of a detachment of ten soldiers in the Pacific Northwest, led by one Lieutenant Sevier M. Rains, as a "massacre." The basic outline of the event was that: "When Rains' detachment…entered a shallow ravine the Indians sprang the trap, pouring a hail of bullets on the cavalrymen." There is absolutely nothing to suggest the Indians violated what would be now considered the "civilized" rules of warfare by killing unarmed prisoners or other acts of that nature. After the initial ambush was sprung, Rains' armed men were eventually killed one at a time by their skilled opponents. Nevertheless, Howard, like other writers, made no effort to explain why armed soldiers killed in mutual combat were considered "massacred."[63]

In 1905, George Bent, the half-Cheyenne, half-white scout and interpreter discussed in a previous chapter, wrote an article about the 1864 killings of the Cheyennes by Colonel Chivington's men at Sand Creek. Although a limited number of these articles were printed, some of them circulated through Denver and were read by old soldiers still living there. Although the "Mile High" city was becoming a symbol of "civilization," it was also home to a ruling elite of the pioneer caste who were unapologetically Indian haters. Nevertheless, they had no interest in reminding people of the public parading of the grisly trophies from the Sand Creek Massacre in 1864, which usually took the form of body parts and scalps as macabre decorations of hats and saddles.

Bent's article on Sand Creek ripped open old wounds; Jacob Downing, a prominent attorney and unrepentant Indian hater and Chivington apologist, lashed out at Bent in the *Denver Times*. Downing spewed his bile at Bent and stated Bent was: "'…[a] cutthroat, and a thief, a liar and a scoundrel, but worst of all a halfbreed.'" Downing claimed Sand Creek was no massacre because according to him only a handful of Indians were killed and: "'…only one squaw and only one papoose [were] in the lot'" that was killed.

In Downing's view, Chivington's infatuation with Indian hating was not particularly unique nor wrong. At the time of Chivington's death, his funeral was the largest in the city of Denver's history. The problems with Bent's article for disciples of Chivington was that it unearthed aspects of the Sand Creek Massacre which they surely must have hoped would remain hidden from public view. Not only had Downing's men, and ultimately Chivington's, mercilessly slaughtered Cheyenne elderly men, women, and children, but as noted, they had shamelessly decorated their hats and saddles with trophies made of every conceivable body part of these victims. At the time of the aftermath of the attack in 1864, the soldiers rode laughing all the way back to Denver and were optimistic they would make it home in time for Christmas. After Bent's article was published some years later, the memory of the laughter and mirth disappeared.[64]

Milo Slaughter, a spokesman for Colorado's Civil War volunteers, pushed for the erection of a monument to be built on the grounds of the state capital in Denver to honor these former soldiers. Beneath the heroic figure of a cavalryman is a list of battles cast in bronze. Among the victories is listed the "Battle" of Sand Creek. In 2017, this monument came under scrutiny for what many believed was the improper promoting of racists as heroes. In an article in the *Denver Post* on August 18, 2017, Glenn Morris of the Colorado American Indian Movement saw the question of the Denver Courthouse monument as part of a larger national question. Morris stated: "All over the country there's tens of thousands of monuments to Indian killers and there's names of towns, there's names of mountains, there's names of rivers." Morris included Chivington in the group of individuals like Columbus when he argued: "If you engage in genocide you forfeit historical honors." Apparently anticipating being accused of engaging in revisionist history, Morris added: "We don't want fantasy or fallacy masquerading as history to go unchallenged."[65]

Fortunately for finding a balanced view of Indian history from the white perspective, not all prominent 19th-century writers nurtured the view Indians were genetically or otherwise predisposed to be savages. At least one, Herman Melville, author of *Moby Dick*, vociferously argued against this bias and asserted, "…our own progenitors…were savages also." In an "anonymous" review of Frances Parkman's *The California and Oregon Trail in the Literary World*, Melville noted for "civilized beings" to regard Indians with "…disdain and contempt" was "wholly wrong." His somewhat stilted criticism of those who held Indians in contempt was framed by the Biblical Gospel stories of the arrogant Publicans and Pharisees. He concluded: "The savage is born a savage; and the civilized being but inherits his civilization, nothing more."[66]

The unthinking use of at best equivocal language concerning Indian history, even if unintentionally done, did not start nor, more problematically, did not end with Helen Hunt Jackson. However, in some respects, since she was considered "Pro-Indian," the impact of her language choice was all the more a Trojan Horse. Well over 100 years later, another seemingly well-meaning writer, Naomi Schaefer Riley, also recommended a more Westernized approach for Indians to adapt for living in her enthusiastic sermon about the glories of free-market capitalism she entitled *The New Trail of Tears*. While for purposes of this book, the bulk of the discussion of Riley's book is contained in the Epilogue, a striking example of how cultural arrogance can be used to obscure placing events in their proper context warrants discussion here. In one of her off-the-cuff proposed solutions to the difficulties found on Indian reservations, Riley, indifferent to any regard to the impact on any remnants of Indian culture, proposes the idea "to make reservations into states." She correctly acknowledged (for the most part): "It would be hard to overstate the political obstacles to creating new states." Then, she casually added: "…are Montana and South Dakota going to voluntarily give up their land?"[67] The theme of Riley's book of ignoring traditional Indian cultural concepts and imposing European ideas could be summed up in one sentence from Prats' *Invisible Natives*. He noted in the films he studied, Indians: "…look[ed] upon the landscape only with the intent to deprive white America of its dream."[68] Since the possibility of a meaningful military action by any Indians is nonexistent, the possibility of Indians remaining Indians seems to be the circumstance depriving Riley of her dream.

Further exploration into the record contained in the written word of the march of history over the dead bodies of Indians in North America reveals the odd cadences used to motivate sojourners on that excursion. In short, Jackson is far from being in exclusive company when phrasing the odd ideas disgorged from her storehouse of rationalizations. In *Andrew Jackson and His Indian Wars*, historian Robert V. Remini stated in the preface that: "We today must remember that in the past a great many normally decent and upright Americans have *repeatedly* mistreated other people: Native Americans, African Americans, and Japanese Americans [emphasis added]." He further explained: "So before anyone today assumes a high moral tone about what happened a century ago, let that person take a long view of American history and remember that fear and mistrust at any time can and probably will lead to despicable crimes that disgrace the nation and blacken its history."[69] The logical fallacy in Remini's argument appears to be the premise Indians and others are not being mistreated now and that all mistreatment of them lies in the past. To borrow a line of reasoning from Helen Hunt Jackson, the current problems on many Indian reservations are so obvious, to list them "…is needless."

In one of the many ironies in analyzing Indian history, it is the eccentric Ward Churchill who provided examples of how absurd Remini's thesis regarding "…decent and upright people…" can appear when applied to specific individuals. M. Annette Jaimes, quoting Churchill, indicated a man named David Nichols rationalized his participation in both the Buffalo Springs and Sand Creek Massacres, by claiming that for the balance of his life, he was a "'good man'" who achieved much of "'socially redeeming value.'" Jaimes argued the same logic could be applied to the legacy of Adolf Hitler since he was instrumental in the creation of the autobahn, Volkswagen, funded museums and opera, etc. like no previous German leader. Jaimes astutely further explained that in the case of Nichols, Hitler, and others it is the evil they participated in which is inextricably bound together with the subsequent good. Much like in the case of the Germans exterminating the Jews and Gypsies in the Ukraine to make way for the settlement of the Germans there, the creation of the State of Colorado was predicated on the physical destruction of most Cheyennes and Arapaho and the forced relocation of the survivors to Oklahoma.[70]

Further, Remini did not elaborate on how his opinion of good people being pressured into committing bad acts is related to the specific topic of his book—Andrew Jackson. Additionally, he did not explain why the "long view" of history as he labels it presents a more flattering picture than what must be the "short view." The examples of brutality and mistreatment outlined in this study are far from an exhaustive list of such occurrences. Would adding to this list present a more optimistic view of human nature, particularly relating to the conquest of North and South America by Europeans and their descendants? Remini and others like him engage in mental gymnastics whose successful execution requires the ability to assume the guise of contortionist rather than athlete.

If Remini considered Andrew Jackson specifically as one of those "normally decent and upright" people committing despicable crimes due to "fear and mistrust," his argument is undercut by his discussion of Jackson's early career. Remini's own writing indicated that rather than being based on "fear and mistrust," the idea of removal was based on the desire to develop a simple solution to the conflict with Indians on the frontier and naked greed for land. Even though the large-scale movement of the Cherokees from Georgia to Oklahoma commenced in the 1830s, as early as 1809, according to Remini himself, Jackson began discussing the concept of removal with Willie Blount. Willie was the half-brother of William Blount who was appointed by President Washington to serve as governor of North Carolina.[71] Although the federal government was preoccupied with fighting the Indians who had defeated General Arthur St. Clair, Governor Blount set the precedent for Jackson as he regularly "pestered" the federal government to remove the "Indian menace" from the Southeastern United States. Remini's outlining of Jackson's early efforts to formulate a removal plan also undermined Helen Hunt Jackson's subtle hints that the "Trail of Tears" was somehow the result of providence rather than the deliberate act or acts of all-too-real flesh and blood men.[72]

Remini's comments do not suggest the identity of whom the "normally decent and upright Americans" are that he is referring to in his soliloquy. However, apparently he was not referring in any way to the inhabitants of the Western Hemisphere at the time of Columbus' arrival. This can be ascertained by noting how Remini described the actions of Cherokees who were hoping (in vain as it turned out) to fend off the seizures by whites of three million acres of land near Muscle Shoals, Alabama, in roughly 1785. Without blinking, Remini labeled the Cherokees engaged in the hostilities "murderers," even after noting what precipitated the killing was white settlers ignoring the Treaty of Hopewell establishing boundaries to Cherokee Territory and labeling those whites "invaders."[73]

This situation was not particularly unique as the wave of "Manifest Destiny" swept over the continent throughout the 19th century. Great debate raged over how best to resolve the "Indian problem." Those living in the eastern United States were believed to favor a gentle approach to this issue whereas those "normally decent and upright Americans" living in western regions advocated more brutal solutions. It simply did not occur to Remini to note from the Indians' perspective, they might have a "white problem." And, fortunately, there are historians who do not hesitate to address head-on the issue of what the "Trail of Tears" was really all about. Eminent historian Henry Warner Bowden plainly stated: "[President Andrew] Jackson had always sided with the white Americans who thought the best way to handle Indians was to push them off any land that white people wanted."[74]

Thus, even when viewing Helen Hunt Jackson's writing in the most favorable light, it is worth considering whether it is as useful, at least in the present day, as some suggest. This is particularly true in the case of debating whether Indians were victims of genocide, which even Cook-Lynn claimed that Jackson considered an "unutterable"[75] word. Thus, when evaluating whether the genocide of Indians occurred in North and/or South America, it is critical to consider in that analysis Lemkin's belief, as interpreted by Michael McDonnell and Dirk Moses, genocide: "…[did] not require the entire physical extermination of the victims, only the elimination of the culture-bearing strata."[76] For example, even if nations like the Cherokee were "strengthened by true Christian principle," is it too much to consider the forced conversion of Indians to Christianity an aspect of the process of genocide? Sadly, it is a question which may seldom be considered in that as Vine Deloria, Jr., stated: "Few Americans have taken the time to learn precisely how the settlement of the continent was justified by the Europeans."[77]

Endnotes

1. John Ehle, *Trail of Tears*, p. 213.
2. Helen Hunt Jackson, *A Century of Dishonor: The Classic Exposé of the Plight of Native Americans* (Mineola, New York: Picador/Farrar, Straus & Giroux, 2016), p. 262. At times, Jackson's writing and attitudes received curious praise. Elizabeth Cook-Lynn argued Jackson: "…denounced treaty breaking and would have condemned the unconstitutional Allotment Act as a solution to dealing with a troublesome population, legislation that caused dire poverty and death to thousands of indigenous people." Cook-Lynn, *A Separate Country*, p. 53. However, Jackson's biographer Valerie Sherer Mathis noted: "She died two years before the passage of the [Dawes] General Allotment Act which divided tribal reservations into small privately held parcels. Her opinion of this legislation remains unknown, although she knew and respected its author, Henry Lauren Dawes. One wonders if she had lived beyond 1885 and continued her membership in the WNIA [Women's National Indian Association], she might have accepted their attitude that only they knew what was best for the Indians. All Indian reform groups, including the WNIA, viewed Indian acculturation as the solution to the problem." Valerie Sherer Mathis, *Helen Hunt Jackson and Her Indian Reform Legacy* (Austin, Texas: University of Texas Press, 1990), p. xvi. As stated in the next quote in the main text, Jackson wrote: "…tribal influences [are] so deleterious to improvement." As will hopefully be made clear in this book, the allotment process was a major factor in the disintegration of tribal cultures and facilitating assimilation.
3. Ibid., p. 174.
4. Ibid., p. 178.
5. Ibid., pp. 184-185.
6. Tinker, *Missionary Conquest*, p. 47.
7. Ibid., p. 74.
8. Jackson, *A Century of Dishonor*, p. 10.
9. Ibid., p. 9. Jackson acknowledged that the "discoverers" of North America could eventually create circumstances where the "lesser right" of occupancy "would be practically denied to our Indians." Nevertheless, in her unflagging belief in the benevolence of the European powers, she stated: "…they could hardly have left more explicit testimony to meet the exigency." Ibid., p. 12. It is noteworthy to point out, as quoted above, that twice in the first two pages of the main text of her book she used one form or another of the word "sentimental" to describe those who questioned the right of "discovering" Europeans nations to take possession of the continent.
10. Bailyn, *The Barbarous Years*, p. 418.
11. Ibid., p. 422.
12. Krech, *The Ecological Indian*, p. 95.
13. Granzotto, *Christopher Columbus*, p. 45.
14. Ibid., p. 74.
15. Ibid., pp. 45, 88.

16 Ibid., p. 46.
17 Wilford, *The Mysterious History of Columbus*, p. 65.
18 Bailyn, *The Barbarous Years*, p. 446.
19 Goetzman, *Exploration and Empire*, pp. 36-37.
20 Joseph Marshall, *The Journey of Crazy Horse* (New York: Viking Books, 2004), p. 280. Interestingly enough, as will be quoted again in the Chapter entitled "Searching for Spiritual Meaning in the Land of John Dunbar—Crazy Horse Redux," Mari Sandoz stated that after the Fetterman Fight Crazy Horse had a: "heart that was cold and black with anger that could not be made good until many more white men died like those scattered naked up there on the ridge." Sandoz, *Crazy Horse*, p. 204.
21 Wilford, *The Mysterious History of Columbus*, p. 177.
22 Jackson, *A Century of Dishonor*, p. 286.
23 (No author listed) "Native History: Potawatamie Removed at Gunpoint, Trail of Death Begins," *Indian Country Today*. September 4, 2014.
24 Jackson, *Century of Dishonor*, p. 262.
25 Bailyn, *The Barbarous Years*, p.68.
26 Remini, *Andrew Jackson and His Indian Wars*, p. 250.
27 Ibid., p. 281. At least one researcher has put this claim into doubt. Jeff Benvenuto, citing Seena Kohl's essay "Ethnocide and Ethnogenesis: A Case Study of the Mississippi Band of Choctaw, A Genocide Avoided" stated: "Kohl's argument is that the Mississippi band of Choctaw, the descendants of those Choctaw who resisted forcible removal by the United States in 1831, managed to narrowly avoid genocide and vitally regenerate their autochthonous society." Woolford, Benvenuto and Hinton, Eds., Jeff Benvenuto, "Resisting Choctaw Ethnocide and Ethnogenesis—The Creative Destruction of Colonial Genocide," *Colonial Genocide in North America,* p. 208.
28 Ibid., p. 280.
29 Ibid., p. 272.
30 Wilson, *The Earth Shall Weep*, p. 323.
31 Powers, *The Killing of Crazy Horse*, p. 82.
32 Wilson, *The Earth Shall Weep*, p. 327.
33 Limerick, *The Legacy of Conquest*, p. 46.
34 Barnett, *Touched by Fire*, p. 328.
35 Rozema, *Voices from the Trail of Tears*, pp. 116-117.
36 Ibid., p. 40.
37 Ehle, *Trail of Tears*, p. 392.
38 Ibid., p. 330.
39 Berg, *38 Nooses*, p. 298.
40 Ehle, *Trail of Tears*, p. 394.
41 Jackson, *A Century of Dishonor*, p. 34, footnote at the bottom of the page.
42 Ibid., p. 33.

43 Ibid., p. 271.
44 Melissa Nelson, Ed., Tirso Gonzales "Re-Nativization in North and South America" *Original Instructions: Indigenous Teachings for a Sustainable Future* (Rochester, Vermont: Bear & Co., 2008), p. 298.
45 Dunbar-Ortiz, *An Indigenous People's History of the United States*, p. 65.
46 Bailyn, *The Barbarous Years*, p. 502.
47 Ibid., pp. 502-503.
48 Leahy, *They Called it Madness*, p.168.
49 Prats, *Invisible Natives*, p. 36.
50 John Woodrow Cox, Scott Clement, and Theresa Vargas, "New Poll Finds 9 in 10 Native Americans Aren't Offended by Redskins Name," *Washington Post*, May 19, 2016.
51 Jacqueline Keeler "On the Shameful and Skewed 'Redskins' Poll," *The Nation*, May 26, 2016.
52 Keila Sypaller, "Mascots Can Reinforce Stereotypes a UM Researcher Finds." *Billings Montana Gazette*, April 15, 2016.
53 David Waldstein, "Cleveland Indians Will Abandon Chief Wahoo Logo Next Year" (*New York Times*, January 29, 2018).
54 Jackson, *A Century of Dishonor*, p. 163.
55 Stearns, *Meaning Over Memory*, p. 46.
56 Jackson, *A Century of Dishonor*, p. 81.
57 Ibid., p. 163.
58 Ibid., p. 81.
59 Eckert, *That Dark and Bloody River*, p. 1.
60 Ibid., p. xliv-xlv.
61 Mathis, *Helen Hunt Jackson*, p. 118.
62 Marshall, *The Day the World Ended at the Little Big Horn*, pp. 232-233.
63 Helen Addison Howard, *Saga of Chief Joseph* (Lincoln, Nebraska: Bison Books/University of Nebraska Press, Revised Edition, 1978), p. 189.
64 Halaas and Masich, *Halfbreed*, p. 339.
65 Danika Worthington, "A History of Racism the KKK and Crimes Against American Indians: Colorado's Struggle with Divisive Monuments Started Long Ago," *Denver Post*, August 18, 2017.
66 Wilcomb Washburn, Ed., Herman Melville, "Melville on Parkman's Indians," *The Indian and The White Man*, pp. 437-438.
67 Riley, *The New Trail of Tears*, p. 181.
68 Prats, *Invisible Natives*, p. 89.
69 Remini, *Andrew Jackson and His Indian Wars*, p. viii.
70 Jaimes, *The State of Native America*, pp. 3-4.
71 Remini, *Andrew Jackson and His Indian Wars*, p. 53.
72 Ibid., p. 32.
73 Ibid., p. 30.

74 Bowden, *American Indians and Christian Missions*, p. 176.
75 Cook-Lynn, *A Separate Country*, p. 53.
76 Woolford, Benvenuto and Hinton, Eds., Keira Ladner, "Political Genocide: Killing Nations through Legislation and Slow-Moving Poison." *Colonial Genocide in North America*, p. 232.
77 Deloria, Jr., *Behind the Trail of Broken Treaties*, p.85.

CHAPTER 8

S. C. Gwynne and Terry Mort
The Savage Indians Got What They Deserved

And it had changed a timid, unaggressive people, the 'good savages' initially hailed by Europe, into fierce defenders of their independence, which had been violated by sailors come from afar whose sudden presence was neither welcome nor desired. The massacre at Navidad marked a turning point in the history of relations between Europeans and Americans. Columbus realized…the colonization of the new lands would henceforth be a long, hard struggle.

Gianni Granzotto, *Christopher Columbus*[1]

While Helen Hunt Jackson's belief in the superiority of white culture is subtle like the winds on the prairie, S. C. Gwynne's bursts forth like the miners who stampeded to and through the Black Hills in 1874 after newspapers reported Custer had found gold there. As a reader might conclude, if S. C. Gwynne's *Empire of the Summer Moon* was the only book about Indians he or she read, that person would certainly be exposed to the point of view that whites were civilized and, in Gwynne's own words, Indians, or at least the Comanches in the mid-19th century, were "Stone Age pagans."[2] *Empire* was a finalist for the Pulitzer Prize and received significant critical praise for its claimed attention to detail. It is an account of the demise of the Comanche nation of the Texas region in the mid-19th century framed by the story of the capture of a white woman named Cynthia Ann Parker by these Indians. It also chronicled the rise to positions of leadership in both Comanche and white society of her half-white, half-Comanche son Quanah Parker.

In commenting on historians such as Samuel Eliot Morison's writings, which set a precedent for writers like Gwynne, historian David E. Stannard noted: "It should come as no surprise to learn professional eminence is no bar against articulated racist absurdities." Stannard's comment was in response to Morison's describing indigenous people as "'…pagans expecting short and brutish lives, void of hope for any future'" and had also, similar to Gwynne, referred to Indians as "'Stone Age savages.'"³ For instance, during the course of this essay, and analyzing the view of the Comanche Indians presented by *Empire of the Summer Moon*, some cursory internet research disclosed an essay entitled "On Racist Discourse in S. C. Gwynne's *Empire of the Summer Moon*." In the article, confirming the viewpoint of this essay that, among other things, *Empire* contained "racist attitudes," the author stated: "The attitudes and beliefs that Gwynne espouses about the Comanche are almost certainly relics of the 19th century." The author noted how this "…racist discourse from the 19th century influenced Gwynne's writing." The author then concluded his article by noting:

> If Gwynne's book were just an isolated piece of poorly written popular history, then there wouldn't be too much of a story here. But S. C. Gwynne's *Empire of the Summer Moon* was actually a finalist for the Pulitzer Prize. This means that a large number of journalists not only did not see a problem with the racism of Gwynne's text, but they believed that this was the sort of historical work worth celebrating. If nothing else, Gwynne's book and its success is an instance of discourse inertia. We like to think that language and ideas are always changing, moving forward and ideally, improving. But the inertia of discourse suggests that backwards concepts from the past will remain with us unless there is a strong concerted effort to push against them.⁴

Although Gwynne's book is primarily about the Comanches of Quanah Parker's era, he managed to take an unnecessary detour to defame the enigmatic Crazy Horse, who, along with other Lakota Indians, is essentially the focal point of this current book. Gwynne continued to lose his way moving from his more or less general take on Comanche history to a specific point about Crazy Horse. Without explanation as to its relevance to Comanche history, Gwynne left that discussion to outline some of his assumptions about Lakota warrior Crazy Horse. In a few paragraphs, he managed to transport readers from the unknown to the absurd. Gwynne argued that Crazy Horse:

> …as an Oglala Sioux…was also a raider, and raiding meant certain very specific things, including the abuse of captives. His great popularity—a giant stone image of him is being carved from a mountain in South Dakota—may have a great deal to do with the fact very little is known about his early life. He is free to be the hero we want him to be.

Gwynne was just getting warmed up: "But certain facts are inescapable: American Indians were warlike by nature and they were warlike for centuries before Columbus stumbled upon them."⁵ That comments like this go unchallenged is astonishing, and that *Empire of the Summer Moon* was a finalist for the Pulitzer Prize is disconcerting. In his BIBLIOGRAPHY, Gwynne has what he called a BIBLIOGRAPHICAL NOTE, which he began with the comment: "As I hope will be apparent to the reader, much of this book was constructed using a large number of firsthand accounts from the era."⁶ The question to be pursued in that regard is, did he put the results of this research to place events in context? Likewise, where did he find firsthand accounts indicating Crazy Horse was an abuser of captives?

Nevertheless, challenging the notion that Crazy Horse was a torturer of his enemies does not require extensive original document research. In *Crazy Horse: The Life Behind the Legend*, Mike Sajna argued: "Torture, except in the form of self-torture in such activities as the sun dance, was not part of plains culture."[7] Likewise, in *Crazy Horse: The Lakota Warrior's Life and Legacy*, claimed to be gathered from information provided by descendants of the great Indian leader, William Matson relayed their thoughts: "The white man had introduced scalping early on to prove they had killed one of us so they could collect a bounty from their head men." Matson further explained their reasoning: "However, by taking a scalp, it also meant in our Lakota way that we would be taking a man's spirit so that he would not be whole on the other side. Crazy Horse wanted no part of that. He just wanted us to keep what had always been ours."[8] And in contradiction to the assertion made by Gwynne and others of many Indians' predisposition towards violence, Joseph M. Marshall clearly stated in *The Day the World Ended at Little Big Horn*: "…contrary to long-held beliefs, the Lakota male did not live for war."[9]

With Gwynne's explanation of source material in mind, at least in the case of Crazy Horse, he does not bother to mention who he thinks Crazy Horse was raiding. The Crow? White settlers? Indian writers unsurprisingly reject the notion Indian warfare was inherently "savage" before the arrival of the whites. Elizabeth Cook-Lynn argued the wars the Indians fought against the whites were unlike anything the Indians had participated in before and that made them: "…seem cruel and heartless and hate-filled and desperate, wars that took away their children and brought death to their communities in such numbers as they had never experienced before."[10] Likewise, Gwynne's portrayal of the Crazy Horse monument as a testament to Crazy Horse's "popularity" is a fundamental mischaracterization of at least how many or maybe even most of the Lakota and other Indian nations view that monstrosity. It's a tough sell to argue all Lakota relish the thought of a giant stone monument of Crazy Horse or of anyone or anything else being blasted out of the sacred Black Hills. Mike Sajna stated Crazy Horse: "…would have been horrified to see such a desecration of his sacred Black Hills."[11]

Gwynne also sidestepped discussing one of the most remarkable aspects of Crazy Horse's leadership, which was his lack of coercive authority over those who followed him but getting them to follow him anyway due to their unthinking savage ways. Lakota writer Joseph Marshall explained Crazy Horse "…rose to leadership because he actually led."[12] Marshall also explained: "The Lakota fighting man of old has long suffered from an image of flamboyance, aggressiveness, and mean spiritedness." He added: "Behind the warrior's accoutrements and habiliments was a man, a thinking, feeling, mortal man with strengths, weaknesses, hopes, dreams, and a family and a strong sense of commitment to cause and country."[13] This does not describe the ingredients for a society promoting leadership based on savagery and brutality as Gwynne claims. Particularly at the Little Big Horn, not only was effective combat leadership required, but also the logistical ability to provide the resources to feed, water, and generally sustain a large village, including a significant number of horses also requiring food and water.

Thus, of all the supercilious comments made by Gwynne regarding Crazy Horse, "He is free to be the hero we want him to be" ranks as one of the most bewildering. Crazy Horse was neither literally nor figuratively free to do much of anything during his life in the face of the encroachment of white settlers and eventual domination by these newcomers to the continent. Unfortunately, well over 125 years after his death, prominent writers such as Gwynne apparently have no compunction regarding portraying the beloved Lakota warrior as an unregenerate savage. Considering the great lengths historians have gone to uplift the reputations of Presidents such as "Sharp Knives" Jackson who allowed the mass killing of Indians in one way or another, Gwynne's remark is not only bewildering, but misguided.

But what indeed about the views of "Sharp Knives" Jackson? Historian Robert Remini supplied readers and students with a flattering snapshot of Jackson, the ultimate facilitator of the "Trail of Tears." Remini argued: "There is no question that in all his dealings with whites and Indians, slaves and free men of color, Jackson always had a deep concern for the 'poor and the sick,'" Remini added: "This regard for the less fortunate was a constant factor in his life and greatly influenced his presidency in later years."[14] The inquisitive reader will of course ponder how Remini came to this interesting conclusion. Does it presume there were no "poor and sick" on the tortuous walk to Oklahoma for those beleaguered souls forced out of their homelands in the Southeastern United States? Further, Jackson was said to be "thrilled" the first major piece of legislation passed during his Presidency was the Indian Removal Act.

Further, who is the "we" Gwynne is referring to in his laughable comment about Crazy Horse and his ability to be: "free to be the hero we want him to be?" As is the case with not knowing who the victims of Crazy Horse's torture were, we just don't know who the "we" was. Whites? Indians? Gwynne and other writers from oil-rich and Comanche-poor Texas? Since he did not explain who the "we" was, Gwynne apparently ascribed to the notion anyone who read his book would grasp that concept.

Nonetheless, the instance of Jackson and his facilitating the "Trail of Tears" provides another opening to discuss the "we" of Gwynne's Crazy Horse comment. To suggest a monolithic view of Indian history, even in the case of the horrendous "Trail of Tears," is to ignore the clear import of the historical record in that case and also highlights the divergence of views for years to come regarding how Indians were to be treated. For example, while Congress passed the Indian Removal Act, it was not done without passionate opposition. Remini presented a synopsis of a fiery speech launched in opposition to the bill by Senator Theodore Frelinghuysen of New Jersey. He passionately exclaimed (as summarized by Remini): "We have treated [the Indians] so badly in the past. Must we continue to do so in the future? We call them 'brothers' and yet we steal their land. They have yielded millions of acres to us 'and yet we crave more.'"[15] Nevertheless, even the vociferous protests of Frelinghuysen against the harsh treatment of Indians and also against Jackson's interference in congressional business could not prevent passage of the bill, which was signed into law on May 28, 1830.[16]

While it may not seem obvious to equate a 21st-century author to the stereotype of a grizzled frontier man, there seems to be the common denominator of Indian hating. The irony, of course, is that men living on the frontier were much more likely to have something in common with Indian men and often ended up taking Indian women as wives. Ultimately, the frontier-dwelling whites and the Indians developed a certain degree of respect for each other. Even Kit Carson, who was famous for Indian killing, argued against atrocities:

> His [Chivington's] men shot down squaws and blew the brains out of little innocent children. You call sich soldiers Christians, do ye? And Indians savages? What der yer 'spose our Heavenly Father, who made both them and us, thinks of these things? I tell you what, I don't like a hostile red skin any more than you do. And when they are hostile, I've fought 'em, as hard as any man. But I never yet drew a bead on a squaw or a papoose, and I despise the man who would. I've seen as much of 'em as any man livin', and I can't help but pity 'em, right or wrong. They once owned all this country yes, Plains and Mountains, buffalo and everything. But now they own next to nuthin' and will soon be gone [spelling as in source].[17]

Nevertheless, Gwynne's polemic portrayed the Comanches as virtually genetically predisposed to violence and displayed this propensity for violence without provocation of any kind. He implied the genocide of Indians was justified because they more or less had it coming. Hampton Sides, a well-known writer on Indian matters and the author of *Blood and Thunder*, his version of the life of Kit Carson quoted immediately above, had this praise for *Empire of the Summer Moon:*

> Man for man, the Comanches were the fiercest and most resourceful warriors in North America, and they held on to their domain with an almost otherworldly tenacity. In this sweeping work, S. C. Gwynne re-creates the Comanches' lost world with gusto and style—and without sentimentality. After reading *Empire of the Summer Moon*, you'll never think about Texas, or the Great Plains, in quite the same way again.[18]

Perhaps writers such as Gwynne, and apparently Hampton Sides, consider the theft of an entire continent as "…either inconsequential or unknown by the Christian intruders"[19] since they are quick to label any show of resistance by the Indians as the acts of "savages"; perhaps even the "wild m[e]n" of medieval legend and art. In this view of the world, the "'wild man'" or "'*wilder Mann*'" in German was: "…a hairy, naked, club-wielding child of nature who existed halfway between humanity and animality." The typical "wild man," or savage, lived: "…a life of bestial self-fulfillment, directed by instinct, and ignorant of God and morality."[20] Thus, if Indians were or are considered little more than beasts, or less than fully human, then chasing them off their land and/or killing them was of no more concern than chasing off or killing a pack of coyotes.

Is it unreasonable to consider Gwynne, Sides, and other writers were engaging in oversized instances of what psychologists term projection by consistently implying Crazy Horse, the Comanches, and other Indians were/are savages/pagans genetically programmed to relentlessly pursue and capture white victims to scalp? Consider this account of an event occurring during the Modoc War in California: "[Captain Ben] Wright's volunteers returned to Yreka sometime before November 29 [1852] with 'Indian scalps dangling from their rifles, hats, and the heads of their horses. Scores of scalps were thus flaunted.'" The exalting in the captured trophies of slaughter was not limited to military men as: "'…the enthusiastic crowd lifted [the soldiers] from their horses and bore them in triumph to…the saloons, and a grand scene of revelry commenced.'"[21] Has a clearer and more succinct description of what was undeniably a pagan ritual ever been written?

In the midst of his zeal to paint Quanah Parker as a "Stone Age pagan," Gwynne missed an opportunity to explore the dynamics of the situation involving Quanah's mother, Cynthia Ann Parker, in relation to both Comanche society and white society. In 1836, after Cynthia Ann was captured at nine years old by the Comanches in a raid where many of her relatives were killed, she was absorbed into Comanche communal life. In 1860, when Quanah was 12 years old, Cynthia and her daughter Prairie Flower were recaptured by whites. Although she never returned to live with her Comanche captors, she had to be constantly watched to ensure she did not try to leave white society. Much like the situation involving the detention of Indians at the Canton/Hiawatha Asylum for Insane Indians, there was no legal basis for holding Cynthia Ann against her will from returning to live with the Comanches.[22]

Thus, what Gwynne could have explored was the fact that Cynthia Ann was not the first female captive of the Indians who indicated her preference for their societies. In 1704, Eunice Williams, the daughter of clergyman of John Williams, was captured by the Caughnawagas during an attack on Deerfield, Massachusetts. After her mother drowned while trying to cross an icy river, Eunice was carried 300 miles by an Indian warrior. Although most of the other captives were eventually ransomed by the French, Eunice never came home. She was adopted by the Caughnawagas and married the warrior who saved her from drowning at the time of her capture. Although years later she visited her former neighbors from Deerfield, after living with the Caughnawagas for so long she was unable to make a social connection.[23]

Lakota writer Elizabeth Cook-Lynn's admonition to place events in their proper context is never more important than in the case of evaluating writing such as S. C. Gwynne's, or those praising his work. For example, when Sides claimed Gwynne wrote about the Comanches "without sentimentality," was he suggesting their demise was ultimately not worth feeling sad about? Fortunately, not all viewed the subjugation of the Comanches as not worth making a fuss about. Although Warren in *Buffalo Bill's America* did not specifically state the situations involved Comanches, he described various conflicts on the frontier being the fault of whites. He noted Captain John Bourke, a veteran of the Army's Apache campaigns, denounced "…reckless, idle, and 'dissolute' settlers for starting Indian wars." In Texas, officer James Parker wrote his mother: "'I would like to go on a scouting expedition after renegade Texans and hang up every scoundrel I caught' for the horse thieving, rapine, and murder they visited upon Indians."[24] Ironically, it seems that throughout Westward Expansion, those closest to Indians, such as these officers and men like Kit Carson, expressed the most sympathetic views of them. At a minimum, it was an indication white culture had moral problems of its own making.

Likewise, Gwynne in particular would be more credible if he noted the Comanches at some level understood Clausewitz's axiom that war was a "continuation of politics by other means." Instead, he described their realization of this brutal fact of life on the plains and acting on the concept that fighting gave them leverage in bargaining as "political terrorism."[25] S. C. Gwynne did not acknowledge that Wilcomb Washburn noted early in his comprehensive book *The Indian and the White Man*: "The unhappy fact remains that those Indian groups that reacted to European intrusion with the greatest hostility survived longest."[26] Similarly, Gwynne did not consider the Comanches (and other Indians) may have fought because they understood and continue to understand:

> ...the United States has sought to destroy Native American culture and nationalism, not only on the battlefields in past centuries, but also through its political and legal institutions from the time of the Declaration of Independence in 1776 up to the present, under a legal principle called the 'Doctrine of Discovery.'[27]

Throughout his discussion of the later years of Quanah Parker's life, Gwynne entertained no doubts whatsoever that Quanah Parker's choice to adopt the ways of white men was the correct one and that the demise of Comanche culture was not worth shedding a tear over. And, as Utley and Washburn noted in *Indian Wars*, surviving encounters with whites even as allies usually ended up being a pretty dicey affair. They explained that during the so-called French and Indian Wars: "Some tribes chose to fight with the French, and some with the English, but all the tribes fought for their own best interests as they saw them."[28] Regardless, even if Indian nations chose the "correct" side, their continued existence was in no way guaranteed.

What Gwynne also failed to explain in his haste to portray the Comanches as "Stone Age pagans" was that they had another, perhaps even singular purpose for displaying aggression—commerce. The Comanches, upon being introduced to the use of the horse, zeroed in on developing trade relationships with the ever-growing number of Europeans attempting to encroach on their territory. Gwynne, to his credit, managed to begrudgingly admit the Comanches were capable of some level of sophistication and noted: "In addition to their prowess in war, the Comanches were great merchants and traders."[29] Historian T. J. Stiles elaborated on the Comanche grasp of commerce as he described a situation where they: "…seized a strategic position on the grasslands between the Spanish, French, and English empires. Comanches traded slaves seized in raids and bison meat and hides in return for iron tools, firearms, and corn."[30]

Thus, while in this expert-addled society, it might seem rude to challenge such writing icons as Hampton Sides, or even Gwynne, it is imperative to question what Sides is talking about when he claimed the Comanches fought with "otherworldly tenacity." Perhaps Sides explained the Comanche attitude in this way rather than just state what he apparently really meant: the Comanches were demon-possessed savages who were so primitive they couldn't understand their obligation to give up their "domain" to the superior "Christian" culture steamrolling over them. Why not state the Comanches fought with intense desperation or similar words rather than hinting the Comanches were demonic, which Sides' colleague Gwynne essentially stated when he noted the killing of a child was: "…an act of almost demonic immorality by any modern standard."[31] Those type of comments exhibit a hypocrisy inhibiting, at a minimum, an understanding of the Indian point of view that they were defending their right to exist, even if their methods did not meet with Gwynne's approval. Gwynne seemed to be one of the few who required people from the past to be judged by a "modern standard."

For example, as explained, Irving claimed when judging Columbus' actions in taking 500 slaves back to Spain: "The customs of the times must be pleaded in his apology." Irving also argued: "…the practice had been sanctioned by the church itself."[32] As noted just above, Remini counseled his readers to "…take a long view of American history and remember that fear and mistrust at any time can and probably will lead to despicable crimes that disgrace the nation and blacken its history."[33] These are just two examples of rationalizing past horrors of whites by arguing the customs/situation of the times justified it. While Gwynne is certainly not responsible for what others wrote, it is difficult to conceive of someone with Gwynne's talents not being aware of this phenomenon and not respond to it more appropriately.

Thus, as should be apparent to readers of *Empire of the Summer Moon*, Gwynne went to great lengths to ensure they received his message of the unrelenting savagery of the Comanches during the 19th century. At one point he stated: "The preceding description [of a Comanche raid] may seem needlessly bloody in its details. But it typified Comanche raids in an era that was defined by such attacks. This was the actual, and often quite grim, reality of the frontier. There is no dressing it up."[34] In that regard, Gwynne did much to exemplify historian Patricia Nelson Limerick's observation that even when whites: "...were trespassers, westering Americans were hardly in their own eyes, criminals; rather, they were pioneers."[35] Likewise, like other authors noted just above excusing the behavior of whites, Gwynne claimed "Chivington was a product of his times."[36] Limerick astutely noted in the case of situations like the whites in combat with the Comanches: "The idea of [whites being] innocent victim[s] retains extraordinary power."[37] In essence, refusing to provide detailed descriptions of white brutality makes it easier to reinforce the myth that "Indians committed atrocities too."

Nevertheless, assigning motives to Gwynne's writing is only speculation. Gwynne, as in the case of Helen Hunt Jackson's refusal to describe the suffering of Indians on the "Trail of Tears," did not elaborate on the reason why he was in such a hurry to get past a description of the Sand Creek Massacre. He opened the door to examining the facts of this horror when he mentioned it, even though it was not directly related to the ostensible topic of his book, which was the Comanches. A somewhat similar phenomenon occurred after Elie Wiesel, the famous Nazi Hunter, reluctantly agreed to review documentation concerning the wholesale slaughter of Aché Indians in Paraguay in the 1960s and 1970s. Churchill stated there was: "...irrefutable evidence perhaps as much as 85 percent of the 25,000 of those Indian people still alive in 1959 were slaughtered by Paraguayan President Alfredo Stroessner's forces." Wiesel stated he: "'...read and reread these documents, these testimonies, with a mixed feeling of horror, disgust, and shame.'" Yet, it was argued by the consistently combative Churchill: "...for all his eloquence of outrage, [he] understated [in his writing] the reality almost entirely. Not only did he overlook the entire genocidal sweep of history in Ibero-America—a process of which the Aché slaughter is only the tiniest of recent parts—he managed to miss many contemporary examples as well."[38]

Gwynne is not the only contemporary author writing "without sentimentality" and promoting the myth Indians were/are savages who got what they deserved. In *Thieves' Road*, Terry Mort had a sharp retort for Red Cloud's famous line: "'They [the whites] made us many promises, more than I can remember, but they never kept but one; they promised to take our land, and they took it.'" Mort, similar to Bordewich's comment regarding Indian aggression in the Introduction, argued that Red Cloud's succinct analysis of Indian history: "'...conveniently ignores the fact that the Sioux got that same land in much the same way—and without payment or negotiation.'" Mort, not satisfied with that tart little bromide, continued: "The Sioux believed in the right of conquest even more fervently than the Americans who were now encroaching upon them." How Mort arrived at this conclusion is left unexplained. To put a *coup de grâce* on his saucy rationalization, and to once again reinforce the Indians were/are savages mantra, Mort opined: "They didn't need a treaty or international law to make it so; they only needed victories and enemy scalps."[39]

Mort either was unaware or unwilling to assess the propensity of *whites* for violence. In the aftermath of the Battle of the Little Big Horn, Texas newspapers joined the chorus of those seeking revenge. One newspaper boasted: "'Ten thousand Texans could be raised to go for the Indians who massacred Custar [sic].'" As an example of the ever-thoughtful writing of that era, the scribes continued: "'Killing a mess of Indians is the only recreation our frontier rangers want.'"[40] Likewise, while Comanche combat may or may not have been singularly ferocious prior to the mid-19th century, it is not a subject Gwynne chose to explore. There is no escaping the conclusion that Gwynne's single-minded effort to paint the Comanches as "Stone Age pagans" and with similar, corresponding adjectives is, at a minimum, suspect, for its failure to analyze this issue.

It is difficult to determine whether Mort came to his belief in the always present, simmering aggression of Plains Indians in the 19th Century through grinding research or rather through sojourns to Saturday afternoon matinees at his local theatre. In explanation, Slotkin noted the films: "*Geronimo, Northwest Mounted Police, Badlands of Dakota,* and *They Died with Their Boots On*" all promoted the theme of military officers' efforts to "*avoid* an Indian war." Slotkin further reported that for those officers to be successful in maintaining the peace: "…they have to fend off the Indians' savage propensity for bloodshed on the one hand, while on the other exposing and defeating the machinations of American politicians, land grabbers, and war profiteers [emphasis in original]."[41]

Mort also did not specify when during the history of Westward Expansion that he believed the Lakota engaged in their displays of genetically encoded violent and aggressive behavior. Therefore, it is a challenge to provide counters to Mort's claims. However, Mike Sajna indicated one source of conflict for the Plains Indians was the forced division of the vast buffalo herd into northern and southern herds by the California and Oregon migrant trails, and the destruction of grasslands and game along those trails in the mid-19th century. As the Lakota and other tribes were forced to seek new hunting grounds, there was a resultant increase in intertribal warfare.[42] Likewise, as noted previously, it is patently obvious United States forces were all too willing to engage in revenge-seeking behavior. In addition to those examples, it was explained: "…the retaliatory Blue Water Creek fight in Nebraska…between Colonel William S. Harney's troops and Brulé Sioux led by Little Thunder and Spotted Tail only portended a disastrous future for the Indians."[43]

In the larger picture, Mort's rationalization stylistically reinforced the choices of earlier historians, as in the case of the descriptions of the Pequot War, to ignore the assessments of John Underhill and other professional soldiers. Underhill noted the Indian allies of the English, the Narragansett and Mohegan Indian nations, admired the English's skill at fighting. However, these same Indian fighters cried: "'Mach it, mach it; that is, it is naught, it is naught, because it is too furious, and slays too many men.'" Underhill had previously stated in his professional military opinion these Indian allies might fight seven years and not kill seven men. He summarized his view of these Indians' attitude toward fighting by stating their wars were "'…more for pastime, than to conquer and subdue enemies.'" Another professional soldier named John Mason agreed with Underhill and quipped sarcastically their: "'…feeble manner [of fighting]…did hardly deserve the Name of Fighting.'" Of course, to include descriptions such as these in books did little to reinforce the "Indians committed atrocities too" conventional narrative so often favored by writers.

Quoting these observations is not intended to comprise an argument that the Woodland Indians, Plains Indians, or most other Indian nations consisted of pacifists. Rather, the point is to reinforce the observations of historian Francis Jennings, as noted by Richard Drinnon, that prior to the arrival of Europeans these Indians were not engaged in "…insane, unending war."[44] Mort's comment about the inherent aggressiveness of the "Sioux" also deflected attention from possible comparisons of the seizing of "Sioux" territory from other instances of Euro-American conquest. Drinnon also noted that at the conclusion of the Pequot War, the essence of John Mason's belief was that: "'Thus was God pleased to smite our enemies and to give us their land for an Inheritance.'" Drinnon wryly commented: "Thus God was a mercantilist…for on the economic level that is exactly what the Pequot War was about: the acquisition of Block Island and Connecticut."[45] Even Mort essentially acknowledged the "Indian Wars" of the Plains started when Custer led his expedition through the Black Hills in violation of the Ft. Laramie Treaty of 1868 unequivocally searching for gold, which: "…even a sight of one of those stones would bring a burning to the brain of white man, a craziness."[46] How the resulting conflicts with the Plains Indians differed from the Pequot Wars in their motivations was left for others to explain, but apparently little interest in doing so exists.

Sides' praise of Gwynne's work and Gwynne's work itself, with the use of the terms "otherworldly" and "demonic," reached further back in time for perspective than either of them seemed to suspect. Slotkin reported an instance in 1675 where some "'rude'" sailors visited Salmon Falls (near the location of the present town of Berwick, Maine, on the New Hampshire border). These men took the infant son of the Sokoki chief Squando and threw him in the river to see if there was any basis to the belief Indians knew how to swim instinctively. The child drowned, and in his understandable fury, Squando immediately joined forces with King Philip in his war against English colonists. Squando later went to Canada and upon his return led braves of the Sokoki tribe in a raid which resulted in the burning of Salmon Falls in 1690.

The actions of these sailors were certainly either sadistic or insane or both, but sadly also reflected the belief prevalent at that time Indians: "…enjoyed a special and more-than-human relationship with nature, which gave them a kind of demonic power." While it would be reprehensible to excuse the behavior of the sailors on that basis, it does provide some feeble basis for explaining it. Individual Indians such as Squanto were not considered real, individual beings, but symbolic "masks" of the demonic wilderness.[47] In an unrelated writing, Wilcomb Washburn's *The Indian and the White Man* contains an essay by Thomas Morton sympathetic to Indian beliefs, the following unusual passage notwithstanding. In writing that seems incongruent to his usually positive views of Indian culture expressed in the rest of the essay (unless he was engaging in satire), Thomas Morton claimed: "…the Powahs are ruled by the Devill, and then you may imagin what good rule is like to be amongst them [spelling as in source]."⁴⁸ It seems Sides and Gwynne held fast to this paradigm.

Fortunately, aspects of the true nature of Indians as human beings and a realistic perspective of the various Indian nations in history are eventually beginning to push through the concrete of myths like flowers that manage to peek through the frozen prairie turf after a harsh winter. James W. Loewen stated in the intriguing *Lies My Teacher Told Me*, again quoting Michael Dorris: "…historically, American Indians have been the most lied about subset of our population." While such comments may not initially seem encouraging, at least they contain a recognition of where the reporting of Indian history actually stands. Loewen also noted, like Frazier's indifference to Indian opinions, that standard history textbooks "…unapologetically present Native Americans through white eyes."⁴⁹

In many respects, after reading comments such as those by Jackson, Gwynne, Mort, and others, it is not only apparent there is little evidence in that writing of the context Elizabeth Cook-Lynn requested, but a complete lack of concern for even considering it. What is most troubling about Mort's comments justifying the aggressive push to take land used, occupied, or otherwise from the Plains Indians is that it negated the claims of white civilization without even realizing it. In and of itself that would be callous but understandable, except it removes all the justifications provided for making Indians farmers, "Christianizing" them, etc. The stark reality of the belief of the *superiority* of white culture is set forth by Robert Berkhofer:

> From the founding of the nation until recent times, and some would include today as well, United States policy makers placed two considerations above all others in the nation's relations with North Americans as Indians: the extinction of native title in favor of White exploitation of native lands and resources and the transformation of native lifestyles into copies of approved White models.⁵⁰

Gwynne and Mort were alike in their suggestions that somehow people on the frontier had the best concept for dealing with the "'Indian problem'" which was just hating them. Gwynne noted: "simple farmers imbued with a fierce Calvinist work ethic…fear[ed] God so much that there was no fear left over for anyone else." Gwynne did not care to reconcile these stalwart Christians' love of God with their loathsome attitudes toward Indians, and noted: "They hated Indians with a particular passion, considering them something less than fully human, and thus blessed with inalienable rights to absolutely nothing."⁵¹ Mort, like Gwynne, did not seem able to reconcile the revulsion many Indians experienced with the idea of converting them to Christianity and the antagonism to those Christian values displayed by many settlers on the frontier. Mort did note the failure of Christian missionaries to convert Indians was likely due to the white men who came before them who "'…stole our [the Indians'] goods and corrupted our women.'" Without pausing for breath, Mort then noted Western settlers: "…were correct when they predicted the failure of the Peace Policy…" supported by President Grant.

In Mort's reasoning, he surmised the rough-hewn characters on the frontier had a better understanding of human nature than the "…well-meaning eastern parsons and their allies in the Quakers."

Mort expressed surprise Grant would support the Peace Policy, and acknowledged many of the problems on the reservations were exacerbated by corruption in the Indian Bureau, the forerunner of the present-day Bureau of Indian Affairs (BIA).[52] Even after the supervision of the Bureau was placed under the Board of Indian Commissioners comprised of "Christian" businessmen and other church leaders, corrupt Indian agents managed to find their way into those lucrative positions on reservations.[53]

Yet, nowhere does Sir Arthur Conan Doyle's warning "there is nothing as deceptive as an obvious fact" apply more than when reviewing the analysis of history writers with agendas. There are many ways to say it with high-sounding phrases, but the simple reason the "Peace Policy" failed in the case of Plains Indians was because they correctly realized the whites wanted to permanently occupy the land they freely roamed. The deceptive argument that the Plains Indians and other bands never really "owned" or "occupied" land is simply a rationalization for outright theft. Once the whites occupied territory in places such as South Dakota, the Lakota had no choice but to stop roaming. Likewise, it is curious Gwynne, who wrote a biography of the life of Thomas "Stonewall" Jackson entitled *Rebel Yell*, would overlook the significance of the Civil War fought primarily in the Eastern United States as the first modern "total war." During this conflict, an entire population located primarily in the Confederate South, not just an army, was subjected to the fury of the invasion by the Union Army which possessed modern weapons of massive lethality. After the conclusion of this first modern, total war, the Plains Indians became the focus of the hurricane of destructive power known as the United States Army. Even though the size of the army was drastically reduced after the War Between the States, the lethality of the weapons employed wreaked havoc during combat. To add to the destructive power of the already powerful army came the Winchester repeating rifle and Richard Gatling's first machine gun, as well as the Hotchkiss rotating cannon. Considering the Comanches were vastly outnumbered to begin with, their complete subjugation was just a matter of time. They had before never encountered violence of such magnitude.

Writers of specific events of Indian history such as Mort, whose ostensible purpose was to write about Custer's 1874 Black Hills expedition in *Thieves' Road*, often propel themselves into intellectual quagmires when they veer off into generalizations about Indian history. (The opposite of what Gwynne did when he tried to make specific comments about Crazy Horse and the Sand Creek Massacre after his more or less general view of 19th-century Comanches.) Mort found his intellectual swamp when he argued that Indians were not the victims of genocide. In that regard, Mort argued that General Sherman's 1872 letter to General Sheridan did not say what it said. General Sherman commented building the Northern Pacific Railroad "'…will help to bring the Indian problem to a final solution.'" Mort explained the letter has a "chilling connotation" since the phrase "'final solution'" is related to the Jewish Holocaust. Mort explained: "…neither Sherman nor most of the professional soldiers favored literal extermination of the Indians." He also based his conclusion on the fact that General James Carleton issued written orders during one of the campaigns he led that "…women and children were not to be killed." Among his other arguments, Mort explained his interpretation in part using a "straw man" argument: "…those [Indians] who surrendered were not then shipped to a concentration camp and murdered."[54] Mort, for whatever reason, did not consider an alternative explanation regarding why there is no written evidence of an actual extermination policy—orders could have been given orally, Carleton notwithstanding.

Tasha Hubbard noted recent scholarship by Sarah Carter suggested the army's policy of buffalo extermination was part: "'...of a well-calculated policy to subdue Native Americans and drive them onto reserves.'" Carter also noted the army engaged in: "'...outfitting civilian hunting expeditions that slaughtered on a massive scale, and...encouraging troops to kill large numbers of buffalo using artillery and cannon.'" Hubbard also explained that David Smits' research indicated General Phil Sheridan had a practice of "...issuing kill orders without written documentation" because it was likely Sheridan: "'...deliberately refused to issue the written orders knowing that orally conveyed orders could be more easily concealed and more plausibly denied.'"[55] Astonishingly, Mort enthusiastically promoted his argument there could not have been genocide even while noting that in 1867, Sherman wrote a letter to then-General Grant stating: "'We are not going to let a few thriving, ragged Indians stop progress. We must act with vindictive earnestness against the Sioux *even to their extermination—men, women and children.*'" Thus, Mort did not explain how those military men did not favor "...literal extermination of the Indians." Mort explained this was the case since: "'Genocide' means extermination of an entire race of people, and no one seriously proposed that." Nevertheless, Mort himself noted: "Their nomadic culture was destroyed, but not the people who gave up their arms [emphasis added]."[56]

Regardless of this misshapen logic, many modern thinkers indicated Mort's argument that destruction of a culture without killing all the people is not genocide misses the mark. A broader definition was provided by Polish jurist Raphael Lemkin in 1944, who stated genocide was a course of action: "'...aiming at the destruction of the essential foundations of the life of national groups...'" and involves: "'...disintegration of the political and social institutions, of culture, language, national feelings, religion, and the economic existence of [the] groups." Lemkin added: "Genocide has two phases: one, destruction of the national pattern of the oppressed group; the other, the imposition of the national pattern of the oppressor."[57] Only intellectual confusion would result in concluding this definition could not be applied retroactively to the situation involving actions against Indians in 19th-century America and beyond.

Mort's statement regarding Indians "...not being shipped to a concentration camp and murdered" is another "straw man" argument, for at least two reasons. First, if reservations are the models for Hitler's concentration camps, as some Indians (and others) claim,[58] there are multiple instances of murders there. A few examples of those murders, of both individuals and groups, are the cases of Crazy Horse, Sitting Bull, and "Big Foot" and his followers at the Wounded Knee Massacre. Even if Mort did not agree with that conclusion, intellectual honesty required at least acknowledgment of this circumstance. The second problem with Mort's claim is the more insidious because it is the more subtle. Essentially, Mort's argument is: since what happened to Indians did not follow the precise pattern of wickedness employed by the Nazis against Jewish people and others, it could not be genocide. Lemkin's definition of genocide highlighted in the preceding paragraph is eminently sensible. The essays from *Colonial Genocide in Indigenous North America* liberally cited in this book are an invaluable reference source for information pertaining to the subject of genocide.

Likewise, unless Mort and others like him have no consciences, and they surely must, they must be uneasy when learning of arguments indicating the Lakota had occupancy of the Black Hills long before the mid-19th century. This assumes, of course, there was any interest in learning of them at all. Lakota Rick Two Dogs noted that the Lakota were indeed a "wandering people" but just because the Europeans first met them in Minnesota does not mean they originated there. Two Dogs, in explaining a central tenet of the Lakota Creation Story, stated: "'Our belief is that we began at the Black Hills thousands of years ago.'"[59]

Reinforcing tenets of Lakota theology, others argued: "As early as the 1800s, the Lakotas began to attach a special significance to the Black Hills—a sacred land from which the first people and buffalo emerged."[60] In response to skeptics who argue at the earliest, the Lakota "discovered" the Black Hills in 1775, Lakota Elders explain there is a fundamental misunderstanding as to American Horse's 1775 winter count. They believe this historical record does not necessarily indicate the "first" discovery of the Black Hills. Frank Fools Crow believed the "Sioux" easily could have come across the Black Hills long before that particular date. He recalled as a boy Elders discussing groups of Lakota making journeys as far west as the Rocky Mountains well before the rest of the nation moved westward.[61] Jeffrey Ostler in *The Lakotas and the Black Hills*, the source of the preceding few facts, believes even if the Black Hills were established as holy ground in the 18th century, as Stephen Big Eagle argued: "'The state has no power, no right, to say it is not permissible for us to have done that.'"[62]

Likewise, rather than speculate on whether Crazy Horse is "…free to be the hero we want him to be," if Gwynne read Elizabeth "Libbie" Custer's *Boots and Saddles,* he would realize there is no doubt she intended that status for her husband General George A. Custer. It might be more accurate to state he was the hero *Libbie* wanted him to be. As Jane Stewart noted in her introduction to *Boots and Saddles,* students of Custer's life believed there: "…would be nothing new on the battle [of Little Big Horn] as long as Mrs. Custer lived." In that regard, Libbie outlived all but one of the officers, Charles A. Varnum, who served in the Little Big Horn Campaign. Stewart concluded: "…George Custer's death and defeat had given him a reputation that no victory could have equaled, and his widow had preserved that reputation to the end." It was also noted Libbie would intervene directly to prevent any negative comments about Custer being made public. Stewart surmised Mrs. Custer: "…literally dedicated herself to keeping the memory of George A. Custer shining and untarnished."[63] At least for many years, George A. Custer was the "…hero we want him to be."

Contrary to Gwynne and Mort's constant direct or indirect aspersions of Indian savagery, even modest searching reveals further evidence of the humanness of Indian leaders. One notable example can be found in the circumstances of Red Cloud's selection at a feast to be "first among equals" in the autumn of 1865. Red Cloud attained this status not through a coup or other violence, but through the decision of the Tezi Tanka, or "big bellies," who were wise leaders who would guide their people through what all believed was the inevitable war with whites. As possible evidence of the all-too-human trait of jealousy found to some degree in most people, it is believed Sitting Bull did not attend this feast due to his envy of Red Cloud's rising prominence. In any event, Sitting Bull's participation was not a factor in the fights the Lakota had with whites over the Powder River Country.[64]

Thus, when reading Mort's book, those concerned about revisionist history can be reassured all is not lost in the realm of not disturbing "conventional" wisdom. In *Thieves' Road*, Mort used some form of the word "hostile" at least 33 times when describing Indians living in or near the Black Hills, using the term even more frequently than Helen Hunt Jackson. This number does not include his use of the words "fierce," "troublesome," "warlike" and "undisciplined savages." Also, like Jackson, Mort seemed to believe the concept of Manifest Destiny had some sort of magical power of its own and relieved the whites of the responsibility for their choices. In the specific case of Custer's 1874 Black Hills Expedition, the subsequent trespassing of gold seekers, and the events that followed, Mort argued, "…the story has the inevitability of a tragedy,"[65] as if the actions of those involved did not require the conscious choice of the participants. As if to anticipate this analysis, Mort claimed, in a style similar to Gwynne's: "Even though they had plenty of excuses to go on the warpath, they didn't need them, it was in their blood." To ensure his point is not misunderstood, he continued: "The Sioux and their allies, therefore, were not blameless victims. Far from it, their culture cried out for war and celebrated the successful warrior."[66]

The counter-argument to this self-serving rationalization arises from an unexpected source—*Great White Fathers* by John Taliaferro, a narrative about the creation of Mount Rushmore. Although published in 2002, 13 years before Mort's *Thieves' Road*, it is almost as if Taliaferro was anticipating Mort's arguments about how a large part of the blame for the so-called "Indian Wars" falls on the Indians involved. Taliaferro noted that the Ft. Laramie Treaty of 1868 prohibited whites from settling or even passing through the Great Sioux Reservation, which was expressly: "'…set apart for the absolute and undisturbed use and occupation of the Indians herein named.'" Taliaferro acknowledged the existence of what he termed "Loophole" language in the treaty, which permitted traveling on or through the Reservation by: "'…officers, agents, and employees of the Government as may be authorized…in discharge of duties.'" Nonetheless, Taliaferro disputed Custer had the right to parade through the Sioux Reservation and argued: "…this provision did not begin to justify Custer's agenda." Taliaferro further noted: "…while surveyors and scientists were arguably a benign presence, the inclusion of miners in the caravan would prove an enormous threat to Indian life and liberty."[67]

Mort's claim of the inherent propensity of Indians toward violence would be more credible if he would at least acknowledge the same pattern of events that occurred in the Black Hills after Custer's 1874 Black Hills Expedition also occurred after the discovery of gold on the Nez Perce Reservation in the Pacific Northwest in 1860. The events surrounding the discovery of "'…the yellow metal which makes Wasichus crazy'"[68] in the Black Hills replicated the events that ultimately resulted in the subsequent war with the Nez Perce in 1877. Just like the situation with the Ft. Laramie Treaty of 1868, by 1861 thousands of miners flocked to the eastern section of the Nez Perce Reservation and outnumbered the population of the entire tribe. And just like the attitude of the Grant Administration a few years later regarding the Black Hills, B. F. Kendall, Superintendent of Indian Affairs for the Washington territory in 1862 whined: "'To attempt to restrain miners would be, to my mind, like attempting to restrain the whirlwind.'"[69]

What is also missing from Mort's proclamation of the inherent savagery of the Lakota is even a flicker of recognition that violence was inculcated in the white culture of the fledgling United States, particularly in Virginia, in the beginning of the 17th century. The colony's official governing council included not only those from the ranks of the highly educated gentry, but: "…tough, experienced soldiers of fortune who had volunteered for, or were drawn into, this open-ended project in search of employment, adventure, and ultimately perhaps exotic riches." Based on the inclination of these mercenaries to be "'headstrong, giddy, and insubordinate,'" it is not surprising that there was conflict among the English themselves, but "…that the settlement they led survived at all." In one instance, a Captain George Kendall was convicted of treason after being accused of planning to desert the colony and/or defecting to the Spanish. Six months after his arrival in Virginia he was executed by gunshot after a "drumhead tribunal" court martial.[70]

It is not surprising Elizabeth Cook-Lynn had a sophisticated response to the type of writing promoted by the likes of S. C. Gwynne and Terry Mort, who failed to take the Indian viewpoint into account. She explained:

> Scholarly tradition in the United States, which this definition [of indigeneity] engages, has become a provider and promoter of the colonizer's status toward indigenous peoples instead of providing recognition of indigeneity as a category of analysis. It has created a body of scholarship unwilling to sacrifice its central place in imperialistic power over the indigene. Instead of eliciting rebuke of its past and discipline for its future, American scholarship generally offers further glorification of expansionism and aggression by a settler-immigrant population.[71]

ENDNOTES

1. Granzotto, *Christopher Columbus*, pp. 207-208.
2. Gwynne, *Empire of the Summer Moon*, p. 319.
3. Stannard, *American Holocaust*, p. 13. Curiously enough, Stannard suggested Bernard Bailyn displayed characteristics of people who belong in this category. Ibid, p. 13.
4. Cober, "On Racist Discourse in S. C. Gwynne's *Empire of the Summer Moon.*"
5. Gwynne, *Empire of the Summer Moon*, p. 44.
6. Ibid., p. 343.
7. Mike Sajna, *Crazy Horse: The Life Behind the Legend* (Hoboken, New Jersey: John Wiley & Sons, 2000), p. 163.
8. Matson, *Crazy Horse: The Lakota Warrior's Life and Legacy*, p. 86. However, Thomas Powers claimed: "About 1855 or 1856 the young man [Crazy Horse], then still known as His Horse in Sight, took part in a fight with Arapahos, returning with two scalps." Powers, *The Killing of Crazy Horse*, p. 7. Nevertheless, Powers clarified his point and noted: "Crazy Horse as a grown man did not take scalps." p. 30.
9. Marshall, *The Day the World Ended at the Little Big Horn*, p. 79.
10. Harjo and Bird, Eds., Elizabeth Cook-Lynn, "Aurelia" *Reinventing the Indian's Language*, p. 222.
11. Sajna, *Crazy Horse: The Life Behind the Legend*, p. ix.
12. Marshall, *The Journey of Crazy Horse*, p. 287.
13. Ibid., pp. 269-270.
14. Remini, *Andrew Jackson and his Indian Wars*, p. 175.
15. Ibid., p. 234.
16. Ibid., p. 237.
17. Sides, *Blood and Thunder*, p. 471.
18. Gwynne, *Empire of the Summer Moon*, Endorsement of Hampton Sides.
19. Cook-Lynn, *Anti-Indianism in Modern America*, p. 47.
20. Berkhofer, *The White Man's Indian*, p. 13.
21. Woolford, Benvenuto, and Hinton, Eds. Benjamin Madley, "California and Oregon's Modoc Indians: How Indigenous Resistance Camouflages Genocide in Colonial Histories." *Colonial Genocide in Indigenous North America*, p. 104. In addition to the other instances of unbridled savagery exhibited by whites throughout the book, Powers noted an instance where scout Baptiste Pourier "'...scalped one of the redskins alive.'" A witness named Valentine McGillycuddy noted: "I well remember him—that bright red hair and beard of his standing on end, he dancing on the hill, swinging the scalp around his head, and howling.'" Powers, *The Killing of Crazy Horse*, p. 211.
22. Gwynne, *Empire of the Summer Moon*, pp. 181-184.
23. Demos, *The Unredeemed Captive*, *passim*.
24. Warren, *Buffalo Bill's America*, p. 202.
25. Gwynne, *Empire of the Summer Moon*, p. 202.

26　Washburn, *The Indian and the White Man*, p. 2.
27　Gonzalez, Mario and Cook-Lynn, Elizabeth, *The Politics of Hallowed Ground*, p. xi.
28　Utley and Washburn, *Indian Wars*, p. 59.
29　Gwynne, *Empire of the Summer Moon*, p. 60.
30　Stiles, *Custer's Trials*, p. 269.
31　Gwynne, *Empire of the Summer Moon*, p. 43
32　Irving, *The Life and Voyages of Christopher Columbus*, p. 351.
33　Remini, *Andrew Jackson and His Indian Wars*, p. viii.
34　Gwynne, *Empire of the Summer Moon*, p. 19.
35　Limerick, *The Legacy of Conquest*, p. 36.
36　Gwynne, *Empire of the Summer Moon*, p. 220. Gwynne's obtuse take on Chivington and the Sand Creek Massacre was in keeping with the jingoistic nature of his writing. While it was noted previously he stated: "There is little point in describing in detail what happened," Ibid., p. 220, he does in fact report a "detail": "Children were shot, point blank, babies were bayoneted." He claimed the: "Saddest of all was the sight of the Indians huddling around a large American flag." p. 221. He left unexplained why this was "sad(der)" than a baby being ripped from a pregnant Indian lady's womb or the sadistic breaking of both arms of the wounded Indian lady described in the Chivington chapter of this book. Halaas and Masich, *Halfbreed*, p. 145-146.
37　Limerick, *The Legacy of Conquest*, p. 37.
38　Ward Churchill, "Genocide in the Americas: Landmarks from 'Latin' America Since 1492," *Since Predator Came*, pp. 53-54. Part of Wiesel's dilemma may have stemmed from him being a: "… proponent of the 'uniqueness of the Jewish experience of genocide.'" Ibid., p. 53.
39　Terry Mort, *Thieves' Road: The Black Hills Betrayal and Custer's Path to Little Big Horn* (New York: Prometheus Books, 2015), pp. 120-121.
40　Paul L. Hedren, Ed., Brian Dippie, "Southern Response to Custer's Last Stand," *The Great Sioux War: The Best from Montana The Magazine of Western History* (Helena, Montana: Montana Historical Society Press, 1991), p. 249.
41　Slotkin, *Gunfighter Nation*, p. 288.
42　Sajna, *Crazy Horse: The Life Behind the Legend*, p. 73.
43　Paul Hedren, Ed., *The Great Sioux War* (Helena, Montana: Montana Historical Society distributed by the University of Nebraska Press, 1991), pp. 2-3.
44　Drinnon, *Facing West*, p. 43 including footnote at the bottom of the page.
45　Ibid., p. 46.
46　Mari Sandoz, *Crazy Horse: The Strange Man of the Oglalas* (Lincoln, Nebraska: University of Nebraska Press, 1942), p. 287.
47　Slotkin, Richard, *Regeneration through Violence*, pp. 118-119.
48　Washburn, Ed., "Thomas Morton of Merrymount (In His Own Eyes)" *The Indian and the White Man*, p. 39.
49　Loewen, *Lies My Teacher Told Me*, p. 93.
50　Berkhofer, *The White Man's Indian*, p. 135.

51 Gwynne, *Empire of the Summer Moon*, p. 20.
52 Mort, *Thieves' Road*, p. 127.
53 Ibid., p. 128.
54 Ibid., pp. 131-132.
55 Woolford, Benvenuto, Hinton, Eds., Tasha Hubbard, "Buffalo Genocide in Nineteenth Century North America," *Colonial Genocide in Indigenous North America*, p. 295.
56 Mort, *Thieves' Road*, pp. 131-132. Newspapers were not shy about advocating genocide. One editorial in the *California Alta* shrieked: "'Either the whole Indian race in California must be exterminated or they must be brought together, organized into a community, made to support themselves by their own labor, and be elevated above the degraded position they now occupy.'" Sides, *Blood and Thunder*, p. 402. There were Army officers such as Lieutenant Fred Calhoun who simply stated: "…I wanted to see them completely crushed, if not exterminated." Powers, *The Killing of Crazy Horse*, p.259.
57 Woolford, Benvenuto, Hinton, Eds., Christopher Powell and Julia Peristerakis, "Genocide in Canada: A Relational View," *Colonial Genocide in Indigenous North America*, pp. 71-72.
58 Simon Moya-Smith, "Ugly Precursor to Auschwitz: Hitler said to have Been Inspired by U.S. Indian Reservation System," *Indian Country Today*, August 27, 2017. Separately, historian David Stannard also noted, citing John Toland: "…the Führer from time to time expressed admiration for the 'efficiency' of the American genocide campaign against the Indians, viewing it as a forerunner for his own plans and programs." Stannard, *American Holocaust*, p. 153. Vicki Rozema stated some historians considered the individual instance of the "Trail of Tears" as genocide. Rozema, *Voices from the Trail of Tears*, p. 10.
59 Ostler, *The Lakotas and the Black Hills*, pp. 183-184.
60 Joseph Agonito, *Lakota Portraits—Lives of the Legendary Plains People* (Guilford, Connecticut: Globe Pequot Press, 2011), p. 11.
61 Ostler, *The Lakotas and the Black Hills*, pp. 9-10.
62 Ibid., p. 184.
63 Custer, *Boots and Saddles*, pp. xxii-xxiii.
64 Drury and Clavin, *The Heart of Everything That Is*, p. 233.
65 Mort, *Thieves' Road*, p. 302.
66 Ibid., p. 299.
67 John Taliaferro, *Great White Fathers: The True Story of Gutzon Borglum and His Obsessive Quest to Create the Mount Rushmore National Monument* (Cambridge, Massachusetts: Perseus Books Group, 2002), p. 24.
68 Mort, *Thieves' Road*, p. 262. Elaborating on what Niehardt wrote in *Black Elk Speaks*: "Pahuska had found there much of the yellow metal that makes the Wasichus crazy…Our people knew there was yellow metal in little chunks up there; but they did not bother with it, because it was not good for anything." p. 79.
69 Helen Addison Howard, *Saga of Chief Joseph*, p. 67.
70 Bailyn, *The Barbarous Years*, p. 46.
71 Cook-Lynn, *A Separate Country*, pp. 3-4.

CHAPTER 9

From Crazy Horse to the Crazy Horse Monument
Who's Kidding Whom?

> They made us many promises, more than I can remember but they never kept but one; they promised to take our land, and they took it.
>
> Red Cloud, Oglala Lakota
Terry Mort, Thieves Road [1]

Black Buffalo Woman was later in her life a central player in one of the most dramatic episodes of Crazy Horse's life, where he was shot in the face by her jealous husband. She was described at the time of her ceremonial coming out feast as "…a beautiful, willowy girl with long, glistening black hair."[2] And although Crazy Horse as a young man earned a reputation as a superb warrior, his family was not considered influential enough to gain the favor of Black Buffalo Woman's family and therefore was not able to obtain approval for him to marry her. Nonetheless, Crazy Horse was not only considered a gifted fighting man but was also deemed capable enough of a leader to be chosen as a "Shirt Wearer." The qualifications of a "Shirt Wearer" were strict:

> To wear the shirts you must be men above all others. You must help others before you think of yourselves. Help the widows and those who have little to wear and to eat and have no one to help them or speak for them. Do not look down on others or see those who look down on you and do not let anger guide your mind or your heart. Be generous, be wise, and show fortitude so that people can follow what you do and then what you say. Above all, have courage and be the first to charge the enemy, for it is better to lie a warrior naked in death than to be wrapped up well with a heart of water inside.[3]

Although Crazy Horse survived being shot in the face, he was removed from his position as a "Shirt Wearer" by the Elders who considered Crazy Horse's pursuit of Black Buffalo Woman selfishly putting his needs before the good of the tribe as a whole. (One source indicated Crazy Horse made this decision voluntarily.)[4]

During his life, Crazy Horse was revered by the Lakota people, at least by those who were not jealous of his charisma. Nevertheless, it is difficult to point out any other single episode in the United States government's dealing with Indians as dishonorable as the circumstances leading up to the senseless murder of this unique man. Sometime after he and his people arrived at Ft. Robinson in northwest Nebraska in May 1877, and prior to his actual killing in September 1877, it is believed a meeting occurred with the likes of General George "Three Stars" Crook, interpreter Frank Grouard, Baptiste Pourier, Red Cloud, American Horse, Lieutenant William Philo Clark, and others. Among the odd happenings of this group, when interpreting Crazy Horse's response when asked if he would fight the Nez Perce, Grouard stated Crazy Horse would fight until no white man was left. It is believed what Crazy Horse actually said is that he would fight until no Nez Perce was left. To add to the sordidness of the whole sleazy affair, Lieutenant Clark offered $300 and a horse to whoever would carry out Crazy Horse's murder.[5] Clearly, the army officers at Ft. Robinson where Crazy Horse was living, at least as represented by this group, had no intentions of dealing with Crazy Horse as a respected and worthy adversary.

Much like Cornplanter of the Senecas has not been left in peace after his death, the quest to capture Crazy Horse's legacy stirs up strong emotions and unusual reactions. It seems to draw out the arrogance of whites as well. Larry McMurtry, who, as noted in the Introduction, won a Pulitzer Prize for his novel *Lonesome Dove*, tried his hand at non-fiction with a book he simply entitled *Crazy Horse*. In this odd book, he noted: "Ian Frazier, in his fine book *Great Plains*, reports correctly that the Crazy Horse Monument is one of the few places on the Great Plains where one will see a lot of Indians smiling."[6]

Sajna, whose comment in the previous chapter contradicts this claim, indicating Crazy Horse would be "horrified" at the prospect of this carving out of the Sacred Black Hills, is not the only researcher who questioned the appropriateness of the Crazy Horse Monument. Elizabeth Cook-Lynn called the work a "blasted monstrosity" and viewed it as "…emblematic of what is so wrong about this place." She added the very idea of: "The so-called sculpture represents a failure to honor the values of Crazy Horse, who refused to have his picture taken during his lifetime because he believed such likenesses could kill the human spirit." She noted Mount Rushmore, the Crazy Horse Monument, and the road connecting them in western South Dakota is known as the "desecration tour."[7]

Further, McMurtry did not disclose whether he is basing his opinion about smiling Indians on personal observation, or solely on what he read in Frazier's book. McMurtry further stated that neither "'writers'" nor "'historians'": "…have convinced many readers—that they have an accurate grip on the deeds—*much less on the soul*, of the Sioux warrior we call Crazy Horse [emphasis added]."[8] McMurtry did not enlighten readers on how the process for getting a "grip" on the soul of Crazy Horse works, which he slyly implied he knows.

Given Crazy Horse's rejection of white culture, there is an unsettling aspect to the claim the Crazy Horse monument grounds is a place where it is possible to see "Indians smiling." A Lakota Indian man explained that when his son worked for the organization, his son and the other youths were told: "…not to speak about the raw truth as it pertains to history."[9] McMurtry's comment is a case study in why Vine Deloria, Jr., as stated throughout this book, advised repeatedly to ask Indians for their opinions instead of just taking what other white people said for granted. The Crazy Horse monument is nothing more than Buffalo Bill's Wild West carved out of stone.

Thus, McMurtry does not indicate any Indian ancestry or extensive study to elaborate on how he obtained such expertise in understanding Crazy Horse's "soul." The background for his confidence in grasping the essence of the long-dead man about whom little has been written in original-type sources is left to speculation. And, as silly as McMurtry's comments might strike a reader, as expected, Deloria, Jr., would not consider them unique in the world of whites writing about Indian history or culture. He noted: "Those whites who dare not claim Indian blood have an asset of their own. They *understand* Indians." Deloria, Jr., continued: "Understanding Indians is not an esoteric art. All it takes is a trip through Arizona or New Mexico, watching a documentary on TV, having known *one* in the service, or having read a popular book on *them*." Deloria, Jr., concluded: "There appears to be some secret osmosis about Indian people by which they can magically and instantaneously communicate complete knowledge about themselves to those interested whites. Rarely is physical contact required." And, in his *coup de grâce*, Deloria, Jr., explained: "Anyone and everyone who knows an Indian or who is *interested* immediately and thoroughly understands them [emphasis in original]."[10]

There is a more problematic aspect to McMurtry's hint that he (and perhaps he alone, although he may not be aware of Kevin Hancock's similar musings in a book written after his, to be explained at length in the following chapter) has somehow captured the "soul" of Crazy Horse than just his arrogance. It's not just plain silly to make such a baseless claim; it's simply another way of labeling this revered Indian leader as a "noble savage" and a back-door way of promoting white superiority over Indians. It is an attitude that suggests Indian accomplishments must be due to solely supernatural intervention, otherwise, how could savages best their betters? After all, why should whites attribute military failures such as the Fetterman Fight of 1866 and the resounding defeat of Custer at the Little Big Horn in 1876 to such human traits as superior Indian tactics, morale, etc. when these failings can be attributed to supernatural intervention?

This observation is not meant to deny Crazy Horse's penchant for pursuing spiritual matters, but rather to question whether historians have done *anything* to avoid acknowledging even the *possibility* Indians *may* have been or are the intellectual equals of whites. It's an attitude that has been long standing, has carried into the 20th century, and has infected recent foreign policy decisions. During the Vietnam War in 1965, General Maxwell Taylor claimed the Viet Cong had the "'recuperative power of the phoenix.'"[11] This is certainly a more palatable explanation for the inability of United States and South Vietnamese forces to defeat the Viet Cong and North Vietnamese Army than admitting the whole premise of the Vietnam War was based on abysmal policy choices and deceiving the American public about the possibility of "success."

Nonetheless, McMurtry's efforts at locating Crazy Horse's soul might have been better spent trying to locate the Great Plains on a world map. He asserted the best description of a gathering of Plains Indians in 1851 was found in: "…Wilfred Thesinger's account of a similar [Zulu] gathering in Adis Ababa in 1916." He described the: "…simple fighting men… [as wearing] lion's mane headdresses, brilliant velvet cloaks stiff with silver and golden ornaments, long silk robes in many colors and great curved swords, etc."[12] This writing is so far off base, it would actually seem necessary to advise McMurtry that Adis Ababa is in Africa. While McMurtry is be commended for suggesting the "Ghost Dance" had Christian overtones, to pass a description of an African tribe off as representative of Plains warriors as part of a biography of Crazy Horse is simply irresponsible. He had to look no further than Libbie Custer's *Boots and Saddles* to find a description of a group of Plains Indian warriors, in this instance led by Iron Horse:

> The war bonnets, shields, and necklaces of bear's claws are all handed down from faraway grandfathers, and only aired on grand occasions. Every available bit of metal that could catch light reflected and shone in the morning sun. The belts were covered with brass nails, shining with many an hour's polishing. They had many weapons, all kept in a brilliant and glistening state.[13]

McMurtry's use of an African gathering to substitute for describing an actual Indian gathering either consciously or unconsciously contains the suggestion serious historians of Indians such as Slotkin, Limerick, and more importantly Mary Crow Dog, try to refute: the experiences of all minorities are the same throughout the history of the United States.

Further, intertwined with describing Indian leaders as mystical creatures is the concept of blaming God or God's wrath for military failures, which has a long, elaborate history in the United States even before the advent of the Plains Wars. In Massachusetts in May 1724, Captain John Lovewell was killed along with 33 out of 47 men from his company after being ambushed by Indian warriors. Reverend Thomas Symmes of Bradford claimed the reason: "'...so many brave men should descend into battle and perish'" was not due to the errors in tactics of a company grade officer but because of the: "...general backsliding and irreverence of New Englanders which had aroused the wrath of a vengeful God."[14] At least by the time the United States became ensconced in the madness of the Vietnam War, God could have been blamed for the mistakes of higher-ranking individuals.

Apparently, McMurtry, in his quest to put himself at the forefront of white people who "understand" the mysterious Lakota leader, overlooked Mari Sandoz's intriguing book *Crazy Horse: The Strange Man of the Oglalas*. In her research on the life of this enigmatic man, Sandoz amassed 5,000 three-by-five index cards that she neatly filed and cross-referenced in her kitchen at the time she was researching her book.[15] It was claimed that during the process of writing the book "The shadow of Crazy Horse fell on Mari Sandoz"[16] just as many claimed it fell on Black Elk. While she received harsh criticism from some critics, others believe: "...she had created an almost perfect work of biographical art."[17] While indeed there appears to be a suggestion Sandoz received otherworldly assistance in generating her book, the use of the thousands of index cards indicates a significant attempt at amassing corporeal information about the man.

Similarly, when an accurate accounting of Crazy Horse's life contains a multitude of significant achievements, it is baffling when writers feel compelled to embellish his record of superb accomplishments. In *Crazy Horse: The Lakota Warrior's Life and Legacy*, William B. Matson possibly mistakenly claims in the *very first paragraph of the foreword* that: "Crazy Horse also led his people in victories over…Captain William Fetterman at the Fetterman Fight at Fort Phil Kearney."[18] While many believe Crazy Horse played an integral role in this battle by drawing the soldiers out of the fort and into the ambush, the overall strategy in the battle belonged to Red Cloud. While it might seem like a minor semantic point, it is not. Likewise, that studying the life of Crazy Horse points to his enigmatic nature is a massive understatement—historian Joe Jackson argued even Crazy Horse's role as a leader of the decoy group is "'uncorroborated.'"[19] Nevertheless, it appears credible to say Crazy Horse was *a* leader in the battle, believed to be if not his first against white soldiers, then one of the first, but not the overall leader of the warriors at that time. To do otherwise is again to suggest his successes in battle were due to almost solely to otherworldly powers. If he was the leader of the overall operation as a young man, it suggests he would not be subject to the growth and development experienced by every other combat leader of worth throughout history regardless of race or nationality.

In his well-done book on Crazy Horse, *Crazy Horse, The Life Behind the Legend*, Mike Sajna provided an interesting perspective on Crazy Horse's combat leadership role. Sajna also indicated Crazy Horse was the primary leader of the Lakota at the Fetterman Fight but hedged his bets by indicating the precise time Crazy Horse completed his evolution into overall combat leader of the Lakota is difficult to state with certainty. Sajna also noted that if Crazy Horse was the overall leader of the Oglala forces at the Fetterman Fight, it is unlikely he would have been part of the decoy force that drew the soldiers out of the fort and into the ambush. Sajna also reiterated a common description of the Lakota fighting style as "independent," emphasizing that following a particular Lakota leader was the result of the individual warrior's choice as opposed to the coercion of that leader. Sajna explained that it was difficult for whites to believe Indians could achieve victory, as they did at the Little Big Horn, had they not possessed "…overwhelming numbers and almost superhuman abilities."[20] To round out the discussion about Crazy Horse's role in the Fetterman Fight, in his quintessentially recognizable book about Sitting Bull, *The Lance and the Shield*, Robert Utley stated: "Leading the decoy party was a brooding, young mystical young Oglala warrior named Crazy Horse."[21]

The subtle, not so subtle, and persistent presentation of the "Noble Savage" narrative/myth hugs far too many descriptions of individual and groups of Indians like the unwelcome grappling and groping from an overly affectionate pet dog. From descriptions of Crazy Horse, the Wounded Knee Massacre, Wounded Knee II, to the underlying premise of the uneven *Dances with Wolves*, there is little hope for escape from the white-created paradigm—there is simply going to be no resolution to the problems and challenges Indians face until they realize being Indian *is* the problem. In the four examples just listed, it is repeated over and over again that the Indians (primarily the Lakota in those instances) have no one but themselves to blame for the near-destruction of their entire cultures. They are reminded they will have no hope until they abandon their savagery, superstitions, etc. As Patricia Limerick explained: "Interpreting Indian-white relations in these terms [of civilized versus savage], Euro-Americans seldom glimpsed the complexity and integrity of Indian cultures."[22]

McMurtry also did not want to be left out of the pantheon of authors of Indian history who omitted details of events involving Indians, apparently because it's not worth the effort to describe them and tell you they're doing it. He bragged:

> I am going to do my best, in this narrative, to avoid blanketing my pages under a blizzard of nomenclature in an attempt to precisely delineate the many bands, groups and villages that flowed back and forth across the Great Plains.[23]

Nonetheless, McMurtry did not elaborate on why writing this "blizzard of nomenclature" was to be avoided. McMurtry's comment did more to illuminate the attitude of the writers of history of the dominant culture than it does to explain the history of those dominated. In the very first sentences of the introduction to his book about another Indian wartime leader, *Little Crow: Spokesman for the Sioux*, Gary Clayton Anderson explained this phenomenon:

> One of the most difficult challenges facing historians today is to write the history of the dispossessed. Such people leave few records and are frequently viewed by the dominant culture as being worthy of nothing more than a footnote in the ever-moving vision of a nation's past.[24]

In short, to head toward the conclusion of this chapter, what McMurtry was most likely really trying to express with his claim that other writers didn't have a grip on the "soul" of Crazy Horse, whether he fully realized it or not, was that Crazy Horse could not be possessed. Cook-Lynn stated Crazy Horse has become an object of white obsession because he refused to participate in white society in every way. She argued that the obsession arose because: "They do it because they must possess what they cannot." To sum up her views on the Crazy Horse monument, Cook-Lynn explained: "…the one distinguishing feature of modern white man-inspired art as it comes face to face with Indians is to reduce the role of art to absurdity. When that happens, social bankruptcy and despair, modern materialism, and mass media are all that's left."[25]

As cogent as Cook-Lynn's arguments about the absurdity of the Crazy Horse carving are, there seems to be no limit to the irresponsibility regarding attempts to describe in one form or another the life and times of the enigmatic Crazy Horse. McMurtry, like Helen Hunt Jackson before him, was drawn like a moth to a flame to the irresistible urge to constantly describe Indians such as Crazy Horse's Lakota in terms of "wildness" or "barbaric." In the next chapter, the other end of the spectrum of describing Indians as being virtually otherworldly beings is reviewed.

ENDNOTES

1. Mort, *Thieves' Road*, p. 120.
2. Marshall, *The Journey of Crazy Horse*, p. 77.
3. Ibid., pp. 140-141.
4. Will Peters, Oglala Lakota, May 11, 2019.
5. Robert A. Clark, *The Killing of Chief Crazy Horse* (Lincoln, Nebraska: University of Nebraska Press, 1988), p. 79. Thomas Powers stated Lieutenant Clark offered $200.00 and his best horse. Powers, *The Killing of Crazy Horse*, p. xi.
6. McMurtry, *Crazy Horse*, p. 2.
7. Cook-Lynn, *Anti-Indianism in Modern America*, p. 27.
8. McMurtry, *Crazy Horse*, p. 13.
9. Anonymous Lakota Elder.
10. Deloria, Jr., *Custer Died for Your Sins*, pp. 12-13.
11. Drinnon, Richard, *Facing West*, p. 370.
12. McMurtry, *Crazy Horse*, p. 21.
13. Custer, *Boots and Saddles*, pp. 174-175.
14. Utley and Washburn, *Indian Wars*, pp. 74-76.
15. Sandoz, *Crazy Horse*, p. xi.
16. Ibid., p. ix.
17. Ibid., p. xiii.
18. Matson, *Crazy Horse: The Lakota Warrior's Life and Legacy*, p. 8. Matson is likely accurate when he stated Crazy Horse led the Indian forces in their victory of Crook at the Rosebud in 1876. Ibid., p.8.
19. Joe Jackson, *Black Elk: The Life of an American Visionary* (New York: Picador/Farrar, Straus, & Giroux, 2016), p. 47.
20. Sajna, *Crazy Horse*, p. 282.
21. Robert Utley, *The Lance and the Shield: The Life and Times of Sitting Bull* (New York: Henry Holt & Co., 1993), p. 71.
22. Limerick, *The Legacy of Conquest*, p. 190.
23. McMurtry, *Crazy Horse*, p. 14.
24. Gary Clayton Anderson, *Little Crow: Spokesman for the Sioux* (St. Paul, Minnesota: Minnesota Historical Society, 1986), p. 1.
25. Cook-Lynn, *Anti-Indianism in Modern America*, pp. 28-29.

Chapter 10

Searching for Spiritual Meaning in the Land of John Dunbar

Crazy Horse Redux

And these ceremonies do not belong to Indians alone. They can be done by all who have the right attitude, and who are honest and sincere about their belief in Grandfather and in following his rules.

Thomas Mails, *Fools Crow*[1]

Perhaps nothing in the history of American Indians created more of a leadership vacuum and confusion about what others saw as the meaning of his life than the murder of Crazy Horse in 1877. Popular Indian writer A. C. Ross, also known as Ehanamani, in his *Crazy Horse and the Real Reason for the Battle of the Little Big Horn*, set out to explain what happened in that famous battle in Montana in 1876 generally through a horoscope analysis of the time of the battle. He accurately stated in the beginning of his book, at least according to a reasonable consensus of historians as touched on in the last chapter, that during the Fetterman Fight of December 21, 1866: "Crazy Horse was selected to lead a group of warriors to decoy the soldiers when they came out of the fort to help the woodcutters."[2] Dr. Ross continued with what could be considered a fairly accurate and interesting argument that the underlying reason for the battle of the Little Big Horn was more or less the lust for gold.[3] Even Terry Mort managed to suggest this conflict between two cultures was exacerbated by national financial problems and noted: "The Great Depression of 1873 was under way in Europe; its contagion would soon spread to the United States, where it would last five years."[4] Nevertheless, later in his book, Dr. Ross stated: "I decided to ask my Astrologer Mary Jayn to do a star map based on the natal or birth time of the battle."[5]

By many accounts Dr. Ross is a well-liked member of the Lakota community. While not directly confronting Dr. Ross' claim of supernatural inevitability regarding the conflict of cultures leading up to the Battle of the Little Big Horn, Elizabeth Cook-Lynn explained, pointing more to Dr. Ross' claims of financial reasons for the famous battle:

> …it was not destiny nor fate nor the hand of the gods that brought about oppressive law or genocidal practice. It was practical American politicians, greedy capitalist developers, the everyday settlers making up the Anglo foundation of the United States in terms of economics and Christianity that masterminded and interpreted these events.[6]

Yet, Ehanamani is not the only writer to "…have gone along with nostalgia rather than politics."[7] Kevin Hancock, whose story was briefly introduced in an earlier chapter and who wrote *Not for Sale*, employed the paradigm of looking to an unrealistic portrayal of bygone days for answers to the complex current challenges facing Indians. *Not for Sale* is his account of his "spiritual" experiences on the Pine Ridge Reservation and what he interpreted as his adventure on the "trail of Crazy Horse."

Like Ehanamani, Hancock placed a heavy reliance on astrology and also did not explain its connection to Lakota spirituality. Hancock seemed well-meaning and he graciously granted permission to quote his book. Without a doubt, Kevin has a generous spirit and has an obvious desire to help the Lakota. However, the logic exhibited by his writing is subject to scrutiny just like any other (including the present writing). And it is unfortunate given Kevin's zeal, it is highly unlikely his perspective is ultimately helpful to the Lakota people. Readers can be excused if they are skeptical of his claims of contact with the revered White Buffalo Calf Woman, the spirits of Crazy Horse and Sitting Bull, his past life as a shaman (or at least as he suspects he was) and other instances of claimed supernatural encounters. Perhaps the hardest to understand statement of all from Kevin, apparently a New England region sports fan, is his comment the Boston Celtics and Los Angeles Lakers played for the 1986 NBA Finals.[8] In 1986, the Celtics played the Houston Rockets in that series and won in six games.

Before evaluating the substance of Hancock's claims of supernatural encounters, readers may get uneasy feelings about how much he awkwardly interjected himself into the stories of Lakota people and history. Of course, this should not be particularly surprising given his clumsy choice of putting a picture of *himself* on the front cover of his book. Granted, Hancock signaled with the title of his book it was a recounting of his personal journey for "Finding Center in the Land of Crazy Horse." Yet, the feel of his book as a whole is one of overfamiliarity with the people of Pine Ridge. How else can it be explained Hancock had no hesitation in tearing a piece of wood off of the venerated Black Elk's cabin?[9]

Like the case with McMurtry, it appears Kevin is one of those individuals described by Deloria, Jr., who has an interest in Indians and who believes he "…immediately and thoroughly understands them."[10] It is highly doubtful Kevin Hancock has any connection to the intricacies of Lakota spirituality. Nevertheless, Kevin needs to understand, if he indeed has a belief in his supernatural leanings, as stated in *Fools Crow*: "To holy men and medicine persons, divinely given power is an awesome and profoundly personal possession, to be handled with the utmost care and concern." Ominously, this explanation was followed by a warning: "A single small mistake or bit of carelessness and it can slip away like an hourglass. One error and the owner of the power might pay for it by a personal disaster, or even the loss of his life."[11]

Also present in *Not for Sale* is Kevin's unfortunately excessive subjectivity. On one page alone of his book, he used the first-person pronoun "I," "me," or "my" 40 times. This page also contained the cringeworthy comment in explaining his attempt to avoid detection by a buffalo herd: "I back off just a few more steps and then use my basketball skills to demonstrate a correct reverse pivot and start running."[12] In another soliloquy, he advised after a hard day of vision questing: "I get out of the truck with a tall can of Budweiser, my binoculars, and my camera." To make sure we don't underestimate the importance of Kevin to the story of the Lakota people, he subsequently advised his readers: "I am wearing my brown wool sweater [of course], jeans, boots, camouflage gloves, and my black Rockin' Seven Ranch wool hat."[13] Why it is important to understand this is not made clear. Apparently not sensing how it sounds in a community suffering a virtual epidemic of alcoholism and drug abuse, he also described another instance where he spent his evening shooting pool and drinking beer at the deplorably named "Million Dollar Cowboy Bar."[14]

Unfortunately, at other times Hancock's book borders on the incomprehensible. His astrologer (see following paragraph) "read" Red Cloud's horoscope that she developed concerning a time near the signing of the Ft. Laramie Treaty of 1868. She reported: "There is a lot of dogma in this chart, even arrogance. I mean, there may be a strong feeling that their culture and their dogma are superior. There is a false sense of power in this chart."[15] An interesting observation indeed, but what this *might* mean has already been explained in Joseph Marshall's *The Journey of Crazy Horse*. Marshall noted that the soldiers prior to the signing of this 1868 treaty let the Indians think they were abandoning the forts along the Bozeman Trail, but explained the federal government in reality: "…could afford to abandon the Bozeman Trail because they were developing an east-west rail line across Montana, a more direct route to the gold fields."[16] In the realm of simple evaluation, Philip Jenkins noted the obvious point regarding such horoscope readings—they simply: "…suffer from the familiar flaws of Western [or Chinese] astrology, namely, the extreme improbability that the human population can be categorized into a dozen or so categories divided according to birth date." Jenkins also made what is unfortunately not as much of an obvious point as it should be that the horoscope system "…has nothing particularly Indian about it."[17] Even conceding there are some indications of a belief in reincarnation among the Northern Algonquin, Cree, Naskapi, Montagnais and perhaps other nations, there is nothing to suggest a reincarnation among Indians would involve an incarnation as a white man.

Yet, first and foremost among the problematic issues regarding *Not for Sale*, is neither Hancock nor any of his supporters make clear the shaky proposition as to how he became the spokesperson for presenting the intricacies of Lakota spirituality to the presumably non-Indian masses. He explicitly outlined that his reason for eventually traveling to the Pine Ridge Indian Reservation for spiritual rejuvenation was receiving discs which: "…were a recording of an astrological reading by an evolutionary astrologer from the San Francisco Bay area." Hancock further explained: "A woman who had never met me was reading my 'natal chart' off nothing more than the date, time, and place of my birth."[18] Although the mechanics of evolutionary astrology are not clearly explained, one internet site proudly proclaimed: "Evolutionary astrology offers tremendous insights into where the soul has been, its current life purpose, and ultimately where the soul is going."[19]

As promising as that may seem to the uninitiated, evolutionary astrology and its twin philosophy of New Ageism ultimately have little, if anything, to offer the Lakota or any other Indian nation attempting to withstand the last assault on Indian culture—cultural appropriation by non-Indians. What made Hancock's attempt to interpret Lakota spirituality particularly odd is his presentation of his "visions" as messages to him as an individual. This is particularly true in the case of "Vision Number 3" where Hancock reported his vision as the directive: "'You don't have to take care of everyone else all the time. It is okay to do things just for you.'"[20] It is likely this "vision" is far off the mark, at least when considering, as Jenkins lucidly explained: "Native traditions are firmly based in the community, and Native religions make no sense except in a communal context, often linked to a particular landscape."[21] In that regard, it is difficult to bridge the gap between a spiritual tradition intertwined with the Black Hills and the idea of applying these concepts to a lumber yard owner from Maine. Hancock also did not explain why the "visions" are delivered in English, complete with the contraction "don't." Stripped of his outward fascination with the superficial symbols of Indian culture and spirituality, it is unclear if Hancock is committed to spreading his spiritual knowledge to the larger Lakota community.

It is also instructive to consider that even when describing spiritual matters in print, there is a limit as to how much information will be disclosed, at least by some Indian people. Frank Fools Crow stated after a vision quest: "I told Stirrup about my vision and he helped me understand it, but *Wakan-Tanka* would not want me to reveal everything I saw. It remains a very personal experience."[22] Curiously enough, as noted in the heading to this chapter, Fools Crow advised: "…[the] ceremonies do not belong to Indians alone. They can be done by all who have the right attitude, and who are honest and sincere about their belief in Grandfather and in following his rules."[23] Whether Hancock is of the type of non-Indian with the "right attitude" Fools Crow is referring to is best left decided by the Lakota themselves. Nevertheless, Hancock could be viewed, perhaps even sympathetically, as one of many: "…ordinary people in modern societies [who] also hunger for a world in which they are more competent or more in control than they are most of the time."[24] Yet, for even well-meaning people to appropriate Lakota or any other type of Indian spirituality for any reason is disheartening.

Kevin also does not explain why a white man approaching middle age pursued a "vision quest" on the "trail of Crazy Horse" when Lakota culture established that spiritual event for male youths, typically around the age of 14. Although Hancock by his own account was not invited to Pine Ridge by the spirits of Sitting Bull or Crazy Horse, he does claim to have received a cameo appearance from these two from spirit land after his participation in a sweat lodge.[25] Unfortunately, the idea of Crazy Horse travelling though space and time in the spirit world to visit a white man is suspect. Unlike Sitting Bull, Crazy Horse had little opportunity and apparently little interest in interacting with white culture. Notably, Mari Sandoz wrote that after the Fetterman Fight in 1866, Crazy Horse had a: "…heart [that] was cold and black with an anger that could not be made good until many more of the white men died like those scattered naked up there on the ridge."[26]

Upon thorough examination, what Hancock's journey actually revealed is a lack of awareness of the totality of actions which created the conditions on Pine Ridge in the first instance. When Hancock disclosed near the conclusion of his epistle: "It would be healthy to consider what would happen if private property rights were strengthened at Pine Ridge,"[27] he seemed to ignore the entire 19th-century history of the Lakota and the disaster created by the Dawes Act of 1887. Much as Helen Hunt Jackson rarely addressed cultural issues and never addressed religious or spiritual ones, Hancock naively did not consider the history of white imposition of private property ownership resulting from Henry Dawes' legislation. George Tinker noted: "In attempting to teach—that is, impose—their own model of civilization on Indian people, the missionaries generated a disintegration of the societal structures of Indian civilization."[28] Additionally, Limerick astutely explained: "In the mission to civilize the Indians, benevolence and acquisitiveness merged; the interests of missionaries who wanted to acquire the souls of Indians and the interests of settlers who wanted to acquire their lands found a paradoxical harmony."[29]

In this age of anti-intellectualism, it is considered rude to point out history does not necessarily bear out the emotional arguments of New Agers and those of that ilk. Hancock would have been well served to recall that in the case of the Cherokee Nation, assimilating white ways was by no means assurance of a long-lasting stable culture. Perhaps those enterprising Indian people achieved the highest known level of adapting white culture, literacy, schooling, etc. In that regard, the Cherokees built houses, developed a written alphabet, built printing presses and a whole host of Euro-styled accoutrements. No matter—government policy overrode any of those considerations of Cherokee sophistication. "Sharp Knives" Jackson, in executing Indian Removal, fulfilled the concept of the removal policy developed by Thomas Jefferson years earlier. It is little wonder some of the full-blooded Indian children in 19th-century Georgia: "…sang hymns but secretly decried what they knew of Christianity and white people, and they were irritated by those mixed-bloods who catered to whites and teachers."[30]

At one point in his book, Hancock, who does not indicate any Indian heritage, revealed that after he: "…[felt] the warrior spirit within me…[he]…let out a mighty Lakota war cry."[31] How he made the transition from his most likely English heritage, who seemingly were genetically predisposed to be those most avid of Indian haters, to that of a Plains Indian warrior, is not entirely clear. The awkwardness of deconstructing this episode, besides the fact Hancock is not a Lakota Indian, is compounded when it becomes evident the best perspective on Hancock's writing is provided by Ward Churchill, who obviously has a plethora of his own issues. Although Churchill has not commented on Hancock's tale directly, he referred to a similar scenario which involved what was popularly known in the 1980s as the "'Men's Movement'" founded by Robert Bly.

Bly's practices included the use of Nordic mythology, his reenactment of what he believed Druidic rituals involved, and of course American Indian symbolism. Bly's advertising circulars centered on men: "'…reclaiming the primitive within us…attaining freedom through use…of appropriate ritual…[and] the rights of all men to transcend cultural boundaries in redeeming their warrior souls.'"[32] Churchill noted: "…to play at ritual potluck is to debase all spiritual traditions, voiding their internal coherence and leaving nothing usably sacrosanct as a cultural anchor for the peoples who conceived and developed them, and who have consequently organized societies around them."[33] Churchill, who seemed adept at channeling *his* true spirit guide—Mark Twain—mocked these poseurs: "Certainly, in a reasonable universe we would be entitled (perhaps required) to assume that no group of allegedly functional adults would take such a farce seriously."[34]

At least Hancock, unlike another sojourner into the realm of Indian spirituality, John Collier, cannot be accused of responding to Lakota spirituality: "…conditioned by the intellectual baggage he was carrying." Whereas Collier in his engagement with Navajo culture was influenced by German intellectual Frederick Nietzsche and "…transferred his Teutonic dreams to living Indian societies,"[35] it is unclear if Hancock utilized any system of thought at all. Yet, neither Collier nor Hancock were willing to attempt to view their respective Indian scenarios without superimposing a European cultural matrix upon them. As George Tinker explained in *Missionary Conquest*, the biggest dilemma for understanding Indian religious practices is: "…Indian spiritual traditions are still rooted in cultural contexts that are quite foreign to white EuroAmericans." Tinker also cautioned that: "…the modern appeal of Indian spirituality to many white people has, I believe, become a major destructive force in our Indian communities."[36]

What is also troubling about Kevin's anti-historical presentation of Indian people is that it reduces them to cartoonish caricatures, or at least cardboard cut-outs. James Wilson explained this well: "During the last quarter of the twentieth century, the Native American world has, arguably, become more contradictory and confusing than at any time in the last 500 years." He added, importantly: "The perennial urge to simplify, to reduce native people to a repertoire of vividly childish images—spiritual nature-lover, tragic victim, feckless bum—only adds to the ever-deepening accretions of irony and ambiguity [punctuation as in original]."[37] No greater example of this phenomenon exists than in the story of Black Elk. While Hancock and others want to turn this historical figure into some type of pure essence of Lakota spirituality, that conclusion can only come at the denial of the profound influence the Catholic Church and religion had on Black Elk's worldview, or at a minimum, his ability to adapt his spiritual practices to Catholic precepts as a mechanism for his efforts at ensuring the survival of the Lakota people.

Vine Deloria, Jr., also cautioned against the hazards of European involvement with Indians, particularly the tendency to over-romanticize them. He stated the following, which Will Peters echoed with his comment about not wanting to return to the "…days of chasing buffalo and living in Tipis":

> I would submit that a great deal of the lack of progress at Pine Ridge is occasioned by people who believe they are helping the Oglalas when they insist on seeing, in the life of the people of that reservation, only those things which they want to see. Real problems and real people become invisible before the great romantic notion that the Sioux people yearn for the days of Crazy Horse and Red Cloud and will do nothing until those days return.[38]

As if to emphasize, albeit inadvertently, Deloria, Jr.'s point, the two entities Hancock claimed his friend advised visited during the sweat lodge, Crazy Horse and Sitting Bull, were hardly a departure from the "typical" idea of what constituted Indians. Hancock's descriptions of the aftermath of the sweat lodge is a stark reminder of Vine Deloria's claim: "American Indians are prohibited from having a modern identity."[39]

Jenkins, a prolific writer on religious matters, advanced many criticisms of New Agers interacting with practitioners of Native religions and whites or non-Indians who presume to speak on behalf of Indians. Echoing Deloria, Jr., and Tinker, Jenkins thus surmised few activities have been as detrimental to American Indians than those which involve non-Indians who claim to know what was in the best interest of Indians. He explained that when "pseudo-Indians" assume the role of spokespersons for Indians, the general public assumes they are speaking on behalf of Indians, whose voices are once again not being heard. In addition to his comment about the connectedness of Indian spiritual practices to specific communities and landscapes, he noted modern "shamans" are "profoundly individualistic" and engaged in personal spiritual pursuits. In the modern view, vision quests are viewed as a device for: "… integration of the individual, and not as originally conceived, the preparation of the individual to fulfill his or her role in the community." Jenkins also noted: "In order to assert the value of Native spirituality, writers consistently idealize their subjects, past and present, ignoring or underplaying those aspects that they might find unsettling."[40]

Continuing his analysis, Jenkins postulated that to promote Native spirituality, writers consistently idealized their subjects in both the past and present and sidestepped aspects of Indian lives and culture that would be contrary to this portrayal. Professor Jenkins made it abundantly clear New Age beliefs in such fringe phenomenon as UFOs had no connection to Indian mythologies. Ironically, however, to counter the resistance of Indian activists to the influx of these New Agers and their often incoherent belief systems, hippie Gary Snyder once claimed: "Spirituality is not something that can be 'owned' like a car or a house."[41] Curiously, Snyder did not note this is precisely the argument many Indian leaders employed when arguing against exclusive white possession of land.

Inexplicably, given all of his misgivings, Jenkins nonetheless provided credibility to New Age believers by asserting: "…a 'real' religion is one that people are prepared to treat as such, regardless of the historical or scholarly grounds on which their views are based. By that standard, the neo-Native religions of the New Age groups are as valid as any other and deserve as much respect."[42] In two sentences, Jenkins has outlined an assertion requiring the implementation of a *reductio ad absurdum* that would require several volumes to properly dissect. Apparently, in short, by Jenkins' logic, followers of Jim Jones from the People's Temple or Branch Davidians, to name a couple of notable examples, are deserving of "respect" regardless of the havoc wreaked in the lives of their adherents because these most often naïve souls treated them as "real" religions.

It might be considered alarmist to devote much attention to Hancock's obscure epistle. Yet, in *Returning to the Lakota Way,* a book Hancock used as a source, Joseph Marshall warned: "Most enormous consequences, though, have innocuous beginnings."[43] An obvious example of that paradigm existed in Columbus' landing in North America in 1492 with his minuscule contingent of fellow sailors and explorers and the subsequent domination of North and South America by Europeans. However, to reassure us all is well, Hancock perhaps unknowingly took Ehanamani's assuredly comforting slogan "We are all related"[44] a step further when he encountered a lone buffalo and claimed: "In Lakota culture, the connection [with animals] is not difficult to make at all, as the buffalo and I are brothers."[45] Interestingly enough, despite Hancock's assurances of the authenticity of his tale, in a moment more revealing than he intended, he blurted out: "I guess, in the end, it is the truth that scares me."[46] One of the aspects of Hancock's tale that is consistently overlooked is how Indians themselves view their over-romanticized images. As Melissa K. Nelson noted: "Certainly Native Peoples are concerned and upset when they are stereotyped and romanticized; this form of racism needs to change."[47]

In regard to Hancock's claim of the authenticity of his experiences, he also claimed (without naming names) that his Lakota friends: "…would not be surprised or skeptical in the least about the vision-quest story I am telling."[48] That would hardly seem to be the case, considering in 1993, approximately 500 representatives from various Lakota bands unanimously voted to pass the *Declaration of War Against Exploiters of Lakota Spirituality*. Some of the provisions pertinent to Hancock's tale included:

> Whereas for too long we have suffered the unspeakable indignity of having our most precious Lakota ceremonies and spiritual practices desecrated, mocked, and abused by non-Indian 'wannabes', hucksters, cultists, commercial profiteers, and self-styled 'New Age shamans' and their followers; and
>
> Whereas non-Indian charlatans and 'wannabes' are selling books that promote systematic colonization of our Lakota spirituality; and
>
> Whereas individuals and groups involved in the 'New Age movement', in the 'men's movement', in "Neopaganism' cults and in 'shamanism' workshops all have exploited the spiritual traditions of our Lakota people by imitating our ceremonial ways and by mixing such imitation rituals with non-Indian occult practices in an offensive and harmful pseudo-religious hodge-podge; and
>
> Whereas the absurd public posturing of this scandalous assortment of pseudo-Indian charlatans, 'wannabes' commercial profiteers, cultists, and 'New Age shamans' comprises a momentous obstacle in the struggle of traditional Lakota people for an adequate public appraisal of the legitimate political, legal, and spiritual needs of real Lakota people;

One of the conclusions of the declaration states:

> We hereby and henceforth declare war against all persons who persist in exploiting abusing and misrepresenting the sacred traditions and spiritual practices of Lakota, Dakota, and Nakota people.[49]

Given the unvarnished hostility to Indians exhibited by L. Frank Baum, author of *The Wonderful Wizard of Oz*, it is ironic that a framework for understanding Hancock's writing can be found in Paul Nathanson's book *Over the Rainbow: The Wizard of Oz as a Secular Myth of America*, cited frequently herein. Hancock's story ran parallel to Nathanson's description of the film version of Baum's book which: "…clearly lends itself to interpretation as a story about the psychological development of individuals."[50] In that regard, Hancock visited Pine Ridge to search for some sort of spiritual recovery because he was, as stated by a U.S.

Senator, "…physically and emotionally exhausted…"[51] Much like Dorothy encountered the Tin Man and the other characters on her journey, Hancock claimed he experienced visits from the spirits of the great Lakota leader Crazy Horse and his ally Sitting Bull.

The teachings of Carl Jung also serve as a useful guide on Hancock's journey of recovery in that he believed religion played a "…helpful role in the development of healthy personalities." He also believed the second phase of life: "…involves initiation into inner reality. This process includes acquisition of deeper self-knowledge or bringing to consciousness what has been hidden in the unconscious."[52] Using the Jungian framework, Nathanson noted in the movie *The Wizard of Oz* the characters Dorothy meets in her dream—the Tin Man with no heart, the Scarecrow with no brain, and the Cowardly Lion—could be argued to represent what Jung classified as "archetypes." Archetypes are highly developed elements of the collective unconscious and can only be understood indirectly using art, myths, religion, etc.[53] It is evident in Hancock's descriptions of encounters with the White Buffalo Calf Woman, Crazy Horse, Sitting Bull and other entities he fervently believed he encountered, that at some level he was dealing with archetypes of Plains Indians.

Perhaps an even more lucid understanding of Hancock's tale about encountering the spirits of Crazy Horse, Sitting Bull and the other assorted adventures described in *Not for Sale* can be found in Armando Prats' *Invisible Natives*. By focusing so intently on Crazy Horse and Sitting Bull as Indian relics from the 19th century, Kevin suggested, intentionally or not, support for the Myth of Conquest where: "…the Indian ceases to have a history, or at least a story worth telling, following the triumph of white civilization." Prats' perspective arrived in the form of his analysis of the movie *Geronimo*, where a Lieutenant Davis expressed outrage at the treatment of the now-captured Indian leader. Prats argued this expression highlighted Davis now has: "…[a] life and a future that the Apaches do not have." Hancock conveyed a similar mindset by taking what he learned from his various "spiritual" experiences involving long-dead Indian men and applying these lessons to his lumber business. Never mind that Indian tribes in Maine were likely displaced to create this enterprise. Unfortunately, even though Hancock appears well-intentioned, he was promoting "mythological historicism" whereby as Prats indicated the supplicant: "…takes it on faith that the last necessary victory over savagery specifies the moment in which the Indian finds his properly paradoxical *place* in 'history' by somehow *disappearing* from it [emphasis in original]."[54]

Like Bishop Henry B. Whipple, it appeared Hancock was: "…genuinely committed to the well-being of Indian people and intended his reform ideas as positive contributions to their survival."[55] Unfortunately, also like Whipple, Hancock based the vast majority of his reform ideas on limited contact with the Pine Ridge community (if he had more training and knowledge, he did not disclose that fact). Like we are led to believe in *Dances with Wolves* that Kicking Bear would have no idea his people were facing an onslaught of settlers had John Dunbar not advised him, Hancock suggested the people on Pine Ridge would not understand they are mired in poverty and dysfunction without his insights. Unfortunately, all the mythmaking or archetype analysis in the world does little to enlighten anyone on the realities of Indian life—past or present. It appears it is easy to hold images of Indians as relics of the past: "What we cannot do is accept…they live with us in a contemporary reality"[56]

While Hancock asserted his ripping a piece off of Black Elk's cabin was a sacred act of some undetermined provenance, he seemed completely unaware for a large portion of his life that Black Elk was nothing more mysterious than a garden-variety Catholic, or at least, according to some, a pretend Catholic. Kevin's act of vandalizing Black Elk's cabin in reality differed only in degree of intrusion from the FBI's ransacking of Pine Ridge residents' homes in the aftermath of the 1973 "occupation."[57] As nasty as the actions of those all-too-earthly guardians of "law and order" were, at least those unrepentant zealots did not make the pretentious claim they were acting on behalf of the "Creator," unless they happened to believe the "Creator" was the spirit of the ruthless and at that time recently deceased J. Edgar Hoover. Kevin Hancock and his musings about spiritual encounters are a prime illustration of Mary Crow Dog's claim: "Sometimes I think the do-gooder types do more harm than the Custer types."[58]

Sadly, despite Kevin's good intentions, in the broader picture of the state of United States society in general, *Not for Sale* is a truly confusing signpost indicating a descent into cultural and historical illiteracy. The only perspective that mattered to Hancock was his belief that all should not be skeptical of his obviously unverifiable claims of consistent supernatural contact and the emotions they produced for him. Like Alden Pyle in *The Quiet American*, Hancock was "'impregnably armored by his good intentions and his ignorance.'"[59] He also preemptively attacked those whom he suspected would question the authenticity of his "experiences." Considering the many laudatory comments about *Not for Sale*, it has become a truly remarkable testament to those who in their desperation would believe just about anything.

Incomprehensibly, Kevin and his supporters in the Pine Ridge milieu and elsewhere appear blissfully unaware of the hazards contained in the unflinching support of a guru (such as Wovoka) whose spirituality is based on non-traditional Lakota concepts. Yet, if any credence is to be given to the explanation that Wovoka's miracle in making ice flow down the Walker River in Utah was based on deception, then it is obvious his status as a shaman of the "Ghost Dance" religion is at least in part based on a lie. And, even though it is an exaggeration to claim the "Ghost Dancers" were a threat to settlers and others, this "religion" based on what some (except for Elizabeth Cook-Lynn) consider Christian beliefs contributed to the turmoil on Pine Ridge and other Plains Indians Reservations.

Careful analysis reveals there is more to be concerned about in Hancock's (fortunately) little known and poorly conceived book (and other books with similar stories of New Age fantasies) than he and his admirers seem willing to acknowledge. One of the obviously troublesome aspects of these New Age-type scenarios is the not-so-subtle suggestion every single event in his and other New Age-types' lives is the result of the intervention of some super charged spiritual energy or force. For example, Hancock described receiving a package of animal crackers from the attendant on a commercial airliner. Although most discerning people would consider this the most mundane of activities, Kevin interpreted this episode as a mystical sign he was to reflect on the use of horses by Plains Indians.

Hancock elaborated on his explanation for this episode by asking rhetorically: "Who else looks at a horse-shaped animal cracker and has such thoughts? I ask myself."[60] The answer, of course, is someone who is thinking about the Lakota culture on a daily basis, which is to a certain extent commendable. Yet, the unspoken question, which Kevin inadvertently and most assuredly unintentionally raises in his book, is: why do seemingly well-adjusted people lose all sense of perspective and evidently the ability to discern reality when it comes to Indians and particularly regarding Crazy Horse? Undoubtedly, a visit to Pine Ridge evokes strong emotions and spiritual yearnings in all but the most hard-hearted. Nevertheless, feelings and emotions are one thing; claiming to have contact with the most sacred entity in Lakota spirituality, the White Buffalo Calf Woman, immediately after exiting a rental car is quite another.

Joseph Marshall, interested in presenting a picture of Crazy Horse as a flesh-and-blood man, had this to say about Crazy Horse: "My Crazy Horse long ago ceased to be a one-dimensional hero impervious to the foibles of being human, I have done my best to make him real."[61] Unfortunately, in the descriptions of Crazy Horse relayed by other writers, the attribution of virtually every single event in Crazy Horse's life and Lakota history to some sort of spiritual intervention or supernatural occurrence becomes a mirror image of the concept of Manifest Destiny.[62] In both instances, the actions and the consequences of the actions of flesh-and-blood men and women are ignored, and assigning responsibility to finite human beings for finite outcomes becomes lost in the haze.

Kevin's book is indeed thought-provoking, but sadly, not in the manner he intended. Unfortunately, to the gullible, with the help of Kevin's overheated imagination, it is a short trip from the land of the absurd to that of pure fantasy. In answering his own question as to why he sojourned to the "Land of Crazy Horse," Hancock advised his story might go something like this:

> I had a past life experience connected somehow to the history of the Lakota people, possibly Pine Ridge. In that past life experience, I was a shaman or spiritual leader of some type, responsible for the well-being of the whole tribe.[63]

Unfortunately, imposing a reincarnation paradigm on Lakota spirituality does nothing to uncover any truths about the Lakota, or few other Indian people. It raises another question—in Hancock's view, was the move from a past life of a Lakota shaman to an Anglo-Saxon lumber yard owner a move up or down the reincarnation hierarchy? Did he have incarnations in between? The questions seem more appropriate for a stand-up comedy routine as opposed to a serious discussion of Lakota spirituality. Although it is questionable whether the position of shaman even existed in Lakota society, historian Robert Utley noted as to the "shadowy" distinction between the shamans and medicine men: "the shamans held higher rank, possessed greater knowledge, and often taught the medicine men."[64]

Hancock's efforts, which unfortunately amount to little more than cultural appropriation, are nothing new. His current attempt to replicate traditional Lakota spiritual practices is simply a return to the practice of white shamanism which was prevalent in the dismal 1960s in the United States. Like unflinchingly vapid actor Peter Coyote and poet Gary Snyder of that earlier era, Hancock's comments on his spiritual experiences did not emanate from years of careful study or acquisition of deep knowledge. Like Gwynne, Hancock missed an opportunity to explore the layers of Lakota culture, in his case by overly romanticizing it. Like Dorothy in the *Wizard of Oz*, Kevin attempted to find happiness in the mythical land "over the rainbow." Ultimately, however, at least in Dorothy's case: "…she realizes that Oz, though colorful, beautiful and fascinating, is also fragmented, illusory, and confusing."[65] Perhaps Hancock would better serve the

Lakota people by attempting to dispel: "…[the] image of the reservation community as intellectually isolated and aliterate, [which is] something of a stereotype, one that might be dispelled by regular reading of *Indian Country Today*."[66] And, although Hancock may convince few he experienced the "spiritual" experiences as he claimed, his romanticized views of Indians prove Bordewich's point that "…Americans still prefer fictional Indians to real human beings."[67]

CHAPTER 10: SEARCHING FOR SPIRITUAL MEANING IN THE LAND OF JOHN DUNBAR

ENDNOTES

1. Mails, *Fools Crow*, p. 51.
2. A. C. Ross (Ehanamani), *Crazy Horse and the Real Reason for the Battle of the Little Big Horn* (Rapid City, South Dakota: Hansen Brothers Printing/Color House Graphics, 2000), p. 18.
3. Ibid., pp. 58-74.
4. Mort, *Thieves' Road*, p. 193.
5. Ross (Ehanamani), *Crazy Horse and the Real Reason for the Battle of the Little Big Horn*, p. 76.
6. Cook-Lynn, Elizabeth, *A Separate Country*, p. 17.
7. Ibid., p. 43.
8. Hancock, *Not for Sale*, p. 31.
9. Ibid., p. 285.
10. Deloria, Jr., *Custer Died for Your Sins*, pp. 12-13.
11. Mails, *Fools Crow*, p. 5.
12. Hancock, *Not for Sale*, p. 376.
13. Ibid., p. 397.
14. Ibid., p. 470.
15. Ibid., p. 461.
16. Marshall, *Journey of Crazy Horse*, p. 52.
17. Jenkins, *Dream Catchers*, p. 189.
18. Hancock, *Not for Sale*, p. 23.
19. Kristin Fontana, "What is Evolutionary Astrology" (https://kristinfontana.com)
20. Hancock, *Not for Sale*, p. 387.
21. Jenkins, *Dream Catchers*, p. 219.
22. Mails, *Fools Crow*, p. 50.
23. Ibid., p. 51.
24. Paul Nathanson, *Over the Rainbow: The Wizard of Oz as a Secular Myth of America*, (Albany, New York: State University of New York Press, 1991), p. 255.
25. Hancock, *Not for Sale*, p. 440. A sweat lodge is a spiritual ceremony that involves several people sitting in an enclosed structure somewhat resembling an igloo where water is poured on hot rocks creating a sauna-type effect. Usually the participants sing or chant sacred songs.
26. Sandoz, *Crazy Horse*, p. 204.
27. Hancock, *Not for Sale*, p. 474.
28. Tinker, *Missionary Conquest*, p. 102.
29. Limerick, *The Legacy of Conquest*, p. 191.
30. Ehle, *Trail of Tears*, p. 136.
31. Hancock, *Not for Sale*, p. 369.
32. Churchill, *Indians Are Us*, p. 209.

33 Ibid., p. 213.

34 Ibid., p. 208.

35 Jenkins, *Dream Catchers*, pp. 89-90.

36 Tinker, *Missionary Conquest*, p. 121.

37 Wilson, *The Earth Shall Weep*, p. 410.

38 Deloria, Jr., *Custer Died for Your Sins*, p. 96.

39 Frederick Hoxie, *This Indian Country*, (New York: Penguin Books, 2012), p. 372.

40 Jenkins, *Dream Catchers*, p. 219.

41 Ibid., p. 250.

42 Ibid., p. 249.

43 Marshall, *Returning to the Lakota Way*, p. 25.

44 Ross, A. C. (Ehanamani), *Mitakuye Oyasin We are All Related* (Denver, Colorado: Wiconi Waste, 1989), passim.

45 Hancock, *Not for Sale*, p. 379.

46 Ibid., p. 268.

47 Nelson, Ed., "Introduction: Lighting the Sun of Our Future: How These Teachings Can Provide Illumination," *Original Instructions: Indigenous Teachings for a Sustainable Future*, p. 13.

48 Hancock, *Not for Sale*, p. 388.

49 Wilmer Stampede Mesteth, et al, "Declaration of War Against Exploiters of Lakota Spirituality" Digital History website 1993. www.digitalhistory.uh.edu.

50 Nathanson, *Over the Rainbow*, p. 78.

51 Hancock, *Not for Sale*, p. 8.

52 Nathanson, *Over the Rainbow*, p. 79.

53 Ibid., pp. 80-99.

54 Prats, *Invisible Natives*, p. 250.

55 Tinker, *Missionary Conquest*, p. 96

56 Wilson, *The Earth Shall Weep*, p. 15.

57 Pine Ridge resident Fannie Carrie Bear Eagle made a statement regarding theft and vandalism dated May 13, 1973, wherein she explained after she returned to her home after a brief absence: "…the rear steps had been broken down and the rear door jamb was forcibly broken. Inside, the house was in total disarray." She noted among missing items: "…were three hand-made star quilts which were locked in a footlocker which had been forced open, ruining the lock on it." She also stated she found a warrant on her bed dated May 10, 1973, for: "All houses and outbuildings at…the Wounded Knee Area formerly occupied by the American Indian Movement." She did not specifically identify the FBI as the perpetrators. However, since the FBI had operational control of the forces surrounding the "occupiers," if they allowed their proxies to conduct harassing searches, it is certainly reasonable to conclude ultimately they were responsible. Fannie Carrie Bear Eagle statement (St. Paul, Minnesota: Minnesota Historical Society, May 13, 1973). It is unknown whether Joseph Trimbach knew about this incident or whether he

would have considered it one of the "…underwhelming tales of FBI depredations." Trimbach, *American Indian Mafia*, p. 383.

58 Crow Dog, *Lakota Woman*, p. 113.
59 Drinnon, *Facing West*, p. 416.
60 Hancock, *Not for Sale*, p. 97.
61 Marshall, *The Journey of Crazy Horse*, p. xx.
62 Powers, *The Killing of Crazy Horse*, p. 5. Powers stated: "Crazy Horse won the battle of the Little Big Horn with a sudden rush at the right moment, splitting the enemy force in two—the kind of masterstroke *explained only by native genius, in answer to a prayer* [emphasis added]." Fortunately, Powers did not seem to succumb to over-romanticizing Crazy Horse. He noted interpreter Louis Bordeaux: "…was struck by the chief's intelligence and calm good sense" and also noted Bordeaux stated Crazy Horse was "a man of more than ordinary mental ability." Powers, *The Killing of Crazy Horse*, p. 394.
63 Hancock, *Not for Sale*, p. 223.
64 Utley, *Last Days of the Sioux Nation*, p. 15.
65 Nathanson, *Over the Rainbow*, p. 275.
66 Holler, *Black Elk's Religion*, p. 184.
67 Bordewich, *Killing the White Man's Indian*, p. 160.

CHAPTER 11

A Short Essay on the Many Faces of Sitting Bull

Sitting Bull agreed to join [Buffalo Bill's Wild West] during the 1885-1886 season at least in part because of the relative freedom it granted him, and he was surely not alone in seeing the show a measure of liberty… A celebrity performer, such as Sitting Bull or the subsequent Wild West spokesmen Red Shirt and Rocky Bear, often received invitations to meet social and political elites wherever the show stopped.

Philip J. Deloria, *Indians in Unexpected Places*[1]

In the annals of Indian history, there is likely no greater divergence of opinion of one man's qualities in the view of Indians in contrast to that of whites than Sitting Bull, who was given the name Jumping Badger at the time of his birth, believed to be in 1831. James Donovan explained that Sitting Bull: "…was that rare warrior who possessed each of the cardinal virtues so valued by the Lakotas: bravery, generosity, fortitude [in regard to both dignity and the ability to endure physical hardship] and wisdom."[2] Indian Agent James McLaughlin offered a much more negative view of the man shortly after Sitting Bull's arrival at Ft. Yates in 1883 as he led his people to reservation life: "'Sitting Bull is an Indian of very mediocre ability, rather dull, and much the inferior of Gall and others of his lieutenants in intelligence.'"[3] That people of two cultures could view one man so differently is not surprising; what *is* surprising is that few seemed to view McLaughlin's remarks as a symbol of the ever-present belief Indians were barely human, and if they were, it was as beings distinctly inferior to whites.

Aside from the conflicting views of Sitting Bull's character, of which the examples above are just a small fraction, it is difficult to overestimate the enormity of Sitting Bull's persona as a larger-than-life character. In *Over the Rainbow: The Wizard of Oz as a Secular Myth of America,* Nathanson described Sitting Bull as one of the real-life individuals being represented by a fictional character in Baum's tale. Nathanson asserted Dorothy: "…is a refugee from the savagery of a demonic being who incarnates the dark, sinister and threatening face of nature in the wild." Referring specifically to the famous Hunkpapa

Lakota warrior, Nathanson added: "The Wicked Witch, ruling this realm from her gloomy castle perched upon a barren crag, is the functional equivalent of Sitting Bull and every other alien tribal chief encountered by white settlers moving West."[4] Those who might consider Nathanson's analysis far-fetched need only review Baum's comments about Sitting Bull and the Wounded Knee Massacre quoted in the introduction. Although Baum described Sitting Bull as "the nobility of the Redskins" as opposed to a witch, he suggested the leaderless Indians were ripe for conquest after Sitting Bull was "extinguished." As such, like the Wicked Witch of the East was no longer a threat after Dorothy's house landed on her and killed her, the settlers of Baum's concern would no longer have to contend with Sitting Bull ever ready to pounce on them after he was assassinated.

Often overlooked in the rush to portray Sitting Bull as a war-mongering savage is that he was: "…best known among the Sioux as a spiritual leader, not a war leader."[5] Some have difficulty with this concept, especially given his participation in the Sun Dance, which many considered the *sine qua non*, or absolute essence, of savagery. Nevertheless, shortly before the Battle of the Rosebud, Sitting Bull participated in a Sun Dance where he had fifty flesh offerings taken from one arm and fifty taken from the other. After dancing for many hours, he fell to the ground unconscious. During this period, Sitting Bull had a vision consisting of: "…a great many white soldiers in the sky—as many as locusts during a plague—but the soldiers were upside down falling into the Indian camp." Sitting Bull also explained: "A voice in this dream told [him] there would be a big fight and the Indians would win. 'I give you these' the voice said, 'because they have no ears'—that is, all the soldiers would die." Although the vision occurred shortly prior to the Battle of the Rosebud, and: "…made a powerful impression on all who heard it described,"[6] it is generally believed the vision concerned the Battle of the Little Big Horn.

Nevertheless, Sitting Bull's name, like that of his ally Crazy Horse, and his enemy George A. Custer, is forever linked to the hot summer days of June 25 and 26, 1876, near Little Big Horn Creek in Montana. Many historians claim Custer and his forces were defeated solely due to being outnumbered by the Cheyenne and Lakota Indians opposing him and his men there. Indians, who remember this conflict by the name Battle of Greasy Grass, argued the answer is not that simple and generally believed their victory was due to the great and able leadership of Sitting Bull, Crazy Horse, Gall and the bravery of the individual warriors. Curiously, some have even argued Sitting Bull did not have an active leadership role in the battle itself. Although many claim Sitting Bull was simply a savage Indian who hated whites, the answer to the question of who the famous leader was, is, in reality, much more complicated than that cliché. As evidenced by his participation in Buffalo Bill's Wild West, many believed Sitting Bull was an intellectually curious individual eager to learn about the wider world outside his Indian culture.

In a modern, presumably culturally diverse world, it may be difficult to comprehend the angst created by the idea "savages" like Sitting Bull and Crazy Horse could orchestrate the defeat of forces led by the iconic George A. Custer. In the immediate aftermath of the Battle of the Little Big Horn, a story began circulating that Sitting Bull was actually a blue-eyed "half breed" named Charlie Jacobs. The story of Charlie Jacobs supposedly began with his birth in Canada near old Ft. Garry, which was located near Winnipeg. The story continued with his conversion to Catholicism at the behest of one Father De Smet and his instruction in French at St. John's College. As a result of his French language skills, the story continued, he was able to absorb Napoleon's tactics in their original language.[7] This concocted story, which was pure fantasy, and which attributed the defeat of Custer to the leadership of a white graduate of an eminent military school, was much easier to accept than the notion that Custer was defeated by "savage" Indians.

Sitting Bull's views of interactions with whites evolved over the years as his contact with them became more extensive. He was initially against conciliation with whites in any way. Later in his life, Sitting Bull traveled with Buffalo Bill's Wild West, and he did have some earlier business dealings with whites, but his initial contacts were essentially in the form of armed conflict. In 1864, Sitting Bull and "his" warriors engaged in a prolonged fight with the forces of General Alfred Sully. Although Sully's forces initially destroyed Sitting Bull's Hunkpapa camp, the following year Sitting Bull returned the favor and chased Sully and his men across Wyoming. In the course of the campaign, Sully's forces lost hundreds of horses and mules due to drought and grasshoppers destroyed grass needed for these animals to graze.

After the Ft. Laramie Treaty of 1868 went into effect, Colonel O. S. Stanley commanded a military escort for a surveying party of the Northern Pacific Railroad. After an initial skirmish with Gall's forces, Stanley was confronted by Sitting Bull and a large number of Hunkpapa, Oglala, Minneconjou, Sans Arc, and Blackfeet warriors. Sitting Bull ultimately tangled with Major E. M. Baker and his 400 men in the valley of the Yellowstone below Pryor Creek on August 14, 1872, although losses on both sides were light. A legendary story from this battle described Sitting Bull getting off his horse, gathering his war pipe and smoking equipment, and sauntering to within rifle range of the soldiers. As bullets whizzed past, he proceeded to smoke his pipe to the bottom of the bowl. After finishing his smoke, he cleaned his pipe, put it back in its bag, and casually strolled back to his warriors. Having proven his lack of fear of the soldiers, he led his warriors back to their camp.[8]

There may have been more complex sociological reasons for Sitting Bull's initial resistance to whites and white culture that might not seem evident upon initial examination. Treaties in particular had serious ramifications for ambitious young Lakota men such as Sitting Bull. This impact first became evident after the Ft. Laramie Treaty of 1851. While older Indian men were content with the possibility of peace, younger men chafed under the treaty's restrictions. It was thought in Plains Indian warrior societies that combat (which consisted in large part of counting coup, i.e. demonstrating bravery by touching the enemy) against other Indian tribes or nations offered the only path to honor, status, and rank. As a young man, Sitting Bull realized if the old men's dreams of peace prevailed, the traditional path of warriors to those honors would be blocked.

There was, of course, Sitting Bull, the flesh-and-blood man. In July 1881, as Sitting Bull led his people out of Canada toward Ft. Buford in what is now North Dakota, it is presumed he experienced a: "…tangle of fear, desperation, bewilderment, dejection, suspension, distrust, uncertainty, helplessness, loathing, and a host of other emotions."[9] This occurred shortly after the Redcoats of the Canadian government had encouraged: "…dissension and encouraging hungry people to abandon Sitting Bull and surrender."[10] Likewise, Sitting Bull had also just experienced the emotional struggle resulting from his beloved daughter Many Horses eloping with a suitor whose dower was previously rejected.[11] Recognizing the cavalcade of emotions experienced by Sitting Bull would be surprising only to those not recognizing his essential complexity and humanness.

However, eminent historian Robert Utley did in fact recognize Sitting Bull's complexity and suggested Sitting Bull possessed three separate and distinct personalities. One was the: "...superlative warrior and huntsman, adept at all the techniques of the war and the hunt, boastful of his deeds, laden with honors and ambition for more, celebrated and rewarded with high rank by his people." Utley then presented the next personality as: "...the holy man, suffused with reverence and mysticism, communing constantly with *Wakantanka* and all the constituent deities, dreaming sacred dreams and carrying out the rites and ceremonies they mandated." Utley continued with his description by noting Sitting Bull the holy man was also: "...entreating for the welfare of his people, offering sacrifices ranging from a buffalo carcass to his own flesh." Utley concluded the third personality was: "...the good tribesman, a man of kindness, generosity, and humility, unostentatious in dress and bearing, composer and singer of songs, friend of children and old people, peacemaker, sportsman, gentle humorist." Utley believed "...the contrasts seem to verge on contradictions."[12]

Nevertheless, it was not simply a matter of Sitting Bull having absolutely no thoughts of interacting with whites; Buffalo Bill's Wild West was not the first time he had business dealings with them. In the early 1860s, Sitting Bull worked for Pierre Garreau, a huge man who ran his trading operation out of Ft. Berthold. In that capacity, Sitting Bull bought furs from other Indians and commented he could make good deals because of his influence with them. Sitting Bull's relationship with Garreau ended after Garreau failed to pay Sitting Bull for his efforts.

It is not much of a stretch to argue the "arrest" of Sitting Bull on December 15, 1890, foreshadowed the Wounded Knee Massacre which occurred two weeks later on December 29, 1890. While thousands and thousands of words have been written about "Custer's Last Stand" and the people involved such as Sitting Bull, rarely do history books make it clear why Sitting Bull was "arrested" in the early morning hours of that cold December morning. Officials of various government agencies described Sitting Bull as a troublemaker and a "threat," which precipitated his arrest. Yet, the question was never clearly answered—a threat to do what exactly? In a fascinating episode in communications, albeit of disputed authenticity, Sitting Bull and Chief Joseph corresponded about the state of their respective nations. Sitting Bull purportedly stated in approximately 1878 that continuing the fight against the whites would be futile.[13] Regardless of the authenticity of the documents involved in this episode, it is difficult to ignore the comment by many scholars about the big picture—by 1877, or 1878 at the latest—the "Indian Wars" were over.

The "arrest" of Sitting Bull and his killing serve as another prime example of Elizabeth Cook-Lynn's axiom regarding failing to place events of Indian history in context. Few, if any, white historians highlight the obvious fact that Sitting Bull was killed, Indians argue assassinated, a mere two weeks before the Wounded Knee Massacre. While there seems to be no documentation linking the two events, it is worth considering he was killed to reduce any possible resistance to the white armed forces ominously gathering near the Pine Ridge Reservation in late 1890. Cook-Lynn put her own perspective on Sitting Bull's killing: "Sitting Bull had to be killed by the U.S. powers because he stood in the way of building a nation utilizing Indian lands. He had to be killed because he was a powerful man with a great following among all the bands of the Sioux Nation, even though subsequent histories have made an effort to diminish his reputation."[14]

Also interwoven with the tale of Sitting Bull is that of the enigmatic Frank Grouard, whose involvement with the drama surrounding Crazy Horse's assassination was outlined in the first chapter on Crazy Horse. Grouard's involvement with Sitting Bull offered no exception to the reasonable conclusion that wherever he was, it was likely to be around trouble of one type of another. At one point Sitting Bull was so angry at Grouard, who he had treated like a son, that he threatened to kill him. Evidently, sometime around 1871 Grouard advised Sitting Bull he was going on a horse-stealing foray and ended up traveling to Ft. Peck instead and lied about it to Sitting Bull. Utley described Grouard as: "…a swarthy mixed blood of twenty-one [at that time], half white and half Polynesian." Utley added Grouard was: "Fathered by a Mormon missionary, Benjamin F. Grouard, [and was] adopted by another missionary, Addison Pratt, and brought to Utah. Mormon life proved too tame for the youth of fifteen, and in 1865 he ran away to Montana." Utley concluded the description of Grouard's life by noting: "Freighting, mail riding, and escapades beyond the pale of the law occupied him until he wound up at Sitting Bull's Tipi." The circumstances of Grouard's arrival remain murky and some claim he was initially a hostage, but it appears his claim of being adopted by Sitting Bull was reasonably valid. Sitting Bull's interest may have been due to the possibility Grouard was a source of information regarding white culture.[15]

What role Grouard played in the assassination of Crazy Horse remains murky. It is also difficult to discern what role, if any, he played in the events surrounding the "Ghost Dance" and ultimately the Wounded Knee Massacre. Considering the oceans of ink thrown on paper regarding the "Ghost Dance" and the blame Sitting Bull was targeted with for its spread among the Lakota, it is curious indeed that Grouard's name is seemingly rarely associated with that event. What makes this episode particularly fascinating is that Grouard had the noted Mormon background. In a letter dated October 14, 1890, a Major Guy V. Henry, identified as the Commanding (Officer) of the 9th Cavalry stated:

> I have the honor respectfully to submit to you for your consideration the following facts, as reported to me this morning by "Scout" Frank Grouard of this Post, whose statements relative to possible Indian Troubles and disaffection I deem worthy to communicate for the consideration of the Department Commander. Grouard reports that a certain 'Medicine Man' connected with one of the several Indian tribes on "Snake River" in Idaho, having assumed to himself the character of the Christ, has by sending emissaries into the Sioux, Crow, and Northern Cheyenne tribes, succeeded in creating an excitement among those tribes. From his extended knowledge of the Indian character, in connection with the matter herein referred to, he deems prospective trouble not improbable, unless measures be adopted to suppress the tendency to a growing excitement among the tribes north of here and elsewhere.[16]

In response, on October 27, 1890, E. R. Kellogg, identified as "Commanding Post" of Ft. Washakie, Wyoming, relayed the letter of Major Henry as an endorsement to an assistant Adjutant General, partially quoted here:

> A band of Cheyennes from the Pine Ridge Agency were here a few months ago, visiting the Arapahos. Last month, Red Cloud, with a small party of men, women and children, was here for a few days… There seems to be no unusual excitement in either tribe [the Shoshones or Arapahos], although emissaries of the Indian "Christ" have been among them; but not, I think, recently. This Indian "Christ" is, I am led to believe, one "Bannack Jim," a Mormon, and it is not unreasonable to suppose that his attempts to stir up strife have been instigated by Mormons. "Bannack Jim" is, I believe, at the Lehmi or the Fort Hall Agency.[17]

Likewise, in a letter dated October 24, 1890, from Catherine Weldon, a friend of Sitting Bull, to Pine Ridge Indian Agent McLaughlin addressing tension on the Pine Ridge Reservation, she stated: "I believe the Mormons are behind it all."[18] Regardless of the origins of the "Ghost Dance" craze, it is undisputed that few if any tears were shed by whites after Sitting Bull's assassination on December 15, 1890, and the Wounded Knee Massacre occurred exactly two weeks later. And like FBI informant Douglas Durham many years later during events surrounding the "occupation," Grouard always seemed to be lurking when trouble arose.

ENDNOTES

1. Deloria, *Indians in Unexpected Places*, p. 69.
2. James A. Donovan, *A Terrible Glory*, 2008, pp. 75-76.
3. Utley, *The Lance and the Shield*, p. 250.
4. Nathanson, *Over the Rainbow*, p. 131.
5. Powers, *The Killing of Crazy Horse*, p. 173.
6. Ibid., p. 174.
7. Connell, *Son of the Morning Star*, p. 227. Similarly, as noted throughout this book, it seems as if every effort is made to portray Indians such as Sitting Bull as unrelenting in their savagery. Yet, historian Stanley Vestal has argued that at the Battle of the Little Big Horn Sitting Bull declined to annihilate all of Custer's forces, specifically the unit led by Captain Reno. Vestal, *Sitting Bull: Champion of the Sioux*, p. 176.
8. Roger L. DiSivestro, *In the Shadow of Wounded Knee: The Untold Final Story of the Indian Wars*, (New York: Walker & Co., 2005), p. 156.
9. Utley, *The Lance and the Shield*, p. 230.
10. Ibid., p. 224.
11. Ibid., p. 226.
12. Ibid., p. 36.
13. Connell, *Son of the Morning Star*, p. 226.
14. Cook-Lynn, *A Separate Country*, p. 140.
15. Utley, *The Lance and the* Shield, p. 94.
16. Maj. Guy V. Henry, October 14, 1890 letter, United States National Archives. Powers noted when Henry was a captain, he was severely wounded by being shot through both cheeks and fell to the ground during the Rosebud/Little Big Horn campaign. Powers, *The Killing of Crazy Horse*, p. 185.
17. E.R. Kellogg, E.R. "Commanding" October 27, 1890 letter, United States National Archives.
18. Smith, *Moon of Popping Trees*, p. 110.

CHAPTER 12

"Libbie" Custer and "Buffalo Bill" Cody: Part II
Ferocious Guardians of George A. Custer's Legacy

God pity the wife who is waiting at home with her lily cheeks and violet eyes dreaming that old dream of love while her lover is walking in paradise.

Libbie Custer, July 5, 1876
Louise Barnett, *Touched by Fire*[1]

On June 25-26, 1876, General George A. Custer and over 265 of his men were killed by Lakota and Cheyenne warriors near the Little Big Horn River in Montana. After Custer's death, his wife, Elizabeth "Libbie" Custer, became the most famous widow in the United States at that time. From 1876 to the time of her death in 1933: "No statement reflecting the slightest discredit upon Custer's ability or reputation was allowed to go unanswered."[2] Her argument counter to his critics' claim of his recklessness and/or incompetence as the cause of his death was that it was due to forces beyond his control. Libbie argued those forces included the vast number of Indians arrayed against Custer and the cowardice of some of the officers under Custer's command. However, as historians are now admitting, the reasons for Custer's defeat are more complicated than simply being outnumbered by desperate Indians defending their families.

    One of the problematic traits Custer possessed was either his inability or unwillingness to conduct meaningful scouting or reconnaissance of the enemy forces he would confront. What makes this failing particularly odd is that George Custer accelerated his career in the Union Army during the Civil War as an aide de camp to George McClellan after McClellan observed Custer's fearlessness in crossing a river to scout enemy positions. Likewise, on a personal level, George Custer and Libbie's relationship involved two flesh-and-blood human beings, not mythical creatures living in a constant state of marital bliss. In the case of the Battle of the Little Big Horn, and especially George A. Custer himself, it is difficult to determine when the myths began, or even how to separate fact from hyperbole. In the case of the relationship between Libbie and George, the notion that they were anything but star-crossed lovers seems particularly difficult to set aside.

An examination of Custer's relationship with Libbie also revealed clues to the insecurities Custer feverishly sought to overcome, or at least hide. Although Custer did little to disguise his flirtations, and even apparently some relationships with other women, any indications by Libbie of interest in other men or from other men exposed gaps in Custer's seemingly impenetrable armor coating of confidence. Custer's remedy for his feelings of insecurity often came in the form of publicity—and usually lots of it. During Custer's 1874 expedition through the Black Hills of South Dakota, publicity about the enterprise became equally as, if not more, important to Custer than the expedition itself. He gave reporters full and prominent access to all phases of the march. One headline crowed: "Custer Expedition Confirms Early Rumors of Gold in Indians' 'Sacred' Black Hills." A subheading noted, "Prospectors Call It a Ten-Dollar Diggin's," which surely helped fuel the desire of the stampede of miners searching for the elusive substance. Most likely the subheading that pleased Custer most was "Fame of Young General Spreading Over World."[3] As is well documented, the miners' flagrant violation of the no-trespass clause of the Ft. Laramie Treaty of 1868 set off a chain of events culminating in Custer's death at the Little Big Horn in 1876. Some military experts have argued Custer's lust for glory and fame caused him to be exposed and isolated from other major units in that battle, making him an easy target for annihilation.

After gold was discovered in the Black Hills, and George set out with his expedition in 1874, a festive and colorful parade proceeded out from Ft. Abraham Lincoln near present-day Bismarck, North Dakota. As the parade passed the officers' quarters, each of the married officers paused to embrace his wife who had accompanied him to this frontier outpost. As Libbie hurried toward Custer, she seemed to swoon, and in exceedingly dramatic fashion. One soldier, observing the scene, commented: "'A very pretty piece of byplay for the men of the command.'"[4] Undoubtedly, George A. Custer was not likely to let an opportunity for a dramatic scene pass him by if he could help it.

As suggested in the Introduction, Fleisher is not the only writer or historian to squander an opportunity to explore the forces in the 19th century unblinkingly sanctioning the utter decimation of Indian culture. The famous author Stephen Ambrose, to employ a useful euphemism, "majored in the minors" when reviewing Libbie Custer's career, or what he apparently considered her lack of a career. In *Crazy Horse and Custer*, he engaged in curious speculation by questioning what kind of career Libbie would have enjoyed had she "been a boy" and bemoaning: "As it was, she was fated to be known only as a wife and then as a widow."[5] Left unexplained is why Ambrose considered Libbie's role as a devoted wife putting her husband's career first would be unusual for that era. Further, Ambrose also left unexplained why Libbie's life in an unquestionably male-dominated society at that time should be viewed through the paradigm of late 20th- and early 21st-century feminism. What is further left unexplained, and more relevant to her story at the time, is why she never questioned, or was never taught to question, the morality of "Manifest Destiny." Ambrose's comment reinforced Patricia Limerick's observation that the conquest of Indians is not taken seriously.

Paradoxically, in *Touched by Fire*, Louise Barnett at times reduced Libbie to a catty, jealous woman, at least insofar as to her views of Indian women. Barnett stated that when Libbie met Monahseetah, a Cheyenne woman who many, including possibly Libbie, suspected of having an affair with George Custer, she told those around her she did not find Monahseetah attractive. However, Libbie's outlook changed when Monahseetah: "'let the blanket fall from her glossy hair, [and] her white, even teeth gleamed as she smiled, and the expression transfigured her.'"[6] On another occasion, she noted a young Indian woman named Miss Spotted Tail was: "'Young, shy, and pretty as Indian girls often are until they become married drudges.'"[7] On another occasion, Libbie apparently noted: "'only extreme youth and its ever attractive charms can make one forget the heavy square shape of Indian faces and their coarse features.'"[8] In none of these instances is any explanation provided as to why Libbie developed such a harsh view of Indian ladies, except to hint the reason may have been jealousy. At least in the instance of Monahseetah, Libbie was prepared to modify her assessment of this young woman when provided other evidence, at least as to her appearance.

Prior to Custer's death, Libbie, who in letters Custer referred to as "My Sunbeam" or "My Sweet Rosebud," was the catalyst for one of, if not the most, infamous episodes of his military career other than the debacle of his "Last Stand" at the Little Big Horn where he was killed. As a prelude to the debacle, after Custer arrived in Kansas in 1866, he led the 7th Cavalry on several fruitless expeditions easily evaded by the resourceful Cheyenne and Lakota warriors. The following year, 1867, Custer led his troops on one particularly fruitless expedition in conditions so harsh even dogs died of exhaustion. Desertions reached such epidemic proportions that at one point between 30 and 40 soldiers left the command in one day, June 6, 1867. Barnett indicated that a few months earlier 40 soldiers deserted in one group. Custer became so frustrated during the June 6 situation he ordered summary executions of those deserters caught, and one of the troopers who had not managed to escape actually died of gunshot wounds at the hands of a 7th Cavalry officer.[9]

Soon after Custer's disgraceful debacle, Libbie arrived in Kansas by train. In his haste to reach his wife, Custer force-marched his troops 155 miles in 55 hours and had left his assigned post at Ft. Wallace on this personal, rather than professional, mission. During this madness, soldiers' mounts broke down and Custer ordered the riders left behind. Indian warriors soon caught up with these isolated soldiers and killed one and wounded another before help arrived. Not surprisingly, Custer was court-martialed for this serious lack of judgment and was found guilty of violating orders and of abandoning his troops to the enemy. He was also found guilty of ordering the execution of a deserter. His sentence was a one-year suspension "of rank and command" and forfeiture of pay during this period.[10] In the next chapter, there will be a fuller discussion regarding this incident in addition to Custer's notable lack of scouting prior to engaging enemy forces.

Given the rousing beginnings of Libbie and Custer's romance, it hardly seems surprising their lives together would be filled with other dramatic episodes of one sort or another. In a little-noticed comparison to his eventual nemesis Crazy Horse, when Custer met the love of his life, Libbie's family—like Black Buffalo Woman's family with Crazy Horse—did not consider Custer worthy of her. Since Custer was the son of a blacksmith, and other suitors came from wealthier families, her prominent judge father was especially hoping her affection would blossom elsewhere. However, the discouragement not only failed to deter Custer, but actually may have sparked Libbie's interest. Unlike the case of Crazy Horse and Black Buffalo Woman, Libbie and Custer eventually wed.[11]

After Custer's death in 1876, even though Libbie was from a prominent family, she struggled financially. Nonetheless, her elegant public persona and charitable service work helped her ascend the social ladder of New York City. Her activities included acting as a trustee of a woman's hospital, functioning as a board member of the Bellevue Training School of Nurses, and also serving as secretary for the New York Society of Decorative Arts. As her actions demonstrated, Libbie was certainly aware of the controversy surrounding the last battle of Custer's career and other aspects of his life, including his sometimes-volatile relationship with her. To redirect the blame for the annihilation of the 7th Cavalry at the Little Big Horn, Libbie: "…lobbied behind the scenes to ostracize surviving junior officers whom she blamed for her husband's destruction."[12] In early 1885, she published a memoir about her marriage to George Custer entitled *Boots and Saddles: Life in Dakota with General Custer* (cited herein). With this book, Libbie attempted to put a gloss on her often-troubled marriage to Custer by portraying it as a bulwark of domestic unity and peace in a life spent on the frequently frightening frontier.

In bolstering the image of Custer after his well-publicized death, Libbie found an enthusiastic ally in William F. Cody, otherwise known as "Buffalo Bill." Cody claimed friendship with Custer even though there was only one documented meeting between the two, which occurred in 1872. Although Cody began his stage career in 1872, in 1874 he served as a scout for federal forces along with several dozen Pawnees during an uneventful campaign in the Big Horn Mountains. Coincidentally, this expedition was executed near the site of Custer's demise two years later. This particular journey was so forgettable the commanding officer of the unit Cody was attached to did not even mention it in his memoirs. At the same time, Custer was leading his highly publicized expedition through the Black Hills and trumpeting the presence of gold in the region the Lakota considered the most sacred. Unfortunately for Custer and many of his men, tromping through the Black Hills in 1874 inflamed Indian passions and touched off the war that ultimately cost Custer and the soldiers he led their lives two years later. After the Little Big Horn battle, Cody was attached to the 5th Cavalry, whose mission was to intercept up to supposedly as many as 800 Cheyenne warriors who left the Red Cloud Agency in Ft. Robinson, Nebraska, heading north. They were believed to be on their way to reinforce Crazy Horse and his warriors. On July 17, 1876, the 5th Calvary encountered a small party of these Cheyenne warriors on Warbonnet Creek, which was located on the current border between Nebraska and Wyoming. The Cheyenne retreated almost immediately and during a running skirmish, no more than three, and possibly only one, warrior was killed.

However, this small fight soon became famous due to Cody, his theatrics, and his knack for publicity by turning it into an episode of revenge for Custer's death. In the story of the actual encounter, inexplicably dressed in a costume of black velvet slashed with scarlet and trimmed with silver buttons, Cody shot and killed a Cheyenne named, ironically enough, Yellow Hair (apparently this was the possible single casualty referred to in historical accounts). Although in reality Cody and Yellow Hair encountered each other quite by chance, in his typical show-business fashion Cody turned the story of the incident into a ritualized duel to the death in his stage play *The Red Right Hand* or *First Scalp for Custer*.[13] Curiously, in a memoir published just prior to his death, Custer was effusive in his praise of a scout named William Comstock but silent about Cody. Cody's play helped neutralize the effects of this publication, as did his fictitious claim of winning a hunting competition against Comstock. Nevertheless, some sources claim Cody even denied he killed Yellow Hair.[14]

Over the years, historians have begun to understand the story of Cody's life was as nuanced as the life of Custer, and not just a cheap imitation of Custer's or possibly "Wild Bill" Hickok's. The actual operation of Buffalo Bill's Wild West ("Show" was not usually considered part of the title in an attempt to demonstrate it *was* the Wild West) proved instructive on the complexity of Indian/white interactions. In addition to the marriages between whites and Indians, the Wild West was considered by many Indians besides Sitting Bull as a chance to make some decent money and see the world. The Wild West was one of the largest employers of Pine Ridge Indians and one of the best paying. When the Wild West would arrive at the reservation, large crowds would show up to greet the tour with individuals hoping to get a chance to gain employment.[15]

As with all famous people including Custer, Cody certainly had his share of critics. Chauncey Yellow Robe, a Lakota educated at Carlisle Indian School in Pennsylvania, denounced Cody for his role in developing the Wild West. Unlike Sitting Bull, and later Indian scholar Vine Deloria, Jr., Yellow Robe believed Cody's enterprise exploited Indians and perpetuated Indian images of "barbarism." Yellow Robe also criticized Cody's participation in a 1913 film that Yellow Robe believed exploited the tragedy at Wounded Knee and the deaths of the "Ghost Dancers." Yellow Robe argued Cody "'…left nothing beneficial to humanity.'"[16] Yet, Yellow Robe himself came under harsh criticism for being an advocate of off-reservation boarding schools which many Indians believed denied, and still believe deny, young Indian children the experience of learning about their history, language, and culture. Essentially, Yellow Robe himself was accused by some Lakota of working for whites and "undermining" Lakota values.[17]

In 1890, as the hysteria surrounding the "Ghost Dance" reached its artificially manufactured crescendo throughout the South Dakota region, Buffalo Bill did his best to take advantage of the situation. General Nelson "Bearcoat" Miles secretly issued an order to Cody to arrest Sitting Bull on the basis Sitting Bull had once been a member of Buffalo Bill's Wild West. As he did regarding Custer, Cody assured Miles he and Sitting Bull were old friends. It was true Cody once defended Sitting Bull's aggressive attitude on the basis Sitting Bull was defending his homeland and stated: "'Their [the Lakota's] lands were invaded by the gold seekers.'" Although Cody did manage to keep his mission to arrest Sitting Bull a secret, sadly, he betrayed his old friend by issuing a press release claiming: "'Of all the bad Indians, Sitting Bull is the worst…if there is no disturbance he will foment one. He is a dangerous Indian.'"[18]

As far as Buffalo Bill's Wild West itself, part of the intrigue of this enterprise was the challenge provided audience members to separate fact from fiction. Interestingly in that regard, in September 1884 Mark Twain wrote an unsolicited letter to Cody praising the authenticity of the production: "Down to its smallest details, the show is genuine—cowboys, Vaqueros, Indians, stage coach, costumes and all; it is wholly free from sham and insincerity and the effects produced upon me by its spectacles were identical with those wrought upon me long ago by those same spectacles on the frontier."[19] Due in part to the belief in the authenticity of the production, the Wild West served the role of "educating" the masses in addition to its entertainment function. Cody's show enthusiastically promoted the myth of Custer as the "unbesmirched" hero of Custer's Last Stand. The reality of Custer's position as a military leader is that he more closely resembled a factory owner who faced the constant threat of revolt of his factory workers; Custer's troops were Italian, German, Irish, and other immigrants as well as poor American-born natives.

To some extent, Buffalo Bill's legacy continued with the emergence of motion pictures as a major form of entertainment. Some "B" Western movie actors adopted his Wild West's practice of borrowing the mystique of the "original" participant by assuming names like "Bob Custer," "Buddy Roosevelt," and, of course, "Buffalo Bill Junior." In the six Westerns he made in 1932-33, John Wayne was always named John in an attempt to somehow promote the idea he was a "real" adventurer. It was in one sense an elaboration of the concept of confusing the mythic and the real life of Buffalo Bill 50 years prior. The difference was that Buffalo Bill attempted authentication by referring the audience to his involvement in the historical "Wild West" whereas John Wayne's: "…'authenticity' is established by confusing an actor with his role and by mistaking references to other movies for references to a world *outside* the movies [emphasis in original]."[20] That John Wayne's lack of military service did not inhibit the success of this ploy is a testament to the Hollywood publicity machine at that time.

ENDNOTES

1. Barnett, *Touched by Fire*, p. 308.
2. Custer, *Boots and Saddles*, pp. xxii.
3. John R. Curtis, "Custer Expedition Confirms Early Rumors of Gold in Indians' Sacred Black Hills," *Chicago Inter-Ocean*, August 27, 1874 (Monroe Michigan: The Custer Collection).
4. T. J. Stiles, *Custer's Trials: A Life on the Frontier of a New America* (New York: Vintage Books/A Division of Penguin Random House, 2015), p. 422.
5. Stephen Ambrose, *Crazy Horse and Custer: The Parallel Lives of Two American Warriors* (New York: Anchor Books/A Division of Random House, 1996), p. 182. In *Touched by Fire*, Louise Barnett commented on Ambrose's statement: "Ambrose, evidently thinking in terms of late-twentieth century career women… [was with] this speculative enhancement…unfairly dismissive of the real Libbie Custer and the meaning of her life." p. 408.
6. Barnett, *Touched by Fire*, p. 196.
7. Ibid., p. 212.
8. Ibid., p. 242.
9. Ibid., p. 136.
10. Stiles, *Custer's Trials*, p. 297.
11. Ibid., p. 147. However, Powers noted that after the episode which resulted in Crazy Horse being shot in the face, Black Buffalo Woman had a baby which: "…was light-haired, like Crazy Horse, and they believed this girl was his daughter." Powers, *The Killing of Crazy Horse*, p. 35.
12. Louis S. Warren, *Buffalo Bill's America*, p. 271.
13. Ibid., pp. 117-118.
14. Ibid., p. 545.
15. Ibid., p. 358.
16. Agonito, "Chauncey and Rosebud Yellow Robe: Living in the White Man's World," *Lakota Portraits*, p. 260.
17. Ibid., p. 258.
18. Warren, *Buffalo Bill's America*, p. 378.
19. Ibid., p. 294.
20. Slotkin, *Gunfighter Nation*, pp. 272-273.

CHAPTER 13

Will the Real George A. Custer Please Stand Up?

> He earned his worst grades in cavalry tactics.
> James Donovan, *A Terrible Glory*[1]

Captain Frederick W. Benteen, never a fan of George Armstrong Custer, sarcastically argued Custer's book *My Life on the Plains* would have more accurately been titled "*My Lie on the Plains.*"[2] Because of his loathing of Custer, Benteen's credibility about accounts of certain episodes in Custer's life and career remains in question to this day. Yet, even in his mostly flattering portrayal of Custer in his interesting book *Son of the Morning Star*, Evan S. Connell colorfully noted that events demonstrating Custer was fully human were often hardly believed. Connell stated the image of Custer as a Christian knight and as a "… dashing cavalier [were] embedded like a fossil in American folklore." Connell further explained: "Why he was esteemed as an Indian fighter is puzzling. None of his frontier campaigns demonstrated any particular skill or insight. Not that they were botched, just that his strategy could not be called brilliant."[3] And, as William Matson declared in his interesting chronicle of the family of Crazy Horse, *Crazy Horse: The Lakota Warrior's Life and Legacy*: "When a story circulates in the public arena long enough, people come to regard it as truth."[4]

One starting point for reviewing the Custer myth is to question whether the battle that resulted in his death and those of his soldiers in 1876 was even the worst defeat of U.S. forces by Indians in United States history, as is commonly claimed. Italian historian Gianni Granzotto explained this phenomenon by stating, "Popular legend…always ignores the subtleties of thought…"[5] That axiom applies especially in the case of Custer, since it is often difficult to look past the "glory" of Custer and analyze what actually happened in history. As a case in point, in 1790 General Josiah Harmar embarked on an expedition with 1,400 men with the intention of engaging Indians in what is now known as the state of Ohio in what was labeled the Northwest Indian War. Harmar drank heavily, had minimal control of his soldiers, and for him and his troops the worst aspect of all was that he had no experience fighting Indians. Little Turtle, a brave and skilled leader of a combined force of Miami, Shawnee, Potawatomi, and Chippewa warriors, nimbly drew Harmar into a trap. His clever plan included burning an occasional village to convince Harmar the Indians were fleeing. Once Harmar's scattered and disorganized forces were trapped deep in the forest, Little Turtle's men surrounded and annihilated 183 of Harmar's soldiers. Little Turtle even chose not to destroy all of Harmar's beleaguered forces, but that was yet to come for the men serving under Harmar.

Yet, after Harmar's debacle, things got even worse for the fledgling United States Indian War efforts. President Washington relieved Harmar as commander of the campaign and replaced him with Harmar's superior, General Arthur St. Clair. Like Harmar, St. Clair fought in the Revolutionary War but lacked experience in Indian warfare. St. Clair's army consisted primarily of militia gathered: "'…from prisons, wheelbarrows, and brothels at two dollars [pay] a month.'" Since St. Clair's quartermaster corps was so corrupt and incompetent, the soldiers often received neither their pay nor food.[6] After his troops confronted Little Turtle, out of 1,000 soldiers participating in combat, it is believed 632 were killed or captured and 264 were wounded; the fates of some remained undetermined. Historian Colin G. Colloway stated: "Proportionately, it was the biggest military disaster the United States ever suffered. It was also the biggest victory American Indians ever won. Yet it was quickly consigned to the footnotes of history."[7] Then again, understanding that Custer's defeat was not the worst defeat by Indians of U.S. military forces in history requires only the "subtlety" of looking at the casualty figures.

Even recent writers of Indian history seem hell-bent on placing their stamps of approval on the actions of whites in the form of arguing that no transgression by Indian killers was too large to be overlooked. In writing about the "mystery" of the Battle of the Little Big Horn, Louise Barnett noted: "…the tactic of envelopment was standard in Indian fighting: in addition to Custer's own victory on the Washita, it had been used successfully by Chivington at Sand Creek."[8] Even though objectively the attacks by both Custer and Chivington were nothing more than slaughters, she noted Generals Sheridan and McClellan both found little fault with Custer's aggressiveness in attacking the Indian village without a full appreciation of its size. It can safely be assumed that, had Custer been more successful at the Little Big Horn, he would have received lavish praise for any type of killing, including the elderly, women, and children. For example, after Custer's attack at the Washita in 1869, General Phil Sheridan praised Custer by claiming: "'Custer had struck a hard blow, and wiped out old Black Kettle and his murderers and rapers of helpless women' who had 'perpetrated cruelties too fiendish for recital.'"[9] Nevertheless Custer, being sensitive to the possibility that the: "…battle of the Washita was merely a repetition of the Sand Creek massacre…conceal[ed] in his initial report of the conflict the vast majority of casualties inflicted were women and children."[10] As noted in the Walter Camp papers: "As wounded Indians were supposed to or known to fight as long as they could all of the wounded Indians in the fight were promptly shot to death without discrimination as to appearance of danger, just exactly as Indians would have treated wounded soldiers."[11]

The rationalization for this uninhibited killing was that it was considered just exactly what Indians would have done to whites, be they men, women, or children. In actuality, the only real mystery is why historians continue to rationalize the actions of men like Custer who died attempting to bring death and destruction to men, women, and children whose only real offense was having the audacity to believe they could live their lives as they saw fit on the Great Plains. There were adjustments made to the image of Custer the man as well. Custer's widow, who appeared to be married to a "…violent, mercurial, and libidinous officer…" transformed him by her lectures and memoirs into: "…an icon of fidelity and chivalric manliness, a man who paced the floor for hours with a sick puppy in his arms and changed the route of his march to protect the nest of a prairie hen and her brood."[12]

What is endlessly fascinating about Custer is he is famous first and foremost for his defeat and *failure* at the Little Big Horn in 1876. Colonel Ranald S. Mackenzie was ruthlessly effective in the mid-1870s during the Red River War in Texas in routing the Comanches. In November 1876 his troops attacked Cheyenne leader Dull Knife's village[13] and Dull Knife eventually surrendered in the spring of 1877. What made Mackenzie's anonymity particularly ironic is Dull Knife-led forces participated in the destruction of Custer's command a few months earlier. Yet, Mackenzie was committed to the Bloomindale Asylum in New York City in December 1882 and eventually died in obscurity.[14]

Further, the mid- to late 1870s contained numerous significant events affecting the entire nation: the great railroad strike of 1877, the formation of Standard Oil as the first of the: "great industrial trusts that would dominate the American economy into the next century," as two examples. At most, Custer's defeat and the corresponding victory of the Lakota and Cheyenne in 1876 delayed the demise of these Plains Indians as an effective fighting force for a year. Yet, in United States culture, the question is why is the "Last Stand" the: "…event whose name and character have been longest remembered and have been invested with the heaviest charge of symbolic meaning? …Don Russell's study of the illustrations of the Last Stand has led him to conclude the Battle of the Little Big Horn is the most frequently depicted moment in all of American history."[15]

During his lifetime, even after his court-martial conviction in 1867 for going AWOL, which was his *second* such conviction, Custer's mythical status remained unchanged in some quarters. The *New York Times* gushed at that time:

> Gen. Custer is, to those who know him intimately, the very *beau ideal* of an American cavalry officer. He is a magnificent rider, fearlessly brave, a capital revolver shot, and without a single objectionable habit. He neither drinks, swears, nor uses tobacco in any form. His weakness, if he has one, is a fast horse, to get all the speed out of which there is no better man than the long-haired hero of the Shenandoah [emphasis added].[16]

As is almost always the case with famous people, the reality of the man or woman being discussed is more complicated—and more interesting than the myth. T. J. Stiles wrote that at General Phil Sheridan's insistence General Grant reinstated Custer to active duty after "'…remission of the balance of his sentence…'" levied after this second court-martial. Stiles also noted: "Grant gave Custer what he wanted most—a chance at redemption."[17] Little did anyone know at that time Custer's "redemption" would arrive after his death through the efforts of his widow, Libbie. Although the public usually viewed Custer as the essence of a noble knight, many who served with him on the Great Plains, and especially under him, saw him as a cruel martinet. This was the result of the harsh and draconian punishments Custer regularly handed down for minor infractions. Critics such as members of the 1st Iowa Cavalry were pleased with Custer's suspension from service as a punishment for his second court-martial conviction. It was noted: "His memory will be a stench in their nostrils, and that of their children's children to the remotest generation."[18]

Many saw hypocrisy in Custer complaining about his punishment for being absent without leave after his conviction by court-martial for leaving his post without permission and traveling hundreds of miles to see his wife. For subordinates during the Civil War committing the same offense, he brought the full force of military justice on them for significantly less serious infractions. In one instance during that period, a soldier at a post nowhere near the front lines of fighting left for five minutes to obtain either some food or some milk. This unfortunate soul was court-martialed and given a dishonorable discharge at Custer's insistence. Tellingly, and to some degree ironically, in a survey conducted at Ft. Leavenworth in 1891, 15 years after Custer's death at the Little Big Horn, the most frequently reported reason for prisoners going AWOL was "'tyrannical superiors.'"[19] Although obviously the survey was conducted long after his passing, an astute observer like Custer could hardly have misinterpreted the motives of men acting in this fashion. Custer conspicuously neglected to report his observations regarding soldier morale as a factor in AWOL situations in his book *My Life on the Plains*.

Yet, the "Custer Myth" lives on. Richard Slotkin suggested part of the appeal of this framework for outlining the dead soldier's life is: "The resonance of the Custer story, and its persistence as an American myth, is thus attributed to its resemblance to the classic myths of heroic sacrifice—especially to the Christian myth of expiatory suffering and death suggested by Vine Deloria, Jr.'s book title *Custer Died for Your Sins*."[20] It could be argued Custer is considered a "Christ figure" as some theology professors might label him. It is intriguing that in explaining the Custer myth Slotkin used Deloria, Jr.'s classic essay since Deloria, Jr., in another section of his book noted: "The most popular and enduring subject of Indian humor is, of course, General Custer. There are probably more jokes about Custer and the Indians than there were participants in the battle." For example, one punchline is that Custer was well dressed for the Battle of the Little Big Horn because he was wearing an "Arrow shirt."[21]

Perhaps the most intriguing of the many facets of Custer's personality is that while he earnestly desired combat against Indians, psychologically he shared the fate of some Indian warrior/hunters (the differences in the types of combat Indians were involved in historically notwithstanding). Like many of those he fought, Custer relished the notoriety performing well in combat provided and, like many Indian men, he enjoyed hunting tremendously. On a deeper level, he ended up being a man unable to find his role in a fast-changing society, as some Indian men found as a bewildering problem as white encroachment progressed. Although Custer was a leader in the Union Army, and helped provide freedom for many slaves, he did not necessarily welcome that freedom for black people and had difficulty adapting to the changes in post-Civil War society. Ironically, his *defeat* at the Little Big Horn brought on an outcry to tame those "hostile" Indians and hastened their banishment to dreary reservations and the stultifying life on those virtual prisons.

Nonetheless, it seems in the case of Custer, the idea that he was a brave and noble knight tragically killed, even murdered, by mindless and heartless savages simply was and is a notion meant to be taken seriously. In contradiction to the pervasive myth of Custer's fame even among the Indians, first and foremost, at least at the Battle of the Little Big Horn, the idea Cheyenne and Lakota warriors specifically targeted, attacked, and killed Custer there is laughable. Out of the Indians present in June 1876, only a few would have recognized him without the presence of the confusion of the smoke and dust of battle. That possibility was almost entirely eliminated because it is almost certain Custer cut his long blond locks before leaving Ft. Abraham Lincoln in North Dakota on his way to his doom. Long hair simply got dirty, made the wearer hot, and was just not worth having in the field. That Custer possibly wasn't scalped was most likely due to the short hair not being worth the effort Indians thought it would take to separate Custer's shortened hair from his head. Nevertheless, as Rain in the Face eloquently stated: "'Why, in that fight the excitement was so great that we scarcely recognized our nearest friends.'"[22]

Some perpetrators of white myths about the conquest of the western frontier, however, simply refuse to let the idea wither away that Indians at the Little Big Horn fought with extra tenacity to destroy the man known to them as "Long Hair." Both Sitting Bull and Gall, another Indian leader, told reporters sometime after the battle they unaware they were fighting Custer. After he was accused of "murdering" Custer, Sitting Bull's terse comment was reported as: "'It is a lie…he was a fool and rode to his death.'"[23] The Indians present in Montana on those hot summer days in June 1876 were simply fighting to protect their families. In actuality, at the Battle of the Little Big Horn, Sitting Bull was perplexed as to why experienced army officers would put their troops and themselves in such precarious tactical situations and actually believed the attacks were merely feints to distract the Indians from a major offensive to take place at another time and location.

Yet, eliminating the Custer myth not only serves to leave those interested in history with an image of a man fully human, but a much more interesting one as well. Far from being a chivalrous knight (whatever that actually means), Custer was a flesh-and-blood man with human desires just like everybody else. Although disputed by historian Stephen Ambrose, multiple sources claimed Custer fathered a child with a beautiful Cheyenne woman named Monahseetah. Of particular interest is the reference to this relationship and birth of a child in *Halfbreed*, the story of George Bent, the half-Cheyenne, half-white son of Cheyenne Pretty Owl and white trader William Bent. The author indicated the belief Monahseetah gave birth to Custer's child in late 1869 as a result of the relationship is based on Cheyenne tradition. The story began after the 7th Cavalry's attack on Black Kettle's village on the Washita River on November 27, 1868.[24]

Regardless of whether he fathered a child or not, the story of Custer at least having a relationship with a Cheyenne woman is not as unlikely as some like Ambrose would suggest. The example of Phil Sheridan is illustrative as to a common practice of that era. Sheridan, who became Custer's benefactor in the later stages of the Civil War and continued in that role once Custer served on the Great Plains, had a very utilitarian view of Indian women, perhaps even of women in general. It was well documented that Sheridan once had a relationship with an Indian woman named Sidnayoh when he was assigned to an army post in the northwest United States as a freshly minted lieutenant out of West Point. For five years, Sidnayoh, known to whites as Frances, kept Sheridan's home, cooked for him, and shared his bed. Although this relationship started out between two human beings, Sheridan eventually exposed if not his cruel streak, at least his cold side. After the Civil War, Sidnayoh, her brother, and two friends came to Washington, D.C., to visit Sheridan, but he refused to acknowledge Sidnayoh or speak to her in any manner, and eventually he married the daughter of a U.S. Army general.[25] Sheridan called the Indians of the Northwest "miserable wretches" and was unconcerned that their desperate plight was due largely to mistreatment by whites. Sheridan famously stated, "The only good Indians I ever saw were dead," which morphed into the even harsher, better-known phrasing, "The only good Indian is a dead Indian."[26]

Whether Custer came to his views on Indians as inferior beings on his own or was simply mimicking his benefactor Sheridan is difficult to assess. In many respects, it is difficult to clearly determine what he thought about his foes on the Plains at all. In his own words in *My Life on the Plains*, Custer mused that the Indian: "'…is, and, so far as all knowledge goes, as he ever has been, a *savage* in every sense of the word; not worse, perhaps than his white brother would be similarly born and bred, but one whose cruel and ferocious nature far exceeds that of any wild beasts of the desert [emphasis in source document].'" Yet, he believed it was incorrect to label them as a group as either "'simple-minded' 'sons of nature'" or individually as: "'…a creature possessing the human form but divested of all other attributes of humanity, and whose traits…and savage customs disqualify him from the exercise of all rights and privileges.'" Custer, however, did not necessarily believe they were the same as white people. He stated they were: "'…a race incapable of being judged by the rules or laws applicable to any other known race of men.'"[27]

Like Sheridan, Custer had a cruel or cold streak as well. In addition to the problem of desertion previously discussed, other disciplinary problems arose as well that required a defter response than Custer displayed. In one notable incident, a popular sergeant with an outstanding Civil War record circulated a petition for the removal of an unpopular officer. Technically this was mutiny and a court-martial sentenced the sergeant to be executed by a firing squad. Custer then had his entire division assembled to witness the execution of the sergeant and a convicted deserter. As both men sat in their coffins, Custer gave the "Ready" and "Aim" commands. Before ordering "Fire," Custer ordered the sergeant to be led away and only the deserter was killed. Although Custer had intended the scene to be an object lesson in discipline, the only thing his men learned from this grotesque and sadistic display was that Custer was a talented yet deeply flawed man who sometimes had exceptionally poor judgment. Custer never regained the nearly unanimous acclaim and loyalty he enjoyed during the Civil War.[28]

Custer's cruel actions were remarkably similar to those of Columbus close to 400 years earlier, although Columbus directed his harsh actions toward indigenous people and not his own men. In 1494, Columbus received news of native unrest in Santo Tomás on the island of Espanola and what is now known as the Dominican Republic. Columbus then ordered the exceptionally aggressive Alonzo de Ojeda to lead a force of 400 men to Santo Tomás to "'spread terror among the Indians to show them how strong and powerful the Christians were.'" Upon his first contact with the Indians, Ojeda ordered the ears cut off men who were merely accused of stealing some Spanish clothing.

In spite of Ojeda's harshness, a cacique who had confidence the Spaniards would not continue to overreact brought the clothes stealers before Columbus, believing they would be released. Foolishly, Columbus ordered the offenders as well as the cacique to be publicly decapitated. Even though Columbus revoked the sentence, Bartoleme de Las Casas wrote the overall actions of Ojeda and Columbus were: "'the first injustice committed under the guise of justice and the beginning of the [era of] shedding of blood which was to flow so copiously from then on all over this island.'"[29] Similarly, Custer's actions sowed discord among his officers and men that created a rift which was never healed before Custer met his fate at the Little Big Horn. For those who have learned about the history of Custer as a cadet at West Point, the manner in which Custer handled the incident with the "mutinous" sergeant is not surprising. Custer was known at this somber institution as a masterful practical joker, and one of his most famous schemes involved the Spanish instructor at the Point at that time. During class, Custer asked this gentleman how to say "class is dismissed" in Spanish, and when the instructor replied accordingly, Custer proceeded to lead his fellow cadets out of the classroom.[30]

Custer's penchant for practical jokes was not limited to victimizing those in the military service. The "jokes" were often cruel, and as in the case with the mock execution of the mutinous sergeant, were barely jokes at all. On July 6, 1870, Custer engaged in a bison hunt with Libbie, Annie Gibson Roberts, Tom Custer, Mary Reno (the wife of newly assigned 7th Cavalry officer Marcus Reno), their son Robert, and some other officer friends. During the hunt, some strangers appeared on the horizon, and Custer, Tom, and a few others rode off to meet them. Libbie, Mrs. Reno, and Robert were left behind with Lieutenant Edward Mathey and Colonel Wesley serving as chaperones. The strangers turned out to be Indians and when Custer reached their location, shots rang out. Someone, those left behind did not know who, fell from his saddle. Mrs. Reno grabbed her son Robert and Libbie cried out, "Auntie will be killed.'" After Mrs. Reno eventually guessed the attack was staged, Colonel Merritt lashed out at Lieutenant Mathey: "'…quit this damned nonsense—don't you see they are frightening the ladies?'" It turned out the Indians were scouts; Mathey admitted the whole production was a "practical joke.'"[31] Few would consider it anything but strange for a husband to stage his own death right before his wife's eyes.

Unsurprisingly, Custer's penchant for poking fun at and even humiliating others was not a trait he welcomed in other people in their actions toward him. Early in Custer's marriage during the Civil War, an army wagon containing Libbie's letters to him and some other personal effects was captured by Confederates at Trevillian Station. After the event, Custer wrote Libbie containing a rigid view of the situation and chided Libbie by stating he did: "'…not relish the idea of others amusing themselves with [her letters], particularly as some of the expressions employed…somebody must be more careful hereafter in the use of *double entendu* [sic].'" Libbie responded she was unconcerned about the discovery of the letters and added: "'…there can be nothing low between man and wife if they love each other.'" In a revealing look at the power Custer seemed to hold over Libbie, in his response to Libbie's letter shaking off his concerns, Custer apologized for his criticism and added this most recent letter of hers: "'…would afford equal amusement to my Southern acquaintances as those now in their hands. Now do not think me too exacting or too particular.'" Curiously, after his apology she retreated from her earlier position of unconcern and replied: "'I am glad you are so particular with me. With my much loved and honored parents, I felt indignant at reproof, but when you express as ever so slightly displeased, I feel grieved and try to do better.'"[32]

At the very end of his time at West Point, Custer's own sense of what was honorable and his disregard of military discipline created considerable anxiety for the almost-new lieutenant. Custer had just barely passed West Point academically, graduating 34th out of 34 cadets and was just eight points shy, 192 out of 200, of the disqualifying number of demerits for his last year (or any year). He remained at West Point while the War Department was finding slots for the new graduates, including himself. He was still considered a cadet and was serving as officer of the guard on June 29 when a fight broke out between cadets Peter Ryerson and William Ludlow.

Custer later wrote: "'I should have arrested the two combatants and sent them to the guard tents, but the instincts of the boy prevailed over the obligation of the officer of the guard.'" Instead, Custer pushed through the crowd of cadets and shouted: "'Stand back boys, let's have a fair fight.'" After failing to act as instructed by the rules of West Point, Custer found *himself* under arrest. As T. J. Stiles aptly and prophetically pointed out: "He finally faced the consequences of being Custer."[33] After hearing testimony about the fight, the court-martial reconvened on July 6, and at some point during the proceedings, Custer pled guilty. He read his final statement to the court in which he did his best to minimize the fight and called it "'merely a scuffle.'" At the conclusion of deliberations regarding his punishment, Custer's sentence ended up being—nothing.[34] The court-martial highlighted the contrast of Custer's personality: individualistic, romantic, and impulsive—against the most rigidly hierarchical and systematic institution in the United States at that time: the United States Army. It is often these types of human flaws which are overlooked in analyzing Custer and his 7th Cavalry's defeat at the Little Big Horn.

Many believe one aspect of practical jokes is some level of cruelty, which Custer demonstrated. In the case of the Spanish instructor early in Custer's career, the cruel aspect involved the embarrassment of this instructor, who was never known as much of a disciplinarian. Perhaps had Custer received a reprimand then, or punishment for his handling of the fight between Ryerson and Ludlow, he might have gotten a grip on his cruel or undisciplined streak. Perhaps then he would have had a reluctance to engage in the thoughtless displays which only earned him the disdain of his troops and officers such as Frederick Benteen. His ability to evade discipline, at least initially in his career, certainly contributed to his sense of invulnerability.

When his life intersected with another famous individual, "Wild Bill" Hickok, he once again revealed a belief that superior humans were to be judged by a different set of rules. It may even be evidence Custer ascribed to the notion of survival of the fittest in one way or another. On July 17, 1870, in Ellis County, Kansas, where Hickok had temporarily served as sheriff, Hickok got in a brawl with two privates from Custer's 7th Cavalry. The brawl ended when Hickok shot them—Jerry Lonergen survived but John Kyle did not. Custer was unfazed by Hickok's actions and stated: "I have personal knowledge of at least a half a dozen men whom he has at various times killed, one [sic] of those being at the time a member of my command." Custer added: "'There was not a single instance in which the verdict of twelve fair-minded men would have not pronounced in his favor.'"[35]

In spite of his penchant for cruelty, at times in Custer's life, his humanity peeked through, even in combat situations. On August 5, 1862, during his Civil War service, Custer encountered two rebels who turned and fled upon seeing Custer and his comrades. Custer proceeded to ride one of the startled Confederates down, who promptly surrendered. Custer then rode back with his prisoner to the spot where he initially encountered the rebel duo. At that point, another rebel officer with 15 or 20 men approached, then fled when they saw Custer and the other Union soldiers. Custer proceeded to chase the rebel officer down in a dramatic scene that involved both officers leaping over a wooden rail fence. After the jump, Custer shouted "'Surrender!'" and "'Surrender or I will shoot!'" After firing and missing with his pistol, Custer again fired, this time with the bullet finding its mark. The rebel officer fell off his horse and died shortly thereafter. The event marked the first time Custer knew he had killed a man. In a letter to his sister and brother-in-law, Custer claimed: "It was his own fault… I told him twice to surrender but was compelled to shoot him." Custer also explained: "'*I tried not to kill him*'" and "'*I tried twice but had no choice* [emphasis in original].'"[36]

Part of Custer's problem during his command time after the Civil War was that few, if any, of his men shared his love of the army, and he could not ever seem to grasp that fact. The troops under his command at the time of the fake execution debacle had volunteered to fight for the Union and were ready to go to their homes, not out to other post-war duties or to fight Indians. His men were in often in surly moods and his efforts to impose his strict style of discipline only created more resentment. He was simply baffled as to why he was so resisted in his efforts to conjure up enthusiasm for Reconstruction efforts in Texas at that time when he was used to accolades for his Civil War exploits.

Nonetheless, while such things are difficult to measure at best, it is quite possible the various aspects of the "Custer Myth" have burrowed so deeply in the collective consciousness of citizens of the United States it may take massive effort to have Custer seen shorn of his mythical trappings. In 1888, Adolfus Busch, president of the newly formed Anheuser-Busch Breweries in St. Louis, bought a saloon displaying a large diorama painting of "Custer's Last Stand." Busch then hired an artist named Otto Becker to paint a smaller version of the battle scene and make a lithograph of it. The 24" x 40" version of the picture showed a long-haired Custer with his sword raised in the center of a furious battle between Indians and cavalrymen. It is believed Becker incorporated some of the fallen figures in the foreground of the painting from Gustav Doré's depiction of Dante's Inferno.

It seems fitting the image of George A. Custer, a known teetotaler, would be an integral aspect of the first national advertising campaign for the sale of beer. In 1896, Anheuser-Busch had 15,000 copies of Becker's picture made and distributed. Eventually over a million copies were distributed and hung behind the counters of taverns and bars. In an irony that would have amused Custer, a notorious practical joker, as many a drinker has sat on a bar stool contemplating his drink while staring at the knightly visage of Custer, it is doubtful it would occur to any of them that Custer completely swore off alcohol after he reached the age of 21. Apparently, after creating a drunken spectacle of himself at that time, Custer decided to swear off drinking for the rest of his life.[37]

It is as if even mistakes by professional historians result in Custer appearing ubiquitous. In *Son of the Morning Star*, Evan Connell claimed: "At Bull Run in October of 1863 he enjoyed supper 'under a stately oak that bears many a battle scar, surrounded by graves, washed by rain so that skulls and skeletons are visible… There is heavy firing to the left.'"[38] The only problem with that description is that First Manassas, known as the Battle of Bull Run, occurred in July 1861 and Second Manassas, or the Second Battle of Bull Run, occurred in August 1862. Perhaps it is nothing more than a misstatement, but it might also be a reminder the myth of Custer's military genius is so pervasive it is stated he fought in battles that didn't even occur.

At the end of this analysis of Custer's life it can be stated the myth of his demise being simply due to being vastly outnumbered by Lakota and Cheyenne warriors has outlived its usefulness, if it ever really served any purpose at all. Part of a realistic explanation for this event is that Custer and the other graduates of West Point did not receive training in the tactics needed to defeat an elusive foe such as Plains Indians warriors. Winfield S. Hancock, who achieved notable success in the Civil War as a Union general, also failed to achieve any significant measure of success on the Plains. Serious study by military analysts would also have revealed, at a minimum, individual Indian warriors were brave and resilient fighters. Similarly, there is no evidence indicating any Department of War, West Point, or any other analysis was ever undertaken of Red Cloud's successful guerrilla war against United States forces in the 1860s.

Nonetheless, a commander more skilled in managing a large, separate command would have at a minimum recognized the importance of reconnoitering. And, appropriate reconnoitering would most likely have disclosed the Indians at the Little Big Horn were indeed present in large numbers and apparently prepared to fight well before the battle began. In that regard, part of Custer's problem was his lack of awareness that while during the Civil War he was *part* of a larger campaign, while fighting (or looking for, mostly) Indians on the Plains he *was* the campaign. However, it is generally believed the idea for engaging the Plains Indians in 1876 was to have: "…three independent forces converge on the hostiles in the Powder and Tongue River country."[39]

Thus, it appears the overall strategy for the campaign was to have Custer's forces operating in conjunction with other units. This was the general concept of cavalry tactics during the Civil War, since for the most part cavalry actions during that war were usually conducted in tandem with larger infantry units, or involved activities such as destroying rail lines. In battle scenarios, such as at Gettysburg, superior officers such as Generals George Meade, Judson Kilpatrick, and David Gregg had responsibility for the larger strategy of the battle, including the overall supervision of cavalry units such as Custer's. That analysis is not meant to diminish Custer's accomplishments in those types of Civil War engagements but only to highlight his activities were usually part of a larger whole. The point is not to debate the effectiveness of cavalry during the Civil War, but to argue that on June 25 and 26, 1876, the 7th Cavalry fought independently of any infantry units or even of other cavalry units and the strategy and tactics on those days was Custer's and Custer's alone.

Interestingly, another aspect of Custer's life which highlighted his lack of interest in management was his sojourn into finance. As Custer "learned" at the cost of his life, appearances alone could not overcome his lack of interest in managing any part of combat operations other than the combat itself. During his time on Wall Street, Custer was taken in by financiers with mistresses, mansions, and theatre boxes. He neglected to notice the work these men put in buying, selling, bargaining, and even bribing to make their fortunes grow. He also failed to notice sometimes things went awry even for the sharpest of them. Jarius Hall, a colonel of the 4th Michigan Infantry during the Civil War, was Custer's partner in the development of the Stevens Lode Silver Mine in the Rocky Mountains west of Denver. Eventually, due to lack of initial financing and lack of silver ore, the prospects of turning a profit in the mine soon fizzled out.[40]

Similarly, one of the consequences of Custer's lack of attention to detail became apparent to historians analyzing the climactic concluding chapter of his life. Likewise, an earlier episode during the initial period of Custer's military career revealed an almost genetic predisposition towards heedless exposure to danger. In May 1862, during the early stages of the Civil War, General George McClellan's chief engineer, General John Barnard, needed to have a reconnaissance of the Chickahominy River to determine its depth prior to its being crossed by a larger force. Barnard ordered Custer to engage in the task and Custer: "Without hesitation…jumped in, exposing himself to the possibility of enemy fire from the opposite bank."[41] In contrast, Mike Sajna noted in his efficient biography of Crazy Horse that the Lakota combat leader was consistently cautious in his approach to enemy encounters. Interestingly, while the 1973 Wounded Knee "occupation" was thought to be the result of impulsivity, Russell Means, a descendant of Crazy Horse, conceived of the strategy well before the event.

The concept of who is an "Indian," addressed earlier in this book, complicated matters for Custer in at least one instance. In 1864, Robert Bent, one of the sons of William Bent and Cheyenne Pretty Owl, led Colonel Chivington to the village at Sand Creek where the Cheyennes were slaughtered in the previously described orgy of violence. Three years later, in April 1867, Ed Guerrier, a survivor of this horror, was ordered to lead George Custer and the 7th Cavalry to another Cheyenne village. It is not clear whether Custer was aware Guerrier was in a romantic relationship with Julia Bent, another child of William Bent and Pretty Owl. Julia lived in the village about to be attacked, along with some hostages taken in Cheyenne raids whom Custer was planning to set free

Although some argue Guerrier should have simply declined to scout for the army like George Bent, he nevertheless had no intention of leading Custer to the Cheyenne village to set hostages free or for any other purpose. When Guerrier spotted a young Cheyenne rounding up ponies in a ravine, the young warrior fled when he got a signal from Guerrier. Guerrier reported to Custer that the trail of the Cheyennes was nearly impossible to follow, particularly since they were not dragging lodge poles. Since Custer lacked experience in Indian warfare, he took Guerrier at his word. During Guerrier's entire service as a "scout," Custer and his 7th Cavalry troops never saw a single Cheyenne.[42]

ENDNOTES

1. Donovan, *A Terrible Glory*, p. 44.
2. Stiles, *Custer's Trials*, p. 371.
3. Connell, *Son of the Morning Star*, pp. 105-106.
4. Matson, *Crazy Horse: The Lakota Warrior's Life and Legacy*, p. 196.
5. Granzotto, *Christopher Columbus*, p. 81.
6. Utley and Washburn, *Indian Wars*, p. 113.
7. Colin G. Calloway, "The Biggest Forgotten Indian Victory," *Zocalo*, June 9, 2015.
8. Barnett, *Touched by Fire*, p. 334.
9. Slotkin, *Fatal Environment*, p. 401.
10. Ibid., p. 400.
11. "Wounded Indians at Washita," Walter Camp Collection, Lilly Library, Bloomington, Indiana.
12. Warren, *Buffalo Bill's America*, p. 272.
13. Hedren, Ed. "The Great Sioux War: an Introduction," *The Great Sioux War 1876-77: The Best from Montana: The Magazine of Western History* (Helena, Montana: Montana Historical Society, 1991). p. 17. Sadly, the urge to describe Indian people in less than human terms is seemingly irrepressible. One writer for this publication described Indian girls running for their lives from onrushing attackers from Mackenzie's unit as "…racing off through the cold like fleeing prairie chickens." Hedren, Ed. Father Peter J. Powell, "High Bull's Victory Roster," *The Great Sioux War*, p. 156.
14. Gwynne, *Empire of the Summer Moon*, pp. 304-305.
15. Slotkin, *Fatal Environment*, p. 14.
16. Stiles, *Custer's Trials*, p. 298.
17. Ibid., p. 305.
18. Ibid., p. 227.
19. Barnett, *Touched by Fire*, p. 81.
20. Slotkin, *Fatal Environment*, p. 27.
21. Deloria, Jr., *Custer Died for Your Sins*, p. 150.
22. Barnett, *Touched by Fire*, p. 400.
23. Connell, *Son of the Morning Star*, p. 232.
24. Halaas and Masich, *Halfbreed*, p. 261. Powers noted after the Battle of Blue Water Creek General Harney "…fathered a girl…" and that: "Some of the Indian women got caught…after a while they were released from the white people, and they all came back pregnant. Some of the squaw women disappeared.'" Powers, *The Killing of Crazy Horse*, p. 100.
25. Donovan, *A Terrible Glory*, p. 17.
26. Ibid., p. 18.
27. Stiles, *Custer's Trials*, p. 367.
28. Ibid., p. 225.

29 Wilford, *The Mysterious History of Columbus*, p. 174.
30 Stiles, *Custer's Trials*, p. 14.
31 Ibid., p. 340.
32 Barnett, *Touched by Fire*, p. 41.
33 Stiles, *Custer's Trials*, p. 26.
34 Ibid., p. 27.
35 Ibid., p. 339.
36 Ibid., pp. 66-67.
37 Frazier, *On the Rez*, pp. 138-139.
38 Connell, *Son of the Morning Star*, p. 353.
39 Powers, *The Killing of Crazy Horse*, p. 196.
40 Barnett, *Touched by Fire*, pp. 263-265.
41 Ibid., p. 28.
42 Halaas and Masich, *Halfbreed*, pp. 221-222.

Chapter 14

The "Lost Bird" of Wounded Knee: Part II

> Kill the Indian and save the man.
> Richard Henry Pratt
> Jake Page, *In the Hands of the Great Spirit* [1]

The story of the "Lost Bird" of Wounded Knee—Zintkala Nuni—a Lakota baby found under a dead Indian woman four days after the Wounded Knee Massacre of December 29, 1890, is compelling in and of itself. Yet, in her book *The Lost Bird of Wounded Knee*, Renée Sansom Flood managed to heighten even more the sense of drama surrounding that dark stain of mass killing splattered on this country's flag. She described in detail the buildup of tensions caused by the uninhibited attacks and often killing by whites of Lakota people in southwest South Dakota during the month of December 1890. Sometimes her descriptions were regarding simple indifference to the needs of fellow human beings.

In one instance, she described that callous indifference as exhibited by parishioners at a log church in response to the needs of the starving, desperate Indian people on their way to Pine Ridge who stopped by for assistance just prior to the Wounded Knee Massacre. As the bedraggled Indians trudged through the bitter South Dakota winter and approached the church, they heard the many hymns being sung. Spotted Elk, otherwise known as "Big Foot," sent a woman to the church door to ask those inside if babies and old people could be brought in to enjoy the warmth of a fire. Instead of being shown Christian hospitality, the minister shouted, "'Go away, outlaws!'"[2] Sometimes, whites simply displayed abject cruelty. There is some indication that the commander on the scene at Wounded Knee where "Big Foot's" people were surrounded by heavily armed federal forces, Colonel James Forsyth: "…ordered the Indian men to stand before the soldiers, then told the soldiers to empty their guns, hold them to the Indians' heads, and pull the trigger."[3]

It is possible these particular followers of "Big Foot" heading to the church were not aware of the malice often directed toward the Indian residents of South Dakota. If they were, the minister's harsh words would have come as no surprise. This is in conjunction with the penchant of many, if not most, historians to promote the idea the horrific events of December 29, 1890, were a consequence of the fear created by the "Ghost Dance." However, Flood argued the desire of ruthless ranchers to maintain possession of the rich grasslands on the opposite side of the Cheyenne River bordering the Pine Ridge Reservation was the primary cause of the slaughter. The ranchers reasoned if the Lakota were provoked consistently enough, the settlers who were offered the opportunity to possess some of these grasslands through an 1889 agreement would be deterred by fear of Indian attacks.

Also, according to Flood, government officials such as then-South Dakota Governor Arthur Mellette contributed to the chaos. Mellette approved the request of Colonel Merritt H. Day to provide him hundreds of rifles and ammunition. Day then organized a two-company militia consisting of a company of 51 men under Captain George Cosgrove and another "home guard" company of 49 men under Captain Gene Atkins and J. B. McCloud. Governor Mellette encouraged and praised Colonel Day for stirring up the Lakota. Mellette's dispatches to Day disclose a cover-up devised (apparently successful at the time) to hide from other military officials and citizens the deliberate attempt to provoke an uprising. One of Mellette's dispatches contained the sly comment: "I was pleased to get your message stating that in a skirmish three Indians had been killed by 'our men' without loss to the whites. Be discreet in killing the Indians." Flood also noted that throughout the month of December 1890, ranchers attacked the Lakota in the hope the resulting strife and tension would scare the settlers away.

Flood also recounted a story of Indian generosity rarely, if ever, related by historians who have argued the killings at Wounded Knee were the result of strife created by the "Ghost Dancers." It also revealed a good part of the treachery surrounding the events leading up to the slaughter was not the result of *any* discernible hostility on the part of the Indians. Around September 1890, Mellette himself and two other sportsmen were hunting on Indian land and managed to get lost. The trio wandered around for three days until they were found—staggering, sick, and nearly starved. Had the Indians carried the hostile intentions supposedly contained in the "Ghost Dance," the trio would not have returned to white society alive.[4] Further, as Magnuson explained: "Most of the Pine Ridge Agency population didn't believe in the Ghost Dance religion."[5] Notably, even though it was claimed Sitting Bull was a leader of the "Ghost Dancers," Stanley Vestal stated that Sitting Bull "…could not swallow such an improbable story" as believed by most of the "Ghost Dance" adherents.[6] Magnuson also commented regarding newspaper accounts of Indians getting stirred up in the region: "And what would soon be called 'yellow journalism' was adding kerosene to a campfire."[7]

If any hostile intentions existed in the Pine Ridge region in the fall and winter of 1890, they were held by the whites, as illustrated by the story of Dead Arm. Initially, Flood's account of the killing of a young Indian man named Dead Arm corresponded to the December 18, 1890, *Rapid City Journal* account but differed significantly as to the motivation for the slaying. The bare outline of the incident is that Dead Arm, apparently so named due to his paralyzed arm, was shot dead on December 17, 1890, on M. D. Cole's ranch. Dead Arm was then unceremoniously scalped by a white man named John Brennan. Accounts of the incident as relayed by Flood and the newspaper story diverged at this point. Flood contended that up until the day Dead Arm was shot dead: "…the rancher [M. D. Cole] had always appeared friendly and the Indians were his frequent customers [at his small trading store]."[8]

However, according to the *Rapid City Journal*, as stated in a quote by Cole, Dead Arm was struck dead by gunfire because: "This morning about four o'clock the Indians made an attempt to run the horses off my ranch." This newspaper account also stated that Dead Arm was found with a Winchester rifle, a Colt revolver, and 44 rounds of (unspecified) ammunition. The *Rapid City Journal* article also contained the obligatory reference to the "Ghost Dance" as it asserted that at the time of his death Dead Arm had on his: "…Ghost Dance shirt, as he was one of the braves who thought this would save his life." The article does not state how the writer arrived at this particular conclusion, since it was written after Dead Arm was killed and no account of an interview with this Indian man exists. Perhaps the newsman had a supernatural source of his own. The *Journal* also noted the rifle ball which struck Dead Arm in the temple made him into a "good Indian,"[9] an obvious reference to General Phil Sheridan's noted harsh comment "The only good Indians I ever saw were dead."[10]

As suggested in the earlier chapter on Crazy Horse, the "Ghost Dance" hysteria was not the first time exaggerated accounts, rumors, and simply outright lies regarding Indian plans for aggression created havoc for the Lakota. On May 6, 1877, Crazy Horse led a contingent of his people to the Red Cloud Agency in northern Nebraska. The situation constituted a foreshadowing to Spotted Elk's profession of peaceful intentions a little over a decade later which could not prevent the Wounded Knee Massacre. As Crazy Horse approached the reservation, he greeted the cavalry officer named Clark, who the Lakota nicknamed "White Hat," by stating: "'I wish to make a peace that will last our whole lives and forever.'"[11]

Sadly, to affirm Crazy Horse's understanding of a vision he experienced himself, peace would never arrive to inhabit his life. After a day of Sun Dancing in early 1876, he had a vision concerning his death which he carved on a rock, now simply called Owl Rock. Part of the carving revealed two stab wounds to his kidney and liver regions and a "death trail" leading to a carving of a soldier holding a bayonet.[12] Yet, in the end, it was the all-too-human trait of jealousy inside of other Indians and the greed and fear gripping the whites which created the circumstances leading to the famous warrior's earthly death.[13]

As such, after Crazy Horse's arrival at the Red Cloud Agency, the military portion of which was known as Ft. Robinson, many sources indicated Red Cloud was jealous of the attention foisted on Crazy Horse. Additionally, shortly after Crazy Horse became a resident of Ft. Robinson, a man named Joe Larrabee brought his young daughter, Nellie Larrabee, to Crazy Horse's Tipi. Nellie's proximity to Crazy Horse created quite a stir within the soldier leadership of the camp. In exchange for all the attention lavished on her, Nellie reported exaggerated tales of Crazy Horse's activities and plans. The soldiers overlooked discounting her stories, failing to consider Nellie was just a teenager. It was also claimed Red Cloud reported to the camp's agent, Dr. James Irwin, that Crazy Horse: "…was a warrior who would turn on him in an instant." Irwin was also told Crazy Horse was planning on using the ammunition the Indian warriors received for hunting to kill all the soldiers and any other white people who accompanied him on any future buffalo hunts.[14] These rumors naturally played on Irwin's fears. Returning to events just prior to the massacre, in relaying the account of Dead Arm's killing as him becoming a "good" Indian, the *Journal* certainly brought into question its ability to report conflicts between whites and Indians in South Dakota with any degree of "objectivity." It would be difficult to imagine these purveyors of news capable of reporting the events in South Dakota on December 29, 1890, a deliberate slaughter when the conventional story was the federal forces reacted appropriately to the menace created by the Lakota people participating in the "Ghost Dance."

What is difficult to understand is what benefit historians now receive by altering even the circumstances of the discovery of "Lost Bird" in the aftermath of the Wounded Knee Massacre. In *American Carnage*, author Jerome A. Greene trotted out the same old canard about the Wounded Knee Massacre being the unavoidable result of the whites' panicked reaction to the "Ghost Dance." For good measure, he added that as far as the perpetrators of the ultra-violence at Wounded Knee themselves: "No pre-meditated intent seems to have existed,"[15] as if any reader who arrived at page 378 of his self-assured discourse would have any doubt it was his view. Inexplicably, he claimed "Lost Bird" was found near an overturned wagon.[16] Although Greene cited Renée Sansom Flood's book for some of the details of "Lost Bird's" life, she made no mention in her book of an overturned wagon being the location of the discovery of "Lost Bird." Greene did not mention a comment Flood *did* make, that in 1992, "Ghost Shirts" were selling for as much as $40,000 each.[17]

Wounded Knee was hardly the first time in U.S. history Indians were blamed under murky circumstances for stirring up the fear and dread which required a response from whites. For example, during the Seminole War in 1817, Andrew Jackson's forces captured "Francis the prophet," who was also known as Hillis Hadjo or Josiah Francis, the son of a Creek woman and a white man. Just prior to his capture, Hadjo and his companion Himollemico observed a gunboat displaying British colors, thinking they found allies, paddled out to it (the type of craft was not stated) and were invited aboard. Unfortunately, the British flag was part of a ruse and they were bound and hauled to St. Marks to be hanged. Alexander Arbuthnot was captured earlier, presumably to be hanged as well.[18] However, as noted by Richard Drinnon, Jackson wanted these men to be "made examples of," therefore: "Evidence that Hillis Hadjo and Arbuthnot…were not 'exciting' the Seminoles to war was thus largely beside the point."[19]

As is also detailed in Flood's gripping account of "Lost Bird's" life, apart from the madness and greed involved in the Wounded Knee Massacre, her life story is filled with unimaginable grief, hardship, and sadness. After her discovery under a dead Indian lady's body, as noted above, "Lost Bird" died 29 years later at the end of a life filled with treachery, neglect, disenfranchisement, abuse, disease, poverty, possible incest or even rape, and perhaps worst of all, indifference. She was originally buried in Hanford, California, the hometown of her husband, Dick Allen. However, as a result of the efforts of Flood herself, "Lost Bird" was disinterred and reburied at Wounded Knee in a grave just outside the gate surrounding the mass grave containing many of the victims of the massacre.[20]

"Lost Bird's" tragic story, perhaps like no other, symbolized the larger story of the Lakota peoples' struggle of the 19th century and the continuing struggles they and other indigenous people continue to face to this day. General Leonard Colby obtained possession of "Lost Bird" in the most offensive way imaginable by dressing in traditional clothes and passing himself off as a mixed-blood Indian. To add to the deception, as he was explaining his story at the home of Indians safeguarding "Lost Bird," who cared for her after she was rescued from the killing grounds of Wounded Knee, he added to the ruse by falsely claiming he and his wife were childless.[21] Similarly, the federal government flagrantly violated the Ft. Laramie Treaty of 1868 that it had no intention of honoring by promoting Custer's Black Hills Expedition of 1874. Likewise, Colby knew little of Lakota customs and traditions, much as the knowledge of Lakota customs, religion, and traditions of other Americans of his day (and likely of this day) was limited to "…the dramatic sun dance ritual."[22] There is no indication Colby had any reluctance in bringing up "Lost Bird" as a white child, and this outlook most certainly reflected a long tradition in the United States. In the 18th century it was the belief, as noted, that: "…third-generation Puritans simply assumed that their religion and culture were destined by Providence to dominate the land."[23] Undoubtedly, this impulse gained strength as Westward Expansion rushed onward.

While it could be claimed Anna Mae succumbed to violent forces generated from outside the Indian community, it could be argued the "Lost Bird" was victimized from within her own "home." Obviously, her "home" was created from outside Lakota culture, and it is sometimes difficult to analyze the sources of violence and hardships with any precision. Nevertheless, given those limitations, Dr. Andrea Smith explained: "…the belief that violence happens 'out there', inflicted by the stereotypical stranger in a dark alley, makes it difficult to recognize that the home is, in fact, the place of greatest danger for women." Dr. Smith added: "…'home' in the U.S. has never been a safe place for people of color."[24]

Particularly problematic in the context of the reporting and writing of such individuals as Robert Novak and Joseph Trimbach is their repeated lie that the problems experienced by Indian people, which obviously includes women, are the result of the doings of the "false heroes of AIM." Engaging in this hollow exercise in deception further obscures the stories of already marginalized indigenous women. While Flood did not specifically state Colby raped "Lost Bird," the belief he impregnated her remained speculation only and no further inquiries were attempted. Even in contemporary times, sexual violence against indigenous women, Lakota or otherwise, past or present, does not appear to be a matter of great concern. Dr. Smith noted:

> …feminist legal scholar Catherine MacKinnon argues that in Bosnia [in the 1990s] 'The world has *never* seen sex used this consciously, this cynically, this elaborately, this openly, this systematically…as a means of destroying a whole people [emphasis mine].' Here, MacKinnon seems to have forgotten that she lives on this land because millions of Native peoples were raped, sexually mutilated, and murdered. Is mass rape against European women genocide, while mass rape against indigenous women business as usual?[25]

Then, there is the individualized terror and fear of the sexual violence experienced by an Indian girl (now woman) who witnessed such depravity at the Carlisle Indian School in Pennsylvania:

> After a nine-year-old girl was raped in her dormitory bed during the night, we girls would be so scared we would jump into each other's beds as soon as the lights went out. The sustained

terror in our hearts further tested our endurance, as it was better to suffer with a full bladder and be safe than to walk through the dark, seemingly endless hallway to the bathroom. When we were older, we girls anguished each time we entered the classroom of a certain male teacher who stalked and molested girls.[26]

Of course, the lack of interest in addressing sexual violence is undoubtedly a subset of the general lack of interest in hearing the point of view of perpetually voiceless Indian women. As Marijo Moore lamented: "Who wants to read books written from an indigenous point of view? Are there people really interested in what I have to say?"[27]

It was stated in an article written by Harriet L. Coolidge in *Trained Motherhood* that "Lost Bird's" "'roving nature'" was said to lead her into "'mischief.'"[28] Similarly, Dr. Smith related how in contemporary times incarcerated Indian women (at least up to the time her book was published in 2005): "…are particularly subjected to medical experimentation programs in order to 'cure' them of the ailment that supposedly led to their incarceration." A former prisoner named Stormy Ogden graphically outlined her ordeal with the medical industry while locked up:

> I was given a combination of 300 milligrams of Elavil, Mellaril, Thorizine, and Chlorhydrate, to keep me calm. What it did was make you stop talking. I still stutter and have problems getting my words out because too much medication has gone through my body. I had to take this. There was no way I could get around taking it; they make sure. And a lot of Indian women are being given Thorazine, to keep us calm, because we are the savages.[29]

Just as "Lost Bird" suffered giving birth to a stillborn baby boy, Indian women on Pine Ridge currently experience a miscarriage rate as high as six times the national average.[30] Yet, perhaps in one respect, "Lost Bird's" life as a Lakota child/woman growing up in white culture differed from that of other Indian women. While Flood does not explicitly state that "Lost Bird" had all the advantages and comforts available to white people at the end of the 19th century and into the beginning of the 20th century, it is reasonable to assume that is the case. In contrast, in *Lakota Women*, published in 1990, Mary Crow Dog described her early life on the Rosebud Reservation near Pine Ridge and explained: "We had no electricity, no heating system, no plumbing. We got our water from the river. Some of the things which even poor white or black ghetto people take for granted we did not even know existed."[31]

ENDNOTES

1. Page, *In the Hands of the Great Spirit*, p. 310.
2. Flood, *Lost Bird of Wounded Knee*, p. 37.
3. Richardson, *Wounded Knee*, p. 266
4. Flood, *Lost Bird of Wounded Knee*, pp. 50-51.
5. Magnuson, *The Death of Raymond Yellow Thunder*, p. 120.
6. Stanley Vestal, *Sitting Bull: Champion of the Sioux* (Norman, Oklahoma: University of Oklahoma Press, 1932), p. 271.
7. Magnuson, *The Death of Raymond Yellow Thunder*, 121.
8. Flood, *Lost Bird of Wounded Knee*, p. 51.
9. "The Indian Problem," *Rapid City Journal*, December 18, 1890. Courtesy of the Rapid City, South Dakota Public Library.
10. Donovan, *A Terrible Glory*, p. 18.
11. Matson, *Crazy Horse: The Lakota Warrior's Life and Legacy*, p. 128.
12. Ibid., p. 98.
13. Ibid., p. 130.
14. Ibid., p. 131.
15. Greene, *American Carnage*, p. 378.
16. Ibid., p. 359.
17. Flood, *Lost Bird of Wounded Knee*, p. 58.
18. Remini, *Andrew Jackson and His Indian Wars*, p. 150.
19. Drinnon, *Facing West*, p. 106.
20. Flood, *Lost Bird of Wounded Knee*, pp. 299-305.
21. Ibid., pp. 75-76.
22. Stiles, *Custer's Trials*, p. 389.
23. Bowden, *American Indians and Christian Missions*, pp. 136-137.
24. Smith, *Conquest*, p. 177.
25. Ibid., p. 28.
26. Harjo, and Bird, Eds Berenice Levchuk, "Leaving Home for Carlisle Indian School," *Reinventing the Enemy's Language*, p. 184.
27. Eric Garnsworth, Ed., MariJo Moore, "Why Do I Continue to Write? An Exhaustive Questioning," *Sovereign Bones* (New York: Nation Books, 2007) p. 47.
28. Flood, *Lost Bird of Wounded Knee*, p. 157.
29. Smith, *Conquest*, p. 115.
30. Ibid., pp. 66-67.
31. Crow Dog, *Lakota Woman*, p. 18.

CHAPTER 15

Henry B. Whipple
"The Do Gooders Do Us More Harm"

In the final analysis, Whipple subscribed to an assimilationist position and helped to implement a cultural imperialism designed to destroy the cultural integrity of the very people he intended to protect... His was the sin of good intentions.

George Tinker, *Missionary Conquest*[1]

In August 1876, Bishop Henry B. Whipple participated in the Manypenny Commission which traveled to the Oglala Lakota Agency on the White River in Nebraska to "negotiate" the relinquishment of the Black Hills to the United States government. When the commission reached the agency on September 7, Whipple opened the proceeding with his "prayer" claiming the Great Father: "'...does not wish to throw a blanket over your eyes, and ask you to do anything without looking at it.'"[2] After Whipple opened with his "prayer," Manypenny read the conditions and, as Dee Brown noted, they were written "...in the usual obfuscated language of lawmakers."[3] When it was Fire Thunder's time to sign the agreement Whipple presented, he came up holding his blanket before his eyes, signing blindfolded in a silent rebuke to Whipple's promise not to throw a blanket over the Lakota's eyes.[4]

In return for giving up the Black Hills, its treasure of gold, and also its unceded territory, according to Whipple, the U.S. government was to provide rations, farming equipment, clothing, etc.: "...until such time you are able to support and care for yourselves."[5] Sadly, many historians believe the Lakota (and other nations) *were* able to care for themselves until the United States government engaged in or at least facilitated the systematic destruction of buffalo herds. Brown commented: "To Bishop Whipple's listeners, this seemed a strange way indeed to save the Indian nations, taking away their Black Hills and hunting grounds, and moving them far away to the Missouri River."[6]

Fire Thunder's approach of holding a blanket over his eyes before signing eventually came to be seen as an eloquent and now long-remembered form of protest.[7] Like Crazy Horse's refusal to have his picture taken during his lifetime, Fire Thunder's nonverbal actions became a prediction of things to come. And Whipple's actions, better than almost any other player on the frontier, again exemplified Mary Crow Dog's belief that the: "…do gooder types do more harm than the Custer types"[8] Dee Brown also noted: "Several members of [the Manypenny] commission were old hands at stealing Indian lands, notably Newton Edmunds, Bishop Henry Whipple, and the Reverend Samuel D. Hinman."[9] American Indian scholar George Tinker explained in part: "Whipple engineered the U.S. government's theft of the Black Hills from the Sioux people which finally broke the back of Sioux resistance."[10] Jake Page, deftly quoting Wilcomb Washburn, summed up the results of the activities of "Christians" in contact with Indians: "By the time the American Indian came face to face with the doctrine of Christ it had hardened into a mold of bigotry, intolerance, militancy and greed which made it the mortal enemy of the American Indian."[11]

Although Whipple's intentions toward the Indians seemed to many outwardly good and heartfelt, his actions played a part in the conquest of Indian people, nonetheless. It has been argued Whipple could not possibly have foreseen the long-term demoralization his mission would have in that regard. Tinker nevertheless believed Whipple thus participated in the "cultural genocide" of the Sioux nation. Tinker also noted Whipple believed: "'Never in the world's history has there been such enthusiasm in all humanitarian work as now,'" yet suggested Whipple: "…would likely be sorely disappointed to see the results of his missionary zeal nearly a half century after his death" and that: "perhaps he would also be open enough to see the modern Indian situation as an indictment of his own best intentions."[12]

Likewise, the career of Bishop Henry Whipple also illustrates the importance of historian Robert Berkhofer's instruction not to overlook other secondary sources when researching Indian history. One glaring example of this phenomenon is found in Scott Berg's *38 Nooses*. In that book, Berg noted Whipple wrote the following Preface to Helen Hunt Jackson's *A Century of Dishonor*:

> Nations, like individuals, reap exactly what they sow; they who sow robbery reap robbery. The seed-sowing of inequity replies in a harvest of blood.[13]

Berg does not mention Brown's comment about Whipple's adroitness at land theft, even to refute it, and even though *Bury My Heart at Wounded Knee* is most likely the most famous and most read book on Indian history ever written. Likewise, in *A Terrible Glory*, James Donovan noted without reservation that to many, Whipple was considered: "…one of the leading voices in the east for Indian rights."[14] Ultimately: "Whipple was a man of his own times and his own cultural heritage,"[15] which inevitably meant he had a bedrock belief in white cultural supremacy as much as he did in his church's teachings of the efficacy of the blood of Christ. Berg did note Whipple supported the Carlisle Indian Industrial School owing to Whipple's: "…belief that the only solution [for Indians] was white customs and white religion."[16]

Whipple was born into a prosperous family from Adams, New York, near Lake Ontario and the mouth of the Saint Lawrence River. Whipple's ancestors included a signer of the Declaration of Independence and his relatives included important personalities of the Civil War era. One of these relatives was Abraham

Lincoln's general in chief, Henry "Old Brains" Halleck. Whipple spent two years at Oberlin College in Ohio before quitting due to a severe bronchial problem. He subsequently became involved in his father's business and an enthusiastic campaigner for the New York Whigs. Curiously, Whipple's political activities caught the eye of Horatio Seymour, a leading Northern Democrat who became governor of New York.[17]

After marrying Cornelia Wright, the daughter of a local lawyer and prominent Episcopalian, and spending time in Florida for health reasons, Whipple eventually returned to New York and entered the priesthood. He enthusiastically pursued saving the souls of the castoffs of society including vagrants, prostitutes, and actresses (considered among the most immoral of people at the time). Even though he loved working in Chicago, in June 1859 he was named the first Episcopal Bishop of Minnesota. After his move to Bashaw, a town about 60 miles south of St. Paul, Whipple found great interest in his church's newfound mission to the Indians in Minnesota. Whipple claimed: "'From my childhood [I] felt a deep interest in these brown children of our Heavenly Father.'" In his memoirs, Whipple noted that in his childhood, his mother told him: "…with her 'gentle hand on my head' 'My dear boy it is always right to defend the weak and the helpless.'" Berg also noted that Whipple's: "…concern for Indians was founded on an intense, emotional paternalism."[18]

Questions about Whipple's attitude toward Indians give rise to questions about the role of religion generally in interactions with indigenous people. If for the sake of argument Columbus is considered the first European to arrive in North America and having contact with Indians, his motives for subjugating them can be assessed with an understanding of his "religious" origin. It has been argued (admittedly perhaps with little substantiated evidence) Columbus' primary motivation for his adventurous activities was financing a: "…crusade to establish a 'New Jerusalem in a New World.'"[19] While this may seem an extraordinary stretch, it has been reported Columbus believed the brutality inflicted upon Indians was justified by this or some other higher purpose, even if that "higher purpose" was merely his promotion to higher status. When Whipple arrived in the Plains region, he brought with him a particular point of view from which he brought forth his idea for the solution to the complications arising from Indian sovereignty which became known essentially as the "'Indian problem.'"[20] It did not appear it ever occurred to Whipple that the Indians might have a "white problem."

In *Missionary Conquest*, George Tinker also sketched the framework of Whipple's views and noted, among other characteristics, that he revealed he had a: "…tendency to heroize any white who died in an Indian-white dispute and always villainize the Indian as the 'savage.'" Tinker also explained that in Whipple's autobiographical *Lights and Shadows*, Whipple referred to the Battle of the Little Big Horn as the "'…massacre of the *gallant* Custer and his heroic soldiers [emphasis in cited material].'" Tinker further explained in 1864, two years after the Little Crow War, Whipple wrote: "'…eight hundred of the most generous people on the earth perished by savage violence…'" due to "'A great crime'" of the Indians. He also called for the execution of the "'guilty'" even though he recognized: "'…[the] war itself was the fault of the U.S. government's blatant violation of its treaty with the Sioux in Minnesota.'"[21] Nevertheless, Whipple failed to comment on the all-too-quickly-conducted capital "trials" of the Indians before military tribunals after this conflict, which came to be known as the Minnesota Uprising of 1862. Most of these "trials" resulted in death sentences for the Indians, to be accomplished by hanging after usually only an hour of testimony and deliberation (at most) in each of the cases. In most cases the "trials" took less than ten minutes.[22]

Nonetheless, Tinker noted Whipple was a: "...genuine friend of Indian people and often spoke out on their behalf throughout his career." Yet, the dilemma suggested previously was that:

> Whipple was a captive of his own culture and its implicit set of values, especially where the priority of white, Euro-American citizens was at stake. Whipple was simply an influential representative of a system which constructed a double standard of justice whereby the 'guilty' must be punished even when it is evident to participants in the system that these 'guilty' are in fact victims.[23]

Much like Whipple's role in the "transfer" of the Black Hills from "Sioux" control to white control is rarely highlighted, the role of Christian churches in the breakup of the "tribal mass" or at least tribal culture through allotment is also largely unknown. In the 1880s, missionaries had visited nearly every tribe in the territory of what eventually became the United States. Especially in remote regions, there was much resistance to Christianizing efforts, and the ability of Indians to fend off the proselytizers existed in large part because the Indians lived in small, united bands or groups within the larger reserves. In this way, the Indians were able to maintain their religious traditions through community religious ceremonies. Siphoning off even a few converts for the little missions was an arduous task for these missionaries. The missionaries thus demanded the reservations be divided into allotments according to the number of individuals in the tribe, thus unraveling the community groups and isolating families from the rest of the tribe, hence making them more vulnerable to conversion efforts.

Even as the "assimilation" of Indians lurched forward, was there an indication the lessons learned from analyzing the effects of Whipple's good intentions gone bad were being put into action? As comprehensive as the 1928 *Meriam Report* appeared to be, it did not contain any analysis or indication of the effects of missionaries functioning essentially as agents of the government. In its chapter entitled *Missionary Activities Among the Indians,* the report suggested the government needed to provide: "...a mechanism for cooperation between the government and the churches doing Indian mission work and between the churches themselves."[24] Likewise, and fundamentally more disconcerting, was the lack of insight or at least the lack of a sense of urgency regarding addressing the problems endemic to boarding schools. Even though the report noted virtually unmanageable problems at these institutions—among many problems was lack of adequate funding—near the report's close, it contained the perplexing conclusion: "...the finest work of the missionaries has unquestionably been in the establishment of mission schools for Indian children."[25]

The *Meriam Report* nonetheless unselfconsciously proclaimed:

> How many a missionary when preaching the white man's religion to the Indians must be embarrassed by the thought of what the white race has done to the Indians? What must be the thoughts of the intelligent Indian when he hears the great precepts of the Christian faith and contrasts them with the actions of the white men toward the Indian race?[26]

But what primarily gets lost in the haze of Indian history is that "Christians," whether they set good examples or not, usually in the guise of missionaries, have always been at the forefront of the white vanguard imposing its collective will on Indians and taking their lands. In addition to Gwynne's previous comments about settlers' views of Indians on the frontier, he also noted:

> They habitually declined to honor government treaties with Native Americans believing in their hearts that the land belonged to them. …they [the Parkers] were militant predestinarian Baptists, severe in their religion and intolerant of people who did not believe as they did.[27]

And, as Paul Nathanson noted in *Over the Rainbow*: "The idea of quest…is built into American identity at a very basic level: the New World was 'discovered' and the United States was 'invented.'" Yet, Nathanson took the concept one step further by suggesting: "…the American quest was early assimilated not only to that of Ancient Israel en route to the Promised Land but also to that of the Christian Church en route to the Heavenly Jerusalem."[28]

How far removed in attitude from more aggressive, frontier, and anti-Indian advocates were more "educated" individuals like Whipple anyway? Newspaper reporters, like missionaries, were in no way immune from energetically rationalizing the conquest of Indians by any and all means. During the early stages of the eventual theft of the Black Hills, *Chicago Tribune* reporter James Howard announced Indians were little more than "'…dusky deadbeats now fattening upon the bounty of government.'" Howard sometimes signed his stories "'Phocion,'" the name of an obscure Athenian statesman, and believed mixed-blood interpreters: "…were inflating Indian hopes for the price gold-hungry whites would pay for the Black Hills." Others, such as West Point-educated General George Crook, believed Indian people who actually had the audacity to cling to the notion they wanted to live according to the dictates of their own culture needed a "'…good sound drubbing.'"

On the frontier "drubbing" was synonymous with "whipping," which had two meanings for these ever-so-thoughtful individuals. Some whites believed a "whipping" meant a: "…crushing and bloody military defeat required to break the Indians' fighting spirit for good and all." Yet, others like "Phocion" hoped Indians would become like those who received literal "whippings" by schoolmasters, "…stupid, uninterested, and learned slowly." As historian Thomas Powers pointed out, "Stupid, uninterested, and slow" describes those with broken spirits, which "Phocion" hoped would be the end result for the "…prideful Sioux." Howard/"Phocion" most likely shared the view of many whites with extermination in mind when he privately stated Indians should be considered in: "'…[the] class known as cumberers of the earth…[who] should be cut down.'" However, in his dispatches to the *Chicago Tribune*, Howard/"Phocion" tamped down his disgust for these human beings and historian Powers explained he urged: "…they be treated firmly as recalcitrant children with heavy recourse to the beech switch."[29]

Of course, "Sharp Knives" Andrew Jackson had a way of symbolizing the unadorned, raw-edged attitude of whites who believed they were entitled to conquest, without the gloss of any religiosity, held by those in contact with Indians. Even to Indians who had been allies, Jackson, to borrow a term from the Gwynne school of thought, exhibited "jaw-dropping" harshness. After the subjugation of the Creek Indians in 1814, Jackson refused to grant even one acre of land to the friendly Indians who had fought with him. Robert Remini explained: "…Jackson was expressing the prejudices, fears, mistrust and hatred of white people living on the frontier toward all Native Americans. Westerners [for example L. Frank Baum later in the century] knew only one thing: the Indian was a threat to their lives, and that danger must be eliminated—permanently."[30] Remini also noted when the Chickasaw Indians requested the market price for land they were being stripped of, Jackson angrily retorted: "'These are high toned sentiment [sic] for an Indian and they must be taught to know that they do not Possess sovereignty, with the right of domain.'" Remini superbly summarized the thinking of those times by concluding: "…the implicit racism of Jackson's remark is still another facet of frontier life, if not American life, in the early nineteenth century. Indians were distinctly inferior to whites, and for them to presume an equality to their 'betters' was offensive and intolerable."[31]

ENDNOTES

1. Tinker, *Missionary Conquest*, p. 110.
2. Ostler, *The Lakotas and the Black Hills*, p. 99.
3. Brown, *Bury My Heart at Wounded Knee*, p. 298.
4. Ostler, *The Lakotas and the Black Hills*, pp. 100-101.
5. Ibid., p. 99.
6. Brown, *Bury My Heart at Wounded Knee*, p. 299.
7. Ostler, *The Lakotas and the Black Hills*, pp. 100-101.
8. Crow Dog, *Lakota Woman*, p. 113.
9. Brown, *Bury My Heart at Wounded Knee*, p. 298.
10. Tinker, *Missionary Conquest*, p. viii.
11. Page, *In the Hands of the Great Spirit*, p. 111.
12. Tinker, *Missionary Conquest*, p. 95.
13. Berg, *38 Nooses*, p. 298. Apparently, this quotation was removed from subsequent editions of *A Century of Dishonor*, at least it is absent from the 2003 edition used for reference in this book.
14. Donovan, *A Terrible Glory*, p. 90.
15. Tinker, *Missionary Conquest*, p. 99. As noted in the Gwynne chapter, this "man of his own times" proposition in one form or another is consistently used by historians, even an Indian one like Tinker, to explain all types of malfeasance.
16. Berg, *38 Nooses*, p. 298.
17. Ibid., p. 51.
18. Ibid., p. 53.
19. Bradley, *The Columbus Conspiracy*, p. 54.
20. Tinker, *Missionary Conquest*, p. 108.
21. Ibid., p. 97.
22. Berg, *38 Nooses*, p. 191.
23. Tinker, *Missionary Conquest*, p. 97.
24. Meriam, *Meriam Report*, p. 813.
25. Ibid., p. 823.
26. Ibid., p. 831.
27. Gwynne, *Empire of the Summer Moon*, p. 20.
28. Nathanson, *Over the Rainbow*, p. 114.
29. Powers, *The Killing of Crazy Horse*, pp. 109-111.
30. Remini, *Andrew Jackson and His Indian Wars*, p. 90.
31. Ibid., p. 171.

Chapter 16

The Mysterious Mormons

The Link between the Mormons and the Messiah Craze is shadowy and probably never will be sharply defined …Some accounts speak of whites participating in Ghost Dances at Walker Lake [Nevada]. It is entirely possible that they were Mormons, for Joseph Smith, founder of Mormonism, had prophesied in 1843 that the Messiah would come to earth in mortal form during the year 1890.

Robert Utley, *The Last Days of the Sioux Nation*[1]

Mentioning the name Mormon or Mormons is likely to evoke numerous and most likely clean-cut images such as pairs of bicycle-riding white-shirt-and-tie-clad young men out to proselytize the masses or even the harmonious sounds of the Mormon Tabernacle Choir. Reinforcing this view in regard to Indian encounters are writers such as Fergus Bordewich, who in his eccentric book *Killing the White Man's Indian* lauded the efforts of Mormons in encouraging Indians to abstain from drinking alcohol.[2] Of course, Bordewich did not indulge the reader of his tome as to his thoughts on the practice of polygamy practiced by a small number of Mormons. Likewise, he did not venture to address the claim by Sitting Bull's friend Catherine Weldon, who in addition to her previously noted statement about Mormons argued: "…I fear some bad white men [Mormons] who are leading you into endless trouble." In this statement, she was referring to those who she was convinced were behind the "Ghost Dance."[3]

Nevertheless, although specifically and not likely a Mormon issue, Bordewich, like so many other historians described in this book, rarely examined drinking by *whites* as a problem for Indians, as explained in the following chapter on Raymond Yellow Thunder and elsewhere. Bacon's Rebellion, considered by many the first revolt against the British crown, had its roots in a drinking bout of Nathaniel Bacon, a cousin of then-governor of Virginia Sir William Berkeley, and an avowed Indian hater. In this conflict, historians Utley and Washburn noted Bacon's victories "…were exclusively against Indians friendly to the colony."[4] The salient point regarding Mormons in relation to Bacon is this: while neither alcohol users nor egregious Indian haters, Mormons still were able to inflict damage on Indian people. The actual amount of damage has yet to be fully explored.

Thus, regarding the specific topic of Mormons, what is there to find when exploring the murky and almost universally unexplored recesses of the dark lagoon of history that is the interaction between these Mormons and Indian people? As noted above and in previous chapters, there have been rumblings for years about the role of the Mormons in the build-up of tensions leading to the Wounded Knee Massacre. Further, it is also instructive to review the attitudes of Europeans toward the end of the 19th century, particularly the belief that Euro-American concepts of Christianity (more or less including those of Mormonism) were the only hope for redeeming Indians in the United States from their savagery and one-way tickets to hell. In an 1884 essay in the *Atlantic Monthly*, writer Charles Leland claimed: "'…there is no proof of the existence among our [sic] Indians of a belief in a Great Spirit or in an infinite God before the coming of the whites.'" William Wassell, in a November 1894 article in *Harper's Monthly* entitled "The Religion of the Sioux," asserted there was: "…hope in the freeing of 'pagan savages' from 'the sorcery and jugglery of weasoned medicine-men' by Christian missionaries who convinced them of 'simple teachings of the Bible.'" Of course, these articles did not explain how a culture that promoted those "simple teachings" justified the slaughter of those same "Sioux" slightly less than four years earlier.

Earlier, in 1891, scholar Alfred Riggs concluded on the basis of the "factual" record that Christian influence was leading the American Indian to: "'a quickened conscience, a strengthened will, the power of self-restraint…power to labor patiently, economy, thrift…a new spiritual impulse, and a new revelation…and the customs of…a social order.'" Similar thoughts were expressed in articles in magazines such as *Popular Science Monthly*, *North American Review*, and others. More than 20 years earlier, Amanda Miller in *Overland Monthly* expressed her exalted view of Christianity over that of Indian paganism: "The contrast between the assemblage of hideously painted savages, whose countenances were rendered still the more revolting by their efforts to intensify their passions of hatred and revenge in their incantations of demonaltry [sic], and the placid and devoted [Christian Indian] congregation at Simcoe, was wonderful and delightful."[5]

In 1857, Mormons, oddly enough, were believed by some sources to be responsible for the massacre in the Mountain Meadows area of Utah of 140 migrants from Missouri heading to California. Apparently, the Mormons concluded these travelers were going to eventually retaliate for the Mormons' refusal to sell the travelling party supplies.[6] Earlier, in 1856, Washington officials were concerned that Mormon "'barbarians'" were forming alliances with Southern agitators and Southwest Indians with the desire to execute a Utah secession. Shoshone support of Mormons during what came to be known as the Utah War heightened suspicions that Mormons were secretly encouraging those Indians to hostilities.[7]

In 1954 Congress passed PL 83-399, known as the Menominee Termination Act, to effectively eliminate the Menominee tribe in Wisconsin as a political entity. As has often been the case with land designated for reservations for Indians "…[the] once useless wilderness in Wisconsin the Menominee had accepted to be left in peace had become valuable to the white man after all."[8] One Menominee spokesman believed a religious dispute was a significant motivating factor behind the push for "terminating" the Menominee tribe: "There were 2 Mormons that come [sic] here to establish a church and build a playground, but the Menominees drove them out."[9] One of the main agents in the push to terminate the Menominee tribe, coincidentally or not, was in fact Mormon Senator Arthur V. Watkins, Republican from Utah.

Watkins presided over hearings on the various "termination" bills introduced in the U.S. Congress in the 1950s. Senator Watkins was described as ruling with an "iron fist" and characterized as "devoutly religious." Yet, it was reported the good senator gave little consideration to the opinions of actual Indians, who would be drastically affected by the "termination" of federal aid, and he pressed on with full-speed-ahead determination. Of all the things that could be said about the "termination" of the Menominee, it being their idea would not be one of them. Behind Watkins' seemingly mild-mannered persona lurked a fierceness that flowed like lava from a volcano through his unrelenting efforts to terminate the Menominee. In that regard, Senator Watkins made it clear to them "termination" was going to happen to them whether they wanted it to or not.[10]

It seems fitting to end the section on Mormons with some information from A. C. Ross' book *We are all Related*. Dr. Ross stated that he was reading a book by mystic Edgar Cayce and noted Cayce claimed: "…in 3000 B.C. the remaining people of the lost tribes of Israel reached America by boat from Lemuria." Dr. Ross then surmised: "Reading this information triggered my memory of a passage in the *Book of Mormon*. The book of Ether [a book within the *Book of Mormon*] states that when the Jaredites first reached the Promised Land [America], 'the whole face of the land northward was covered with inhabitants.'"[11] Dr. Ross' statements are fascinating for so many reasons.

Endnotes

1. Utley, *The Last Days of the Sioux Nation*, p. 65, footnote 6.
2. Bordewich, *Killing the White Man's Indian*, p. 264.
3. Roger L. Di Silvestro, *In the Shadow of Wounded Knee*, pp. 71-72.
4. Utley and Washburn, *Indian Wars*, p. 28.
5. Churchill and Jaimes, Ed., *Fantasies of the Master Race*, p. 27. Jugglery is the art or practice of a juggler. The definition of weasoned is uncertain.
6. Fleisher, *The Bear River Massacre*, pp. 36-37.
7. Ibid., p. 33.
8. Shames, Ed., *Freedom with Reservation*, p. 4.
9. Ibid., p. 5.
10. Ibid., pp. 7-14.
11. A. C. Ross, *Mitakuye Oyasin "We Are All Related"* p. 81. Wilford made a similar comment: "Perhaps these [Indians] were descendants of the lost tribes of Israel, an idea that in the nineteenth century became a central part of the Book of Mormon." *The Mysterious History of Columbus*, p. 152.

Chapter 17

Raymond Yellow Thunder

There had been a few instances of plunder by the Spanish and a few thefts by the Indians. Ojeda had the thieves' hands cut off, but only the hands of Indian thieves.
        Gianni Granzotto, *Christopher Columbus*[1]

He was just a drunken Indian, after all
Stew Magnuson, *The Death of Raymond Yellow Thunder*[2]

In early 1972, the sad case of the vicious beating and eventual death of Raymond Yellow Thunder put drunken, cruel violence against Indians at center stage in the town of Gordon, Nebraska. The town is located in the northwest part of the state about 50 or so miles south of the Pine Ridge Indian Reservation. Raymond's story exemplifies the belief there is a unique brand of nastiness lurking in the shadows of small-town America that on special occasions is paraded through its main streets like cherry red, mint-condition '57 Chevys. In the specific cases of whites living in small towns in proximity to Pine Ridge, Raymond's home town, author Ian Frazier noted: "Some people in South Dakota [and presumably nearby northern Nebraska] hate Indians, unapologetically, and will tell you why; in their voices you can hear a particular American meanness that is centuries old."[3] Renée Sansom Flood in *Lost Bird of Wounded Knee* noted: "In South Dakota many white people either despise Indians or completely ignore them as if they don't exist."[4] Putting a broader perspective on the topic, Elizabeth Cook-Lynn argued: "It is the view of some that Indian-hating has always been deeply embedded in the American character."[5]

Mary Crow Dog, born on the Rosebud Reservation near Pine Ridge, endorsed the idea of rampant racism existing in southwest South Dakota. She claimed: "In South Dakota, white kids learn to be racists almost before they learn to walk."[6] She recalled being in a grocery store looking at oranges, when a *wasicu* teacher blurted out: "'Why can't those dirty Indians keep their hands off this food? I was going to buy some oranges, but they put their dirty hands on them and I must try to find some oranges elsewhere. How disgusting."[7] Leonard Crow Dog, Mary's husband, related: "If you were a teenager and an Indian and were found someplace away from home, you had to be guilty of something."[8]

Oddly, Gutzon Borglum, the creator of the nearby Mount Rushmore monument, and the son of a Mormon-indoctrinated father, had a remarkably similar view of the citizens of South Dakota. In the midst of one of his constant flaps over the financing of the Mount Rushmore project, similar to those he experienced during his creation of the Stone Mountain, Georgia, Confederate Memorial, he unleashed his vitriolic descriptions of the populace of South Dakota. The genesis of his complaint was his belief these people did not appreciate his genius. He bitterly complained: "I am thoroughly disgusted with the way I have been taken advantage of right and left in Rapid City" and added he was frustrated with the: "…total lack of gratitude, intelligent understanding or appreciation of the sacrifices [I have] made."

Borglum lamented to the internationally famous architect Frank Lloyd Wright: "'[E]ighty percent of the [Black Hills] population, including their best, belong to the unburied dead, and that part of them that is alive…is only concerned with the most ordinary of material things.'" Borglum was just getting warmed up. He added: "'My biggest fight in the Black Hills has not been with the granite, but [with] the stupid people.'" As a parting shot, Borglum explained to newly elected South Dakota Governor Leslie Jensen: "'I hardly need to point out [even though he gladly did] what I have done in bringing the name of South Dakota out of the swill barrel.'" Borglum's litany of insults ended with his coup de grace of calling the denizens of South Dakota "'oxen-minded.'"[9]

Like it or not, Borglum had more in common attitude-wise with the Nebraska native killers of Raymond and the "oxen-minded" inhabitants of South Dakota than he might have cared to admit. Although apparently not well-publicized, Borglum was at least for part of his adult life an avid supporter of the Ku Klux Klan. This was especially true during his days of working on the Stone Mountain Confederate Memorial near Atlanta, Georgia. In actuality, the Klan experienced a rebirth of interest in 1915 at Stone Mountain. The Klan wholeheartedly endorsed the concept of the monument after the idea was proposed by the United Daughters of the Confederacy.[10]

While documentation that Borglum officially joined the Klan is lacking, that circumstance is a mere formality. Borglum attended Klan rallies, served on Klan committees, mediated disputes (often unsuccessfully to no one's surprise due to Borglum's ego), and simply viewed the burgeoning, highly organized Klan network throughout the South as a source of funds for his pricey Stone Mountain project. Although he did not specifically articulate his views on Indians in the United States, past or present, on September 4, 1923, Borglum noted: "Before I went to bed last night, I wrote 2,500 to 3,000 words on the evils of alien races." He also noted regarding the issue of slavery and in a tour de force of victim-blaming that: "While Anglo-Saxons have themselves sinned grievously against the principle of pure nationalism by illicit slave and alien servant traffic, it has been the character of the cargo that has eaten into the very moral fiber of our race character, rather than the moral depravity of Anglo-Saxon traders."[11]

Raymond Yellow Thunder's killers committed a brutal crime against an individual human being. Although not equal in depravity by comparison, Borglum insulted an entire culture by carving the likenesses of four white presidents out of sacred Black Hills' granite. Likewise, in his recounting of the creation of the Mount Rushmore sculpture, *Great White Fathers,* John Taliaferro, to his credit, does point out how sacred the Black Hills region is considered by the Lakota people. Unfortunately, Taliaferro did not make any mention of how the nearby Crazy Horse monument is considered by more than a few Lakota to be an affront to the memory of that Indian leader, particularly since Crazy Horse refused to have his picture taken during his lifetime. Of course, Taliaferro could not leave it at that. In the tradition of many conventional historians, he described one of the first known instances of Crazy Horse's combat experiences as the "Fetterman *Massacre* [emphasis added]."[12] And like those historians, Taliaferro did not explain how the combat deaths of the United States soldiers involved in that event, who were most likely *better* armed than their Lakota victors, constituted a massacre. It seems like a habit that just cannot be broken to describe mutual combat where non-Indians got the worst of it as "massacred," as previously noted in the case of *The Saga of Chief Joseph.*[13]

Borglum warrants further comparisons with the citizens of Gordon, Nebraska, particularly at the time of Raymond's senseless murder. Again, to his credit, as noted, Taliaferro went to great lengths to describe Borglum's connections to the Ku Klux Klan and his xenophobic viewpoints and noted the Lakota consider the Black Hills sacred. Further, Taliaferro explained that Borglum seemed to grasp how Mount Rushmore is a significant symbol of white conquest and the subsequent decimation of Lakota culture. While Taliaferro also noted that Borglum was concerned with the desperate state of the Lakota people, he implied Borglum's gift of cattle, sheep, clothing, and blankets and their honoring him with membership in the Lakota tribe balanced out the desecration created by his stone carvings of the four presidents in the sacred Black Hills.[14]

Similarly, Reva Evans, the editor and publisher of the *Gordon Journal,* denied the town of Gordon's harsh treatment of Indians and claimed the citizens of Gordon "'treated their Indians good'" and: "'These things they're saying about discrimination just aren't true. Indians are treated just like everyone else in this town.'"[15] Evans did not mention, however, that intoxicated Indians were smacked with the billy club and shoved into the back of the squad car of "big bad John Paul."[16] She also did not explain why only the names of Indians arrested for public intoxication were printed in the *Journal* while the names of whites were omitted.[17]

What is also curious about Taliaferro's Borglum and Gordon, Nebraska, is that there is little record of either helping the Lakota in any sustained way. While Borglum argued Mount Rushmore put South Dakota on the map, Taliaferro himself noted there is no indication the residents of Pine Ridge, Rosebud, etc. benefitted financially in any significant way from this enterprise. There were those from Gordon who argued some of the Indian people gained from an effort to provide them with more stable housing, but there is no sense they were welcomed into the mainstream of that community's life. As far as the Crazy Horse monument, putting aside the question of its appropriateness, Taliaferro did not explain how the Lakota were to benefit from this curiosity, particularly since it was and remains for the most part a privately financed venture.

Considering the name Gordon, Nebraska, where Raymond lived, is itself a celebration of sorts for white people violating the Ft. Laramie Treaty of 1868, that his senseless murder would be downplayed seems congruent with its history. John Gordon, the town's namesake, was an expedition leader for gold-crazed treasure seekers and had an extensive knowledge of the Black Hills region. Expeditions for gold, or encroachment of the Black Hills in general, were prohibited by the celebrated and ultimately meaningless Ft. Laramie Treaty of 1868; that is, meaningless at least as far as the whites were concerned. Gordon's last expedition was intercepted by federal troops, who, in addition to burning the wagons in the caravan, arrested Gordon.[18] Nonetheless, even though Gordon was convicted of violating the treaty, he was given only token punishment. In honor of the persistent and law-breaking Gordon, an 1885 expedition led by a Methodist minister named a town Gordon in northwest Nebraska about 20 miles from where Gordon's expedition was stopped. As Stew Magnuson aptly stated, naming the town Gordon "…was a rare honor to bestow upon a lawbreaker."[19]

Raymond Yellow Thunder, a less conspicuous presence during his life in Pine Ridge reservation lore than others such as SuAnne or Anna Mae, was born there in 1921. However, like those two more well-known individuals, Raymond's life encapsulated the struggles of Indians living in this isolated region of South Dakota and northwestern Nebraska. At the time World War I broke out seven years before Raymond's birth, beef and leather prices skyrocketed due to the increased demands of the military.[20] Yet, there was a "belief" by the various surrounding ranching concerns in South Dakota and Nebraska that much of the land would "go to waste" on the reservation if not used by these noble men. Adding to the dilemma was that so many of the Oglala Lakota men were off fighting for democracy (perhaps for others) in the trenches of France and Belgium. These ranching concerns, utilizing the Dawes Act of 1887 as the mechanism, made a deal with a corrupt Indian agent there to "lease" this land. The agent then decided the politically powerless Lakota people should be responsible for collecting the grazing fees from the white ranchers, who conveniently forgot to put their checks in the mail. The white ranchers had little concern when their herds trampled gardens, tore down fences, and fouled previously clear streams with cow dung. It is sad to note the once-thriving Oglala Lakota livestock industry was left in ruins.

The story of Raymond Yellow Thunder is by and large another tragic story that puts a face on the otherwise anonymous suffering that often occurs on or near reservations. Raymond left high school in the ninth grade, but with his gift for working with animals, was able to eke out a living breaking horses on various ranches throughout the Pine Ridge area. He married a childhood friend, Dora Cutgrass, but the marriage ended after Raymond's drinking increased beyond Dora's ability to cope with it. After the divorce, Raymond began drinking even more heavily. However, Raymond was not an obnoxious drunk and became quieter the more he drank; he was quite generous to his sisters and their families. He was essentially a peaceful man who ironically did not attract much attention throughout his life until it was ended by murder.[21]

Raymond's senseless beating on the night of February 12, 1972, catapulted his life story to the forefront of stories of the dismal treatment of Indians. On that cold night in northern Nebraska, where Raymond was staying at the time, he had a fateful encounter with several mean, drunken Nebraska rednecks: Les and Melvin Hare, Robert "Toby" Bayliss, Bernard "Butch" Lutter, and Janet Thompson, although Thompson did not participate in the crimes. As these small-town punks got increasingly drunker as the night wore on, they spotted Raymond climbing into the cab of an old pickup truck to try to grab some sleep. In their drunken fog, the group decided Raymond was a suitable candidate to provide the group some "entertainment." Les opened the cab door and yanked Raymond out into the cold night air. One account of the subsequent savagery is as follows, "'I got him' he [Les] yelled to the others." As Butch came running: "…he saw Les on the other side of the truck, hopping up and down, grabbing the panels for leverage. 'I'm really stomping him!' Les said." The story continued: "Toby arrived next, with Pat on his heels. Toby grabbed [Raymond] by his hair, lifted his head, and punched him in the mouth twice. 'Come on Butch this is a lot of fun' Toby said. The beating shocked Butch."

The drunken men then de-pantsed Raymond and carried him toward the car. Toby ran ahead to open the trunk as he declared, "'That stinkin' Indian ain't riding in front!'" They then drove the beaten man to the Gordon Legion Hall and shoved him inside. Raymond left the Legion Hall after declining an inquiry about medical assistance from people in the Legion Hall. He was again later spotted by the drunken, redneck savages and again shoved into the trunk by these barbarians. After driving for a while, the drunken group spotted the place where Raymond was originally accosted by noting his clothes laying there. In a moment to match any thoughtless cruelty perpetrated against Indians, Butch Lutter took 35 cents out of one of Raymond's pockets and put it into his own—35 cents. At the time this was barely enough to buy a soda and a candy bar.[22]

Raymond was let out of the trunk of the hoodlums' car and he crawled into the back of a pickup truck once again. Eight days later Raymond was found dead inside the same cab. From the time Raymond suffered the beating until he was found eight days later, the veins on the outer layer of his brain had been dripping microscopic amounts of blood, which eventually pooled together to become an amount large enough to stop his brain from fulfilling its functioning regarding other body parts. At some point from the time Raymond sustained his beating until he was found dead over a week later, he slipped into a coma and contracted pneumonia as well.[23] Two autopsies indicated Raymond had not been tortured, as some believed. When this specific information was released, a white woman callously stated: "'It wasn't as bad as they made it out to be.'" An Indian woman's insightful response to this absurd comment was, "Oh, is he then still alive?'"[24]

In what was a common practice in the area surrounding Pine Ridge, including northern Nebraska, the Hares and their friends were not charged with the most serious charge of murder—since the victim was an Indian—but with manslaughter and false imprisonment. In 1973, the year following Raymond's slaying, Darld Schmidtz, the man who stabbed Wesley Bad Heart Bull to death in the aftermath of a barroom incident in Rapid City, was charged with just manslaughter.[25] Ironically, while Schmidtz did not spend a single day in jail, Wesley's mother spent five months in jail after she was convicted for her part in what became known as the "Custer Court House Riots," which were protests about the lack of enthusiasm evident in prosecuting Schmidtz. Yet, overlooking the killing of Indians was not a phenomenon limited to the 20th century or to the South Dakota region.

According to Helen Hunt Jackson, D. Balinska was acquitted of killing a Winnebago Indian man, Henry Harris, because "…it was only an Indian that was killed."[26] Throughout the time of the conquest of the United States, it was thought the average settler considered the presence of Indians was no more an obstacle to conquest than "…a fox or a coyote…"[27] It was noted by Henry Adams that in the early 1800s no jury in the Indiana territory ever convicted a white man of murdering an Indian.[28] Sadly, Allan Eckert contended the avoidance of charging whites with the killings of Indians went even further back than the early 1800s. He noted that in the latter stages of the 1700s, Indians attacked whites: "…in retaliation for the murders of Indians that were being committed, murders that not only went unpunished but were applauded by other whites."[29] Charging whites with any offenses at all was some improvement over doing nothing at all. As Robert F. Berkhofer, Jr. noted: "…local agencies and courts refused frequently to find White criminals guilty when committing crimes against Indians… White murderers and thieves went scot-free after the clearest evidence of their guilt [was established]."[30]

Conversely, when it was believed an incident involved Indians committing crimes against whites, local militia often rushed in to punish Indians presumed to be murderers and thieves, without any regard to the infliction of mortal wounds on innocent Indians. At a council discussion during the movement of the Nez Perce from Oregon in the late 1870s, a young man named Walaitits left in anger during talks of peace regarding the whites. The source of his anger was his father's murder by a white settler named Larry Ott who was not punished for his act of murder. Likewise, the murderers of We-lot-yah were not punished for killing this Indian man who was mistakenly believed to be stealing horses.[31]

Thus, in the past the application of the law regarding those who hurt and even killed Indians was at best minimal and at worst disgraceful. Providing the most basic of due process rights for Indians required monumental effort, if it even happened at all. This attitude was far-reaching and was found on the eastern side of the United States as well. Prior to removal in the 1830s, the Georgia legislature passed laws forbidding Indians to dig for gold. Indians were also denied the right to testify in court and any court case regarding a contract dispute involving Indians required two non-Indian witnesses. The various Georgia laws were challenged in the United States Supreme Court as infringing on treaty rights, but the laws were upheld in the July 18, 1831, ruling of *Cherokee Nation v. Georgia* on the basis the Cherokee nation was a "domestic, dependent nation." As a further result, a Georgia law was upheld requiring whites living within the Georgia portion of the Cherokee nation to obtain a license to live there or be imprisoned for four years.

Thus, even as to whites whose general motivation was to promote Indian well-being, the law could be a cruel tool. While it is certainly debatable whether mission work was ultimately helpful to Indians, the law requiring the obtaining of the license applied almost exclusively to these men of the cloth. Missionaries Reverend Samuel Worcester and Reverend Elizer Butler were convicted of violating this law and sentenced to four years hard labor each. Fortunately for Worcester, at least initially, the judge in his case set aside his conviction on the basis he was an authorized agent of the United States government. However, he was later rearrested for this same offense, and given the same time—four years—and served his time with Butler.[32]

In addition to highlighting the shaky relationship between justice and Indians, Raymond's story also perhaps exemplified the relationship between alcohol and Indians—or at least how the relationship between alcohol consumption and Indians was perceived. In *All the Real Indians Died Off*, Roxanne

Dunbar-Ortiz noted that recent studies have challenged the stereotypical thinking that mixing Indians and alcohol led to "'instant personal and cultural devastation.'" Momentarily putting aside the disdain Indians usually have for anthropologists, in 1971 anthropologist Nancy Lurie hypothesized drinking became a way for Indians to: "…validate and assert their Indianness in the face of negative stereotypes."[33] Of course, as with anything else involving Indians, there is no indication anyone ever bothered to ask Raymond why he drank. Stew Magnuson, as noted, surmised Raymond began drinking early in his life and increased his drinking after Dora divorced him.

Although drinking alcohol to excess is considered a problem for many Indians, Raymond's death was not caused by the alcohol *he* consumed. Rather, Raymond died as a result of the blows rained on him by *others* who were drinking—in this case whites—the Hares and their friends. Raymond's story is not the first time it was reported that drinking by white or partly white people caused significant problems for Indians living in or near southwest South Dakota. As described in the William Henry Harrison chapter, it is believed what is now referred to as the "Grattan Massacre" was precipitated at least in part by a mixed-blood interpreter named Wyuse who chose to fill his canteen with whiskey instead of water. Even when sober, Wyuse often twisted the Lakota's words to make trouble for them.[34]

Nevertheless, drinking by white soldiers not only caused problems for Indians, but for the soldiers themselves. What is often overlooked about life on the frontier, and soldiering in general, is that even in combat situations, brief moments of terror are often bookended by long stretches of boredom. Statistics for the 19th century are hard to come by, but an incident during the Black Hills Expedition is instructive. One Private Ewert sought medical attention for one of his comrades and engaged the help of a young lieutenant in doing so. The first doctor they encountered was passed out from drinking. They proceeded with Ewert's comrade to the other doctor who was also drunk, but who managed to examine Ewert's fellow soldier. The doctor pronounced the soldier fit for duty and the soldier proceeded to die that night. The title of "doctor" was dropped by members of Ewert's Company and the two physicians became known as "Butcher Allen" and "Drunken Williams."[35]

The belief that drunkenness and/or alcohol abuse was a self-inflicted condition of the Indians has a long, sordid history in the United States. For example, the venerated Benjamin Franklin once suggested that rum was: "'The appointed means' of fulfilling 'the design of Providence to extirpate these savages in order to make room for the cultivators of the earth.'"[36] Franklin's quote contains more than a suggestion that Indians would "extirpate" themselves by drinking too much and that "Providence," who in Franklin's mind had no use for Indians, would use "demon rum" as the instrument of conquest. Perhaps watching Indian culture disintegrate through excessive drinking was not as dramatic as the Israelites slaying the hated Philistines on the way to the "Promised Land," but the method of annihilation by alcohol contained the possibility of fewer casualties on the side of the "Lord's Chosen People."

Fittingly, the stilted reporting on the history of alcohol consumption relating to situations involving Indians careens through the decades and centuries like a drunken sailor on shore leave. Josiah Cotton's *Vocabulary of the Massachusetts (or Natick) Indian Language* contained multiple references to the virtues of refraining from indulging in alcohol consumption. For example, one recorded exchange of dialogue (although it is difficult to determine if it actually occurred since it is not attributed to specific individuals) proceeded in this manner: "And why don't you work hard?" "So I would with all my heart, but I am sickly." "But it may be work will cure you, if you would leave off drinking too." Another pithy piece of dialogue claims: "A great deal of praise that Indian deserves that keeps himself sober."[37] There is no indication of any dialogue indicating Indians would have been better off had alcohol not been introduced to them in the first instance, often as a major component of trade situations with whites.

If there is any good to be gained from the sad story of Raymond Yellow Thunder, perhaps it is the opportunity to examine one of the most deeply ingrained myths of Indian history and or culture—that Indians are naturally predisposed to alcoholism. If there is anything whites think they know about Indians, the belief that Indians are going to become alcoholics if exposed to alcohol at all is one of the most ingrained. To be sure, alcoholism is a problem in places like Pine Ridge. But what if excessive alcohol consumption is not a cause of the destruction of Indian culture, but a symptom? This myth may be one of the most difficult of all to look at objectively. Similar to Vine Deloria, Jr., Dunbar-Ortiz argued: "Non-Natives thus position themselves, either wittingly or unwittingly, as being the true experts about Indians and their histories—and it happens at all levels of society, from the uneducated all the way up to those with advanced college degrees."[38] Dunbar-Ortiz also argued: "Few images of Native peoples have been as intractable and damaging as the trope of the drunken Indian."[39]

Raymond Yellow Thunder's life and death also provides a prism to view Indian culture and the effects of more subtle forms of weapons of destruction used against it and the people in it. The violence of the Hares against Raymond was an obvious form of destruction while others were not. Mary Crow Dog argued the use of boarding schools was a significant factor in destroying Lakota culture and fueled (and fuels) the excessive use of alcohol on reservations such as Pine Ridge:

> The kids were taken away from their villages and pueblos, in their blankets and moccasins, kept completely isolated from their families—sometimes for as long as ten years—suddenly coming back, their short hair slick with pomade, their necks raw from stiff, high collars, their thick jackets always short in the sleeves and pinching their arms, their tight patent leather shoes giving them corns, the girls in starched white blouses and clumsy high-buttoned boots—caricatures of white people.

Mary then explained the worst aspect of all for the Indians caught up in the process: "When they find out—and they find out quickly—that they were neither wanted by whites nor by Indians, they got good and drunk, many of them staying drunk for the rest of their lives."[40]

Archie Fire Lame Deer, who like Mary Crow Dog was born on the Rosebud Indian Reservation, echoed her memories of the horror of Indian boarding schools. Lame Deer recounted the first day Lakota children were taken to these institutions designed to indoctrinate Indian children into white culture was called *anpetu sicha*, the "worst of all days," or "the day of doom." These descriptive phrases dispel the notion these Indian people viewed white culture as something to be desired, at least when force fed. It is said Indian mothers would generally tell their misbehaving children: "*Hoksila*, if you are bad, the white man will come and take you away—*wasichu amgnikte!*" This is told to the children if the threat of the *chichiye*, considered a truly horrible creature, coming to get them, is not enough to get their attention. Lame Deer considered his "day of doom" to have arrived in the form of both a *chichiye* and a white man—Catholic priest Father Buechel.

Although Lame Deer's boarding school, the Catholic Boarding School at St. Francis, was only ten miles away from where he lived on the Rosebud Reservation, he claimed: "…the distance might as well have been a hundred thousand miles." He believed this was the case because he and the other Lakota children, like other Indian children around the country, "…were totally cut off from their families." Lame Deer learned Father Buechel was a decent man who spoke Lakota, but discovered other priests and nuns were not so flexible.[41] Lame Deer soon learned he was forbidden to speak his native Lakota language. Failure to abide by this restriction, if discovered by the priests or nuns, could lead to a lashing with the intimidating leather straps. He also learned the priests and nuns wanted the Indian children to forget about the White Buffalo Calf Woman and the Sacred Pipe she bestowed upon the Lakota people. If the children did not show enough love for the white gods, Lame Deer noted: "…they would try to beat the love into us with a strap or a ruler." Although later in life Lame Deer found Christ's teachings beautiful, he never accepted Christianity because for him and other boarding school survivors: "…the word 'Jesus' always conjured up memories of the leather strap."[42]

Endnotes

1. Granzotto, *Christopher Columbus*, p. 212.
2. Magnuson, *The Death of Raymond Yellow Thunder*, p.46.
3. Frazier, *On the Rez*, p. 207.
4. Flood, *Lost Bird of Wounded Knee*, p. 300.
5. Cook-Lynn, *A Separate Country*, p. 58.
6. Crow Dog, *Lakota Woman*, p. 22.
7. *Ibid.*, p. 21. The term *wasicu* is a slang term generally believed to mean something to the effect of "taker of fat." It is usually used to describe European invaders who took Indian land.
8. Leonard Crow Dog with Richard Erdoes, *Crow Dog: Four Generations of Sioux Medicine Men* (New York: Harper Collins Publishers, 1995), p. 80.
9. Taliaferro, *Great White Fathers*, p. 262.
10. Ibid., pp. 185-194.
11. Ibid., p. 192.
12. Ibid., p. 37.
13. Howard, *Saga of Chief Joseph*, p. 189.
14. Taliaferro, *Great White Fathers*, p. 321.
15. Magnuson, *The Death of Raymond Yellow Thunder*, p. 151.
16. Ibid., p. 45.
17. Ibid., pp.45-46.
18. Ibid., p. 35.
19. Ibid., p. 36.
20. Ibid., p. 172. Anna Mae was not born on Pine Ridge, but her story is inextricably bound to its history.
21. Ibid., p. 43. In contradiction of Magnuson's claim Raymond was a heavy drinker, Akim D. Reinhardt stated: "Friends and family remembered him as humble, sober, and hard working." Reinhardt also indicated Raymond was a grandson of American Horse, the famous nineteenth century Lakota warrior. *Ruling Pine Ridge: Oglala Lakota Politics from the IRA to Wounded Knee* (Lubbock, Texas: Texas Tech University Press, 2007), p. 127.
22. Ibid., p. 20-23.
23. Ibid., p. 48.
24. Smith and Warrior, *Like a Hurricane*, p. 116.
25. Ibid., p. 183.
26. Jackson, *A Century of Dishonor*, pp. 254-255.
27. Valerie Sherer Mathis, *Helen Hunt Jackson and Her Indian Reform Legacy*, (Austin, Texas: University of Texas Press, 1990), p. 69.
28. Washburn, Ed., Henry Adams, "Tippecanoe and Tyler Too! "*The Indian and the White Man*, p. 359.
29. Eckert, *That Dark and Bloody River*, p. 20.

30 Berkhofer, *The White Man's Indian*, p. 147.
31 Howard, *Saga of Chief Joseph*, pp. 107, 137.
32 Ehle, *Trail of Tears*, pp. 248-249.
33 Dunbar-Ortiz and Gino-Whitaker, *All the Real Indians Died Off* (Boston, Massachusetts: Beacon Press, 2016), p. 131.
34 Smith, *Moon of Popping Trees*, pp. 18-21.
35 Connell, *Son of the Morning Star*, p. 245.
36 Weinberg, *Manifest Destiny*, p. 77.
37 Washburn, Ed., Josiah Cotton, "What is the Matter That Indians Very Often No Speak True." *The Indian and the White Man*, pp. 198-199.
38 Dunbar-Ortiz and Gino-Whitaker, *All the Real Indians Died Off*, p. 2. In a speech to a Congressional Committee in April 1972 concerning a Navajo-Hopi Land dispute, Annie Wauneka admonished: "You wonder why the problem never gets solved. It's because every white man is an expert on Indian problems, but nobody listens to the Indians." Niethammer, *I'll Go and Do More*, p.184.
39 Ibid., p. 130.
40 Crow Dog, *Lakota Woman*, p. 30. John (Fire) Lame Deer explained: "When we enter the school we at least know we are Indians. We come out half red and half white, not knowing what we are." John (Fire) Lame Deer and Richard Erdoes, *Lame Deer—Seeker of Visions* (New York: Simon and Schuster, A Touchstone Book, 1972), p. 35.
41 Archie Fire Lame Deer and Richard Erdoes, *Gift of Power: The Life and Teachings of a Lakota Medicine Man* (Rochester, Vermont: Bear & Co., 1992), pp. 45-46.
42 Ibid., p. 49.

CHAPTER 18

Russell Means and His Strange Journey to the Heart of the American Dream

After I joined AIM, I stopped drinking. Others put away their roach clips and airplane glue bottles. There were a lot of things wrong with AIM. We did not see these things or did not want to see them. At the time these things were not important. What was important was getting it on.

Mary Brave Bird, "We Aim Not to Please" *Reinventing the Enemy's Language*[1]

The only way to deal with these kinds of people [AIM members] is to put a bullet in their heads. Put a bullet in a guy's head and he won't bother you anymore.

Bill Janklow (then candidate for South Dakota Attorney General)
The Unquiet Grave[2]

When Bill Janklow was a candidate for attorney general of South Dakota, his quote about shooting AIM members in their heads encapsulated his raw emotional reaction on how to deal with American Indian Movement leaders like Russell Means, Dennis Banks, and others. Stanley Lyman, Superintendent of the Bureau of Indian Affairs for Pine Ridge in the early '70s, said he could not "'…keep back the hatred and the glee'" when he saw Means in handcuffs during the "occupation."[3] Like the parable of the blind men describing an elephant as each holds a different part of the behemoth, the reaction to Russell Means depended on the point of view of the person dealing with him. Yet, regardless of the reaction or viewpoint of the observer, it is generally agreed upon he was a bold, creative individual and: "When it came to charisma Russell Means had few peers. He made many people think of Crazy Horse, Sitting Bull, Touch the Clouds, American Horse. Even his enemies conceded his moments of brilliance."[4] Nevertheless, like

Janklow, Joseph Trimbach, a high-level former FBI agent present at the beginning of the 71-day standoff at Wounded Knee in 1973, saw Means as nothing more than a bullying, violent thug. Criticism from individuals like Trimbach and Janklow must be evaluated carefully to determine if there is an agenda behind the criticism. Conversely, many Indians who personally knew Means believed he was a "brutally honest"[5] individual whose friendship and leadership is missed by many since his death due to esophageal cancer in October 2102.

As obviously articulate and intelligent as Russell Means was, it is still surprising people like Trimbach did not understand Indian leaders like him recognized being passive often cost Indian leaders their lives. Crazy Horse was lured into surrendering at Camp Robinson and stabbed from behind while unarmed. Even being aggressive was no guarantee of safe passage—when Sitting Bull was being "arrested" on December 15, 1890, he was shot after putting up a struggle. Prior to that occasion Sitting Bull himself noticed most "'accidents'" which befell Indian leaders were caused by: "…soldiers, agents, licensed traders—*all of them official representatives of the Grandfather* [emphasis in original]."[6] According to numerous eyewitnesses, on January 14, 1973, Means was arrested without explanation by law enforcement officials in riot gear, thrown to the ground, and clubbed several times. Witnesses also indicated the caravan of police power included 15 police cars. Even though he was later charged with carrying a concealed weapon, none of these witnesses observed Means with a weapon.[7]

Trimbach's uninhibited scorn directed against AIM and Russell Means accomplished Means' objectives of the 1973 "occupation" in a way it is unlikely either man anticipated. It would seem highly unlikely a representative of the FBI, official or not, would make a contemptuous statement about Indian people as Gwynne did regarding Crazy Horse being "…free to be the hero we want him to be." Yet, Trimbach did exactly that by constantly insulting Means, Banks, etc. and by complaining about the ultimately trivial matter of AIM people ransacking the Gildersleeves' store at Wounded Knee. By many accounts, this establishment contained only crappy, knock-off souvenirs anyway, and used highly questionable business practices such as cashing the checks of Indians without authorization.[8] The trashing of AIM and Means absolutely proved Means' point of how politically powerless Indians in the United States really were and still are. It is indeed fitting that Means had roles in movies about Indians after his days of protests since during the height of his activism on behalf of Indians he was anything but "faceless and voiceless." Perhaps government officials like Joseph Trimbach and Stanley Lyman generated scorn for Means because he did not understand as they believed he should that Indian history ended December 29, 1890. Certainly, Russell Means made it clear, particularly in his autobiography, *Where White Men Fear to Tread* that he (rightfully) believed that Indians needed an autonomous voice in how their lives should be governed.

In his Pulitzer Prize-winning book *Custer's Trials,* T. J. Stiles stated regarding Custer's personality: "The search for [a] unifying theme is complicated by the astonishing number of roles he played."[9] It could also easily be stated it is difficult to find a "unifying theme" for Russell Means' larger-than-life personality. In Means' life he was a professional dancer, accountant, barroom brawler, father, grandfather, husband, ex-husband, brother, son, community organizer, convict, internationally known Indian activist, subject for an Andy Warhol painting, author, and movie actor. Also, like Custer, Means experienced a tempestuous personal life. Even though Custer was married only once, he was linked romantically to a Cheyenne woman, and it is rumored he fathered a child with her. Means was married multiple times and fathered several children. Like Custer, who more than anything is remembered for his failure at the Little Big Horn, Means and AIM's effort at the 1973 "occupation" of Wounded Knee is often viewed as a failure, at least by white journalists.

Deloria, Jr., argued Indian history did not end on December 29, 1890, and Means and his allies in AIM worked hard to drive home that point. AIM's actions along with Deloria, Jr.'s commentaries highlight a debate not satisfactorily resolved to this day—whether or not to support and promote Indian self-government. In the 19th century, the self-appointed "Friends of the Indian" found themselves defending Indian actions against the hostility of the United States general public when it was learned Indians attacked and sometimes killed settlers. At the opposite end of the spectrum were those who agreed with Teddy Roosevelt as he stated in *The Winning of the West* that: "'The war against merciless savages was the most ultimately righteous of all wars.'"[10] Accepting as valid those Indian rights would have delayed obtaining valuable tracts of land needed by railroads and desired by miners or farmers. Yet, without allowing some degree of Indian self-government, it is understandable if Indians fail to see reservations as anything other than open-air prisons.

When ferreting out the myths deployed and which often assign roles to the various actors at WKII, it is fascinating to note Means played Chingachgook in the film adaptation of James Fenimore Cooper's book *Last of the Mohicans*. Richard Slotkin pointed out Chingachgook and his son: "…do not share Magua's weak predilection for all things white." Yet, while far from a perfect analogy, it is undeniable the real-life Means also possessed some of the same traits as Magua. As such, Magua was a: "…warrior chief who is drawn to the whites because of his admiration for their apparent superiority in weaponry and wealth." Joseph Trimbach, the FBI Agent in Charge during the initial phase of WKII, would fulfill the role of Munro, since "Munro and Magua simply do not understand each other's ways, and the result is tragedy."[11] Trimbach accused Means and his allies of being "false heroes" who were responsible for the perpetuation of decades-old problems on Pine Ridge. As would be expected, Elizabeth Cook-Lynn had a different take on the situation and bristled at the notion of not giving AIM and Russell Means the credit she believes they deserved. She argued the Wounded Knee "occupation":

> …story, with the potential to become the inflammatory story of our time, has become, instead, a story of failure told mostly by white writers who want to take up the whitewashed Plains Indian history of 'how the West was won' and discuss the divisions on Indian Reservations between half-breeds and 'traditionals.'[12]

Although Russell Means was born November 10, 1939, it often feels as if his story began long before that date. It could be argued it began when the Lakota Nation rose up long ago out of what is now known as Wind Cave in South Dakota. It could be credibly stated Means' story began in 1492 when Europeans began their process of separating Indians from their occupation of North America. Perhaps it began in 1868 with the Ft. Laramie Treaty of that year. Means' story possibly started in 1887 with the Dawes

Act which legislated the breaking up of communal Indian land into allotments to be devoured by white piranhas. However, it is perhaps best to suggest Means' story began with the opening of the Canton/Hiawatha Asylum for Insane Indians described in the earlier chapter on Manifest Destiny.

To some, it might appear as a major stretch or exaggeration to relate the history of the Canton/Hiawatha Asylum with the biography of Russell Means. Yet, the connection of the sadistic efforts by the "medical staff" at the Canton/Hiawatha Asylum to suppress traditional Indian culture and Means' rebirth as a flawed but spiritual leader is more logical than might appear on initial examination. In some respects, Means' somewhat later-in-life enthusiasm for a return to traditional Indian values resembled Apostle Paul's conversion to Christianity on the road to Damascus, as neither were likely candidates for their respective experiences. Means was a hard-drinking, hard-partying brawler and Paul was a persecutor of the early Christians. Although perhaps Means' transformation was more gradual than Paul's, both men became fervent advocates for their respective faiths. Undoubtedly, Means was more involved in politics.

That AIM, the organization in which Russell Means was once a prominent member, was slandered by claiming it had success which was "…contingent upon [its] ability to capitalize on tragedy and violence"[13] should come as no surprise to those who analyze Indian history. A description of Eagle Woman, born in 1820 in South Dakota, resonated like it could have been written by Helen Hunt Jackson, who favored Indians who absorbed European values. It was indicated Eagle Woman was a: "'…good Catholic and an excellent person, a striking example of what the influence of religion and civilization can accomplish for the welfare of the Indians.'"[14] It was noted a reporter for the *New York Herald* who had described her as a "'…prophetess and real chieftainess [sic] …a civilized and educated lady'" had fallen into the same pattern as other white commentators on Ms. Galpin (Eagle Woman): "…the more they perceived her willingness to defend white civilization, the more effusive their praise of her."[15] Elizabeth Cook-Lynn saw the aggressive Means in a more positive light, and maintained her credibility by acknowledging his flaws: "Means is, admittedly…discredited very often by his own less than stellar personal behavior, but he is a man who insisted for two decades that his people defend themselves against grinding poverty and racism in this country."[16]

Cook-Lynn did not specifically state what actions by Means constituted his "…less than stellar personal behavior." However, the claims of Means' misbehavior in what was titled a "press statement" issued by the American Indian Movement February 20, 1999, provided some possible insight. The "statement" contained an allegation Means had assaulted his father-in-law, Omaha and Dine (Navajo) elder Leon Grant. The "statement" also alleged he misappropriated $15,000 out of a $35,000 settlement from a 1983 lawsuit against the Cleveland Indians for discrimination in that the organization used Chief Wahoo as a mascot (as noted, the Cleveland Indian organization discontinued the use of the mascot in 2019). Other comments in the "statement" related to what was considered Means' challenge to the concept of Indian sovereignty and the jurisdiction and authority of the Dine (Navajo) Nation's Criminal Courts (apparently in connection to the assault charge).

The February 20, 1999, "press statement" also contained attachments of statements listing arguably much less troubling behavior and gave a glimpse into some of the infighting inside AIM.

One comment was before leaving AIM, Means condemned James Fenimore Cooper's novel *Last of the Mohicans*, then after appearing in the film version of that novel as well as voicing the title character's father in the animated feature *Pocahontas*, claimed they were the two best Indian movies ever made. The "statement" also criticized his portrayal of a Navajo medicine man in Oliver Stone's film *Natural Born Killers*.[17]

Likewise, Means' book *Where White Men Fear to Tread* was criticized for, ironically, among other things, its "petty attacks" on people. Means was also questioned for allowing himself to be "manipulated" by Miskito Indians and basically anti-revolutionary Contras. Nevertheless, nothing described in this press release confirms Trimbach's claims Means was a murderer, etc. Thus, Trimbach's charge that Means was involved with the murder of Anna Mae Aquash remains unproven speculation at this point. Additionally, as outlined in a previous section, the weight of conventional history militates against considering the possibility that instead of the FBI containing the "savages" during the "occupation," the beleaguered AIM Indians and their allies presented legitimate grievances. Nevertheless, Cook-Lynn argued regarding Means' book, *Where White Men Fear to Tread*: "…even if one admits it has flaws, is a political document that deserves study if one is to understand the violence done to Indian peoples by the federal government and the powers that be."[18]

Means and other members of AIM certainly had detractors within the Indian community, as evidenced by the interactions at the Dakota Conference held at Augustana College in April 2012. Even though the conference was held within ten months of the 40th anniversary of the "occupation," the animosity between some of the participants was still very evident. Some of the people arguably held hostage by AIM members, the Gildersleeves, who claimed at least partial Indianness, accused the AIMsters of rough treatment. Adrienne Fritze, a cousin of AIM leader Clyde Bellecourt, stated: "'I am shaking so much it is unbelievable. The brutality happened. You guys perpetrated it. Some of us believed that you could bring freedom, but you took it away from us.'"[19] Even people not directly involved with the "occupation" and not at the conference still harbor resentments against AIM. David Treuer, author of *Rez Life*, related that his father said: "AIM was too polarized and too explosive to build anything. They couldn't build power lines or consensus or community. They just used people. They were all a bunch of Al Sharptons. And you can quote me on that."[20]

Nevertheless, as the Indian activism in the latter half of the 20th century came into focus, for many Indians being an "Apple"—red on the outside and white on the inside—became an intolerable state of being. White indifference to the needs of Indians as simply human beings invigorated the urge of many to seek solace in traditional Indian values, and most importantly, community. In describing official reaction to a family tragedy, Ms. Jim-James in the *Dine Way* noted that white officials: "…talked about my [murdered] aunt as if she was no one and her children were to be nothing more than problems for the system to handle." Trimbach's constant spewing of negative comments about Means, naming him a "dissident," "criminal," etc., revealed an identical viewpoint of seeing him and his allies as nothing more than "…problems for the system to handle." Jim-James eloquently explained how Indian "dissidents" came to view living in the United States:

> From this experience, I have come to see that White America will not give me justice, and will not give my people, the American Indian justice. I must command justice, and my people must command justice.[21]

Undoubtedly, Means never shied away from conflict or controversy and even appeared to relish them. Many criticized him and other members of AIM as being concerned only with personal glory and not with seeking long-term solutions to problems on reservations and elsewhere. However, as Lakota Mary Brave Bird noted: "Some things were done by AIM, or rather by people who called themselves AIM, that I am not proud of. But AIM gave us a lift badly needed at that time."[22]

The story of Russell Means' life has a more subtle meaning as well. He chafed against the theme of Indian cluelessness as depicted in *Dances with Wolves*—it takes a white guy to show Indians not only which end is up, but what it means to be a real Indian. One of the pivotal scenes in *Dances* is where Costner/Dunbar explains to Kicking Bear the vast number of whites soon to be heading west, as if the Lakota hadn't figured that out by the time Costner/Dunbar arrived on the scene. As Mike Sajna noted in *Crazy Horse: The Life Behind the Legend*, Plains Indians did not need anyone to explain the coming onslaught of the white population. At least by the 1840s, the Lakota recognized whites were coming in endless numbers. We know the setting of *Dances with Wolves* is some time after the Civil War owing to the opening scene where Costner/Dunbar displays his heroism/recklessness in riding up and down on his horse in front of massed and firing Confederate rifles (aren't the "bad guys" always poor shots?). Sajna noted that well before the conclusion of the Civil War, to the Indians (presumably the Lakota and perhaps the Cheyenne), the: "…trails leading to Oregon and California became sources of confusion and concern." Sajna also explained, quoting the well-known Jesuit missionary Father De Smet, the Indians also: "…conceived a high idea of the countless White Nation, as they express it."[23]

Means also resented white experts such as anthropologists and sociologists; he felt like they made judgments based on superficial observations. Means also questioned a major premise of the best-selling book *Bury My Heart at Wounded Knee* concerning the circumstances regarding the Wounded Knee Massacre and the "Ghost Dance." He argued:

> [Brown] repeated the myth that the Sioux had embraced the teachings of the 'Pauite Messiah Wovoka, who had founded the religion of the ghost dance'…Whites are taught that followers of the Ghost Dance 'religion' believed bullets would bounce off their ghost shirts, also believed they would become invincible supermen and were getting ready to attack settlers… [it is] bullshit—U.S. military propaganda lies to excuse the mass murder of Pauite, Shoshone, Nez Perce, and Sioux people.[24]

Other Lakota agreed with Means. One current Pine Ridge resident stated, "It was a planned massacre."[25] Means further stated that Lakota men Kicking Bear and Short Bull went to what is now Nevada to learn about Wovoka the Pauite Medicine Man and the "Ghost Dance," not to learn how to start another war.

The tendency never to give Means or any of the other Indian activists credit for their efforts marches on today. In *Killing the White Man's Indian*, Fergus Bordewich surmised that even though the 1970s was: "…one of the most active periods of Indian legislation in American history…the political landscape of Indian Country would be profoundly altered, less by the attention getting dramatics of the radical American Indian Movement…than by deliberations of the United States Congress."[26] This overgeneralization ignored the reality of the growth of Indian activism in the latter half of the 20th century at least. Elizabeth Cook-Lynn criticized Bordewich's book itself as "…a very bad book on Indian affairs.[27] To some extent the savvy Means used his penchant for planning and executing protest events, which drew much media attention, to capitalize on the activism that had its roots on college campuses in the late 1950s. At that time, student groups had been working on these campuses and in communities, producing cohorts of college-educated tribal officials and administrators. Simultaneously, traditional Indians, local poor, and working-class people had been staging protests long before the Wounded Knee "occupation," even if these early events were largely ignored by the mainstream press and other media.

One of the leaders of Indian activism to emerge during this period was the aptly named Clyde Warrior. Clyde was born in 1939 near Ponca City, Oklahoma, and grew up immersed in the Ponca language and culture. His personal growth and evolution into an activist accelerated during his participation in workshops at the University of Colorado at Boulder where he was provided up-to-date information on the current state of Indian affairs. Like Means would react later, Warrior bristled publicly at the notion that Indian people were backwards and the crux of the problem was Indian culture itself. And, also like Means, some considered Warrior an arrogant blowhard. Yet, many secretly agreed with Warrior and admired his outspoken nature, much as many admired Means without necessarily publicly acknowledging it.

In 1960, Warrior was voted President of the Southwest Regional Indian Youth Council. When he mounted the podium to make his campaign speech just prior to the election, he rolled back his sleeves, pointed to his bare arms, and simply said: "'This is all I have to offer. The sewage of Europe does not flow through these veins.'" By the end of the summer of 1961, Warrior and some Indian students from Boulder, Colorado, met in Gallup, New Mexico, and formed the National Indian Youth Council (NIYC). As would be expected, Warrior became one of the leaders of the group. One of the early signals as to the direction Warrior would take the NIYC was his bringing actor and civil rights activist Marlon Brando to the NIYC meeting at Ft. Duchesne, Utah, in 1963. Brando's message was that the NIYC needed to become more involved with civil rights protests. At this same meeting, Hank Adams, a 19-year-old "Sioux/Assiniboine," joined with Warrior to urge direct action for activists to promote Indian issues. Adams helped focus one of the earliest planned protests on a simple straightforward target—fishing rights in the Pacific Northwest.

Although the idea was simple, the genesis of the issue was Public Law 280, and it was anything but simple. Public Law 280 was intertwined with the termination push of the mid-20th century; in its simplest terms termination was the federal government's attempt to end the reservation system by eliminating funding. Public Law 280 paved the way for states to assume jurisdiction over many Indian matters on ostensibly Indian land. Of particular concern to Adams was how Public Law 280 paved the way for the state of Washington to allow alcohol sales on the Quinalt Reservation where he was raised by his mother and stepfather. These sales had previously been prohibited by the tribal council as an attempt to limit young people's access to these substances, which was considered a means of inhibiting the suicide rate of Indian youths there. Teen suicide, some of it fueled by alcohol dependency, has been a major public health issue on many Indian reservations.[28] Sadly, alcohol abuse became a major issue for Adams' colleague Clyde Warrior as well, and he died of liver failure just short of his 29th birthday.[29]

In 1964, the National Congress of American Indians (NCAI) elected the transcendentally intellectual Lakota Vine Deloria, Jr., as its executive director. Earlier in the 1960s, Deloria, Jr., had worked at the United Scholarship Service, a group located in Denver that had supported American Indian and Mexican American college students. Thus, Deloria, Jr., became another intellectual voice in the Indian activist world along with Hank Adams, Warrior, and Mel Thom.[30] Deloria, Jr., had already achieved a high degree of notoriety and fame after publishing his acerbic book *Custer Died for Your Sins*. In this scathing commentary on the situation of Indians in the United States, he noted: "For many Indians the white had no culture other than one of continual exploitation."[31]

Interestingly, as previously noted, Deloria, Jr., much like Dee Brown with *Bury My Heart at Wounded Knee*, endured much scorn from academia for being highly critical of the theory that Indians arrived in North America by crossing the Bering Strait from Asia after the waters receded. Curiously, Deloria, Jr., did not seem interested in addressing the issue of the population of indigenous people at the time Columbus and other Europeans arrived in North America. Nonetheless, Deloria, Jr., was steadfast in his criticism of the Bering Strait theory that Indians or their ancestors traveled from Asia to North America on a land bridge. Deloria, Jr., stated that when a theory such as the land bridge theory is: "…published, it is treated as if it was *proven* and then it is popularized by people who rarely read the original documents, and vigorously defended by scholarly disciplines more fiercely than they would defend our country [emphasis in original]."[32] Nevertheless, the Bering Strait theory itself has come under increasing scrutiny and criticism since Deloria, Jr., first raised the issue and aroused the scientific community's ire.

Warrior became president of the NIYC in 1966, but he was becoming increasingly frustrated with the lack of control Indians exercised over their futures. He harshly criticized the efforts of the War on Poverty in Indian communities by noting that: "'We know that no one is arguing that the dispossessed, the poor, be given any control over their own destiny.'" He argued Indian people "'…are not free. We do not make choices.'" Warrior further argued: "'…programs must be Indian creations, Indian choices, Indian experiences. Even the failures must be Indian experiences because only then will Indians understand why a program failed and not blame themselves for some personal inadequacy.'"[33] Unfortunately, as noted, Warrior died one month short of his 29th birthday. Like Lakota Will Peters commenting he was not advocating a return to buffalo hunting, but essentially a respect for traditional values, Mel Thom, Hank Adams, and Warrior prior to his death envisioned a world: "…in which the necessities of modern culture could exist alongside elaborate, old-fashioned, community and family-centered feasts and ceremonies."[34]

At the end of November 1969, not quite a year and a half after Warrior's death, members of an organization named Indians of All Tribes occupied Alcatraz Island in San Francisco Bay. Ultimately, the federal government's response to the occupation (this is not in quotes since it does not appear it was specifically designated Indian land at the time, at least in the sense by treaty rights) was managed at senior levels in the Nixon White House as opposed to being considered a minor trespass handled by law enforcement. Leonard Garment, a relatively long-time Nixon friend and ally, believed the occupation was a political opportunity for the administration to showcase its desire to develop programs for the betterment of Indian lives.

Although it was apparently not well known, Nixon himself had a soft spot for Indians due to his friendship with an Indian man named Wallace "Chief" Newman, the football coach at Whittier College near Los Angeles where Nixon attended and played football. Nixon and Newman thrived on their mutual respect; Newman enthusiastically supported his former player and Nixon revered Newman and showcased him at fundraisers, political picnics, and in electoral victory parades through the town of Whittier itself. Nixon was further open to changes in Indian policy simply due to his indifference to dealing with domestic affairs. Under Eisenhower's tutelage while Nixon was his Vice President, Nixon realized Presidents wielded far-reaching power in foreign affairs compared to the "arcane" battles with Congress over such topics as agriculture, transportation, and crime. Thus, in the realm of Indian affairs, his friend Garment was given free rein in handling them as long as he didn't embarrass the President.[35]

About eight weeks into the occupation of Alcatraz, some of the Indians involved in the protest began pressing for the United States government to transfer title to them, but Robert Robertson, another Nixon operative, explained to these individuals the only matters open for discussion were the issuance of medical supplies and some safety issues. Nevertheless, another item of discussion desired by the Indians was funding for a cultural center and staff to explain the story of Indians of All Tribes. The government instead proposed improvements to the physical plant of the former prison, but the Indians were skeptical in that they believed this concept was already in the planning stages before the occupation even began. It was alleged that during one meeting arranged to discuss these issues, an Indian man named David Leach tried to spike Robertson's coffee with mescaline. One of the other Indians on the island thought this was an exceptionally poor idea, although another said he was glad Leach made the attempt.[36]

As a historical footnote, it wouldn't necessarily be productive to argue turnabout is fair play, but many believe that in 1661, Alexander, son of Wampanoag Chief Massasoit, was poisoned during a meeting with the governor of Plymouth, Massachusetts. One of those who strongly suspected Alexander was poisoned was Metacom, Alexander's brother, known to the English as Philip. In 1675, after the English found three Wampanoags guilty of killing a Harvard-educated Indian man named John Sassamon, the trio was executed. King Philip had no love for the English to begin with due to what he suspected they did to his brother. He was further angered at them for what he believed was their meddling in what was a strictly Indian affair. Subsequent events spiraled out of control and the ensuing hostilities were named King Philip's War. It is difficult to credibly argue events essentially set in motion by poisoning another human being (if indeed Alexander was poisoned) ever turn out well, regardless of whether the poisoner believes there is justification.[37]

In a prepared response to the government's proposal to more or less create an Indian theme park on Alcatraz, the Indian leaders stated, among other things, they nonetheless: "…will no longer be museum pieces, tourist attractions, and politician's playthings."[38] As with many situations involving conflict, problems and issues are often resolved with negotiations. Unfortunately, like many other groups, the Indians on Alcatraz lacked experience in this area. Vine Deloria, Jr., noted: "…only ten Indians in the country are qualified to negotiate with the federal government" and he made it clear he did not believe that group included any of the Indians of All Nations members on Alcatraz Island.[39] In May 1971, the federal government began the process of transferring the Alcatraz property to the Department of the Interior and the National Park System. Although the Indians on Alcatraz talked of their resolve to continue the protest, their efforts were thwarted by one of the federal government's most effective tactics—indifference. Compounding this issue were divisions within the Indian community itself—some Indians from California labeled the Alcatraz occupiers themselves as colonizers since they had not sought permission to enter the island from the descendants of the people who originally lived in the area.

Subsequently, on June 11, 1971, 30 federal agents landed on Alcatraz Island deployed from three boats and a helicopter. In less than an hour, and without any resistance, they located, frisked, and arrested the last of the fifteen occupiers of the island. The *San Francisco Chronicle*, originally a supporter of the occupation, in the end blasted the concept of the event and argued it did "'…little to create sympathy for the Indians' claim.'"[40] What many in the media failed to address was that "sympathetic media and guerrilla theatre" could generate immediate attention and place Indian issues on the front pages of major newspapers in the United States and around the world. While Indian activism most certainly did not begin with the Alcatraz occupation, not until that moment: "…had anyone tapped the potential of media-fueled, spectacular protest on such a grand scale."[41] And while this lesson may have been lost on many, it is fair to conclude Russell Means was not one of them.

A situation at the Alcatraz occupation which went largely unnoticed, even to Indians, may have been one of the most significant symbols of the unheralded sophistication of Indians: a Tipi that didn't blow over. During the occupation, the Indian protesters erected a Tipi on that perpetually windy piece of rock in San Francisco Bay that served as a federal penitentiary. The authors of *Like a Hurricane* expressed their surprise the Tipi could withstand the weather conditions there: "During winter storms, wind ripped through the place with such ferocity you could practically hear the concrete being ripped from the iron foundations. But when the storm passed impossibly there it was: defiant, hanging tough, and standing tall. That tepee [sic] never blew over, not once."[42] However, the amazing aerodynamics of the Tipi were not lost on Russell Means:

> Architects the world over have ascertained that the Tipi is the finest mobile home ever devised. A Tipi can withstand higher winds than a dome or any other shape. Due to the Tipi's conical design, an increase in wind causes stronger down-force on the poles, making the Tipi free of the need for a foundation, and making it grip the earth more securely as the weather gets stormier.[43]

Like the Tipi, another conical or round design which served the Lakota well was the round shield, at least until they were confronted with enemies possessing firearms. Initially, the round design of the shield attracted the eye of those shooting arrows and away from other, exposed areas of the body. And, even if struck, the arrows simply could not penetrate the shield. Unfortunately, the round shape of the shield also attracted the attention of those shooting firearms and the shields could not repel bullets. Author Stanley Vestal noted the impact of firearms on Lakota culture as well: "Firearms put a terrific strain upon the science—or art—of the Sioux shaman," since the destruction caused by these weapons "broke their [the shamans'] medicine."[44]

What critics of Russell Means and AIM seem to consistently lose sight of, at least during the late 1960s and early 1970s, is that like the round design of the shield focused the attention of enemy arrow shooters in earlier times, civil disobedience was an effective tool to focus attention on issues that mattered to many Indians. While ultimately the protest at Alcatraz faded from memory, in other instances the results of Indian activism were remarkable. In 1970, a University of California, Davis (UC Davis) professor named Jack Forbes, a Powhatan and Lanape Indian, became aware a 640-acre Strategic Air Command base was due to become surplus property. Forbes believed that unlike Alcatraz, the site offered usable structures, good agricultural land, and as a bonus offered views of the sacred sites of Pupiana (Mt. Diablo), Maidu Buttes (Three Peaks) and the Sierras.

Professor Forbes and other Indians believed the site was ideally suited for the development of an indigenous university. The name chosen for the university was Deganawida-Quetzalcoatl University (or DQ for short), which reflected the Native American-Chicano partnership in this situation. Deganawida was an Iroquois or Six Nations prophet and leader, and Quetzalcoatl was an Aztec deity. Forbes and his allies organized a board of trustees for DQ University, followed federal procedures, and applied for the property. Ignoring this effort, the federal government awarded the property to UC Davis instead. At this juncture, things really got interesting after the feds rejected the request of DQ University for the property. Some UC Davis Indians who were veterans of the Alcatraz occupation and some Chicano students climbed the property fence and began an occupation (as in the case of Alcatraz and the BIA, this was not necessarily Indian land, at least by treat rights). Ultimately, the protesters succeeded in convincing UC Davis to withdraw its application and the property was designated for use by DQ University, which operated from 1971 to 2005. Clearly Indian activists were entitled to take pride in the success of their efforts.[45]

Likewise, Dennis Banks, one of the leaders of AIM at the time of the Wounded Knee "occupation," viewed the efforts of those confronting the federal government as an unqualified success:

> We were the prophets, the messengers, the fire starters. Wounded Knee awakened not only the conscience of Native Americans, but also of white Americans nationwide. We changed an attitude of dependence on the BIA and the government, of 'give me a handout,' to 'I can do it, you can do it, we can do it!' We changed our people's lifestyle.

Banks went on to proudly note there was a revival of respect for Indian culture handed down for generations, and a new group of writers, poets, etc. arose to celebrate this revival. Banks added: "We no longer needed whites to 'interpret' our culture."[46] Vine Deloria, Jr., while not speaking directly about the occupation, stated in 1969 (yet almost prophetically about the "occupation" to occur four years from then) regarding what might be loosely described as Indian "activism": "We will never have a powerful lobby or be a smashing political force. But we will have the intangible unity which has carried us through four centuries of persecution and we will survive. We are a people unified by our humanity; not a pressure group unified for conquest."[47]

Without taking the long view of Indian history at least back to the time of Columbus into consideration, "authors" such as former FBI agent Joseph Trimbach do a disservice by neglecting to even outline events which occurred six months or so prior to the Wounded Knee "occupation" itself. A review of these events reveals the 71-day standoff between AIM and its allies and the federal forces bearing massive firepower was the culmination of the federal government ignoring the requests of Indians to address longstanding problems and the frustration of Indians this neglect fueled. Thus, the "occupation" itself was the ultimate expression of dissatisfaction building up from at least the "Trail of Broken Treaties" which itself resulted in the occupation of the Bureau of Indian Affairs headquarters in Washington, D.C., in the fall of 1972 (as in the case of Alcatraz and DQ University, the BIA building was not specifically designated Indian land by treaty). The original purpose of the four-mile-long caravan was to draw attention to the "Twenty Points" which were a list of demands for action by the federal government to be presented to the Nixon Administration. The pattern of events was duplicated by the white and Indian actors a few months later in the remote Pine Ridge Reservation in southwest South Dakota.

The concept for the "Trail of Broken Treaties" was conceived at a Sun Dance in August 1972 at Crow Dog's Paradise on the Rosebud Sioux Reservation. It is believed Bob Burnette, former chairman of the Rosebud Tribe, near Pine Ridge, came up with the name.[48] In its execution, the "Trail" was a caravan of cars filled with Indian people which originated at such diverse points as Seattle, San Francisco, and Los Angeles. As the various caravans progressed from the West Coast, they made stops at 33 different reservations and visited sacred sites such as Wounded Knee along the way. Dennis Banks, an AIM leader harshly criticized by Trimbach in his book *American Indian Mafia*, insisted that each of the separate caravans, which ultimately converged near Minneapolis, be led by a medicine man carrying a sacred pipe and drum. The drums were beaten night and day to symbolically remind people of the 372 treaties broken by the federal government throughout its history. As a harbinger of things to come very shortly, when the Dennis Banks-led caravan approached the Pine Ridge reservation in South Dakota, Dick Wilson, Pine Ridge Tribal Chairman, declared: "'…open season on all AIM members daring to set foot on *his* reservation [emphasis in original].'"[49]

Later, as the caravans converged in St. Paul, adjacent to Minneapolis, Reuben Snake conducted a large meeting attended by representatives of 150 different tribes. At this meeting, the "Twenty Points" representing the various demands of Indian people were formulated. After driving all night from Minneapolis, the four-mile-long caravan entered Washington, D.C., just before dawn on November 2, 1972. Trouble greeted the Indians immediately upon their arrival. Prior to the Indians reaching Washington, D.C., Burnette, who was leading one of the caravans, received promises of help and good lodgings from various individuals and organizations. It was believed, however, that due to government pressure, these parties reneged on their offers of assistance. A church the AIM group was ultimately offered for lodging had, among other problems, rats. Clyde Bellecourt, a strong-willed AIM leader, encouraged the other members to action by shouting: "'Enough of this bullshit! Let's get out of here! Let's go have a talk with the BIA.'"[50]

Eventually, somewhere between 600 and 700 Indians ended up at the BIA headquarters building. In reality, the original intent of the organizers of the event did not include occupying the BIA building, but the group had nowhere else to congregate. AIM leaders such as Bob Burnette, George Mitchell, and Anita Collins had originally arranged meetings with officials from the Department of the Interior, Department of Labor, Department of Commerce, and other officials involved in Indian matters. However, Burnette relayed that even though the appointments had been confirmed, all the government officials involved canceled their respective meetings. Burnette reasoned the officials disengaged due to "'…some kind of threat from the [Nixon] administration.'" Then the Indians called elected officials they knew, such as Senators Edward Kennedy, Hubert Humphrey, and Walter Mondale, but none were willing to take meetings.[51]

As the frustrations of the Indians escalated, at around 2:00 p.m. on November 2, some minor BIA officials arrived and announced to the group: "'…it's official. The government agencies don't want to meet with you at all.'" Increasingly agitated, shouts went out to have someone compel the Commissioner of Indian Affairs to meet with the group. Louis Bruce, the half-Sioux, half-Mohawk Commissioner of Indian Affairs, arrived and expressed his sympathy for the hungry, cold, and weary travelers, but explained his boss, Assistant Secretary of the Interior Harrison Loesch, ordered him not to provide any assistance. Subsequent to this announcement, chaos broke out with Indian people yelling and screaming their frustrations about the federal government. After Bruce then expressed his sympathy for his fellow Indians and announced, "'This building will remain open to all Indians,'" he was relieved from his position as Indian Commissioner. When Dennis Banks and Russell Means inquired further about facilities for the Indians to stay in, they were told by a man: "'[from] Housing'…'that's your problem. We didn't invite you. We didn't tell you to come here. We're not in the housing business.'"[52]

After some discussion about the housing dilemma, Martha Grass said: "'…this is the BIA building. This is an Indian building. This is our building, and we're going to stay right here.'" Shortly after this proclamation, a scuffle broke out when Henry Wahwassuck tried to prevent the Washington, D.C., police from entering the BIA building. Shortly thereafter, a platoon of heavily armed guards with helmets and billy clubs forced their way into the building and clubbed everyone who tried to resist. Some of the Indians had blood running down their faces where they were struck by the police's blows, so to defend themselves from future attacks some of them tore legs from chairs and tables to use in self-defense. Eventually, the Indians forced the police out. Someone put up a sign over the entrance to the building exclaiming "AMERICAN INDIAN EMBASSY." Additionally, the Indians erected a Tipi on the lawn in front of the building and raised an upside-down American flag up the flagpole.[53]

After the Indians took control of the building, the next morning the press arrived and interviewed some of the group. Chief U.S. Marshal Colburn, who would be in charge of the U.S. Marshals at Wounded Knee a few months later, arrived with a court order stating the Indians must vacate the building by midnight. In addition to the table legs taken for use as weapons, the Indians gathered up loose roof tiles and filled trash cans with boiling water to drop on police who tried to evict the "occupiers." Banks believed the police outside the building understood they were: "…not facing a bunch of flower children or student anti-war protestors" and that the Indians were "dead serious."[54]

While inside the BIA building, some of the "occupiers" found files indicating how some individuals were stealing reservation oil and natural gas out of reservations in Oklahoma and Wyoming. Initially, the primary aim of leaders such as Dennis Banks was simply to have senior officials of the federal government meet with them to discuss Indian concerns. Nonetheless, on the morning of November 4, Secretary of the Interior Rogers Morton issued a statement claiming those inside the building were "'a splinter group of militants'" and added: "'it is obvious to me that the seizure and continued occupation of the building are nothing more than a form of blackmail by a small group which seeks to achieve, through violent means, objectives which are not supported by a majority of reservation Indians.'"[55] Since there is no record of Morton meeting with those inside the BIA building during the confrontation, it is not clear how he determined what the goals of the group were or what analysis he undertook to determine those goals were "'not supported by a majority of reservation Indians.'" Vine Deloria, Jr., noted that at the "occupation" of Wounded Knee a few months later, there was: "…a strong contingent of Sioux traditional people…[and]…Revered medicine men and several well-known holy men…taking part."[56]

Finally, more senior Nixon administration officials Leonard Garment and Brad Patterson met with some members of the occupying group. Unsurprisingly, the talks proved unproductive. On November 5, the Indians demanded to see President Nixon himself along with top aide John Erlichman, but instead the White House sent the usual "low level flunkies." Later in the day on November 6, Frank Carlucci, who Banks described as the "head of the Office of the Management and Budget," Garment, and Morton arrived at BIA headquarters. As a consequence, the White House agreed to set up a task force to seriously consider the "Twenty Points." The government also provided $66,000 cash to pay travel expenses for the group to get to their various homes.[57]

Ultimately, the federal government reneged on its promise to seriously consider the "Twenty Points" and labeled them "'impracticable.'" Much like Trimbach would later complain about the destruction of the Gildersleeves' trading post during the Wounded Knee "occupation," the government castigated the "occupiers" of the BIA headquarters for their "radicalism" and for the damage done to the BIA building. Additionally, the government convinced: "…a number of tribal chairmen, Uncle Tomahawks and Hang-Around-the Fort types" to condemn AIM as a: "splinter group that did not represent Indian people in general." Much like it would be claimed regarding the Wounded Knee "occupation" at its conclusion a few months later, the press claimed the BIA headquarters "occupation" was a "failure." The press also claimed it moreover "'…a defeat for the radicals who achieved nothing.'" Nonetheless, the Indians themselves involved in the takeover believed it was indeed a victory.[58]

ENDNOTES

1. Joy Harjo and Gloria Bird, Eds., Mary Brave Bird, "We AIM Not to Please," *Reinventing the Enemy's Language.* pp. 339-340. Mary Brave Bird is also known as Mary Crow Dog.
2. Hendricks, *The Unquiet Grave*, p. 151.
3. Lyman, *Wounded Knee 1973*, p. 65.
4. Smith and Warrior, *Like a Hurricane*, p. 134.
5. Will Peters, Oglala Lakota.
6. Stanley Vestal, *Sitting Bull: Champion of the Sioux*, p. 229.
7. Dale Means and numerous other signatories, untitled typed statement describing the arrest of Russell Means (St. Paul, Minnesota: Minnesota Historical Society, January 14, 1973). An account of this incident also appeared in the February 27, 1973, edition of the *Akwesasne Notes*.
8. In a typed, unsworn statement, it was claimed: "In the summer of 2970 [sic] Eddie [White Dress] needed a small amount of money to buy groceries. He had a porcupine quill traditional headress [sic] which he took to Jim Czywczynski at the Trading Post to pawn. Czywczynski took the headress [sic] and gave Eddy $6.00 for it. About one month later Eddie went back to the Trading Post with $6.00 to retrieve the headdress. Czywczynski took the $6.00 but refused to return the headdress. He said he give [sic] Eddie his headdress back when he [Eddie] paid all his bills. Eddie never recovered his headdress [spelling as in source]." Sand Brim, Statement of Eddie White Dress re: Pawn at Trading Post (St. Paul, Minnesota: Minnesota Historical Society, undated). The Czywczynski family also owned an interest in the trading post. Hendricks, *The Unquiet Grave*, p. 61.
9. Stiles, *Custer's Trials*, p. xvi.
10. Cook-Lynn, *Anti-Indianism in Modern America*, p. 6.
11. Slotkin, *Fatal Environment*, p. 91.
12. Cook-Lynn, *Anti-Indianism in Modern America*, p. 206.
13. Trimbach, *American Indian Mafia*, p. 62.
14. Agonito, Joseph, "Eagle Woman: A Woman's Voice for peace," *Lakota Portraits—Lives of the Legendary Plains People*, p. 144.
15. Ibid., p. 148.
16. Cook-Lynn, *Anti-Indianism in Modern America*, p. 207.
17. American Indian Movement Grand Governing Council, "Press Statement" (Minneapolis, Minnesota: February 20, 1999).
18. Cook-Lynn, *Anti-Indianism in Modern America*, p. 207.
19. Stew Magnuson, *Wounded Knee 1973: Still Bleeding—The American Indian Movement, The FBI, and Their Fight to Bury the Sins of the Past* (Arlington, Virginia: Court Bridge Publishing, 2013), p. 84.
20. David Treuer, *Rez Life: An Indian's Journey Through Reservation Life* (New York: Grove Press, 2012), p. 133.
21. Sonslata Jim-James, Joy Harjo and Gloria Bird, Eds., "Dine Way," *Reinventing the Enemy's Language*, p. 489.
22. Brave Bird, *Reinventing the Enemy's Language*, p. 344.

23 Sajna, *Crazy Horse*, p. 53.
24 Means, *Where White Mean Fear to Tread*, p. 285.
25 Anonymous Lakota Elder.
26 Bordewich, *Killing the White Man's Indian*, p. 84.
27 Cook-Lynn, *Anti-Indianism in Modern America*, p. 91.
28 Smith and Warrior, *Like a Hurricane*, pp. 43-46
29 Ibid., p. 57.
30 Ibid., p. 46.
31 Deloria, Jr. *Custer Died for Your Sins*, p. 185.
32 Vine Deloria, Jr., *Red Earth, White Lies: Native Americans and the Myth of Scientific Fact* (Golden, Colorado: Fulcrum Publishing, 1997), p. 211.
33 Smith and Warrior, *Like a Hurricane*, p. 55.
34 Ibid., p. 58.
35 Ibid., pp. 69-70.
36 Ibid., p. 80.
37 Utley and Washburn, *Indian Wars*, p. 47.
38 Smith and Warrior, *Like a Hurricane*, p. 81.
39 Ibid., p. 82.
40 Ibid., p. 109.
41 Ibid., p. 111.
42 Ibid., p. 64.
43 Russell Means and Bayard Johnson, *If You've Forgotten the Names of Clouds, You've Lost Your Way: An Introduction to American Indian Thought and Philosophy* (Porcupine, South Dakota: Treaty Publications, 2012), pp. 13-14.
44 Stanley Vestal, *Sitting Bull: Champion of the Sioux*, p. 31.
45 Smith, *Hippies, Indians, and the Fight for Red Power*, p. 157.
46 Banks and Erdoes, *Ojibwa Warrior*, p. 360.
47 Deloria, Jr., *Custer Died for Your Sins*, p. 221.
48 Smith and Warrior, *Like a Hurricane*, p. 139.
49 Banks and Erdoes, *Ojibwa Warrior*, p. 130.
50 Ibid., p. 132.
51 Ibid., p. 133.
52 Ibid., pp. 133-135.
53 Ibid., pp. 135-137.
54 Ibid., pp. 138-139.
55 Ibid., p. 140.
56 Deloria, Jr., *Behind the Trail of Broken Treaties*, p. 75.

57 Banks and Erdoes, *Ojibwa Warrior*, pp. 141-143. Actually, Carlucci was Undersecretary of the Office of Health Education and Welfare.
58 Ibid., pp. 143-144.

CHAPTER 19

J. Edgar Hoover, the Guardian of "Freedom," and His Federal Bureau of Imperialism: Part I

> Presidents came and went, but over the decades Hoover remained.
> Seth Rosenfeld, *Subversives*[1]

On May 3rd through 4th, 1972, the days immediately following his death on May 2, J. Edgar Hoover's body lay in state in the U.S. Capitol Rotunda in Washington, D.C. Few in the history of the United States, including Presidents, had been afforded that honor. Up until the time of his passing, Hoover was the only FBI director in the history of the organization, a span of 48 years. In Sacramento, California, Ronald Reagan gushed that no man had meant more to America in the 20th century than this powerful bureaucrat.[2] Hyperbole aside, Reagan was most likely projecting onto the American populace his unspoken, undoubtedly heartfelt, conviction no one had been more instrumental in *his* political success. Throughout the years, the two men, both intensely allergic to combat duty early in life, later turned their public personas into war hawks and forged a bond as self-styled defenders of "…the American Way of Life."

Like most legends, as exemplified in the case of George A. Custer, simply mentioning the name J. Edgar Hoover inevitably evokes debate—for good reason. Some believe Hoover created a virtually mythical entity—the FBI—molded in his image to be: "…the most respected and effective law enforcement organization the world had ever seen."[3] Nonetheless, in the nitty-gritty of the real world it was discovered one of Hoover's last directives was to destroy his personal office files. In that regard, immediately after his death, Hoover's longtime secretary, Helen Gandy, removed 35 file cabinet drawers from his office and had them shredded. Although Gandy later testified all the files concerned private and/or personal matters, author Seth Rosenfeld explained: "…some documents survived having been recently transferred to other files. They concerned illegal black bag jobs and other highly sensitive matters."[4]

Thus, although Hoover died just over nine months prior to the AIM-led "occupation" of Wounded Knee, his impact on the thought processes as the event unfolded was evident, nonetheless. At this point in time, it appears no directives exist stating Hoover or any subsequent FBI director ordered the destruction of AIM. Yet, only those who never grow weary of digesting the "…propagandistic qualities of American history"[5] would refuse to consider that the motives and ethics of the FBI regarding AIM were less than admirable. Steve Hendricks, in *The Unquiet Grave*, put it more bluntly:

> Had the FBI not sabotaged the rights movements of the postwar era, had it not sent Doug Durham and Gi and Jill Schafer and John Stewart and Virginia DeLuce and others of their kind into AIM, had it not added the virus of informers A and B to the paranoia it had already created, had it investigated crimes against AIMers on Pine Ridge, had it stanched the perjury and coercion and framing that its agents practiced as a matter of course, had the Justice Department not gone along with every step of this, had the BIA not let Dick Wilson run his own impeachment trial, steal an election, and jerry-rig voter rolls to save his government, had the courts held the FBI or prosecutors accountable for their sins, or had Congress done so, Anna Mae Aquash would not have been killed. To read the news reports of the last few years is to be told Aquash was murdered because AIM thought she was an infiltrator. This is only half the truth. Aquash was murdered because the government of the United States waged an officially sanctioned, covert war on the country's foremost movement for Indian rights.

Hendricks was not oblivious to the shortcomings of AIM and declared that as to the conflict between the FBI and AIM, AIM "…must shoulder its share of the blame."[6]

Ronald Reagan, the devoted admirer of Hoover, developed his close relationship with the FBI and ultimately Hoover starting as an informer as to the "Communist" activities of his fellow actors belonging to the Screen Actors Guild. Even as president of the SAG, Reagan continued his informant activities, providing information to the FBI about the activities of a number of actors. He also provided extensive assistance to the United States House of Representatives Un-American Activities Committee (HUAC), which held hearings proving destructive to a number of actors' careers.[7]

Including the history of the FBI's (and Ronald Reagan's) involvement with thwarting student dissent at Cal Berkeley in the present analysis of Indian history serves a key function. As Stearns noted: "Individual groups must be given their own pasts, but also their often-complex relationships to larger power structures and larger value systems" must be considered. As with African-American history, Indian history: "…is not just the story of separate values and reactions, and therefore it must be taught in balance with larger forces." Stearns added the admonition: "Multiculturalism need not, indeed should not, be an excuse for randomness."[8] Thus, it appears the United States government's confrontation with AIM spearheaded by the FBI was not particularly out of the ordinary for that era.

Nevertheless, aspects of the Wounded Knee "occupation" were distinctive relative to at least the federal response to the activities of other "subversive" groups. Even considering the harsh rhetoric employed against the Black Panthers, the FBI seemed to publicly raise even higher the level of rhetoric regarding

AIM. Joseph Trimbach, whose *American Indian Mafia* was a not-so-subtle rant against what he described as the "false heroes" of AIM, claimed he was surprised he: "…would experience so much violence firsthand, along with my fellow Agents who likewise found themselves in a war with militant Native Americans."[9] But what did Trimbach actually reveal with this comment?

First and foremost, much like many of his other comments and those of many other writers whose work is discussed herein, he apparently did not understand the implication of his word choices, particularly "war," in the context of Lakota history. He and others would have been well served to consider the situation involving Lakota Indian Plenty Horses' killing of Lieutenant Edward Casey on January 7, 1891. On that date, a little over a week after the Wounded Knee Massacre, Casey rode toward Indian leader Two Strikes' camp near White Clay Road on the Pine Ridge Reservation. Apparently, Casey's mission was to conduct some type of reconnaissance. En route, Casey encountered Plenty Horses; accounts vary regarding the substance of their conversation, but it was thought to be generally friendly. At some point it is believed Plenty Horses did warn Casey not to go any closer to the Lakota camp which contained vulnerable women and children.

Some accounts of the encounter suggest Casey did state he was returning later. Nevertheless, as Casey was riding away from Plenty Horses, Plenty Horses fired a round from his Springfield rifle which crashed through Casey's skull and killed him instantly.[10] Plenty Horses was charged with murder and his first trial in federal court in Sioux Falls, South Dakota, surprisingly ended in a hung jury. As DiSilvestro commented: "A hung Indian, not a hung jury, had been the anticipated result of the trial."[11] Before jury deliberations began in the subsequent trial, the judge ordered the jury to bring in a verdict of not guilty. (This may have been an order of dismissal or acquittal). In explanation, Judge Shiras stated: "…on the day Lieutenant Casey met his death there existed in and about the Pine Ridge Agency a condition of actual warfare of the United States…and the Indian troops occupying the camp." The judge further stated: "While the manner in which Plenty Horses killed Lieutenant Casey was such as would meet the severest condemnation, nevertheless we cannot deny the fact Lieutenant Casey was engaged in an act of legitimate warfare against the Indians."[12] Understandably, many military men were relieved at this outcome, fearing that if Plenty Horses was found guilty of murder there was a possibility of murder charges for events occurring at the Wounded Knee killings in December 1890 and the surrounding timeframe. As an editorial writer for the *Sioux Falls-Argus Leader* cautioned from the white perspective: "'If the Sioux trouble was not a war, the Indians killed at Wounded Knee were simply murdered by our soldiers.'"[13]

Perhaps Trimbach was disclosing nothing more than an unwillingness to accept the truth about white/Indian history as so many others have done. Philip Deloria explained that eventually: "American history took shape, not as a frontiersman's struggle with wild lands, but as one long Indian war, a violent contest in which Americans were shaped by constant struggle with a dangerous and challenging adversary."[14] More specifically regarding the situation at the Wounded Knee "occupation," perhaps Trimbach was indicating surprise that he was at war with AIM because AIM had not previously been involved in firefights. Certainly, there was a confrontation between police forces and Indians at the conclusion of the "Trail of Broken Treaties" during the occupation of BIA headquarters, but that did not involve using firearms.

ENDNOTES

1. Rosenfeld, p. 16.
2. Ibid., p. 489.
3. Trimbach, *American Indian Mafia*, p. 34.
4. Rosenfeld, *Subversives*, p. 489.
5. Stearns, *Meaning Over Memory*, p. 93.
6. Hendricks, *The Unquiet Grave*, p. 360. Hendricks noted: "Durham either never found evidence of important crime, or he did but the government did not pursue prosecution." Id at 194. For an excellent discussion of Durham's activities as an informant, including spying on the Means and Banks Defense team at their Wounded Knee Trial, see Yvonne Bushyhead, "In the Spirit of Crazy Horse: The Case of Leonard Peltier" 2 Yale J.L. & Liberation (1991).
7. Rosenfeld, *Subversives*, pp. 127-150.
8. Stearns, *Meaning Over Memory*, p. 104. Nevertheless, it is useful for a solid understanding of Indian history to keep in mind that Indian experiences in North and South America throughout history are not necessarily always similar to other groups, as noted by Slotkin. *Fatal Environment*, p. 321.
9. Trimbach, *American Indian Mafia*, p. 13. Obviously, Trimbach's statement in this specific instance was written some years after the actual events.
10. Di Silvestro, *In the Shadow of Wounded Knee*, pp. 97-100. I highly recommend Di Silvestro's book for anyone interested in a succinct explanation of complex legal issues surrounding warfare involving the Plains Indians. It is interesting Plenty Horses' case did not appear to be used in the defense of Leonard Peltier, who was convicted in 1976 of killing two FBI agents during a shootout on the Pine Ridge Reservation. This seems particularly curious in light of Trimbach claiming the FBI and U.S. Marshals were at "war with militant Native Americans." Trimbach, *American Indian Mafia*, p. 13.
11. Ibid., pp. 176-177.
12. Ibid., p. 192.
13. Ibid., pp. 198-199.
14. Deloria, *Indians in Unexpected Places*, p. 62.

Chapter 20

Joseph Trimbach and the Federal Bureau of Imperialism: Part II

"…totally unacceptable"…both the hearing and report: "…seem to have no other purpose than to discredit…the American Indian Movement."
        Committee Chair Senator Birch Bayh commenting on the hearing and report of
        Senator James Eastland's Senate Subcommittee on Internal Security, 1976
        Peter Matthieson, *In the Spirit of Crazy Horse*[1]

We took more bullets in seventy-one days than I took in two years in Vietnam.
        Roger Iron Cloud, Oglala Vietnam combat veteran
        commenting on Wounded Knee "occupation"
        Ward Churchill and Jim Vander Wall, *Agents of Repression*[2]

For reasons known only to him, in his anti-American Indian Movement screed *American Indian Mafia*, former high-ranking FBI Agent Joseph Trimbach, among other expositions, clumsily attempted to explain how the United States troops surrounding "Big Foot's" band on December 29, 1890, at Wounded Knee, South Dakota, were justified in slaughtering those desperate and freezing souls. Perhaps by labeling this group of Indians as instigators of trouble, it helped him rationalize the overwhelming force directed against the "occupiers" of this same remote village by him and other federal agents 83 years later in 1973. One explanation for his hostility is found in Stew Magnuson's *Wounded Knee 1973: Still Bleeding*. Magnuson believed that over the years, Trimbach's "…hatred of AIM leaders appeared to fester." According to Magnuson, historian Rolland Dewing wrote: "'FBI insiders say Trimbach's conduct at Wounded Knee plus his substandard performance at the ensuing trial at St. Paul blighted his chance of advancement. He was transferred to Memphis, Tennessee in 1975 and retired in 1979.'"[3]

What is particularly unsettling is Trimbach seemed content to consider his utter and naked contempt for any notions of due process and fair play for the less than powerful as the best of what the United States has to offer. He continuously ridiculed Russell Means and his allies in the American Indian Movement without even a flicker of recognition that a majority of those polled in the United States at the time of the "occupation" were sympathetic to the "occupiers" of Wounded Knee. Equally as unsettling are the uninhibited endorsements of influential public figures such as William Webster and Oliver North to the observations of Trimbach, which at best can charitably be labeled as callous and juvenile. Having no filter whatsoever, he even trivialized the suffering of the federal judge assigned to the Means/Banks trial in St. Paul, Minneapolis, who lost a daughter in a car accident. Hopefully, Trimbach's overly bombastic blaming of AIM for: "…bring[ing] further misery to a community whose only failing was to pin their hopes on a small group of false heroes"[4] represents the nadir of the abysmal and misguided recounting of events in the United States involving traditionally-minded Indians. Particularly baffling is Trimbach's inability to grasp that it was the FBI's ham-handed handling of the autopsy and other matters surrounding the death of Anna Mae Aquash which generated so much suspicion regarding who committed her murder.

Unfortunately, Trimbach and other U.S. government officials never seemed to grasp that their view of the complicated situation of Indians diverged significantly from that of the Indians themselves and was an underlying burr generating much of the discord on Pine Ridge. Although it is not necessarily identical to the Indian Reorganization of 1934, an analysis of Canada's Indian Act of 1876 is instructive. Kiera Ladner wrote:

> Under the Indian Act band councils were not provided with the tools, jurisdictions, and structures of accountability that are typically associated with government. As a result few would disagree with the statement that the Indian Act did not and does not provide for a system of good governance. Rather the Indian Act's system of government was created to aid the federal government in administering Indian reserves [Reserves is the Canadian term for reservation].[5]

Rather than acknowledge the deficiencies of the analogous Indian Reorganization Act of 1934 and the lack of accountability in that legislation, Stanley Lyman, Trimbach, Robert Novak and others blame the "false heroes" of AIM for creating chaos in places like Pine Ridge.

Similarly, Elizabeth Cook-Lynn's analysis of the oversight of the United States government is that it: "…has been a 'trustee' of Indian lands and it holds a 'fiduciary' responsibility to its treat co-signatories, the United Sioux Tribes." Instead, she explained that the federal government has foregone its legal responsibility and along with states has been: "…draining the assets of the tribes to which it owes treaty obligations." She explained when the feds fail in that capacity: "It's like an estate lawyer selling off his client's assets to enrich himself. For such actions in the real world, lawyers go to jail!! Only in Indian cases is the fiduciary rewarded for such illegal behavior." She asked where is the "free press" in instances where the theft of Indian lands and assets is occurring?[6]

Trimbach's aggressive verbal attacks on the American Indian Movement and its leadership may not have had the effect he intended. His angry, illogical, and often sophomoric comments should come as no surprise to readers considering the almost clever title of his book *American Indian Mafia* which is an obvious slap at the name American Indian Movement. He undermined his own credibility by making the silly and flippant comment that his son John performed many tasks including writing the manuscript "To the great detriment of his golf game,"[7] as if golf somehow had more importance than writing about Indians fairly. Considering the bitter and amateurish tone of Trimbach's book, his son may indeed have been better served sticking with playing golf. The Trimbach father-and-son duo proved perpetually incapable of presenting their arguments logically and without ad hominem attacks. At a conference on the "occupation" in 2012, John Trimbach argued concerning events surrounding the 1973 Wounded Knee "occupation": "…AIM leader Dennis Banks became increasingly paranoid about spies in his midst."[8] Yet, Trimbach did not explain how Banks succumbed to a state of being "paranoid" when Trimbach himself acknowledged an individual named Douglas Durham was an FBI informant. Durham's nefarious deeds, including possible involvement in Jancita Eagle Deer's death, were spread out through the entire Pine Ridge region, and "Durham had been Dennis' right hand man."[9] Trimbach's statement that Banks was "paranoid" because he was concerned there were "spies in his midst" when there was actually at least one spy in the AIM camp was condescending and absurd.

Trimbach complained that Peter Matthiessen, who wrote *In the Spirit of Crazy Horse*, was a "'Yale-trained New York Blueblood'" without acknowledging Matthiessen at one point in his career worked for the United States Central Intelligence Agency (CIA). Trimbach frequently and vehemently insinuated the involvement of AIM people in various crimes without any supporting evidence, such as implying Leonard Peltier had something to do with Anna Mae Aquash's murder. Yet, he seemed miffed that someone like Matthiessen had written a book "…sprinkled with underwhelming tales of FBI depredations."[10] Unfortunately, Trimbach's and the FBI's own myopia contributed to the "paranoia" described by Hendricks. He bellowed that: "In the aftermath of duel murders, it was only prudent that when agents raided AIM strongholds, they should do so with superiority of manpower and weapons."[11] Yet, he chastised Matthiessen a few pages earlier for implying the FBI erred when they: "…knew that fugitive Peltier was on the reservation and thus sent two poorly armed agents to go in after him."[12] This inconsistency in the Trimbach father-and-son writing team is one of the many triple-bogeys or worse that show up on their "golf" scorecard.

To a large extent, Trimbach's anger at the Indians would be better directed at social programs which resulted in reservation Indians moving to cities such as Los Angeles, Chicago, and ironically for Trimbach, Minneapolis. It has been argued that in these urban environments, Indians became adept at understanding modern society. In the case of Minneapolis specifically, Indian "militants" who eventually became the core of the American Indian Movement initially organized to thwart police brutality by sending AIM members out on "patrol" to monitor police activities. Through AIM's efforts, incidents of abuse of Indians by police dropped dramatically in number. Ultimately these AIM members organized the "occupation" of Wounded Knee which brought worldwide publicity to the plight of Indians in the United States. James Wilson is one of those who believed living in urban areas made Indians more savvy in dealing with modern culture. He opined: "Living in the cities, they were less hampered both by BIA control and by inter-tribal frictions…their [urban] experience, according to previous Commissioner of Indian Affairs Philleo Nash argued… had turned them into 'street wise people' who 'understood the amount of leverage that would be obtained by being bad instead of being good.'"[13]

Curiously, some within the Indian community itself blamed "the false heroes of AIM" for a variety of chronic reservation issues, particularly the lack of economic and infrastructure development. It was postulated "economic development people" in other locations outside South Dakota were said to be uneasy about the "…effects of Wounded Knee on the industrialization of reservations." C. Mac Eddy, director of the Navajo tribal council's division of Program Development, argued industrial leaders: "'…feel the economic gains and labor advantages [on reservations] are offset by the animosity their people and families receive.'" Eddy added the problem stemmed from: "'…the fear of having their facilities taken over or destroyed, and the fact that no housing is available on a local level for key personnel.'" Eddy stated the National Rifle Association (NRA) was planning on locating a $20 million headquarters facility on a Navajo reservation, but NRA officials balked after learning of the takeover of the BIA building in Washington, D.C. Eddy claimed "'several other [unnamed] industrial companies have developed a sudden lack of interest as the various militant operations take place.'" Eddy did not explain how AIM or other activists were responsible, for example, for the claimed lack of "'housing available for key personnel.'"[14]

The hollowness of these claims is laughable since they are so easy to rebut. Particularly in the instance of Pine Ridge, it has been over 45 years since the end of the 1973 "occupation" and nearly that long since the FBI decimated AIM's ability to function as a viable political entity in the mid-1970s through lengthy and costly court battles. Thus, now that "militants" no longer "occupy" the BIA headquarters or barren ground outside the mass grave at Wounded Knee, what is now retarding industrial development on reservations? By Eddy's logic, would businesses never consider a storefront, warehouse, or manufacturing facility anywhere near Washington, D.C., since pop star Madonna asserted, in a protest speech after Donald Trump's inauguration in 2017, she felt like "blowing up" the White House? Of course not.

The accusations that Indian activism thwarted industrial or economic development on reservations had an unintended, albeit little publicized, consequence of raising questions about the seamier underside of business dealings on the reservations. And, "activists" highlight what Vine Deloria, Jr., argued was: "The real issue, white control of the reservation [which] was overlooked completely."[15] It also had another unintended effect of defusing the claims Indian activists were little more than thugs and hustlers and revealed many, if not most, were thoughtful and articulate advocates for Indian rights. For example, in 1972, "activist" Hank Adams issued a comprehensive white paper dealing with Indian economic and social issues entitled *REVIEW STUDY OF A MODEL FOR FAILURE IN THE BIA'S INDUSTRIAL DEVELOPMENT PROGRAM: An Abstract Discussion on Economic Development Projects on the Sisseton-Wahpeton Sioux Tribes of South Dakota (1971-72)*.[16.]

Adams' Review Study exposed the interest and grasping of white "businessmen" for projects on Indian reservations suspect for integrity, if not simply fraudulent, at least in one lurid example. In his report, he indicated on November 2, 1972, President Richard Nixon signed a bill authorizing a $5,870,000 land claim settlement originally awarded to the Sisseton-Wahpeton Sioux Indians of the Lake Traverse

Reservation. On that same day, more than two dozen Sisseton-Wahpeton Indians, mostly junior and senior high school students, arrived in Washington, D.C., and became participants in what became known as the "occupation" of the Bureau of Indian Affairs (BIA) headquarters discussed previously. Federal officials denied the rural, small town, and reservation backgrounds of people like the young Sisseton-Wahpeton students, and further argued the Indians occupying the building were: "'...urbans without valid interests to assert'...and were 'bloody revolutionaries' being led by criminal elements [consisting of] ex-convicts having the most sordid of backgrounds." Federal officials considered the claims of these "criminal elements" so "frivolous and invalid," an assistant secretary of the Interior declared to the students and other Indian people they would have "'to beg' him to listen to their views."

Earlier that year, in April 1972, BIA officials met with an individual named John W. Cabot regarding a proposed business deal with the Sisseton-Wahpeton Tribe. Cabot possessed a 30-year history outlined in an FBI report of: "...almost continuous arrests and prosecutions, periodic imprisonments, and almost twenty different aliases used in his repetitious schemes of confidence, fraud, forgery, robbery, and other offenses in twenty different cities prior to 1962." Apparently, the ten-year gap without detected criminal activity from 1962 to 1972 was assurance enough of Cabot's reformed character for BIA officials to grant a $25,000 loan to him and/or his company named the "Lake Traverse Paint and Chemical (LTPC) Corporation." Cabot formed this enterprise in cooperation with Sisseton-Wahpeton tribal officials after first meeting with them in October 1971. At the April 1972 meeting in the same auditorium occupied by the Indian "criminal" elements a month later, none of the BIA officials involved generated enough curiosity to inquire about Cabot's shaky background.

BIA representatives at the October 1972 meeting were apparently unconcerned about Cabot's colorful background since he had: "...gained the confidence of the Lake Traverse Tribal leaders and was willing to 'help them out.'" Although repayment of Cabot's $25,000 loan was to be taken from "future profits of the paint company" in case of default, the loan would be repaid from the Indian claims funds approved for distribution by Nixon earlier that year. The structure of the loan was "engineered and advocated" by an individual named George W. Hubley, Jr., who worked in the BIA's Industrial Development Program (IDP). The IDP was considered to be a "major" program effort initially developed in 1957 to attract industry to Indian reservations.

According to Adams' report, the "Lake Traverse Paint Company" became a major headache for the Sisseton-Wahpeton Tribe almost from the time it first met with Cabot in October 1971. A prospectus for this noble "'partnership'" effort indicated the Tribe would receive 51 percent of the profits from the company and Cabot would enjoy 49 percent. It was stated the total cost to the tribe would be $300,000. In establishing his business credentials, Cabot claimed he was president of a paint firm named "Plastic Shield Products Corporation" (PSPC). He also claimed this company produced a product called "'Save Stone,'" which he further claimed was sprayed on the Lincoln Memorial and the Acropolis in Greece to prevent these structures from further deterioration from air pollution.

After the Articles of Incorporation for the "Lake Traverse Paint and Chemical Corporation" were signed on December 15, 1971, Cabot escalated his ambitions. On December 18, 1971, Cabot was appointed president of the company and granted full voting rights at future board of directors' meetings. Cabot then requested the "par value" of the 1,000 shares of corporation stocks issued to be raised from a value of $100 to $250 per share, which raised his holdings from $100,000 to $250,000, at least on paper. The "'Joint Venture Contract'" developed at the December 18 meeting established the value of the "good will and all its assets" of the underlying PSPC corporation at $400,000. This "Joint Venture Contract" also provided for the "absorb[tion]" of the PSPC into LTPC.

As if the actions and mechanisms developed by the participants at the December 18 meeting weren't convoluted enough at that point, several other Byzantine proposals approved earlier, on October 7, were modified. A Charles F. Klopp, Jr., was appointed at that October meeting as the "non-Indian Tribal Information and Education Officer." Klopp drafted both the Articles of Incorporation and the so-called "Joint Venture Contract." At the December 18, 1971, meeting Klopp was given the position of vice president of LTPC. At one point, Klopp suggested an ownership "split" be made in LTPC and that BIA Agency Superintendent Dennis Peterson be awarded one-third ownership in the company. Klopp's reasoning was that this share for Peterson would be his "'finder's fee'" for contacting the American Paint Corporation of Duluth, Minnesota, and arranging for production of paint products which LTPC might sell. Peterson wisely declined to accept the offer.

In his report, Adams also indicated that on December 4, 1972, a BIA area office industrial development specialist involved with the project since 1971 discovered less than reassuring information about Cabot's PSP corporation. This specialist's investigation revealed PSP was also named the "Savestone Corporation" and actually only ever existed on paper. In spite of the revelation of the fraudulent nature of Cabot's activities concerning LTPC, the Sisseton-Wahpeton Tribe, and his problematic criminal history, the BIA employee indicated "there were no claims of wrongdoing" against Cabot. Although the BIA employee expressed no concern regarding Cabot's possible fleecing of the tribe, he did warn Adams against making any public disclosure of Cabot's activities since Cabot might seek "legal remedies" against whoever made the disclosure. That the interests of the Sisseton-Wahpeton Tribe appeared to be neglected seemed of no concern to this BIA employee, according to Adams.

In effect, the transaction providing Cabot $1.00 and 49 percent of all LTPC profits was given in exchange for the "assets" of Cabot's nonexistent corporation and his "'good will.'" Under the already nefarious circumstances of his dealings with the tribe, his introduction of Robert Kubinak as "manager and chemist" for LTPC had the feel of a punchline for a bad joke. A contract to pay Kubinak's salary was signed March 6, 1972, with a provision the agreement was to expire within six months if LTPC failed to generate profits. However, on May 5, 1972, the contract was canceled after Kubinak became ill and was hospitalized. Nonetheless, Kubinak received a "'severance fee'" for his "services" up to that point. The ever-enterprising Klopp was selected to replace Kubinak as manager, although his title was "Liaison and Public Relations Director." It was never explained why a paint company of that size needed a "Public Relations Director" or if LTPC ever turned a profit at any time during its existence.

At the end of July 1972, tribal member and company secretary Rosebud Marshall wrote Cabot a letter inquiring about his efforts in creating a successful paint company and included a confidential report regarding Cabot's past criminal history. After receiving the letter Cabot quickly left the reservation. However, Cabot was never one to easily give up on the idea of personal enrichment with minimal effort. In a letter to the tribal representatives dated August 7, 1972, he offered to work for the Executive Council of the Sisseton Tribe for a fee of $2,500/month while living in Chicago. Cabot's offer was refused by the tribe, although inexplicably Tribal Chairman Moses Gill was opposed to cutting ties with Cabot. Gill believed without Cabot: "'…the paint company might as well fold up since there will be no one to run it.'" Adams' report does not indicate whether there was a discussion with Gill concerning the reality there was actually no paint company to run.

Cabot's refusal to willingly cut ties with the Sisseton-Wahpeton Tribe must have seemed to be an unending bad dream. In his August 7 letter he pompously explained he chose to work with the Sisseton-Wahpeton Tribe because: "[the] Council members seemed to be the most alert and intelligent I had dealt with…" After Cabot was no longer associated with the tribe, "critics" among the tribal members were blamed for the failure of the "…paint company to 'really get off the ground.'" Rather than supporting the efforts of tribal members having appropriate questions about the legitimacy of Cabot's efforts, tribal and federal officials questioned the motives of those sincere tribal members and expended considerable energy "…protecting the questionable reputation of John W. Cabot."

Adams astutely noted in his report how the government put forth minimal energy and effort to ensure Indian interests were properly protected, particularly in the case of the BIA's Industrial Development Program and the Commerce Department's Economic Development Administration. Adams claimed these government entities took advantage of the Sisseton-Wahpeton Tribe's lack of business experience to promote and sell the tribe on a multitude of losing business ventures and "questionable, off-the-wall, and failing companies." It was no surprise the key attraction for "'business and commercial interests'" to the Sisseton-Wahpeton Tribe was the availability of the claims award monies. In the legislation authorizing disbursement of these funds were provisions indicating 30 percent of the amount was to be used for industrial and commercial development projects. Counting interest, that established an amount in the neighborhood of two million dollars for that purpose. Again, to no one's surprise Cabot and some federal officials encouraged the tribes to make loans out of the claims award monies before they received official permission to disburse the money.

It was not only outsiders who succumbed to the temptation to abuse governmental processes. After the Tribal Council became essentially one and the same as the LTPC Board of Directors, the LTPC Board voted to create for itself five-year terms, three more than the two-year terms for the Sisseton-Wahpeton Tribal Council itself. The non-profit Industrial Development Corporation, having the same executive officers as LTPC, unhesitatingly voted to loan LTPC $250,000 against the claim's money. In their interchangeable roles as officers of the Tribal Industrial Development Corporation, Planning Development Corporation and LTPC, these men were introduced to a number of businessmen from a variety of states with proposals to develop industry on the reservation. By mid-year 1972, plans were accepted for developing a steel manufacturing and fabrication plant, a mattress-producing firm, an eight-track tape equipment and machines assembly operation, and a number of other enterprises. Unfortunately, the common denominator for all the proposed enterprises was that they were without funds or financial solvency. Additionally, the tribal approvals were based on the advice of the BIA's Industrial Development Program, Economic Development Administration, and the "omnipresent 'business consultant' John W. Cabot." Although no business proposal was rejected by tribal officials, most enterprises failed simply for the noted lack of funds or financial solvency.

Another $250,000 loan was arranged for the development of an electronics operation on the Sisseton-Wahpeton Reservation by the "Belair Corporation of California" without conducting any due diligence as to the financials of the corporation by anyone with input for approval for the project. Conventional banks denied loans simply on the basis Belair was a poor financial risk. The Belair proposal called for more than a million dollars in tribal and federal grants, expenditures, and loans. However, the Belair Corporation was not asked to invest any of its own assets as collateral or otherwise for the project. Somehow the "Belair" name and its "line of credit" was to be valued at $125,000 in connection with any "business" venture. Although BIA Superintendent Dennis Peterson declined the offer of an ownership interest in LTPC, he did recommend the development of the Belair project. Adams' report did not indicate whether the Belair project ever materialized.

Adams' report also revealed there were always advocates for projects considered worthy of the investment in tribal funds regardless of how much opposition arose. "Larklain Products, Ltd" desired to develop a "'pet carrier'" and plastics molding company, but a feasibility study conducted by the federal government contained a recommendation against it. Additionally, Booz-Allen, a private consulting firm retained by the EDA technical section of the BIA, also recommended not initiating the project. However, Washington, D.C., attorney Owen Donley, a longtime staff and campaign aide to then-South Dakota U.S. Senator George McGovern lobbied on behalf of "Larklain." Donley's influence was quite considerable in that at that time Senator McGovern was chairman of the United States Senate Indian Affairs Subcommittee and Donley was considered particularly close to Senator McGovern. Donley also claimed he had been in contact with officials at the United States General Services Administration (GSA) and they assured him the GSA would have an interest in purchasing a variety of plastic products from a Sisseton plant, at best a questionable claim. It was also recommended that an individual named Art Chapman be contracted to serve as a consultant on the project for $350,000.

Another loser of a project was supporting the "Grow Chemical" company of New York City, which lost more than $50,000 in its first year of operation. Grow Chemical's president, Russell Banks, blamed the Small Business Administration (SBA) and GSA for this failure because they didn't purchase Grow's products in the amount of hundreds of thousands of dollars. Adams, however, noted the federal government consistently failed to provide sound advice and assistance and that the federal government supported tribal officials when they were involved with these shaky deals. Additionally, in an April 22, 1973, radio interview on station WCBN, the challenges of developing businesses on Pine Ridge were discussed with several of that reservation's residents. One individual reported that during the tribal administration of Gerald One Feather, the Oglala Sioux Construction Company was started. The company was managed by a Pine Ridge man and had successfully built some houses. However, when Dick Wilson became tribal president, he fired all the individuals working for the company and apparently disbanded its board.

Subsequently, Wilson contracted the work to vendors outside the reservation. Around this time period, several members of the reservation organized the Oglala Sioux Civil Rights Organization independently from any influence from the American Indian Movement, even though their goals overlapped at times.[17]

Recently, commentators on the centuries-old struggle for Eurocentric dominance and ultimately the elimination of Native American culture have recognized the "'false heroes'" in the history of the conquest of what became known as the United States were those other than beleaguered AIM members. Going all the way back to the 15th century, novelist and essayist Hans Konig wrote in the *New York Times* in 1990 about this history and accused Columbus of instigating: "…an extermination of Native Americans and of being as mean, cruel and greedy in small matters as he was in vast ones." In what could certainly be considered a rebuttal to Trimbach's constant mocking and trivializing of Indian culture, Konig concluded: "We must end the phony baloney about the white man bringing Christianity, and about Columbus the noble son of the humble weaver. Our false heroes and a false sense of the meaning of courage and manliness have too long burdened our national spirit."[18]

Like Jake Page, Deloria, Jr., had harsh criticisms of the state of Christianity in the United States: "…any higher deity exists for Americans only insofar as he or she can guarantee great sex, lots of money, social prestige [read celebrity], a winning football team, and someone to hate." Just getting warmed up, he added: "It is impossible to sin today because all of the really good sins have become Christian virtues, much as Greed, once one of the Seven Deadly Sins, has become the chief American and Republican virtue." Unsurprisingly, Deloria, Jr., believed Christianity offered no solutions for Indians:

> Christianity has been the curse of all cultures into which it has intruded. It has offered eternal life somewhere else and produced social and individual disintegration. Even today its chief personalities fall one after another into disrepute. Catholic Priests prey on their parishioners; televangelists engage in fraudulent financial practices or are seen in the seedy parts of town on sexual escapades. Clergy extol the virtues of 'the church' but rarely speak of God, and today we have large numbers of them desperately trying to get into Indian ceremonies to experience 'spirituality.'[19]

Whether or not the United States government created a public relations disaster in its handling of the Wounded Knee "occupation" in 1973 has been the subject of considerable debate over the years. Assuming for the sake of argument that Trimbach's individual participation was less than stellar, he is certainly not alone in the annals of "warfare" in his attempt to turn the perception of his poor performance as a representative of a government entity into a propaganda victory. In April 1754, George Washington was ordered to the Ohio Valley at the helm of 159 troops and a construction force to enhance the military position of the English King. Much like it appeared in Trimbach's case in 1973, Washington found himself in a position that "'…proved both politically and militarily far beyond his depth.'" Earlier in the year in the wilderness Washington was nearly killed on two occasions—once by a group of "French Indians" who fired at him—and missed—at close range—and a second time nearly freezing to death in an icy river.

As the April 1754 expedition progressed, Washington learned of a French force of about 30 soldiers camped in a ravine near Ft. Duquesne. As Trimbach would commit a major error in judgment on how to proceed almost 220 years later, Washington made a glaring error in judgment in overlooking the simple fact the English and French were not at war in deciding to attack. As a result of the attack, Washington eventually realized a French ambassador had been assassinated.[20] In 1973, Trimbach and other federal officials similarly overlooked the Posse Comitatus Act of 1878. This legislation was intended to prohibit the federal government's ability to use military personnel in the role of domestic law enforcers unless expressly authorized by the President. Nevertheless, even long after the event, Trimbach expressed much bitterness towards U.S. Army Colonel Volney Warner's resistance to using army troops to quash the "occupation."[21]

There is a little-known precedent for using military forces in a domestic situation which occurred in the World War II era. Although the existence of shameful internment camps for Japanese living in the United States is relatively well known, the use of military police to quell dissent there is not. Some resistance arose in 1943 in the Japanese population of these camps to answering loyalty questionnaires which pertained to a "registration program." Harvey Coverly, the director of the field office in San Francisco which supervised the Tule Lake Camp, requested assistance from the FBI. N. J. L. Pieper, the special agent in charge of the San Francisco office, responded: "'…this office had no authority to summarily arrest or incarcerate any individuals or groups of individuals to assist in the camp's registration program.'" Undaunted, Coverly enlisted the aid of army military police soldiers to arrest the "troublemaker(s)."[22]

At one point in the dismal history of the Japanese internment camps, teams of two or three WRA "Caucasian" policemen investigated the murder of Yaozo Hitomi, the pro-government manager of a cooperative store. The investigation involved ransacking barracks in search of "evidence," forcible searches and seizures similar to those conducted by the army in the past, and just general mistreatment of the Japanese-Americans. To compound the problem, some likened the renewed commitment to Japanese heritage to the Lakota enthusiasm for the "Ghost Dance" religion that garnered so much attention from federal authorities in the latter part of the 19th century. The "cultural revivalism" also initiated an interest in repatriation of Japanese people to Japan, a homeland many of them had never even visited. During the period of growing conflict, younger Japanese men began wearing sweatshirts decorated with the "Rising Sun" emblem. Gangs of toughs assaulted or menaced "administration stooges" which brought added misery to the lives of detainees.[23] (In the situation of Pine Ridge in the 1970s, the Guardians of the Oglala Nation, known as GOONS, expended their efforts at intimidating *opponents* of the government and their policies.)

Returning to the story of George Washington's ill-fated encounter, after the attack, on July 3, 1754, about 1,100 French and Indian troops surrounded Washington's troops at Ft. Necessity, which in reality was nothing more than a small rectangular ammunition shed surrounded by a small circle of rough-hewn upright log poles about seven feet tall. After the French and Indians unleashed a fusillade of rifle fire against Washington's position, on July 4, Washington decided to surrender along with his starving, rain-soaked, and increasingly drunken troops who had broken into a storage area containing kegs of rum. What Washington did not appear to understand was that when he signed the parole papers presented by the French, he admitted to assassinating the French diplomat. Yet, in the end, Washington's superiors convinced Virginia leaders to recognize Washington and his men for "'gallant and brave behavior'" as a heroic stand against the French and their "'savage'" allies.[24] (Of course, similar descriptions were attributed to the actions of Custer and his men after their defeat at the Little Big Horn.)

Adding to the oddness of Trimbach's journey into authorship is the majority of the "DISCLAIMER" included at the beginning of *American Indian Mafia*:

> The information in this book is believed to be a true and accurate recounting of events. The opinions, observations, and recommendations herein are those of the authors alone and do not necessarily represent the views of the United States Department of the Interior, the Indian Health Service, the United States Justice Department, or the Federal Bureau of Investigation. Furthermore, they do not necessarily represent the views of the editors, endorsers, publisher, or the many FBI Special Agents and other persons who furnished information for this book.
>
> The events actually happened as described and are a factual part of our history. The FBI policies mentioned in this book were the policies in effect, as we understood them to be, in the early 1970s. The policies of the FBI today may or may not be the same. Unless otherwise noted, photographs are borrowed from private collections or else widely available in the public domain.[25]

That Trimbach would expend his disdain for the Lakota people generally is not hard to imagine after reading his book. It's as if when reading Trimbach's account of the history of events in South Dakota, one imagined John Wayne as: "…he gazes across the Texas prairie [substitute South Dakota Plains] in *The Searchers*, [and] he sees a land where he believes that civilization and savagery, good and evil, beauty and foulness collide in a clear and apocalyptic struggle."[26] Or, perhaps Trimbach envisioned himself as the flesh-and-blood embodiment of one of the fictional hard-boiled detectives or Western heroes of the likes created in books written by Edgar Rice Burroughs, Zane Grey, Dashiel Hammett, and others.[27]

Before exploring the parallels of Trimbach to these imaginary sleuths, it is critical to note, as will be explored in the following chapter, the attitudes regarding race some claim were exhibited by his real-life colleagues. And while Trimbach extolled the virtues of the man synonymous with the FBI—J. Edgar Hoover—the story of Hoover's FBI indeed has itself been suggested to contain a hidden history of racism. According to some sources, Hoover once stated as long as he was director, he would never have a black as an agent. When pressed by Bobby Kennedy during the Church Select Committee hearings on Intelligence as to how many black agents he had, Hoover told Kennedy he did not categorize people by race, creed, etc. Kennedy further pressed for an answer and Hoover said five. Unbeknownst to Kennedy or the five black men who functioned as chauffeurs, by Hoover's answer they had received instantaneous promotions to Special Agents during the hearing. And while its sister organization, the CIA, had a fondness for labeling secret missions and activities as "black" ops, it was not until it ran operations in Africa in the 1960s that it employed black people as agents. Prior to that time, black employees at the CIA only performed menial tasks such as cleaning offices or driving shuttle buses.[28] Unfortunately, it does not seem Trimbach's xenophobic views were unique in the federal law enforcement/counterintelligence community in the mid-20th century.

Endnotes

1. Peter Matthieson, *In the Spirit of Crazy Horse: The Story of Leonard Peltier and the FBI's War on the American Indian Movement* (New York: Penguin Books, 1983), p. 318.
2. Churchill and Vander Wall, *Agents of Repression*, p. 151.
3. Magnuson, *Wounded Knee 1973: Still Bleeding*, p. 126.
4. Trimbach, *American Indian Mafia*, p. 9.
5. Woolford, Benvenuto and Hinton, Eds., Kiera Ladner, "Political Genocide—Killing Nations through Legislation and Slow-Moving Poison," *Colonial Genocide in North America*, p. 237.
6. Cook-Lynn, *Anti-Indianism in Modern America*, pp. 162-163.
7. Trimbach, *American Indian Mafia*, p. 534.
8. Kelsey Goplen, Jasmine Graves, Amy Nelson and Harry Thompson, Compilers, John Trimbach, "Wounded Knee 1973: Forty Years Later: Papers of the Forty Fourth Annual Dakota Conference—A National Conference on the Northern Plains" (Center for Western Studies, 2012), p. 130.
9. Ibid., p. 136.
10. Trimbach, *American Indian Mafia*, p. 383.
11. Ibid., p. 461.
12. Ibid., p. 421.
13. Wilson, *The Earth Shall Weep*, pp. 393-394.
14. "Akwesasne Notes" April 23, 1973. Ironically, during research for this book, the only documented instance discovered regarding housing shortages on Indian Reservations was a March 22, 1973, statement describing how federal agents displaced Wounded Knee residents during the "occupation" in 1973. The statement from these ousted people included the comment: "The persons now outside their home of Wounded Knee have been forced into terrible living conditions, due to the shortage of space, and the fact that the outside Officers and agents have taken up so much of the available space in Pine Ridge and around reservation communities." Statement of various Wounded Knee residents (St. Paul, Minnesota: Minnesota Historical Society, March 22, 1973).
15. Deloria, Jr. *Custer Died for Your Sins*, p. 94.
16. Hank Adams, *REVIEW STUDY OF A MODEL FOR FAILURE IN THE BIA'S INDUSTRIAL DEVELOPMENT PROGRAM: An Abstract Discussion on Economic Development Projects of the Sisseton-Wahpeton Sioux Tribes of South Dakota (1971- 1972)* (St. Paul: Minnesota Historical Society, December 6, 1972).
17. Wounded Knee Information and Defense Fund, *Transcript of Rest of the News Tape* (St. Paul: Minnesota Historical Society, April 22, 1973).
18. Hans Koning, "Don't Celebrate 1492, Mourn It," *New York Times*. August 14, 1990.
19. Deloria, Jr., *Red Earth, White Lies*, p. 10.
20. Davis, *America's Hidden History*, pp. 107-108.
21. Trimbach, *American Indian Mafia*, p. 107.

22 Drinnon, *Keeper of Concentration Camps*, p. 86.
23 Ibid., pp. 126-127.
24 Davis, *America's Hidden History*, pp. 109-110.
25 Trimbach, *American Indian Mafia*, unnumbered page.
26 Bordewich, *Killing the White Man's Indian*, p. 114.
27 Slotkin, *Gunfighter Nation*, pp. 194-228.
28 Drinnon, *Facing West*, p. 385, footnote.

CHAPTER 21

Joseph Trimbach and the Federal Bureau of Imperialism: Part III

If we are be constrained to lift the hatchet against any tribe we will not lay it down until that tribe is exterminated (1807). The American Government has no choice before it than to pursue the Indians to extermination (1813).

Thomas Jefferson quotes
Elizabeth Cook-Lynn, *A Separate Country* [1]

Whites who attempt to help Indians are constantly frustrated by their tragic lack of understanding of Indian people.

Vine Deloria, Jr., *Custer Died for Your Sins* [2]

Although the "occupation" was ultimately a bold move for AIM and its supporters, for the FBI, it was business as usual, if you happened to be a group on which the FBI declared *"war."* If there is anything American Indians can be grateful for in the aftermath of the "occupation" it is that AIM was treated like any garden-variety "subversive" group of that era and not necessarily singled out because of its Indian characteristics. As evidence and as previously noted, in *Subversives: The FBI's War on Student Radicals and Reagan's Rise to Power*, Seth Rosenfeld outlined Ronald Reagan's role as informant against colleagues in the Screen Actors Guild during the 1950s and 1960s and also his efforts as governor during the student-protest era at Cal Berkeley. Interestingly enough, in the case of his zeal to thwart "Communism," Reagan fulfilled two roles later filled by two separate individuals related to events in Pine Ridge, South Dakota—Doug Durham and Bill Janklow.

As with Reagan during his years as informant while serving as a member of the Screen Actors Guild, Douglas Durham was a well-placed informant within AIM during the time surrounding the "occupation" in 1973. Like Reagan, who clearly had much authority as governor of California, Bill Janklow exercised considerable power as attorney general of South Dakota and later as governor. Also, as Reagan considered the work of campus protesters evidence of the evils of Communism, Janklow believed "Communism" was the driving force behind the "occupation" and protests at Wounded Knee. During the 1960s, "Communism" was seen as the driving force behind virtually anything not considered to mesh with the "American Way of Life."

In the aftermath of the especially serious rioting and subsequent destruction in Detroit and Newark during the "long, hot summer of 1967," Reagan suggested the underlying cause of the trouble was a "Communist" plot and publicly stated: "'It would be pretty naïve to believe these riots are just spontaneous,'" and added "'I believe there is a plan.'" FBI agents closely surveilled black militants, campus activists, and Communist Party members and to their credit reported no evidence of communist involvement and did not try to manufacture any. President Johnson appointed the bipartisan National Advisory Commission on Civil Disorders, which concluded that not only was there no communist plot, but rather stated: "…ingrained white racism created the conditions that fueled the riots, namely pervasive discrimination in housing, employment, and education." The commission also found: "…black violence had been greatly exaggerated by the police and the press."[3]

Nonetheless, during the period of unrest at Cal Berkeley, the FBI was relentless in pursuing the notion of "Communist" involvement. A few weeks after Reagan was inaugurated as California's governor, FBI Agent Don Jones submitted a report dated January 23, 1967, containing the incorrect claim that a prominent activist named Mario Savio had attended communist "educational classes" of the Cal Berkeley branch of the Communist Party in August 1966. Jones suggested Savio was thus more involved with the Communist Party than previously known. The FBI reiterated the allegation in internal documents and additionally forwarded the incorrect information about Savio to Army Intelligence. Unfortunately, at the root of the problem was a transcription error of an informant's comments which was never corrected.

To further compound the problem, there is no indication at any time the FBI sought to correct the error. As a result, Savio's position on the FBI's surveillance schemes was upgraded from the Reserve Index to the Security Index. This meant Savio was believed to be one of the people the FBI considered: "…most dangerous to national security in the event of a national emergency, to be detained indefinitely without judicial warrant." FBI agents at that time also issued a "'Security Flash'" for Savio, which meant field offices would be alerted whenever a police agency inquired about him.[4]

Similarly, much effort was exerted in painting the "occupation" of Wounded Knee as being the result of communist organizers. A "Newsletter" dated March 26, 1973, urged Lakota Indians to "Unite against the American Indian Movement and their planned takeover of our Reservation." The "Newsletter" goes on to explain: "What has happened at Wounded Knee, is all part of a long-range plan of the Communist Party." Like Reagan's earlier charges of a communist conspiracy in the attempted takeover of Hollywood, no factual evidence of the conspiracy is provided. Nonetheless, the "Newsletter" explained:

> The supporters of AIM come in all shades and the national Council of Churches are (sic) very vocal because the Liberal Press and the T.V. News media is (sic) right at their elbow. No news

reporter or t.v. camera man has ever won a war, but they can destroy a Nation by the propaganda of lies and hate that they broadcast for every Crackpot, Screwball, and Communist-front organization who wants to take a swat at our American way of life.[5]

Another handout or letter argued that the Wounded Knee "occupation" was: "…just a small part of a much bigger picture; a picture of America in trouble." This document invited the recipient to the showing of a film entitled "An Overview of Our World."[6]

Thus, in a parallel to its approach to dealing with protesters at Cal Berkeley in the 1960s, the actions of the FBI and U.S. Marshals during the "occupation" exacerbated what could just have easily been close to a benign situation. No satisfactory explanation has ever been provided as to why federal forces deployed such overwhelming firepower to that scenario. Richard La Course, considered the "Dean of Indian Journalism," quoting Secretary of the Interior Rogers Morton, described the actions of AIM as "symbolic rather than substantive."[7] However, due to the heavy-handed tactics of the federal government, the situation became a needless virtually out-of-control shootout. Likewise, just as the Free Speech Movement (FSM) was losing steam after a sit-in on campus fizzled out, FBI ally and *San Francisco Examiner* reporter Ed Montgomery ran front-page stories claiming communists were behind the campus unrest. The stories ended up increasing pressure on campus administrators to crack down on students, which in turn caused the Cal Berkeley leaders to issue discipline to FSM leaders. As a result, the students involved bristled and the campus reexperienced turmoil.[8]

Whether or not the FBI was the bastion of racism as suggested, reports ring true of Hoover's FBI's penchant for manhandling "dissidents" long before the encounter at Wounded Knee. No doubt, the FBI's enthusiasm for thwarting the tranquility of these individuals and groups was Hoover's belief that: "…radicals not only held dangerous political theories…but were 'intellectual perverts.'" In the early part of the 20th century, he oversaw a program to round up and deport "…noncitizen immigrants whom he concluded were radicals." The ultimate result of the process meant these unfortunate souls could be deported even if they never had committed acts of violence or threatened to do so. It is no stretch to conclude Hoover carried this type of thinking forward when he became Director of the FBI.

For example, in 1919, Hoover oversaw a Justice Department program designed to: " …round up and deport noncitizen immigrants whom he had concluded were radicals." Based on Hoover's "evidence" police and immigration agents conducted raids in 12 cities on November 7, 1919. Four hundred mostly poor people with little ability to speak English were arrested without the slightest indication of having committed crimes of violence. These people were guilty only of the technical charge of being aliens and members of suspect organizations. Soon thereafter, Emma Goldman, a famous "radical" caught up in the sweep along with 248 other aliens, was on a boat headed to Russia. Hoover followed up on this massive raid with raids on members of the American Communist Party and the American Communist Labor Party.

As a result of a second set of raids in January 1920, some 6,000 "alien radicals" from 33 different cities were detained. Together, these raids ultimately came to be known as the "Palmer Raids." Although initially Hoover and Attorney General A. Mitchell Palmer received praise for these mass arrests, the activity eventually resulted in scandal. The detention facilities were inadequate, unsanitary, and many detainees were held incommunicado for days. Contrary to Hoover's claims, most members of the American Communist Labor Party who were arrested did not know the organization professed the violent overthrow of the government. Louis Post, the Assistant Secretary of Labor who would rule on whether the arrestees should be deported, called the raids a "'gigantic and cruel hoax'" and condemned Hoover's use of informers and agents provocateurs. Ultimately, out of the thousands arrested, only 556 were deported.[9]

Likewise, it only takes reading a few pages of *American Indian Mafia* before it is clear Trimbach is not going to be reflective and consider the instances when the FBI itself became a threat to the ability of Indians to exercise their Constitutional rights. This is never more evident than when he engaged in the virtual deification of the two agents killed in June 1976 on the Pine Ridge Reservation, Ron Williams and Jack Coler. Trimbach, as well as most other writers, failed to mention Williams was involved in one of the FBI's most infamous episodes involving its conduct relating to the trials of Dennis Banks and Russell Means: taking witness for the prosecution Louie Moves Camp on a drinking spree. Williams' performance at less than acceptable standards for an FBI agent during this litigation was another episode that aroused the ire of federal judge Fred Nichol. There was a fairly complicated procedural situation with the trial; but, as noted, essentially Nichol eventually dismissed all the charges against Means and Banks for their involvement in the Wounded Knee "occupation" due to his view the government engaged in significant misconduct.[10]

As mentioned throughout this book, it is becoming more well recognized that Indian populations in North and South America were decimated by the diseases Europeans brought with them one way or another. Likewise, historians of Indian matters, of which Trimbach apparently fancied himself, have often been infected with the inability to see events through anything other than a very narrow and Eurocentric focus. Rather than parse out the circumstances of specific events, many historians and other writers consider any paradigm other than blaming the victim, in this case Indians, as virtual blasphemy. Likewise, Trimbach's ignorant and dismissive attitude towards Indian culture permeated his book. As suggested in the Introduction, he took childish delight in recounting FBI Special Agent Robert Heafner's "cowboy [sic] and Indian cartoons" and Heafner's description of how the federal forces: "…formed a semi-circle of vehicles as our perimeter defense just like in the old movies."[11] Although Trimbach may have considered these humorous comments, in the context of all of his harsh comments about AIM and their supporters, his story comes off as mean-spirited, particularly when he again stated he and his agents were in a "war" with the Indian people at Wounded Knee.[12] His descriptions of Indians is thus a sad reminder it is acceptable to trivialize and even dehumanize Indians in the United States. His thoughtless comments exemplified Patricia Limerick's belief: "…to most twentieth-century Americans, the legacy of slavery was serious business, while the legacy of conquest was not."[13]

It was often the case that whites did not consider Indians savages until the whites betrayed them. A lady named Allie Hanson lived near the Shoshone tribe in Idaho and believed interacting with them was a significant educational experience. As a result, she learned: "'…they weren't savage with whites until the whites betrayed them'" and "'…they are not the glorified "Cowboy and Indian" Indian. They think differently, traditions are different.'" Although she is not a trained historian or anthropologist, unlike Trimbach, she recognized issues between whites and Indians could arise due to "'cross-cultural miscommunication.'"[14]

What Trimbach also neglected to mention was the FBI's actions in precipitating the situation that resulted in the deaths of the two agents on the Jumping Bull Ranch. As Dennis Banks argued: "They [the FBI] *had* to know if they ventured into AIM territory they would surely invite trouble." Banks continued: "The initial arrival of the two agents at Tent City [on the Jumping Bull Ranch] always seemed to me to be a case of calculated provocation." Banks surmised the resistance by the Indians of the two agents might have "give[n] them an excuse to wipe out our camp." Banks then concluded: "The FBI might not have intended for the two agents to die, but they deliberately put them in harm's way. The Feds apparently went looking for trouble and they found it [emphasis in original]."[15] As noted, Trimbach himself believed the FBI was in a "war" with AIM.

Trimbach also neglected to describe the utter ruthlessness exhibited by the FBI in laying siege to the Wounded Knee "occupation" area in 1973. In addition to the abysmal conditions existing inside the compound caused by the lack of food and proper sanitation, the FBI extended its tentacles across the entire United States. The organization was determined to thwart any attempts at providing the basic necessities for life to the "occupiers." As mentioned in the Introduction, Scott Burgwin described his arrest in Bend, Oregon, after picking up a U-Haul van in Eugene, Oregon, over 1,200 miles from Wounded Knee, filled with clothing and food:

> As we were leaving Bend at about 4 p.m. on Sat[urday] March 24, about 10-15 FBI agents, in several vehicles, a State Trooper, local police officers [Bend, Oregon] including a matron, caused us to stop near a shopping center. We were ordered out of the truck by FBI agents, who proceeded to have 5 [five] of us searched and then handcuffed. [Two FBI agents] asked me what the food was for, where it was going, why the 5 of us were taking the food. I told them I was taking the food to the Pine Ridge and Rosebud Indian Reservations. They told me it was against the law to do what we were doing.

Burgwin went on to say he was asked about having weapons and he said he had none. He then stated he was taken to the county jail, booked and fingerprinted. Subsequently, he was placed in an unmarked FBI car, handcuffed, and driven to Portland. Burgwin's bond was initially $10,000, then reduced to $1,000 after being told he was being charged with intent to aid and abet a riot by using interstate commerce (highways). Burgwin was arraigned on Monday, March 26, and on Tuesday, March 27, he was advised the charges were being dropped.[16]

It is unclear how the FBI became aware of the proposed food delivery; presumably through some sort of wiretap or informant. Likewise, it is not evident what became of the food and clothing, but it is reasonable to assume the items were destroyed. However, the largest question remaining unanswered by Trimbach is why did the FBI have such a keen interest in the Pine Ridge Reservation in the first place? Other than the oft-maligned Ward Churchill and Peter Matthiessen, few writers seem willing to investigate the subject and do not question people like Trimbach when they claim the FBI and U.S. Marshals were there to suppress the activities of "militants."

It is hardly surprising Trimbach assumed Means was incapable of comprehending the history of the hammer blows of conquest rained down on indigenous people in both North and South America for centuries. Obviously, the issues raised by the whites violating the Ft. Laramie Treaty of 1868 were of the most immediate concern to the Plains Indians such as the Lakota and Trimbach appeared unwilling to delve deeply into that discussion. Nonetheless, whether Trimbach or anyone else chose to face the issues head-on or even acknowledge them, those unresolved treaty violations inevitably loomed large in the encounters between whites and Indians throughout history. Further, some of these breaches of agreement occurred well before the United States, as the prime energizer behind the tidal wave of Manifest Destiny, became a distinct political entity. For example, after a period of combat between the British and the Indians which included the intense Battle of Bushy Run in western Pennsylvania on August 5, 1763, the British Board of Trade issued the Royal Proclamation of 1763.

The Royal Proclamation of 1763 was not necessarily a well-known treaty like the Ft. Laramie Treaty of 1868, yet violation of this edict had a profound effect on the region. The proclamation negated the Lancaster Treaty of 1744 and created a "…hard and fast" boundary between the whites and Indians, primarily the Shawnees. At a minimum, it was a formal promise reduced to writing. This document claimed: "…everything west of the heads of the streams that ultimately empty into the Atlantic are to be, for the present and until our further pleasure be known, reserved for the tribes." The formal treaty was concluded in the summer of 1764, but the peace didn't last but a moment in the sun. As thousands of immigrants arrived from England, Scotland, Wales, and Ireland, the "need" for Westward Expansion grew even greater. Much like Means' thought process a little over 200 years later: "…when continued appeals to British authorities failed to curtail the invasion and oust the intruders, the Indians took matters into their own hands."[17] The situation facing the AIM members and their allies in 1973 and that facing the Shawnees and their allies in 1763 were different only in the aspect the more modern foes of the Indians had weapons that were much more accurate and fired at much higher rates.

Trimbach's real-life FBI expended considerable resources combatting "white collar" crime, the no-nonsense imaginary detectives of Edgar Rice Burroughs and others gloried in exposing the corruption of defalcating bankers and crooked speculators. Yet, their greatest aspirations were realized in battling the urban criminal underworld, which could explain his constant referencing of Means and his allies as crooks, thugs, etc. and ignoring or distorting the history leading up to the "occupation." Trimbach's inability to overlook the youthful indiscretions of individuals like Clyde Bellecourt, who spent time in prison for robbery, morphed into a condemnation of AIM in its entirety as a criminal enterprise. It did not register with Trimbach that while many Indians did indeed view AIM leaders as nothing more than glory-seeking publicity hounds, other Indians saw AIM as a symbol of restored pride in Indian heritage, a view also held by Clyde Warrior, who rejected the notion that being an Indian was in and of itself at the core of Indian issues.

In Dashiel Hammett's *The Big Knockover* in particular, the hero dispatched a series of characters whose racial and class characteristics are readily identifiable by their names: "the 'Dis and Dat' Kid, Sheeny Holmes, Spider Giraci, Nigger Vojan, and Paddy the Mex." Likewise, Slotkin summed up those characterizations when applied to non-whites, particularly Indians on the frontier: "These are Indians whom our scout-detective 'knows,' and his understanding teaches him that in the end we will have to use violence against them. *Black Mask* detectives approached this necessity more or less in the spirit of the Indian-hater."[18]

Yet, Trimbach reflected a perhaps commonly held, subconscious belief that darker-skinned foes were less than worthy adversaries, even though by 1973, it was apparent the United States' effort in Vietnam was hurtling toward failure, a debacle ultimately symbolized by North Vietnamese forces capturing the U.S. embassy in Saigon in 1975. Thus, Trimbach seemed hypnotized by the myth of Frontier which also guided the planning and execution of the Vietnam War as an extension of the Frontier, which, as described by Slotkin: "…that myth taught us that historical progress is achieved only by the advance of White European races/cultures into and against the terrain of 'primitive' non-White natives." Further, fleshing out his analysis of the Frontier Myth applied to Vietnam-era policies, Slotkin noted that myth also contained the core belief: "The native races are inherently lacking in the capacity to generate 'progress.'" And clearly specifying what Russell Means was *not*, Slotkin added in regard to those subject to domination to whites according to the "Frontier Myth": "The best of them are seen as passively willing to subordinate themselves to the progressive Whites." Trimbach would endorse the view of Means as Slotkin would explain in general terms: "The worst are seen as savagely opposed to progress, preferring extermination to either civilization or subjugation."[19]

Years later, in addition to unresolved debates over the character and morality of AIM leaders, and like the first Wounded Knee event in 1890, versions of what happened unsurprisingly vary widely. Trimbach argued that U.S. Marshal Lloyd Grimm, who was initially paralyzed and later died from a gunshot wound, was struck by a bullet fired by a "…gunman positioned in the small tower of the 'Little Church'" outside the mass grave. Trimbach further claimed the round was that of: "…[a] large caliber hunting rifle possibly stolen from [Gildersleeve's] trading post."[20] In a contrary version of the source of Grimm's ultimately mortal wounds, Bob Anderson in *Akwesasne Notes* indicated unattributed sources noted: "…it is widely believed that [Grimm] was caught in crossfire and hit by a U.S. bullet." (Remarkably, the explanation is similar to the one provided for U.S. soldier casualties at Wounded Knee [83 years earlier].) Grimm himself did not shed any light on the topic when he told reporters before he died that he held no ill will toward the Indians and added: "'I knew somebody would get shot somehow, some way.'"[21]

Returning to the Vietnam paradigm as the model for dealing with "militant" Indians, Trimbach's spiritual father could be seen as Edwin Geary Lansdale, the (ironically) famous CIA special operative from the Vietnam War era. Lansdale began his activities in Southeast Asia before a significant number of ground combat troops were deployed there. Just as Trimbach would shortly display his ignorance of Lakota culture shortly after arriving at Pine Ridge, Lansdale: "…not only knew no Vietnamese [language] but little or no French and next to nothing about Indochina's history and cultures." Unsurprisingly, Lansdale was fond of playing "cowboys and Indians" with the children of then-South Vietnamese Premier Ngo Dinh Diem in his official palace. Like Trimbach's efforts in 1973, Lansdale's energy was expended in an enterprise with a significantly less than satisfactory ending when South Vietnam was overtaken by North Vietnamese soldiers in 1975.[22]

Unfortunately, the fantasies of Lansdale and Trimbach of Europeanizing people they knew next to nothing about had real-life consequences for these people, which often meant they suffered untimely and violent deaths. Lansdale funded Diem's plan to "divide and conquer" the armed sects the French had previously relied upon to stave off the Viet Minh's effort to "conquer" South Vietnam in the 1950s. Likewise, Trimbach's FBI supplied Dick Wilson's Guardians of the Oglala Nation (GOONS) with weapons and other military equipment. The GOONs used these materials to, among other things, help the FBI surround the AIM-led "occupiers" who were desperately seeking protection from the blizzard of gunfire in their makeshift fortifications on the Wounded Knee burial grounds. One of the casualties of one of the many firefights between the FBI/U.S. Marshals and the "occupiers" was Buddy Lamont, Jr. Buddy had served as a Marine in Vietnam only to die on the Pine Ridge Indian Reservation doing his best to assert his right to embrace his Indian heritage and identity.[23]

Trimbach's view of Indian history in South Dakota also suggested he adhered to another musing of Tolstoy, regarding world events, who: "…viewed history as a kind of mysterious force following predetermined paths the human mind is slow to grasp."[24] Trimbach's fantasy-filled explanation for the Wounded Knee Massacre of 1890 included a belief that he viewed the incident as mutual combat where the killing of women and children was likely caused by a "mysterious force" as well. Trimbach argued (in his account) an unnamed Indian, possibly the son of "Big Foot," fired on the soldiers, and that: "His shot was followed by many others from the Indians. The soldiers did not fire until they were actually compelled to, and after the Indians had fired many shots." Trimbach explained: "If women and children were killed in the shelling of this camp [by the Hotchkiss guns], the Indians who caused [the ambush] are to blame." In his never-ending quest to tarnish the reputation of the Minneconjou Lakota involved, he claimed they were "…severely condemned by the Brulés and Oglalas."[25]

Before Trimbach got all misty-eyed about the virtue of the federal troops at Wounded Knee on that cold December morning in 1890, a review of the history of conflicts between Indians and whites would have been edifying to determine if it followed the pattern of other incidents. While analysis of the Sand Creek Massacre provides some insight into the thinking of those with military authority, the "Columns of Vengeance" conducted in the aftermath of the Minnesota Uprising of 1862 set the precedent for conduct that was to a large extent replicated at Wounded Knee and other incidents. As has been argued regarding the motives for the 7th Cavalry's behavior at Wounded Knee, the main reason for the expeditions of 1863-1864 was a desire to seek revenge for the whites killed in 1862 in Minnesota. Apparently, the mass hanging of 38 Indians on December 26, 1862, after summary trials was not a sufficient pound of flesh to satisfy this desire for revenge.[26] As a counterpoint, Elizabeth Cook-Lynn noted that there were no mass hangings of Confederate soldiers during or after the Civil War, which obviously took place during that same era.[27]

Unquestionably during and after the 1862 uprising, violence in Minnesota emanated from both Indians and whites. The "Sioux" executed an attack on the Wiseman farm where three white children were killed and two were "mortally wounded."[28] Indians also attacked a small boat on the Missouri River, killing twenty-one men, three women, and an unknown number of children.[29] Actions by whites exhibited at least an equivalent level of ferocity and intensity. As an example, when men from the 6th Minnesota learned that Mounted Rangers had 31 scalps in their possession, the soldiers of the 6th replied they had "'…forty of their topknots in our possession.'" While initially repulsed by such barbarism, General Alfred Sibley rescinded his earlier order prohibiting scalping and allowed the "Sioux" to be "…treated like wild animals to be hunted and skinned."[30]

In another instance to be replicated at Wounded Knee (which in that instance involved the use of Hotchkiss guns, a type of revolving cannon firing large caliber shells), and employing tactics he learned in the Civil War, General Alfred Sully used artillery against Indian civilian targets. Specifically, during the Battle of Kildeer Mountain in North Dakota in 1864, Sully employed these lethal weapons on high hills, giving them a wide range of fire. During direct contact with Sioux warriors, canister shot was used. Later in the battle, as the soldiers approached about a mile from the Indian encampment, they noticed hundreds of women, children, and elderly people on a butte watching the progress of the battle. Sully ordered eight artillery pieces to open fire on these non-combatants. While the initial volley fell short, the second and subsequent volleys found their targets. Putting aside Sherman's concept of total war against the South, while civilians during the Civil War found themselves subjected to cannon fire, it would not seem (although it is possible) it was done so as the result of intentional orders as was the case in this instance. A soldier named Minor Thomas described the destruction unleashed upon these helpless human beings as a "'magnificent sight.'"[31]

Certainly, it can be argued Indians attacked civilians as well. In that regard, however, one characteristic of what ultimately separated the conduct of the whites from Indians was the level of bloodthirsty rhetoric employed by white soldiers. At the end of Sibley's first campaign in 1863, he issued General Order 51, which foreshadowed comments like Baum's previously noted, and stated in part:

> You have routed the miscreants who murdered our people last year…and driven them in confusion and dismay across the Missouri River…[and]…it would be gratification if these remorseless savages could have been pursued and utterly extirpated, for their crimes and barbarities merited such a full measure of punishment.[32]

In contrast, as author Paul Beck explained: "Never in the history of the Lakotas had they fought a war with the intended [purpose of the] eradication of an entire tribe or nation."[33]

Likewise, owing to his lack of specific knowledge of the Lakota and Indian history generally, when Trimbach more or less claimed Black Coyote and some of the other Indians surrounded by roughly 500 federal troops (with thousands more in the immediate vicinity) were planning an ambush with weapons hidden in blankets,[34] he may have been confusing the situation with an episode involving the Cheyennes a little over 12 years earlier. On September 9, 1878, Dull Knife, Little Wolf, and other Cheyennes left the

Darlington Agency in Oklahoma and headed north; they left their Tipis up and fires burning to slow the soldiers' ability to detect their departure. After several weeks battling freezing temperatures and lack of food, Dull Knife and his group split off from Little Wolf and came into Camp Robinson in late October. After two months army representatives advised Dull Knife his group would be required to return to Oklahoma instead of being allowed to stay at the Red Cloud Agency as promised.

Dull Knife advised the soldiers he and his people would rather die than return to Oklahoma (and his people agreed they would fight to stay). The soldiers then cut off the Indians' water supply and put chains across their doors in hopes the Indians would give up. The Cheyennes advised the soldiers they were giving up, but they had previously hidden some weapons in women's clothing. Children wore some of the smaller pieces of the weapons as jewelry. On the night of January 9, 1879, the Cheyennes assembled the weapons and ended up with a grand total of five rifles and 11 pistols.

Whether or not the Lakota actually hid the weapons under blankets on December 29, 1890, as well, there is no distinction between the outcomes for both groups—annihilation. Just as it happened to the Lakota a little over 12 years later, the Cheyenne men, women, and children were gunned down. Although several members of Dull Knife's family were killed during the melee, he managed to lead a group of them up some nearby rocky cliffs and to safety.[35] Trimbach did not venture into what is slowly leaking out over time as one of, if not the, primary cause of the massacre—drunkenness of the federal troops. Eli Ricker, a lawyer originally from the East, reported the Indians at Wounded Knee: "'…were attacked, wantonly, cruelly, brutally, and what little fighting they did was in self-defense. The affair at Wounded Knee was a *drunken slaughter*—of white soldiers and innocent Indians—for which white men were responsible—solely responsible. A little reason and patience and forbearance would have avoided the murderous clash [emphasis added].'"[36] Rex Smith indicated a Pine Ridge storekeeper, James Asay: "…brought along a small keg of whiskey to toast the capture of Big Foot" and added defensively: "According to all reports, the celebration was neither lengthy nor particularly boisterous."[37] Interestingly enough, in addition to Flood's comment about the keg of whiskey as noted in the Introduction, Heather Cox Richardson also indicated a keg of whiskey was brought out to the soldiers' camp, but did not indicate it was "small."[38]

If it is difficult for some to grasp the possibility of drunkenness as a major cause of the Wounded Knee Massacre, there is much evidence to support the prevalence of soldiers heavily drinking on the frontier, as outlined in the chapter on Raymond Yellow Thunder and elsewhere. Drinking was a primary method for alleviating the boredom and harsh conditions found there. There are other examples of extreme abuse of alcohol noted throughout the history of soldiers on the Plains as well. One of the early epicenters of drunkenness was Ft. Union, built around 1828 a few miles upstream from where the Missouri River joins the Yellowstone River. Indians came there from all over the upper Missouri watershed to trade furs, beaver skins, and buffalo robes mainly for alcohol. At that time in the mid-1800s beaver hats in particular were considered fashion designators of high status, usually for doctors or lawyers. Ian Frazier stated bluntly: "…the history of the confluence area [around Ft. Union] since white men first came is the history of a binge."[39] Drunken murders of Indians were so common that less than wholesale slaughter garnered little attention. In December 1863, a group of drunken soldiers from Company B, 7th Iowa Cavalry murdered three Ponca women and a girl, and wounded at least two others near Niobrara, Nebraska. Even though Ponca agent J. B. Hoffman called the actions of the soldiers "'murder'" and army officials promised the Poncas the soldiers would receive punishment, none was ever administered.[40]

Likewise, what adds to the credibility of Ricker's account is that he did not arrive on the "frontier" with a predisposition to be sympathetic to the plight of the Indians. Quite the opposite was true. In early 1890, citizens in the South Dakota region called on the federal government to: "…restore their confidence by taking steps to stop the Indians from rising once and for all." The group from Washington issued resolutions calling for harsh measures up to and including death for Indian "…'criminals'…traitors, anarchists, assassins." Ricker was one of the signers of these resolutions which were sent to Secretary of War Redfield Proctor in November, 1890.[41] Nevertheless, in an about-face for reasons never made entirely clear, Ricker considered publicizing what he considered the unvarnished truth about what happened at Wounded Knee on December 29, 1890, his life's work.[42]

Speculation aside, Trimbach never explicitly made clear his reasons for undertaking his shaky journey into analyzing late 19th-century events on the Great Plains. For example, Trimbach stated that: "By the end of 1890, the year 150 Indian men, women, and children died near Wounded Knee Creek, a way of life came to an unhappy end for the Plains Indians and most every other tribe in America."[43] Curiously, in a different section of his screed, Trimbach agreed with a more commonly accepted figure of 300 as the number of Indians killed during the massacre.[44] Trimbach's comment that a "…way of life came to an unhappy end" is a misnomer in that the "way of life" he speaks of actually developed in the latter portion of the 19th century, primarily through the Plains Indians being introduced to a revolutionary tool, the horse. He also neglected to mention how the Lakota incorporated firearms into their culture after being introduced to them by the Europeans. While for about 20 years, from 1850 to 1870, Plains Indians were dominant on the Plains, by approximately 1870 they were living sedentary lives on reservations. It is arguable they were no longer self-reliant as early as 1855. It has also been asserted the frontier closed in 1869 when the transcontinental railroads were joined at Promontory Point in Utah. James Wilson explained the big picture:

> It was the defeat of the Plains tribes that seemed to consign the Indian irreversibly to history and finally put the stamp of 'civilization' on the entire continent. There is something deeply ironic—though somehow strangely fitting—about this. To begin with, far from pre-dating contact, the Plains Indian culture of the nineteenth century was a relatively recent phenomenon which depended, in part, on innovations introduced by Europeans [punctuation as in original].[45]

In *Son of the Morning Star*, Evan Connell noted as early as 1876, shortly after Custer's defeat at the Little Big Horn: "As the [London] *Times* shrewdly predicted, a way of life was ending." The *Times* had also commented that: "… Indians would be driven backward to death or to yet more distant and barren reservations."[46] Sitting Bull, also as early as 1876, stated it was futile for the Plains Indians to continue fighting against the whites, in essence conceding that the Lakota would soon be dominated by white culture. It is difficult to argue that the timing of the military defeat of the Plains Indians or at least acceptance of the futility of continued fighting is a separate issue from the end of a "'way of life,'" particularly in the case of the "Sioux." Military dominance by the whites meant confinement to reservations.

Other sources confirm the perspective that Custer's defeat at Little Big Horn in 1876 provided only a brief interruption from the onslaught of Western settlement and was the beginning of the end for Lakota and Cheyenne forces. As stated in *The Great Sioux War of 1876-1877*: "For the Sioux and Cheyennes… the victory over Custer provided only a brief respite. By the autumn of 1877, their war had ended."[47] Likewise, Sitting Bull believed at this juncture in history, "The time for use of warlike arms is past."[48] Other historians suggest that as early as 1868, after the signing the Ft. Laramie Treaty of 1868, for the Indians, the United States government implemented policies which lead Indians to believe: "…the old life of wandering was coming to an end, the government stressed."[49]

In terms of the specific situation existing at the time Spotted Elk's band encountered the federal forces outside Pine Ridge in 1890, it is important to dig through the detritus of history to arrive at discovering what Spotted Elk reportedly said. The likely validity of the comments is high in that they correspond to those outlined above regarding the likelihood of the "Sioux" going to war. It is worth repeating and more fully stating the exchange Spotted Elk and a man from the reservation had on December 28, 1890, the day prior to the massacre: "'I [Spotted Elk] have come to this reservation to avoid trouble and I will take the main road to the agency and join the peaceable people there.' and the Oglala man said he thought it would be a satisfactory movement."[50]

Another measure of "a way of life" coming to an end long before the Wounded Knee Massacre is found in examining the number of settlers moving through Ft. Laramie in the 18th century. It has been estimated that by the time Crazy Horse, then known as Curly, entered his second decade of life in 1850, more than 55,000 migrants had passed through this frontier outpost. At that time, 55,000 was roughly three times the population of the entire Lakota nation. Another 10,000 traversed this territory in 1851; 50,000 in 1852; 20,000 in 1853; and 10,000 in 1854. Sajna noted: "Even as Curly was learning to hit a moving target with an arrow…the most basic elements of [Lakota] life were unalterably changing."[51] Likewise, by the end of the 1840s, more than 9,000 miles of railroad track had already been laid in the West.[52]

What Trimbach also left out of his soliloquy on the End of Life as Plains Indians knew it was what some considered the systematic starving of Pine Ridge residents by Indian agents from approximately the late 1870s to just prior to the Wounded Knee Massacre. The Lakota were forced to attempt farming since buffalo hunting as a means of sustaining the population was no longer possible. As evidence of this circumstance, Agent McLaughlin from the Standing Rock Agency stated there was no rain at all there from August 1889 to June 1890. Agent McChesney from the Cheyenne River Reservation reported: "This is not farming country and until some means is found to overcome the effects of the hot, drying winds it never will be." Waves of influenza, whooping cough, and measles killed large numbers of the population. At the Cheyenne River Reservation alone 25 to 30 children died from whooping cough in the spring of 1890.[53]

Trimbach, like Gwynne and Mort, joined the pantheon of American writers who Richard Slotkin argued: "justify their (or justify on behalf of settlers) title to the land they took for their own." Trimbach had the added need to attempt the justification for the heavily armed force of FBI agents and U.S. Marshals surrounding the significantly outmanned and outgunned group of Indians temporarily "occupying" the sacred ground around Wounded Knee in 1973. The overall handling of the situation at Wounded Knee created discomfort, if not downright embarrassment, for the Nixon Administration which was already coming under siege for the Watergate mess. Trimbach's odd commentary about the circumstances at Wounded Knee 83 years earlier was what Slotkin would also call justification "through imaginative reconstruction of events." Slotkin uncannily summarized the writing of Gwynne, Mort, and Trimbach: "who more or less deliberately sought to create a unified and compelling version of the total American experience—an American myth."[54]

It appears some Indian writers such as Cook-Lynn see Trimbach's writing as little more than propaganda.[55] Adding to the list of what Trimbach failed to recognize was that by 1895, life had also changed dramatically for the non-Indian farmers and others who were eking out meager existences on the frontier during the time of rapidly rising power of corporations in the United States. Much earlier than even the 1890s, the outline of what was to come was already taking shape.

And like so many others, Trimbach repeated like an uncritical drudge the fable the "Ghost Dance" was the primary reason federal forces surrounded Big Foot's band and killed most of them, much like Sitting Bull was supposedly killed while "resisting arrest" a mere two weeks earlier. Considering the bile he unleashed against the Wounded Knee "occupiers" in 1973, it is understandable Trimbach would resort to the "Ghost Dance" fable in explaining the reason for the 1890 massacre. Yet, the purpose of Indian dances in general is misinterpreted in "academic" circles as are many other myths about Indians and their motivations. Drinnon explained: "From Sculptor Borglum and from interpreter Stevens there was not the hint of an understanding that the Indians might have been using their bodies as instruments of prayer."[56] Barely below the surface of this flimsy belief about the threatening nature of Indian dances, if it is below the surface at all in the national consciousness, was (and perhaps still is) the belief: "…westward expansion could provide an inexhaustible stimulus to economic growth."[57] There was (and again may still be): "…the association of economic development with agrarian expansion on the borders of society."[58] The real dancing at Wounded Knee was performed by whites who were seduced by the siren song of unending wealth to be gained at any cost in lives, particularly those of "savages" who were nothing more than impediments to "progress."

The sad and desolate region of South Dakota where this dark stain on the American flag occurred is the eternal shrine for an event that resonates throughout history like no other except the "Trail of Tears" or perhaps the Sand Creek Massacre of 1864. How much the memory of that day in 1890 affects Indian people, particularly the Lakota, is difficult to grasp for outsiders. Nonetheless, in the dark and grisly arena of categorizing which atrocities committed against Indians were the most despicable, Wounded Knee is the measuring stick against which the evil of all other events is measured. Accordingly, one author remarked regarding the Bear River Massacre which occurred on January 29, 1863, it was: "…the worst massacre west of the Mississippi, worse than Wounded Knee."[59]

Unfortunately, Trimbach's approach to the confrontation at "Wounded Knee II" replicated the approach of Defense Secretary Robert McNamara's misguided notions of how to "win" the Vietnam War.

As noted, what makes Trimbach's position even more problematic is that by 1973, it was evident to even the casual observer the Vietnam War was a debacle in concept from the very beginning. Richard Drinnon quoted McNamara's astonishing admission, similar to Lansdale's: "'I had never visited Indochina...nor did I understand or appreciate its history, language, culture, or values.'"[60] Drinnon added that: "McNamara [did] not grasp that his imperial ignorance of other cultures and peoples, especially colored [sic], is as American as the Pledge of Allegiance."[61] After reading *American Indian Mafia*, there would be little credibility to any argument Trimbach, like Lyman, exhibited any greater degree of understanding of the "history, language, culture, or values" of the Lakota than McNamara did of the Vietnamese.

And while Trimbach and Lyman zealously heaped scorn upon Russell Means and the other members of AIM by labeling them little more than criminals and troublemakers, the reality of the situation was (and most likely still is) corruption festered unaddressed on Pine Ridge and other reservations for decades. In January 1918, Makah, believed to be one of Crazy Horse's surviving relatives, drove in his buckboard to the Cherry Creek ration point to retrieve rations for his family. After arriving, Makah complained to the workers distributing the rations he was tired of seeing his people getting shorted on their ration allotments. He further warned he was going to go to Washington, D.C., to expose corruption on the reservation and request officials there take control of the situation. On Makah's return to Bear Creek, four masked white men shot him six times in the chest and he died at a place known as Rudy Creek on January 19, 1918, without his murderers ever being convicted of the crime and apparently never even being charged.[62]

Trimbach also left unexplained how Douglas Durham never provided the FBI information as to a single instance of any serious crimes committed by AIM members. For 18 months, Durham had virtually unlimited access to AIM files, and more importantly, its leadership. Yet, it is not disclosed whether a single indictment against any AIM personnel was ever issued based on information provided by Durham. Likewise, Steve Hendricks noted: "Since the 'Trail of Broken Treaties,' the FBI had cultivated moles inside both AIM and the Oglala Civil Rights Organization, and the moles kept the Bureau informed of the activists' movements."[63] Nevertheless, even though these informants also failed to provide information linking Means or Banks to any murders such as Anna Mae's, Trimbach and others such as Robert Novak have apparently never felt any qualms about labeling Russell Means, Dennis Banks and others as "false heroes." As a counterpoint to Trimbach's mendacious claims, superb investigative journalist Steve Hendricks pointedly noted: "By giving *carte blanche* to murderers—and to rapists, batterers and thieves—the FBI permitted crime to flourish on Pine Ridge as nowhere else in the country [emphasis in original]."[64]

Endnotes

1 Cook-Lynn, *A Separate Country*, p. 64.
2 Deloria, Jr., *Custer Died for Your Sins*, p. 212.
3 Rosenfeld, *Subversives*, pp. 382-383.
4 Ibid., p. 407.
5 "Lelo," *Newsletter*, March 26, 1973 (St. Paul, Minnesota: Minnesota Historical Society, March 26, 1973).
6 William Rooks, untitled document inviting Pine Ridge residents to watch a film strip entitled "An Overview of Our World," (St. Paul, Minnesota: Minnesota Historical Society, undated).
7 Richard LaCourse, *The FBI's 'Racial Intelligence' and the American Indian Militants*, (St. Paul, Minnesota: Historical Society: undated essay), p. 3.
8 Rosenfeld, *Subversives*, pp. 212-213.
9 Ibid., pp. 17-18.
10 Hendricks, *The Unquiet Grave*, pp. 137-141.
11 Trimbach, *American Indian Mafia*, pp. 309-310.
12 Ibid., p. 310.
13 Limerick, *The Legacy of Conquest*, p. 18.
14 Fleisher, *The Bear River Massacre*, p. 178.
15 Banks and Erdoes, *Ojibwa Warrior*, pp. 294-295.
16 Scott Burgwin, Affidavit dated March 31, 1973, (St. Paul, Minnesota: Minnesota Historical Society, March 31, 1973).
17 Eckert, *That Dark and Bloody River*, p. xvi.
18 Slotkin, *Gunfighter Nation*, p. 223.
19 Ibid., p. 446.
20 Trimbach, *American Indian Mafia*, p. 148.
21 "Akwesasne Notes" April 23, 1973.
22 Slotkin, *Gunfighter Nation*, *passim*.
23 Crow Dog, *Lakota Woman*, p. 143.
24 Morgan, *Lions of the West*, p. xx.
25 Trimbach, *American Indian Mafia*, p. 558.
26 Beck, *Columns of Vengeance*, *passim*.
27 Cook-Lynn, *Anti-Indianism in Modern America*, p. 163.
28 Beck, *Columns of Vengeance*, p. 142.
29 Ibid., p. 149.
30 Ibid., p. 109.
31 Ibid., p. 211.
32 Ibid., p. 126.
33 Ibid., p. 237.

34 Trimbach, *American Indian Mafia*, p. 559.
35 Matson, *Crazy Horse: The Lakota Warrior's Life and Legacy*, p. 149.
36 Richardson, *Wounded Knee*, p. 311.
37 Smith, *Moon of Popping Trees*, p. 179.
38 Richardson, *Wounded Knee*, p. 262.
39 Ian Frazier, *Great Plains*, New York, Picador, 1989, p. 23.
40 Beck, *Columns of Vengeance*, p. 173.
41 Richardson, *Wounded Knee*, p. 213.
42 Ibid., p. 309.
43 Trimbach, *American Indian Mafia*, p. 51.
44 Ibid., p. 72.
45 Wilson, *The Earth Shall Weep*, p. 248.
46 Connell, *Son of the Morning Star*, p. 332.
47 Paul L. Hedren, Ed. Michael Malone and Richard B. Roeder, "1876 on the Reservations: The Indian Question," *The Great Sioux War: The Best from Montana: The Magazine of Western History*, p. 63.
48 Connell, *Son of the Morning Star*, p. 226. Connell noted, however, that the poem from which this line is taken is unlikely to have actually been written by Sitting Bull.
49 Jackson, *Black Elk*, p. 52.
50 Walter Camp, Interviews with Andrew Good Thunder, Little Hawk, No Flash, Louis Bordeaux (Bloomington, Indiana: Walter Camp Papers, Lilly Library), p. 524, Envelope 90.
51 Sajna, *Crazy Horse*, p. 58.
52 Ibid., p. 38.
53 Greene, *American Carnage*, pp. 58-59.
54 Slotkin, *Regeneration through Violence*, pp. 18-19.
55 Cook-Lynn, *A Separate Country*. Cook-Lynn called Trimbach's *American Indian Mafia*: "…a 652-page diatribe by a former FBI agent" and further argued: "… it provides legitimacy for the actions of the federal government which was attempting to carry on its two hundred years of foreign hegemony on this poverty-stricken reservation of the Oglala Sioux," p. 204, footnote 1 under Chapter 11.
56 Drinnon, *Facing West*, p. 337.
57 Slotkin, *Fatal Environment*, p. 40.
58 Ibid., p. 36.
59 Fleisher, *The Bear River Massacre*, p. 202. It is unclear on what source Fleisher's comment was based. Although Fleisher claimed Churchill did not comment on the Bear River Massacre, as noted, he did state that 500 Shoshones were slaughtered at the Bear River Massacre. Churchill, "Like Sand in the Wind: The Making of an American Indian Diaspora in the United States," *Since Predator Came*, p. 175.
60 Drinnon, *Facing West*, p. vii.
61 Ibid., p. viii.
62 Matson, *Crazy Horse: The Lakota Warrior's Life and Legacy*, p. 160.

63 Hendricks, *The Unquiet Grave*, p. 63. Nevertheless, Hendricks queried during a conversation with Means, "'Did AIM kill Anna Mae?'" Means answered: "'Anna Mae is a victim of the war between the FBI and AIM. In war, strange things happen, whether it's My Lai or friendly fire. There are victims of war who are totally innocent, and that's what Anna Mae was.'" Hendricks wrote after this conversation he believed: "This statement…was probably true, but it also had the echo of a troubled conscience." p. 356.

64 Ibid., p. 332.

CHAPTER 22

Black Elk

An Unrecognized Symbol of Cultural Survival

He's a funny old Man.
Flying Hawk's description of Black Elk
Joe Jackson, *Black Elk*[1]

Nowhere else in Indian history does the phrase "...the man behind the curtain" from the *Wizard of Oz* more aptly apply than in the case of Lakota holy man Nicholas Black Elk. John Neihardt's *Black Elk Speaks* serves as a focal point in the debate over who exactly this enigmatic man was and essentially presents Black Elk as America's "archetypical Indian" holy man completely engrossed in traditional Lakota spirituality. While Neihardt does not explore the question of Black Elk's Catholicism, in *Fools Crow,* Thomas Mails quoted Frank Fools Crow as stating: "...I want to point out...that my uncle Black Elk, became a Roman Catholic in 1904, and I am certain his first name, Nicholas, was given to him at that time." Fools Crow also explained he "...was very interested in the teachings of the Roman Catholic Church, and spent many hours talking to the priests about it...Black Elk told me that he had decided the Sioux religious way of life was pretty much the same as that of Christian churches."[2] Mails further related Fools Crow was surprised to learn the book *Black Elk Speaks* even existed.[3]

Nevertheless, it is vital to an understanding of the historical Black Elk to puncture through several layers of myth to arrive at anywhere close to a picture of the real man. As a starting point for that analysis, Damian Costello explained: "More than fifty years after Nicholas Black Elk's death, modern academics struggle to understand Black Elk's conversion to Catholicism and its relationship to Lakota tradition." Costello further commented that: "[Raymond] Demallie wrote in 1984 that 'Black Elk's Catholicism represents the biggest gap in our understanding of him as a whole human being.' This 'gap' assumes that there is a division between Christianity and Native American identity."[4] Likewise, the gap existing in virtually any discussion of Indian religion is the gap between the description of it as virtually an otherworldly phenomenon and the reality of Lakota religion as both a political and religious force. Similarly, Costello contended Neihardt's depiction of Black Elk in *Black Elk Speaks* was Neihardt's artistic interpretation of his interviews with the holy man and were heavily influenced by Neihardt's Social Darwinist views.[5]

Then again, there is a gap in Holler's analysis of Black Elk's view of Indians as one of or the "Lost Tribe[s] of Israel." If the Exodus from Egypt is viewed as the pivotal episode in the Old Testament story of the Israelites, then there would seem to be a belief in a future liberation of the Lakota. Some might suggest the "Ghost Dance" was intended to be a predicate to this future glorious time. One explanation for this lack may be a belief the Lakota are already living in the Promised Land—the Black Hills region of South Dakota. As Joe Jackson argued: "Like another culture that had considered themselves God's Chosen People, they'd reached their Promised Land."[6] Nevertheless, what makes Holler's view of Black Elk fascinating, and ultimately instructive, is his description of Black Elk as forward-thinking. In contrast Hancock, like the more prominent writer John Neihardt, viewed Black Elk with nostalgia and as essentially a relic of a bygone era. Holler energetically urged readers to "disentangle" their views of Black Elk as a defeated old man and consider him as leading his people into the future, even one that was heavily constrained by the dominant white culture.[7]

The failure to explore Black Elk's Catholicism and the usual corresponding promotion of Black Elk as an archetype is to reinforce the notion "The only true Indian [is] a vanishing Indian."[8] Neihardt's *Black Elk Speaks* is the encapsulation of a comment from part of a letter quoted in *Shades of Hiawatha*: "'The Indian is not to be forgotten, I hope, because Mr. Wannamaker is going to erect a statue of him.'"[9] Unfortunately, more contemporary writers like Hancock and Trimbach, whose writing has been reviewed above, and to some extent Neihardt, present virtually ahistorical, i.e., lacking in historical perspective, and simplistic accounts of Black Elk and the lives of other Lakota. In contrast, Holler argued Black Elk was a "complex and captivating"[10] figure who was affected by "…rapid and forced cultural change."[11] Costello asserted the Lakota saw Black Elk's Christianity as: "…a typical manifestation of Lakota culture of the early reservation period."[12]

And, while John (Fire) Lame Deer provided a portrait of Black Elk as: "…[a] buffoon by characterizing him as a 'catechism teacher' and 'cigar store Indian,'"[13] Holler further contended: "…it is a giant step in the right direction to see Black Elk as the creative religious thinker that he really was, rather than as a pitiful old man consumed with a longing for a past that never was."[14] Pursuing that line of thought even further, Holler's portrayal of Black Elk, from a strictly intellectual or historical perspective, was: "…infinitely more interesting than Neihardt's portrayal or the romantic stereotype."[15] Those recent superficial portrayals of Indians such as Black Elk hearken back to the works of George Catlin, who created: "…the image—[of] the noble, happy, pristine, uncontaminated Indian [which] had always been a great deal easier to deal with than the diverse and complicated human beings who had come to be known as Indians."[16] It is a challenge to those who desire to interact with Indians to overcome the obstacles created by Catlin's and others' over-romanticized version of these real human people.

Perhaps what is most challenging for entering the debate about Black Elk's Catholicism is it turns the question of Indian savagery on its head. Hancock uninhibitedly described his peculiar story of how he tore off a piece of Black Elk's cabin in his act of vandalism and then proceeded to place it in a "wedge between branches." During this process, Hancock paid homage with his own imagination to Lakota spirits or deities in his self-conjured "ceremony" which included, of course, a "conversation" with Black Elk (although Kevin did all the talking).[17] As noted, at a later juncture which may or may not be related to his image of Black Elk, Hancock felt "…the warrior spirit within me" and he let out "…a mighty Lakota war cry." He added: "After five or six full-throttle war cries, I stop and listen to my own sounds reverberate and die out."[18]

The juxtaposition of Hancock's fevered imagination with Black Elk's sophisticated approach to the Catholic faith in Lakota culture could not create more of a stark contrast. Many scholars who have given a great deal of thought to Black Elk's circumstances concluded he tried to harness the Catholic faith to help his people adapt to the power of white society overwhelming the Lakota. Hancock, on the other hand, appeared to have viewed his spiritual journey to Pine Ridge as: "…a new beginning for [him as] someone who cannot cope with the complexities and restrictions of industrial civilization."[19] In an odd way, both Black Elk and Hancock were similar in that each was attempting to cope with white society.

It is difficult to overstate how the infusion of Western spiritual traditions created a murky prism through which to view even contemporary Lakota culture, much less trying to reconstruct Black Elk's religious and/or spiritual philosophy. While Black Elk appeared to have been a sincere convert to the Catholic faith, the purpose for embracing this tradition for him and Lakota society as a whole could certainly have had multiple objectives. Holler noted: "…the Lakota were in effect driven to the Christian churches as the only available alternative for religious community."[20] An additional factor to consider was the "'shattering emotional blow'" administered to the Lakota by the banning of the Sun Dance. Clearly this prohibition was another step in the process of whites attempting to foist assimilation upon the Lakota, but Holler explained that this aggressive approach to cultural change was "…largely responsible for the widespread disintegration of Dakota society."[21] If Black Elk embraced Catholicism as a means to help provide structure to enable his Lakota people to cope with this disintegration, it is at a minimum understandable, and is for the open-minded admirable.

While history books are replete with dramatic and not so dramatic battles between whites and Indians, particularly the Battle of the Little Big Horn, the lesser known government/missionary campaign to eliminate traditional Indian ceremonies and the roles of medicine and holy men and women had significantly more far-reaching consequences on Indian culture. Historian Joe Jackson noted:

> This war on identity would be the most protracted experiment in social engineering ever conducted in American history, a multigenerational attempt to 'kill the Indian in the Indian' for his own good—a failed endeavor to replace the soul of one people with another, the ramifications of which still resonate today.[22]

Specifically, in the instance of the Lakota, the significance of the influence of Catholic (and other) missionaries gets lost in the virtually all-encompassing symbols of Wounded Knee I and II. This is particularly ironic in that many commentators, as pointed out by McMurtry, have noted the "Ghost Dance" and associated beliefs claimed to be the "cause" of the massacre are similar to the type of Christian beliefs that point to the promised return of the Messiah at the end of history. Likewise, while "Big Foot" was considered the leader of the slaughtered Minneconjous, and Russell Means and Dennis Banks were thought to be the leaders of Wounded Knee II, little thought is given to the significant leadership role of Black Elk as a cohesive force in Lakota culture. Many seemed content to relegate Black Elk to a role as some hoary symbol of the past, perhaps as a "noble savage."

The debate over the legitimacy of Black Elk's devotion to Catholicism can be viewed as an encouraging installment in the push to erase the narrative of Indians as uncomprehending, superstitious savages incapable of sophisticated views of the world around them. It is a reminder the Lakota have a long history of developing strategies—some successful and some not—of coping with the onslaught of white settlement and its corresponding seizure of Lakota territory. It further illustrates, much like the conflict between various Lakota factions during the 1973 "occupation," there is no monolithic "Indian" view of situations, even within people of the same tribe or nation, much less Indians in the United States as a group. This, of course, is nothing new. In the case of Lakota scouts leading Sully's troops through the Badlands in 1864 in search of the larger Lakota nation, these men at times encouraged the Lakota to keep fighting. And while it is difficult to understand, at other times the scouts brutally killed Indians who became prisoners. Paul Beck explained the actions of these scouts was: "…an example of the deep divisions and conflicts the warfare had caused for the entire Sioux nation."[23] Earlier, at the Battle of Kildeer Mountain, Lakota warriors taunted the mixed-blood and full-blood scouts who accompanied the federal troops and "'abused them terribly.'"[24]

ENDNOTES

1. Jackson, *Black Elk*, p. 11.
2. Mails, *Fools Crow*, p. 45.
3. Ibid., p. 5.
4. Costello, *Black Elk*, p. 51.
5. Ibid., p. 8.
6. Jackson, *Black Elk*, p. 31.
7. Holler, *Black Elk's Religion*, p. xiii.
8. Alan Trachtenberg, *Shades of Hiawatha: Staging Indians, Making Americans, 1880-1930* (New York: Hill & Wang, A Division of Farrar, Straus, & Giroux, 2004), p. 176.
9. Ibid., p. 246.
10. Holler, *Black Elk's Religion*, p. 1.
11. Ibid., p. xix.
12. Costello, *Black Elk*, p. 70.
13. Holler, *Black Elk's Religion*, p. 3.
14. Ibid., p. 38.
15. Ibid., p. 22.
16. Limerick, *The Legacy of Conquest*, p. 185.
17. Hancock, *Not for Sale*, pp. 296-299.
18. Ibid., p. 369.
19. Nathanson, *Over the Rainbow*, p. 236.
20. Holler, *Black Elk's Religion*, p. 132.
21. Ibid., p. 133. Holler appeared to use the names Dakota and Lakota interchangeably.
22. Jackson, *Black Elk*, p. 7.
23. Beck, *Columns of Vengeance*, p. 234.
24. Ibid., p. 212.

Epilogue

SuAnne Big Crow
The "Shooting Star" of Pine Ridge: Part II

Maybe it was a good thing that they would not let us Indians keep that land. Think what would have been missed: the motels with their neon signs, the pawn shops, the Rock Hunter's Paradise, the Horned Trophies Taxidermist Studio, the giftie shoppies, the Genuine Indian Crafts Center with its beadwork from Taiwan and Hong Kong, the Sitting Bull Cave—electronically lighted for your convenience… If that land belonged to us there would be nothing here, only trees, grass and some animals running free. All that *real estate would be going to waste* [emphasis in original].

John (Fire) Lame Deer, *Lame Deer-Seeker of Visions* [1]

In *The New Trail of Tears*, journalist and commentator Naomi Schaefer Riley shared with the unwashed and unwary proponents of socialism and its recipients of unearned government largesse her belief: "The truth of the matter is that Dawes was right - *private property is an almost magical force* [emphasis and punctuation as in original]."[2] She argued throughout her peppy travelogue that the lack of private property ownership is the major component of the economic woes of reservation Indians. Riley was not the first, and most likely will not be the last, to promote this ill-conceived and apparently hypnotic mantra. In the 1830s, James Hall, known as "Judge" Hall, proposed that the military force Indians to live in villages where they would be "…taught to understand the importance of private property."[3] The Dawes Act of 1887 was legislation which placed a gloss of legitimacy around the idea of turning communal Indian property into individual plots of land through the process known as allotment. Ultimately, the Dawes Act taught the Indians they could be separated from their land without the whites firing a single shot at them in anger. Riley's suggestions for how to cure the ills of Indians is reminiscent of the situation of the doctor who prescribed to a man attacked by a bear to pour: "'…a mixture of salt, red pepper, and vinegar as an antiseptic upon [the patient's] exposed brain.'"[4] One astute critic of Riley's "ahistorical" book stated:

Unsurprisingly, Riley hearkens back to the allotment policies enshrined in the Dawes Act, a federal program in the 19th century that mandated the confiscation of Indian reservations by the federal government followed by the liquidation of those assets at pennies on the dollar of their market value and their public sale to non-Indians on the cheap. It was a state sponsored land grab of unprecedented proportions with negative effects on Indians still felt to this day. What a model for a property rights advocate.[5]

When considering Riley's idea to just turn poverty-stricken Indian reservations into parcels of land up for grabs for earnest capitalists, those familiar with Indian history are reminded of the tenure of Thomas Morgan, Commissioner of Indian Affairs from June 10, 1889, to April 17, 1893. It was said of Morgan that: "…the man who presided over the first stages of the social experiment to determine the Indians' fate admitted he did not understand them."[6] Throughout the 198 pages of her Reagan-era type fantasy, Riley preached that if only given a chance, free market forces could turn SuAnne's hometown of Pine Ridge into a New York suburb like the one from which Riley hails. According to Riley, all the residents of that remote South Dakota region need to do is shed their lazy reliance on the unearned gifts provided by the near-socialistic United States government.

Riley's book appears to be an expansion of the diatribe of James Watt, Reagan's first Secretary of the Interior and ultimate overseer of the Bureau of Indian Affairs. Watt complained in 1983: "If you want an example of the failure of socialism, don't go to Russia. Come to America and go to the Indian reservations.'" As if anticipating people like Riley would echo Watt, Patricia Limerick explained: "Bewildering as it was, Watt's remark was also a dazzling demonstration of the power of ideology to overrule an understanding of history."[7] Watt's comment also did not take into account the long history of private business people taking advantage of Indians, such as those outlined in Hank Adams' report on the Sisseton-Wahpeton tribe. Amazingly, Riley managed to appropriate the tired and stilted arguments of Bordewich's *Killing the White Man's Indian* and make them even more irrelevant to the actual circumstances of Indians living in the United States today. As Robert Wintour wrote in 1635, which Riley updated in contemporary terms: "Where can witt and worth be more truly exprest then in conquering nations to enrich them, subduing people to make them men, subjecting wild savages to make them free, taking nothing from them but barbarous nakednes and in counterchange adorning them with decent civility [spelling as in source]?"[8]

Never mind the 500-plus-year history of Indian people combatting the forces of colonialism and Westward Expansion that have often crushed the spirits of these misunderstood folks, many of whom were nomadic, and ultimately horse riding, and forcing them onto the bite-sized pieces of unwalled prisons called reservations. Riley's lofty sermon on the benevolent fruits of capitalism is her nifty and subtle reminder to Indians that at the end of the day, the inescapable conclusion they must face is that the problem for Indians is that they *are* Indians. Riley's beliefs are similar to the odd explanation in the 1928 Meriam Report apparently indicating the Dawes Act was the real culprit behind poor reservation conditions. The report noted: "The actual poverty of the Indians is, as a matter of fact, much greater than figures regarding the value of their property would seem to indicate because the property is often not effectively used for the production of income."[9]

Riley moaned Indians such as those living in Wounded Knee Village on the Pine Ridge Reservation participate in: "…[a] rhythm of life…surprisingly dependent on the timing of government subsidies."[10] Further, Riley unblinkingly and incredulously suggested: "It's not the history of forced assimilation, war, and mass murder that have left the American Indians in a deplorable state; it's the federal government's policies today."[11] Riley forgot this is similar to William T. Sherman's advocating during the wars against the Plains Indians in the 1870s for replacing the wild buffalo with herds of docile cattle and: "'…substituting for the useless Indians the intelligent owners of productive farms and cattle ranches.'" Sherman was the government agent recommending his recipe for solving the "Indian Problem,"[12] which still exists in large part today—especially for Indians trying to revitalize traditional cultures while living in a modern world.

General Phil Sheridan, Sherman's obedient disciple, observed the Indians, those "'…wasteful and hostile occupants'" of lands useful for agriculture, containing valuable minerals, etc., were "'…forced upon reservations under the supervision of the government.'" As a consequence, in his view, Indian children came: "'…under instruction in a better life than the vagabond existence to which they were born.'" Likewise, the vast area: "'…over which the wild and irresponsible tribes once wandered, [was] redeemed from idle waste to become a home for millions of progressive people.'"[13] The simple and dominant concept in vogue at the end of the 19th century was Indians must either conform to the expectations of white culture, or, as stated by one Indian Commissioner, "'be crushed by it.'"[14] Limerick explained that George Catlin, the early 19th century painter, believed Indians: "…simply could not survive, unadapted, in the modern world. In Catlin and his emotional descendants, the depth of one's concern for Indians correlated to the intensity of one's desire to remake them according to one's own standards of improvement."[15]

Fortunately, for those who desire an optimistic outlook for the survival of Lakota culture, it is almost a certainty that what is colloquially known as the "death of the dream" speech at the end of *Black Elk Speaks* was never uttered by him.[16] However, it has been repeated many times as an authentic statement of Black Elk indicating more or less his belief in the inevitable disappearance of the Lakota culture. Thus, Riley was not the first, nor anywhere close to the most prominent, figure to imply the ultimate fate of Indians was to vanish as an independent culture through either attrition or being absorbed into white culture. Of course, some believe Indians simply lacked or lack the fortitude to be successful in white society. In a letter to Peter Collinson dated May 9, 1753, Benjamin Franklin offered a harsh assessment of Indians' perceived lack of industriousness: "The proneness of human Nature to a life of ease, of freedom from care and labour appears strongly in the little success that has hitherto attended every attempt to civilize our American Indians [spelling as in source]."[17] And, in the second half of her book, Riley, oddly for a Jewish person, perhaps unintentionally revealed her true intentions when she proclaimed: "Saint Labre [a Catholic school in Montana] exposes its students to life off the reservation."[18]

There is nothing in that comment indicating Riley was interested in finding real answers to challenges faced by Indians living on reservations. Riley noted without hesitation the other mission besides education of Saint Labre was: "To proclaim the Gospel of Jesus Christ according to the Catholic Tradition by providing quality education which celebrates our Catholic faith and embraces Native American cultures"[19] etc. Although there have been many advances in technology since 1492, Riley's comments indicated the mission of Europeans in what is now North America has not changed at all—total domination of Indians. There is little acknowledgment that Catholics and other Western religions have had presences on Indian reservations for decades. Riley also did not make any mention of the now well-known issues regarding the abuse of Indian children at Catholic boarding schools.

Riley's ode to free enterprise and how it will finally lift Indians out of poverty ignored, as do most proponents of this viewpoint, one of the dirty little secrets of capitalism as outlined by Kevin Phillips in *Wealth and Democracy*. Phillips, a former speech writer for Richard Nixon, basically argued all wealth creation is the result of government policy.[20] Riley admitted as much without seemingly being aware she had done so, at least in one example. She noted Senator Claire McCaskill of Missouri protested Boeing Aircraft Company was unfairly pushed out of receiving federal contracts by Alaskan native corporations. In contradiction to her major premise that Indian people should develop economic programs, rather than praising the initiative of these hardy folks, Riley explained without elaboration: "Certainly non-Native companies like Boeing [headquartered in Missouri] have complained that they're losing federal contracts to companies that are hardly disadvantaged [even if the ancestors of the people at the helm were historically subject to discrimination]."[21] As a corollary to this proposition, the lack of government provision of infrastructure ensures the possibility of meaningful economic growth is virtually nonexistent. In the case of SuAnne's hometown of Pine Ridge, no major highway or rail line exists to provide a means of shipping goods even if they were produced there.

Yet, Riley careens at warp speed into explaining the invincible power of the free market to solve all the woes of those unique people she barely restrains herself from labeling shiftless reservation Indians. Her essay called to mind, among other things, Lewis Lapham's transcendent essay published in *Harper's* magazine prior to the invasion of Iraq, in October 2002—"The Road to Babylon." Lapham's essay, which included many precise observations, condemned the proponents of that ill-fated "preemptive" fiasco for only considering the logistics of the enterprise and failing to contemplate its essential morality. The question Lapham raised was how could we justify the invasion of Iraq when it "had done [the United States] no demonstratable harm."[22] Riley's attempt at explaining the morality of imposing Western values on Indians relied on the obnoxious but tried-and-true mantra that Indians got what they deserved and bemoaned the fact American school children "…rarely hear about the brutalities that Indians committed against white settlers."[23] What she neglected to mention, among many things, is that Indians are usually mentioned in the context of United States history, if at all, only as props in the mythical Thanksgiving story so effortlessly spouted every November.

Contrary to the enthusiastic proponents of capitalism such as Riley (and Kevin Hancock), optimism about turning the Great Plains region into a bastion of capitalistic success is not universal. In fact, some researchers are singularly pessimistic about the prospect of economic growth for the region not only for Indians, but for anyone. Rutgers researchers Frank and Deborah Popper calculated the 140,000 square miles of the Great Plains contained a total non-Indian population of approximately 400,000 (a lower population density than existed in many parts of North America at the time of Columbus' arrival). The Poppers argued any type of economic growth was impossible since the time the land was seized from the Indians in the 19th century. Interestingly, the Poppers cited Ward Churchill as a source for arguing the area could not be supported "'[w]ithout considerable federal subsidy.'" The Poppers, in stark contrast to Riley and spiritual seeker Hancock, argued the entire region should be abandoned and bison should once again be allowed to roam freely.[24]

What the "Indians got what they deserved" historians, or whatever people like Riley fancy themselves to be, failed to mention is that white slaughters continued long after Indians were capable of even remotely organizing even small-scale attacks on *anyone*. Riley did not condescend to explain, for example, why a federal force wiped out "Big Foot's" followers on December 29, 1890, when to borrow a phrase from Lapham, they "had done it no demonstrable harm." Riley also did not note, unlike Mike Sajna and Renée Sansom Flood, that in many cases "Indian raids" on white settlers in the 18th century were executed by renegade whites, in what some might now label "false flag" operations. Curiously enough, the situation created by these "false flag" practitioners was precarious enough in some frontier settings that one leader in an 1854 editorial in the *Desert News* warned his followers to be wary of: "…numerous and well organized band of white highwaymen, painted and disguised as Indians."[25] Sajna further argued that the accounts of Indian depredations were "usually fictitious."[26]

As such, Riley's work did not take into account Patricia Limerick's advice about putting forth the effort needed to understand the situation of Indians: "The ethnic diversity of Western history asks only that: pay attention to the parts, pay attention to the whole. It is a difficult task, but to bemoan and lament the necessity to include minorities is to engage, finally, in intellectual laziness." And as a useful rebuttal to people like Riley's and Bordewich's various claims of "political correctness," etc., Limerick stated: "The American West was a complicated place for its historical participants; and it is no exercise in 'white guilt' to say that it is—and should be—just as complicated for us today."[27] Nevertheless, Riley languidly summarized what has been loosely labeled the "conventional" view of history as she noted: "Tribes agreed to give up the land they occupied and move to reservations in exchange for payments and other benefits." Whether or not the tribes actually "agreed" to "give up" the land in question has been the subject of what can only be politely labeled considerable debate for decades.

Riley appeared incapable of shifting her view that the annuity payments were and are a form of welfare even though she begrudgingly and specifically admitted these payments were compensation for land. She managed to note, "Often of course these promises weren't kept." This acknowledgment of the failings of the federal government is a setup for the punchline for her biggest joke: "In principle, there's no reason that tribes couldn't have adapted themselves again to a more sedentary life on the reservation, however unjust the reason they'd wound up there in the first place."[28] Perhaps Riley took solace in John Adams' claim: "'I see not how the Indians could have been treated with more equity or humanity than they have been in general in North America.'"[29]

As has been previously noted as a theme throughout this book, it is entirely in line with typical reporting or writing about matters affecting Indians not to solicit their views on the matters at hand or even to refer to books written by Indians. Even if it could be argued that Indian treaties were not obtained by force or coercion, it can be credibly argued it is unlikely Indian leaders understood the ramifications of many, if not all treaties. Mike Signa noted the Ft. Laramie Treaty of 1851 was the: "…first major attempt by Congress to directly interfere in the government of the Plains tribes." Unsurprisingly, problems with the translation of the treaty were downplayed. A. B. Chambers, the editor of the *Missouri Republican*, stated: "At the insistence of some of the Chiefs, portions of it were read several times, for their better understanding. Every effort was made, and successfully too, to give them the full and just import of each article."[30]

Riley would certainly argue she made an effort to engage Indian people in discussions about their economic futures. Yet, the arguments ring hollow in that little is said about the larger issue of preserving Indian culture and heritage. As Alan Trachtenberg forcefully stated in *Shades of Hiawatha*, the critical point often overlooked by scholars is that Indians: "…seemed to matter only in relation to the invading settlers." Trachtenberg outlined this paradigm after analyzing Frederick Jackson Turner's essay "The Significance of the Frontier in American History."[31] Turner promoted the idea that the originating act of becoming an American is becoming an Indian. However, the pioneer/Indian eventually mastered the wilderness and its transformation into territory controlled by these settlers meant the Indians have been moved off the land and the new arrivals have seized and plundered it. In essence, in this world view, the proper sequence of becoming an American is becoming an Indian, and then becoming master of the Indian. Trachtenberg astutely registered one of the most salient points in understanding the march of westward conquest—in the forward movement of white civilization, scholars such as Turner flip the script and argue the frontier became for those whites: "'…a military training school, keeping alive the power of resistance to aggression.'" Trachtenberg also noted that in this paradigm: "Indians have become aggressors, an alien force in their own land.'"[32]

Another question related to the one raised by Trachtenberg, unsurprisingly ignored by Riley, and posed by eminent historian Richard Drinnon and noted previously is: "How have we [as white people] become so alienated from ourselves and from the land?"[33] Many Indians and others understandably express frustration over those who are often referred to as "wannabes," "white shamans," etc., i.e. whites who try to appropriate Indian culture; those living in that weird world of imposters. Yet, trying to become an Indian is one tactic used to overcome that sense of alienation which often permeates Western culture. Luther Standing Bear quipped: "'The white man does not understand the Indian for the reason he does not understand America.'" Standing Bear added: "'The roots of the tree of his life have not yet grasped the rock and soil… The man from Europe is still a foreigner and an alien. And he hates the man who questioned his path across the continent.'"[34]

Riley, however, was not troubled by the subtleties of Indian spirituality and how accepting them might alter her single-minded obsession with the secular. Riley seemed to have an inexhaustible zeal for crying out for the exorcism of what she apparently perceived as the demon of federal government socialism. Nonetheless, she expended little of that effort analyzing the *state* of South Dakota's involvement in Pine Ridge affairs. She argued about white-Indian cooperation without providing supporting facts: "If the Indians of South Dakota were to support a charter law, it would probably pass."[35] This seems doubtful, at least based on white-Indian relations in that state throughout the years, as explained in the Ward Churchill chapter. In addition to the examples provided there, the "Pony Congress" of South Dakota passed a law 27 years *before* South Dakota became a state banning Indians from traveling from their reservations without a pass. This same group of lawmakers provided for a militia to protect settlers against "Confederate or Indian attacks."[36] Not an auspicious beginning for those concerned with finding faith that South Dakota has a track record of protecting Indians or promoting their rights. Of course, Indian-despising William Janklow based his mostly successful career in South Dakota politics in part on his palpable disdain of Indians and their culture. As Cook-Lynn wrote: "Anyone who has examined the trajectory of Indian law of the past two centuries knows that states' rights, state governmental and legislative influence, is at the heart of anti-Indian law."[37]

And just as McMurtry deployed the description of a Zulu nation gathering to convey the image of a Lakota gathering, Riley devotes a large chunk of her brief 198 pages to outline the challenges of *Canadian* Indians. Although that applies to this writing to a small degree as well, she specifically stated on her cover jacket, "How Washington is destroying American Indians" (and this book does state in its title it is about North American Indians). Perhaps Riley is a descendant of the renowned explorer Columbus and is a little hazy when it comes to geography. It is a curious phenomenon, at least as exhibited by some of the authors referred to in this book, that their lack of attention to detail suggests they believe telling an accurate description, or even acknowledging their lack of information, of the histories of the Indian nations in the United States is barely worth the effort.

Likewise, dissecting Riley's flippant equating Indian problems to those of black Americans causes her belief system to crash like a tray of overpriced food carried by an overworked waiter in a too-crowded restaurant. Vine Deloria, Jr., explained whites: "…systematically excluded blacks from all programs, policies, social events, and economic schemes. With the Indians the process was simply reversed… Indians were subjected to the most intense pressure to become white." Deloria, Jr., concluded: "The white man forbade the black to enter his own social and economic system and at the same time force-fed the Indian what he was denying the black."[38] Patricia Limerick concluded: "A minority by conquest [Indians] is not the same as minority by immigration [as in the case of imported slaves]."[39] And, as she astutely noted: "Freeing blacks meant freeing them from slavery and slaveholders. If the reformers wanted to free the Indians, from whom did they want to free them?"[40] Consciously or not, Riley also echoed the assumption of German philosopher Max Weber who surmised native people were incapable of rational behavior. In Riley's terms, that would mean she, like Fleisher, is not capable of understanding that some Indians may not want to live like her. Mary Crow Dog explained: "The blacks want what the whites have, which is understandable. They want *in*. We Indians want *out*. That is the main difference [emphasis in original]."[41] Vine Deloria, Jr., recounted the story of Alex Chasing Hawk testifying at a Congressional hearing. In response to the question, "'Just what do you Indians want?'" he replied, "'A leave-us-alone law!'"[42]

Perhaps most telling of all, Riley described a city (in Canada) named Kamloops that: "…has the feel of a middle-class oasis where people have found the right balance of work and play."[43] It is unclear what she considered the "right balance" and who was deciding of what that state of existence consisted. Apparently, this town is occupied by Kamloops Indians, although she did not make this entirely clear. Certainly, Riley envisioned one of the refreshments to be made available at this "middle-class oasis" is rampant materialism. Her description of this earthly paradise is reminiscent of Donald Rumsfeld's use of the word "fabulous" when describing the glories resulting from the invasion of Iraq. Lapham aptly asked, "fabulous for whom?"[44]

If SuAnne's life had not ended with her untimely death, and she chose to attend college, perhaps on a basketball scholarship, what then? Would she have learned about Indian people in contemporary society? Riley herself noted a study by University of Missouri Professor Sarah Shear indicated 87 percent of the time American Indians were "…portrayed…in a pre-1900 context."[45] What sources being studied Riley did not say, but it is not a particularly surprising finding. Nevertheless, Riley's patronizing views can be summarized by Berkhofer's argument that: "…most Whites still conceive of the 'real' Indian as the aborigine he once was, or as they imagine he once was, rather than he is now." Berkhofer also noted: "Indians who remained alive and who resisted adoption of civilization appeared to accept White vices instead of virtues and so became those imperfect creatures, the degraded or reservation Indian."[46] Riley also did not address the previously raised question of logic regarding European resettlement in the Western Hemisphere: "If [the] Christian civilization [of Europe] was so wonderful, why were its inhabitants all trying to settle somewhere else?"[47] A similar way to frame the question would be to ask—if European culture was so superior, why did settlers and explorers so often depend on Indians for their very survival? Yet Riley's writing, as well as that of many other authors, contained the supposition of European superiority over Indian culture.

Given this paradigm has been passed down through generations, perhaps Riley can be forgiven for her desire to impose her version of the "American Way of Life" on what she most certainly viewed as unenlightened people who usually have dark skin. While it is often claimed baseball is the national pastime, it can be argued that attempting to impose some form of Jeffersonian Democracy on these supposedly uninformed and pagan masses is the national obsession. If they can be converted to "Christianity," all the better. These endeavors are much more satisfying if the banner carriers of this new, improved way of life have not had to expend any energy learning even the most basic facts about the cultures they are "saving." This process has been employed since Columbus' arrival in the Western Hemisphere in the 15th century and has continued to the present day.

Before any real outward "progress" is made toward "improving" conditions on Pine Ridge and other reservations, white culture is obligated, as Morton provided with his example some 500 years ago of: "…entering into the lives of the victims of colonial aggression and of sympathizing with how they felt as persons."[48] Frazier's writing about SuAnne provided one example of this framework. According to local legend, the Lady Thorpes, SuAnne's team, went to Lead, South Dakota, for a game in the fall of 1988. The game in Lead was an opportunity for interaction between Indians and whites at a town where unfortunately the Lady Thorpes regularly encountered harassment. On this particular night, before the game, some of the fans were yelling fake-Indian war cries, a "woo-woo-woo" sound. As the Lady Thorpes were lining up and waiting in the hallway outside the locker room leading to the court, the yelling intensified and some of the spectators also spit out "squaw!" or "where's the cheese?" (a reference to Indians lining up to receive government-issued cheese). What followed is the substance of mythology:

> SuAnne came running onto the court dribbling the basketball, with her teammates running behind. On the court, the noise was deafeningly loud. SuAnne went right down the middle; but instead of running a full lap, she suddenly stopped when she got to the center court. Her teammates were taken by surprise, and some bumped into one another. Coach Zimiga at the rear of the line did not know why they had stopped. SuAnne turned to Doni De Cory and tossed her the ball. Then she stepped into the jump-ball circle at center court, in front of the Lead fans. She unbuttoned her warm-up jacket, took it off, draped it over her shoulders, and began to do the Lakota shawl dance. SuAnne knew all the traditional dances—she had competed in many powwows as a little girl—and the dance she chose is a young woman's dance, graceful and modest and show-offy all at the same time. 'I couldn't believe it—she was powwowin' like, "get down!" Doni De Cory recalled. 'And then she started to sing.' SuAnne began to sing in Lakota, swaying back and forth in the jump-ball circle, doing the shawl dance, using her warm-up jacket for a shawl. The crowd went completely silent. 'All that stuff the Lead fans were yelling—it was like she reversed it somehow,' a teammate said. In the sudden quiet, all you could hear was her Lakota song. SuAnne stood up, dropped her jacket, took the ball from Doni De Cory, and ran a lap around the court dribbling expertly fast. The fans began to cheer and applaud. She sprinted to the basket, went up in the air, and laid the ball through the hoop, with the fans cheering loudly now. Of course, Pine Ridge went on to win the game [spelling as in source].

Yet Ian Frazier, in his wonderful book *On the Rez* where this account of SuAnne's life appeared, hedged his bets against the reality of this tale. He stated that even though a newspaper story reported the events as retold above, no one actually remembers SuAnne performing the dance, that she was actually in the eighth grade at the time the event supposedly occurred in Lead, and that the Lady Thorpes lost the game.[49] However, Frazier believed the account of SuAnne's dance captured her pride in being an Indian, her spirit, and reflects the admiration her fellow tribe members had for her.

There is more to the maybe-real, maybe-fictional story of SuAnne's dance than Frazier lets the reader know, or perhaps even he knows. For ultimately, what is SuAnne's story if not of hope, even if it is unfulfilled? And what symbolizes hope in any language or culture better than dancing? Whether it is a nervous prom dance in a high school gym in Any Town, U.S.A., or the desperate symbol of the longings of a besieged people in 19th-century South Dakota, dancing is a symbol of hope for better things to come. As stated in Matson's *Crazy Horse—the Lakota Warrior's Life and Legacy*: "Although most of us did not believe in the powers of the Ghost Dance, we agreed with what it was trying to accomplish. We wanted the nightmare of what the white people were doing to our people and our way of life to end." Adding an even more somber note, Matson added: "The dance had given some of our people hope. Echoing Black Elk, the [Wounded Knee] massacre killed that hope for many of them."[50]

Frazier also left unanswered the question to be asked by this reported mini-drama—symbolic or not—is the sole function of Indians, even "assimilated" ones, to prove to whites they are harmless? Better yet, to serve as curiosities and entertainment? As sincerely supportive of Indians and Indian culture as Frazier appeared to be, he did not note the lesson suggested by SuAnne's dance is that at times Indians are safest, despite the gains made by Indian "activism," when they serve as animated "cigar store Indians." Louise Barnett explained in *Touched by Fire,* the insightful biography of Custer and events on the 19th-century Plains frequently previously cited herein, that as trade and dependence with white culture grew, Indians increasingly danced more for spectators and less for reasons "intrinsic to their culture."[51] If conventional accounts of the causes of the Wounded Knee Massacre are to be believed (which they shouldn't), even "dancing" can be hazardous to Indians' health. Likewise, what device can Indians not as talented and charismatic as SuAnne use to deflect hostility and harassment? As Raymond Yellow Thunder discovered in the waning hours of his life as it seeped out of him, even in contemporary times simply being an Indian can be hazardous and even fatal.

It is fair to ask how many current authors, historians, anthropologists, and especially "religious" thinkers follow Morton's example of perceiving: "…at its inception the stereotype of the treacherous savage and reject[ing] it out of hand." Morton proceeded one step further and: "…asserted the superior humanity of the Indians and then went dangerously far toward establishing that claim by living among them in amity." Additionally: "As a living example he undermined, just as they were establishing it, the colonizers' notion of the treacherous savage and their need to see themselves as a tightly knit armed band of Christians perched on the edge of hostile territory." As a reward for what might now be labeled promoting diversity, the "Christian" magistrates of 1631 New England had Morton's house: "…burnt downe to the ground in the sight of the Indians." Although these outstanding religious leaders claimed this harsh act was executed for the: "…many wrongs hee [Morton] hath done them [the Indians] from tyme to tyme,'" Drinnon argued it was for the "…many *rights* he had done from time to time [emphasis and spelling as in source]."[52]

Although many consider themselves advocates of "modern" or "new" thinking, in essence Riley's arguments are nothing more than reformulations of time-worn and crusty rationalizations. She proposed a slick combination of the "survival of the fittest" motifs and some mantras seeping up through the writings of James Fenimore Cooper. In *The Last of the Mohicans,* as Slotkin noted, the race tension between whites and Indians is resolved by the: "…death of the mediating figures and the 'vanishing' of the Indian." In *The Prairie,* written after *The Last of the Mohicans,* it is the elimination of the lesser developed whites, i.e, "the primitive enemy," although the squatters are only "*partly* exterminated [emphasis in original]."[53] If extrapolated to Riley's worldview, these undesirables would be incapable of functioning in her "capitalistic" paradise since they would be incapable of joining those anointed as the "fittest." And, as Slotkin also noted, in terms of what might serve as what modern people believe is representative of all Indian nations: "The Great Plains are represented as so arid and intractable to agricultural development that they constitute a permanent barrier to the continuation of the frontier [Interestingly, as noted previously, contemporary researchers such as the Poppers have essentially concluded just that]." This might explain why individuals such as Kevin Hancock visit places like Pine Ridge to try to find Indian culture frozen in some type of time warp with buffalo hunters and Tipi dwellers. But, what Slotkin somewhat ambiguously proposes, and a concept with which the Poppers apparently agree, is that: "…it is nature that determines the social fate of the region."[54]

Riley hinted at but did not specifically state her unspoken premise—the one that has led to one foreign policy fiasco after another from Vietnam to Iraq—darker-skinned people are simply incapable of self-government. In the early 20th century, Senator Henry Cabot Lodge, Jr., judged the Filipinos as having "'utter unfitness' for self-government." Similarly, like his grandfather six decades earlier, Ambassador Henry Cabot Lodge was "congenitally unprepared" to believe the Vietnamese were capable of self-government. In 1966, General Taylor added: "It is obviously true that the Vietnamese are not today ready for self-government."[55] While Riley did not explicitly argue this point, her conclusions about what needs to be done to assist Indians are most certainly a continuation of this paradigm and ironically the paradigm of the interfering Washington, D.C., crowd of which she complains.

What accounts for these naïve and ultimately futile attempts to conform the rest of the world into a vision of the world seemingly concocted during a drunken binge in Georgetown bars and recorded on official versions of cocktail napkins? Drinnon warned that not only does the rest of the world need protection from our adolescent longings to create worldwide conformity, but we need protection from our own innocence. Citing the narrator from Graham Greene's *The Quiet American*, Drinnon related that: "…innocence 'always calls mutely for protection when we would be so much wiser to guard ourselves against it; innocence is like a dumb leper who has lost his bell, wandering the world, meaning no harm.'"[56] The salient question to be considered is what does protecting ourselves from our own innocence ultimately mean?

Riley's attitude also incorporated the noxious fumes emanating from Richard Pratt's foul ode to genocide and used in the heading to the chapter on the "Lost Bird": "Kill the Indian, and save the man."[57] Pratt's attitude, of course, is itself based on the notion of Indians' predisposition to savagery. As Slotkin noted: "The present forms in which the myths appear embody not only the solutions to past problems and conflicts; they contain the questions as well, and they reflect the conflicts of thought and feelings and actions that were the mythmakers' original concern."[58] It is a fair conclusion to state the "mythmakers' original concern" was to justify the conquest of Indian territory, primarily through the argument the soon-to-be-vanquished Indians never really occupied the territory in question. Since they were non-Christian and less-than-human savages, their possession didn't really count anyway. And if the promoters of these arguments were not wholly convinced of their veracity, they can numb their consciences and take comfort when contemplating the extent of the slaughter of Indians. After all, those who question the morality of Westward Expansion must be informed their concerns are due to the "…overwhelming sense that political correctness pervades our conversation about American Indians."[59]

Whether or not past injustices to Indians can ever be rectified remains to be seen. What form that reparation or reparations should take is not a question easily answered and should not be answered without significant input from the Indians themselves. Nonetheless, Slotkin provided a lens through which myths about Indians should be viewed: "If we can understand when and how in history the rules of the game originated, what real human concerns and social relationships the rules conceal or distort and what the historical consequences of playing the game have been, we may be able to respond more intelligently the next time an infantry captain or a president invokes [a myth]."[60]

As *The New Trail of Tears* stumbled to its brittle conclusion, Riley quoted a psychologist, Joni Renberger, as having argued: "'The idea of forgiveness is unheard of for some people'…which is unfortunate because 'hanging on to the anger about the white man does no good, and it perpetuates a lot of the issues affecting Indians.'"[61] This statement is as outrageous and absurd as Trimbach's claim the "false heroes of AIM" were behind the chaos and poverty existing on Pine Ridge. Of course, Riley, who is Jewish, apparently has not considered the implications of asking Jewish people to just forget about the Holocaust. Neither Riley nor Trimbach cite any valid empirical evidence to support the suggestion anger at the "white man" or the "worship of the false heroes of AIM" are the main reason, or even *a* reason, for the poverty and chaos existing in many Indian communities. On Pine Ridge, at least, if the question of poverty is a focus, it is difficult to imagine anger or any other emotion is a greater cause of absence of economic growth than the lack of a manufacturing base or reliable ground transportation. As one Pine Ridge citizen stated, all the roads on Pine Ridge "lead out."[62] The amount of nonsense spewed out by people like Trimbach, Riley and others who think they have the answers to the challenges facing Indians in the United States is truly astonishing. They do not seem to recognize: "No acid ever worked more mechanically on a vegetable fibre than the white man acted on the Indians. As the line of American settlements approached, the nearest Indian tribes withered away."[63]

Reinforcing the urge to advise Indians to "forget" past slaughters, thefts, and cruelty inflicted upon them is what historian George F. Kennan cited was a special weakness in Americans' lack of ability to clearly see themselves. He explained, as noted, the American psyche contained a: "…certain moralistic and legalistic posturing on our part—a desire to appear, particularly to ourselves, as more wise and noble than we really were."[64] Adding to this elixir are the comments of historians such as Rex Alan Smith who thoughtlessly and speciously advised concerning events such as Wounded Knee: "…it is time we stopped concerning ourselves with the blame anyhow."[65] Perhaps underwriting this mindset is the notion Indians were and still are savages who got what they deserved. Plains Indian Emma LaRoque commented: "Like most children in North America, I grew up with comic books and movies, which is to say, I grew up with the glorified white man locked in moral [sic] combat against the much dehumanized 'Indian.'" She added: "…the cowboys were not only innocent victims of the irrational violence of bloodthirsty savages, but always the winners."[66]

Further, Riley's elixir for healing the emotional scars of Indians, i.e. to just forget about them, is nothing new. Fergus Bordewich, who Riley heavily relied on for intellectual structure in her treatise, in *Killing the White Man's Indian*, suggested: "…historical guilt, like romanticism or mindless pity is a narrow and cloudy lens through which to view present day realities, including that of Native Americans." Even though it is undeniable that over the decades a tsunami of acts of murder, theft, and other cruelties were perpetrated against Indians, or at least allowed to be perpetrated, Bordewich claimed: "Indian policy has embodied the nation's unending struggle to apply moral standards to the conduct of public policy."[67] Bordewich, quoting Charles Wilkinson, further stated: "'For all its many flaws, the policy of the United States toward its native people is one of the most progressive of any nation.'"[68]

Likewise, there may be some truth in the suggestion that welfare systems inhibit self-reliance. However, claiming that government assistance for such places as Pine Ridge is indeed welfare is deceptive in that it is believed the provisions were initially promised in exchange for giving up territory, at least by some. Nevertheless, to humor Riley and her penchant for using Canadian examples, it is noted that two Canadian researchers, Mark Zannis and Robert Davis, made the following finding concerning the welfare system in Canada: "The welfare system is a form of pacification. Combined with political and physical repression, it keeps people alive at a subsistence level but blunts any attempt to revolt while turning them into captive consumers of industrial products." They added: "For the past two to three decades, a kind of enclosure movement has taken place, brought on by the very nature of the welfare system and the dictates of corporate profits."[69] Unfortunately, Riley's perfunctory suggestions overlook the simple fact adherence to principles of private property accumulation or the doctrines of Catholic boarding schools have been tried and been found wanting. Riley, as do many commentators of Indian history, also overlooked the need to respect Indian culture when considering what "solutions" are needed to "help" Indians.

As such, as pointed out by Cook-Lynn: "The failure to contextualize honestly the facts of history, then, must be identified as one of the main kinds of anti-Indianisms in literary expression " and is best addressed by Indian writers. Separating specific facts from their larger context is the historical equivalent of the saying about statistics, "Figures don't lie, but liars figure." Vine Deloria, Jr., framed it like this:

> We have been taught to look at American history as a series of land transactions involving some three hundred Indian tribes and a growing U.S. government. This conception is certainly the picture that emerges when tribal officials are forced to deal with federal officials, claims commissioners, state highway departments, game wardens, county sheriffs, and private corporations. Yet it is hardly the whole picture. Perhaps nearly as accurate would be the picture of settlement phrased as a continuous conflict of two mutually exclusive religious views of the world.[70]

Unfortunately, Riley's ode to capitalism ignored the paradigm proposed by Deloria, Jr., and varies little from the rationalization for seizing Indian lands that Indians have been flagellated with over many years, decades, and centuries. And like those previous proponents of conquest, Riley attacked Indian culture and society from the vantage point of "friendship." Luke Lea, a corrupt supporter of mid-19th-century fur companies and appointed Indian Commissioner in 1851, issued his report in 1852 containing lengthy strictures on why: "'enlightened and Christian' whites were justified in taking Indian lands." Lea wrote: "'When civilization and barbarism are brought in such relation they cannot coexist together, it is right that the superiority of the former should be asserted and the latter compelled to give way.'" To make sure future generations would not wallow in what is now called "political correctness" Lea continued: "'It is, therefore, no matter of regret or reproach that so large a portion of our territory has been wrested from its aboriginal inhabitants and made the happy abodes of an enlightened and Christian people.'" Of course, no discourse on the rightness of Manifest Destiny would be complete without reminding those with uneasy consciences about demolishing Indian culture—"Indians Committed Atrocities too."

As Lea lurched toward his self-assured conclusion he added: "'Much of the injury of which the red man and his friends complain has been the inevitable consequence of his own perverse and vicious nature.'"⁷¹ Further, Riley's analysis of issues regarding the education of Indians can best be charitably described as superficial and chaotic. At one point, she referred to the Stuart Buck book *Acting White,* which outlined the negative aspects of the experiences of black students attending school in the southern United States. She claimed: "All evidence suggests that Indians experienced many of the same problems."⁷² Although Riley's comment seems like common sense, Indian writers and other writers noted herein have differentiated the experiences of Indians from other groups, sometimes significantly.

Nevertheless, Riley may see herself as an "expert" on Indian issues and the morphing of issues facing African-Americans and Indians as reality. In truth, her self-appointment as an innovator to solve the issues facing Indians because of an "understanding" of the issues facing other cultures or groups is not new in any respect. A study of "dependent classes" in cities conducted by J. B. Harrison borrowed extensively from the "vocabulary of white-Indian relations." As a consequence of his efforts at studying urban matters he was deemed to have sufficient "…expertise relative to dealing with Indians" and in 1880 he embarked on a tour of Indian reservations. Likewise, Vincent Collyer, a businessman and philanthropist involved with reconstruction efforts during the Civil War era, was appointed to serve as a negotiator with the Plains Indians during the formulation of the "Peace Policy" in 1868-69. Thus, during the noted period in the 19th century, it was believed issues confronting poor, urban whites, blacks, and Indians were so similar it was assumed any knowledge or expertise gained in dealing while interacting with one group were transferable to any of the other three.⁷³ Vine Deloria, Jr., similarly stated: "The most common attitude Indians have faced has been the unthoughtful Johnny-come-lately liberal who equates certain goals with a dark skin." Deloria, Jr., added these academic types: "…have not wanted to show their ignorance about Indians. Instead, they prefer to place all people with darker skin in the same category of basic goals, then develop their programs to fit these preconceived ideas."⁷⁴

However well-intentioned those efforts were, they gave birth to the octopus of greed whose tentacles eventually grew into the Dawes Act—legislation which just about strangled the life entirely out of Indian culture. In 1872, President Grant appointed Francis A. Walker Commissioner of Indian Affairs. Walker supported the Act of 1871 (see comment in endnote) which eliminated the vestiges of Indian culture Indian people had developed over many generations and designated tribes "'wards of the nation.'" The unmistakable momentum created by the Act of 1871 and Walker's support was the "…possibility of an assault on Indian tribal land-title." Speculators sought to take advantage of the poverty of the Indians and the greed of government officials seeking to acquire more land. The naïve reformers had visions of creating small independent farmers out of community-oriented individuals and Walker was under the illusion the government would protect the Indians from the avarice of the land speculators. He also believed the government's power and resources would facilitate the transformation of the Indians into productive United States citizens who would be self-reliant, economically independent, and would vote. Ultimately, underpinning Walker's optimism regarding the transformation of Indians into veritable copies of Europeans was his unshakeable belief in the superiority of white culture.⁷⁵

Additionally, lurking monumentally larger in the history of encounters of whites with Indians than the issue of economic development is the question that will just not go away—the question of genocide. In 1948, the United Nations General Assembly passed the "Genocide Convention," but ratification by the Senate Foreign Relations Committee was upheld until 1988. Leo Kuper, an exceptional student on the subject of genocide, queried did the United States: "'...fear that it might be held responsible, retrospectively, for the annihilation of Indians in the United States, or its role in the slave trade, or its contemporary support for tyrannical governments engaging in mass murder?'"[76] Will peace come to the psyche of the United States unless this question is honestly answered?

It is not necessary to imagine the understandable revulsion which would accompany any response to the writings and teachings of those who are charitably labeled "holocaust deniers." Yet, Riley's comments about the overuse of political correctness concerning Indian issues generated little concern. Further, it is open season on anyone who suggests the problems and challenges facing Indians are not all self-created; many who suggest Indians in North America were and still are the victims of genocide are urged to understand they are mistaken.

Riley took note that in 2008, the Canadian prime minister issued an apology on behalf of the Canadian government for its treatment of Indians in its residential school system. Leonard Peltier, convicted of killing the two FBI agents during the Pine Ridge shootout in 1975, quoted an earlier general "Statement of Reconciliation" issued by the Canadian government in 1998 in his book *Prison Writings*:

> As a country, we are burdened by past actions that resulted in weakening the identity of aboriginal peoples, suppressing their languages and cultures, and outlawing spiritual practices... The government of Canada today formally expresses to all aboriginal people in Canada our profound regret for past actions of the federal government which have contributed to these difficult pages in the history of our relationship together.[77]

In keeping with the tone-deafness of her writing, Riley neglected to mention that no similar comprehensive statement has been issued by the United States government. As Melissa K. Nelson adeptly noted in *Original Instructions*:

> Many diverse thinkers, writers, and native Elders have asserted that the collective consciousness of Native American communities and of the dominant American society will not be at peace until modern Americans acknowledge the past treatment of American Indians and the fact that this country was built on genocide and slavery. There must be an acknowledgement of the truth, an apology, a reconciliation, restitution, and a healing.[78]

Additionally, Peltier, from his confinement in a federal penitentiary, filled in the gaps in Riley's presentation. He noted Canada established what it called a "Healing Fund" to assist victims of the physical and mental abuse experienced in those chambers of horrors labeled boarding schools. Peltier also argued that in the United States: "Economic reparations to Native Americans are absolutely essential for a just future, as is the return of sacred sites and pieces of ancestral territory, as well as a fair share of natural resources on lands taken in violation of treaties." Peltier added: "Native Americans, and indigenous peoples everywhere, should be given a special stewardship over the land."[79]

Yet, even efforts at simple apologies to Indians in the United States have fallen woefully short of anything remotely approaching those noted in Canada. In a state of affairs crying out for at a minimum a meaningful apology, there is the unresolved matter of addressing the Wounded Knee Massacre. As noted in an earlier chapter, in *The Politics of Hallowed Ground*, the deception and indifference involved in the attempt to formulate a specific amends for that one episode of nastiness, the Wounded Knee Massacre, which created a stain on the American flag that has yet to be addressed, was chronicled.[80] Riley, who is herself Jewish, is not content to leave it at that. She hinted that Americans can't be bothered to take time out from watching mindless television programs to take a few moments to seriously ponder whether indeed Indians were the victims of genocide.

Part of the answer to the question to what has happened to Indians after the onslaught of white settlers arrives at the end of this book, appropriately, from the author who wrote of SuAnne's story outlined at the beginning of this book. Ian Frazier wrote in *Great Plains*:

> This, finally, is the punch line of our two hundred years on the Great Plains: we trap out the beaver, subtract the Mandan, infect the Blackfeet and the Hidatsa and the Assiniboin, overdose the Arikara; call the land a desert and hurry to get across it to California and Oregon; suck up the buffalo, bones and all; kill off nations of elk and wolves and cranes and chickens and prairie dogs; dig up the gold and rebury it someplace else; ruin the Sioux and Cheyenne and Arapaho and Crow and Kiowa and Comanche; kill Crazy Horse, kill Sitting Bull; harvest wave after wave of immigrants' dreams and send the wised-up dreamers on their way; plow the topsoil until it blows to the ocean; ship out the wheat, ship out the cattle, dig up the earth itself and burn it in power plants and send the power down the line; dismiss the small farmers, empty the little towns; drill the oil and natural gas and pipe it away; dry up the rivers and springs, deep-drill for irrigation water as the aquifer retreats.[81]

Frazier concluded with this melancholy note: "And in return we condense unimaginable amounts of treasure into weapons buried beneath the land which so much treasure came from—weapons for which our best hope might be that we will someday take them apart and throw them away."[82]

As it is now, so it was in the beginning. In Irving's ponderous book on Columbus, cited frequently throughout this one, he noted: "Such is the tragical [sic] history of the delightful region of Xarangua and of its amiable and hospitable people—a place which the Europeans by their own account, found a perfect paradise, but which, by their vile passions, they filled with horror and desolation."[83]

Riley inadvertently identified the obstacle to a thoughtful approach to assisting Indian people— identifying "…indigeneity itself as a problem to be solved."[84] Unfortunately, it appears the young Riley is part of what Duncan Riley Scott described as an: "…intelligentsia [that] conceives of its mission as the dragging of a technically backward, unschooled, subsistence-oriented population into the 20th century, [which makes] its self-assigned cultural role as educator of its people…doubly grandiose."[85] Knowingly or not, she endorsed: "[r]esidential schooling [which] for Aboriginal peoples is particularly remarkable in that it represented a rationally planned form of social engineering that envisaged the elimination of *Aboriginal difference* itself [emphasis in original]."[86] Unfortunately, Riley did not even hint that she recognized what some have labeled "historical trauma" is considered by many to be: "…an explanatory frame for rampant substance abuse, trauma, violence, depression, pathological grief, and suicide in present-day American Indian communities."[87] While exploring the concept of historical trauma is a subject worthy of extensive and continuing study, in the short term, people like Riley need to understand private property, like many other hare-brained schemes devised by Euro-Americans, is not the "magical force" needed to sustain indigenous culture.

Endnotes

1. Lame Deer, *Lame Deer: Seeker of Visions*, pp. 19-20.
2. Riley, *The New Trail of Tears*, pp. 14-15.
3. Drinnon, *Facing West*, p. 208.
4. Marks, Paula Mitchell, *Precious Dust*, p. 242.
5. Matthew L.M. Fletcher, "Repeating the Mistakes of the Past in 'The New Trail of Tears,'" *Los Angeles Review of Books*, October 21, 2016.
6. Jackson, *Black Elk*, p. 348.
7. Limerick, *The Legacy of Conquest*, p. 336.
8. Bailyn, *The Barbarous Years*, p. 128.
9. Meriam, *The Meriam Report*, p. 438.
10. Riley, *The New Trail of Tears*, p. 83.
11. Ibid., p. xiii.
12. Barnett, *Touched by Fire*, p. 323.
13. Ibid., p. 324.
14. Ibid., p. 326.
15. Limerick, *The Legacy of Conquest*, p. 186.
16. Costello, *Black Elk*, p. 9.
17. Washburn, Ed., Benjamin Franklin, "Send us Your Children and We Will Make Men of Them," *The Indian and the White Man*, p. 60.
18. Riley, *The New Trail of Tears*, p. 117.
19. Ibid., p. 116.
20. Kevin Phillips, *Wealth and Democracy: A Political History of the American Rich* (New York: Broadway Books, 2002), *passim*.
21. Riley, *The New Trail of Tears*, pp. 59-60.
22. Lewis H. Lapham, "The Road to Babylon: Searching for Targets in Iraq," (*Harper's*, October, 2002).
23. Riley, *The New Trail of Tears*, p. xi.
24. Wilson, *The Earth Shall Weep*, p. 249.
25. Sajna, *Crazy Horse*, p. 63.
26. Ibid., p. 65.
27. Limerick, *The Legacy of Conquest*, p. 292.
28. Riley, *The New Trail of Tears*, p. 8. Curiously, earlier on page 8 Riley used the phrase "land they occupied" when the justification often used in westward expansion was Indians roamed so much they never "occupied" the land. Interestingly, Deloria, Jr., stated: "The argument of the federal government that the treaties were documents recording political surrender by the tribes in return for annuities from the government and reservations on their traditional homelands is a strong one, but the facts do not bear out that conclusion." *Trail of Broken Treaties*, p. 118.

29 Drinnon, *Facing West*, p. 76.
30 Sajna, *Crazy Horse*, p. 81.
31 Trachtenberg, *Shades of Hiawatha*, p. 36.
32 Ibid., p. 35.
33 Drinnon, *Facing West*, p. xxix.
34 Trachtenberg, *Shades of Hiawatha*, p. 306.
35 Riley, *The New Trail of Tears*, p. 137.
36 Robert Karolevitz, *Challenge: The South Dakota Story* (Sioux Falls, South Dakota: Brevet Press, 1975), p. 62.
37 Cook-Lynn, *A Separate Country*, pp. 66-67.
38 Deloria, Jr. *Custer Died for Your Sins*, p. 173.
39 Limerick, *The Legacy of Conquest*, p. 211.
40 Ibid., p. 196.
41 Crow Dog, *Lakota Woman*, p. 77.
42 Deloria, Jr. *Custer Died for Your Sins*, p. 33.
43 Riley, *The New Trail of Tears*, p. 23.
44 Lapham, "The Road to Babylon: Searching for Targets in Iraq."
45 Riley, *The New Trail of Tears*, p. x.
46 Berkhofer, *The White Man's Indian*, pp. 29-30.
47 Mann, *1491*, p. 52.
48 Drinnon, *Facing West*, p. 19.
49 Frazier, *On the Rez*, p. 209.
50 Matson, *Crazy Horse: The Lakota Warrior's Life and Legacy*, p. 157.
51 Barnett, *Touched by Fire*, pp. 209-210.
52 Drinnon, *Facing West*, pp. 19-20.
53 Slotkin, *Fatal Environment*, p. 100.
54 Ibid., p. 98.
55 Drinnon, *Facing West*, p. 448.
56 Ibid., p. 417.
57 Page, *In the Hands of the Great Spirit*, p. 310.
58 Slotkin, *Fatal Environment*, p. 20.
59 Riley, *The New Trail of Tears*, p. 168.
60 Slotkin, *Fatal Environment*, p. 20.
61 Riley, *The New Trail of Tears*, p. 168.
62 Anonymous Lakota Elder.
63 Washburn, Ed., Henry Adams, "Tippecanoe and Tyler Too," *The Indian and the White Man*, p. 357.
64 Morgan, *Lions of the West*, p. xxiii.
65 Smith, *Moon of Popping Trees*, p. 203.

66 Harjo and Bird, Eds., Emma LaRocque, "Tides, Towns, and Trains," *Reinventing The Enemy's Language*, p. 360.
67 Bordewich, *Killing the White Man's Indian*, p. 311.
68 Ibid., p. 312.
69 Jaimes, Ed., Ward Churchill and Winona LaDuke, "The Political Economy of Radioactive Colonialism," *The State of Native America*, p. 245.
70 Deloria, Jr., *God is Red*, pp. 237-238.
71 Sajna, *Crazy Horse*, p. 94.
72 Riley, *The New Trail of Tears*, p. 100.
73 Slotkin, *Fatal Environment*, pp. 311-312.
74 Deloria, Jr., *Custer Died for Your Sins*, p. 171.
75 Slotkin, *Fatal Environment*, pp. 311-313. It appears Slotkin was referring to the Indian Appropriations Act of 1871. Slotkin also noted that the push to "assimilate" Indians during the period from 1869-1875 created a: "…policy [which] attacked and ruined tribal structure and the sustaining concepts of moral and personal value that were supported by tribalism. These were replaced with nothing: since Indians could not be trusted to govern themselves." Ibid., p. 319.
76 Stannard, *American Holocaust*, p. 256.
77 Leonard Peltier, *Prison Writings* (New York: St. Martin's Griffin, 1999), p. 204.
78 Melissa K. Nelson, Ed. "Introduction: Lighting the Sun of Our Future: How These Teachings Can Provide Illumination," *Original Instructions: Indigenous Teachings for A Sustainable Future*, p. 16.
79 Peltier, *Prison Writings*, pp. 203-204.
80 Gonzalez and Cook-Lynn, *The Politics of Hallowed Ground*, *passim*.
81 Frazier, *Great Plains*, pp. 209-210.
82 Ibid., p. 210.
83 Irving, *The Life and Voyages of Christopher Columbus*, p. 649.
84 Woolford, Benvenuto and Hinton, Eds., Jeremy Patzer, "Residential School Harm and Colonial Dispossession," *Colonial Genocide in Indigenous North America*, p. 169.
85 Ibid., p. 174.
86 Ibid., p. 168.
87 Woolford, Benvenuto, Hinton, Alexander, Eds. Joseph P. Gone, "Colonial Genocide and Historical Trauma in Native North America," *Colonial Genocide in Indigenous North America*, p. 274.

Afterword

The real aim…[of this policy] is to get at the Indian lands and open them up to settlement… If this were done in the name of greed it would be bad enough; but to do it in the name of humanity, and under the cloak of an ardent desire to promote the Indian's welfare by making him like ourselves, whether he will or not, is infinitely worse.
United States House of Representatives Indian Affairs Committee
James Wilson, *The Earth Shall Weep*[1]

Someday, someone, who may not yet be born, will have a mission: to change all the history texts to read that 'Columbus was the first European to land on American shores.' If that person is truly successful, the sentence will be followed by another: 'It was a sad day for Indian people.'
Kenneth Stern, *Loud Hawk: The United States versus the American Indian Movement*[2]

Prior to April 2014, I gave American Indians little thought. Little did I know that from that time forward, I would read over 125 books on Indian history, visit such places as the National Archives in Washington, D.C., and become friends with people who experienced the hard lives offered to Indians in this country, especially those living on the Pine Ridge Reservation in South Dakota. Yet, as I drove with my oldest son from Dayton, Ohio, toward Wyoming that spring, those events were yet to come. At that time I also did not know that a few years later I would understand Clyde Holler's comment: "…my encounter with native North America has been the greatest intellectual challenge and adventure of my adult life," and would be "…an endeavor that greatly repays serious thought."[3] In that regard, if there is anyone interested in more information about sources, I will be happy to assist in providing it.

However, before recounting my journey leading up to writing this essay, and the actual writing of it, a few comments about my point of view are in order. First and foremost, I clearly had (and have) a point of view as I researched and wrote about my observations of the Pine Ridge Reservation and other aspects of Indian history that I would consider "pro-Indian." To pretend otherwise would be to engage in the pretension that presentations of history are "objective." After driving through the Pine Ridge Reservation on Good Friday, 2014, there was little doubt in my mind that whatever it was that was happening there was unacceptable in what is virtually the geographic center of the continental United States—the-self-proclaimed greatest country in the world. When I saw on a subsequent trip an upside-down United States flag on a flagpole outside of a run-down trailer near the Wounded Knee Massacre site, I did not become angry as former BIA area director Stanley Lyman said he did. How could anyone with any compassion mistake that symbolic act as anything other than a cry of desperation? From the moment I left Pine Ridge on that day in April 2014 I set out to understand why there was virtually a developing, poverty-stricken country existing in the middle of the United States, which possesses so much wealth. I was not at all satisfied that what little I knew about Indian history could explain what I saw in that remote region of South Dakota.

Italian historian Gianni Granzotto argued that: "What was new about Columbus [more specifically his interpretation of how the world worked] was his passionate spirit of inquiry and the quickness with which he managed to explain facts and phenomena that hitherto had not only gone unexplained, but had been accepted and unquestioned."[4] I hope by reading this book, the reader of this volume has to some extent developed or a continued "passionate spirit of inquiry" about Indian history. Equally as important, I hope readers are ready to reconsider aspects of Indian history that previously "…had been accepted and unquestioned," not necessarily take my word for it, and come to their own conclusions if they vary from mine. Nevertheless, hopefully, thinking and feeling people arrive at similar destinations. During my sales pitch to a publisher about why she should be interested in another book about the mistreatment of Indians, she told me these things had already been explained in some detail and why would anyone be interested? About two weeks later, while reading *The Legacy of Conquest*, author Patricia Limerick provided a pithy answer to me, noted in the Preface: "Because the message has not gotten through."[5]

Just prior to my first encounter with people on the Pine Ridge Reservation, I knew so little about Plains Indians, I bought a book about Chief Joseph of the Nez Perce Nation at the Mount Rushmore bookstore the day before my arrival at Pine Ridge. I had no idea who Chief Joseph was or that other than a brief encounter with Sitting Bull, he had no connection with Plains Indians. However, I did recall from my high school days the worldwide interest in the "occupation" of Wounded Knee and that it took place somewhere in South Dakota. I also recalled thinking at the time of the "occupation" the guys (I didn't know then women such as Anna Mae Aquash were involved) who did the "occupying" were pretty "cool" and brave. After reading my book, it should be obvious that view hasn't changed, although I now have more specific reasons for my admiration. Life in general has taught me sometimes great men such as Russell Means have correspondingly great flaws, but those flaws do not diminish the magnitude of their accomplishments. As Irving said about Columbus, a hero does not need to possess "… all the good qualities under the Sun." Nonetheless, before arriving at Pine Ridge, I had little recognition that perhaps the most famous warriors and leaders in Indian history, Sitting Bull and Crazy Horse, were of the Lakota Nation—Sitting Bull being of the Hunkpapa band and Crazy Horse of the Oglala band.

Before furthering the discussion of the development of this book, it is appropriate to, in the words of the King in *Alice in Wonderland*, "begin at the beginning."[6] In April 2014, as I drove with my oldest son from Dayton, Ohio, to what I knew than as Devil's Tower, Wyoming, I had no idea the Lakota Indian name for this amazing geological formation was translated into English as Bear's Table. The plan for the trip was to also visit Mount Rushmore, the Crazy Horse monument, and then Pine Ridge. We also had a plan to visit St. Joseph's Indian School on the Good Friday of our trip, but by the time we arrived the school was closed for the holiday. Along with my lack of knowledge of Lakota history, I had minimal understanding of the current state of affairs involving Pine Ridge residents, or any other Indians for that matter. For starters, I did not realize some Indian people referred to the Mount Rushmore monument, Crazy Horse monument, and the road between them the "Desecration Tour." The nickname was derived for the most part due to these stone behemoths being carved out of what the Lakota considered the sacred Black Hills. To add to the freakishness of the scenario, the carving and construction of the Crazy Horse monument began in 1948 and it does not appear it will be finished anytime soon.

Thus, in the interest of full disclosure, Pine Ridge was not even the primary stop or main consideration for a visit when we planned the trip. The main goal of our trip was to see Devil's Tower, Wyoming, and we would stop by Wounded Knee on the way back from Wyoming, time permitting. Before taking the trip, I was also very much interested in stopping by St. Joseph's Indian School in eastern South Dakota. Ironically, since that trip, I have thought the most about Pine Ridge and Wounded Knee. As I stated above, as it turned out, by the time my son and I reached St. Joseph's on that Good Friday, it was closed.

Of course, my first visit to Pine Ridge was a monumental revelation. I could not, and still cannot, understand how such a place as Pine Ridge exists virtually in the geographic center of the United States. When I let my imagination reach its outer limits, I wondered if we had driven through some kind of black hole and ended up in a developing country. I was so taken aback by what I witnessed that when I returned to my home in Dayton, Ohio, I wrote Senator John Thune from South Dakota and asked him if there was anything I could do to help the situation. Of course, and as I soon found out was typical, I received no response. In the interest of fairness, I received no response from Representative Kristi Noem (now governor of South Dakota in 2019) either when I wrote her.

As I reflect back on that day in the spring of 2014, I really think the "experience" of Wounded Knee began as we were driving up Route 18 to the village of Pine Ridge. Although the housing was dilapidated, there were some young Indian people riding horses in that area. In spite of the pervasive symbols of poverty such as run-down cars and worn-out housing, the scene was simply majestic. As we pulled into town, we stopped at a place called "Big Bat's Shell." After getting gasoline, I went inside to take a break. A gentleman named Pierre asked me if I wanted to buy some handmade earrings, for ten dollars a set. I told him I needed to attend to some matters, but that I would be right back. As I headed toward another area of Big Bat's, I noticed a group of about 20 Indian youths sitting in the corner. I wondered how so many young people could be idle at that time of the day. I initially thought their presence was due to the day being Good Friday; I subsequently learned that the unemployment rate on Pine Ridge is estimated to be as high as 80 percent. Sadly, the rate of alcoholism is estimated to be at a similar number.

As I was walking through this area of Big Bat's, one of the young men in the group, a 20-something Indian man, walked toward me. He gave me with a look that I can best describe as a mixture of pride, anger, and frustration. It was as if his look was saying, Are you just another tourist that's going to look at us like we're zoo animals or are you going to do something about the situation? I subsequently learned that some Indians believe that white people come to Pine Ridge to see "poverty porn"—getting titillation from the desperation of the situation. When I came back out to Pierre, he said something to the effect that, "We're just like everybody else," and I have been pondering that comment ever since. I offered to buy the one set of earrings for ten dollars. Pierre said I could have both sets for that amount (I should apologize for that). As my son and I left Big Bat's and headed for the Wounded Knee burial ground, I still, though, had no idea that one of the biggest questions for me would become: what is the truth of the history of the Pine Ridge Indian Reservation and the various events surrounding the Wounded Knee Massacre of December 29, 1890, and the 1973 "occupation" (as noted, sometimes referred to as Wounded Knee II)?

As we headed toward the gravesite, we unknowingly passed the Re-Member complex to which I would subsequently make multiple trips. After arriving at the Wounded Knee Massacre site, as we got out of our car, a large Indian man approached us and asked if I wanted to buy a dream catcher. I asked how much? He said, "20 bucks." I said sure and handed him 20 dollars, and he handed me a beautiful blue dream catcher. After getting the dream catcher, my son and I got in our car and drove across the highway and parked in the gravel parking lot near a round building I was to understand some called the Wounded Knee Museum. To illustrate how little signage exists instructing people where things were located, my son and I had an animated discussion about where to park to give us access to the burial ground. We then walked up to the summit of the hill where the mass burial site is located. What I found on top of the hill could not have symbolized the history of American Indians any better.

Given the massive significance of the grounds of Wounded Knee, it was sad to see how nondescript at least the physical trappings of the area were. In fact, the area borders on appearing abandoned. On the side of the road where the mound itself is located pavement is nonexistent. The arch on the east signifying the entrance to the burial ground is in a state of disrepair (I discovered on my third trip to South Dakota that on the reverse side of the arches, someone took a marker of some kind and listed many of the infamous episodes in the history of European settlers dealing with Indians including a list of broken treaties. On a later trip I found out the list had been erased).

If you choose to walk through the arch, you come upon a fence similar to which you would find surrounding a yard in a working-class neighborhood. Yet, of all the physical attributes of Wounded Knee that are noteworthy, the one that I now ponder over the most is the cross at the top of the arch. It seems ironic, given the application of the tenets of "Christianity" to the relationship between whites and Indians, that this symbol appears where it does. As a casual student of history must admit, the basic guidelines of Re-Member, which I did not know at the time I would become involved with, as an organization that facilitates service projects on Pine Ridge, has the sensible restriction against proselytizing while volunteers attend one of their week-long service trips. The restriction is understandable. Dee Brown ends his iconic *Bury My Heart at Wounded Knee* with a comment that after the indiscriminate slaughter of Indian men, women, and children at Wounded Knee on December 29, 1890, was concluded, some of the decimated and dazed remnants of "Big Foot's" band were brought to the Episcopal Mission on Pine Ridge and laid under a "crudely lettered banner" which proclaimed PEACE ON EARTH, GOOD WILL TO [sic]

MEN.[7] Nonetheless, as is undeniable, Christian churches of all denomination maintain significant visible presences on the Pine Ridge Reservation.

As I walked toward the back of the fenced area surrounding the mass grave, an Indian lady whose name I also didn't get charged up the hill in a tan SUV. She asked if I wanted to buy a dream catcher, so I asked how much. She answered, "Twenty bucks," so I said sure and handed the twenty dollars to her. After she handed me the dream catcher, she said something to the effect of: "Good, now I'll be able to buy some gas." This lady also mentioned to me about how the musician Neil Young performed some type of benefit concert the previous year to help finance some type of protest. As I was to discover later, the event she described related to opposition to the construction of the proposed Keystone II pipeline. At the time I purchased the various items of jewelry from these people I had no idea of the future extent of my interest in the subjects of Pine Ridge and Wounded Knee, so I did not record their names.

There are many events subsequent to my first visit to Pine Ridge and Wounded Knee which shaped my perceptions of Indian history. Hopefully, that point of view is evident in the previously written pages. Nevertheless, my story is insignificant in the larger picture except to note I am not surprised when I experience joy or sadness regarding family events. However, my continuing reaction to the events of that Good Friday on Pine Ridge seemed to come out of nowhere—a desire to understand people as of that time I knew next to nothing about.

That understanding was greatly enlarged on my July 2019, trip to Pine Ridge, just prior to (the first) submission of the manuscript of this book to the publisher. As my youngest son and I arrived at the Re-Member facilities on the morning of July 14, 2019, that week's volunteers were getting ready to depart on a tour of the reservation, including the Wounded Knee Massacre site. We decided to go with the group and unpack our rental SUV later. It proved to be a fortuitous choice.

The tour school bus transported us to the Wounded Knee Massacre site, where we were joined by a young Lakota man named Dakota High Hawk who presented information concerning events surrounding the massacre. I had heard Dakota's presentation before, but this time he mentioned a fact which solidified my view (and that of many Lakota) that the killing was a planned massacre and the claim the troops were sent to Pine Ridge to suppress the "Ghost Dance" was a pretext. Dakota stated that the Catholic priest Father Francis Craft read the Minneconjou Lakota their last rites the night before they were killed. Suffice it to say I have not read or heard about this fact in other non-Indian sources.

Dakota also stated well over 400 Indian men, women, and children were shot dead on that cold December morning. That is well over twice the number of people claimed to have died according to some sources. For example, in *Moon of the Popping Trees*, Rex Alan Smith reported: "…the total number of Indians who died in the *battle* of Wounded Knee that day was no fewer than one hundred seventy and no more than one hundred ninety [emphasis added]."[8] Ironically, even though Trimbach made the absurd and ahistorical claim Spotted Elk was leading his people: "…in the hope of joining forces with Chief Red Cloud in the south,"[9] his number (or at least one of them) of "…close to 300 Indians died, mostly women and children"[10] more closely aligns with Dakota's.

Later that evening, another speaker whom I had also heard on previous visits to Re-Member made the interesting claim the White Buffalo Calf Woman was an incarnation of the Virgin Mary. He also stated Christ appeared to Lakota Elders sometime around 1150 A.D. to warn them that strange people were coming to Turtle Island and would cause them intense suffering. On Monday evening my friend Will Peters spoke of the need to treat children as sacred beings. He also said we are all related, which sounded like it came from someone who had given the idea considerable thought.

On Tuesday evening another Lakota presenter explained to our group there is no such thing as a hereditary medicine man. He further explained the idea of a male "chief" was a concept implemented to enable the Lakota to interact with the whites advancing across the continent. In his discussion of Lakota spirituality and spiritual practices, just like the previous four occasions I heard him speak, the concept of reincarnation was not mentioned at all. It would seem anyone, particularly those outside Lakota culture, who suggests a reincarnation paradigm as an element of Lakota spirituality is confused.

Later that evening, I spotted a copy of Raymond J. DeMallie's book, *The Sixth Grandfather*, in the Re-Member day room. One of the significant takeaways from this book was the comment: "…when Black Elk was away in Europe, Jesuits had established a Roman Catholic mission in response to an invitation of Chief Red Cloud. Black Elk's practice of traditional healing ceremonies quickly brought him into conflict with the missionaries."[11] Nevertheless, on our second tour of the reservation on Wednesday, in the foyer of the Holy Rosary Church hung a tapestry with the caption: "Servant of God—Nicholas Black Elk 1866-1950." Again, Black Elk's involvement with Catholicism is evidence refuting the notion Indians are nothing but relics of the past. Obviously, Black Elk's legacy is complex and points to the idea he had the *future* of the Lakota people as a preeminent consideration.

Another unexpected discovery of information was finding the book *Ruling Pine Ridge—Oglala Lakota Politics from the IRA to Wounded Knee* by Akim D. Reinhardt in the Oglala Lakota College bookstore. Before leaving for the trip to Pine Ridge, I had concluded I had no more need of source material. However, I was intrigued by the title and why the book was wrapped in plastic, so I purchased a copy. Again, a fortuitous choice. The book's contents solidified my belief in the many conclusions about Lakota history (and indirectly other aspects of Indian history) I previously made.

One of Reinhardt's astute observations regarding Stanley Lyman, the Pine Ridge BIA superintendent in the early 1970s, was especially illuminating considering how many historians and others depict Indian-white relations in such simplistic terms. Reinhardt stated Lyman: "…proved himself incapable of understanding the complexity of the situation"[12] on Pine Ridge. It is an observation applicable to many involved in past and current events on Pine Ridge, particularly Joseph Trimbach and his inability to grasp the "occupation" was not a "cowboy and Indians" movie.

Regarding Trimbach specifically, contrary to his claim the "occupation" was nothing more than an AIM publicity stunt operated by "militants" with no connection to Pine Ridge, Reinhardt explained AIM did in fact have support from the locals. In that regard, Reinhardt quoted Ellen Moves Camp: "'Most of the reservation believes in the AIM, and we're proud to have them with us.'"[13] Another prominent supporter included Tribal Vice-President David Long, which created a rift between him and Tribal President Dick Wilson. Wilson's animosity toward Long became so intense he "suspended" Long even though he had no authority to do so.[14] Coincidentally, Dakota High Hawk's great uncle, William High Hawk, was one of the council members who made a motion to lift the "suspension" of David Long.

Ruling Pine Ridge also helped me fill in the blanks concerning other details regarding this writing. Reinhardt identified William Rooks, who distributed the flyer announcing the showing of the film strip "An Overview of Our World" as discussed in the chapter of this book entitled Joseph Trimbach and the Federal Bureau of Imperialism—Part III. Rooks and his brother Eugene were identified by Reinhardt as "…conservative, anti-AIM, mixed-blood members of the John Birch Society."[15] Reinhardt also suggested the FBI placed a phone call to reporter Lyn Gladstone of the *Rapid City Journal* advising her that a rally for the purpose of protesting charging Darld Schmidtz with second degree manslaughter instead of murder in the knifing death of Wesley Bad Heart Bull was canceled.[16]

Reinhardt's book also contained insight regarding another stop on the tour that day following the Oglala Lakota Community College—the Singing Horse Trading Post—although I did not know it at the time. The Singing Horse Trading Post is owned by a German woman named Rosie, who is featured in Hancock's book *Not for Sale*. Reinhardt noted: "…of 124 total businesses on the reservation in 1972, only twenty-one of them were Indian-owned, with another six co-owned by Indians. The other ninety-six, or nearly 80 percent were owned by non-Indians."[17] There is no reason to believe this ratio has changed significantly since that time. In the interest of full disclosure, I bought my wife a decorated T-shirt at this establishment without considering the ramifications of patronizing a business owned by a non-Indian. While Hancock may be sincere in his desire to assist Lakota people, it would be beneficial for him and others like him (and also me) to recognize the lack of Indian-owned businesses on Pine Ridge.

Perhaps Kevin's lack of awareness of Indian needs is an outgrowth of his view of Indians in general. Although he reported being given an Indian name "Chun Ota,"[18] it did not seem to occur to him all the Indians he encountered in the spirit world were voiceless. Crazy Horse, Touch the Clouds, Sitting Bull and Rain-in-the Face, and Black Elk were *all silent*. In his attempt to depict Black Elk as an archetypical "medicine man" in his "conversation" with him, Kevin did not discuss with him his conversion to Catholicism, as evidenced by, among other things, the aforementioned tapestry in the Holy Rosary Church on the Red Cloud Indian School campus. Although it occurred after Kevin wrote his book, the Vatican as of 2016 was considering Black Elk for sainthood. Nevertheless, this circumstance provides a fitting end to this book, which hopefully suggests to its readers the complexity of Indians and Indian culture. When asked about Black Elk's Catholic faith, Charlotte Black Elk, his granddaughter, stated "…she views the Catholic Church as a cult…" and: "When asked if he should be made a saint, she said no, she doubted he ever truly held Catholic beliefs."[19]

ENDNOTES

1   Wilson, *The Earth Shall Weep*, pp. 301-302.
2   Stern, *Loud Hawk*, p. iv.
3   Holler, *Black Elk's Religion*, p. xviii.
4   Granzotto, *Christopher Columbus*, p. 55.
5   Limerick, *The Legacy of Conquest*, p. 31.
6   Lewis Carroll, *Alice in Wonderland* (New York: Goldsmith Publishing, 1865).
7   Brown, *Bury My Heart at Wounded Knee*, p. 445.
8   Smith, *Moon of Popping Trees*, p. 196.
9   Trimbach, *American Indian Mafia*, p. 71.
10 Ibid., p. 72.
11 Raymond J. DeMallie, *The Sixth Grandfather: Black Elk's Teachings Given to John G. Niehardt* (Lincoln, Nebraska: University of Nebraska Press, 1984), p. 12.
12 Akim D. Reinhardt, *Ruling Pine Ridge: Oglala Lakota Politics from the IRA to Wounded Knee* (Lubbock, Texas: Texas Tech University Press, 2007), p. 162.
13 Ibid., p. 163. Sherry Smith stated a reporter for the Unicorn News Radio Network insisted: "AIM...had enormous support on Pine Ridge." Smith, *Hippies, Indians, and the Fight for Red Power*, p. 191.
14 Ibid., pp. 156-157.
15 Ibid., p. 165.
16 Ibid., p. 169.
17 Ibid., p. 120.
18 Hancock, *Not for Sale*, p. 440.
19 Kirk Peterson, "Vatican Considers Sainthood for Black Elk," *National Catholic Reporter*, August 25, 2018.

Bibliography

Indiana Historical Society
Hedges, Charles, Ed. "General Harrison's letter of Acceptance," September 11, 1888. *Speeches of Benjamin Harrison - Twenty Third President of the United States.* (New York: National Book Co., 1892), p. 111.

Lilly Library—Indiana University Bloomington
Camp, Walter, Interviews with Andrew Good Thunder, Little Hawk, Louis Bordeaux (Transcript).

"Wounded Indians at Washita" (Transcript).

Minnesota Historical Society, St. Paul, Minnesota
Adams, Hank, REVIEW STUDY OF A MODEL FOR FAILURE IN THE BIA's INDUSTRIAL DEVELOPMENT PROGRAM: An Abstract Discussion on Economic Development Projects of the Sisseton-Wahpeton Sioux Tribes of South Dakota 1971-72, December 6, 1972.

Akwesasne Notes, February-April 1973.

Bear Eagle, Fannie Carrie, Statement regarding theft and vandalism, May 13, 1973.

Brim, Sand, Statement of Eddie White Dress re: Pawn at Trading Post, undated.

Burgwin, Scott, Affidavit dated March 31, 1973 outlining FBI arrest in Oregon for attempting to bring food to Indians at Wounded Knee, South Dakota in 1973.

LaCourse, Richard, "The FBI's 'Racial Intelligence' and the American Indian Militants." Undated essay.

"Lelo" *Newsletter* (warning against the perils of communism facing Pine Ridge) March 26, 1973.

Rooks, William, Untitled, undated document inviting Pine Ridge residents to watch a film strip entitled "An Overview of Our World."

Thornburgh, Richard L., July 12, 1976, letter to Arthur Fleming, Chairman of the United States Civil Rights Commission.

Tilsen, Attorney Kenneth, April 15, 1976, letter to FBI Director Clarence Kelly.

Wood, William B., FBI Agent March 8, 1976, Affidavit describing events in the Anna Mae Aquash Homicide Investigation.

Wounded Knee Information and Defense Fund, Transcript of *Rest of the News* program, April 22, 1973.

Wounded Knee Legal Defense/Offense Committee and North American Media, Memorandum describing the success of the Wounded Knee "occupation," undated.

MONROE COUNTY MICHIGAN PUBLIC LIBRARY CUSTER COLLECTION

Curtis, John R., "Custer Expedition Confirms Early Rumors of Gold in Indians' Sacred Black Hills," *Chicago Inter-Ocean*, August 27, 1874.

McMurry, Captain George J. (Chaplain 7th Cavalry), "The Seventh Cavalry at the Fiftieth Anniversary of the Little Big Horn." Undated.

RAPID CITY, SOUTH DAKOTA PUBLIC LIBRARY

"The Indian Problem," *Rapid City Journal*, December 18, 1890.

UNITED STATES NATIONAL ARCHIVES, WASHINGTON, D.C.

Henry, Major Guy V., October 14, 1890, letter.

Joint Resolution of the South Dakota Legislature Regarding Indian Outbreak, January 20, 1891.

Kellogg, E. R., "Commanding," October 27, 1890, endorsement.

Miles, General Nelson A., March 2, 1891, 2d Endorsement regarding women and children killed at Wounded Knee Creek.

OTHER SOURCES

Allen, Samantha, "Tribes Blast 'Wannabe' Native American Professor," *The Daily Beast*, July 11, 2015.

American Indian Movement Grand Governing Council "Press Statement," Minneapolis, Minnesota, February 20, 1999.

Brown, Thomas, "Did the U.S. Army Distribute Smallpox Blankets to Indians? Fabrication and Falsification in Ward Churchill's Genocide Rhetoric," *Plagiary*, Ann Arbor, Michigan, University of Michigan Library, Vol. 1, 2006.

Bushyhead, Yvonne. "In the Spirit of Crazy Horse: The Case of Leonard Peltier" 2 Yale J.L. & Liberation, 1991.

Calloway, Colin G., "The Biggest Forgotten Indian Victory," *Zocalo*, June 9, 2015.

Cary-Alvarez, Jana, "Media Interpretations of Wounded Knee II: Narratives of Violence versus Sympathetic coverage," *Sound Ideas*, Washington University of Puget Sound, 2013.

Chasing Hawk, Ernestine, "Did Nawaziwin Orchestrate the Death of Anna Mae?" *Native Sun News*, March 30, 1976.

Choi, David and Collman, Ashley, "'Inappropriate and Wrong' Cherokee Nation Official Throws Cold Water on Elizabeth Warren's DNA Test of Native American Heritage," *Business Insider*, October 15, 2018.

Churchill, Ward, "Spiritual Hucksterism: The Rise of the Plastic Medicine Men," *Cultural Survival Quarterly*, June 2003.

Cober, D., "On Racist Discourse in S. C. Gwynne's *Empire of the Summer Moon*," *Ration of Common Humanity*, September 20, 2013.

Cox, John Woodrow, Clement, Scott and Vargas, Theresa, "New Poll Finds 9 in 10 Native Americans Aren't Offended by Redskins Name," *Washington Post*, May 19, 2016.

Dewing, Roland, "South Dakota Newspaper Coverage of the 1973 Occupation of Wounded Knee," *South Dakota Historical Society*, Undated.

Fletcher, Matthew L. M., "Repeating the Mistakes of the Past in *The New Trail of Tears*," *Los Angeles Review of Books*, October 21, 2016.

Fugleberg, Jeremy, "Can Oglala Sioux Tribe ban Gov. Kristi Noem from reservation? Here's What the law says," *Sioux Falls Argus Leader*, May 7, 2019.

Goar, Allison Marie, "A Critical Examination of Non-Native Practice of Native American Religion," Fort Collins, Colorado State University, Spring, 2016.

Goplen, Kelsey; Graves, Jasmine; Nelson, Amy; and Thompson, Harry Eds. John Trimbach, "Wounded Knee 1973: Forty Years Later," Papers of the Forty-Fourth Annual Dakota Conference—A National Conference on the Northern Plains, Center for Western Studies, 2012.

Keeler, Jaqueline, "On the Shameful and Skewed Redskins' Poll," *The Nation*, May 26, 2016.

Klein, Rebecca, "Native American School Mourning 4 Student Suicides gets Emergency Federal Aid," *HuffPost*, June 19, 2015.

Koning, Hans, "Don't Celebrate 1492, Mourn It," *New York Times*, April 14, 1990.

Lind, Neeta, "Pine Ridge: American Prisoner of War Camp #334," *Daily Kos*. June 4, 2010.

Mesteth, Wilmer Stampede et al., "Declaration of War Against Exploiters of Lakota Spirituality," *Digital History* website, 1993.

Moya-Smith, Simon, "Ugly Precursor to Auschwitz—Hitler Said to have been inspired by U.S. Reservation System," *Indian Country Today*, August 27, 2017.

"Native History: Potawatamie Removed at Gunpoint, Trail of Death Begins," *Indian Country Today*, September 4, 2014.

Nelson, McKenzie, KEVN Fox News Report, April 5, 2005.

"Oceti Sakowin/Seven Council Fires," Akta Lakota Museum and Cultural Center Website.

Robideau, Robert, "John Trudell, A profile of Cowardice—An FBI Informant Covers His Tracks in the Murder of Anna Mae Aquash," *Independent Media Center*, July 18, 2007.

Ross, Gyasi, "Leaving the Reservation—Modern Day Assimilation," *Huffington Post*, updated May 19, 2014.

Shorter, David, "Four Words for Andrea Smith: 'I'm Not an Indian,'" *Indian Country Today*, July 1, 2015.

Sypaller, Keila, "Mascots can Reinforce Stereotypes, a UM Researcher Finds," *Billings, Montana Gazette*, April 15, 2016.

Waldstein, David, "Cleveland Indians Will Abandon Chief Wahoo Logo Next Year," *New York Times*, January 29, 2018.

Weaver, Christopher, Frosch, Dan, and Johnson, Gabe, "Pedophile Doctor Left Trail of Suspicions—and Abuse," *Wall Street Journal*, February 9-10, 2019.

Worthington, Danika, "A History of Racism, the KKK and Crimes Against American Indians: Colorado's Struggle with Divisive Monuments Began Long Ago," *Denver Post*, August 18, 2017.

BOOKS

Agonito, Joseph. *Lakota Portraits: Lives of the Legendary Plains People*. Guilford, Connecticut: Guilford Pequot Press, 2011.

Ambrose, Stephen. *Crazy Horse and Custer: The Parallel Lives of Two American Warriors*. New York: Anchor Books/A Division of Random House, 1996.

Anderson, Gary Clayton. *Little Crow: Spokesman for the Sioux*. St. Paul: Minnesota Historical Society, 1986.

Bailyn, Bernard. *The Barbarous Years: The Peopling of British North America: The Conflict of Civilizations*. New York: Alfred A Knopf/A Division of Random House, 2012.

Banks, Dennis and Erdoes, Richard. *Ojibwa Warrior: Dennis Banks and the Rise of the American Indian Movement*. Norman, Oklahoma: University of Oklahoma Press, 2004.

Barnett, Louise. *Touched by Fire: The Life, Death, and Mythic Afterlife of George Armstrong Custer*. New York: Henry Holt & Co., 1996.

Beck, Paul. *Columns of Vengeance: Soldiers, Sioux, and the Punitive Expeditions 1863-1864*. Norman, Oklahoma: University of Oklahoma Press 2013.

Berg, Scott. *38 Nooses: Lincoln, Little Crow, and the Beginning of the Frontier's End*. New York: Pantheon Books, 2012.

Berkhofer, Robert. *The White Man's Indian: Images of the American Indian from Columbus to the Present/* New York: Vintage Books/A Division of Random House, 1979.

Bordewich, Fergus. *Killing the White Man's Indian*. New York: Anchor Books/A Division of Random House, 1997.

Bowden, Henry Warner. *American Indians and Christian Missions*. Chicago, Illinois: University of Chicago Press, 1981.

Bradley, Michael. *The Columbus Conspiracy: An Investigation into the Secret History of Christopher Columbus*. Willowdale, Ontario, Canada: Hunslow Press, 1992.

Brand, Johanna. *The Life and Death of Anna Mae Aquash.* Toronto: James Lorimer & Co., 1978.

Brown, Dee. *Bury My Heart at Wounded Knee: An Indian History of the American West.* New York: St, Martin's Press, 1970.

Churchill, Ward and Vander Wall, Jim. *Agents of Repression: The FBI's Secret War Against the Black Panther Party and the American Indian Movement.* Boston: South End Press, 1988.

Churchill, Ward, *A Little Matter of Genocide: Holocaust and Denial in the Americas 1492 to the Present* (San Francisco: City Lights Books, 1997).

Churchill, Ward. *Fantasies of the Master Race.* Monroe, Maine: Common Courage Press, 1992.

Churchill, Ward. *Indians Are Us: Culture and Genocide in Native North America.* Monroe, Maine: Common Courage Press, 1994.

Churchill, Ward. *Perversions of Justice.* San Francisco: City Lights, 2003.

Churchill, Ward. *Since Predator Came.* Oakland, California: AK Press, 1995.

Clark, Robert A. *The Killing of Chief Crazy Horse.* Lincoln, Nebraska: University of Nebraska Press, 1988.

Coleman, William S. E. *Voices of Wounded Knee.* Lincoln, Nebraska: Bison Books/University of Nebraska Press, 2000.

Connell, Evan. *Son of the Morning Star.* New York: Harper and Row Publishers, 1984.

Cook-Lynn, Elizabeth. *Anti-Indianism in Modern America: A Voice from Tatekeya's Earth.* Chicago: University of Illinois Press, 2001.

Cook-Lynn, Elizabeth. *A Separate Country: Postcoloniality and American Indian Nations.* Lubbock, Texas: Texas Tech University Press, 2012.

Cordova, Gilbert. "Senate Bill Allocates Millions to Address Missing and Murdered Indigenous Women Epidemic" Anchorage, Alaska: Channel 2, KTUU, 2019.

Costello, Damian. *Black Elk: Colonialism and Lakota Catholicism.* Maryknoll, New York: Orbis Publishing, 2005.

Crosby, Alfred W. Jr., *Ecological Imperialism: The Biological Expansion of Europe—900-1900.* Cambridge, England: Cambridge University Press, 1986.

Crosby, Alfred W., Jr. *The Columbian Exchange: Biological and Cultural Consequences of 1492.* Westport, Connecticut: Greenwood Press, 1972.

Crow Dog, Leonard and Erdoes, Richard. *Crow Dog: Four Generations of Sioux Medicine Men.* New York: Harper Collins Publishers, 1995.

Crow Dog, Mary. *Lakota Woman.* New York: Harper Collins Publishers, 1990.

Custer, Elizabeth R. *Boots and Saddles: Or Life in Dakota with General Custer.* Norman, Oklahoma, University of Oklahoma Press, 1961.

Davis, Kenneth C. *America's Hidden History: Untold Tales of the First Pilgrims, Fighting Women, and Forgotten Founders Who Shaped a Nation.* New York: First Smithsonian Books/Harper Collins Publishers, 2008.

Deloria, Philip J. *Indians in Unexpected Places.* Lawrence, Kansas: University Press of Kansas, 2004.

Deloria, Vine, Jr. *Behind the Trail of Broken Treaties: An Indian Declaration of Independence.* Austin, Texas: University of Texas Press, 2000.

Deloria, Vine, Jr. *Custer Died for Your Sins: An Indian Manifesto.* New York: Avon Books, 1969

Deloria, Vine, Jr. *God is Red: A Native View of Religion.* Golden, Colorado: Fulcrum Publishing, 1994.

Deloria, Vine, Jr. *Red Earth, White Lies: Native Americans and the Myth of Scientific Fact.* Golden, Colorado: Fulcrum Publishing, 1997.

DeMallie, Raymond J. *The Sixth Grandfather: Black Elk's Teachings Given to John G. Neihardt.* Lincoln, Nebraska: University of Nebraska Press, 1984.

Demos, John. *The Unredeemed Captive: A Family Story from Early America.* New York: Vintage Books/A Division of Random House, 1995.

Di Silvestro, Roger L. *In the Shadow of Wounded Knee: The Untold Final Story of the Indian Wars.* New York: Walker & Co., 2005.

Donovan, James. *A Terrible Glory: Custer and the Little Big Horn: The Last Great Battle of the American West.* New York: Back Bay Books/Little Brown & Co., 2008.

Doyle, Arthur Conan. "Adventure IV: The Boscombe Valley Mystery." *The Adventures of Sherlock Holmes.* London: George Newnes, 1892.

Drinnon, Richard. *Facing West: The Metaphysics of Indian-Hating and Empire Building.* Norman, Oklahoma: University of Oklahoma Press, 1980.

Drinnon, Richard. *Keeper of Concentration Camps: Dillon S. Myer and American Racism.* Berkeley, California: University of California Press, 1987.

Drury, Bob and Clavin, Tom. *The Heart of Everything That Is: The Untold Story of Red Cloud, An American Legend.* New York: Simon & Schuster, 2013.

Dunbar-Ortiz, Roxanne. *All the Real Indians Died Off.* Boston, Massachusetts: Beacon Press, 2016.

Dunbar-Ortiz, Roxanne. *An Indigenous Peoples' History of the United States.* Boston: Beacon Press, 2014.

Eckert, Allan W. *A Sorrow in Our Heart: The Life of Tecumseh.* New York: Bantam Books, 1992.

Eckert, Allan W. *That Dark and Bloody River: Chronicles of the Ohio River Valley.* New York: Bantam Books, 1995.

Ehle, John. *Trail of Tears: The Rise and Fall of the Cherokee Nation.* New York: Anchor Books/A Division of Random House, 1988.

Fleisher, Kass. *The Bear River Massacre and the Making of History.* Albany, New York: State University of New York Press, 2004.

Flood, Renée Sansom. *Lost Bird of Wounded Knee: Spirit of the Lakota.* New York: Scribner, 1995.

Frazier, Ian. *Great Plains.* New York: Picador, 1989.

Frazier, Ian. *On the Rez.* New York: Picador, 2000.

Garnsworth, Eric, Editor. *Sovereign Bones: New Native American Writing Volume II.* New York: Nation Books, 2007.

Goetzmann, William H. *Exploration and Empire: The Explorer and Scientist in the Winning of the American West.* New York, The Norton Library/W.W. Norton & Co., 1966.

Gonzalez, Mario and Cook-Lynn, Elizabeth. *The Politics of Hallowed Ground: Wounded Knee and the Struggle for Indian Sovereignty.* Chicago: University of Illinois Press, 1999.

Granzotto, Gianni. *Christopher Columbus: The Dream and the Obsession.* Garden City, New York: Doubleday & Co., 1985.

Greene, Jerome A. *American Carnage: Wounded Knee, 1890.* Norman, Oklahoma: University of Oklahoma Press, 2014.

Grua, David W. *Surviving Wounded Knee: The Lakotas and the Politics of Memory.* New York: Oxford University Press, 2016.

Gwynne, S. C. *Empire of the Summer Moon: Quanah Parker and the Rise and Fall of the Comanches, the Most Powerful Tribe in American History.* New York: Scribner, 2010.

Halaas, David Fridtjof and Masich, Andrew. *Halfbreed: The Remarkable True Story of George Bent: Caught Between the Worlds of the Indian and the White Man.* Cambridge, Massachusetts: Da Capo Press/A Member of the Perseus Books Group, 2004.

Hancock, Kevin. *Not for Sale: Finding Center in the Land of Crazy Horse.* Casco, Maine: Seventh Power Press, 2015.

Harjo, Joy and Bird, Gloria Eds. *Reinventing the Enemy's Language: Contemporary Native Women's Writings of North America.* New York: W.W. Norton & Co., 1997.

Hedren, Paul L. Ed. *The Great Sioux War: The Best from Montana—The Magazine of Western History.* Helena, Montana: Montana Historical Society Press, 1991.

Hendricks, Steve. *The Unquiet Grave: The FBI and the Struggle for the Soul of Indian Country.* New York: Thunder Mouth's Press, 2006.

Holler, Clyde. *Black Elk's Religion: The Sun Dance and Lakota Catholicism.* Syracuse, New York: Syracuse University Press, 1995.

Howard, Helen Addison. *Saga of Chief Joseph.* Lincoln, Nebraska: Bison Books/University of Nebraska Press, Revised Edition, 1978.

Hoxie, Frederick. *This Indian Country.* London: Penguin Books, 2012.

Irving, Washington. *The Life and Voyages of Christopher Columbus.* Hertfordshire, England: Wordsworth Editions Limited, 2008.

Jackson, Helen Hunt. *A Century of Dishonor: The Classic Exposé of the Plight of Native Americans.* Mineola, New York: Dover Publications, 2003.

Jackson, Joe. *Black Elk: The Life of an American Visionary.* New York: Picador/Farrar, Straus, & Giroux, 2016.

Jaimes, Annette Ed. *The State of Native America: Genocide, Colonization, and Resistance.* Boston: South End Press, 1992.

Jenkins, Philip. *Dream Catchers: How Mainstream America Discovered Native Spirituality.* New York: Oxford University Press, 2004.

Joinson, Carla, *Vanished in Hiawatha: The Story of the Canton Asylum for Insane Indians.* Lincoln, Nebraska: University of Nebraska Press, 2016.

Josephy, Alvin. *1492: The World of Indian People Before the Arrival of Columbus.* New York: Vintage/Penguin Books, 1993.

Karolevitz, Robert. *Challenge: The South Dakota Story.* Sioux Falls, South Dakota: Brevet Press, 1975.

Katz, William Loren. *Black Indians: A Hidden Heritage.* New York: Atheneum Books, 1986.

Kinew, Wab. *The Reason You Walk.* New York: Penguin Random House Co., 2015.

Krech III, Shepard. *The Ecological Indian.* New York: W.W. Norton & Co., 1999.

La Duke, Winona. *The Militarization of Indian Country.* East Lansing: Makwa Enewed, 2013.

Lame Deer, Archie Fire and Erdoes, Richard. *Gift of Power: The Life and Teachings of a Lakota Holy Man.* Rochester, Vermont: Bear and Company, 1992.

Lame Deer, John (Fire) and Erdoes, Richard. *Lame Deer: Seeker of Visions: The Life of a Sioux Medicine Man.* New York: Touchstone Books/Simon & Schuster, 1972.

Lazarus, Edward. *Black Hills, White Justice: The Sioux Nation Versus the United States 1775 to the Present.* New York: Harper Collins, 1991.

Leahy, Todd. *They Called It Madness: The Canton Asylum for Insane Indians 1899-1934.* Baltimore: Publish America, 2009.

Light, Steven Andrew and Rand, Kathryn R. L. *Indian Gaming and Tribal Sovereignty: The Casino Compromise.* Lawrence, Kansas: University of Kansas Press, 2005.

Limerick, Patricia. *The Legacy of Conquest: The Unbroken Past of the American West.* New York: W.W. Norton & Co., 1987.

Loewen, James. *Lies My Teacher Told Me.* New York: Touchstone/A Division of Simon & Schuster, 1995.

Lyman, Stanley. *Wounded Knee 1973: A Personal Account.* Lincoln, Nebraska: University of Nebraska Press, 1991.

MacArthur, John. *The Vanishing Conscience: Drawing the Line in A No-Fault, Guilt Free World.* Dallas, Texas: Word Publishing, 1994.

McGaa, Ed. *Spirituality for America: Earth Saving Wisdom from the Indigenous.* Hill City, South Dakota: Four Directions Publishing, 2013.

McGregor, James. *The Wounded Knee Massacre from the Viewpoint of the Sioux.* Rapid City, South Dakota: Fenske Printing, Inc., 1940.

McMurtry, Larry. *Crazy Horse.* New York: Viking/Penguin Group, 1999.

Magnuson, Stew. *The Death of Raymond Yellow Thunder and Other True Stories from the Nebraska- Pine Ridge Border Towns.* Lubbock, Texas: Texas Tech University Press, 2008.

Magnuson, Stew. *Wounded Knee 1973: Still Bleeding: The American Indian Movement, the FBI, and Their Fight to Bury the Sins of the Past.* Arlington, Virginia: Court Bridge Publications, 2013.

Mann, Charles C. *1491: New Revelations of the Americas Before Columbus.* New York: Vintage Books, A Division of Random House, 2005.

Mann, Charles C. *1493: Uncovering the New World Columbus Created.* New York: Vintage Books/A Division of Random House, 2012.

Marks, Paula Mitchell. *Precious Dust: The Saga of the Western Gold Rushes.* Lincoln, Nebraska: University of Nebraska Press, 1994.

Marshall III, Joseph. *Returning to the Lakota Way.* New York: Hay House, 2013.

Marshall III, Joseph. *The Day the World Ended at the Little Big Horn.* New York: Penguin Books, 2007.

Marshall III, Joseph. *The Journey of Crazy Horse.* New York: Viking Books, 2004.

Mathis, Valerie Sherer. *Helen Hunt Jackson and Her Legacy of Indian Reform.* Austin, Texas: University of Texas Press, 1990.

Matson, William. *Crazy Horse: The Lakota Warrior's Life and Legacy.* Layton, Utah: Gibbs Smith, 2016.

Matthiessen, Peter. *In the Spirit of Crazy Horse: The Story of Leonard Peltier and the FBI's War on the American Indian Movement.* New York: Penguin Books, 1992.

Means, Russell and Johnson, Bayard. *If You've Forgotten the Names of Clouds, You've Lost Your Way: An Introduction to American Indian Thought and Philosophy.* Porcupine, South Dakota: Treaty Publications, 2012.

Means, Russell and Wolf, Marvin. *Where White Men Fear to Tread.* New York: St. Martin's Griffin, 1995.

Messerschmidt, Jim. *The Trial of Leonard Peltier.* Boston: South End Press, 1983.

Morgan, Robert. *Lions of the West: Heroes and Villains of the Westward Expansion.* Chapel Hill: Algonquin Books, 2011.

Mort, Terry. *Thieves' Road: The Black Hills Betrayal and Custer's Path to the Little Big Horn.* New York: Prometheus Books, 2015.

Nabokov, Peter Ed. *Native American Testimony: A Chronicle of Indian-White Relations from Prophesy to the Present, 1492-2000 (Revised)*. New York: Penguin Books, 1978.

Nathanson, Paul. *Over the Rainbow: The Wizard of Oz as a Secular Myth of America*. Albany, New York: State University of New York Press, 1991.

Neihardt, John G. *Black Elk Speaks*. Lincoln, Nebraska: University of Nebraska Press, 1961.

Nelson, Melissa K. Ed. *Original Instructions: Indigenous Teachings for a Sustainable Future*. Rochester, Vermont: Bear & Co., 2008.

Nerburn, Kent. *The Girl Who Sang to the Buffalo: A Child, an Elder, and the Light from an Ancient Sky*. Novato, California: New World Library, 2013.

Niethammer, Carolyn. *I'll Go and Do More*. Lincoln, Nebraska: University of Nebraska Press, 2001.

Olson, James and Wilson, Raymond. *Native Americans in the Twentieth Century*. Chicago: University of Illinois Press, 1986.

Ostler, Jeffrey. *The Lakotas and the Black Hills: The Struggle for Sacred Ground*. New York: Penguin Books, 2010.

Page, Jake. *In the Hands of the Great Spirit: The 20,000-Year History of American Indians*. New York: Free Press/A Division of Simon and Schuster, 2003.

Peltier, Leonard. *Prison Writings*. New York: St. Martin's Griffin, 1999.

Phillips, Kevin. *Wealth and Democracy: A Political History of the American Rich*. New York: Broadway Books, 2002.

Powers, Thomas. *The Killing of Crazy Horse*. New York: Vintage Books/A Division of Random House, 2010.

Prats, Armando. *Invisible Natives: Myth and Identity in the American Western*. Ithaca, New York: Cornell University Press, 2002.

Price, Catherine. *The Oglala People 1841-1879*. Lincoln, Nebraska: University of Nebraska Press, 1996.

Pritchard, Evan. *No Word for Time*. Tulsa, Oklahoma: Council Oaks Books, 1997.

Reinhardt, Akim. D. *Ruling Pine Ridge.* Lubbock, Texas: Texas Tech University Press, 2007.

Remini, Robert. *Andrew Jackson and His Indian Wars.* New York: Viking Press, 2001.

Richardson, Heather Cox. *Wounded Knee and the Road to an American Massacre.* New York: Basic Books/A Member of Perseus Books Group, 2010.

Riley, Naomi Schaefer. *The New Trail of Tears: How Washington is Destroying American Indians.* New York: Encounter Books, 2016.

Rosenfeld, Seth. *Subversives: The FBI's War on Student Radicals, and Reagan's Rise to Power.* New York: Farrar, Straus, & Giroux, 2012.

Ross, A. C. (Ehanamani). *Crazy Horse and the Real Reason for the Battle of the Little Big Horn.* Rapid City, South Dakota: Hansen Brothers Printing/Color House Graphics, 2000.

Ross, A. C. (Ehanamani). *Mitakuye Oyasin—We are all Related.* Denver, Colorado: Wiconi Waste, 1989.

Rozema, Vicki. *Voices from the Trail of Tears,* Winston-Salem, North Carolina: John F. Blair, Publisher, 2003.

Sajna, Mike. *Crazy Horse: The Life Behind the Legend.* Hoboken, New Jersey: John Wiley & Sons, 2000.

Sandoz, Mari. *Crazy Horse: The Strange Man of the Oglalas.* Lincoln, Nebraska: University of Nebraska Press, 1942.

Shames, Deborah, Ed. *Freedom with Reservation: The Menominee Struggle to Save Their Land and Their People.* Madison, Wisconsin: Impressions, Inc., 1972.

Sides, Hampton. *Blood and Thunder: The Epic Story of Kit Carson and the Conquest of the American West.* New York: Anchor Books/A Division of Random House, 2006.

Slotkin, Richard. *Fatal Environment: The Myth of the Frontier in the Age of Industrialization 1800-1890.* New York: Atheneum Publishers, 1985.

Slotkin, Richard. *Gunfighter Nation: The Myth of the Frontier in Twentieth-Century America.* Norman, Oklahoma: University of Oklahoma Press, 1998.

Slotkin, Richard. *Regeneration Through Violence: The Mythology of the American Frontier 1600-1860.* Norman, Oklahoma: University of Oklahoma Press, 1973.

Smith, Andrea. *Conquest: Sexual Violence and American Indian Genocide.* Durham, North Carolina: Duke University Press, 2005.

Smith, Paul Chaat and Warrior, Robert Allen. *Like A Hurricane: The Indian Movement from Alcatraz to Wounded Knee.* New York: The New Press, 1996.

Smith, Rex Alan. *Moon of Popping Trees: The Tragedy at Wounded Knee and the End of the Indian Wars.* Lincoln, Nebraska: University of Nebraska Press, 1988.

Smith, Sherry. *Hippies, Indians, and the Fight for Red Power.* New York: Oxford University Press, 2012.

Stannard, David E. *American Holocaust: The Conquest of the New World.* New York: Oxford University Press, 1992.

Stearns, Peter. *Meaning Over Memory: Recasting the Teaching of Culture and History.* Chapel Hill: University of North Carolina Press, 1993.

Stern, Kenneth. *Loud Hawk: The United States versus the American Indian Movement.* Norman, Oklahoma: University of Oklahoma Press, 1994.

Stiles, T.J. *Custer's Trials: A Life on the Frontier of a New America.* New York: Vintage Books/A Division of Penguin Random House, 2015.

Taliaferro, John. *Great White Fathers: The True Story of Gutzon Borglum and His Obsessive Quest to Create the Mount Rushmore National Monument.* Cambridge, Massachusetts: Perseus Books Group, 2002.

Tinker, George. *Missionary Conquest: The Gospel and Native American Cultural Genocide.* Minneapolis: Augsburg Fortress, 1993.

Trachtenberg, Alan. *Shades of Hiawatha: Staging Indians, Making Americans, 1880-1930.* New York: Hill and Wang, A Division of Farrar, Straus & Giroux, 2004.

Treuer, David. *Rez Life.* New York: Grove Press, 2012.

Trimbach, Joseph. *American Indian Mafia.* Denver, Colorado: Outskirts Press, 2009.

United States Department of Justice/Federal Bureau of Investigation. *The F.B.I: A Centennial History: 1908-2008*. Washington, D.C.: United States Government Printing Office, 2008.

Utley, Robert M. *The Lance and the Shield: The Life and Times of Sitting Bull*. New York: Henry Holt & Co., 1993.

Utley, Robert M. *The Last Days of the Sioux Nation*. New Haven, Connecticut: Yale University, 1963.

Utley, Robert and Washburn, Wilcomb E. *Indian Wars*. Boston: Houghton Mifflin Co., 1977.

Vestal, Stanley. *Sitting Bull: Champion of the Sioux*. Norman, Oklahoma: University of Oklahoma Press, 1956.

Warren, Louis. *Buffalo Bill's America: William Cody and the Wild West Show*. New York: Vintage Books/A Division of Random House, 2005.

Washburn, Wilcomb, Ed. *The Indian and the White Man*. Garden City, New York: Anchor Books, 1964.

Weatherford, Jack. *Indian Givers: How Indians Transformed the World*. New York: Fawcett Books, 1988.

Weinberg, Albert K. *Manifest Destiny: A Study of Nationalist Expansionism in American History*. Chicago: Quadrangle Paperbacks, 1963.

Welch, James (with Paul Stekler). *Killing Custer: The Battle of the Little Big Horn and the Fate of the Plains Indians*. New York: Penguin Books, 1995.

Wernitzig, Dagmar. *Going Native or Going Naïve: White Shamanism and the Neo-Noble Savage*. Lanham, Maryland: University Press of America, 2003.

Wilford, John Noble. *The Mysterious History of Columbus: An Exploration of the Man, the Myth, the Legacy*. New York: Knopf Doubleday Publishers, 1991.

Wilkinson, Charles. *Blood Struggle: The Rise of Modern Indian Nations*. New York: W.W. Norton & Co., 2005.

Wilson, James. *The Earth Shall Weep: A History of Native America*. New York: Picador, 1998.

Woolford, Andrew; Benvenuto, Jeff and Hinton, Alexander Laban, Eds. *Colonial Genocide in Indigenous North America.* Durham, North Carolina: Duke University Press, 2014.

Yenne, Bill. *Indian Wars.* Yardley, Pennsylvania: Westholme Publishing, 2006.

Aberdeen South Dakota *Saturday Pioneer*, 2
Ache Indians, 138
Acting White (book), 310
Adams, Hank, 243, 244, 262, 263, 264, 265, 266
Adams, John, 93, 301
Adams, John Quincy, 15
Adams, New York, 214
Adis Ababa, 153, 154
Afghanistan, XVII 11, 103
A Frontier Lady: Recollections of the Gold Rush and Early California (book), 63
Agents of Repression: The FBI's Secret Wars Against the Black Panther Party and the American Indian Movement (book), 84
Akwesasne Notes, 279
Alcatraz, 244, 245, 246, 247
Alexander, son of Chief Massaoit, 245
Alexander, William, 93
Alice in Wonderland (book), 318
Allen, Dick, 208
All the Real Indians Died Off (book), 231
Alvarado, Captain, 100
Ambrose, Stephen, 12, 184, 195
American Carnage (book), 22, 83, 208
America's Hidden History (book), 18
American Indian Embassy, 249
American Indian Mafia (book), 34, 36, 83, 248, 257, 259, 261, 269, 276, 286
American Indian Movement (AIM), 33, 34, 39, 42, 47, 56, 74, 75, 80, 122, 237, 240, 243, 259, 260, 262, 267, 274
Anacaona, 58
Andrew Jackson and His Indian Wars (book), 123
anpetu secha, 232
Apostle Paul, 112, 240
Aquash, Anna Mae, X 13, 33, 34, 36, 37, 38, 39, 41, 42, 209, 228, 241, 256, 260, 261, 288, 318
Anthony, Susan B., 7

anthropologists, 104, 231, 242, 277, 306
Anti-Indianism in Modern America (book), IX 1
Arana, Julio Cesar, 55
Arapaho, 97, 98, 100, 105, 123, 180, 312
Arbuthnot, Alexander, 208
Arcoren, John and Yvonne, 39
Arizona, 153
Arizona Daily Star, 76
Army Corps of Engineers, 20
Arsenic, 53
Ash Hollow, Battle of (also known as Battle of Blue Water Creek), 4, 139
Assistant Secretary of the Interior Harrison Loesch, 249
Atkins, Captain Gene, 206
Atlantic Monthly, 222
Augustana College, 241

Badlands of Dakota (film), 139
Badlands, South Dakota, 294
Bailyn, Bernard, 6, 10, 16, 110, 114, 118
Balinska, D., 229
Banks, Dennis, 33, 36, 37, 38, 40, 41, 77, 237, 247, 248, 249, 250, 260, 261, 276, 277, 286, 294
Banks, Russell, 266
Barnett, Louise, 12, 13, 185, 192, 306
Bashaw, Minnesota, 215
Battle of Bushy Run, 278
Baum, L. Frank, 2, 3, 166
Bear River Massacre and the Making of History, The (book), 7
Bear's Table, 319
Beata Island, 56
Bear Creek, 286
Beck, Paul, 281, 294
Bedinger, Representative, 63
Beef Industry on Pine Ridge, 228
Belisarius, Count, 100

Belgium, 228
Bellecourt, Clyde, 241, 249, 278
Bend, Oregon, 13, 277
Berg, Scott, 117, 214
Berwick, Maine, 140
Bissonnette, Gladys, 34
Black Buffalo Woman, 151, 185, 186
Black Elk, Ben, IX
Black Elk, Grace, 34
Bly, Robert, 163
Boots and Saddles (book), 3, 144, 154, 186
Bordeaux, Catherine, 40
Bordewich, Fergus, 19, 30, 22, 24, 25, 138, 170, 221, 243, 298, 301, 308
Borglum, Gutzon, 226, 227
Bosque Redondo, 106
Boston Celtics, 160
Bozeman Trail, 161
Bradley, Michael, 10, 11, 49
Brady, Sam, 91
Branch Davidians, 165
Brackenridge, Henry M., 102
Brennan, John, 206
British Board of Trade, 278
Brown, Dee, 5, 38, 213, 214, 242, 244, 320
Brown, Thomas, 84, 85
Bruce, Louis, 249
Brule, X, 4, 139, 280
Bryan, William Jennings, 68
Buck, Stewart, 310
Buffalo, XV, 1, 55, 68, 98, 101, 105, 120, 135, 139, 143, 144, 178, 207, 213, 244, 282, 284, 299, 307, 312
Buffalo Bill Cody, 186, 187, 188
Buffalo Bill's America (book), 136
Buffalo Bill's Wild West, XV, 3, 23, 104, 153, 175, 176, 178, 187, 188
Buffalo Springs Massacre, 123

Bukey, Hezekiah, 91
Bullock, William "Billy", 24
Bullock, William G., 24
Bull Run, Battle of, 199, 200
Bureau of Indian Affairs, 21, 35, 36, 37, 39, 41, 142, 247, 248, 249, 250, 256, 257, 262, 263, 264, 265, 266, 298
Burgwin, Scott, 13, 277
Burkin, Carol, 18
Burnette, Robert ("Bob"), 75, 248, 249
Burroughs, Edgar Rice, 269, 278
Burton, J.R., 3
Bury My Heart at Wounded Knee (book), 38, 98, 214, 242, 244, 320
Busch, Adolfus, 199
"Butcher Allen', 231
Butler, Dr., 116
Butler, Reverend Elizer, 230
By Our Hand, Through the Memory, 68

Cabot, John W., 263, 264, 265, 266
Caciques, 57, 58
Caitlin, George, 104
Caldwell, Agnes, 67, 68
Calhoun, James, 64
California and Oregon Trail in the Literary World (book), 122
Calley, Lieutenant William, 97
Camp, Walter, 82, 192
Canadian Indians, 303
Canton Asylum /Hiawatha Asylum, 66, 67, 68, 136, 240
Carib Indians, 49
Carlton, General James Henry, 106, 142, 143
Carlyle Industrial School, 214
Carson, Kit, 105, 134, 135, 136
Cary-Alvarez, Jana, 76
casinos, 65, 66, 79, 80, 105

castilla elastic, 54
Caughnawaga Indians, 136
Cavalry, United States Seventh, X, 1, 3, 4, 64, 116, 185, 186, 195, 197, 198, 200, 201, 280
Central Intelligence Agency (CIA), 261
Century of Dishonor (book), 109, 214
Chambers, A.B., 302
Chasing Hawk, Alex, 303
Chattahoochie Valley, 115
Cherokee Indians, X, 52, 64, 81, 109, 113, 116, 117, 124, 125, 163, 230
Cherokee Nation v. Georgia, 230
Cheyenne Dog Soldiers, 99
Cheyenne Indians, 3, 13, 81, 97, 98, 99, 99, 100, 105, 122, 176, 180, 183, 185, 186, 193, 195, 200, 201, 239, 242, 281, 282, 284, 312
Cheyenne River Reservation, 284
Chicago Tribune, 217
Chickahominy River, 201
Chickasaw Indians, X, 218
Chief Wahoo, 119, 240
Chingachgook, 239
Chivington, Colonel John, 17, 47, 97, 98, 99, 100, 101, 121, 122, 135, 138, 192, 201
Choctaw Indians, X
Christians/Christianity, 6 12, 42, 47, 50, 51, 57, 64, 69, 82, 85, 93, 109, 110, 111, 113, 116, 121, 125, 135, 137, 141, 142, 154, 160, 163, 168, 191, 194, 196, 205, 214, 216, 217, 222, 233, 240, 267, 291, 292, 293, 294, 304, 306, 309, 320, 321
Churchill, Ward, 9, 22, 23, 38, 47, 48, 73, 74, 79, 81, 83, 84, 85, 123, 138, 163, 164, 259, 277, 301, 303
Church Select Committee, 269
Clark, Lieutenant William Philo, 152
Cleveland Indians, 119, 240
COINTELPRO, 36, 84

Colby, Clara, X
Colby, Leonard, X, 208, 209
Colburn, Marshall, 249
Coleman, William, 20
Cole, M.D., 206
Coler, Jack, 41, 276
Collier, John, 164
Collinson, Peter, 299
Collyer, Vincent, 310
Columbian Exchange, The (book), 18, 85
Columbus Conspiracy, The (book), 10, 49
Columbus Day Parade, Denver 1992, 47
Columns of Vengeance (book), 77, 85, 280
Comanche Indians, 17, 98, 101, 105, 131, 132, 135, 136, 137, 138, 139, 142
Comanche the Horse, 116
Commerce, Department of, 249
Comstock, William, 187
Communist/Communist Party, 75, 256, 274, 275, 276
concentration camps, 20, 143
Connell, Evan S., 191, 199, 283
Contras, 241
Cook-Lynn, Elizabeth, IX, XI, 1, 5, 18, 22, 35, 42, 124, 125, 133, 136, 141, 146, 152, 156, 160, 168, 178, 179, 225, 239, 240, 241, 260, 273, 280, 285, 303, 309
Coolidge, Harriet, 210
Cooper, James Finnimore, 239, 241, 306
Cornplanter, 20, 152
Costello, Damian, 291, 292
Count Balasarius,
Coverly, Harvey, 268
Crazy Horse, XVIII, 21, 56, 84, 113, 132, 133, 134, 135, 142, 143, 144, 151, 152, 153, 156, 159, 160, 162, 164, 167, 169, 176, 179, 185, 186, 191, 201, 207, 207, 214, 227, 237, 238, 286, 312, 318, 319, 323

Crazy Horse (book), 5, 152
Crazy Horse and Custer (book), 184
Crazy Horse—the Lakota Warrior's Life and Legacy (book), 13, 133, 191, 154
Crazy Horse—the Life Behind the Legend (book), 133, 155, 242
Crazy Horse and the Real Reason for the Battle of the Little Big Horn (book), 159
Crazy Horse—the Strange Man of the Oglalas (book), 154
Cree Indians, 14
Creek Indians, 64, 113
Critical Race Theory: The Key Writings that Formed the Movement (book), 81
Crosby, Alfred W. Jr., 18, 57, 85
Crow Dog, Leonard, 18, 57, 85
Crow Dog, Mary (aka Mary Brave Bird), XI, 7, 8, 9, 154, 168, 210, 214, 225, 232, 237, 242, 303
Crow Indians, 103, 133, 179, 312
Cuba, 56
Cuppy, John, 91
Curly, 284
Curtis Act, 115
Custer Court House Riots, 229
Custer Died for Your Sins (book), 21, 194, 244, 273
"Custer Expedition Confirms Early Rumors of Gold in Indians' 'Sacred' Black Hills", 184
Custer, Elizabeth "Libbie" Bacon, 13, 144, 154, 183, 184, 185, 186, 193, 197
Custer, George, 1, 3, 4, 12, 13, 21, 38, 56, 57, 61, 62, 64, 66, 109, 113, 131, 140, 142, 144, 145, 153, 168, 176, 183, 184, 185, 186, 187, 188, 191, 192, 193, 194, 195, 196, 197, 198, 199, 200, 201, 209, 214, 215, 238, 239, 255, 269, 283, 284, 306
Custer, Tom, 197
Custer's Trials (book), 238

Dakota Indians, 7, 10, 77, 119
Dances with Wolves (film), 155, 167, 242
Dark and Bloody River, That (book), 92
Darlington Agency, 282
Darwin, Charles, XVII, 63, 66
Davis, Captain, 118
Davis, Kenneth C., 18
Davis, Lieutenant, 167
Davis, Robert, 309
Dawes Act of 1887, 20, 103, 115, 163, 228, 239, 240, 297, 298, 310
Day the World Ended at the Little Big Horn, The (book), 133
Day, Colonel Merritt H., 206
Dead Arm, 206, 207
Declaration of Independence, 91, 137, 214
Declaration of War Against Exploiters of Lakota Spirituality, 166
DeCory, Doni, 305
Deganawich-Quetzalcoatl University, 247
de Langlede, Charles Michael, 120-121
Delano, Columbus, 61
De las Casa, Bartolome, 54, 197
Delaware Indians, 85, 117
Delaware River, 23
Deloria, Philip, 10, 77, 82, 175, 257
Deloria, Vine Jr., XI, XVII, 6, 10, 14, 21, 22, 48, 77, 82, 104, 125, 153, 164, 187, 194, 232, 244, 246, 247, 250, 262, 273, 303, 309, 310
DeLuce, Virginia, 256
DeMallie, Raymond, 291, 322
Demos, John, 17, 18
Denevan, William, 12
Denneson, Johnson, 80
Denver Opera House, 47, 97, 100
Denver Daily News, 3
Department of the Interior, 41, 246, 249, 269
DeSmet, Father, 176, 242

"Devil's Tower", 318, 319
Dewing, Roland, 74, 75, 259
Did the U.S. Army Distribute Smallpox Blankets to Indians—Fabrication and Falsification in Ward Churchill's Genocide Rhetoric, 84
Discourse Inertia, 6
Dis 'n Dat Kid, 279
Dominican Republic, 196
Donovan, James, 65, 175, 214
Doolittle, Senator James, 100
Dorothy *Wizard of Oz*, 167, 169, 175, 176
Dorris, Michael, 83, 141
Downing, Jacob, 121
Doyle, Sir Arthur Conan, 74, 142
Dream Catchers (book), IV
Dred Scott v. Sandford, 93
Dresden Zoo, 104
Drinnon, Richard, XVII, 2, 6, 10, 13, 82, 93, 94, 140, 208, 285, 286, 302, 306, 307
Dull Knife, 193, 281, 282
Dunbar, John, 167
Dunbar-Ortiz, Roxanne, 101, 102, 103, 104, 117, 118, 231, 232
Durham, Douglas, 41, 180, 256, 261, 273, 286

Eagle Deer, Jancita, 39, 40, 41, 261
Eagle Woman (Ms. Galpin), 240
Earth Shall Weep, The (book), 85, 317
Eckert, Allan, 92, 230
Ecological Imperialism: The Biological Expansion of Europe 900-1900 (book), 57
Ecuyer, Captain Simeon, 85
Eddy, C. Mac, 262
Edmunds, Newton, 214
Ehanamani, 159, 160, 165
Ehle, John, 116, 117
Eisenhower, President Dwight David "Ike"/ Eisenhower Administration, 21, 245

Eisler, Kim, 80
Elizabethan Lumber Room (book), 6
Ellis, George, 62
Emigdiano Indians, 106
Empire of the Summer Moon (book), 17, 38, 84, 98, 131, 132, 135, 138
England, 110, 112
Espanola, 196
Eugenics, "science", of 66
Eugene, Oregon, 13, 277
Europeans, 6, 7, 10, 12, 16, 20, 24, 48, 50, 51, 52, 53, 54, 65, 80, 85, 110, 111, 112, 117, 118, 119, 124, 125, 131, 137, 140, 165, 222, 239, 244, 283, 300, 310, 312
Evans, Reva, 227
Evans, Roland, 77, 78
Ewert, Private, 231
Exploration and Empire (book), 62, 112

"Fame of Young General Spreading All Over the World", 184
Fatal Environment (book), 8, 12
Father Buechel, 233
Federal Bureau of Investigation (FBI), 9, 11, 13, 33, 34, 36, 37, 38, 39, 40, 41, 75, 76, 77, 78, 83, 84, 168, 238, 239, 241, 248, 255, 256, 259, 260, 262, 269, 273, 274, 275, 276, 277, 278, 280, 285, 286, 311, 323
Fetterman Fight, 6, 153, 155, 159, 227
Fifth Cavalry, 186
Filipinos, 68, 307
Fire Thunder, 213, 214
First Iowa Cavalry, 194
First Scalp for Custer (see also Red Right Hand), 187
Fitzcarrald, Carlos, 54, 55
Five Civilized Nations, 114
Fleisher, Kass, 7, 8, 9, 42, 184, 303
Fleming, Arthur, 41

Flying Hawk, 291
Flood, Renee Sanson, 7, 73, 205, 206, 208, 209, 210, 225, 282, 301
Fools Crow, Frank, 102, 162, 291
Fools Crow (book), 102, 159, 291
Forbes, Jack, 247
Forsyth, Lieutenant Colonel George, 5, 61, 205
Fort Buford, North Dakota, 177
Fort Duchesne, Utah, 243
Fort Duquesne, Pennsylvania, 268
Fort Garry, Winnepeg, Canada, 176
Fort Laramie Treaty of 1851, 177, 302
Fort Laramie Treaty of 1868 66, 109, 140, 145, 161, 177, 184, 209, 228, 239, 278, 284
Fort Leavenworth, Kansas, 194
Fort Necessity, Pennsylvania, 268
Fort Peck, Montana, 179
Fort Pitt, Pennsylvania, 117
Fort Riley, Kansas, 3
Fort Tejon, California, 106
Fort Union, North Dakota, 282
Fort Wahakie, Wyoming, 180
1491, 49, 50
1492, 49
1493, 24
Franklin, Ben, 231, 299
Frantz, Joe B., 81, 82
Frazier, Ian, XVI, 6, 141, 152, 225, 282, 305
Freedom With Reservation (book), 21
Free Speech Movement, 275
French, IX, 18, 112, 120-121, 136, 137, 177, 267, 268, 269, 280
French and Indian Wars, 137
Friends of the Indian, 239
"Frontier Myth", XVII, 68, 279
Gall, 176, 177, 195
Galton, Sir Francis, 66
gambling, 65, 66, 80

Gandy, Helen, 255
Garment, Leonard, 245, 250
Garraeu, Pierre, 178
General Order, 51, 281
Genghis Khan, 100
Genoa, Italy, 48, 112
genocide, XI, XVII, 8, 19, 22, 25, 47, 49, 68, 79, 81, 116, 122, 125, 135, 143, 209, 214, 311, 312
Gensler, C.H., 67, 68
Germans, 104, 123
Geronimo (film), 139, 167
"Ghost Dance", 1, 5, 6, 15, 17, 20, 23, 24, 106, 154, 168, 179, 180, 187, 206, 207, 208, 242, 268, 285, 292, 294, 305, 321
Giago, Tim, 80
Gianzotto, Gianni, 57, 111, 131, 191, 225, 318
Gifford, Oscar, 66
Gildersleeves, 78, 238, 241, 279
Gill, Moses, 265
Giraci, Spider, 279
Goar, Allison Marie, 81
Godfrey, Captain, 82
gold, 11, 25, 38, 48, 50, 51, 52, 54, 57, 66, 131, 140, 145, 159, 161, 184, 186, 187, 213, 217, 228, 230, 312
Goldman, Emma, 275
Gordon Journal, 227
Gordon, John, 228
Gordon, Nebraska, 225, 227, 228
Gordon, Nebraska Legion Hall, 229
Goshoot Indians, 103
Grant, Leon, 240
Grant, Ulysses S., 61, 66, 94, 141, 143, 145, 193, 310.
Grass, Martha, 249
Grattan, John L. 4, 92
"Grattan Massacre", 4, 5, 92, 231
Great Britain, 63

Great Plains, 13, 19, 55, 120, 135, 152, 153, 156, 193, 195, 283, 300, 306
Great Plains (book), 152, 312
Great Sioux War 1876-1877, The (book), 284
Great White Fathers (book), 145, 227
Gregg, General David, 200
Greene, Jerome, 1, 83
Grimm, Marshall Lloyd, 279
Grouard, Benjamin F., 179
Grouard, Frank, 152, 179, 180
Gualpa, Diego, 52
Guardians of the Oglala Nation (GOONS), 268, 280
Guerrier Ed., 201
Gunfighter Nation (book), 10, 14
Gwynne, S.C., 10, 17, 19, 67, 81, 84, 98, 100, 101, 131, 132, 133, 134, 135, 136, 137, 138, 139, 140, 141, 142, 144, 145, 146, 169, 217, 218, 238, 284.

Hadjo, Hillis, 208
Haefner, Robert, 83
Halfbreed, 122
Halfbreed (book), 195
Hall, Jarius, 201
Halleck, Henry "Old Brains", 215
Hancock, Kevin, 9, 84, 153, 160, 161, 162, 163, 164, 165, 166, 167, 168, 170, 292, 293, 300, 301, 306, 323,
Hancock, Winfield S., 200
Hanford, California, 208
Harper's Monthly, 222
Harrison, J.B., 310
Harrison, William Henry, 91, 92, 94, 231
Haudenosee Indians, 2
Hayward, Richard "Skip", 80
"Healing Fund", 312
Hendricks, Steve, 38, 40, 41, 78, 256, 261, 286

Henry, Major Guy V., 179
Hickok, "Wild Bill", 187, 198
Hidatsa Indians, 312
High Foretop, 4
Higuena-mota, 58
Himollemico, 209
Hinman, Reverend Samuel D., 214
Hispaniola, 56
Hitler, Adolf, 20, 123, 143
Hitomo, Yoaza, 22
Holler, Clyde, 102, 292, 317
Holmes, Sheeny, 279
Hoover, J. Edgar, 168, 255, 256, 317
Horseshoe Bend, Battle of, 100, 113, 114
Hoskin, Chuck Jr., 81
Hotchkiss guns, 1, 142, 280, 281
House of Representatives Un-American Activities Committee, 256
Houston Rockets, 160
Howard, Helen, 121
Hummer, Harry, 67, 68
Humphrey, Hubert, 249
Hunkpapa Lakota, X, 2, 175, 177, 318
Huth, Hans, 93

Indian Country Today (publication), 170
Indians in Unexpected Places (book), 175
Indians of All Tribes, 244
Indigenous People's History of the United States (book), 101
Indian Wars, 4, 63, 82, 115, 117, 136, 140, 145
Indian Wars (book), 137
Ingalls, Rufus, 12
Interior, Department of the, 249
In the Hands of the Great Spirit (book), 205
In the Spirit of Crazy Horse (book), 259, 261
Invisible Natives (book), 118, 123, 167
Irish, 188

Iron Hail (aka Dewey Beard), 1
Irving, Washington, 11, 48, 49, 50, 51, 56, 57, 58, 312, 318
Irving, William "Bronco", 24
Irwin, 207
Israel/Israelites, 66, 217, 223, 231, 292
Italy/Italian, 48, 111, 188, 191, 318

Jackson, Andrew, 19, 53, 64, 92, 100, 113, 114, 123, 124, 134, 163, 208, 217, 218
Jackson and the Course of American Freedom (book), 114
Jackson, Helen Hunt 10, 67, 106, 109, 110, 111, 113, 114, 115, 119, 120, 121, 122, 123, 124, 125
Jackson, Joe, 155, 292, 293
Jackson, Thomas "Stonewall", 142
Jacobs, Charlie, 176
Janklow, William, 39, 40, 41, 237, 238, 274, 275, 303
Jaimes, M. Annette, XVIII, 123
Japanese, 11, 21, 123, 268
Jefferson, Thomas, 14, 66, 91, 94, 163, 273
Jeffersonian Democracy, 304
Jenkins, Philip, 162, 165
Jennings, Frances, 140
Jensen, South Dakota Governor Leslie, 226
Jesuits, 322
Jim-James, 241
Jones, Don FBI Agent, 274
Jones, Jim, 165
Josephy, Alvin, 49
Journey of Crazy Horse, The (book), 161
Jumping Badger (Sitting Bull), 176
Jumping Bull Ranch, 33, 42, 277
Jung, Carl, 167

Kansas City Chiefs, 74
Kellogg, E.R., 180
Kelly, FBI Director Clarence, 39
Kendall, B.F., 145
Kendall, Captain George, 146
Kennan, George F., 22, 308
Kenosha Agency, Wisconsin, 67
Keogh, Captain Miles, 116
Kennedy, Bobby, 249
Kennedy, Senator Edward, 249
Keystone Pipeline, II 76, 321
Kieft, Willem, 16, 17
Kicking Bear, 167, 242
Kildeer Mountain, Battle of, 281, 294
Killing Custer: The Battle of the Little Big Horn and the Fate of Plains Indians (book), 12
Killing the White Man's Indian (book), 19, 24, 221, 243, 298
Killsright, Joe Stuntz, 33
Kilpatrick, Judson, 200
King Philip, 140, 245
King Philip's War, 23, 245
Kinzua Dam, 20
Klopp, Charles F. Jr., 264
Koster, John, 75
Kubinak, Robert, 264
Ku Klux Klan, 226, 227
Kuper, Leo, 311
Kyle, John, 198

Lac du Flambeau Agency, 67
La Course, Richard "Dean of Indian Journalism", 265
Ladner, Kiera, 260
Lady Thorpes, Pine Ridge High School, XV, 304, 305
Lake Traverse Paint and Chemical Corporation (LTPC), 263, 264

Lakotas and the Black Hills, (book) 144
Lame Deer, Archie Fire, 232, 233
Lame Deer, John Fire, 292, 297
Lamont, Buddy Jr., 280
Lancaster Treaty of 1744, 278
Lance and the Shield, The (book), 155
Lansdale, Edwin Geary, 279, 280, 286
Lapham, Lewis, 300, 301
LaRoque, Emma, 308
Larrabee, Joe, 207
Larrabee, Nellie, 207
Last Days of the Sioux Nation (book), 221
Last of the Mohicans (film), 239, 241, 306
Lea, Luke, 309, 310
Leach, David, 245
Lead, South Dakota, 304
Legacy of Conquest (book), 61, 115, 318
Lies My Teacher Told Me (book), 47, 83, 141
Life and Voyages of Christopher Columbus, The (book), 11, 49
Lights and Shadows (book), 215
Like a Hurricane (book), 246
Limerick, Patricia Nelson, XVIII, 6, 10, 61, 115, 138, 155, 163, 276, 298 299, 301, 303, 318
Lincoln, Abraham 214, 215
Lions of the West (book), 18, 79
Little Big Horn Battle (see also Battle of the Greasy Grass), 3, 4, 57, 109, 116, 133, 139, 144, 153, 155, 159, 160, 176, 183, 184, 185, 186, 192, 193, 194, 195, 197, 198, 200, 215, 239, 269, 283, 293
Little Crow War, 215
Little Crow—Spokesman for the Sioux (book), 156
Little Thunder, 4, 139
Little Turtle, 191, 192
Little Wolf, 281, 282
Lodge, Ambassador Henry Cabot, 307
Lodge, Senator Henry Cabot, 307

Loesch, Interior Secretary Harrison, 249
Loewen, James, 47, 83
London Times, 283
Lonergen, Jerry, 198
Looking Cloud, Arlo, 38
Lord De la Ware, 117
Los Angeles, California, 39, 245, 248, 261
Los Angeles Lakers, 160
Los Angeles Times, 75
"Lost Bird", X, 7, 33, 39, 73, 74, 205, 208, 209, 210, 307
Lost Bird of Wounded Knee (book), 73, 205, 225
Lovewell, Captain John, 154
Lowry, Rich, 105
Ludlow, William, 198
Luiseno Mission Indians, Pechanga Band, 79
Lutter, Bernard "Butch", 228, 229

MacArthur, John F., 14, 35
McClellan, General George, 183, 192, 201
McCloud, Janet, 8
McCloud, J.B., 206
McDowell, Representative, 63
Mackenzie, Colonel Ranald, 193
McLaughlin, Agent James, 175, 180, 284
McMurtry, Larry, 5, 6, 152, 153, 154, 156, 160, 294, 303
McNamara, Robert, 193
Madonna, 262
Magaw, Ed, 102
Magnuson, Stew, 15, 206, 225, 228, 231, 259
Magua, 239
Maidu Buttes, (Three Peaks) 247
Manhattan, 17
Manifest Destiny, 3, 14, 19, 62, 63, 64, 65, 66, 67, 68, 69, 92, 93, 120, 124, 145, 169, 184, 240, 278, 309
Manifest Destiny (book), 26

Mann, Charles C., 11, 12, 48, 49, 50
Marshall, Joseph, 22, 113, 121, 133, 161, 165, 169
Marshall, Rosebud, 264
Mashco Indians, 55
Massachusetts, 81, 136, 154, 245
Massaoit, 245
Mathey, Lieutenant, 197
Matson, William, 13, 133, 154, 191, 305
Matthiesen, Peter, 261, 277
Mayflower, II 36
Meade, General George, 200
Meaning Over Memory (book), 119
Means, Lorelei, 7
Means, Russell, IX, XI, 5, 36, 37, 41, 47, 75, 77, 78, 101, 104, 201, 237, 238, 239, 240, 241, 243, 246, 247, 249, 260, 276, 278, 286
Media Interpretations of Wounded Knee II: Narratives of Violence versus Sympathetic Coverage, 76
Medicine Men, 169, 241, 250
Mellette, Governor Arthur, 76, 206
Melville, Hermann, 122
Memphis, Tennessee, 259
Menominee Indians, 21, 222, 223
Menominee Termination Act P.L., 83-399 222
Men's Movement, 163, 166
Mercury, 53, 54
Meriam Report, XVII, 76, 216, 298
Metacom, 245
Mex, Paddy the, 279
Mexican War, 15
Miles, General Nelson "Bearcoat", 16, 17, 82, 187
Militarization of Indian Country, The (book), 103
Miller, Amanda, 222
Mills, Billy, XVI
Minneconjou Indians, X, 1, 15, 177, 280, 294, 321
Miskito Indians, 241
Missionary Activities Among the Indians, 216

Missionary Conquest (book), 164, 213, 215
Missouri Republican, 302
Miss Spotted Tail, 185
Mitchell, George, 249
Monahseetah, 185, 195
Mondale, Walter, 249
Monmouth, 116
Montagnais Indians (see also Innu Indians), 161
Month of the Freezing Moon (book) (see also the Sand Creek Massacre of November, 1864), 81
Montgomery, Ed 275
Moon of Popping Trees (book), 16, 17
Moose, Warfield, XVI
Morgan, Robert, 18
Morgan, Thomas, 298
Mormons, 10, 23, 179, 180, 221, 222, 223
Morris, Glen, 74, 122
Morton, Rogers, 250, 275
Morton, Thomas, 93, 140, 304, 306
Mort, Terry, 19, 81, 138, 139, 140, 141, 142, 143, 144, 145, 146, 159, 285
Mountain Meadows Area Massacre, 222
Mounted Rangers, 281
Mount Rushmore, 226, 227
Moves Camp, Ellen, 34, 322
Moves Camp, Louie, 276
Myer, Dillon S., 21
My Lai Massacre, 98
"My Lie on the Plains", 191
My Life on the Plains (book), 191, 194, 196
Mysterious History of Columbus, The (book), 48, 57
Myrick, Andrew, 86

Nakota Indians, IX, 166
Napolean, 177
National Advisory Commission on Civil Disorders, 274
National Archives, 23, 318

National Commission on the Causes and
    Prevention of Violence, 14
National Congress of American
    Indians (NCAI), 244
National Football League, 118
National Indian Youth Council (NIYC), 243, 244
National Park Service, 22, 83
National Review, 105
National Women's Association of Canada, 38
*Nature and the American: Three Centuries of
    Changing Attitudes (book)*, 93
National Rifle Association, 262
Natural Born Killers (film), 241
Nelson, John Y., 24
Nelson, Melissa K., 166
New Age, 162, 163, 165, 166, 168
New Amsterdam, 16
New England, 2, 18, 23, 111, 117, 118,
    154, 160, 306
New English Canaan, (book) 93
Newman, Wallace "Chief", 245
New Trail of Tears, The (book), 8, 122, 297, 308
New World, 11, 47, 48, 51, 57, 62, 111,
    112, 215, 217
New York Herald, 4, 240
New York Morning News, 62
New York Society of Decorative Arts, 186
New York Times, 35, 193, 267
Nez Perce, 52, 145, 152, 230, 242, 318
Nichols, David, 123
Nichols, Judge Fred, 37
Niehardt, John, 291, 292
Niethammer, Carolyn XI
Nietszche, Frederick, 164
Ninth Cavalry, 179
1948 United Nations Convention on Punishment
    and Prevention of the Crime of Genocide, 47

Nixon, President Richard, 56, 245, 262,
    263, 285, 300
Noem, Congresswoman Christi, 76, 319
Noqoilpi, 80
North American Review, 222
Northern Algonquin, 161
Northern Pacific Railroad, 142, 177
North, Oliver, 260
North Vietnamese, 11, 153, 279
Northwest Indian War, 191
Norton, Jack, 18
Not for Sale (book), 84, 160, 161, 167, 168
Novak, Robert, 77, 78, 79, 209, 260, 286

Oberlin College, Ohio, 215
Oglala Lakota Agency, 213
Oglala Lakota Community College, 323
Ohio Valley, 267
Ojeda, Alonzo de, 196, 197
Ojibwa Warrior (book), 33
"On Racist Discourse in S.C. Gwynne's Empire of
    the Summer Moon", 132
On the Justice of Roosting Chickens—Reflections
    and Consequences of U.S. Imperial Arrogance
    and Criminality, 85
*On the Origin of Species or The Preservation
    of Favoured Races in the Struggle for Life
    (book)*, XVII, 66
On the Rez, XVI, 305
Oregon Territory, 63
Orifino Creek, 25
Original Instructions, 311
Orwell, George, 84
Osawatomie, Kansas, 113
O'Sullivan, John, 61, 64
*Out of Many: A History of the American
    People (book)*, 113
Ovando, 57, 58

Over the Rainbow—The Wizard of Oz as a Secular Myth of America (book), 166, 175, 217
Ovieda, 111
Owl Woman, 98, 99
Ozema River, 56
Page, Jake, 51, 83, 214, 205, 267
Palmer, Attorney General Mitchell A., 275
"Palmer Raids", 275
Palos, 112
Paria, 54
Parker, Cynthia Ann, 131, 136
Parkman, Francis, 122
Patterson, Brad, 250
Pauite tribe, 21, 242
"Peace Policy", 61, 141, 310
Peltier, Leonard, 38, 261, 311, 312
Penn, William, 23
People's Temple, 165
Pequots,
Pequot War,
Peterson, Dennis, 264, 266
Peters, Will, XV, 105, 244, 322
Philadelphia, Pennsylvania, 23
Phillipine Insurrection, 68
Pickering, Kathleen, 104
Pieper, N.J.L., 268
Pine Ridge Indian Reservation, IV, IX, X, XV, XVII, 1, 5, 8, 13, 15, 24, 33, 34, 35, 37, 38, 40, 41, 74, 78, 83, 84, 160, 161, 162, 163, 164, 168, 179, 180, 187, 205, 206, 210, 225, 227, 229, 232, 237, 239, 242, 248, 256, 257 (Agency) 260, 262, 266, 268, 273, 276, 277, 280, 282, 284, 286, 293, 298, 299, 300, 302, 306, 308, 309, 311, 317, 318, 319, 320, 321, 322, 323
Plastic Shield Product Corporation, 263
Plenty Horses, 257
Pliny the Elder, 54
Plymouth, Indiana, 113
Plymouth, Massachusetts, 245
Pocahontas (film), 241
Politics of Hallowed Ground, The (book), 312
Poppers, Deborah and Frank, 300, 301
Popular Science Monthly, 222
Portland, Oregon, 277
Posse Comatatus Act of 1878, 268
Post, Louis, 276
post traumatic stress disorder, 103
Potawatomi Trail of Death, 113
Potosi, 53, 54
Poverty, XV, XVI, XVII, 12, 19, 48, 77, 80, 103, 111, 167, 208, 240, 244, 298, 300, 308, 318, 319
"poverty porn", 320
Pourier, Baptiste, 152
Powder River, 144
Powhatan Indians, 247
Prairie, The (film), 306
Prats, Armando, 63, 118
Pratt, Addison, 179
Pratt, Captain Richard, 307
Pretty Owl, 195, 201
Prison Writings (book), 311
Proctor, Secretary of War Redfield, 283
Promontary Point, Utah, 283
Propriety of Pennsylvania, 23
Pueblo Indians, 55, 80
Pupiana (Mount Diablo), 247
Pyle, Alden, 168
Quang Nai Province, Vietnam, 97
Quiet American, The (book), 168, 307
Quinalt Reservation, 244

Rain in the Face, 195
Rains, Lieutenant Sevier M., 121
Rapid City Journal, 206, 207, 323
Rapid City, South Dakota, 226, 229

Raritan Indians, 16
Reagan, Ronald, 84, 255, 256, 273, 274, 298
Red Right Hand, (First Scalp for Custer)(play), 187
Red Cloud, 24, 138, 144, 151, 164, 321
Red Cloud Agency, 186, 207, 282
Red River War, 193
Reinhardt, Akin D., 322, 323
Reinventing the Enemy's Language (book), 237
Re-Member, XVI, 105, 320, 321
Remini, Robert, 114, 115, 116, 123, 124, 134, 137, 218
Renberger, Joni, 308
Reno, Marcus, 197
Reno, Mary, 197
Reno, Robert, 197
Returning to the Lakota Way (book), 165
Revenge of the Pequots (book), 80
Review Study of a Model for Failure in the BIA's Industrial Development Program, 262, 263, 264, 265, 266, 267
Ricker, Eli, 282, 283
Riggs, Alfred, 222
Riley, Naomi Schaefer, 8, 19, 81, 122, 123, 297, 298, 299, 300, 301, 302, 303, 304, 306, 307, 308, 309, 310, 311, 312, 313
Road to Babylon, The, 300
Road to Wounded Knee, The (book), 75
Roberts, Annie Gibson, 197
Robideau, Robert, 38
Roubideaux, Ramon, 35
Roman Catholic, 291, 322
Rooks, Eugene, 323
Rooks, William, 323
Roosevelt, Buddy, 188
Roosevelt, Theodore, "Teddy", 65, 68, 239
Rosebud, Battle of the Rosebud, 176
Rosebud Reservation, 8, 40, 74, 102, 225, 227, 233, 248, 277

Rosebud Tribal Court, 40
Rosebud Tribal Hospital, 8
Rosenfeld, Seth, 84, 255, 273
Rosewood, Florida, 8
Rosewood (film), 8
Ross, A.C., 159, 160
Ross, Gyasi, 106
Roughing It (book), 103
Royal Proclamation of, 1763 278
Royce, Sarah, 63
Rozema, Vicki, 116
Rudy Creek, 286
Ruling Pine Ridge (book), 303, 304
Rumsfeld, Donald, 304
Russell, Don, 193
Ryerson, Peter, 198

Sacramento, California, 256
Saga of Chief Joseph (book), 121, 227
St. Clair, General Arthur, 124, 192
St. Labre, 299
St. Marie, Buffy, 14
St. Tammany, John, 72
Sajna, Mike, 133, 139, 152, 155, 201, 284, 301
Salmon River County, 52
Sanchez, Alonso, 112
Sand Creek Massacre, Colorado, 9, 47, 81, 97, 98, 99, 100, 101, 121, 122, 138, 142, 192, 201
Sandoz, Marie, 154, 162
Sandoz, "Old Jules", 105
San Francisco Chronicle, 246
Sans Arc, X
Santo Tomas, 196
Savestone Corporation, 264
Savio, Mario, 274
Schafer, Gi, 256
Schafer, Jill, 256
Schmidtz, Daryld, 229, 323

Schroeder, Edith, 67, 68
Schultz, Diane, 81
Schwarzenegger, Arnold, 65, 66
Scott, Randy, 41
Scott, Winfield, 62, 116
Screen Actors Guild, 84, 256, 273
Searchers, The (film), 269
"Security Flash", 274
Seminole Indians, 8
Seminole War, 208
Senate Foreign Relations Committee, 311
Seneca Indians, 20, 94, 152
Seventh Iowa Cavalry, 282
Seymour Horatio, 215
Shades of Hiawatha (book), 292, 302

Shamans, 14, 160, 165 166, 169, 247, 302
Sharpton, Al 242
Shear, Professor Sarah, 304
Sheridan, General Phil, 86, 142, 143, 192, 193, 195, 196, 207, 299
Sherman, General William T., 13, 19, 142, 143, 281
Shirt Wearers, 151
Short, Elizabeth, 39
Sibley, General Alfred, 281
Sides, Hampton, 38, 105, 106, 135, 137
Sidnoyah, 195, 196
Sierras, 247
Significance of the Frontier in American History, The (book), 302
silica, 53
Since Predator Came (book), 9
Singing Horse Trading Post, 323
Sioux City, South Dakota, XV
Sioux Falls Argus Leader, 75, 76, 257
Sisseton-Wahpeton Reservation, 262, 263, 264, 265, 298

Sitting Bull, XVIII, 2, 16, 21, 56, 143, 144, 155, 160, 162, 164, 167, 175, 176, 177, 178, 179, 180, 187, 195, 206, 221, 237, 238, 283, 284, 285, 297, 312, 323
Six Nations, 247
Slaughter, Milo, 122
Slotkin, Richard, XVII, 6, 8, 10, 12, 14, 15, 65, 81, 82, 103, 139, 140, 194, 239, 279, 285, 307
Smith, Andrea, 12, 38, 209
Smith, Rex Alan, 16, 17, 308, 321
Snake, Reuben, 248
Snyder, Gary, 14, 165, 169
Son of the Morning Star (book), 191, 199, 193
Sorrow in Our Hearts—the Life of Tecumseh (book), 92
South Dakota Newspaper Coverage of the 1973 Occupation of Wounded Knee, 74
Spotted Elk (Big Foot), X, 2, 6, 15, 205, 207, 284, 321
Standing Bear, Chief Luther, 302
Stanley, Colonel O.S. ,177
Stannard, David, 8, 97, 131
Stanton, Elizabeth Cady, 7
Staten Island, 16
Stearns, Peter, 8, 12, 119, 256
Stevens Lode Silver Mine, 201
Stewart, Jane, 13, 144
Stiles, T. J., 137, 193, 198, 238
Stirrup, 162
Stone Mountain Georgia, 226
Strategic Air Command, 247
strychnine, 85
Subversives—The FBI's War on Student Radicals and Reagan's Rise to Power (book), 84, 255, 273
sulfer, 53
Sully, General Alfred, 19, 92, 177, 281, 294
Sun Dance, 51, 102, 176, 209, 248, 293
Swisshelm, Jane Grey, 7
Symmes, Reverend Thomas, 154

Taliaferro, John, 145, 227
Taylor, General Maxwell, 153
Teton tribes, 55
Termination, 21, 115, 223, 243
Terrible Glory, A (book), 65, 190, 214
Tetonwan, X
Thanksgiving, 36, 300
That Dark and Bloody River (book), 92
Thesinger, Wilford, 153
Thieve's Road (book), 138, 142, 145
38 Nooses (book), 214
Thom, Mel, 244
Thornton, Russell, 116
Thune, Senator John, 319
Tienhoven, Cornelius van, 17
Tilsen, Ken, 39
Tinker, George, 110, 121, 164, 165, 213, 214, 215, 216
Tippecanoe, 93
Tipis, 105, 121, 164, 179, 207, 246, 249, 282, 307
Tolstoy, Leo, 18, 25, 61, 280
Touched by Fire (book), 12, 183, 185, 280
Trachtenberg, Alan, 302
"Trail of Broken Treaties", 36, 248, 257, 286
"Trail of Tears" X, 20, 52, 64, 106, 113, 114, 115, 116, 117, 124, 134, 285
Trail of Tears (book), 109
Trevillian Station, 197
Trimbach, Joseph, 9, 10, 11, 34, 35, 36, 37, 41, 74, 75, 77, 78, 83, 85, 209, 238, 239, 241, 248, 250, 257, 259, 260, 261, 268, 269, 276, 277, 278, 279, 280, 281, 282, 283, 284, 285
Trudell, John, 38
Truman, Harry, 21, 94
Trump, Donald, 80, 81, 262
Tule Lake Camp, 268
Turner, Frederick Jackson, 302
Turtle Island, 119, 322

Turtle Island (book), 14
Twain, Mark, 103, 164, 187
"Twenty Points", 248, 250
Two Dogs, Rick, 144
Two Kettles, X
Two Strikes, 257
Tyler, 93

Ukraine, 123
Underhill, John, 17, 139
Unemakemi, 121
United Nations, 47, 311
United Daughters of the Confederacy, 226
United States Magazine and Democratic Review, 62, 63, 64
"Unknown helmsman", 111, 112
University of California, Berkeley, 84, 256, 274, 275
University of California, Davis, 247
University of Colorado, Boulder, 22, 83, 243
University of Montana, 119
Unquiet Grave, The (book), 237, 256
Unredeemed Captive (book), 17
Utah, 21, 103, 168, 179, 222, 223, 243, 283
Utley, Robert, 23, 82, 137, 155, 169, 178, 179, 221

Van Buren, Martin, 114
Vanishing Conscience, The (book), 14, 35
Varnum, Charles A., 144
Vattel, Emerich, 6
Vestal, Stanley, 206
Viet Cong, XVII
Vietnam War, XVII, 11, 97, 103, 153, 259, 279, 280, 285, 286
Vincent, Philip, 2
Vocabulary of the Massachusetts (or Natick) Indian Language (book), 231
Voices from the Trail of Tears (book), 116

Voices of Wounded Knee (book), 20
Vojan, Nigger, 279
Volkswagen, 123
Wakantanka, 178
Walatits, 230
Walker, Francis A., 310
Walla Walla, Washington, 52
Wall Street Journal, 79, 105
Wampanoag Indians, 245
Wannamaker, 292
War and Peace (book), 19
Warhol, Andy, 238
Warner, Colonel Volney, 268
War Relocation Authority, 21
Warren, Senator Elizabeth, 81
Warrior, Clyde, 243, 244
Washburn, Wilcomb, 136, 140, 214, 221
Washington, D.C., 13, 36, 37, 61, 67, 79, 196, 222, 248, 249, 255, 262, 263, 283, 286, 303, 307, 317
Washington, George, 2, 56, 93, 124, 192, 267, 268
Washington Post, 119
Washington Redskins, 118
Washington State, 145, 244
Wassell, William, 222
Washita, Battle of the, 192, 195
Watkins, Senator Arthur V., 223
Watt, James, 298
Wauneka, Annie Dodge, XI
Wayne, General "Mad Anthony", 91
Wayne, John, 188, 269
Wealth and Democracy (book), 300
Weasal Bear, Louise, 1
Weber, Max, 303
Webster, William, 260
Welch, James, 12
Weldon, Catherine, 180, 221
Wesley, Colonel, 197

Westchester County, New York, 17
West Point Military Academy, 195, 197, 198, 200, 217
Wheelock College, 36
Where White Men Fear to Tread (book), IX, 238, 241
Whipple, Bishop Henry, 167, 213, 214, 215, 216, 217
White Buffalo Calf Woman, 160, 167, 169, 233, 322
White Man's Indian, The (book), 15, 118
White Nation, 242
White River, Nebraska, 213
White Thunder, 98
Whittier College, 245
Wicked Witch (of the West), 176
Wiesel, Elie, 138
"Wild Bill" Hickok, 187, 198
"Wilder Mann", 135
Wilford, John, 48, 57, 112, 113
Wilkinson, Charles, 104, 308
Williams, Eunice, 136
Williams, Ron, 276
Wilson, James, XVII, 85, 164, 261, 283
Wilson, Richard "Dick", 34, 35, 38, 248, 256, 266, 267, 280, 322
Wind Cave, 239
Winnepeg, Canada, 176
Wintour, Robert, 298
Without Reservation (book), 80
Women's National Indian Association (WNIA), 112, 121
Wonderful Wizard of Oz (book), 2, 3, 166, 169
Wood, FBI Agent William, 37
Woody, Elizabeth, 68
Woolf, Virginia, 6
Worchester, Reverend Samuel, 231
Wounded Knee Massacre, X, XI, 1, 4, 6, 7, 10, 15, 16, 17, 20, 21, 23, 73, 74, 76, 98, 132, 187, 205,

206, 208, 242, 257, 279, 280, 281, 282, 284, 285, 301, 320, 321

Wounded Knee "Occupation", X, 9, 11, 34, 36, 37, 55, 74, 75, 76, 78, 83, 168, 180, 201, 237, 238, 239, 241, 243, 247, 248, 250, 256, 257, 262, 267, 273, 274, 275, 276, 277, 285, 294, 318, 320, 322

Wounded Knee Legal Defense Committee, 78

Wounded Knee Massacre from the Viewpoint of the Sioux (book), 74

Wounded Knee 1973: A Personal Account (book), 35

Wounded Knee 1973: Still Bleeding (book), 259

Wovoka, 21, 23, 168, 242

Wright, Frank Lloyd, 226

Xarangua, 57, 312

Xenophon, 100

Yankton Sioux Reservation, 92

Yellow Bird Steele, John, XVI

Yellow Hair, 186, 187

Yellow Robe, Chauncey, 187

Yellow Thunder, Dora, 228

Yellow Thunder, Raymond, 5, 92, 225, 226, 227, 228, 229, 230, 231, 232, 282, 306

Yellow Woman, 99

Yellow Wood, Troy Lynn, 37, 38

Young, Neil, 321

Zannis, Mark, 309

Zimiga, Coach, 305

Zulu, 153, 303

About the Author

David Fierst is an attorney living in Dayton, Ohio. He is married with two adult sons.

Hidden Disgrace is his first book and the result of a visit to Pine Ridge Indian Reservation in South Dakota in April 2014, after which he grappled with understanding the reasons for the harsh living conditions there.

Hidden Disgrace is further the result of researching the history of Indians generally in the United States and gauging whether that history is accurately depicted. It incorporates the views of Indian writers and intellectuals, both men and women, whose views often seem to be drowned out by those failing to understand the challenges of Indians in the United States as unique.

To learn more about David Fierst or to connect with him about his books and research, visit his website at:
www.DavidFierst.com

www.ingramcontent.com/pod-product-compliance
Lightning Source LLC
Chambersburg PA
CBHW080330170426
43194CB00014B/2511